SIXTH EDITION

REAL ESTATE LAW

James Karp

Elliot Klayman

Dearborn™
Real Estate Education

This publication is designed to provide accurate and authoritative information in regard to the subject matter covered. It is sold with the understanding that the publisher is not engaged in rendering legal, accounting, or other professional service. If legal advice or other expert assistance is required, the services of a competent professional person should be sought.

President: Roy Lipner
Vice-President of Product Development and Publishing: Evan M. Butterfield
Associate Publisher: Louise Benzer
Development Editor: Elizabeth Austin
Director of Production: Daniel Frey
Production Editor: Leah Strauss
Creative Director: Lucy Jenkins

Published by Dearborn™ Real Estate Education,
a division of Dearborn Financial Publishing, Inc.®
30 South Wacker Drive
Chicago, IL 60606-7481
(312) 836-4400
http://www.dearbornRE.com

Printed in the United States of America.

06 07 08 10 9 8 7 6 5 4 3 2

Library of Congress Cataloging-in-Publication Data

Karp, James.
    Real estate law / James Karp, Elliot Klayman.— 6th ed.
        p. cm.
    ISBN 1-4195-1133-5 (case)
1. Real property—United States. 2. Real estate business—Law and legislation—United States.
I. Klayman, Elliot I. II. Title.
    KF570.G5 2006
    346.7304'3—dc22

                                                                        2005026673

Dedication:

To a future of sustainable development.

To Norman and Annette, two extraordinary people,
who have been a source of encouragement throughout my life.
–EK

To Edlyn, Greg, Deb, Beth, and Kari
for sharing their love with me.
–JK

CONTENTS

PART ONE

Nature of Real Estate Law

PART TWO   Legal Interests in Real Estate

CHAPTER 4
Estates in Land 62

CHAPTER 5
Co-Ownership 78

CHAPTER 6
Condominiums, Cooperatives, Time-Shares, and Real Estate Investments 100

PART FIVE

Financing the Transaction

CHAPTER 21
Mortgages 464

CHAPTER 22
Land Installment Contracts 498

CHAPTER **27**
Green Development 610

The fundamental principles of real estate law are developed because of land's historic importance as a source of wealth. Many of the principles are difficult to group because they were formulated under different environmental, social, and economic conditions. The vocabulary is often antiquated and hardly part of our daily lexicon. To add to the complexity, attitudes regarding some areas of real estate law are shifting because of changing environmental and social perspectives.

To overcome these obstacles to learning, we have tried to write in a non-technical style. We have provided key terms and review questions to reinforce understanding. We have presented legal cases with a simplified statement of the facts, while at the same time preserving the accuracy of the dispute. We have tried to anticipate the future directions through The Changing Landscape pieces in each chapter.

■ THE SIXTH EDITION

Content

We have updated text material and cases, where newer cases better illustrate the legal issues. Contemporary topics such as limited liability companies, condominiums, the Fair Housing Act, and many more are explored in great depth, ensuring that Real Estate Law continues to provide the most up-to-date and comprehensive coverage possible.

The Changing Landscape commentaries in each chapter continue to present a big-picture framework for envisioning the larger context of the issues presented in the text, and we have updated these sections to reflect the state of the legal world today. With The Changing Landscape, we are asking the reader to step back from the nitty-gritty of existing rules to reflect on the big picture in the hope that, as the architects of the future, you will see the proverbial forest and not just the individual trees.

Pedagogy

- Textual and case material has been updated.
- Tables and charts have been added to help clarify material.
- Web sites facilitate learning more about the subject matter in the chapter.
- Key terms are listed at the end of the chapter with the page on which they are discussed.
- The short case examples, longer legal cases, review and discussion questions, case problems, and glossary features of the prior edition have been retained.

Instructor Support

For instructors, we have developed an extensive package of support materials that can be accessed and downloaded (with password) from the publisher's Web site at *www.dearbornre.com.* These support materials include

- detailed lecture notes, including Chapter Purpose, Learning Objectives, and a Lecture Outline in Microsoft PowerPoint and PDF format for each chapter;
- suggested answers to the end-of-chapter Review and Discussion Questions;
- suggested answers to the end-of-chapter Case Problems in the text;
- a vast multiple-choice test bank for creating customized assignments and examinations.

In addition, the test-building software Diploma™ is available to instructors by contacting your sales representative.

New Student Study Guide CD-ROM

Included in the back of the book is a Student Study Guide CD-ROM for students to use on their own or as a group exercise. There are two sections of the study guide: Interactive Case Studies and Case Study Reviews. Each case study covers a certain set of chapters, and the following icon at the end of the appropriate chapters indicates when it is time for the reader to work through one of the case studies:

■ ACKNOWLEDGMENTS

First, we wish again to recognize the contribution of Emeritus Professor Frank Gibson, the first author and the visionary of this work. It is upon his vision that we continue to build.

We owe a debt of gratitude to others who helped in the research and preparation of the book, along the way. Thanks to Edlyn Karp, Carolyn Hilleges, Joyce Klayman, Sandy Yoakam, John Wilson, and Amanda Runyon, a third year student at the Ohio State University College of Law.

Finally, we sincerely thank all of the people who provided comments and suggestions that have greatly improved this edition of the text. Our reviewers included Mitchell L. Appelrouth, Richmond Association of REALTORS® School of Real Estate; John G. Banner, J.D., College of Business, University of Cincinnati; Stanley J. Lieberman, Esq., Polley Associates, Newton Square, PA; Mariam J. Masid, Colorado State University; Ward F. McDonald, University of Illinois; Raymond A. Salco, Cuyahoga Community College; Susan C. Tarnower, GMAC Commercial Mortgage Corp. We also wish to thank Sandi Kellogg for her work in preparing Chapter 21 and Veronica Micklin for her help with the preparation of the Instructor's Manual.

■ ABOUT THE AUTHORS

James P. Karp, J. D.
Professor of Law and Public Policy, Emeritus
Syracuse University
Whitman School of Management

Elliot Klayman, J.D., L.L.M.
Associate Professor of Business Law
The Ohio State University
Fisher College of Business

PART ONE

Nature of Real Estate Law

1 Introduction to Law and Legal Systems

■ LAW AND THE REAL ESTATE BUSINESS

Many aspects of the real estate business are closely associated with law. In fact, only the world of finance may be more closely controlled by law. Almost any professional activity of a broker, salesperson, appraiser, or investor involves certain legal restrictions. Thus, people in these positions and many others in real estate have a genuine need to know about the law and legal systems; the more extensive their knowledge, the more effective their job performance will be.

Real estate professionals deal not only with lawyers but also with recording clerks, building inspectors, tax officials, planning board members, and personnel from state and federal housing agencies. All of these people have specialized functions in the legal system. Understanding what they do and some of the responsibilities of their jobs increases the real estate professional's ability to work effectively with them. Many private sector individuals with whom salespeople and brokers come in contact also have specialized knowledge of the law; loan officers and appraisers are examples. Real estate professionals who have similar knowledge will be able to work more effectively with other specialists and improve their professional image at the same time.

Legal knowledge is especially important to professionals engaged in the buying and selling of real estate. They are involved in the real estate transaction at a critical point, as far as legal input is concerned. Clients and customers will often question them about legal matters or the advisability of consulting an attorney. Although sales personnel should never give legal advice, a knowledge of law will help them develop an awareness of situations in which a lawyer should be consulted. Because legal knowledge is considered so important, some states require that salespeople and brokers engaged in selling real estate complete a formal course in real estate law.

Although this book is devoted to a study of real estate law, to some extent that designation is misleading. Real estate law cannot really be separated from other types of law. A famous jurist once said, "Law is a seamless web"; nevertheless, because of the complexity of law, people who want to understand it often consider it in small segments. The boundaries of these segments are never exact, nor is there general agreement on what each segment includes. So the reader must realize that although much of what is said about real estate law applies to law in general, some strands of the "seamless web" are more important to the real estate business than others. This book deals primarily with these strands.

Most of this book discusses specific rules important to people involved in real estate transactions. In this first chapter, however, the book takes a broader look at law and the legal system. This chapter attempts to clarify the law by looking at where law is found and the structure within which it operates.

■ SOURCES OF LAW

Knowledge concerning many legal questions comes from life's experiences. As a person learns in school, on the job, or through daily living, laws important to that person become part of his or her knowledge of the manner in which things operate. Sometimes legal questions arise that are not answerable from experience. How does one find the answers to these questions? To what source does the student, the real estate professional, the lawyer, or the judge turn to find out what the law is?

One of the prevailing myths about law is that all laws are found in nicely indexed, officially published volumes of statutes enacted by a legislative body. According to this belief, all a person has to do to answer a legal question is to locate the correct page in the right book, and the law will be there in clear black letters. Unfortunately, few legal questions are answered this simply.

Thousands of cases, statutes, and administrative regulations are published each year. As a result, determining what the law is has become increasingly difficult. Computers have, during the past 25 years, provided a tool that enhances the potential for legal professionals and the general public to access the sources of law more effectively. The speed and manipulative power of the computer allow increased control over the burgeoning quantities of legal information.

To answer a legal question involving real estate, a person might have to examine one source or a number of different sources. Sometimes an answer will be found in a state constitution or the federal Constitution. Most often, however, people find the answer to real estate law questions in court opinions (often referred to as *precedents*), in statutes, and in the regulations of administrative agencies. The different sources of law are discussed in the paragraphs that follow.

Constitutions

A basic source of law, **constitutions** provide the framework within which the federal and state governments must operate. Ordinarily one does not associate real estate law with constitutional problems, but at least two functions of constitutions are important to the real estate business. First, the U.S. Constitution allocates power between the states and the federal government. Because the states generally have retained power over local matters, most real estate law is state law. However, because the states have given the federal government power to regulate businesses affecting interstate commerce, numerous federal statutes apply to the real estate business. At present, many people in the field are concerned about how federal statutes relating to antitrust concerns, such as the Sherman Act and the Clayton Act, are affecting real estate. Bankruptcy statutes and consumer protection laws such as Truth-in-Lending, the Real Estate Settlement Procedures Act, and environmental protection legislation are other examples of federal law that apply to real estate.

A second function of constitutions—both state and federal—is the protection of individual rights, including private property. Constitutional provisions require that the law be applied equally to all; in addition, they prohibit government from depriving a person of life, liberty, or property without due process. This means that an individual's property can be taken by government only under limited circumstances. But the protection accorded the individual is far from absolute. Both the power of eminent domain and the police power allow government to restrict private property.

Precedent

■ *A published opinion of an appellate court that serves as authority for determining a legal question in a later case with similar facts.*

A distinctive feature of the law of English-speaking countries is its reliance on cases decided by appellate courts as a source of law. Reports of these cases are published as opinions, which provide the answers to many legal questions.

CASE EXAMPLE

Clayborne and his adult daughter lived in a house that Clayborne owned. At the request of the daughter, Dexter painted the house. Clayborne did not authorize the work, but he knew that it was being done and raised no objection. Clayborne refused to pay Dexter, arguing that he had not contracted to have the house painted.

Dexter asked his attorney if Clayborne was legally liable to pay him. The attorney told Dexter that in their state several published appellate court decisions had established that, when a homeowner allows work to be done on his home by a person who would ordinarily expect to be paid, a duty to pay exists. The attorney stated that, based on these precedents, it was advisable for Dexter to bring a suit to collect the reasonable value of the work that he had done.

In the legal system of countries that follow the English system, judges are obligated to follow principles established by prior cases (precedents). This obligation, also referred to as *stare decisis*, is ingrained in our system. The extent to which a court is governed by precedent is difficult to assess. Although the practice of following precedent is not a legal duty, it is definitely more than a tradition. A judge who failed to follow precedent would not be convicted of a crime, but he or she ordinarily would be reversed and in extreme cases, censured or possibly impeached. People trained in our system generally consider reliance on precedent an effective and fair way to reach a decision, and the concept is fundamental to U.S. law.

The obligation to follow precedent is limited by a number of factors. A court need not follow precedent established in another state, although in reaching decisions courts sometimes consider case decisions from other states when their own state has no case law on the subject. Lower courts are bound to follow decisions rendered by higher courts of their state. Again, failure to do so may result merely in the lower court's decision being reversed. The highest appellate court in a state can overrule its own precedent. Although this occurs on occasion, most state appellate courts overrule reluctantly because they believe that certainty is a desirable characteristic of law. The reluctance to overrule is often seen in private areas such as real estate law, because certainty is deemed very important where property rights are involved. A court will overrule a prior decision when the rule of law was applied incorrectly in the first place or when the rule is not considered applicable because of a change in circumstances. In addition, only that part of a court's opinion that is *necessary* to resolve the dispute between the parties, called the *holding*, creates a precedent for future cases. Any discussions not necessary to settle the legal issue in question are *dicta*, and need not be followed in subsequent decisions.

Courts and attorneys frequently avoid the effect of a previous case by distinguishing it from the case under consideration. A case is distinguished when a significant factual difference can be pointed out between the two situations. For example, assume that, in defending Clayborne in the suit brought by Dexter, Clayborne's attorney asks the court to dismiss the case because she has found the published decision of a case with like facts where the appellate court held that the homeowner was not required to pay. Dexter's attorney argues that in that case the homeowner was on vacation and did not know the work was being done. As Clayborne knew that his house was being painted, the two cases are different and can be distinguished. If the court agrees the two cases are significantly different, that is, can be distinguished, it will decide that the earlier decision is not precedent and therefore not controlling in deciding the case before the court.

Law that evolves from published opinions of appellate courts, or precedent, is often called **judge-made law** or *decisional law*. In England, reliance on previous decisions or cases and on custom and tradition created a law that was common to the entire country. Therefore, the law based on prior opinions is often referred to as *common law*. Sometimes people have difficulty accepting the idea that in these opinions statutes are not involved in any manner. In fact, often no statute exists that can be used to settle the dispute. The United States adopted the English common-law approach. Most of the non-English speaking nations have civil law systems relying exclusively on statutory or code law.

A modern example of judge-made law is found in those appellate decisions that impose responsibility on builders of defective homes. Before World War II, the builder of a defective home had little legal responsibility for injury or property damage once the home was sold. The buyer was required to make his or her own inspection of the premises. On the basis of this inspection, the buyer accepted responsibility for all defects, relieving the builder of responsibility for any defective construction. The courts were applying the ancient doctrine of *caveat emptor—let the buyer beware*.

During the 1950s and the 1960s, courts began to recognize the unfairness of this rule. They began to allow buyers of new homes to recover for personal injury and property damage resulting from defective construction. In numerous states, this modification of the law from caveat emptor to *caveat venditor (let the seller beware)* was accomplished without legislation. As one state court commented:

> If at one time . . . the rule of caveat emptor had application to the sale of a new house by a vendor-builder, that time is now past. The decisions and legal writings herein referred to afford numerous examples and situations illustrating the harshness and injustice of the rule when applied to the sale of a new house by a builder-vendor. . . . Obviously, the ordinary purchaser is not in a position to ascertain when there is a defect in a chimney flue, or vent of a heating apparatus, or whether the plumbing work covered by a concrete slab foundation is faulty.

The caveat emptor rule as applied to new houses is an anachronism patently out of harmony with modern home buying practices. It does a disservice not only to the ordinary prudent purchaser but to the industry itself by lending encouragement to the unscrupulous, fly-by-night operator and purveyor of shoddy work. *Humber v. Morton*, 426 S.W.2d 554 (Tex. 1968).

Statutory Law

Law enacted by local and state legislative bodies and by Congress.

The Role of Statutes. Although for many years the opinions of courts were the chief source of real estate law in English-speaking countries and for the legal system generally, during the past 100 years statutes have gradually assumed this role. Among the many reasons for this trend are that statutes are more comprehensive, statutes can modify the law more rapidly, statutes can treat an entire problem rather than just a part, and statutes are usually more understandable than cases.

During the past 75 years, statutes have been used to bring greater uniformity to state law. Economic expansion since the Civil War has been characterized by the growth of regional and national markets. States, however, have often adopted different laws to solve common problems occurring in these markets. This practice has increased the cost of doing business and caused confusion and uncertainty.

In 1890, the National Conference of Commissioners on Uniform State Law was established to alleviate this problem. The commission is charged with determining what uniform laws are necessary, drafting a uniform statute, and trying to get states to adopt it. More than 100 uniform laws have been recommended, although few have been adopted by all or even a majority of the states.

The commission has proposed a number of laws that deal with real estate. These include a uniform condominium act, a uniform residential landlord-tenant act, a uniform simplification of land transfers act, and a uniform eminent domain code. However, the impact of these uniform laws on real estate has been minimal to date.

Court Interpretation of Statutes. Despite the growing importance of statutes as a source of law, court opinions continue to play a significant role in shaping the law. Many statutes are broadly written. Often their meaning is not clear until they have been interpreted by a court. It is probably safe to say that in a majority of instances, a lawyer looking for the answer to a legal question will first check for an appropriate statute and then review relevant court opinions interpreting that statute.

Codification of Appellate Judge-Made Law. Another reason that court opinions continue to be important is that statutes often are merely a codification of the cases dealing with a particular legal problem. When a legislative body codifies the law, it adopts a statute that reflects the decisional law. For example, when the courts in some states decided that the act of selling real property implied a warranty of fitness for habitation, the state legislature passed statutes mirroring the court's decisions.

Administrative Rules and Regulations

In our dynamic, complex society, much of the work of government is done by administrative agencies. Both Congress and state legislatures create administrative agencies as part of legislation that aims to cure some social ill. The agency is empowered to enforce and implement the goals of the legislation. A substantial number of administrative agencies significantly influence the real estate business. Among such federal agencies are the Department of Housing and Urban Development, the Environmental Protection Agency, and the Federal Home Loan Bank Board. State administrative agencies also have a far-reaching influence on the real estate business. They are the source of rules pertaining to such matters as licensing and disciplining real estate sales personnel, zoning, safeguarding the environment, and landlord and tenant rights.

Administrative agencies perform several functions. They are authorized to settle disputes and, in doing so, act like courts; this is called *administrative adjudication*. The procedures used in administrative adjudication are generally much less formal than those used by the courts, making reaching a settlement less time-consuming and costly. Another benefit of administrative adjudication is that the agency personnel resolving the dispute are experts in the subject area of the dispute and can therefore resolve the case more effectively than is sometimes possible in a court.

Many agencies also have the power to make rules and regulations that have the force of law. In this respect they act as legislatures. An agency's authority to make rules and regulations is granted in the legislation that created the agency. If the rule or regulation issued by the agency is constitutional, if proper procedures have been followed, and if the agency has not exceeded the power and authority granted to it by the legislature, the rule or regulation is immune from modification or invalidation by the courts.

■ COURT STRUCTURE

People in the real estate business sometimes become involved in litigation, so it is helpful for them to know something about the structure of the system that applies the law.

Trial and Appellate Courts

Two types of courts are fundamental to the operation of the legal system: trial and appellate courts.

Trial Courts. The function of a **trial court** is to determine the facts and to apply the relevant law to these facts. A jury usually makes the factual determination, but in some cases the parties are not entitled to a jury or they waive this right. Disputed facts are then decided by the judge. Whether a judge or jury makes the factual determination, findings are based on evidence. In most instances evidence is the oral testimony of witnesses who are questioned by attorneys for the parties, and documents admitted into the proceedings.

The testimony of most witnesses is valuable because the witness has personal knowledge of the facts. One important type of witness often does not have personal knowledge of the situation, but does have expertise related to a disputed fact. This person is the expert witness. The testimony of the expert witness is not permitted until the trial court judge is convinced that the witness is qualified. When qualified, the expert witness may answer a hypothetical question that covers technical aspects of a disputed fact. Real estate brokers and appraisers often testify as expert witnesses in cases involving disputed land values.

Appellate Courts. If either party thinks that a legal error has been made by the trial court judge, the party may ask a higher court to review the case. This procedure is called an *appeal*, and the court hearing the case is an **appellate court**. The function of the appellate court is quite different from that of the trial court. This court is not concerned with deciding disputed facts; rather, it corrects legal mistakes. For this reason, there is no jury in an appellate court; there is a panel of judges. Instead of hearing the testimony of witnesses, the judges read briefs in which the parties explain what they believe the law to be. The attorneys may also present oral arguments. After the judges decide which party is correct, one of the judges will write an opinion presenting the views of the majority. If the court finds that an error has been made, the court may, in its opinion, order the lower court to correct its mistake. These opinions constitute the judge-made law explained earlier.

State and Federal Courts

A first step in understanding the American legal structure is to recognize that both the federal government and each of the states have their own systems of trial and appellate courts. Each of the systems—state and federal—in most instances is the final authority within its own **jurisdiction**. One exception to this principle is that federal courts do have authority over state courts in questions involving the federal law.

Jurisdiction of State Courts. The authority of state courts is extensive. It includes cases involving violations of the state's criminal statutes as well as statutes that involve matters as diverse as divorce, education, public health, and social welfare. Most contract cases and those involving personal injuries are also heard in state courts. In fact, state courts have jurisdiction over all matters except those the Constitution or Congress has given exclusively to the federal courts or has denied to the states.

Jurisdiction of Federal Courts. The jurisdiction of federal courts is limited to that given to them by the Constitution and the federal statutes that create them. As a result, federal courts hear only cases that involve the Constitution, treaties between the United States and a foreign nation, federal statutes, and citizens of different states. In the following case, the jurisdiction of the federal courts to decide a case brought against New Orleans real estate brokers is questioned.

McLain v. Real Estate Board of New Orleans, Inc.
U.S. Supreme Court
444 U.S.232 (1980)

Background. McLain and others (petitioners) brought a class action on behalf of real estate purchasers and sellers. The action was against real estate trade associations, firms, and brokers (respondents). The complaint stated that the respondents had engaged in a price-fixing conspiracy in violation of the Sherman Act, a federal statute.

The petitioners' complaint alleged the following: (1) that respondents' activities were "within the flow of interstate commerce and have an effect upon that commerce"; (2) that respondents assist their clients in securing financing and insurance involved with the purchase of real estate and that much of this financing and insurance comes from outside the state. The purpose of these allegations is to show the interstate connection of the respondents' activity, thereby raising a federal Sherman Act issue.

The U.S. District Court dismissed the complaint, finding that respondents' activities involving real estate were purely local in nature and did not substantially affect interstate commerce. The U.S. Court of Appeals affirmed, and the petitioner appealed.

Decision. The U.S. Supreme Court remanded the case for trial.

Mr. Chief Justice Burger. The question in this case is whether the Sherman Act extends to an agreement among real estate brokers in a market area to conform to a fixed rate of brokerage commissions on sales of residential property.

* * *

The broad authority of Congress under the Commerce Clause has, of course, long been interpreted to extend beyond activities actually in interstate commerce to reach other activities that, while wholly local in nature, nevertheless substantially affect interstate commerce. During the near century of Sherman Act experiences, forms and modes of business and commerce have changed along with changes in communication and travel, and innovations in methods of conducting particular businesses have altered relationships in commerce. Application of the Act reflects an adaptation to these changing circumstances.

The conceptual distinction between activities "in" interstate commerce and those which "affect" interstate commerce has been preserved in the cases, for Congress has seen fit to preserve that distinction in the antitrust and related laws by limiting the applicability of certain provisions to activities demonstrably "in commerce." It can no longer be doubted, however, that the jurisdictional requirement of the Sherman Act may be satisfied under either the "in commerce" or the "effect on commerce" theory.

Although the cases demonstrate the breadth of Sherman Act prohibitions, jurisdiction may not be invoked under that statute unless the relevant aspect of interstate commerce is identified; it is not sufficient merely to rely on identification of a relevant local activity and to presume an interrelationship with some unspecified aspect of interstate commerce. To establish jurisdiction, a plaintiff must allege the critical relationship in the pleadings and, if these allegations are controverted, must proceed to demonstrate by submission of evidence beyond the pleadings either that the defendants' activity is itself in interstate commerce or, if it is local in nature, that it has an effect on some other appreciable activity demonstrably in interstate commerce.

To establish the jurisdictional element of a Sherman Act violation, it would be sufficient for petitioners to demonstrate a substantial effect on interstate commerce generated by respondents' brokerage activity. Under the Sherman Act, liability may be established by proof of either an unlawful purpose or an anticompetitive effect.

* * *

On the record thus far made, it cannot be said that there is an insufficient basis for petitioners to proceed at trial to establish Sherman Act jurisdiction. It is clear that an appreciable amount of commerce is involved in the financing of residential property in the Greater New Orleans area and in the insuring of titles to such property. The presidents of two of the many lending institutions in the area stated in their deposition testimony that those institutions committed hundreds of millions of dollars to residential financing during the period covered by the complaint. The testimony further demonstrates that this appreciable commercial activity has occurred in interstate commerce. Funds were raised from out-of-state investors and from interbank loans obtained from interstate financial institutions. Multistate lending institutions took mortgages insured under federal programs which entailed interstate transfers of premiums and settlements. Mortgage obligations physically and constructively were traded as financial instruments in the interstate secondary mortgage market. Before making a mortgage loan in the Greater New Orleans area, lending institutions usually, if not always, required title insurance, which was furnished by interstate corporations. Reading the pleadings most favorably to petitioners, for present purposes we take these facts as established.

At trial, respondents will have the opportunity, if they so choose, to make their own case contradicting this factual showing. On the other hand, it may be possible for petitioners to establish that, apart from the commerce in title insurance and real estate financing, an appreciable amount of interstate commerce is involved with the local residential real estate market arising out of the interstate movement of people, or otherwise.

To establish federal jurisdiction in this case, there remains only the requirement that respondents' activities which allegedly have been infected by a price-fixing conspiracy be shown "as a matter of practical economics" to have a not insubstantial effect on the interstate commerce involved. It is clear, as the record shows, that the function of respondent real estate brokers is to bring the buyer and seller together on agreeable terms. For this service the broker charges a fee generally calculated as a percentage of the sale price. Brokerage activities necessarily affect both the frequency and the terms of residential sales transactions. Ultimately, whatever stimulates or retards the volume of residential sales, or has an impact on the purchase price, affects the demand for financing and title insurance, those two commercial activities that on this record are shown to have occurred in interstate commerce.

We therefore conclude that it was error to dismiss the complaint at this stage of the proceedings. The judgment of the Court of Appeals is vacated, and the case is remanded for further proceedings consistent with this opinion.

Vacated and remanded.

Today, would it be possible to operate a purely intrastate real estate market, thereby avoiding federal jurisdiction?

The power of federal courts to hear cases that arise under the Constitution, treaties, and federal statutes is called *federal question jurisdiction*. Most federal question matters involve the application or interpretation of one of the many federal statutes, such as the Clean Water Act, the Civil Rights Act, or the Internal Revenue Code.

The power of federal courts to hear cases involving citizens of different states is called **diversity jurisdiction**. Diversity jurisdiction exists because at the time the Constitution was adopted, many people believed that a citizen of one state would not get a fair trial if sued in another state. Consequently, those who drafted the Constitution included in it a provision extending federal judicial power to disputes between citizens of different states. Diversity jurisdiction places a substantial burden on the federal courts because they are often applying state law; therefore, Congress has limited the diversity jurisdiction of these courts to cases in which the dispute involves more than $75,000.

> **CASE EXAMPLE**
>
> Able was a resident of New Hampshire and Baker a resident of New York. The two entered into a contract in which Baker agreed to purchase a large resort hotel in New Hampshire from Able. Baker breached the contract, and Able sued her in the New Hampshire courts for $850,000 in damages. Baker may transfer the case to the federal district court because the parties are residents of different states and the amount in controversy exceeds $75,000.

State Court System

As there are 51 independent court systems operating within the United States, understanding the structure of American courts might seem an impossible task. The task is, however, simplified by the existence of a pattern common to both the federal and the 50 state systems. This structure can be visualized as a pyramid with two or sometimes three levels. (See Figure 1.1.)

State Trial Courts. Trial courts are at the base of the structural pyramid. Trial courts can be classified into three broad groups. This classification is based on the court's power to hear a case, which is termed its *jurisdiction.*

Courts of general jurisdiction. Each state usually has a trial court of general jurisdiction. In some states these are called *superior courts.* Other states call them *county courts, district courts, circuit courts,* or *courts of common pleas.* These courts have the power to hear a wide variety of civil and criminal cases. Ordinarily, there are no limits on the court's monetary jurisdiction, and the court has the power to grant extraordinary remedies, such as the injunction and specific performance. An *injunction* is an order forbidding a person to do a particular act. Conversely, an order for *specific performance* commands that a particular act be performed.

In a number of states these courts hear appeals from administrative agencies and courts of limited jurisdiction. (See Figure 1.1.) Trial by jury is available for most cases. The court generally has statewide jurisdiction but is organized on a district or county basis. These courts are generally considered the cornerstones of judicial administration.

Courts of limited jurisdiction. Many of the more populous states have created trial courts that are limited to hearing cases in which the damages are less than a certain amount, fixed by statute. Depending on the state, this amount ranges from a few hundred to thousands of dollars. These courts also generally have criminal jurisdiction over cases involving petty crimes and misdemeanors. *Municipal courts* is a common name for these courts. Other states call them *justice courts, magistrates' courts,* or *district courts.*

Generalizations about courts of limited jurisdiction are difficult to make. Their authority differs widely from state to state. In metropolitan areas their monetary jurisdiction is sometimes extensive, and the courts are manned by full-time judges with large staffs. In some rural areas these courts hear only the most trivial cases and may be presided over by part-time judges with no legal training. Courts of limited jurisdiction

FIGURE 1.1   A Typical State Judicial System

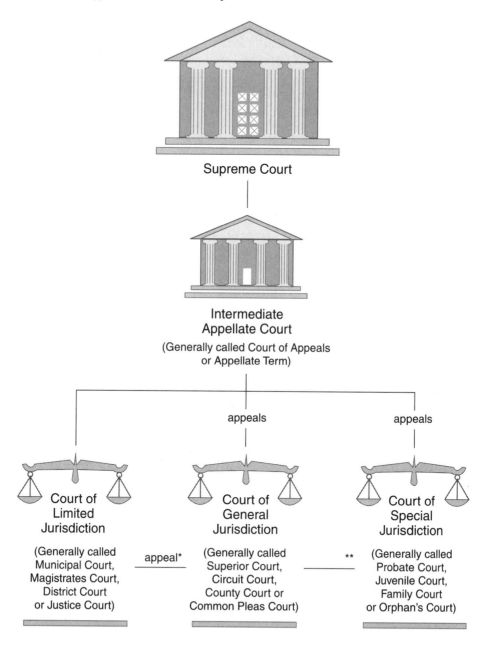

Supreme Court

Intermediate
Appellate Court
(Generally called Court of Appeals
or Appellate Term)

appeals   appeals

Court of
Limited
Jurisdiction

Court of
General
Jurisdiction

Court of
Special
Jurisdiction

(Generally called
Municipal Court,
Magistrates Court,
District Court
or Justice Court)

appeal*

(Generally called
Superior Court,
Circuit Court,
County Court or
Common Pleas Court)

**

(Generally called
Probate Court,
Juvenile Court,
Family Court
or Orphan's Court)

* In a number of states, courts of general jurisdiction consider appeals from courts of limited jurisdiction.
** In many states these courts are part of the court of general jurisdiction.

are important to the legal system because they take some of the pressures off the courts of general jurisdiction.

Courts of special jurisdiction. Either because of tradition or because of the peculiar needs of judicial administration, many states have established special courts to resolve a wide variety of disputes. Traffic offenses are one type of case often tried in a court of special jurisdiction. Traffic cases are generally tried in a special court or a special division of a trial court, as so many traffic offenses are processed that they would clog the regular judicial machinery.

Juvenile and domestic relations cases are also heard by special courts. These courts provide privacy and informal procedures that are effective in dealing with juvenile and family matters.

Numerous states also have separate probate courts that exercise jurisdiction over the administration of decedents' estates. When a real estate broker or sales associate is involved in a transaction that has to do with a decedent's real property, the broker or sales associate often has to deal with a probate court. In some states, probate courts have jurisdiction in guardianship, adoption, and competency proceedings.

State Intermediate Appellate Courts. About half the states have, by constitution or statute, established an intermediate level of appellate courts. The purpose of these courts is to lighten the burden of the state's supreme court. Some intermediate appellate courts have limited powers to act as trial courts. Usually this involves the power to issue extraordinary writs. However, the primary function of these courts is to provide appellate review. Although the extent of appellate jurisdiction is generally broad, some states place limits on the appeals that can be heard, possibly on the type of case or the maximum monetary amount. An intermediate appellate court might be permitted to hear all civil appeals or civil appeals only in cases wherein the amount in controversy is under $30,000.

State Supreme Courts. At the apex of a state's judicial system is the state supreme court, which in most states hears appeals in all civil and criminal matters. This jurisdiction is often concurrent with that of the intermediate appellate court. Because of the extensiveness of the review process and the large number of appeals, most states allow their court of last resort to accept for review only cases that the justices or judges consider important. Appeals as a matter of right may, however, often be taken in important cases, such as those that involve constitutionality of a state or federal statute or the death penalty.

Federal Court System

U.S. District Courts. The U.S. District Courts are the trial courts of the federal system. The United States is divided into 94 districts, each with a single district court. Almost all federal cases are initiated in these courts, as they have the power to hear all types of federal cases except those assigned by Congress to special courts such as the tax court.

U.S. Courts of Appeal. The federal intermediate appellate courts are called *U.S. Courts of Appeal.* In 1985 the United States was divided into 12 geographic areas called *circuits*, with a court of appeals for each. Each court hears appeals from the federal district courts that are included in its circuit. They also hear appeals from administrative agencies. In addition, there is a Court of Appeals for the Federal Circuit that hears special appeals, for example, those from the Court of International Trade.

U.S. Supreme Court. The United States Supreme Court is the final appellate court in the federal system. Most of the cases the Supreme Court reviews come from the U.S. Courts of Appeal and from the state supreme courts. The Supreme Court may review state supreme court decisions involving the federal Constitution or a federal statute.

In certain cases the Supreme Court must hear an appeal. One example is a case in which a U.S. Court of Appeals has held a state statute unconstitutional. Another is when a lower federal court has held a federal statute unconstitutional and the United States is a party. In most cases the party seeking review must first ask the Supreme Court to hear the case by petitioning for a *writ of certiorari*. This is a writ in which a superior court orders a lower court to supply a record of a particular case. The Supreme Court denies most petitions for certiorari because it does not consider a case important enough to hear.

Alternative Dispute Resolution

■ *A means of settling legal disputes without using the courts.*

Alternative dispute resolution (ADR) can take many forms. For instance, it can take the form of *mediation,* when a neutral third party listens to both sides and tries to facilitate a compromise. The mediator cannot force the parties to reach a compromise. The mediator focuses the parties on what they are willing to do to settle the dispute. The mediator may adopt a facilitative posture, urging the parties to find their own solution; or the mediator may provide the parties with an advisory opinion giving a proposed solution to the dispute. Many people argue that ADR is faster, cheaper, and less emotionally draining than traditional litigation.

Arbitration is another form of ADR. It may involve the formal submission of the dispute to a nonjudicial third person. The expertise of the arbitrator may be as a business professional. The expertise of the judge in litigation is the law. A person may get into arbitration by way of a contractual agreement, by statute, or by court order. Usually the arbitrator's decision is binding on the parties. A contractual agreement to arbitrate a dispute is the most common situation today.

Frequently, arbitration clauses are included in contracts dealing with development and sale of real estate, especially in construction contracts. The following case illustrates the use of a mediation/arbitration clause in a real estate sales contract.

Lee v. Heftel
Supreme Court of Hawaii
911 P.2d 721 (1996)

Background. In May 1990, the Lees purchased a home from Cecil and Joyce Heftel for the purchase price of $3,100,000.

On May 23, 1990, the parties executed a Deposit Receipt, Offer, and Acceptance (DROA) con-tract for the sale of the aforementioned residential property. Paragraph 5.3 of the DROA's Addendum No. 1 provides:

continued on next page

Mediation and Arbitration. If any dispute or claim in law or equity arises out of this DROA, Buyer and Seller agree in good faith to attempt to settle such dispute or claim by mediation under the Commercial Mediation rules of the American Arbitration Association. If such mediation is not successful in resolving such dispute or claim, then such dispute or claim shall be decided by neutral binding arbitration before a single arbitrator in accordance with the Commercial Arbitration rules of the American Arbitration Association. Judgment upon the award rendered by the arbitrator may be entered in any court having jurisdiction thereof.

On July 7, 1992, the Lees filed a complaint in circuit court alleging intentional or negligent misrepresentation, fraudulent concealment, breach of warranty, dual agency, and malicious and wanton conduct. On September 1, 1992, the Heftels filed their motion to stay and contended that the DROA expressly provided that "any dispute or claim in law or equity must first be submitted to mediation and then, if necessary, binding arbitration under the rules of the American Arbitration Association." The Lees opposed said motion and argued that "when a [p]laintiff seeks 'revocation' of a contract, Hawaii [S]tatutes expressly provide that an arbitration clause will not be enforced."

On January 6, 1993, the circuit court filed its order granting the Heftels' motion to stay.

"[W]hen presented with a motion to compel arbitration, the court is limited to answering two questions: (1) whether an arbitration agreement exists between the parties; and (2) if so, whether the subject matter of the dispute is arbitrable under such agreement."

Decision. The Hawaii Supreme Court affirmed the lower court granting the Heftels' motion to stay the proceedings pending arbitration.

Justice Nakayama. In this case, there is no dispute between the parties as to the existence of the arbitration clause provided in Addendum No. 1, paragraph 5.3 of the DROA. Rather, the controversy

exists as to the determination of the second prong of the two-part test. The Lees argue that, because they were fraudulently induced into purchasing the transferred property, mere allegations of such fraud revoke the contract, including the arbitration clause.

Because the pertinent language of HRS s 658-3 is virtually identical to the language of the federal arbitration statute, and due to the absence of [Hawaii] law regarding the scope of the trial court's role when faced with a motion to compel arbitration, we look to federal authority for guidance. In *Prima Paint Corp. v. Flood & Conklin Manufacturing Co.,* (1967), the United States Supreme Court heard a case involving circumstances analogous to those in the present case. The contract in *Prima Paint,* as in the present case, contained an arbitration clause, providing that "[a]ny controversy or claim arising out of or relating to this Agreement, or the breach thereof, shall be settled by arbitration." One party in that case alleged that the other had committed fraud in the inducement of the contract, although not of the arbitration clause in particular, and sought to have the claim of fraud adjudicated in court. The Supreme Court held that, notwithstanding a contrary state rule, consideration of a claim of fraud in the inducement of a contract "is for the arbitrators and not the courts." Accordingly, if the claim is fraud in the inducement of the arbitration clause itself—an issue which goes to the "making" of the agreement to arbitrate—the federal court may proceed to adjudicate it. But, the statutory language does not permit the federal court to consider claims of fraud in the inducement of the contract generally . . . . We hold, therefore, that in passing upon a[n] application for a stay while the parties arbitrate, a federal court may consider only issues relating to the making and performance of the agreement to arbitrate.

Thus, absent a state law to the contrary, arbitration clauses are separable from the contracts in which they are embedded, and where no claim was made that fraud was directed to the arbitration clause itself, a broad arbitration clause will be held to encompass arbitration of the claim that the contract itself was induced by fraud.

Like *Prima Paint*, no claim has been advanced by the Lees that the Heftels fraudulently induced them to enter into the agreement to arbitrate any controversy or claim arising out of or relating to this agreement, or the breach thereof. Additionally, there is no Hawaii statute contrary to the holding in *Prima Paint*. Thus, because the Lees' general allegations were based on fraud in the inducement of the contract as a whole, rather than fraud in the inducement of the arbitration clause, we hold that the claim should be decided first by mediation, and then, if necessary, by arbitration, in accordance with the terms of the DROA contract.

In reaching this conclusion, we emphasize the importance of utilizing alternative methods of dispute resolution in an effort to reduce the growing number of cases that crowd our courts each year. This court has long recognized the strong public policy supporting Hawaii's arbitration statutes.

Affirmed.

If you had a contractual dispute, would you favor using the courts or ADR?

THE CHANGING LANDSCAPE

It may be enlightening to picture the law as a series of overlay maps. The base map for all law is the federal Constitution. Its words, and the values underlying the words, provide a framework into which all other law must fit. Statutory law and its judicial interpretation, followed by common-law precedents, are maps overlaid onto the constitutional base map.

Anyone who reads the federal Constitution can only be amazed at the ambiguity of the words and phrases used to express our most fundamental values. Phrases such as "equal protection," "due process," and right to "bear arms" are notoriously unclear and controversial. One can argue that the words and the values underlying them are often perverted by those who interpret them, courts and citizens alike. For example, until the middle of the twentieth century the statement that all people were created equal was perverted by the Supreme Court's pronouncement that public facilities could be kept racially separate as long as they were equal. The interpretation met the needs of the dominant sector of society. Unfortunately, racially separate facilities were seldom equal. Fortunately, separate but equal and many other perversions of the Constitution have been reinter-preted over time to give meanings more consistent with the true intent of the words and phrases of the constitution.

If one focuses a lens on the part of the maps dealing with real estate law, one sees a similar phenomenon. If you go back 50 years and more to examine the laws dealing with real estate, they were very protective of private property rights, especially of those who had significant investments in property. No doubt one of the prime values of the time was encouraging real estate development. The growing country implemented that value by breaking down new frontiers, generating personal wealth, and building a great nation. The values supported by law were successful.

Our success has led to new values rising up to compete. Today, there is less concern about protecting private investment at all cost. At one time the law was stretched to protect landlords in disputes with tenants. As you will see in later chapters, today there is more balance in protecting the rights of both. The landowner, who at one time could build almost anything on the land as long as it was not a blatant nuisance, must now

continued on next page

conform to zoning laws, laws protecting wildlife, and even laws protecting a neighbor's ability to get sunlight on his or her solar panels. As real estate development and use created greater stress on the earth's natural systems, our values shifted. What lies ahead?

Some years ago law professor Christopher Stone proposed giving a legal right to sue to forests, oceans, rivers, and other natural objects so that they would be protected from destruction or modification by human development. Of course, a human would have to file the suit on its behalf. Does this idea have any merit? Do you see it gaining support from people in the future? What events might precipitate that support? Can real estate developers alter their conduct to avoid this change in the law?

■ KEY TERMS

alternative dispute resolution 15	diversity jurisdiction 11	precedent 5
appellate court 9	judge-made laws 6	statutory law 7
constitutions 4	jurisdiction 9	trial court 8

■ INTERNET RESOURCES

General Real Estate Information

www.lawsource.com/also (sources of U.S. law)

www.uscourts.gov/understand02/content_4_0.html (federal courts)

www.judicial.state.ia.us./students/overview.asp (state court systems)

■ REVIEW AND DISCUSSION QUESTIONS

1. Name the courts in your state having (a) general jurisdiction, (b) limited jurisdiction, and (c) final jurisdiction.

2. (a) Define the doctrine of precedent. (b) Indicate limitations on the use of precedent.

3. During the past 50 years, statutory law has gradually replaced some judge-made or decisional law. Explain the reasons for this.

4. Do you think that the courts' recognition of binding arbitration clauses in contracts will undermine the "right to a day in court"? Explain.

■ CASE PROBLEMS

1. Sorensen, a licensed real estate broker, entered into a listing agreement with Schomas. Sorensen located a buyer who submitted a purchase offer. Schomas refused to accept the offer or to pay Sorensen the commission that was clearly owed. Enraged, Sorensen threatened to "take the case to the United States Supreme Court, if necessary." Explain why Sorensen probably would be unable to do this.

2. Taylor was involved in litigation involving a real estate problem. Taylor's friend Bennett testified in Taylor's behalf at the trial. Bennett's testimony was critical to the outcome of the case. Taylor lost the case and decided to appeal. When Taylor informed Bennett of his intention to appeal, Bennett told him that he could not testify a second time as the experience had drained him emotionally. Taylor told Bennett that it would not be necessary for him to testify again. Explain why.

3. Stanley Beck purchased a remote farm to which he moved with his family. After living there for a time, Beck became disturbed because his children had a long walk to the school bus. The walk was especially dangerous during the winter because there were no sidewalks and the road was often icy. Beck asked an attorney whether the purchase could be rescinded on the grounds of fraud. Beck contended that the seller, knowing Beck had school-age children, should have informed him that the walk to the bus stop could be dangerous in winter.

   The attorney told Beck that, in their state, silence could not be the basis for fraud unless the seller, knowing of a hidden defect in the property that could cause injury, failed to disclose it. The attorney stated that there was no precedent for the proposition that a long walk on an icy road to a school bus is a hidden defect that a seller is bound to reveal. Explain what the attorney meant by *precedent* and why the fact that no precedent existed was significant.

4. Harvey's house burned down. When he demanded payment from his insurer, Allstate, it refused to pay, accusing him of arson. Harvey sued Allstate in Texas state court to recover under his insurance policy. Subsequently, Allstate made a motion to remove the case to a federal district court. Federal law permits a defendant to remove a case from state to federal court, provided the plaintiff could have brought the suit in federal court at the start. What would Allstate have to show in order to remove to federal court? *Harvey v. Allstate Insurance Company*, 243 F.3d 912 (2001).

2

Real and Personal Property

■ PROPERTY

■ *Legal rights that an individual possesses with respect to a thing; rights that are themselves of economic value.*

In traditional legal usage, **property** generally refers to an aggregate, or "bundle," of rights that people have in tangible items. People often refer to the items—the automobile, guitar, or home—as their property; from a legal point of view, however, the items themselves are not significant. What is important are the rights the person has in these items. These rights include the right to use the item, sell it, or even destroy it if the person wishes. In his famous *Commentaries on the Law of England*, Blackstone describes property as an "absolute right, inherent in every Englishman . . . which consists in the free use, enjoyment, and disposal of all his acquisitions, without any control or diminution, save only by the laws of the land." Today, the term *ownership* is often used as a synonym for *property*.

The concept of property is readily understood when related to something tangible like an automobile or land. A person can, however, own something that is related only indirectly to a tangible item. An example would be a lease. The tenant of a commercial building has a right to occupy space. This right is valuable because of the building's existence, but the right itself is intangible. *Property* also is used to refer to rights that people possess independent of anything tangible. Contracts, trademarks, copyrights, and patents are examples. They are all property, as they establish rights that the owner can enjoy, sell, give away, or deny to others.

The protection of property rights is a function of the government. State and federal laws provide guarantees and protections creating and maintaining the bundle of rights that the legal system refers to as *property*. For example, in our society property interests exist in land because numerous laws allow individuals to do certain things with land, such as sell it, dispose of it to their heirs, or exclude others from it. On the other hand, although one's right to vote is important, it is not property. The state provides no aggregate of rights related to a person's right to vote. All that the individual can do is vote or refrain from voting. Whether or not something is a property right has important constitutional implications because the Bill of Rights prohibits government from taking property without due process of law. Thus, in taking property, government must follow legal procedures that safeguard the owner's rights, the property must be taken for public use, and the owner must be compensated adequately.

It is important to understand that property is a dynamic concept that is continually being reshaped to meet new economic and social needs. In the United States today, appreciable legislation and case law are developing that modify traditional property rights, or at least reevaluate them, in relation to civil rights. Many good examples can be found in cases and legislation protecting fundamental interests of minorities.

CASE EXAMPLE

Shelley, an African-American man, purchased real estate from Fitzgerald. The sale violated a recorded restriction on which former owners of this parcel and a number of other owners had agreed. This restriction prohibited occupancy by "any person not of the Caucasian race." Kramer and others who owned real property subject to the restriction sued to restrain Shelley from taking possession and to divest him of title. When the Missouri courts granted the relief requested, the United States Supreme Court reversed. The court held that state courts are prohibited by the equal protection clause of the Constitution from enforcing a private agreement denying a person because of his race the right to own real property. *Shelley v. Kramer*, 334 U.S. 1 (1948).

Although one clearly visible trend in the law is to limit property rights when weighed against civil rights, in other areas property rights have been expanded. In a number of cases, plaintiffs have contended that they have a property interest in their employment or in the facilities necessary to practice a chosen profession and even in their status and reputation. At present the movement of the law in this direction is slow, but the trend is discernible.

Real Property Rights

■   *Ownership or proprietary rights in land and anything permanently affixed to land.*

Legal institutions reflect dominant economic, political, and social values. Laws and the legal system sustain the existing order and are used to attain objectives that society considers important. Throughout the history of England and the United States, land and law have been closely interwoven. In both countries, as well as in most other nations of the Western world, land has been an important form of wealth. In addition, for many hundreds of years in England, not only was land the major source of wealth but the possession of land, even particular tracts of land, determined an individual's social position. Possession or ownership of land also had important political connotations in both England and the United States. For many years in England and in most of the United States, only landowners were permitted to vote.

One result of the historic importance of land is a distinction in the law of English-speaking countries between it and other forms of wealth. Because of land's economic significance, the early common law provided extensive protection to landowners. A landowner ousted from possession could immediately bring an action to recover the land (called an *action in ejectment*). In contrast, the right of an owner of personal property against one who wrongfully took that property was limited to a lawsuit for money (called *damages*). Legal actions such as ejectment that protected the rights of owners in their land were known as *real actions*, and that is the reason land is called **real property** or *real estate*. The lawsuit for money by a person who lost control of something of economic value other than land, usually a movable item, was known as a *personal* *action* because the items involved were personal property. In modern law, as will be discussed later, the distinction between real and personal property continues to be recognized in many areas.

Personal property generally is characterized as being movable, and is normally transferred by a bill of sale. Historically, the items of personal property of importance were tangible things such as cattle, farm equipment, and the tools of a person's trade. Today, many intangible forms of wealth exist. An example would be a franchise. These intangible rights are also personal property. Over the centuries these forms of personal property have expanded, and personal property has become more equivalent to real property as wealth. One result has been a narrowing of the legal distinctions between the two, but differences continue to exist and to influence American law.

Real and Personal Property: Legal Problems

The fact that real and personal property continue to be treated differently in the law of English-speaking countries causes many problems. For example, a deed, the written document transferring ownership of real estate, conveys only real property, separate from personal property. This sometimes results in confusion when a home or business is sold. The potential buyer of a home, an apartment for investment, a factory, or a farm examines the premises from a functional, not a legal, viewpoint. If the real estate is a residence, the buyer is thinking about a place to live, not about the distinction between real and personal property. Items such as the stove, refrigerator, storm windows, and perhaps a bar are functionally related to the reason for the purchase. The buyer understandably considers these items integral parts of the building. At the same time the seller, perhaps having purchased the items separately, often thinks of them as independent of the structure. If the law considers these articles part of the real estate, they pass to the buyer by deed unless specifically excluded by agreement. If the items are deemed personalty and hence not part of the real estate, they are not covered by the deed, and the buyer does not get them.

CASE EXAMPLE

David, by deed, conveyed land to Bessie. A hay barn containing equipment for unloading hay was located on the land. The equipment consisted of a track, hangers to support the track, a carrier, a hay harpoon, two pulleys, and rope. The hangers were bolted to the rafters, and the track was attached to the hangers. David removed the equipment. Bessie demanded that he return it, claiming that it was real estate, as it was a part of the barn. Although a court would find for Bessie if David refused to return the equipment, the problem could have been avoided if David and Bessie had agreed in the contract how the equipment was to be treated.

The distinction between real and personal property is also significant in real estate financing. A debt secured by a mortgage is secured only by the real estate. Personal property is not part of the security. For example, if a bank takes back a mortgage on a motel as security for a debt, the furniture that is integral to successful operation of the business is not covered. Of course, the furniture could also be used as security if designated as such by a separate security agreement.

CASE EXAMPLE

National Bank lent funds to a small manufacturing company and took back a mortgage on realty owned by the company. On the premises was a 2,000-gallon tank set on concrete blocks. The tank was used to store gas and was connected to a garage by lines that ran above ground. The bank was forced to foreclose because the debt was not paid. Both the bank and the company claimed the tank. If the court held the tank to be part of the real estate, the tank could be sold at the foreclosure sale.

Whether an item is real or personal property also raises important insurance, tax, and inheritance questions. For example, when a business acquires or erects buildings, for accounting purposes it may choose to separate out the cost of personal property, like office furniture, from the costs of items that become part of the realty. The personal property can be depreciated as a business expense much more rapidly than real estate can. This process of "cost segregation" can lead to a significant reduction in taxes paid. Sometimes state statutes help provide answers to these questions, but most continue to be settled by case law. Contracts and mortgages should make clear what property the parties intend to be personal property and what they intend to be real property. Sometimes, as in the case that follows, the parties do not have an opportunity to reach an agreement regarding the status of the property. The subject matter is this case and its value may seem trivial by today's standards, but the legal analysis and conclusions are useful in deciding modern cases.

Haslem v. Lockwood
Supreme Court of Connecticut
37 Conn. 500 (1871)

Background. On the evening of April 6, 1869, Haslem employed two men to gather into heaps manure that lay scattered on and along the side of a public road. The men piled the manure into 18 heaps between 6:00 P.M. and 8:00 P.M., and then left without removing them. The manure was made chiefly by horses hitched to posts on the street alongside a Borough of Stamford park. Lockwood discovered the heaps the next morning, and after unsuccessfully trying to find out who made them, removed the heaps around noon. Neither party requested permission from the Borough, from whose land it was scraped, to take the manure. No sign was left on the heaps by Haslem's men. The value of the manure was estimated to be $6. Haslem sued Lockwood for the value of the manure. The trial court ruled for Lockwood.

Decision. The Connecticut Supreme Court reversed the judgment of the trial court and ordered that the plaintiff be given a new trial.

Judge Park. The plaintiff claimed that the manure was personal property which had been abandoned by its owners and became by such abandonment the property of the first person who should take possession of the same, which the plaintiff had done by gathering it into heaps, and that it was not and never had been a part of the real estate of the borough. He further claimed that if it was a part of the real estate, it was taken without committing a trespass, and with the tacit consent of the owners of such real estate, and that thereby it became his personal property.

The defendant claimed that the manure being dropped on and spread out over the surface of the earth was a part of the real estate, and belonged to the owner of the fee, subject to the public easement; and that, unless the heaps became personal property, the plaintiff could not maintain his action. The defendant further claimed that if the manure was always personal estate, or became personal estate after being scraped up into heaps, the plaintiff, by leaving it from eight o'clock in the evening until noon the next day, abandoned all right of possession which he might have had, and could not, therefore, maintain his action.

We think the manure scattered on the ground, under the circumstances of this case, was personal property. The cases referred to by the defendant to show that it was real estate are not in point. The principle of those cases is, that manure made in the usual course of husbandry on a farm is so attached to and connected with the realty that, in the absence of any express stipulation to the contrary, it becomes appurtenant to it. The principle was established for the benefit of agriculture. It found its origin in the fact that it is essential to the successful cultivation of a farm that the manure, produced from the droppings of cattle and swine fed on the products of the farm, and composted with earth and vegetable matter taken from the land, should be used to supply the drain made on the soil in the production of crops, which otherwise would become impoverished and barren; and in the fact that manure so produced is generally regarded by farmers in this country as a part of the realty and has been so treated by landlords and tenants from time immemorial.

But this principle does not apply to the droppings of animals driven by travelers on the highway. The highway is not used, and cannot be used, for the purpose of agriculture. The manure is of no benefit whatsoever to it, but on the contrary is a detriment; and in cities and large villages it becomes a nuisance.

The manure originally belonged to the travelers whose animals dropped it, but it being worthless to them was immediately abandoned; and whether it then became the property of the Borough of Stamford which owned the land on which the manure lay, it is unnecessary to determine; for, if it did, the case finds that the removal of the filth would be an improvement to the borough, and no objection was made by any one to the use that the plaintiff attempted to make of it. At all events, we think the facts of the case show a sufficient right in the plaintiff to the immediate possession of the property as against a mere wrong doer.

The defendant appears before the court in no enviable light. He does not pretend that he had a right to the manure, even when scattered on the highway, superior to that of the plaintiff; but after the plaintiff had changed its original condition and greatly enhanced its value by his labor, he seized and appropriated to his own use the fruits of the plaintiff's outlay, and now seeks immunity from responsibility on the ground that the plaintiff was a wrong doer as well as himself.

It is further claimed that if the plaintiff had a right to the property by virtue of occupancy, he lost the right when he ceased to retain the actual possession of the manure after scraping it into heaps.

We do not question the general doctrine, that where the right by occupancy exists, it exists no longer than the party retains the actual possession of the property, or till he appropriates it to his own use by removing it to some other place. If he leaves the property at the place where it was discovered, and does nothing whatsoever to enhance its value or change its nature, his right by occupancy is unquestionably gone. But the question is, if a party finds property comparatively worthless, as the plaintiff found the property in question, owing to its scattered condition on the highway, and greatly increases its value by his labor and expense, does he lose his right if he leaves it a reasonable time to procure the means to take it away, when such means are necessary for its removal?

A reasonable time for the removal of this manure had not elapsed when the defendant seized and converted it to his own use. The statute regulating the rights of parties in the gathering of seaweed, gives the party who heaps it on a public beach twenty-four hours in which to remove it, and that length of time for the removal of the property we think would not be unreasonable in most cases like the present one.

continued on next page

Judgment is reversed, and a new trial granted.

The horses in the case ate oats and grass and turned them into horse. The manure is the part of oats and grass not made into horse. Would it make more sense to treat the manure as real property because it came from and will return to the land?

Would it make better social sense?

Fixtures

■ *Separately identifiable items that were once personal property but that have become real property generally through annexation to land or buildings.*

Chandeliers, carpeting, electric hot water heaters, and shrubbery are common examples of **fixtures** associated with residential real estate. All these items are personal property while part of the seller's inventory, but when annexed to land or buildings they are generally considered part of the real estate. On a farm, items such as cattle stanchions, water pumps, and fencing would ordinarily be fixtures. Many items associated with industrial or commercial real estate are also classified as fixtures. How would you classify the mirror behind the bar in your favorite restaurant or the overhead track for moving heavy material in a factory? Both could be readily detached without harm to the building, and they appear movable, as is personal property, but they, too, are probably fixtures.

In a residence, the built-in stove, window treatment rods, towel racks, and built-in microwave oven are generally considered to be fixtures. The reason is most homeowners intend that these items become part of the house, the items are actually affixed to the house, and usually the items are part and parcel of any residence. The picture becomes murky when the item is a toaster oven or microwave oven that sits on the kitchen counter, or window curtains that hang on the affixed rods. Generally, homeowners expect to take these items with them when they leave, they are not fastened to the structure of the house, but nevertheless are common to most homes. As a rule, courts would conclude that these items are personalty and do not go to the buyer of the house. There are other items that cause confusion when a house is sold, such as the clothes washer and dryer, the dishwasher, and the refrigerator. If these questions go to courts, as seen in the *Schwend* case that follows, judges will apply the threefold test:

■ What was the intention of the annexing party?

■ Was the item physically attached to the realty?

■ Was the item peculiarly adapted to the use being made of the realty?

Courts will amass the facts presented to them, weigh them, and reach a conclusion. It is risky to let questions of fixtures go to the courts when it is easier and safer to state exactly what items are included in the sale.

The chief test in determining whether an item is a fixture is the intention of the party who attached it to the real estate. Intention will, however, be determined by the manner in which the one who affixed the item acted, not by his or her secret intention. In the case that follows, intention is clearly established by the evidence.

Schwend v. Schwend
Supreme Court of Montana
983 P.2d 988 (1999)

Background. Albert Schwend and Sons, a partnership, was a family ranch with assets consisting of real property and ranch equipment. On the death of the father, Albert, two sons, Marvin and Charles, filed actions to dissolve the partnership. A settlement was reached in which Marvin and Charles received several of the ranch's real property parcels. The remainder of the ranch properties and equipment went to Dan and Les, the two other sons and members of the partnership.

Despite the settlement agreement, part of the ranch's irrigation system came into dispute. The irrigation system consisted of an underground main line to which segments of plastic and aluminum irrigation pipe could be attached at various points. The above-ground pipe can be picked up and moved by one person. Marvin took the pipe and stacked it on his property, called *Jones Place*, for winter storage. Subsequently, Dan and Les removed the above-ground pipe from Marvin's property but did not disturb the underground portion. Marvin and Charles brought a motion in District Court asking it to order that the pipe be returned. The District Court denied the motion, and Marvin and Charles appealed.

Decision. The Montana Supreme Court affirmed the judgment of the District Court.

Justice Trieweiler. Marvin and Charles contend that the District Court erred when it concluded that the irrigation pipe was not a fixture, pursuant to § 70-15-103, MCA. Martin and Charles contend that because the irrigation pipe removed by Dan and Les was affixed to the Jones Place, it was distributed to them as part of the real property by the property settlement agreement, rather than distributed to Dan and Les, as the ranch equipment. Real Property includes: "(1) land; (2) that which is affixed to land; (3) that which is incidental or appurtenant to land; (4) that which is immovable by law." Section 70-15-101, MCA.

Personal property and equipment may become a fixture, permanently attached to the real property, pursuant to § 70-15-103, MCA, which provides: "A thing is deemed to be affixed to land when it is: (1) attached to it by roots, as in the case of trees, vines, or shrubs; (2) imbedded in it, as in the case of walls; (3) permanently resting on it, as in the case of buildings; or (4) permanently attached to what is thus permanent as by means of cement, plaster, nails, bolts, or screws. To determine whether an object has become a fixture or not, we consider the following factors: (1) annexation to the realty, (2) an adaptation to the use to which the realty is devoted and (3) intent that the object become a permanent accession to the land. Of those three, the intent of parties has the most weight and is the controlling factor." Pacific Metal Co. v. Northwestern Bank of Helena (1983).

This Court has never addressed the specific question of whether an irrigation system is a fixture. However, there are several other jurisdictions which have done so, and from our analysis of those cases it is clear that other jurisdictions continue to apply the annexation, adaptation, and intent factors of the fixtures test, with special emphasis on the intent of the person who originally brought the personalty to the property, and to the specific facts of each case.

The Supreme Court of Wyoming addressed a question similar to the issue in this case, in Wyoming State Farm Loan Board v. Farm Credit System Capital Corp. (Wyo. 1988). The Wyoming Court first examined whether real or constructive annexation of the pipe to the land occurred. It concluded that because the pipe was attached to the riser pipes only intermittently during the irrigation season and stored away from the field when not in use, it had never undergone a real annexation. It further concluded that the irrigation pipe was not constructively annexed to the land because it was not a necessary and integral part of the land, nor was it of little or no value if separated from the land.

continued on next page

The majority concluded that the adaptation factor was the weakest part of the fixture by virtue of its "necessity" for continuing to put the land to that use. Finally, the Court concluded that there was no evidence that the appellants intended to make the pipe a fixture, but that there was some evidence that they thought of the pipe as equipment because it was listed in security agreements as after acquired machinery and equipment.

In this case, Les and Dan removed plastic and aluminum irrigation pipe which had been stored on the side of the field for the winter. From our review of the record, the characteristics of the equipment they removed appear to be the most similar to the gated irrigation pipe described in the Wyoming State Farm Loan Board case. There, and here, the equipment at issue was primarily: [P]lastic pipe with gates, or windows on one side that can be opened to regulate water flow onto a field. This pipe comes in lengths of twenty or thirty feet and diameters of six, eight, and ten inches. A farmer or rancher uses the pipe by moving the needed lengths to the field on a special trailer and laying them out end-to-end in the proper location. The pipe is then connected to riser pipes that are permanently attached to water lines buried underground. While the installation of the water mainline and the riser pipes clearly involves substantial earthwork, the gated pipe is specifically designed to be lightweight and portable for use in more than one field. A farmer or rancher using this system needs the gated pipe to irrigate. However, any farmer or rancher with a riser pipe connection could attach the gated pipe and irrigate his field with it. The pipe remains above ground at all times, and it is stored away from the field when not in use.

The clearest cases of annexation are those in which the equipment has some characteristic of permanent physical attachment to the land, such as being buried within the land, or consisting in part of concrete slabs partially buried within the land. Several parties in this case testified that the pipe removed by Les and Dan was portable and easily moveable.

We conclude that because the pipe was attached to the riser pipes only during the irrigation season and stacked when not in use, there was never a real annexation of the pipe to the land. Nor was the pipe constructively annexed to the land, because it was useful apart from the land, as evidenced by Les'[s] testimony that the pipe was used on other ranch properties. It was also easily and readily replaceable with other pipe, as evidenced by the fact that pipe borrowed from a cousin was used in combination with the rest of the irrigation system. Thus the pipe was not annexed to the land.

Nor can we conclude that the irrigation pipe was adapted to the land. The Jones property was irrigated farm land, and its irrigation system was a necessity for the continued use of the land for irrigated crops; however, the pipe at issue was not an integral part of that system, nor was it adapted to the particular ground being farmed in the way that the remainder of the system was.

The pipe was apparently used on other properties, and from this we conclude that there was no objective manifestation of intent to affix the individual lengths of pipe to the Jones property.

We conclude that the plastic irrigation pipe in this case does not meet the definition of a fixture, and we affirm the judgment of the District Court which awarded the pipe to Les and Dan pursuant to the terms of the property settlement agreement.

Affirmed.

The Court makes clear the intent of the annexor is the most important of the three elements. Suppose the pipe was neither annexed to the realty nor adapted to the site, but the annexor's intent clearly was to make it part of the realty. What would be the outcome?

Trade Fixtures

■ *Items annexed to land or buildings by a tenant to be used in the tenant's trade or business.*

We have seen that items of personal property, annexed to realty with the intention that the item become part of the realty, are fixtures. *Fixtures are real estate* and usually may not be removed or treated separately unless the parties agree. It is clear, however, that a business firm leasing real estate would be seriously hampered if this rule applied to items needed to operate a plant or shop effectively. Therefore, the legal system differentiates between *fixtures* and **trade fixtures**, the latter being personalty attached to real estate in order to carry on a trade or business. A tenant may generally remove trade fixtures. Agricultural fixtures have been treated in a similar manner. To remove a trade or agricultural fixture, the tenant must restore the premises to their original condition and remove the trade fixture before the lease terminates.

Allowing tenants to remove trade fixtures has social benefits. It encourages both the use of land and efficiency in business. Tenants are more likely to invest in new and improved equipment if they can remove these items after they have been attached to the realty. Statutes in a number of states establish tenants' rights to remove trade fixtures.

Although the law allows tenants to remove trade fixtures at the end of a lease, even if the lease does not mention this point, parties to a commercial lease should include provisions that express their agreement as to how trade fixtures will be treated when the lease ends. They might agree that the tenant shall not remove items that ordinarily would be trade fixtures. On the other hand, a lease provision stating the tenant's right to remove those items added to carry out the business or trade shows the intention of the parties and lessens possibilities for disagreement and litigation as to whether the items may be removed.

Growing Crops

Traditionally, courts classified growing crops in two categories. An annual crop that was the product of human effort was referred to as **fructus industriales**. This classification included crops such as wheat, corn, oats, cotton, and rice. Crops that were produced on perennial roots, such as trees, bushes, and vines, were categorized as **fructus naturales**. Fructus naturales were crops such as citrus fruits, apples, berries, and grapes. As a general rule, fructus industriales were considered personal property and fructus naturales real property.

Today, in most states, for most purposes the classification of fructus industriales has been broadened considerably. In general, it includes any crop that owes its value to human care and labor. Thus, fruit and berry crops as well as crops such as hay are classified as fructus industriales. In a limited number of states the courts consider the produce of perennial roots fructus industriales, although the trees, vines, and bushes that produce the crop are fructus naturales.

Although these classifications continue to be of importance when a dispute arises involving growing crops, modern courts consider a number of other factors when determining whether a crop is realty or personalty.

One significant factor in some states is the maturity of the crop. The more mature the crop, the more likely courts are to consider it personal property. In addition to maturity, courts often consider factors such as the relationship of the parties, their intentions and the type of transaction. Many present-day legal problems involving growing crops are solved by statutes that individual states have adopted because of the uncertainty of the case law.

One of the most significant of these statutes is the Uniform Commercial Code (UCC), which has been adopted by all states. Article 2 of the UCC deals with the sale of goods. "Goods" under the UCC are always personal property. Furthermore, the UCC defines growing crops as goods, whether they are grown on annual or perennial roots. This definition eliminates the traditional legal distinction between fructus industriales and fructus naturales, at least for UCC purposes. The UCC also states that growing crops become goods if they can be removed without harm at the time buyer and seller contract for their sale, even if they are part of the real estate at the time. Thus, Christmas trees and sod grown on the land become personal property before severance if they are identified as the subject of a contract.

Although statutes such as the UCC bring some certainty to the law, the real estate practitioner should realize that the most effective method of preventing controversy is to have the parties agree how the crops are to be treated. This agreement should then be included in the lease, deed, purchase offer, or other written documentation that covers the transaction.

■ SECURED TRANSACTIONS

> ■   *A transaction in which the parties agree that personal property or fixtures will secure a loan or the purchase of an item on credit.*

Lenders use various types of personal property to secure repayment of loans. Sellers, too, often retain an interest in goods being sold on credit to ensure payment of the purchase price. Secured transactions of this nature are very important to the economy of the United States. They range from relatively minor purchases of appliances and television sets by consumers to extensive financing of inventory and equipment by business firms. These secured transactions frequently involve real estate, inasmuch as fixtures are often used as collateral, or security for the loan. Common examples would be air-conditioning equipment and industrial machinery. Even after these are installed in a building, the credit seller may retain a security interest until the purchase price is paid.

The law pertaining to secured transactions is found in Article 9 of the UCC. Article 9 applies to all personal property and fixture security interests created by agreement. For Article 9 to protect a creditor effectively, both attachment and perfection must occur.

Attachment

■ *The process by which a secured party acquires a security interest in collateral.*

A security interest is not effective between the parties until it has attached to the collateral. Three events must take place for a security interest to attach. Although these events usually occur in the following order, no particular order is required. The security interest attaches when the last event occurs.

1. The debtor and secured party (creditor) agree that a security interest attaches.
2. The secured party (creditor) gives value to the debtor.
3. The debtor has or acquires rights in the collateral.

In most secured transactions, the agreement must be in writing, including an electronic agreement with an electronic signature; however, if the secured party retains possession of the security, an oral agreement is sufficient. The written agreement is known as a *security agreement*. The UCC defines a security agreement as "an agreement which creates or provides for a security interest." In those situations in which the secured party retains possession of the security, the transaction is known as a *pledge*.

Ordinarily, a security agreement is initiated when the secured party supplies a standard form that is to be completed by the borrower or buyer. This form is usually labeled "Security Agreement," but other terms such as "Conditional Sales Contract" are also used. Whatever the form is called, if it includes the necessary information, a security agreement exists under the UCC.

Perfection

■ *The process by which the secured party establishes priority in the collateral over claims of third parties.*

The purpose of **perfection** is to notify third parties of the existence of a security agreement. Under general legal principles, when a third party knows of or has available information as to the existence of a security interest, the third party's rights are subordinate to that security interest. Two principal methods for perfecting a security interest under the UCC are (1) *public filing* of a notice, called a *financing statement*, that such an interest exists and (2) *possession* of the collateral by the secured party. A good example of the latter is the security interest a pawnbroker has in articles of personal property taken as collateral for loans. (This is a pledge, as defined earlier.)

State law must be checked to determine the proper place for filing a financing statement for most items, but the UCC specifically states that to properly perfect a security interest in a fixture, the secured party must file in the office where real estate mortgages are recorded. This *fixture filing* must contain the name of the real property owner and the address of the property.

Sometimes there is a question as to whether an item is a fixture. In this event, the secured party should file twice. The second filing should be made as state law directs for items other than fixtures.

Fixture Filing

■ *A section of the UCC that allows a security interest to persist in goods (personal property) that later become fixtures.*

With few exceptions, a security agreement that has been perfected by filing a financing statement provides the secured creditor with priority over claims of third parties. This sometimes results in problems where fixtures are involved. For example, conflict can occur between a mortgage lender who has a security interest in the real property and a second party who has a security interest in a fixture located on the same real property.

> **CASE EXAMPLE**
>
> Fran's Pizza needed a new oven. One was purchased on credit from Only Oven, Inc., which had Fran sign a security agreement. The oven was installed in the pizza parlor, which was owned by Fran but heavily mortgaged to the Bank of Durango. Despite the new oven, Fran's business was unsuccessful, and she became bankrupt. Only Oven tried to remove the oven, but the bank argued that it was a fixture and should be sold as a part of the building.

Recent changes to the UCC propose a uniform national financing statement form, and permits electronic filing of financing statements. Financing statements must be filed in the jurisdiction where the debtor is located.

Under the current provisions of the UCC, Only Oven would have priority over the Bank of Durango if it had properly perfected its security interest. Perfection requires filing of a financing statement covering the fixture described in the security agreement before the goods become fixtures or within ten days thereafter. The ten-day grace period given to the creditor applies only against prior recorded interests in the real estate. A fixture filing has priority against subsequent interests as of the date of filing. If the Bank of Durango had advanced funds after the manufacturer had installed the oven (i.e., after it had become a fixture), Only Oven would not enjoy a priority unless its security interest were already perfected by a fixture filing.

Fixture security interests are subject to an exception when a construction mortgage is involved.

> **CASE EXAMPLE**
>
> Claude Real Estate is building an office on land that it owns. The construction is being financed by Central Bank, which has agreed to advance funds as the work progresses. The bank has recorded a construction mortgage. Claude purchases plumbing fixtures from Little John, which perfects a security interest by filing a financing statement. Soon after the building is completed, Claude fails, and Little John attempts to remove the fixtures. Central Bank objects, claiming a prior interest on the basis of its construction mortgage.

In this situation, Little John would not be able to remove the plumbing fixtures. The UCC expressly gives priority to a *construction mortgage* recorded before the filing of a fixture security interest. In addition, the UCC provides that no fixture security interest exists in ordinary building materials such as bricks and lumber once they are incorporated into a structure, for obvious reasons.

THE CHANGING LANDSCAPE

It is very easy to fall into the trap of viewing the current state of affairs as immutable. If the common law today states that fixtures require annexation and adaptation to the realty and an intention by an annexor is to make a mobile home part of the real property, it is assumed that this has and always will be the rule. In general, this is not true. Also, in the chapters in this book we focus primarily on narrow legal rules, and seldom try to put the entire body of real estate law into the context of "Does it make sense in the wider world of law and living?"

If you examine property rights created by real estate law in a macro context, it is a mechanism for regulating relations among people by distributing powers to control valued resources. It is a tool for promoting autonomy, security, and privacy. If one *owns* real property, one has a bundle of rights, including the rights to use it, to exclude others from it, and to pass it on to heirs on death. The usual perception is that if one owns land and has normal property rights, a nonconsensual loss of any part of those rights is to be frowned on.

Yet in reality nonconsensual loss of parts of an owner's bundle of rights is fairly common. Since ancient times, nuisance law has prohibited use of real property in a manner that unreasonably interferes with a neighbor's use of land. More recently, governments have curtailed private land use through zoning codes and other land use regulations. Some statutes provide that one cannot exercise the right to exclude others if the exclusion is based on race or other characteristics that constitute legally protected classes. In reality, the bundle of rights can be and often is limited. In short, property rights are dependent on the needs of the time and the effects the exercise of those rights have on others.

Looking down the road, what limits to private property rights do you see coming? Will private landowners be restricted from cutting a forest on their land because the trees are ancient redwoods? In addition to extensive rights, will landowners acquire some responsibilities to others when using their land? For example, will landowners have a responsibility to be stewards of the land when the land has attributes important to the larger community? Will they have to protect those redwoods, preserve an endangered wildflower, save nutrient-rich agricultural soil from erosion, or maintain a scenic vista? Do you think such changes would be for the better?

■ KEY TERMS

■ INTERNET RESOURCES

General Real Estate Information

http://dictionary.law.com/default2.asp?selected=2143+bold=%7c%7c%7c%7c (defines legal terms)

http://straylight.law.cornell.edu/topics/secured_transactions.html (overview secured transactions)

www.answers.com/real%20property (articles on real property topics)

www.realtor.com (home page of the National Association of REALTORS®)

■ REVIEW AND DISCUSSION QUESTIONS

1. Define trade fixture and explain how the law relating to trade fixtures differs from the law relating to fixtures generally.

2. What legal problems might arise because American law distinguishes between real and personal property?

3. Explain the difference between attachment and perfection of a security interest.

4. Discuss the factors courts consider when attempting to determine if an item is a fixture.

■ CASE PROBLEMS

1. Stephens purchased a steel grain-drying bin from B. C. Manufacturing and executed a conditional sales contract and a financing statement. The financing statement was filed in the county clerk's office but not in the office of the registrar for deeds. The bin was placed on a concrete base on property owned by Newman Grove Grain Company. This property was later mortgaged to Battle Creek Bank. The mortgage was foreclosed, and Tillotson purchased the real estate at the foreclosure sale. B. C. Manufacturing sued for the value of the bin. Would B. C. Manufacturing be successful? Discuss. *Tillotson v. Stephens*, 195 Neb. 104, 237 N.W.2d 108 (1975).

2. In November 1991, Charles and Rosa Parker were married. Shortly thereafter they purchased as joint tenants a manufactured home (mobile home). The home was placed on real estate owned solely by Charles. The axles and wheels were removed and it was placed on a permanent cinder-block foundation. Subsequently, Charles died and a dispute arose over whether Rosa or Charles' children by a previous marriage were entitled to the manufactured home. If the home is real property the children will succeed, but if it remains personal property Rosa will keep the home. The state has a statute that states the owner of a mobile home may convert it to real property by attaching it to a permanent foundation owned by the manufactured home's owner, and the if removal of the transporting apparatus makes it impracti-

cal to reconnect it to the manufactured home. The common law of the state uses the traditional three-pronged test of annexation and adaptation to the realty and intent of the annexor. Who is entitled to the mobile home? *In re: Estate of Parker*, 25 SW3d 611 (2000).

3. Stanley King purchased an old Victorian residence from its owner, Helen Floyd. After King took possession of the home he discovered that Floyd had taken drapes that had been tailored to fit an odd-sized window, a window air conditioner, and an antique bathtub. The tub had been replaced by a new tub of excellent quality. The contract of sale signed by both parties did not mention any of these items. Is King entitled to recover damages? Support your answer.

4. Thatcher was interested in buying a business. She finally located a gift shop and agreed to buy it. The business was located in a building that Thatcher leased for three years. To increase the shop's business, she purchased several new display cases. These were attached to the floor. The business was successful; however, the landlord notified Thatcher that the lease would not be renewed. Does Thatcher have the right to remove the display cases? Support your answer.

3

Land, Water, and Air Rights

■ LAND

■ *The solid surface of the earth and the natural elements (water and minerals) associated with it.*

It is the **land**, air, and water in combination that make planet Earth different from other planets, and a place where humans can live. Until recently, the idea that people could exist for any length of time apart from land was inconceivable. Even today, when the idea of human beings living out their lives on islands in space is a possibility, human destiny remains linked with land. Since time immemorial, humans have taken their living directly or indirectly from the land. Because land and people have always been inseparable, the ways in which land has been viewed are as diverse as the world's communities.

Much of the conflict between the Native Americans and Europeans who settled this hemisphere resulted from attitudes toward land. Land, to the Native Americans, was a resource possessed by the tribe. It was not subject to individual ownership. Some native groups in Africa, Australia, and South America hold similar views today. In western Europe during the late Middle Ages, the idea of community ownership in some lands existed, but by the time major colonization occurred in North America, the concept of individual property rights prevailed. Most settlers who came to this country after 1700 wanted to own their own land. Although themes other than individual ownership can be discerned in the way Americans regard land, a majority, especially those living in the United States, continue to consider it a commodity to be owned individually.

Probably the most important factor in viewing land as a commodity is rooted in our economic philosophy. Our pioneer ancestors were individualistic in economic matters. The men and women who wrested arable land from the great forests of the East and from the prairies of the West were acquiring wealth for themselves and their families. They saw land, like any commodity, as something that could be bought and sold or passed on to their children. These people also believed in personal freedom. They regarded private ownership of land as a bulwark against both the intrusion of the state and the inquisitiveness of their neighbors. Finally, traditional economic theory in the Western world includes land as an important factor of production. Land is an important good that, with labor and capital, can be put to work to provide profit for the owner.

Real Estate

■ *Land and its improvements; mines, minerals, and quarries under the land; air and water rights associated with land; and other rights and privileges related to land.*

Although it is a commonly used term, the meaning of *real estate* varies from place to place and from situation to situation. For example, in a number of states, leases are not considered real estate. In some states, the duration of the lease determines whether the tenant's interest is real estate; in other states it does not. In addition, *real estate* sometimes has more than one statutory definition within a single state, some definitions being broader than others. It is difficult to give real estate one definition because the sense in which it is used in everyday speech does not always correspond to its specific legal meaning.

In some contexts the terms *real estate* and *land* are used interchangeably; however, the meaning of *real estate* is generally broader than the meaning of *land*. *Real estate* includes not only land but also improvements on the land, such as a house, a barn, and other structures. Many rights and privileges associated with land are considered to be real estate as well. For example, if one has a right-of-way from his or her own land across the land of a neighbor to reach a road, that right-of-way is real estate and can be sold or transferred as such in many instances. Water rights, mines, minerals, and quarries are also considered real estate for most purposes.

Real property is a term lawyers and judges often use as a synonym for real estate. This chapter discusses real estate, or real property, principles in greater detail.

Land as a Natural Resource

Although the view of land as a commodity has been dominant in the United States, this is but one view of land. A contrasting view of land as a natural *and* social resource that must be preserved for future generations has gained increasing acceptance in recent years. As a result of this trend, vast areas of our nation have been set aside as a public domain, and governments at all levels have adopted legislation to control land use for the benefit of society. Some commentators are urging that the nature of land as essential for human survival necessitates that we cultivate a duty of stewardship toward the land, along with our emphasis on private property rights.

> Stewardship is an essential concept that helps to define appropriate human interaction with the natural world. An ethic of stewardship builds on collaborative approaches; ecosystem integrity; and incentives in such areas as agricultural resources management, sustainable forestry, fisheries restoration, and biodiversity conservation.[1]

Land has become the subject of a large body of law as our nation tries to cope with the problems involved with its use and disposition.

As traditionally defined by courts and commentators, *land* encompasses the surface of the earth, everything above that surface and all that is below. Land has been described as an inverted pyramid extending upward indefinitely into space (air rights) and downward to the center of the earth. Many items such as water, minerals, oil, and gas can be separated from the land. Because these things are both scarce and desirable, they are often severed and treated as independent commodities. The result has been that detailed laws regulating their use have developed throughout the United States. These laws differ from place to place and from time to time as they reflect the needs of people in a particular area during a particular era. Consider how life today would have been affected had the opposite result been reached in the *Thrasher* case.

Thrasher v. City of Atlanta
Supreme Court of Georgia
173 S.E. 817 (1934)

Background. Thrasher lived adjacent to the municipal airport. Though it was the advent of the age of the airplane, the flights across Thrasher's land were low and becoming more frequent. The plaintiff sued the City of Atlanta as the owner of the airport from which the flights originated. The plaintiff contended that the flights constituted an illegal trespass, violated his constitutional rights to private property, and perpetuated a nuisance on him and his family. The portion of the case reproduced here focuses on the issue of the trespass only. The trial court found for the defendant.

Decision. The appellate court affirmed the decision for the defendant.

Justice Bell. The Civil Code (1910), sec. 3617, declares that "the right of an owner of lands extends downward and upward indefinitely." In section 4477 it is stated that "the owner of realty having title downwards and upwards indefinitely, an unlawful interference with his rights, below and above the surface, alike gives him a right of action." These statements as to ownership above the surface are based upon the common-law maxim *cujus est solum ejus est usque ad coelum*—who owns the soil owns also to the sky. These provisions of the code should therefore be construed in the light of the authoritative content of the maxim itself. As a matter of fact, the language of the code that the title to land extends upwards indefinitely would seem to be a limitation upon the **ad coelum doctrine,** indicating by implication that the title will include only such portions of the upper space

as may be seized and appropriated by the owner of the soil. Such a construction of the code provisions would materially minimize the difficulties in the present case; but even if the code was intended to express the ad coelum theory in its entirety, and this we assume in the present case, it remains true that the maxim can have only such legal signification as it brings from the common law.

What is the sky? Who can tell where it begins or define its meaning in terms of the law? When can it be said that a plane is above the sky or below it? How can there be an unqualified tangible right in a thing so indeterminate and elusive? What and where is the res [thing] of which a court may assume jurisdiction in a case involving a private claim of title? Possession is the basis of all ownership and that which man can never possess would seem to be incapable of being owned. In order to recover for a trespass it is necessary to show title or actual possession. The space in the far distance above the earth is in the actual possession of no one, and, being incapable of such possession, title to the land beneath does not necessarily include title to such space. The legal title can hardly extend above an altitude representing the reasonable possibility of man's occupation and dominion, although as respects the realm beyond this the owner of the land may complain of any use tending to diminish the free enjoyment of the soil beneath. The maxim to which reference has been made is a generalization from old cases involving the title to space within the range of actual occupation, and any statement as to title beyond was manifestly a mere dictum. For instance,

continued on next page

a court in dealing with the title to space at a given distance above the earth could make no authoritative decision as to the title at higher altitudes, the latter question not being involved. The common-law cases from which the ad coelum doctrine emanated were limited to facts and conditions close to earth and did not require an adjudication on the title to the mansions in the sky. Accordingly, the maxim imported from the ancient past consists in large measure of dicta, and to that extent cannot be taken as an authentic statement of any law. It follows that the literal terms of the code sections referred to must be discounted or qualified in like measure.

But the space is up there, and the owner of the land has the first claim upon it. If another should capture and possess it, as by erecting a high building with a fixed overhanging structure, this alone will show that the space affected is capable of being possessed, and consequently the owner of the soil beneath the overhanging structure may be entitled to ejectment or to an action for trespass. However,

the pilot of an airplane does not seize and hold the space or stratum of air through which he navigates, and cannot do so. He is merely a transient, and the use to which he applies the ethereal realm does not partake of the nature of occupation in the sense of dominion and ownership. So long as the space through which he moves is beyond the reasonable possibility of possession by the occupant below, he is in free territory—not as every or any man's land, but rather as a sort of "no man's land." As stated above, however, the occupant of the soil is entitled to be free from danger or annoyance by any use of the super-incumbent space, and for any infringement of this right he may apply to the law for appropriate redress or relief.

Affirmed.

Suppose this court and others took the "ad coelum" doctrine seriously. What would have happened to the Age of Aviation?

■ WATER

Water is an element essential to human survival. Without water, land is of little value. Consequently, lands adjacent to water or having water readily available are usually more valuable than other lands. Because of water's importance, disputes sometimes develop between property owners attempting to take advantage of this valuable resource. Efforts to solve these disputes have led to an extensive law of water rights.

Whatever the legal system, several factors appear to have a major influence on water rights law. The most significant is water's scarcity or abundance. The influence of this condition is clearly evident in U.S. law. Another important factor is the type of economy prevailing in the area. Climate and technology are also significant in determining rights of individuals to water. Historically, water rights law in the United States has been concerned mainly with problems of surface water. In more recent times, however, legal questions have also arisen concerning water that flows underground and water that percolates into the subsurface from rain and snow melt. (See Figure 3.1.)

Surface Water

■ *Water upon the surface of the earth in flowing streams and lakes.*

Lakes and streams that are the subject of water rights can be navigable or nonnavigable. A navigable body of water is one that has the capacity to be useful for commerce or travel. The U.S. Constitution allocates power to Congress to regulate navigable

| FIGURE 3.1 | The Water Cycle |

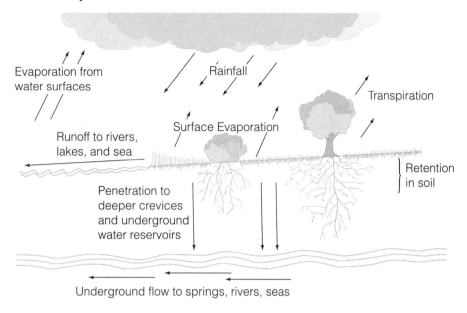

waters, but until Congress acts, the states also may regulate. Although Congress frequently has taken actions that involve navigable waters, it has not, except in limited instances, such as the Clean Water Act, restricted the rights of owners of land along these waterways. As Congress has not asserted all its powers over navigable waters, the power of the state over waters within its jurisdiction is paramount, just as it is for non-navigable waters.

Riparian Land. Riparian lands are those that border on a stream, river, or watercourse. Riparian lands extend away from the stream, including the stream's drainage area or watershed, although all of the drainage area is not necessarily riparian land. The riparian area of the watershed is only that portion under ownership of a person whose property fronts on the waterway. A landowner's property might be in the watershed of a stream, but the landowner is not a riparian owner unless his or her property fronts on the stream.

Littoral Land. Littoral lands are those that border on an ocean, a sea, or a lake. In some states *littoral* applies only to lands that border on a tidal body such as an ocean or a sea. Other states use the term to describe lands that border on lakes as well. In many states the term is not used at all: *riparian* is used to designate lands bordering on lakes, oceans, and seas, as well as those bordering on flowing streams.

In general, the rights of owners of littoral lands are the same as those of the owners of riparian lands. These rights are discussed in the paragraphs that follow. However, at least one difference exists between riparian owners and littoral owners. Littoral owners do not own the land to the water. They own only to the line to which the high tide rises. This is called the *high-water mark*. From the high-water mark to the water (the *low-water mark*), the property is owned by the state. Therefore, the states have the power to control and regulate from the high-water mark to the low-water mark.

Surface Water Rights Theories

At present, two distinct theories of surface water rights exist in the United States. They are *riparianism* and *prior appropriation*. The riparian rights doctrine is the foundation of water rights law in most of the eastern United States. All states east of the Mississippi River follow this theory to some extent, although the theory has been greatly modified by statute in Mississippi. Riparian rights are also the basis of water rights law in a number of states west of the Mississippi River. Generally, these states, such as Minnesota, Arkansas, and Louisiana, have an abundance of water.

Prior appropriation is the basis of water rights law in the more arid regions of the western United States. A number of the western states, however, use both doctrines. This is generally the case in those large states that are arid in certain sections but have sufficient water in others, such as California, Washington, Oregon, Texas, and Oklahoma.

■ **Riparianism (Riparian Rights Eastern States).** *Water rights doctrine based on the idea that all owners of riparian lands are entitled to share equally in the use of water.*

Riparianism has two basic principles. First, ownership of the land bordering on water establishes a right to use the water equally. This right cannot be lost by disuse, but it is clearly limited to use, not ownership.

> **CASE EXAMPLE**
> Kerley owned land on the upper end of a lake. The upper and lower ends of the lake were connected by a narrow neck of water about 18 inches deep. Wolfe, who owned the land on both sides of this passage, erected a fence to prevent rowboats and other small craft from passing through. Kerley, claiming that he was a riparian owner, brought an action to have the fence removed. The court ordered Wolfe to remove the fence as it interfered with the rightful use of the lake by other riparian owners. *Kerley v. Wolfe*, 349 Mich. 350, 84 N.W.2d 748 (1957).

Second, as the abutting landowner has no proprietary right in the water itself, any control over flowing water is lost once it passes the riparian tract. Conflicts concerning right of use that sometimes arise between upstream and downstream owners have generally been solved in one of two ways: natural flow doctrine or reasonable use doctrine.

Natural flow. The riparian rights principle that each riparian owner possesses the right to the ordinary flow of water along his or her land undiminished in quantity and unimpaired in quality is called the **natural flow doctrine**. In a natural flow jurisdiction, a downstream or lower riparian owner can limit the use of water by the upper riparian owner if the upper riparian owner interferes with the stream's natural flow. This doctrine developed in England at a time when the English economy was primarily agrarian. Rainfall was abundant, and even extensive use of water by farm owners did not ordinarily decrease the natural flow of the stream. In the United States, the natural flow principle was adopted in eastern states with abundant rainfall when they were primarily agrarian. The natural flow principle, however, is not conducive to effective use of water in an industrialized economy. Thus, in most states the principle is greatly modified by legislation and judicial decision. It is doubtful that the original principle exists in pure form anywhere in the United States today.

Reasonable use. The riparian rights principle that allows a riparian owner to make reasonable use of the water that flows by his or her land is called the **reasonable use doctrine**. The doctrine of reasonable use dominates water rights law in the riparian states. It permits the riparian owner to make any use of water that does not unreasonably harm a lower riparian owner. The upper owner thus may reduce the natural flow of the stream as long as this does not unreasonably injure the lower owner. The test of reasonable use turns on the circumstances of each case. Many factors are considered, including the intended use, its extent, its duration, and the necessity for it. Other factors that courts consider are the needs of other riparian owners, climate conditions, the nature of the stream, and the customs of the area.

The doctrine of reasonable use thus does not concern itself with impairment of the natural flow or quality of the water but allows full use of the water in any beneficial manner, provided it does not unreasonably interfere with its beneficial use by others. In some states the riparian owner's beneficial use of water is restricted to riparian lands; others permit the use on or off the land if this does not cause damage to other riparian owners.

Most jurisdictions following the reasonable use doctrine have established a hierarchy of uses as a means of determining reasonable use. Domestic uses have priority over agricultural uses, and agricultural uses have priority over industrial and commercial uses.

CASE EXAMPLE

Deetz and Carter owned land along the Cold Creek. The creek followed a natural course through the Carter ranch down to the Deetz property. Cold Creek, although small, had a steady year-round flow, and the Deetz family obtained all its domestic supply of water from it. Carter diverted water from the creek for irrigation and livestock. This action so lowered the level of the creek that the Deetz family could not use the water for domestic purposes. An appellate court affirmed a decree restricting Carter's agricultural use of the water to permit Deetz's domestic use. *Deetz v. Carter*, 232 Cal. App. 2d 851, 43 Cal. Rpr. 321 (1965).

Riparian rights are subordinate to navigation and to regulation by state and federal governments. Where the public has access to navigable streams or lakes, most states permit the use of these waters without obstruction or restriction by abutting landowners.

■ **Prior Appropriation (Western States).** *A water rights doctrine giving primary rights to the first users of water.*

The doctrine of riparianism is not suited to the conditions in the arid states of the West, especially where irrigation is necessary. In these states the principle of prior appropriation developed. In general, a system of **prior appropriation** creates a superior right in the person who is the first to use a body of water for economic purposes. The recording of a permit may be needed to establish this priority.

Prior appropriation was originally based on custom and necessity and eventually became a part of the positive law. Today, prior appropriation is recognized in either the constitutions or statutes of all the western states. Several of these states have rejected riparian rights completely. Colorado was the leader in this move, and absolute rejection of riparianism is referred to as the *Colorado doctrine*. California and other states with areas of abundant water combine riparian rights with prior appropriation principles.

CASE EXAMPLE

Hunter was the first settler in a valley in Washington. A sizable creek flowed through the valley, but Hunter's land was not on the creek. Sogle settled in the valley shortly after Hunter. In 1882, the two began construction of an irrigation ditch from the creek to Sogle's land. Later the ditch was to be extended to Hunter's land, but the two had a dispute and the ditch was not extended.

In 1883, Hunter began to construct his own ditch. This ditch was finally completed in 1885. In litigation during the 1920s involving conflicting claims to water rights from the creek, the court held that owners with title through Sogle had superior rights to those holding title through Hunter. The court also held that Hunter's claim commenced from 1883, when he started his own ditch. It ruled that the time of diversion relates back to the beginning of work when the work has been pursued with reasonable diligence. *Hunter Land Co. v. Laungenour*, 140 Wash. 558, 250 P. 41 (1926).

Beneficial use. The right of prior appropriation is limited to the extent that the water can be used beneficially. However, once an appropriator has established priority, the right to have water exists except for changes that are the result of natural causes. Like the riparian system, prior appropriation does not create title but merely invests a right to use the water.

Generally, **beneficial use** is construed liberally, and ordinarily one beneficial use is not preferred over others. There may, however, be constitutional or statutory guidelines for determining preferential uses. Where such guidelines exist, domestic use is invariably preferred. A change of beneficial use is permissible but cannot be used as an excuse for enlarging an appropriation.

In addition to beneficial use, the applicant for a permit must

- establish that the water is subject to appropriation;
- show that it can be taken without injury to others;
- actually divert water by means of an artificial structure; or
- apply the water to a beneficial use within a reasonable time.

Statutory Permit Systems

The prior appropriation systems of the western states evolved through local customs and regulations. As population increased, states replaced local regulations and common-law rules with comprehensive state legislation. This legislation, although based on the prior appropriation principle, treats water resources as a public trust. Today in the West, state agencies allocate water resources through permit systems that attempt to ensure the orderly distribution of water so that the public interest is served.

Statutory permit systems require that a person seeking to obtain unappropriated water file an application for a permit with a state agency. The application includes the information necessary to determine whether granting the permit is in the public interest. Notice of the application is provided to the public; people who object to granting the permit have an opportunity to present their arguments at a public hearing.

Evidence at the hearing is provided by a state official, often the state engineer, who has reviewed the facts stated in the application. Objectors also have a right to present their case against issuing the permit. All state statutes provide for judicial review of the agency's determination.

A number of eastern states have also adopted statutory permit systems. Permit systems in the eastern states limit the rights of riparian owners. These systems are based on the riparian principle of reasonable use of water. Administrative officials who issue permits consider factors such as the purpose of the use, the suitability of the use to the watercourse or lake, and the harm the use might cause as well as its economic and social values. The future development of real estate in the East will be increasingly affected by permit systems.

Subterranean Water

Subterranean water is an important resource in many areas of the United States. In recent years litigation involving subterranean water has increased. One reason is that methods for obtaining it have improved. Another is that population has expanded in many areas of the country that lack adequate supplies of surface water. This has led to increased dependence on subterranean waters in these areas. Subterranean water is divided into two classes: percolating waters and underground streams.

■ **Percolating Waters.** *Water that passes through the ground, not flowing in a clearly defined underground stream or supplied by streams flowing on the surface.*

Percolating waters may be rainwater infiltrating the soil or water from a stream that has seeped or oozed from the streambed and is no longer part of the flow. Percolating waters include underground lakes, artesian basins, and veins and rivulets that flow in a course not discoverable from the surface without excavation.

Percolating waters are involved in more legal disputes than underground streams. The reason is that underground streams are difficult to identify as such, and courts in many states presume that the water is percolating unless it can be shown to flow in a clearly defined channel.

Common-Law Rule. In the traditional English common law of subterranean water rights, percolating waters belong absolutely to the owner of the land in which they are found. This traditional English rule is followed in many areas of the United States. Where this common-law rule is followed, the landowner may deal with percolating water without regard to the manner in which his or her actions affect others. For example, the landowner may divert the percolating waters completely, to the detriment of adjoining landowners. Conversely, if an owner does something on his or her property that inhibits the drainage of percolating waters, he or she is not responsible for damage caused to neighbors by the backup.

Reasonable Use Rule. Because of injustices resulting from the application of the common-law rule, a number of state courts and legislatures have modified it. The most common modification is the substitution of a rule based on reasonable use. This rule has been recognized in states as diverse as Florida, Minnesota, New Jersey, and Washington.

According to this rule, each owner of land has the right to use the percolating waters to fulfill the reasonable needs and necessities of the land.

> **CASE EXAMPLE**
>
> The City of Shawnee purchased 20 acres of land about eight miles from the city. It drilled 12 wells on the tract and transported the water in pipelines to the city. This action caused wells on farms to dry up, and the residents sought an injunction. The trial court refused to grant the injunction. Upon appeal relief was granted, the appellate court stating "the rule of reasonable use is that each landowner is restricted to a reasonable . . . use of his own property, in view of the similar rights of others." *Canada v. City of Shawnee*, 179 Okla. 53, 64 P.2d 694 (1937).

Reasonable use does not prevent the proper use of percolating waters by landowners in manufacturing or agriculture. The landowner is immune from liability to the extent that the use of the water was reasonably necessary in connection with the use or improvement of the land. The reasonable use rule does prohibit, as the previous case example illustrates, the withdrawal of percolating waters for distribution or sale for uses not connected with property ownership if this use damages neighboring owners.

Correlative rights doctrine. California courts have rejected both the common-law and reasonable use rules as they apply to percolating waters. Instead, these courts have adopted a doctrine that requires that landowners share percolating waters in proportion to their ownership of the surface area. A property owner may not extract more than his or her share even if the water is being used beneficially on the land. This **correlative rights doctrine**, as it is known, is similar to that applied by some states to the extraction of oil and gas. However, because the correlative rights doctrine is hard to apply, it has not been accepted outside California. The following case illustrates the seriousness of water shortage in some areas of the West, and offers one possible approach for dealing with it.

◼ **Underground Streams.** *Subterranean waters that flow in a clearly defined channel discoverable from the earth's surface.*

Water rights in subterranean streams are relatively less important than those involving percolating waters, for the two reasons previously mentioned. First, establishing that an underground stream exists is difficult. The person asserting that water is flowing in an underground stream must establish *from the surface* the direction and course of the stream and that the stream has a definite bed, bank, and current. Excavation to prove this is not permitted. Second, the courts in most cases presume that subterranean water is percolating water.

Legal disputes involving underground streams are ordinarily solved by applying the surface water law of the jurisdiction. If the state applies riparian rights to surface water problems, riparian rights will be applied to underground streams. When prior appropriation is the rule for surface water, it will be applied to underground streams as well.

■ MINERAL RIGHTS

■ *The right to extract minerals from under the land, which may be legally assigned to or owned by someone other than the surface owner.*

The common law envisioned the surface owner's rights as extending upward indefinitely into the sky and downward to the center of the earth. Until the industrial revolution, this definition was adequate to solve most legal questions. Except for a limited number of metals such as gold and silver, minerals were not of great concern to society. Consequently, problems involving subsurface rights were rare. The industrial and technological revolutions changed this situation; the demand expanded for many minerals found below the surface. This led to an increase in the value of these minerals and of the subsurface in which they were found.

Early industrialization depended on coal as a source of energy. Metals such as iron, copper, tin, and lead also contributed to commercial growth. Technological developments of the 20th century have further increased dependence on these and other minerals as well as on gas and oil. As these resources became more valuable, real property law adapted to provide solutions for legal problems created by their increased use.

Land was recognized as a commodity that could be divided horizontally for the purposes of ownership. One person could own the surface, while others had rights in the subsurface. An owner could grant the right to extract minerals, lease land with the right to take minerals, or convey title to the subsurface in which valuable resources were located. U.S. law clearly allows a surface estate and one or more subsurface estates to be carved separately out of a single tract and held in entirely separate ownership.

Acquisition Of Mineral Rights

Mineral rights may be acquired by four different means: (1) mineral deed, (2) mineral reservation, (3) mineral lease, and (4) mineral rights option.

Mineral Deed. A *mineral deed* is similar to a deed used to transfer title to surface estates, which is discussed in Chapter 16. For example, Daniels conveys rights to the minerals on her tract of land to Deep Hole Mining Co., reserving to herself rights to the surface lands. Although the mineral deed transfers title to only mineral rights, the laws relating to the two, mineral rights and surface estates, have many of the same features. The person acquiring mineral rights by deed ordinarily acquires absolute title, just as one would who acquired a surface estate. The deed grants in express terms a mineral estate, describing the size and kinds of minerals acquired. The deed or other document conveying the mineral rights should also grant all rights necessary to conduct a mining operation. These would include rights related to access, development, processing, and transportation.

Mineral Reservation. Absolute title to mineral rights is often acquired by a *mineral reservation* in a deed. In this situation the owner, on disposing of the surface, retains the mineral rights. In each instance, the grant or the reservation, the owner of the mineral rights has an interest that can be conveyed without regard to surface ownership.

Mineral Lease. Mineral rights are often acquired by *mineral lease*. The lessee obtains an exclusive right to carry out mining operations and title to the ore. Unlike the absolute sale of mineral rights, the lessor usually retains a present or future right in the mineral estate. In a lease arrangement, the owner of the property is compensated by royalty payments. These payments are based on a fixed percentage of the value of extracted minerals. A mineral lease should contain provisions setting forth the duration of the lease, renewal rights of the lessee, any rights to suspend lease provisions, and responsibilities of the lessee relative to the surface condition of the property.

Mineral Rights Option. A *mineral rights option* provides the holder, usually a mining company, with the right to explore the property for the presence of minerals. The agreement establishes a period of time within which the exploration must take place. Before the period ends, the mining company must decide whether to lease or purchase the land at the price stated in the option.

■ OWNERSHIP OF OIL AND GAS

During the latter half of the twentieth century, the U.S. began to rely very heavily on oil as the primary source of energy to fuel its growing economy. The use of oil led to large increases in unwanted by-products being emitted into the atmosphere in the form of sulfur dioxide, nitrous oxides, carbon dioxide, and particulate matter. These by-products were identified as creating major health and environmental problems. Despite these problems, consumption of oil has remained high. Natural gas, which is environmentally cleaner, has begun in part to replace oil. The tables on the facing page illustrate the changing consumption levels of these two natural resources.

U.S. courts have not been consistent in their treatment of the nature of the landowner's interest in oil and gas under the surface. (See Tables 3.1 and 3.2.) Some courts have attempted to solve legal disputes involving oil and gas ownership by applying principles developed in cases involving ownership and mining of solid minerals. The theory that evolved is known as the *ownership theory*. Other courts recognized that oil and gas migrate under the ground from high-pressure to low-pressure areas. These courts applied rules similar to those applied to questions involving the ownership of wild animals and migratory birds. This theory is called the *nonownership theory*. A discussion of the two theories follows.

Ownership Theory

■ *The theory under which oil and gas are minerals and are therefore as subject to absolute ownership as coal or any other solid mineral.*

"Absolute" is the key to this theory. In fact, the term *absolute* is often used in place of *ownership*. The **ownership theory** is not applicable logically to gas and oil because they are migratory within the earth. However, many states apparently have adopted this theory. In addition to Texas (see the following Case Example), states following this

TABLE 3.1	Annual Consumption and Production of Petroleum in the United States		
Year	Consumption (millions of barrels)	Domestic Production (millions of barrels)	Imports as percent of consumption (%)
1920	434	443	2
1930	862	898	4
1940	1,285	1,353	5
1950	2,375	1,974	17
1960	3,611	2,575	29
1970	3,365	3,517	34
1974	5,900	3,500	40
1980	6,250	3,500	45
1990	6,500	3,400	48
2000	6,900	3,400	51

Source: Dorf, Richard C., *Technology, Humans, and Society: Toward a Sustainable World* (San Diego, Calif.: Academic Press, 2001).

TABLE 3.2	Natural Gas Consumption in the United States, 1920–2020	
Year	Consumption (millions of cubic feet)	Consumption (EJ)*
1920	0.8	0.9
1940	2.7	3.0
1960	12.8	14.0
1980	20.0	21.8
2000	22.0	24.0
2020	30.0†	32.7†

*Exajoules = EJ 10^{18}J; I cubic foot of natural gas = 1.09 MJ.

†Projected.

Source: Dorf, Richard C., *Technology, Humans, and Society: Toward a Sustainable World* (San Diego, Calif.: Academic Press, 2001).

principle include Arkansas, Colorado, Kansas, Pennsylvania, Tennessee, and West Virginia.

CASE EXAMPLE

S. R. Hill executed a lease of oil and gas rights to Mid-Kansas Oil and Gas Co. The county assessed a tax against the company based on the lease. At the time, no oil or gas had been taken from the ground. The company argued that it could not be taxed because oil and gas in place cannot be owned. This argument was based on the premise that, until oil or gas is brought to the surface, owners of adjacent land may lawfully appropriate the oil or gas.

The question of tax liability was decided in favor of the county. The court stated: "[G]as and oil in place are minerals and realty, subject to ownership, severance, and sale while embedded in the sands or rocks beneath the earth's surface, in like manner and to the same extent as coal or any other mineral." *Stephens County vs. Mid-Kansas Oil and Gas Co.*, 113 Tex. 160, 254 S.W. 290(1923).

Under the ownership theory, the landowner may sever oil and gas by deed just as he or she could sever solid minerals or a portion of the surface itself. The person who acquires the oil or gas gets the same property rights that are acquired when buying a lot on the surface.

Nonownership Theory

■ *The theory that oil and gas are not the subject of ownership because of their migratory nature.*

Under this theory, the landowner has no ownership of oil and gas in place. Each landowner has an exclusive right to drill on the land and becomes the owner when the oil is brought to the surface. The right can be transferred by sale or otherwise. Although the right to search for oil and gas is an interest in land, it is not real property. Some states by statute attribute to this interest many rules applying to real property. Ohio, Louisiana, New York, Alabama, Indiana, and Kentucky are among the states in which courts generally adhere to the nonownership theory.

Although the nature of oil and gas ownership differs under these two theories, many significant aspects of oil and gas law are the same under both. For example, although drilling near the boundary line of one's land in most states is not an illegal interference with the rights of owners of adjoining land, a slanted well that goes under the surface of another's land is a **trespass.** Under both theories, government has the power to regulate operating and production practices, waste is not permitted, and no driller may unreasonably injure the reservoir. Additionally, the important *rule of capture* is recognized under both.

Rule Of Capture

■ *The rule that states that the owner of the surface has the right to appropriate all oil and gas from wells on his or her land, including oil and gas that have migrated from the land of another.*

Whether a jurisdiction recognizes the ownership or the nonownership theory, as oil and gas migrate under the ground, the person whose wells produce the oil and gas owns it. This principle is applied in jurisdictions accepting the ownership doctrine, even though oil brought to the surface does not always originate beneath the land of the driller. Similarly, ownership of oil and gas that migrate away from the surface owner's lands is lost. The **rule of capture** is a logical approach to ownership of oil and gas. It is impossible to distinguish oil that has seeped from under the land of another from that originally under the surface on which the well is located.

CASE EXAMPLE

Hastings owned 165 acres of land in northern Ohio. The Ohio Oil Co. owned oil and gas rights in several large parcels of land partially surrounding Hastings's acreage. Although the company had ample space to locate wells elsewhere, it drilled several wells at 400-foot intervals 25 feet from the Hastings property line. Hastings sought an injunction prohibiting the company from operating oil wells at any point within 200 feet of Hastings's farm. He argued that much of the oil produced from the company's wells percolated from under his land. Ohio courts refused to grant the injunction, thus recognizing the rule of capture. *Kelley v. The Ohio Oil Co.*, 57 Ohio St. 317 (1897).

The rule of capture allows each landowner to appropriate oil and gas produced by all wells on his or her property. Early cases even permitted the wasteful disposal of whatever these wells produced. In some states an operator may increase flow from wells by pumping, although this practice draws oil from adjoining land. The only protection available to a neighbor is to drill and pump on his or her own land. The following case discusses the rights of parties to dispose of the by-product of a gas storage facility.

Boudreaux v. Jefferson Island Storage & Hub
Fifth Circuit Court of Appeals
255 F. 3d 271 (2001)

Background. Jefferson Island operates an underground gas storage facility. It was granted the requisite permits by the Louisiana Department of Natural Resources to create two underground storage caverns by injecting fresh water into a layer of salt over 5,000 feet beneath the surface, hollowing out several salt caverns. These operations produced saltwater as a by-product that Jefferson Island disposed with by injecting it into the underground "saltwater sea" a mile below the land surface. Boudreaux, a neighboring landowner, sued Jefferson Island claiming its operations trespassed on their land. The Boudreaux plaintiffs contended that the saltwater by-product from Jefferson Island's operations migrated onto their land, precluding Boudreaux from possible future injections of saltwater into the ground without having to trespass on its neighbors. The trial court found for Jefferson Island.

Decision. The Circuit Court affirmed the lower court's decision.

Judge Jolly. We hold that these facts do not constitute a trespass under Louisiana law. In Louisiana, a trespass is "an unlawful physical invasion" upon the property of another. Assuming saltwater usually migrated beneath the Boudreaux plaintiffs' property, the question is whether Jefferson Island's saltwater injection was "unlawful" under Louisiana law. Jefferson Island contends that its actions were in accordance with state and federal law, and therefore not unlawful. In *Nunez v. Wainoco Oil & Gas Co.*, the defendant drilled a well on property adjacent to Nunez's property, and the well extended under the plantiff's property two miles beneath the surface. Both parcels of land were included within a "drilling unit" created by the Louisiana Conservation Commission. The *Nunez* court held that the plaintiff's trespass claim was not actionable because the process of unitization superseded individual property rights to establish a common interest in the hydrocarbon deposit.

continued on next page

Judge Mentz applied *Nunez*'s rationale to hold that migrated saltwater, disposed of pursuant to the authority of the State of Louisiana, cannot constitute a legally actionable trespass. Although *Nunez*'s specific holding was that no legally actionable trespass occurs "when a unit has been created by order of the [State]," the court did repeatedly defer to the "important state interest in developing its resources fully and efficiently." Louisiana's natural resources conservation law gives the Commissioner of Conservation the "authority over all persons and property necessary to enforce effectively the provisions of this Chapter and all other laws relating to the conservation of oil and gas." Here, Jefferson Island was granted authorization by the Department of Conservation to drill its saltwater disposal wells. Under these circumstances, the district court properly followed in finding no trespass claim under the facts of this case.

As a final point, we should observe that, despite the Louisiana Supreme Court's rejection of the particular trespass claims in *Nunez*, a plaintiff can still recover if he can show that his property was actually damaged. However, no evidence of any measurable damages or inconvenience exists in this case. If saltwater injected by Jefferson Island did migrate beneath the Boudreaux plaintiffs' property a mile underground, that fluid did nothing more than displace existing saltwater and in no way affected the use or enjoyment of the land.

Affirmed.

Is there any way that the actions of Jefferson Island could have interfered with the "use and enjoyment of the land" by Boudreaux?

State Statutes

During the past 25 years, court opinions and statutes in a number of states have extended the rights of all landowners to share in a common source of oil and gas. Waste is prohibited, and each landowner is permitted a reasonable opportunity to obtain a just and equitable share of the oil or gas in the pool. This is known as the *doctrine of correlative rights*. The gas under the ground may go wherever it will, but an operator may not draw off gas from a neighbor's land in a manner that will unnecessarily deplete a common pool.

A few states have adopted legislation defining the amount of land that must surround a well or requiring a specific distance between wells. These are known as *spacing statutes*. Their purpose is to prevent waste and to give each surface owner an opportunity to take from the common pool.

Other states attempt to control production so that each owner has a reasonable opportunity to recover a fair share of the oil and gas under his or her tract by pooling or prorating the allowable production of oil. Extensive regulation by the state is a fact of life where oil is involved.

■ AIR RIGHTS

Until recently, the traditional theory that whoever owns the soil owns to the heavens (the **ad coelum doctrine**) was sufficient to solve most disputes involving invasion of airspace. Airspace problems, which usually concerned overhanging branches, bushes, or eaves, were important to the parties but of little significance to society. With the advent of the airplane as a major means of transportation, courts and legislative bodies had to reconsider the old concept of absolute control of airspace. The early English rule that airspace was an appurtenance to land, giving absolute and exclusive right to the owner "to the highest heavens," was repudiated. In general, the courts recognize that the public interest in efficient transportation outweighs any theoretical trespass in airspace. As long as air flight does not interfere with the owner's right to the effective use of the space above his or her land, airplanes passing through this space are not trespassing. In brief, a landowner's exclusive domain extends at least to a height that makes it possible for the land to be used in a reasonable manner. To this extent the owner of the surface has absolute ownership of the space above his or her land.

Recently some important developments in real estate have been possible because the ownership of airspace may be separated from ownership of the surface. As population has expanded, investors have turned to space above land to satisfy both commercial and residential needs. When an individual purchases a highrise condominium, that person is acquiring title to airspace. In metropolitan areas such as New York City and Chicago, railroads owning downtown property have separately conveyed airspace above the tracks to be used for commercial buildings. The purchaser acquires air rights above the area needed by the railroad for its trains and a surface easement sufficient to support construction and facilities. As interest has grown in recent years in alternative, renewable sources of energy, questions arose regarding air rights to sunlight and to wind. The following case illustrates the point.

Prah v. Maretti
Supreme Court of Wisconsin
321 N.W.2d 182 (Wis. 1982)

Background. Glenn Prah constructed a house in a subdivision, installing a solar system, including roof collectors, to supply energy to heat his house and water. Later, Richard Maretti purchased an adjoining lot for the purpose of building a house and acquired all the requisite government approvals to commence construction. Prah requested that Maretti move his proposed house further south on the lot than he planned so that it would not shade Prah's solar panels. Maretti refused the request and commenced construction.

Prah sued Maretti claiming that he was entitled to unrestricted access to the sun for solar power under the doctrine of private nuisance and sought to enjoin construction. Maretti moved for summary judgment for failure to state a cause of action. The trial court granted the motion for summary judgment.

Decision. The Wisconsin Supreme Court reversed the trial court holding that Prah had stated a valid claim for relief and should be granted a trial to prove the claim.

Justice Abrahamson. This state has long recognized that an owner of land does not have an absolute or unlimited right to use the land in a way which injures the rights of others. The rights of neighboring landowners are relative; the uses by one must not unreasonably impair the uses or enjoyment of the other. When one landowner's use of his or her property unreasonably interferes with another's enjoyment of his or her property, that use is said to be a private nuisance.

The private nuisance doctrine has traditionally been employed in this state to balance the conflict-
continued on next page

ing rights of landowners and this court has recently adopted the analysis of private nuisance set forth in the Restatement (Second) of Torts. The Restatement defines private nuisance as "a nontrespassory invasion of another's interest in the private use and enjoyment of land." The phrase "interest in the private use and enjoyment of land" is broadly defined to include any disturbance of the enjoyment of property.

Although the defendant's obstruction of the plaintiff's access to sunlight appears to fall within the Restatement's broad concept of a private nuisance as a nontrespassory invasion of another's interest in the private use and enjoyment of land, the defendant asserts that he has a right to develop his property in compliance with the statutes, ordinances and private covenants without regard to the effect of such development upon the plaintiff's access to sunlight. In essence, the defendant is asking this court to hold that the private nuisance doctrine is not applicable in the instant case and that his right to develop his land is a right which is per se superior to his neighbor's interest in access to sunlight. This position is expressed in the maxim, "cujus est solum, ejus est usque ad coelum et ad infernos," that is, the owner of land owns up to the sky and down to the center of the earth. The rights of the surface owner are, however, not unlimited.

The defendant is not completely correct in asserting that the common law did not protect a landowner's access to sunlight across adjoining property. At English common law a landowner could acquire a right to receive sunlight across adjoining land by both express agreement and under the judge-made doctrine of "ancient lights." Under the doctrine of ancient lights if the landowner had received sunlight across adjoining property for a specified period of time the landowner was entitled to continue to receive unobstructed access to sunlight across the adjoining property. Under the doctrine the landowner . . . could prevent the adjoining landowner from obstructing access to light.

Although American courts have not been as receptive to protecting a landowner's access to sunlight as the English courts, American courts have afforded some protection to a landowner's interest in access to sunlight. American courts honor express easements to sunlight. American courts initially enforced the English common law doctrine of ancient lights, but later every state which considered the doctrine repudiated it as inconsistent with the needs of a developing country. Indeed, for just that reason this court concluded that an easement to light and air over adjacent property could not be created or acquired and has been unwilling to recognize such an easement.

This court's reluctance in the nineteenth and early part of the twentieth century to provide broader protection for a landowner's access to sunlight was premised on three policy considerations. First, the right of landowners to use their property as they wished, as long as they did not cause physical damage to a neighbor, was jealously guarded.

Second, sunlight was valued only for aesthetic enjoyment or as illumination. Since artificial light could be used for illumination, loss of sunlight was at most a personal annoyance which was given little, if any, weight by society.

Third, society had a significant interest in not restricting or impeding land development. This court repeatedly emphasized that in the growth period of the nineteenth and early twentieth centuries change is to be expected and is essential to property and that recognition of a right to sunlight would hinder property development.

Considering these three policies, this court concluded that in the absence of an express agreement granting access to sunlight, a landowner's obstruction of another's access to sunlight was not actionable. These three policies are no longer fully accepted or applicable. They reflect factual circumstances and social priorities that are now obsolete.

First, society has increasingly regulated the use of land by the landowner for the general welfare.

Second, access to sunlight has taken on a new significance in recent years. In this case, the plaintiff seeks to protect access to sunlight, not for aesthetic reasons or as a source of illumination but as a source of energy. Access to sunlight as an energy source is of significance both to the landowner who invests in solar collectors and to a society which has an interest in developing alternative sources of energy.

Third, the policy of favoring unhindered private development in an expanding economy is no longer in harmony with the realities of our society. The need for easy and rapid development is not as great today as it once was, while our perception of the value of sunlight as a source of energy has increased significantly.

Courts should not implement obsolete policies that have lost their vigor over the course of the years. The law of private nuisance is better suited to resolve landowners' disputes about property development in the 1980s than is a rigid rule which does not recognize a landowner's interest in access to sunlight. "What is regarded in law as constituting a nuisance in modern times would no doubt have been tolerated without question in former times."

Yet the defendant would have us ignore the flexible private nuisance law as a means of resolving the dispute between the landowners in this case and would have us adopt an approach favoring the unrestricted development of land and of applying a rigid and inflexible rule protecting his right to build on his land and disregarding any interest of the plaintiff in the use and enjoyment of his land. This we refuse to do.

Private nuisance law, the law traditionally used to adjudicate conflicts between private landowners, has the flexibility to protect both a landowner's right of access to sunlight and other landowner's right to develop land. Private nuisance law is better suited to regulate access to sunlight in modern society and is more in harmony with legislative policy and the prior decisions of this court than is an inflexible doctrine of non-recognition of any interest in access to sunlight across adjoining land.

We therefore hold that private nuisance law, that is, the reasonable use doctrine as set forth in the restatement, is applicable to the instant case. Recognition of a nuisance claim for unreasonable obstruction of access to sunlight will not prevent land development or unduly hinder the use of adjoining land. It will promote the reasonable use and enjoyment of land in a manner suitable to the 1980s. That obstruction of access to light might be found to constitute a nuisance in certain circumstances does not mean that it will be or must be found to constitute a nuisance under all circumstances. The result in each case depends on whether the conduct complained of is unreasonable.

We do not determine whether the plaintiff in this case is entitled to relief. In order to be entitled to relief the plaintiff must prove the elements required to establish actionable nuisance, and the conduct of the defendant herein must be judged by the reasonable use doctrine.

Reversed.

Given the reasoning of the court, can we state with confidence that the right to access to sunlight is permanently settled in Wisconsin?

Who Owns The Sky Anyway? *For a fascinating read, see a book by that title written by Peter Barnes (Island Press, 2001).*

The Historic Preservation section in Chapter 25 discusses another aspect of air rights. Transferable development rights have been used by some communities to allow air rights to be traded between nearby landowners to achieve the social goal of historic preservation or some similar goal.

■ COMMON-LAW LIMITATIONS

There are limitations created by the common law on the rights of owners to unrestrictively use their land. Such common-law limitations are imposed by the law for the benefit of surrounding landholders.

Nuisance

■ *An unreasonable interference by one party with another's use or enjoyment of his or her land.*

The notion of **nuisance** is an ancient creation to protect landowners from unfettered and wrongful use of land by a neighbor. It does not require a physical invasion of the complainant's land, as does trespass. Such things as noise, dust, vibration, and odors may constitute a nuisance. A party who is victimized by a nuisance will be able to get compensatory damages and may be able to enjoin the nuisance. Most states, however, will grant an injunction only after balancing the equities between the parties and determining that the benefit of the injunction will outweigh the ensuing detriment to the perpetrator of the nuisance. As a result of this balancing process, injunctions are not readily available to small landowners complaining about a nuisance created by a large industrial or commercial facility. For instance, in a case entitled *Boomer v. Atlantic Cement Co.*, 26 N.Y.2d 219, 257 N.E.2d 870 (1970), New York's highest court was unwilling to enjoin the operation of the $45-million plant, though admitting that there was a substantial nuisance to several nearby landowners. Prior to this case, New York had been more liberal than most states in granting injunctions in nuisance cases.

Trespass

■ *A wrongful, physical invasion of the property of another.*

A common-law remedy may be available to the landowner to put a stop to physical encroachments, whether they occur on the land's surface, in the air above, or on the ground beneath.

Actual damages need not be shown to recover for a trespass to land, but as a practical matter the landowner is likely to get only nominal damages when he or she does not actually show loss.

■ NOTE

1. The President's Council on Sustainable Development, *Sustainable America: A New Consensus for Prosperity, Opportunity, and a Healthy Environment for the Future* (Washington D.C.: GPO, 1996), 109

THE CHANGING LANDSCAPE

When someone uses the term *real estate*, we normally think of developers, brokers, banks, houses, apartment buildings, factories, and even farm fields. These have an economic orientation. All of these people and uses of real estate are critical to our economic development for the generation of individual and national wealth. A few years ago, John Sawhill, past president and CEO of The Nature Conservancy, had a contrasting and sobering reflection regarding land. He said, "(I)n the end, our society will be defined not only by what we create but by what we refuse to destroy." Sawhill is suggesting that land has value beyond that reflected in the calculations of economists.

In the 1940s Aldo Leopold expressed similar reflections in his book *A Sand County Almanac*. In a portion of the book entitled "The Land Ethic," he bemoaned the fact that Americans did not have an ethical approach to land. Our relationship to land, he asserted, is strictly economic, entailing privileges but no obligations toward the land itself or the role it plays in the larger community. We see ourselves as consumers of land (i.e., we pay money for it and an array of rights are born), rather than as citizens of it (i.e., having a series of rights and obligations in using the land). In reality, buying land is more like purchasing a TV set than living in and creating a community.

Though writing more than 50 years apart, are Sawhill and Leopold on the same track? They are urging us to see land as multidimensional. When seeking approval for a development proposal and asked the question "What is on the land?" how many owners, having no prior construction existing on the site, would respond "nothing"? Most? Leopold would respond by describing the soils, waters, plants, and animals on the land. The land ethic, he argues, simply enlarges the boundaries of our human community to encompass these other elements. If that was done, the persons owning the land and the ones approving the development would examine the ecological, economic, and aesthetic characteristics of the land. Do you think Leopold's land ethic makes sense? Since Leopold's day, have we begun to move in the direction of viewing land as a community of natural elements? Do we consciously "refuse to destroy" some land areas, as suggested by Sawhill?

■ KEY TERMS

■ INTERNET RESOURCES

www.ncrs.usda.gov/technical/land
(Provides maps and information on various natural resource uses of land)

www.waterwatch.org/water_law.htm
(Critique of prior appropriation theory)

http://medicolegal.tripod.com/pureaircases.htm
(Advocates for common law right to fresh air and lists many cases decided on related issues)

■ REVIEW AND DISCUSSION QUESTIONS

1. Outline those arguments supporting individual ownership of land. Evaluate these arguments.

2. Compare the riparian doctrines of reasonable use and natural flow. What limitations exist on reasonable use? From a public policy viewpoint, which doctrine is most valuable? Why?

3. (a) List the four methods of acquiring mineral rights. (b) What are the major legal differences among them?

■ CASE PROBLEMS

1. Richards and Schneider owned adjoining land. Richards drilled several oil wells on his property very close to the boundary between the two parcels. When Richards began to pump substantial quantities of oil from these wells, Schneider sought an injunction. At the hearing Schneider's witnesses, all expert geologists, testified that most of the oil came from under Schneider's land. (a) In a state that had no correlative rights legislation, would Schneider's injunction be granted? (b) Would your answer differ if the state's oil and gas law were based on ownership theory? Discuss.

2. Gilliam owned an airplane that he used for crop dusting. While he was flying over Shrock's property to reach a field that was to be sprayed, crop dusting material was released. Although it was not clear how this occurred, Gilliam clearly was not negligent. At the time the dust was released, Gilliam was flying at a safe altitude. Shrock sued for damages, as the poison dust destroyed valuable nursery stock. Would Shrock be successful? Discuss.

3. In 1968, Coffin purchased land along St. Vrain Creek. He built a dam and used water from the creek to irrigate his farm. Several years prior to Coffin's purchase, the Left Hand Ditch Co. had constructed a ditch diverting water from St. Vrain Creek to James Creek and then to Left Hand Creek, where it irrigated land adjacent to that stream. None of this land was adjacent to St. Vrain Creek. When a drought

struck, the Left Hand Ditch Co. tore out a portion of Coffin's dam, which was impeding the flow of water to land irrigated by Left Hand Creek. Coffin sought damages and an injunction. Although this was a prior appropriation jurisdiction, he argued that he had a better right to the water because his land was adjacent to St. Vrain's Creek. (a) Explain prior appropriation. (b) Discuss the validity of Coffin's argument.

4. Nilsson and Latimer both owned land that bordered on the Little Cossatot River. In an exceptionally dry year, Latimer's irrigation pumps pumped dry two or three holes on the river. This action deprived Nilsson of occasional recreational fishing at these particular pools. Nilsson sued Latimer for damages based on Latimer's unreasonable use of the water. Would she be successful? Support your answer. *Nilsson v. Latimer,* 664 S.W.2d 447 (1984).

5. Harris had title to 11 acres of vacant land. Unknown to her, the Wabash Coal Co. had recorded mineral rights in the land. A state statute provided that a person having apparent title or "a semblance of title" to vacant land who pays taxes on the land for seven successive years becomes the legal owner. When Harris discovered the existence of the mineral rights, she claimed title to them; she argued that the payment of taxes on the property constituted payment of taxes on the mineral rights that had been separated from it. The taxing authorities had not assessed separate taxes against the Wabash Coal Co., owner of the mineral rights. Would Harris be successful? Discuss.

Go to the Student Study Guide CD-ROM and work through Case 1.

PART TWO

Legal Interests in Real Estate

Estates in Land

■ ALLODIUM

■ *Absolute ownership of land where the holder owes no obligation to a superior.*

Interests in land existing in the United States today are the result of two different systems of ownership. For several centuries, both systems existed side by side in Europe. One of these systems was *feudalism*, in which everyone holding land, except the sovereign, owed rents and services to a "land lord." Contrastingly, in the *allodial system* all land was owned absolutely. The holder had no obligation to pay rents or services to another.

Absolute ownership was the basis of Roman real property law. After the collapse of the Roman Empire, feudalism gradually became dominant in most of Europe except in some sections where Roman influence persisted. In many of these areas, the Roman idea of absolute ownership continued as the basis for holding land. The owner had an absolute title to the land with few limitations or restrictions on the right to use or dispose of it.

Today, the allodial concept of ownership—private ownership—is the distinguishing feature of real property ownership in the United States. Private ownership of land is free and absolute, subject only to governmental and reasonable private restrictions. However, traces of the feudal system continue to influence English and American law.

■ FEUDALISM

The fundamental principle of **feudalism** was tenure; all land was held on the condition that certain duties and services be performed for a superior "landlord."

Tenure

In the tenurial system, the king owned the land and parceled it out. Land was not owned in the sense that we think of ownership today. There were a number of legal restrictions that made it more like a tenancy. Under certain situations, the land would revert to the king or the "landlord." One such case was when innocent blood was shed on the property as the result of a homicide.

As a tenant, the occupant owed certain services to his immediate overlord that arose because he had possession; for example, he was required to provide "rents" and military service. In turn, the overlord protected the landholder. (See Figure 4.1.) Under feudalism, the land was always to have an occupant; otherwise, it would not serve the purpose of producing rents and services. Lords who possessed large tracts of land would transfer smaller tracts by the ceremony of *livery (delivery) of seisin* to sublords.

FIGURE 4.1   Ancient System of Tenure

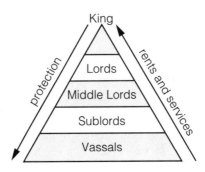

This ceremony involved the transfer of a clod of earth or twig from the lord to the sublord. All the witnesses at the ceremony would remember the transfer in the event they were called on to testify as to ownership. This ceremony was later replaced with transfer by deed.

Tenure in the United States

In the eastern part of the United States, some of the early colonial grants were based on tenure. The proprietor held land directly from the king. The small monetary payment required as a token of this relationship was called a *quitrent*. When the proprietor of a colony granted smaller tracts to individual settlers, each owed a quitrent by an extension of the feudal theory. These quitrents were very often ignored because of the ready availability of land on the frontier. In Massachusetts, Rhode Island, and Connecticut, the tenurial system never existed; land there was held privately. After the Revolution, quitrents were abolished, and the notion prevailed that a person who owned land had an absolute title limited only by the state.

Vestiges of feudalism and tenure are retained in U.S. real property law. One example is the law of *escheat*, with land reverting to the state if a person dies without heirs. Probably more important is the English concept of estates in land, for our legal system continues to recognize the idea that separate divisible interests may exist simultaneously in the same piece of land.

■ ESTATES

■   *The extent and character of a person's possessory rights and interests in land.*

The feudal notion of tenure is the foundation of the doctrine of **estates** in land. This doctrine has substantially influenced the rights that individuals may have in real property. The term *estate*, as used in this context, has a restrictive and technical meaning. Estate is derived from the word *status*, connoting the status that the king conferred on a favored subject of the realm by conferring property on him. This use of the term *estate* should not be confused with the more common usage, as a synonym for all of a person's assets.

As there are many possible interests in land, estates have numerous dimensions. Several classifications of estates have developed, reflecting these differences. (See Figure 4.2.) This chapter distinguishes between two types of estates characterized by the duration of the owner's right to possession: *freehold* and leasehold estates, *nonfreehold estates*. Nonfreehold estates are discussed in full in Chapter 7. Freehold estates, including future estates, are discussed in this chapter.

■ FREEHOLD ESTATE

■ *An estate of uncertain duration.*

A number of freehold interests exist in land. Although all freehold estates are of an uncertain duration, other rights of the owners differ. The holders of most freehold estates may pass their interests along to their heirs. These are generally called *freehold estates of inheritance,* or *heriditaments.* The most common is the **fee simple absolute**, sometimes referred to as *fee simple.* Life estates are also freehold estates because their duration is uncertain. Life estates, however, are not considered estates of inheritance because they ordinarily terminate on the owner's death.

Some estates are created for a fixed period of time. The principal estates of this nature are the estate, or tenancy, for years and the tenancy from period to period. At common law, these nonfreehold estates were distinguished from freehold estates. For many purposes, they were treated as personal, not real, property. The holder of a nonfreehold estate did not have the same status or legal rights as the holder of a freehold estate. Tenancies at will and tenancies at sufferance are other nonfreehold estates, and are discussed in Chapter 7.

FIGURE 4.2   Estates in Land

Fee Simple or Fee Simple Absolute

■   *The most extensive interest in land that a holder might possess.*

Most land in the United States is held in fee simple absolute. A *fee simple* is a freehold and the most extensive estate known to the law. It is the greatest quantum of interest one may own. The holder of a fee simple title possesses the whole "bundle of rights" commonly associated with property or ownership. Possession is one of these rights. Subject to limitations by the state, the owner may sell the estate or give it away during his or her lifetime. The owner may direct the disposition of the estate by will; however, if the owner dies without a will, the fee simple will be disposed of according to the laws of the jurisdiction in which the fee simple is located. Creditors may levy against the estate, or the owner may use it as security for a loan. The holder of a fee simple may voluntarily limit uses to which it may be put or carve out lesser estates from it. Use limitations will be recognized by the courts if they do not violate public policy. Although the term has its roots in feudal times, in most respects, the holder of a fee simple today has the fullest rights of private ownership.

Except in cases of conveyances to institutions such as corporations or the government, the common law required the grantor to use specific words to create a fee simple. The words "and his heirs" continue in common use today, although in most states any words that indicate an intention to create a fee simple are sufficient. Thus, the granting clause in a deed will generally state "to [grantee] and his heirs." The phrase "and his heirs" does not grant an interest to the grantee's heirs but simply describes the estate conveyed to the grantee, which in this case is a fee simple. In some parts of the country, this estate is referred to simply as a *fee*.

Defeasible Fee

■   *A fee simple that terminates on the happening of some future stated event.*

The holder of a fee simple or lesser estate has the right to create other estates in the land, which may be limited in several ways. Although this factor has complicated the property law of English-speaking countries, it has also provided variety in the uses to which real property may be put. A grantor, by using the **defeasible fee**, is often able to benefit society and, at the same time, protect self-interests. The two types of defeasible fees next discussed have been used for self-serving and narrow-minded purposes, but they also have been used in a manner benefiting the entire community. In this context, it is important to remember that until a defeasible fee terminates because the stated condition has occurred, the interests of the owner are the same as those possessed by the owner of a fee simple absolute.

CASE EXAMPLE

Mrs. Zahn, who is an environmentalist, owns a large tract of land in Wisconsin on which she desires to establish a wildlife sanctuary. She proposes to do this by giving the land to the National Wildlife Society. Although the directors of the society have agreed to administer and maintain the sanctuary, Mrs. Zahn fears that, as time passes and the land becomes more valuable, her original intent might be forgotten.

The law provides a number of methods, by which Mrs. Zahn can accomplish her objective and ensure that her intentions are honored. One of these would be to limit the future use of the land by imposing conditions in the deed. This task may be accomplished by creating either a fee simple determinable or a fee simple subject to condition subsequent.

Fee Simple Determinable. The **fee simple determinable**, sometimes called a *fee simple with a special limitation*, is a fee simple that *automatically* terminates when a stated condition is fulfilled. If the granting clause in the deed to the wildlife society states, "To the National Wildlife Society and its successors and assigns so long as the property is used as a wildlife preserve," a fee simple determinable would be created. The fee is indefinite in duration because it is a fee simple, but the grantee's interest terminates automatically and reverts back to the grantor or her heirs on the occurrence of the event, in this case when the property ceases to be used as a wildlife preserve. The grantor is said to have a *possibility of reverter.* The language creating such a fee will ordinarily include words of limitation such as "so long as," "as long as," or "until."

Fee Simple Subject to Condition Subsequent. The **fee simple subject to condition subsequent** is a fee simple that *may* be terminated by the grantor or the grantor's successor when a stated condition is fulfilled. This estate is very similar to a fee simple determinable. The major difference is that termination is not automatic. The estate continues when the stated condition occurs unless the grantor or the grantor's successors take steps to terminate it. The grantor or successor is said to have a *power of termination*, or *right of reentry*. The environmentalist might create an estate of this nature by stating in the deed: "to the National Wildlife Society and its successors and assigns forever on condition that the land is used as a wildlife preserve, but if the land is used for any other purposes, Mrs. Zahn and her heirs shall have a right of reentry and repossession." The language creating such a fee will ordinarily include words of limitation such as "subject to the following," "subject to the conditions and restrictions," or "but if. . . ."

Life Estate

■ *An estate measured by a life or lives.*

Granting an estate to an individual for life has been a common practice in the United States. A **life estate** typically is measured by the life of the owner, but it may be measured by the life of some other person. If the holder of a fee simple absolute makes a grant "to A for life," A has an estate that terminates with his or her death. If the grant were "to A for the life of B," A's estate would terminate on the death of B. This type of life estate is called an **estate *pur autre vie***. An estate *pur autre vie* (for the life of another) does not expire on the death of the owner; it continues in the owner's heirs until the death of the "other" measuring life. In modern practice, estates *pur autre vie* are seldom created.

Rights and Duties of Life Tenants. The holder of a life estate, usually called the life tenant, has an ownership interest in the land. This interest may be sold, mortgaged, or leased, but it is not very marketable because any interest a buyer, mortgagee, or lessee acquires ordinarily ends with the death of the life tenant. Life tenants are entitled to rents and profits from the property while their tenancy lasts, but they may not use the property in a manner that will permanently reduce its market value. If they do so, the eventual owner of the fee may bring an action against the life tenant for *waste*, as occurred in the previous case.

McIntyre v. Scarbrough
Supreme Court of Georgia
471 S.E.2d 199 (Ga. 1996)

Background. In 1988 Russell and Sally Scarbrough purchased a 16.59 acre tract of land from Dellie McIntyre. Ms. McIntyre reserved a life estate in 1.2 acres, which included a mobile home, porch, and shed. Under the terms of the reservation, she was to pay the real estate taxes.

Ms. McIntyre was 90 years old. The Scarbroughs alleged, under oath, that she had not been seen on the property for two years; that there was no water or gas service to the mobile home, nor a mailbox on the property; and that the property taxes were not paid. A fire marshal swore under oath that the premises were in a state of decay and disrepair and that it posed health hazards and was unfit for habitation.

In response, Ms. McIntyre swore under oath that she was unable to recently occupy the premises due to health problems and that she was in the process of renovating the home to make it fit for habitation. Her son signed an affidavit stating that his mother had been confined away from home for medical reasons, that she intended to return, and that she had never removed her belongings.

The Scarbroughs (the plaintiffs) requested the court to grant them a forfeiture of the life estate based on the sworn statements. The court granted judgment in plaintiffs' favor, holding that Ms. McIntyre was not "occupying" the estate and that she committed waste.

Decision. The Supreme Court of Georgia affirmed the trial court decision.

Justice Thompson. "Occupy" is more expansively defined in *Black's Law Dictionary* . . . as "to hold possession of; to hold or keep for use; to possess." Because one may occupy a residence by holding it or keeping it for use, the court erred in imposing a requirement that permanent physical presence was necessary to fulfill the occupancy requirement of the warranty deed. Evidence that Ms. McIntyre had never removed any of her personal belongings during the time she had been away for medical reasons, as well as her stated ongoing intent to occupy the residence until her death, raises a question of fact as to whether she continued to occupy the residence while residing elsewhere for medical recuperation.

The trial court, however, correctly determined that the plaintiffs were entitled to judgment as a matter of law under plaintiffs' alternative theory of recovery, that the life estate was extinguished under the doctrine of waste.

A life tenant is entitled to the full use and enjoyment of the property if in such use he or she exercises the ordinary care of a prudent person for its preservation and protection and commits no acts which would permanently injure the remainder interest. . . . In the present case, not only was the defendant obligated by law to maintain taxes on her portion of the property, but she also specifically agreed to pay . . . taxes as a condition of the . . . deed. Although the question of waste is generally one for a jury, the undisputed facts show that the defendant failed to exercise ordinary care for the preservation of the property, and to comply with a condition of the . . . deed, resulting in forfeiture of the life estate as a matter of law.

Chief Justice Benham Dissenting. I agree fully with the first division of the majority opinion. . . . I do not believe, however, that [the defendants] are entitled to judgment as a matter of law, so I must dissent from the majority opinion's affirmance . . . on the issue of waste.

As the majority opinion correctly notes, the question of waste is generally one for a jury. That is especially so in a case such as the present one where there is evidence presented in defense of the life estate to the effect that any damage to the estate has been unintentional and due to the circumstances of the holder of the life estate rather than

from disregard of the estate. . . .

In the present case, there is evidence that Ms. McIntyre has made some efforts, through the agency of her son, to reverse the deterioration of the property and that she has been ill and unable to care for the property adequately, although she has always intended to return to it. That evidence, if believed, does not show the wilful behavior required to warrant a forfeiture. . . .

The question of whether Ms. McIntyre's conduct with regard to the life estate she holds has been so egregiously wasteful as to warrant forfeiture of her interest in the property should be submitted to a jury.

Which opinion do you favor? The majority or the dissent? Explain why.

Life tenants must make ordinary repairs to the property. They are responsible for annual property taxes, but for only a proportionate share of special assessments for sewers, sidewalks, and other permanent improvements. As a general rule, the life tenant is required to pay the interest on a mortgage, but not the principal.

The reversionary or remainder interest holder is generally entitled to receive the property in substantially the same condition it was when the life tenant took possession. However, when the surrounding conditions have substantially changed so as to affect the usefulness of the property, even razing the "residence" may be an improvement rather than being regarded as waste.

CASE EXAMPLE

Pabst Brewing owned a life estate and the Melms owned a future reversionary interest in fee simple. The property contained a dwelling house. The neighborhood changed in such a way that the use of the property as residential became valueless. Factories, railway tracks, and brewery buildings dominated the surrounding area, and the residence became isolated. It would not rent for enough to pay the taxes and insurance. Consequently, Pabst removed the dwelling house on the life estate and graded the property to prepare it for construction of business property. This increased the value of the estate substantially.

The Melms contended that Pabst committed waste. Because of the radical change in the neighborhood, rendering the residential property valueless, the removal was an improvement and probably not a commission of waste. See *Melms v. Pabst Brewing Co.*, 79 N.W. 738 (Wisc. 1899).

Life estates frequently cause legal problems. In many cases, these problems involve the relationship between the life tenant and the holders of the estate to be enjoyed on the termination of the life estate.

CASE EXAMPLE

Bridges owned a life interest in realty on which there was a building worth $10,000. She insured the building, using her own funds. The building was destroyed by a hurricane and the proceeds of the policy paid to Bridges. The court approved a petition by the owner of the remainder that Bridges be ordered to rebuild or hold the insurance proceeds for the remainderman with interest going to Bridges for life. *Crisp Lumber Co. v. Bridges*, 187 Ga. 484, 200 S.E. 777 (1939).

In modern practice, the use of the life estate in the disposition of real property is gradually being replaced by use of the trust. Lawyers have found that the trust provides a more effective and flexible method of disposing of wealth. A trustee may be given legal title to land to hold for the life of a beneficiary. Proceeds from the land are paid to the beneficiary. On the death of the beneficiary, the land or proceeds from the sale of the land are distributed as the creator of the trust directed. The trustee may also be given additional authority, such as power of sale, which would permit disposal of the property should a profitable opportunity arise. Trusts are discussed in greater detail in Chapter 5.

Despite the potential legal problems, the life estate concept has been used in some states to provide security for one spouse upon the death of another. In some states, the law grants the surviving spouse a life interest in the real property of the deceased. Life estates of this nature are called *legal life estates*.

Legal Life Estates. In common law, several types of life estates in land were created as a result of marriage. A primary objective of these estates was to provide support for the wife upon the death of her husband. A husband also had a life interest in the wife's real property in the event of her death. In some states, features of these marital life estates continue as important elements of real property law. A considerable number of states, however, have abolished them and substituted a statutory plan to provide for the widow or widower. These plans provide that the surviving spouse be entitled to choose what is called an *elective share*.

■ **Dower.** *Life estate of a widow in one-third of any real property to which her spouse had legal title during marriage.*

For many generations, **dower** was an important right that a widow acquired in her husband's real property upon his death. This right minimally entitled her to a one-third interest in his lands for life. The widow was entitled to dower as well as any gifts made in the husband's will, unless the will clearly stated that the gifts were in *lieu of dower*. If it was clear that the bequests were in lieu of dower, the widow had to elect one or the other.

While the husband was alive, the wife's right, which did not materialize unless the husband died before she did, was protected against both the husband's acts and claims of his creditors arising after the marriage. The wife's interest, which was called *inchoate dower,* was a potential estate. She acquired a legal estate only if she survived her husband.

CASE EXAMPLE

Mary and Ed were secretly married in 1994. At that time, Ed owned a large office building. In order to modernize the building, Ed borrowed a substantial amount of money in 1996 and gave a mortgage to secure the loan. As a result of depressed economic conditions, Ed could not meet payments on the loan, and the mortgage was foreclosed. Any purchaser at the foreclosure sale would be subject to Mary's inchoate right of dower.

For dower to be allowed, the parties must have been legally married at the time of the husband's death. Consequently, in most states, the right to dower is terminated by divorce. A wife may ordinarily release her inchoate right of dower by joining in on any conveyance of the husband's real property. In the event a husband mortgages his property, the wife will release her inchoate right of dower if she signs the mortgage, but dower is restored on payment of the debt. In old England a husband had a right similar to dower, called *curtesy*. Curtesy has been abolished by most states and dower has been extended to protect the husband as well as the wife. For more information about the history of dower, go to *http://vi.uh.edu/pages/bob/elhone/rules.html*.

Future Estate

■ *An interest in an estate that may become possessory in the future.*

In the system of tenure as it developed in England, land was separated from interests that might exist in it. Because land was one thing and interests in it another, several people could possess interests or estates in the same piece of land. This idea continues to be a feature of the law of English-speaking countries. Although a complete estate in land may exist at the present moment, it may be divided into various slices in such a way that each slice is regarded as existing now, even though possession may not occur until the future.

CASE EXAMPLE

Lansing Thomas owns a large farm. He directs by will that on his death, the property would pass to Beverly Lane, his only daughter, for life and then to her oldest son. When Lansing dies, two estates exist in the land simultaneously.

Lansing's daughter Beverly has a *life estate*. This is a possessory estate because she is entitled to the rents and profits from the farm for her life. Beverly's oldest son has a *future estate*. On his mother's death he is entitled to the farm, but he can claim nothing in possession until she dies.

Although the nature, quality, and extent of their interests often differ, each holder of an estate invariably has a present or future right of possession. During his mother's life, the son in the preceding example does not have a right to occupy the land or profit from it. He does, however, possess an interest, or estate, that would be recognized in American courts as it was in medieval England. His is a future interest. However, he does have the right to prevent *waste* of the property by the life tenant now.

The common law accepted the idea that several estates of different duration could exist in land at the same time. (See Figure 4.3.) Our legal system continues to recognize this concept. Only one of these interests is possessory, but because of the estate concept,

| FIGURE 4.3 | Future Interests |

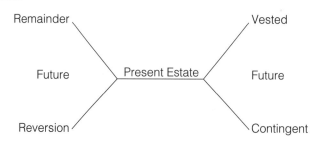

the party in possession does not necessarily have all interests associated with owner-ship. If *A*, the holder of a fee simple, grants a life estate to *B*, *B*'s interest terminates with death and something obviously is left over. As *A* has a fee simple, *A*'s estate, from which the grant to *B* was carved, is indefinite in duration. If *A*'s grant to *B* said nothing about what was left after *B*'s death, *A* has a future interest. This is an interest that entitles *A* to possession at that time in the future when *B* dies. This particular type of future interest is called a *reversion*, as the residue reverts back to *A* or his heirs.

Suppose, however, that *A*'s deed is worded "to *B* for life, remainder to *C* and her heirs"; in such case, then *C* has a future interest. Although *C* has no present right to possession, her future interest is probably more valuable than *B*'s life estate, for on the death of *B*, *C* acquires a fee simple absolute. *C*'s interest is called a *remainder*. As *C*'s interest is not subject to any contingency except *B*'s death, the remainder is said to be *vested*.

In addition to the reversion and the remainder, other future interests also exist. An example is the previously mentioned fee simple determinable. In creating this estate, the holder does not make an absolute grant of the entire interest. When the condition limit-ing the grant is fulfilled, the interest of the party in possession automatically terminates. The grantor and his or her heirs thus have a possibility of regaining possession at some time in the future. This future interest is called a *possibility of reverter* and is a contin-gent interest.

The creation of a fee simple subject to a condition subsequent also creates a future interest. This future interest is referred to as a *right of reentry for condition broken,* or a *power of termination*. When the possessory estate terminates because the condition is fulfilled, the holder of the right of reentry may acquire the property by filing suit. Like the possibility of reverter, the right of reentry is a contingent interest, because the pred-icate condition may never occur.

Current Status of the Future Interest

The acceptance of the concept of possessory estates in land followed by a future inter-est lends flexibility to the disposition of real property. In many instances, however, future interests exist because a grantor wishes to limit the free transferability of land. Often the creator of the estate wishes to control the use of the land, not only during his or her lifetime but after death as well. Conditional and defeasible fees have been used in the past for this purpose and continue to be so used today.

The right of reentry and the possibility of reverter cause especially serious problems. The fees that give rise to these interests are created to last forever and often do last for many years. As a result, the right of reentry and the possibility of reverter are merely expectant interests with almost no present economic value. Often the current possessors of these interests are remote descendants of the original creator. Frequently they are unaware that this interest exists. When a title search reveals the existence of these interests, a person attempting to clear the title is presented with a difficult, if not insoluble, problem arising from the fact that often it is impossible to contact the parties who might retain an interest in the land because of the future interest.

A growing number of states have attempted to solve this problem through legislation. This legislation often places limitations on the time a future interest can last. Another type of legislation places limitations on the time during which a future interest may be enforced. Other states have adopted legislation that ensures that a person who has an unbroken chain of title extending over a given number of years has a fee simple free of future interests.

The next case illustrates the propensity of a court to interpret language, so as not to effect a forfeiture, or reversion of the property.

Mitchell v. Jerrolds
Tennessee Court of Appeals
1991 Tenn. App. Lexis 201

Background. The Jerrolds conveyed developed real estate to the Turkey Baptist Church as a gift. The deed stated: "LIMITATIONS. This land is given by us to the Church for the purpose for the home for the Missionary Baptist Pastor and no Pastor shall occupy said place as a home unless he preaches that you are saved by Grace through Faith in Jesus Christ and not by works. And in the event he refuses to preach such doctrine he will not be permitted to reside in said pastorium." The church sought permission from the court to sell the property in order to purchase new property and construct a new pastorium. Heirs of the cograntor contended that the property under the language of the deed must revert to them. The trial court held in favor of the church and the heirs of the cograntor appealed.

Decision. The Tennessee Court of Appeals affirmed the trial court decision.

Judge Williams. It is the insistence of the defendants that because the subject language begins with the word "limitations," such fully describes the intent of the grantors to create a determinable fee. . . .

Under the now well-accepted rule in construing a deed, we determine the estate conveyed in the deed by trying to determine the intentions of the parties. . . .

In [*Bailey v. Eagle Mountain Telephone, Inc.*], the Tennessee Supreme Court spelled out the long and well-established principles of law and rules of construction to be employed by the courts in determining whether the language in a deed established a determinable fee . . . or merely a statement of purpose for the grant and not sufficient to create a determinable fee. The question presented in *Bailey* was whether the following language created a determinable fee with a possibility of reverter to the heirs

continued on next page

of the grantor, "In consideration of love and interest we have in Education, we this day deed, transfer and convey a certain lot or parcel of land . . . To have and to hold for school purposes . . . so long as the aforesaid lot of land is used for the aforesaid purposes."

In holding that the language did, indeed, create a fee simple determinable subject to a possibility of reverter, the Supreme Court proceeded to contrast examples of when a determinable fee was created and when not.

Old examples of determinable fees are limitations to one and his heirs "as long as the Church of St. Paul shall stand" or "until the grantee go to Rome"; the most appropriate words to create a determinable fee being, during, so long as, till, until, whilst, etc., such words fitly prefacing a limitation.

A determinable fee may either arise from and be dependent on a condition, or arise from a limitation, the essential difference being that in a case of a condition the estate is not terminated [automatically] by the happening of the event on which it may be defeated, while in the case of a limitation it passes at once by way of reverter to the grantor. . . . It results from this distinction that the usual technical words by which a limitation is expressed relate to time, differing from those expressing a condition. . . .

It is plain that the subject language for construction in the Jerrolds' deed does not contain any apt word expressing a limitation in relation to time. Compare the words in the Bailey case which state,

"to have and to hold for school purposes . . . so long as . . . the aforesaid lot of land is used for the aforesaid purposes." The language in the Jerrolds' deed states in pertinent part: "This land is given by us to the Church for the purpose for the home for the Missionary Baptist Pastor." Nothing else appears.

Defendants also strenuously contend that the word "LIMITATIONS" [automatically] proves the grantor's intention to create a determinable fee. . . . We agree with the learned trial judge . . . that the grantor's use [of] the word, "LIMITATIONS" as a word of reference for the purpose of calling specific attention to the proviso that they were limiting the pastor to preaching the doctrine of "Grace through Faith" and nothing more, else the pastor and his family could not live in the pastorium.

We therefore hold that the subject matter words contained in the Jerrolds' deed to the church . . . on which the pastorium was erected were merely words stating the purpose of the gift and did not constitute a determinable fee with possibility of reverter or a condition subsequent. We therefore hold that . . . the subject matter deed conveyed in fee simple absolute the title to the property described in said deed to the original named trustees. . . .

Affirmed.

Craft language in the deed that would lead to the result that the church property reverts to the grantors on a breach of the stated condition.

THE CHANGING LANDSCAPE

Estates in land hearken back to the medieval days of lords, knights, squires, and English chivalry. Our system of estates draws heavily from that period in English history when the King ruled, and land was the power over the people. Land was, indeed, status and security. Because of its importance, the aristocracy sought ways to gather land and keep it within the family. The fee tail was the preferred estate that accomplished this goal. Through the fee tail "to the heirs of my body," the land would theoretically continue *ad infinitum* in lineal descendants of the grantor. The English Parliament, seeking to perpetuate the concentration of land in the hands of the wealthy, legislated means of restricting land transfers and thus favored the fee tail, which presumably promoted family cohesiveness and wealth. At the same time the common-law courts, which were common-people minded, in reaction to Parliamentary feudalism, decided cases in such a way as to promote a more egalitarian system of landholding. The common-law courts, thus, preferred the fee simple absolute, and found ways to disentail the restrictive

estates. Then Parliament would respond in attempts to counter the courts.

Today, in the United States, although we have adopted much of the ancient nomenclature, land tends to be freely alienable. Like a commodity it may be readily sold for residential, commercial, or investment purposes. Estate-holding today is designed to fit the needs of today's society and the individualized need of the landholder. For some it is an estate-planning tool to pass down the land to family members, while minimizing tax impact. For others the objective is to use land as a vehicle of investment by buying, renovating and selling, or developing. And for still others, estates are an opportunity for enjoying condominium living, "time-share vacations" and other creative uses discussed more fully in Chapter 6.

In a changing society, what will estates in land mean in the future? Will there be greater regulatory restrictions or will private landholding and free alienability rule the day? What direction do you envision the future holds and why?

■ KEY TERMS

■ INTERNET RESOURCES

To learn about the history of feudalism, see

www.fidnet.com/~weid/feudalism.htm

www.factmonster.com/cele/history/A0818585.html

www.historyguide.org/ancient/lecture21b.html

■ REVIEW AND DISCUSSION QUESTIONS

1. What is the difference between how land was held in feudal times and how it is held in the United States today?

2. (a) What is the chief characteristic of an estate? (b) Explain how the concept of estates has influenced the development of real estate law.

3. Distinguish between a freehold estate and a nonfreehold estate. Give an example of each.

4. Explain *dower* and its purpose.

5. Explain the difference between a *fee simple subject to condition subsequent* and a *fee simple determinable*.

6. What is the tendency today with regard to restrictions on the title of real estate?

■ CASE PROBLEMS

1. John F. McElveen conveyed to the trustees of Central Common Free School a tract of one acre. The deed contained the following provision:

   > Provided, always nevertheless notwithstanding, that in case it should so happen at any time that a free common school shall not be maintained on the described premises for a period of three consecutive years, then the said premises shall be considered abandoned and revert back to John F. McElveen.

   Describe the interest of John F. McElveen in the one-acre tract. Does he have a right to sell his interest? Discuss.

2. Sterner, by his last will and testament, granted a life estate in his residence to Virginia Sullivan. Other than the residence, the estate had few assets. Sullivan paid the real estate taxes for the current year and a special sewer assessment. She filed a claim against the estate for reimbursement. Is she entitled to recover? Support your answer.

3. In 1965 Maricopa County executed two quitclaim deeds to the City of Tempe. The deeds contained the following provision:

   > Subject to the restriction that the . . . real property shall be operated and maintained solely for park, recreation, public accommodation, and convenience purposes.

   No words creating a right of reentry or indicating a reversionary interest in the county were used. The city leased the land to Baseball Facilities, Inc. (BFI). In 1973 BFI applied for a sales tax permit to conduct activities such as a music festival and evangelical meetings on the land. None of these uses was prohibited by the lease. The city, however, denied the permit on grounds that the use for these purposes would create a right in Maricopa County to recover the property. The city argued that the provision in the deeds created a defeasible fee. Was the city correct?

Discuss. *City of Tempe v. Baseball Facilities, Inc.*, 23 Ariz. App. 557, 534 P.2d 1056 (Ct. App. 1975).

4. Melody Davis purchased a farm from Boyd Bishop, who was very ill. After Melody and her son Don moved into the farmhouse, Don discovered an old deed that conveyed the farm to "Boyd Bishop and his heirs forever." As Bishop had several children, Don was concerned that the children might, as heirs, have a claim to the farm when Bishop died. Explain to Don what these words mean.

5. Ronald Guard was married to Loretta Guard in a state that had abolished dower. Loretta was a successful investor in real estate. She owned several multifamily buildings, appraised at $500,000. In addition, she held securities valued at $100,000. When Ronald and Loretta quarreled, she destroyed her will, under which Ronald had been left her entire estate. What claim, if any, might Ronald have against Loretta's estate if she dies before he does?

5   Co-Ownership

■ CO-OWNERSHIP

■ *A form of ownership in which two or more persons have undivided interests in the same property.*

Rights and interests in real estate may be divided in various ways. A number of different interests often exist simultaneously in the same parcel. A horizontal division of interests is common. As discussed in Chapter 3, one person might own the surface while others own the minerals below or the airspace above the surface. Rights and interests are sometimes divided over time. For example, in Chapter 4 we learned that a *life estate* might be followed by a *remainder in fee*. Both estates are valuable. The owner of the life estate has a present possessory interest. Simultaneously, the owner of the remainder in fee has a present interest, but the right to possession will not materialize until the life estate terminates in the future. A third division of rights exists when several people own undivided interests in a parcel of land at the same time. Generally, in this type of ownership, each person is entitled to a specific fraction of the parcel but also shares with the others a single right to possession and *profits* from the land. This is generally referred to as *concurrent ownership* or **co-ownership.**

Co-ownership was important to the common law, and the various concurrent estates that developed at common law remain important today. (See Table 5.1.) A number of legal problems are associated with these common-law estates. Many of these problems are reduced or eliminated if multiple owners use a partnership, corporation, limited liability company, or trust to hold title to the property. As a result, these devices are becoming increasingly important in real estate holdings, and, to a degree, are replacing the common-law forms of multiple ownership. This chapter discusses the traditional concurrent estates: joint tenancy, tenancy in common, tenancy by the entirety, and tenancy in partnership. State laws regarding community property are considered briefly, as are some alternative organizational structures for multiple ownership of real estate.

■ JOINT TENANCY

■ *A form of co-ownership where the entire estate passes to the survivor on the death of the other joint tenant(s).*

The principal feature of the **joint tenancy** is the *right of survivorship*. On the death of one of the co-owners, that person's interest passes automatically to the surviving joint owners.

| TABLE **5.1** | Forms of Co-ownership: Comparison |

	Joint Tenancy	Tenancy in Common	Tenancy by the Entirety	Tenancy in Partnership
Survivorship Interest	Yes	No	Yes	Yes
Equal Right to Possession	Yes	Yes	Yes	Yes
Husband and Wife Only	No	No	Yes	No
Severable by One Co-owner Conveying Interest to a Third Party	Yes	Yes	No	Yes
Subject to Dower Rights	Yes	Yes	Yes	No

CASE EXAMPLE

Tom Casicollo conveys Blackacre in fee simple to his wife Helen and son Tony "as joint tenants." Helen dies. As this is a joint tenancy, Helen's interest in Blackacre does not become part of her inheritance estate but automatically becomes Tony's sole property.

Joint tenancy with the right of survivorship is an additional example of the manner in which law tends to reflect existing economic and social conditions. During the feudal period, when English property law was developing, ownership of an estate by a single individual facilitated the lord's collection of the rents and services to which he was entitled. As a result, when a deed or will created rights in co-owners, the common-law courts presumed that a joint tenancy was intended unless some other form of co-ownership was clearly indicated. In those days, even if Tom had not stated that Helen and Tony were to hold as joint tenants, the law would have presumed that they did. The survivor possessed the entire fee.

Additional forms of co-ownership developed during the feudal period, and after feudalism ended, the joint tenancy with its right of survivorship continued to meet the needs of English society. Throughout the 17th and 18th centuries, the wealth and power of the English aristocracy was based on large landholdings. Land was a principal source of political power, the chief source of wealth, and the basis of social status. If the landholding had become fragmented because of too much division of property among multiple owners or through inheritance, the power of the English upper class would have been diluted. Because joint tenancy helped to prevent this dilution of power, it continued to be the dominant form of co-ownership and the form assumed by the courts to have been selected when the grantor's intention was not clear.

Although joint tenancy played a role in colonial American real property law, it was never as important in this country as it was in England. The reason for this was the marked difference in social and economic conditions between the two countries. As forms of wealth other than land became important, joint tenancy was gradually replaced by other types of co-ownership. Most of these developed because they were more readily adaptable to modern society's need for the free transferability of property.

Rights of Joint Tenants

Each co-owner who holds as a joint tenant has an equal right to possession of the entire property. This is referred to as an *undivided interest*. Although a joint tenant may not exclude other joint tenants from possession, strangely enough, the law considers occupancy by one as occupancy by all. In the previous example, if Tom Casicollo occupied Blackacre as a residence without his mother's objection, he would not be obligated to pay her a proportionate share of the rent; neither would he be required to share income with her if Blackacre were a farm or commercial real estate. Helen Casicollo, however, has the same rights; hence, if each tenant is to benefit, all must agree to share the proceeds of the property. Where agreement cannot be reached, the tenancy must be severed.

Severance of Joint Tenancy

A number of different methods exist to sever or terminate a joint tenancy. Traditionally, for a joint tenancy to be created or to continue, four "unities" are required. (See Table 5.2.) First, the *unity of possession* requires that each have an undivided right to possession. Second, the *unity of interest* requires that each receive the same type of estate and each have an equal fractional interest. For example, one joint tenant cannot hold as a life tenant while the other holds in fee simple; neither can one hold a 1/4 interest and the other a 3/4 interest. Finally, the interests in the estate must be received at the same time (*unity of time*) and from the same instrument (*unity of title*). If any of these unities terminates, the joint tenancy also ends. The new form of ownership is *tenancy in common*, a form in which the right of survivorship does not exist.

■ TENANCY IN COMMON

▨ *A form of concurrent ownership in which each owner possesses an undivided right to the entire parcel of land, with each owner's rights similar to those possessed by a sole owner.*

In the United States today, the **tenancy in common** is probably the most frequently occurring form of concurrent ownership. Although tenancy in common developed contemporaneously at common law with joint tenancy, the joint tenancy was for centuries

TABLE 5.2	Unities of Joint Tenancy	
	• Possession	equal rights
	• Interest	identical fraction
	• Time	same title
	• Title	same instrument

the favored form of multiple ownership. This is no longer true. Today a tenancy in common is implied unless a joint tenancy is clearly indicated by the instrument creating the concurrent estate. Hence, the tenancy in common is now in many states the "default."

> **CASE EXAMPLE**
>
> By a provision in his will, Patrick Cross gave all his property to his sons, Thomas and William, to "share and share alike, or to the survivor of them." William died before Thomas, and Thomas's heirs claimed the property, arguing that their father was a joint tenant with the right of survivorship. The court held that William and Thomas were tenants in common, not joint tenants. As a result, each son was entitled to an equal share of the property which, on their death, became part of each son's separate estate. *Cross v. Cross*, 324 Mass. 186, 85 N.E.2d 325 (1949).

Rights of Tenants in Common

Like joint tenants, each tenant in common has an undivided right to possession of the entire parcel. Normally, a tenant in common will not be responsible to the co-owners for any benefits obtained through exclusive occupancy unless he or she excludes the others from participating. At the same time, no tenant in common is entitled to the exclusive use of any part of the land. The result is that problems arise when one cotenant wrongfully excludes the others or when it is impractical for the property to be occupied by more than a single tenant. Under the circumstances, in a number of states, the cotenants not in occupancy will be entitled to a fair compensation for the use of the property. Similar problems arise where a cotenant not in possession receives benefits from the property exceeding those of the co-owners. These types of problems may best be solved by agreement among the parties, as may problems involving liability of cotenants for upkeep and improvements. When agreement cannot be reached, partition of property may be the only solution.

■ PARTITION

> ■ *An action by which a co-owner obtains a division of property terminating any interest of other co-owners in the divided portion.*

Partition is the historic method by which unwilling concurrent owners of real property may terminate the interests of fellow co-owners. Courts traditionally ordered partition even when no statute authorized them to do so. Today partition exists in some form by statute in every state. Many states make the remedy available to some holders of future interests.

Partition may be voluntary or compulsory. Voluntary partitions are the result of agreement among the co-owners to end the relationship. They are usually carried out by deeds in which each co-owner is allocated a described portion of the realty by all the other co-owners. It is also possible for all the co-owners to convey to a third party, the third party in turn conveying to each former co-owner the agreed-on parcel. Although a few states recognize oral voluntary partitions, a written instrument is usually required, primarily to permit recording in the public records. Voluntary partition requires not only the consent of all the parties to the act but also agreement as to the specific division of the estate. Compulsory partition by judicial action is necessary when one or more of the multiple owners desire to terminate the relationship and agreement cannot be reached.

The right to partition appears to be absolute unless the parties themselves have agreed that they will not use the remedy. A co-owner may demand partition without regard to the size of his or her share. The fact that the interest of a co-owner is subject to a mortgage or other lien, though it is a complicating factor, will not defeat the right. So extensive is the right to partition that state condominium statutes must specifically prohibit the right of condominium owners to seek partition of the condominium elements that are owned in common.

Partition is accomplished in one of three ways. The preferred method is by a physical division of the property. The court orders the property divided, allocating a share to each co-owner. Often, however, physical division is not appropriate or desirable, and in these cases the property will be sold and the proceeds divided among the co-owners in relation to their interests. The determination of the allocation of interests may not be easy, especially because factual scenarios vary. Common sense often prevails and the allocation may be based on the amount that each contributed to the purchase price or the percentage that each contributed to the household expenses. The third method effectively results in one or more of the co-owners purchasing the interests of the other co-owners.

■ TENANCY BY THE ENTIRETY

■ *Co-ownership of property by husband and wife that is nonseverable without the consent of both; on the death of either, the survivor remains as sole owner.*

About one-half of the states recognize **tenancy by the entirety,** a type of co-ownership existing only between husband and wife (see *www.smartagreements.com/bltopics/ bltopics38.html*). This type of co-ownership is based on an ancient legal fiction by which the common law regarded husband and wife as a single legal person. One result was that if the two acquired equal interests in real estate by the same instrument, the property was considered owned as an indivisible legal unit. On the death of either, the survivor remained as the parcel's sole owner. This result has long been accepted by modern law. Today, a right of survivorship similar to that existing for the joint tenancy exists for the tenancy by entirety. This right benefits the surviving spouse, as it avoids the necessity and cost of probate proceedings and involves only a simple administrative transfer.

CASE EXAMPLE
Jim Seaver and his wife, Helen, purchased an apartment building and took title in both their names. Jim died without making a will, and children by a former marriage claimed that a part interest in the property vested in them. They argued that Jim and Helen were tenants in common. The court held that Helen was the absolute owner because when a husband and wife take title in both their names, a tenancy by the entirety is created unless otherwise indicated.

The result would not be the same in all states that recognize a tenancy by the entirety. Most states that accept this type of tenancy do so only if it is expressly stated in the granting instrument.

Termination

A tenancy by the entirety is a more stable type of co-ownership than joint tenancy. Because the marital partners are considered a single unit, neither husband nor wife can sever the tenancy without the other's consent. Unlike joint tenancy, a sale by either the husband or the wife does not terminate the tenancy or end the right of survivorship.

In many jurisdictions, a tenancy by the entirety cannot be terminated by the forced sale of the husband's or wife's interest. This means that if either spouse individually incurs debts and then refuses to pay them, the creditor cannot *execute on*, that is, judicially seize and sell, the property. This rule has been criticized because it permits the debtor to escape responsibility while owning an interest in a valuable asset. For this reason a number of states have abolished the tenancy by the entirety. Some states permit the separate creditors of either spouse to execute on and sell the share of the debtor, whether husband or wife. If the nondebtor spouse survives, the creditor loses any rights to execute on the property. If the creditor holds a judgment against both spouses, resulting from an obligation both incurred, the creditor may execute on the estate held by the entirety.

Tenancies by the entireties are terminated by divorce because the marital relationship is essential to this form of co-ownership. On divorce the parties become tenants in common, unless the divorce decree provides for the transfer of one party's interest to the other.

The common law allowed the husband almost complete control of all of his wife's property. This included her individual share in a tenancy by the entirety. Thus, the husband, was entitled to all the income from the estate, and he had sole discretion as to occupancy and use. In fact, the husband could even unilaterally sell the real estate, although sale was subject to the wife's right of survivorship.

A husband's absolute power over his wife's property was terminated by the passage of a number of married women's acts during the past century. These statutes entitle the wife to control, and benefit from, her property. Today, in states that recognize tenancy by the entireties, the wife has the same rights in the property as her husband.

■ TENANCY IN PARTNERSHIP

> ■ *A form of co-ownership in which each partner owns partnership property together with the other partners; each partner's share is treated as personal property; partnership property of a deceased partner passes to the surviving partners.*

The common law did not recognize the partnership as a legal entity. As a result, property could not be held in the partnership name. This not only caused confusion but also frequently led to complex legal problems when a partner died or experienced financial difficulty. Creditors of an individual partner could then get a specific partnership assets; on the death of a partner, that partner's share in specific partnership property passed through that partner's estate.

CASE EXAMPLE

Kane and Waldron entered into a partnership agreement to operate a creamery. Partnership funds were used to purchase real estate to operate the business. Title was taken in both Kane's and Waldron's names. A short time later, Kane died. At common law, his interest in the real estate would pass to his heirs, not to the surviving partner.

Most states have now adopted the Uniform Partnership Act, which creates the tenancy in partnership. Specifically, the Uniform Partnership Act permits the firm to buy, hold, and sell real estate in the partnership name. Individual partners share ownership in particular property only as members of the firm. Spouses, heirs, and creditors of individual partners have no rights in partnership property.

Individual partners may not assign partnership property unless the assignment involves the rights of all partners. Although an individual partner may transfer partnership real property, any such transfer is made only as an agent for other partners of the firm.

On death, a partner's share passes to the surviving partners. In the previous example, Waldron, as the surviving partner, acquires Kane's share. Waldron, however, possesses this property only for the purpose of liquidation, as Kane's death terminates the partnership. During liquidation, Waldron may operate the business without interference from Kane's legal representatives.

Kane and his heirs—in fact, any partner—all have a valuable interest in the partnership. The interest stems from the individual's right to share in the profits and surplus of the firm. The interest is not in specific firm property. Under the Uniform Partnership Act, this interest is regarded as personalty, not realty. The partner's interest is unlike the interest of a joint tenant or a tenant in common. When the partner's interest is sold separately, the partnership is destroyed and the interest is not subject to partition.

■ COMMUNITY PROPERTY

■ *A form of co-ownership between husband and wife in which each has a one-half interest in property acquired through the labor of either during the marriage.*

Several jurisdictions in the United States apply the doctrine of **community property** to real estate owned by a husband or wife. Generally, the community property states are those located in the West and Southwest. The law of these states was influenced by the laws of France and Spain, countries that have traditionally used the concept of community property in determining property rights of married persons. The states in which community property is an integral part of the legal system include Arizona, California, Idaho, Louisiana, Nevada, New Mexico, Texas, Wisconsin, and Washington. Other states have from time to time adopted some of the community property ideas. Because community property ownership is statutory, each state varies the characteristics of the system to fit its own purposes.

Community property is based on the marital relationship. In community property jurisdictions, the husband and wife are regarded as partners. Each spouse becomes a co-owner with the other in all property acquired through the labor or skill of either or both while the two are married. This fact applies even if title to the property is held individually by the husband or wife.

CASE EXAMPLE

Tanya and Bob Blunt, residents of California, were married in 1949. Tanya, following the traditional role of homemaker, managed the domestic establishment and cared for the family. Bob successfully practiced his profession as a doctor. From 1979 until 1997, Bob's practice prospered, and he earned a great deal of money. Some of this was invested in real estate, which was held in Bob's name. When Bob died in 1997, one-half of this real estate, which was community property, belonged to his wife; the other half would be in Bob's estate.

Control of community property in most states has been given to the husband. The rationale appears to be the traditional view that the husband is the head of the family. Both the statutes that allocate this power to the husband and numerous judicial opinions require that the husband deal with the property in good faith. Recent statutory developments in several community property states have expanded protection of the wife against abuse of the husband's power to manage and control community property.

Community property is at odds with the law in other states, which recognize that property held in the name of one of the spouses is solely the property of that person. Even in those states, however, the other spouse usually has some rights in relation to the property on the death of the owner and on the termination of the marriage by divorce.

Separate Property

■ *Property owned by the husband or wife prior to marriage and property acquired during marriage by gift or inheritance.*

Not all property owned by husband and wife in the community property states is community property. The parties retain separate title to property owned separately before marriage and to property each acquired by gift or inheritance during marriage.

CASE EXAMPLE

The will of John Earles, who died in 1983, gave a one-third interest in a 1,600-acre ranch to his son, Jesse. The remaining two-thirds was given to Helen Earles, John's wife. Jesse was married in 1990. In 1998 Helen Earles, retaining a life interest in her two-thirds share, transferred title to her portion of the ranch to Jesse. On Jesse's death the ranch would pass as a part of his separate estate, not as community property.

Real property purchased with the separate property of one spouse who takes title in his or her name remains separate property. In the example above involving Tanya and Bob Blunt, if Bob had inherited money from his mother and invested it in real estate, the real property acquired would be separate property. In some community property states, rents and profits from separate property are considered separate property. In others, rents and profits from separate property become community property. Nonetheless, the property may lose its separateness if its character changes, as the next case illustrates.

In Re Walrath
Court of Appeals of California
51 Cal. App. 4th 1504 (1997)

Background. Gilbert and Gladys Walrath were married in 1992 and separated three years later. The parties filed for a dissolution of the marriage. Before the marriage, the husband deeded property (known as the Lucerne property) to himself and his wife. At that time the property had a value of $228,000, an $82,000 mortgage, and equity in the amount of $146,000. The wife later paid $20,000 out of her separate marital property to reduce the mortgage further.

At the time of the separation, the Lucerne property was valued at $240,000. The couple refinanced the home, borrowing $180,000. They used $60,000 of the loan proceeds to pay off a portion of the first mortgage, another $62,000 to pay off the mortgage on another piece of property in Nevada, and another $40,500 to acquire and improve an investment property in Utah. They placed another $16,000 in a joint savings account.

The husband sought reimbursement for the amount he contributed to the Nevada and Utah properties and the amount placed in the joint savings account, arguing that this was part of his separate property. The trial court disagreed, ruling that the husband had no claim to reimbursement from the assets acquired with the loan proceeds. The case was appealed to the California Court of Appeals.

Decision. The Court of Appeals affirmed the decision.

Judge Corrigan. [U]nder the Family Code, spouses who make separate property contributions to a community asset are entitled to reimbursement on dissolution of the marriage. Here we encounter an issue of first impression. When the original community asset is leveraged and loan proceeds are used to acquire new community properties, may a spouse seeking reimbursement for his original separate property contributions look to these new community properties acquired with loan proceeds?

Here, it is undisputed that the Lucerne property was transmuted to community property, and thus acquired by the community, when [the] Husband converted title to joint tenancy. Thereafter, the proceeds of the refinanced loan secured by the Lucerne property were community property. If, instead of refinancing, the parties had divorced, each would have been entitled to reimbursement for their separate property contributions to the Lucerne property. The parties did not divorce. Instead they made a joint decision to borrow against their community asset, thus reducing its value. They took the money gained and acquired new community assets. The community would profit or suffer loss as those new assets rose or fell in value. Each party retained the right to reimbursement from "the property" to which they had made their separate property contributions. That property was the Lucerne home, the value of which the parties had consciously diminished.

Section 2640, subdivision (h) provides that the contributing spouse shall be reimbursed for contributions to the acquisition of the property "to the extent the party traces the contributions to a separate property source." Husband contends he is entitled to reimbursement from the new community assets because he can trace the moneys used to acquire those assets to the value of the Lucerne residence in 1993, which in turn can be traced to his 1992 contribution to the Lucerne property of $146,000.

Tracing methods are necessary when separate and community funds have been commingled. These tracing methods are of no benefit to Husband, because the new community assets were not purchased with funds from a commingled source. The proceeds of the Lucerne loan did not have

continued on next page

a separate property and a community property component. Instead, the loan proceeds were 100 percent community property.

... The assets from which Husband seeks reimbursement were not acquired with his separate property, but with community property loan proceeds obtained by refinancing a community property home. The $118,500 in loan proceeds Husband seeks to recover from the Nevada and Utah properties and the joint savings account are community assets. ... Husband presented no evidence that the lender relied on his separate property in approving the Lucerne refinance. Indeed, at the time of the refinance, the Lucerne property had already been transmuted to a community asset; the community property served as collateral for the loan. Thus, the community property presumption governing the loan proceeds was not rebutted. ...

Husband was entitled to reimbursement for his separate property contributions to the acquisition of the community asset, limited by the net value of the asset at the time of division. Thereafter, when the community asset is used to acquire new community properties, Husband may not seek reimbursement for his original separate property contributions from these newly acquired community assets, because he made no separate property contribution to the acquisition of those assets.

Affirmed.

How could you alter the facts to achieve a separate property result?

■ REAL ESTATE SYNDICATE

■   *A group of investors who combine funds and managerial resources to develop, manage, or purchase real estate for a profit or as a tax shelter.*

As a syndicate is not a form of ownership, the investors involved must organize in some legal form. To answer legal questions involving a real estate syndicate, a lawyer needs to know in what legal form the syndicate holds the realty. Probably the simplest form for the organization of a syndicate is the tenancy in common. More important forms of ownership today are the S corporations, general and limited partnerships, joint ventures, and limited liability companies. (See Table 5.3.) Each of these forms will be discussed in the following pages. Chapter 6 provides additional discussion of real estate investment trusts (REITs) and other forms of real estate investments.

Corporation

The **corporation** is a desirable business association as an investment vehicle because the investors, called *shareholders*, enjoy limited liability. They cannot lose more than their investment, regardless of the corporation's indebtedness or liability. The corporation enjoys perpetual life, and its continuity is not interrupted because of changes in stock ownership. It may freely purchase and sell real property, and dower interests do not attach. The big downside to the general corporation is that there is "double taxation." The corporation is taxed on its profits at corporate rates, and the shareholders are taxed on the income they receive in the form of dividends from the corporation.

Federal law authorizes syndicates to use a modification of the corporate form. The modification allows investors to escape the double taxation of a corporation. The **S corporation** allows the syndicate to pass income through without being taxed at the corporate level. Thus, the owners are not subject to the double burden associated with the ordinary corporation. S corporations are limited to 75 shareholders, and some limitations are placed on the type of income allowed. Losses that a shareholder may take are also restricted. Additionally, the corporation must elect the S corporate status with the IRS; failure to do so results in the organization's being taxed as a general corporation. Because of these limitations and additional complex tax problems, S corporations are used only for relatively small, but sophisticated, syndications.

Partnership

■ *An association of two or more persons to organize a business venture and divide the profits.*

Many syndicates are organized either as general or limited **partnerships**. Both partnership forms also avoid double taxation—the nemesis of incorporation. A partnership is not taxed on its income; any income is taxed directly to the partners as individuals.

Investors who syndicate as a general partnership face three legal handicaps. Probably the most serious is the unlimited liability of the partners. Each partner is personally responsible for all partnership obligations, and his or her property, both real and personal, may be reached if the partnership assets are insufficient to satisfy the claims against it. This risk may be shifted by obtaining appropriate insurance. A second handicap is the power of individual partners to make agreements binding the firm that may prove harmful. Every partner is an agent of the partnership for the purpose of its business, and the act of every partner binds the partnership. To some extent, this risk may be mitigated by the use of restrictive language in the partnership agreement. Finally, death, withdrawal, or bankruptcy of one of the partners automatically terminates the partnership. To continue, the syndicate must be re-created by a new agreement. To facilitate securing capital for business ventures, many states have legislation that allows the creation of partnerships in which some of the members have limited liability. Partnerships of this kind are called *limited*, or *special*, *partnerships*. They are a popular form of organization for real estate syndicates.

Limited partnership. State laws providing for the creation of limited partnerships are based either on the *Uniform Limited Partnership Act* (ULPA) or on a 1976 revision of that act, known as the *Revised Uniform Limited Partnership Act* (RULPA), and amended in 1985. Only a few states have not as yet adopted the amended act.

Both acts define a **limited partnership** as a partnership having as members one or more general partners and one or more limited partners. Under most circumstances, a limited partner's liability to creditors of the partnership is limited to that person's capital contribution. Under the provisions of both acts, to be considered a limited partner, the individual must be designated as such in a certificate filed with a designated state official or agency. A limited partner enjoys limited liability.

CASE EXAMPLE

Anna, Ben, and Carla Lane formed a limited partnership to invest in real estate. Anna, the general partner, invested $10,000 and agreed to manage the property. Ben and Carla, as limited partners, contributed $25,000 each. The project failed after accumulating debts of $65,000. Individual assets of Anna could be reached to cover any claims of creditors not satisfied on liquidation. Ben's and Carla's individual assets could not be reached by the syndicate's creditors beyond the amounts of their initial investment.

When limited partners participate in the "control of the business," they lose their defense against liability to creditors. However, the ULPA does not define what constitutes "taking part in control." This has been left to the courts. Generally, they have interpreted "taking part in control" in a manner that significantly restricts the limited partner's ability to participate without forfeiting limited liability. In addition, under the ULPA, if the limited partner's name appears in the partnership name, the limited partner becomes liable as a general partner. This is intended to protect creditors who extend credit to the business on the basis of the financial resources of a person who is actually only a limited partner.

The RULPA specifically allows a limited partner to act in a number of situations for the business without forfeiting limited liability. For example, the revised act permits a limited partner to be a contractor for, or an agent or employee of, the limited partnership. A limited partner can also consult with and advise a general partner, act as a surety for the partnership, and approve or disapprove an amendment to the partnership agreement without losing the "limited partner" status. In addition, the act permits a limited partner to vote on the:

■ dissolution and winding up of the business;

■ sale, exchange, lease, mortgage, pledge, or other transfer of all or substantially all of the assets of the limited partnership;

■ incurrence of indebtedness by the limited partnership other than in the ordinary course of business;

■ change in the nature of the business; and

■ admission or removal of a general partner.

More important, under the RULPA, a limited partner is liable only to persons who transact business with the partnership who have actual knowledge of the limited partner's participation in control. Additionally, to recover, a plaintiff must be misled into reasonably believing the limited partner is a general partner. If, however, the limited partner's participation is substantially the same as that of a general partner, the limited partner will be liable to any person who transacts business with the partnership. The next case illustrates the need for limited partners to be extremely careful to avoid any semblance of "control" that may expose them to liability.

| TABLE 5.3 | Comparison of Business Organizations | | |

Type	Liability	Taxation	Number of Investors
Sole proprietor	Unlimited liability. Personally liable for all obligations of the business.	Taxed only once. Income is reported on the owner's personal tax return.	One
Corporation	Limited liability. Shareholders are liable only up to the amount that they have invested in the stock.	Double taxation. Profits are taxed once at the corporate level, and then the profits of the individual shareholders are reported on their personal income tax returns.	Unlimited
Subchapter S Corporation	Limited liability. Shareholders are liable only up to the amount that they have invested in the stock.	Taxed only once. Income passes through and is reported on individual shareholder's tax return.	75 or fewer
General Partnership	Unlimited liability. The personal assets of all partners can be reached to satisfy the obligations of the partnership.	Taxed only once. Income passes through and is reported on individual shareholder's personal tax return.	Unlimited
Limited Partnership	Limited liability for the limited partners. Unlimited liability for the general partner.	Taxed only once. Income passes through and is reported on individual partner's personal tax return.	Unlimited
Limited Liability Company (LLC)	Limited liability. Owners are liable only up to the amount that they have invested in the stock.	Taxed only once. Income passes through and is reported on individual owner's personal tax return.	Unlimited

Tapps of Nassau Supermarket, Inc. v. Linden Boulevard L.P.
Supreme Court of New York, Appellate Division
242 A.D. 2d 235, 661 N.Y.S. 2D 223 (1997)

Background. Tapps subleased certain premises from Linden Boulevard, Inc. (Linden), a Delaware limited partnership. Shopping Center of America (Shopping Center) was initially the general partner and Aviva Neuman, a limited partner. Under the sublease agreement Tapps was required to pay common area maintenance charges, and a share of the real estate taxes to Linden, who was to turn over the monies to their Landlord. Allegedly, Linden failed to turn the monies over; as a result, Linden and its subtenant, Tapps, were evicted.

Tapps filed suit against Linden and Neuman, personally, alleging that they wrongfully and fraudulently withheld the monies from the Landlord. It sought $14 million in damages. Neuman moved to have the suit against her dismissed on the grounds that she was a limited partner and was shielded from personal liability for the debts of the limited partnership. She also denied any wrongdoing.

The Court granted Neuman's motion to dismiss on the grounds that Neuman's acts as representative of Linden were insufficient to justify a reasonable belief by Tapps that she was acting in a way that would expose her to liability, that in fact, she was not exerting control over Linden.

Decision. The Appellate Division reversed the decision.

Opinion. The rules concerning the liability of limited partners are set out in Delaware's partnership law, " . . . A limited partner is not liable for the obligations of a limited partnership unless he is also a general partner or, in addition to the exercise of his rights and powers as a limited partner, he participates in the control of the business. However, if the limited partner does participate in the control of the business, he is liable only to persons who transact business with

the limited partnership reasonably believing, based upon the limited partner's conduct, that the limited partner is a general partner."

Subdivision (b) provides a laundry list of protected activities that a limited partner may engage in that do not constitute participation in the control of the limited partnership. These activities include acting as an agent or contractor for the limited partnership or the general partner; being an officer, director or shareholder of a corporate general partner; . . . [and] advising a general partner, or causing the general partner to take or refrain from any action . . . . Further, division (c) states that the enumeration of protected activities in subdivision (b) does not mean that the exercise of other activities by a limited partner necessarily constitutes participation in the control of the business. . . .

While some of Neuman's activities on behalf of Linden fall within the statute's protected activities, Tapps relies on other factors to support its belief that Neuman ignored the general partner and acted in her individual capacity. The affidavits of Tapps' president and chief financial officer establish that Neuman initially introduced herself as the "landlord" during lease negotiations, she negotiated the sublease on behalf of Linden, and acted as its attorney, she alone met with Tapps' representatives during a dispute concerning overcharges and she was the sole representative of Linden who collected the rent and arranged for repairs on the premises. Tapps asserts that these activities by Neuman, to the exclusion of all other Linden representatives, justified its reasonable reliance that Neuman was acting as Linden's principal. Neuman disputes this, and notes that the sublease was signed by . . . the president of Shopping Center, and that she signed all correspondence with Tapps as "Linden. . ., by Aviva D. Neuman, Vice President."

The New York Court of Appeals, however, in a factually similar case, has held that a "limited partner who 'takes part in the control of' the limited partnership's business should not automatically be insulated from individual liability merely by benefit of status as an officer and sole owner of the corporate general partner." In *Gonzalez v. Chalpin* plaintiff Gonzalez was hired as a superintendent of a building owned by Excel Associates, a limited partnership. Excel consisted of one general partner, one corporate general partner, Tribute Music, Inc., and one limited partner, defendant Chalpin, who was also the president and sole shareholder of Tribute [the corporate general partner]. Chalpin had been the person who hired Gonzalez, and after a dispute arose, Chalpin terminated Gonzalez's employment. Thereafter, Gonzalez commenced an action against the general partners and Chalpin for unpaid compensation.

The Court of Appeals held that Chalpin had lost his limited liability protection because "he failed to prove that he acted as an officer of Tribute on behalf of Excel rather than individually." The Court explained: "A limited partner who assumes such a dual capacity rightly bears a heavy burden when seeking to elude liability. For once a plaintiff meets the threshold burden of proving that a limited partner took an active individual part in effectuating the limited partnership's interest ... the fulcrum shifts. The limited partner in such a dual capacity must then, at least, prove that any relevant actions taken were performed solely in the capacity as officer of the general partner."

It is true that the Gonzalez Court relied in part on the fact that Chalpin offered no evidence, other than his own self-serving statements, that he was acting in his representative capacity for the partnership, unlike Neuman here, who did sign some correspondence in her representative capacity. However, in other acts, such as negotiating the lease and in meeting with Tapps' representatives to resolve financial disputes, Neuman made no such disclosures.

Accordingly, Neuman's motion . . . should have been denied.

Reversed.

What specifically should Neuman have done to have clearly avoided liability?

Joint Venture

■ *A business entity in which two or more persons have agreed to carry out a single undertaking for a profit.*

A **joint venture** is a form of business organization very similar to the partnership. Most of the law that applies to partnerships also applies to the joint venture. Like a partnership, the joint venture is based on agreement, and the members have a fiduciary relationship to each other. They share profits and losses; each enjoys the right to manage and direct the venture; and the venture is treated as a partnership for federal tax purposes.

The major difference between the partnership and the joint venture is that the latter is usually created to carry out a single transaction. Although some limited partnerships are created for a single purpose, most partnership operations are more extensive, carrying out a general business for a period of years. Other differences also exist between a partnership and joint venture. In a joint venture, each participant has limited power to bind the others. However, the participants may agree that each will have full power to bind. Finally, death of a joint venturer does not automatically dissolve the joint venture.

Limited Liability Company (LLC)

■   *A business entity that resembles, and is usually taxed, like a partnership, but offers the advantages of limited liability for the owners, like a corporation.*

A **limited liability company (LLC)** has characteristics of both the partnership and the corporate forms of ownership. It is a type of hybrid. LLCs offer an alternative to the limited partnership because the LLC form does not require at least one general partner with unlimited liability. Instead, all partners enjoy limited liability.

Investors in an LLC are called *owners* and the managers are called *members*. Like a corporation, an LLC is a separate legal entity with very few ownership restrictions. There is no limitation on the number of owners. Owners are not restricted to individuals; they may be corporations, partnerships or other LLCs, as well as certain trusts. The owners' interests may be divided into classes, not unlike the classes of stock in a corporation, for example, common and preferred.

There are several ways in which an LLC is more like a partnership than a corporation. An LLC is taxed like a partnership, not like a corporation. Instead of being taxed twice (once at the corporation level and once at the individual owners' level), the LLC's profits or losses "pass through" to the individual owners. In that way each owner preserves his or her own autonomy for tax purposes. Also, while a corporation must adhere to certain corporate formalities, such as annual shareholders' meetings, the LLC does not have such obligations. The transfer of stock can be more difficult in an LLC than a corporation because the usual rule is that the owners of an LLC must obtain approval of the other owners before ownership may be sold or transferred. Finally, an LLC can be managed by owners, in which case management is much like that of a partnership, or it can be managed by members, in which case it is more like a corporation.

For many, LLCs are the preferable choice as a means of holding real estate. One reason for this is the liability protection that it affords. Even when an owner has excellent insurance coverage, there are still many risks associated with owning property. LLCs provide owners with limited liability, meaning that only the LLC's assets may be reached by creditors of the LLC. The owners' personal assets are beyond the reach of the LLC's creditors. The taxation benefits discussed above are also important in the real estate context, especially when property is sold or converted to personal use. The owners of the LLC would still have to pay a capital gains tax on their share of the property, but at a lower rate than a corporation. Additionally, if the LLC members wanted to convert the property to personal use or trade it for property of similar value, there are no tax consequences. For a corporation, however, these transactions would be treated as a sale, with the attendant tax liability.

Trust

■   *A legal relationship in which a grantor transfers legal title to property to a trust (or a trustee), which holds the property for the benefit of third parties, or beneficiaries.*

The trust is a device that has been used in the United States and in England for several centuries. It has been an important instrument in law reform and the legal basis for some significant economic innovations.

CASE EXAMPLE

Elaine Morgan, a successful business executive, was married to Carl Morgan, a well-known musician. Carl had little interest in financial matters. To ensure that Carl had adequate income throughout his life, Elaine irrevocably transferred certain securities and real estate to Central Trust Company to be administered by the company with the income going to Carl for life. On Carl's death, the property was to go to the Juilliard School of Music.

Elaine has created a living, or *inter vivos*, trust. If she had made these provisions in a will, on her death a *testamentary trust* would have been created. Today, trusts are used for many different purposes. They are used extensively in family estate planning of the type mentioned in the example, but they are also important in business. Trusts are frequently utilized to finance real estate ventures and to protect bondholder creditors of a corporation. Many large charities are organized as trusts; wealthy individuals convey assets to a trustee, who administers them for some designated public benefit.

In a trust, one person or an institution, the *trustee*, is given title to specific property that is managed for the benefit of others. The property may be real or personal. In the example, Central Trust Company legally owns the securities and real estate, but it must administer them for Carl Morgan's benefit.

With few exceptions, trusts involving real property must be in writing. Some states permit *inter vivos* trusts of personal property to be created orally. All testamentary trusts, whether the property is real or personal, must be in writing and executed in a precise manner. Testamentary trusts that are frequently part of an estate plan often supplement a will.

Fiduciary Duty. Every trust must have a trustee to hold and manage the property. The trustee has a **fiduciary duty**, the responsibility for the utmost good faith and undivided loyalty, to the beneficiaries.

The doctrine of fiduciary responsibility applies to numerous legal relationships. Because some of these—such as the attorney-client and broker-seller relationships—are very important to real estate transactions, a brief outline of the duties common to all fiduciaries is in order. A fiduciary (1) must act for the benefit of the other party in matters within the scope of the relationship, (2) must not profit at the other party's expense, and (3) must make full disclosure of all information affecting transactions with the other party. In a case involving a trustee's fiduciary duties, Justice Benjamin Cardozo once said:

> Many forms of conduct permissible in a workaday world for those acting at arm's length are forbidden to those bound by fiduciary ties. A trustee is held to something stricter than the morals of the marketplace. Not honesty alone but the punctilio of an honor the most sensitive is then the standard of behavior. As to this there has developed a tradition that is unbending and inveterate. Uncompromising rigidity has been the atti-

tude of courts of equity when petitioned to undermine the rule of undivided loyalty by the "disintegrating erosion" of particular exceptions. Only thus has the level of conduct for fiduciaries been kept at a level higher than that trodden by the crowd. *Meinhard v. Salmon*, 164 N.E. 545 (N.Y. 1928).

Under the terms of most trusts, trustees are usually granted extensive powers. Sometimes these powers are statutory, but they are also included in most well-drawn trust instruments. A trustee's powers will usually include, but not be limited to, making new investments, managing real estate, carrying on a business, selling property, borrowing money, reviewing mortgages, settling litigation, voting stock, collecting income, and making distributions.

The fiduciary responsibility of the trustee protects the trust beneficiary. As a result, trusts continue to be important in personal financial planning. Since World War II the trust has been one of several devices used by investors to organize real estate syndicates.

■ KEY TERMS

community property 85	limited liability company 94	S corporation 89
co-ownership 79		tenancy by the entirety 83
corporation 88	limited partnership 89	tenancy in common 81
fiduciary duty 95	partition 82	tenancy in partnership 84
joint tenancy 79	partnership 89	trust 94
joint venture 93	real estate syndicate 88	

■ INTERNET RESOURCES

For a general guide to estate planning issues, see

www.estateplanninglinks.com

For an estate planning site connected with joint tenancy and tenancy in common, see

www.oklawyers.com/bas1002.htm

THE CHANGING LANDSCAPE

During the late nineteenth century, the American economy was expanding rapidly. Large sums of money were needed for investment in many segments of the economy. Real estate was no exception. Unfortunately, the corporate form of business organization that was used to attract capital into most business activity could not be used in real estate because most of the states prohibited ownership of real property by corporations. The business, or Massachusetts, trust evolved to circumvent this prohibition. The trust had many advantages over the corporation, such as limited liability, ready transferability of shares, and continuous existence. Because the trust was not a corporation, it was a permissible form of enterprise for real estate investment.

With the passage of time, state prohibitions against corporate ownership of real property were abolished, but the business trust continued to be important. It provided investors with a major tax advantage over the corporation. For tax purposes the trust was treated as a conduit through which income passed. Income it earned was not taxable to it as long as the income was distributed to the trust beneficiaries. Corporate income is not treated in this favorable manner but is taxable to the corporation and also to the shareholder when distributed. The tax advantage enjoyed by the business trust was eliminated by a number of court decisions that emphasized the corporate characteristics of the trust and held these sufficient to classify the trust as an association taxable as a corporation.

These rulings had little immediate impact because of the depressed economic conditions of the 1930s and, later, the influence of World War II. The need for capital in the real estate market was limited. Conditions changed late in the 1940s, as the postwar U.S. economic boom created a need for large sums of money to be invested in real estate. About this time, an effort was made to restore to the business trust the tax advantage that it had previously enjoyed. This effort was finally successful in 1960, when Congress approved legislation that allowed business trusts and investment trusts dealing in real estate to once again serve, under certain prescribed conditions, as a conduit through which income could pass without being taxed twice. There are rigid income, asset, and distribution requirements that are necessary to satisfy IRS qualifications.

Most recently, another tool for investment syndication has arisen. It is the limited liability company (LLC), which seeks the best of all worlds. A majority of the states have legislated the limited liability company into existence. The LLC enjoys the limited liability of a corporation and the single taxation of a partnership. There are no limitations on the number of shareholders (called *members*), the number of classes of stock, or the types of entities that may be members.

Perhaps there are too many organizational structures from which to choose. Can you suggest one structure that would eliminate the disadvantages of all of the existing structures? What would be its features?

■ REVIEW AND DISCUSSION QUESTIONS

1. Compare and contrast a *joint tenancy*, a *tenancy by the entirety*, and a *tenancy in common*.

2. Under what circumstances will a court order the property owned by tenants in common to be partitioned?

3. During the past 15 years, the S corporation and the limited partnership have been used extensively in real estate syndication. More recently, the LLC has become the darling of the business association world. What factors account for this?

4. Outline some of the problems that real estate sales personnel face as a result of co-ownership of real property.

5. Define a real estate syndicate and the various business forms through which it may organize.

■ CASE PROBLEMS

1. Lars Olsen is a general partner and Swen Nielson a limited partner in Olsen and Sons, a limited partnership engaged in the construction and sale of bowling alleys. Nielson had been in the construction business for many years but had retired because of ill health. Olsen has been in the construction business for a short time but had served as Nielson's accountant for a number of years. Although Olsen makes all business decisions, he frequently phones Nielson for advice. When asked for advice, Nielson usually replies, "Lars, I'm not telling you how to do it, but if I were doing it, I would do it this way." Olsen generally follows Nielson's advice. (a) If the venture fails, could Nielson be held liable as a general partner? Discuss. (b) Would the result be different if the business had been run by Nielson prior to his retirement? Explain.

2. Matilda Schomas owned a small apple orchard, which was operated by her son. Matilda did not wish to write a will, but she wanted her son to succeed to the property on her death. Without the aid of counsel, she decided that she and her son should hold the orchard as joint tenants. Matilda then conveyed the orchard to herself and her son "as joint tenants, not as tenants in common." When she died, the son claimed the orchard by right of survivorship. Was a joint tenancy created? Explain why or why not.

3. Marie Rodesney and Fred Rowlett owned property as tenants in common. They had acquired the property for speculative purposes, each agreeing to use his or her best efforts to sell it at a profit. While they owned the property, Rowlett rented it to a Mr. Wood for a used-car lot. Rentals under the agreement amounted to $5,230. Rowlett disbursed $3,511.52 for taxes and improvements, leaving a net balance of $1,718.48; however, the reasonable rental value of the property while it was owned by Rodesney and Rowlett was $15,900. On sale of the property, Rodesney contended that in addition to her share of the proceeds she was entitled to one-half of the reasonable rental value. Is her contention correct? Discuss. *Rodesney v. Hall*, 307 P.2d 130 (Okla. 1957).

4. James Huff and Carol Burns owned a condominium as tenants in common. From February 1978 until September 1985, they lived in the condominium as a family with Burns's minor child. During this period, Huff paid the maintenance expenses on the condominium. In 1985, the two quarreled and Burns changed the locks to the condominium, excluding Huff. Huff petitioned to partition the condominium, and the property was sold. In addition to his half share from the sale, Huff argued that he was entitled to half of the maintenance expenses and half of the rental value during the period that he was excluded from the property until the judicial sale. Is Huff correct? Discuss each claim separately.

5. A partition statute in Missouri reads:

    In all cases where lands . . . are held in joint tenancy, [or] tenancy in common . . . it shall be lawful for any one . . . of the parties interested therein . . . to file a petition . . . asking for . . . the partition . . . if the same can be done without great prejudice to the parties in interest; and if not, then for a sale of the premises, and a division of the proceeds thereof among all of the parties, according to their respective rights and interests.

Doyal Lemay and Esther Hardin, unmarried, entered into a real estate transaction in which both of them appeared as joint tenants, with right of survivorship, in the deed. They were hopeful that their relationship would ripen into marriage. Hardin did not contribute any monies to the purchase of the home; however, she did paint and clean it. Lemay contributed 100 percent of the monies. Lemay and Hardin broke up. Lemay contends that he owns the entire interest in the property. Hardin contends that she is entitled to an amount of money that will compensate her for the work that she did on the property. She files an action in partition. Will she be successful? Explain. See *Lemay v. Hardin*, 48 S.W. 3d 59 (Missouri Ct. App. 2001).

6. Catherine (Cathy) Sack and Rickey Tomlin started living together in March 1984. Shortly thereafter, Cathy obtained a divorce from her husband, William. She received fee simple ownership to a house in Carson City, pursuant to the divorce decree. In return she gave William a promissory note in the amount of $43,082, due and payable September 30, 1990. As that date approached, Cathy deeded the house to herself and Rickey as tenants in common, and they refinanced the house, borrowing $126,000 to pay off William. Each undertook an indebtedness of $63,000. Cathy and Rickey split up in February 1991 after differences arose, and Rickey continued to make one-half the mortgage payments. All told, Rickey contributed 36 percent of the funds applied toward the total expenditures of both parties during the period of cohabitation. In April 1992, the house was sold. Cathy made the final five mortgage payments. The sale of the house, for $185,000, netted equity in the amount of $46,278. A dispute arose regarding the apportionment of that equity between Cathy and Rickey. Rickey contended that Cathy intended to make a gift of one-half of the property to Rickey. Cathy denies this and contends that Rickey's contributions were for payment for rent and a fair share of the household expenses. How should the proceeds from the sale be split? What are the possibilities? Explain. See *Sack v. Tomlin*, 871 P.2d 298 (Nev. 1994).

7. Ellen and Jack Slaney lived in a community property state. Jack was employed as an accountant. Ellen managed the home. When Ellen became pregnant, they decided to build a home and purchased land on which to do so. After the baby was born, Jack changed his mind, as he preferred apartment living. Several years later, Ellen inherited money from an uncle. She used the inheritance for the construction of a home on the land. Is the land community property? What about the home? Support your answers.

8. Excel Associates was a limited partnership consisting of one individual general partner (Lipkin), one corporate general partner, Tribute Music, Inc., and one limited partner, Chalpin. Chalpin is the president, sole shareholder, and director of Tribute.

Chalpin hired Gonzalez to do maintenance and renovation work on Excel's apartment building. Chalpin paid Gonzalez with checks that he signed in his own name. Thereafter, Chalpin dismissed Gonzalez from the work, and Gonzalez sued Chalpin for pay allegedly owed. Under what theory is Chalpin liable in his individual capacity? What is Chalpin's argument for limited liability? What questions would you pose to help you better answer the question of individual liability versus limited liability in this case? *Bernabe v. Gonzalez,* 565 N.E. 2d 1253 (New York, 1990).

6

Condominiums, Cooperatives, Time-Shares, and Real Estate Investments

The condominium and the cooperative afford techniques for obtaining an ownership interest in a dwelling or office. They are in many ways similar, but they also have marked differences. This chapter focuses initially on the condominium and then describes and contrasts the cooperative.

The chapter also discusses various types of time-share agreements and real estate syndications.

■ CONDOMINIUM

■ *The fee simple ownership of one unit in a multiple-unit structure, combined with an ownership of an undivided interest in the land and all other parts of the structure, held as tenants in common with the owners of the other individual units in the structure.*

The concept of **condominium** ownership has blossomed in the United States since the mid-1960s. Condominiums often take the physical form of multi-unit high buildings or semi-detached town house type units. The notion of fee ownership, coupled with a release from the repair and maintenance chores of home ownership, made condominiums attractive to many people, especially to the elderly and to single-person households.

Condominiums did not present any fundamental legal problem. The common law had long recognized separate ownership of individual rooms or floors in a structure, which in essence is the nature of a condominium. Common or joint ownership of land and building was equally well established. Condominium ownership as a specific form, however, not only was new but also was a complex form of residential ownership. Describing the co-ownership, joint management, cross-easements, and enforcement of individual responsibilities was part of the complexity. To provide some clarity and uniformity for this new area, states quickly began to adopt permissive condominium legislation. By 1968 all the states had adopted some form of condominium law. Although the terminology differs, there is a great deal of similarity in the statutes adopted by the various states.

This chapter discusses condominium ownership as it applies to residential units. The condominium form is also being used in commercial and some industrial property. The legal principles are the same, regardless of the use to which the condominium unit is put.

Formation of a Condominium

The developer may purchase an existing multiple-family apartment building for conversion into a condominium. Alternatively, he or she may purchase land and obtain a construction mortgage for erecting the condominium structure. The completed condominium units are then sold to individuals. The individual purchasing the condominium unit attains a fee simple interest in the apartment unit. In addition, the individual becomes a tenant in common with the other unit owners of the land and all structures outside the walls of the individual apartments. These are known as the common elements.

The condominium owner, if necessary, obtains a mortgage on his or her individual unit. Payment at the time of purchase is made to the condominium developer, who in turn pays off the construction mortgage as it pertains to that individual unit and its appropriate share of the common elements and has them released from the lien of the construction mortgage.

CASE EXAMPLE

Greg and Helene Burnside purchase a condominium unit from Condo Developers Inc. for $128,000. They obtain a mortgage on the unit for $110,000 from Security Bank, provide $18,000 of their own cash, and deliver a check for $128,000 to Condo in exchange for a deed to the unit. Condo pays its mortgagee an amount sufficient to obtain a release for the Burnsides' unit and for 1 percent of the common elements. (There are 100 units of equal value in the development.)

Declaration

■ *A document required by state law, which must accompany and be recorded with the master deed for the condominium development.*

The **declaration**, one of three documents commonly mandated by state law, contains a description of the property, restrictions on use, and the detailed legal requirements that attach to ownership of a condominium unit. The other two documents are the bylaws and the deed to each individual unit.

The declaration is required for both new construction and for conversion of an existing building. It is filed in the county where the property is located, and it is maintained by the county clerk in the condominium records for the county. The declaration must contain a legal description of the property; a general description of each unit, including square footage and identification by floor and unit number; a description of any area that is subject to limited control, such as carports and garages; and a description of the common areas and each apartment's fractional interest in the entire condominium regime. Any changes or alterations to these declarations must be filed with the county clerk.

Declarations can also contain other matters, such as restrictive covenants. Restrictive covenants are discussed in Chapter 24, and the law discussed there is as applicable to condominiums as it is to other types of real property. Sometimes the condominium declaration will state that the association has a *right of first refusal* so that it can screen potential buyers of condominium units. When the existing owner of a unit has a willing buyer, the association is given a limited time in which to determine whether the prospective owner is satisfactory to the association. If not, the association can purchase the unit under the same terms as those offered by the buyer.

In addition, provisions are made for the contingency that the buildings might be substantially destroyed by fire or some other disaster. The declaration usually provides for its own amendment by a majority of the unit owners. Some states allow the purchaser the right to rescind a condominium contract for a period of time after receiving the documents.

Bylaws

▣ *The rules governing the internal operation of the condominium development.*

The bylaws of a condominium development are not unlike the bylaws of any organization. They provide for the selection of the board of directors of the association, meetings, regulations for the common elements, rights and responsibilities of unit owners, assessment and collection of monthly charges, and other relevant matters.

The bylaws are very important to the property owners because they establish the rights and responsibilities of each with respect to the condominium regime. Prior to the purchase of a unit, the bylaws as well as the declaration should be read carefully. The courts strictly enforce the bylaws and will uphold action taken by the council of owners pursuant to the bylaws.

Rules and Regulations

▣ *Rules and regulations complement and add specificity to the bylaws.*

The board of directors of a condominium will usually adopt a set of **rules and regulations** to give more detail to the bylaws. The rules and regulations must be in conformity with the bylaws. Their purpose is to protect the architectural integrity and harmony of the community, to promote the welfare of the residents, and to maintain an acceptable quality of life for the community. The primary governing document of the condominium continues to be the bylaws, and, in case of conflict, the bylaws supersede the rules and regulations.

The rules and regulations apply to property owners, their guests, tenants, and vistors, and are enforced by the board of directors. The restrictive nature of the rules and regulations should be tempered by an effort to ensure that they do not interfere with the reasonable use and enjoyment of the owners. The board of directors may change the rules and regulations by resolution at any time. An example of a rule and regulation would be the following:

> Common areas: The lawns and walkways shall not be used for storage or parking or be obstructed in any way. No bicycles, toys, trash cans or recycling bins or other personal property shall obstruct entrance ways, parking, or other common areas.

Individual Unit Deed

■   *The deed for each individual condominium unit in the development.*

Because the interior of each condominium apartment, along with a share of the common elements, is owned in fee simple by the unit owner, the deed must be recorded to protect the unit owner from a fraudulent conveyance by the seller. In addition, it provides a chain of title that can be relied on by a subsequent purchaser to ensure the marketability of the title. Each individual unit owner is entitled to apply for a mortgage to help finance the purchase.

Common Elements

■   *The parts of the development property that are necessary or convenient for the residents of the condominium and are owned in common by all the condominium residents.*

Each condominium unit owner has a tenancy in common in the land and buildings and other structures not constituting the interior of his or her individual condominium unit. This ownership interest is undivided; that is, all unit owners have an equal right to all the common elements.

The common elements generally include hallways, elevators, recreational facilities, land, stairways, exterior of the buildings, and so on. Most state statutes specifically designate what items are included in the common elements. Where not so provided, they should be described carefully in the declaration.

The percentage of the common elements ascribed to each apartment unit may be equal where the units are quite similar. Where significant differences exist among the units, however, the percentage may be based on the differing values of the individual units. In any event, the amount attributable to each unit is designated in the declaration.

The highrise condominium has caused a distinction to be created between two kinds of common elements. *General common elements* are those previously described, in which all the unit owners share. In a condominium made up of townhouses all the common elements are usually general. *Limited common elements* that are shared by more than one unit owner but less than all of them may include stairways, balconies, and elevators in divided sections of a highrise condominium.

The state statutes generally provide that the expenses of administering, maintaining, repairing, and replacing the common elements be borne by an assessment of the unit owners made by the board of directors of the association. The board of directors is then responsible for repairing and operating the common elements. Unit owners are bound by the terms of the declaration to pay their shares of the assessment. Payment of the expenses cannot be avoided by waiving the right to use certain parts of the common elements. For example, a nonswimmer cannot reduce the monthly assessment by deducting an amount that would cover maintenance of the swimming pool.

If the association that administers the common elements is unincorporated, the individual unit owners are liable as principals for all authorized and apparently authorized acts of the association. Incorporation of the association, however, limits the unit owners' liability to the assets of the corporation.

Condominium Association

■ *The organization stipulated by statute to administer the operation of the common elements of the condominium.*

The association, and its board of directors on a day-to-day operational level, carries out the business of caring for the condominium. Members of the board of directors are the representatives of the unit owners and bear a fiduciary relationship to those owners. Their responsibility to the unit owners is multifaceted. For instance, their fiduciary duty to the unit owners requires that the board deal fairly and carefully with the business interests of the unit owners. It must avoid participation in decisions that present conflicts of interest for individuals. In short, board members can be held legally liable for mismanagement or for secretly profiting from that management. Board members are not relieved of liability merely because they are "volunteer" or unpaid. It is advisable that the board member have the association provide liability insurance coverage.

Because the association is generally mandated by state law, it is quasi governmental in nature. Its actions may be treated as "state action" and thus subject to the proscriptions in the constitution. For instance, when a unit owner is subjected to sanctions provided in the declaration for nonpayment of an assessment, the unit owner is entitled to due process (notice and hearing). Similarly, the right of first refusal cannot be utilized by the association to exclude prospective purchasers on the basis of race, religion, color, sex, national origin, familial status, or handicap. Although the boundaries of constitutional responsibility of associations are unclear, it appears certain that some restrictions such as those mentioned above will be imposed.

Assessments

■ *The regular monthly payments for upkeep of the common elements, as well as payments required for special expenses or improvements to those common elements.*

State legislation generally provides that the bylaws establish the rules for regular and special assessments. The association's board of directors, or a project manager appointed by the board, normally collects the assessments and uses them in maintaining the condominium property. The original setting of the amount of the regular assessment, the changing of that amount, and the imposition of a special assessment are determined by the terms of the bylaws. The bylaws are likely to place responsibility for establishing these assessments with the association or its board of directors.

CASE EXAMPLE
The newly elected board of directors of a highrise condominium discovered that the building had serious structural defects and that the association was in debt. The board of the Tower West Condominium discussed the woes at length and then levied a $100,000 special assessment to be paid proportionately by the unit owners. Papalexion and several other unit owners refused to pay the assessment contending that according to the bylaws a vote of the full association was necessary unless there was "an extreme emergency." They argued that this was not such an emergency.

The court held that the unit owners had to pay the assessment. Based on the structural problem and the poor financial condition of the condominium association, the board acted reasonably in concluding that this was an extreme emergency as intended under the bylaws. *Papalexion v. Tower West Condominium*, 167 N.J. Super. 516, 401 A.2d 280 (1979).

When a unit owner refuses or is unable to pay an assessment, he or she is subject to enforcement procedures that are usually stated in the bylaws. In at least two states, the statute permits the association to cut off utilities ten days after notice of delinquency is given. The normal route, however, makes any unpaid assessment a lien on the property with priority over all other liens except those designated in the statute. Generally, the liens designated in the statute are the most common forms: tax liens, prior mortgages, mechanics' liens, and the like.

The procedure for foreclosing on this lien is the same as that followed under the state's mortgage foreclosure law, unless otherwise stated. At the foreclosure sale, the association is permitted to purchase the delinquent unit unless the practice is proscribed by the declaration. The main disadvantage of the foreclosure procedure is that the other unit owners must bear the expense of the delinquency during what may be a protracted foreclosure action.

The association also has the option of bringing an action for money damages, and this action does not preclude the subsequent lien foreclosure action described above. If delinquency is caused by a unit owner's shortage of funds, generally an action for money damages is not advisable.

In states that have homestead laws, seizure of the place of residence may be prohibited. Often the residential condominium qualifies as the homestead. A second lien method that circumvents these laws is the trust and lien on sale technique. This technique permits recovery of the delinquent amount from the proceeds at the time the delinquent unit is sold. Because the proceeds are considered to be in trust, the assessment lien must be satisfied prior to any distribution to the seller of the condominium unit. The legal implications for the buyer are unclear. A cause of action may lie against the buyer who receives the proceeds prior to a satisfaction of the assessment lien.

Again, this technique may force the other unit owners to bear the burden of the delinquency for an extended period of time. However, it should circumvent the difficulty under the homestead laws existing for the previously described lien technique.

The *Beachwood Villas* case that follows provides a good insight into the roles that the state condominium statute, the declaration, and the board of directors play in regulating condominium use.

 ### Beachwood Villas Condominium v. Poor
District Court of Appeal of Florida
448 So.2d 1143 (1984)

Background. The board of directors of Beachwood Villas Condominium adopted two rules regulating unit rentals and the occupancy of units by guests during the owner's absence. Earl and Iris Poor, owners of a condominium unit, were unhappy with the rules and sued to have them declared invalid because they exceeded the scope of the board's authority. The trial court agreed with the Poors, deciding that the board exceeded its authority.

Decision. The District Court of Appeals reversed the judgment of the trial court.

Judge Hurley. Rule 31, the rental rule, requires that: (1) the minimum rental period be not less than one month, (2) the number of rentals not exceed a specified number which is calculated to the size of the unit, (3) tenants not have pets without the approval of the board, and (4) a processing fee of $25.00 be paid. Rule 33, the guest rule, requires: (1) board approval for the "transfer" of a unit to guests when the guests are to occupy the unit during the owner's absence, (2) the number of transfers (either by rental or guest occupancy) not exceed six per year, and (3) that the occupancy rate not exceed a specified number which is calculated to the size of the unit.

Hidden Harbour Estates, Inc. v. Basso, (1981), suggested that condominium rules falling under the generic heading of use restrictions emanate from one of two sources: the declaration of condominium or the board of directors. Those contained in the declaration "are clothed with a very strong presumption of validity . . . ," because the law requires their full disclosure prior to the time of purchase and, thus, the purchaser has adequate notice. Board rules, on the other hand, are treated differently. When a court is called on to assess the validity of a rule enacted by a board of directors, it first determines whether the board acted within its scope of authority and, second, whether the rule reflects reasoned or arbitrary and capricious decision making.

The reasonableness of rules 31 and 33 was not questioned below and, therefore, we are concerned only with the scope of the board's authority. Inquiries into this area begin with a review of the applicable statutes and the condominium's legal documents, i.e., the declaration and by-laws.

By express terms in the statute and in the declaration, the association has been granted broad authority to regulate the use of both the common element and limited common element property.

In general, that power may be exercised as long as the exercise is reasonable, is not violative of any constitutional restrictions, and does not exceed any specific limitations set out in the statutes or condominium documents.

Since there has not been any suggestion that either rule violates the Condominium Act, Section 718, Florida Statutes (1983), we begin by viewing the Beachwood Villas declaration of condominium. Article X provides that "[t]he operation of the condominium property shall be governed by the By-Laws of the Association which are . . . made a part hereof." In turn, Article IV of the by-laws states that "[a]ll of the powers and duties of the Association shall be exercised by the board of directors. . . ." More specific is Article VII, Section 2, which states that "[t]he Board of Directors may, from time to time, adopt or amend previously adopted rules and regulations governing and restricting the use and maintenance of the condominium units. . . ."

It is obvious from the foregoing that the board of directors is empowered to pass rules and regulations for the governance of the condominium. The question remains, however, whether the topics encompassed in rules 31 and 33 are legitimate subjects for board rulemaking. Put another way, must regulations governing rental of units and occupancy of units by guests during an owner's absence be included in the declaration of condominium? A declaration of condominium is "the condominium's constitution." Often, it contains broad statements of general policy with due notice that the board of directors is empowered to implement these policies and address day-to-day problems in the condominium's operation through the rulemaking process. It would be impossible to list all restrictive uses in a declaration of condominium. Parking regulations, limitations on the use of the swimming pool, tennis court, and card room—the list is endless and subject to constant modification. Therefore, we have formulated the appropriate test in this fashion: provided that a board-enacted rule does not contravene either an express provision of the declaration or a right

continued on next page

reasonably inferable therefrom, it will be found valid, within the scope of the board's authority. This test, in our view, is fair and functional; it safeguards the rights of unit owners and preserves unfettered the concept of delegated board management.

Inasmuch as rules 31 and 33 do not contravene either an express provision of the declaration or any right reasonably inferable therefrom, we hold that the board's enactments are valid and plainly within the scope of its authority. Accordingly, we reverse the order on appeal and remand the cause for further proceedings consistent with this opinion.

Reversed and Remanded.

It seems as if the bylaws give this condominium association very broad authority. What are its limits? Can it make the minimum rental period two months? Or six months? Can it limit the renters to adults, or to two adults? If there are limits to the association's authority, what are the boundaries of permissible and impermissible rules?

■ COOPERATIVE

> ■ *A form of ownership in which the land and buildings are (usually) owned by a corporation; individual unit residents own stock in the corporation and have a proprietary lease in a specific unit or apartment.*

Unlike the condominium unit owner, the **cooperative** owner or tenant does not have a fee simple interest in the apartment. Instead, the owner has shares of stock in the corporation that owns the land and building, along with a long-term *proprietary lease.* Occasionally, the cooperative ownership is in a trust or partnership form rather than a corporate form.

The notion of a proprietary lease connotes that, unlike typical tenants, the cooperative tenants participate in the running of the cooperative through their stock interest in the corporation. The participation may be direct, when an individual is elected as a member of the board of directors, or indirect, when voting for directors or giving opinions to the elected directors. Despite the proprietary nature of the lease, however, it continues to be a lease and is governed by landlord-tenant law. One must be cautious, however, because the state may choose to treat a proprietary lease differently from a traditional lease.

CASE EXAMPLE

Drew Associates, a cooperative developer, challenged the New Jersey Cooperative Recording Act as unconstitutional. One of Drew's grounds was that the statute created an illegal restraint on the alienation of land by requiring that all transfer documents be recorded and that they contain the consent of the board of managers of the cooperative. These conditions are not placed on other leases or even condominium transfers.

The Court upheld the statute stating that cooperative ownership is a "hybrid" form of property and does not fall within traditional notions of either realty or personalty. It is reasonable, therefore, for the state to impose conditions on cooperative transfers not imposed on other forms of transfer. *Drew Associates of N.J. v. Travisano*, 122 N.J. 249, 584 A.2d 807 (1991).

Financing a Cooperative

In a typical situation, an investor purchases a multiple-unit dwelling to convert it into a cooperative. To finance the conversion, the investor takes out a mortgage with a bank for 80 percent of the dwelling's value. The remaining 20 percent is paid initially by the investor but is recouped through the issuance of stock in the cooperative corporation to the future tenants. Future tenants pay their share of the 20 percent by purchasing stock when they enter the cooperative. In addition, each makes monthly payments that cover his or her share of the mortgage payment as well as operating expenses.

In addition to the mortgage share, each tenant as part of the monthly rent will pay a share of any other debt, taxes, and operating expenses. As in a condominium, the share of these expenses may be on a per-unit basis or may vary with the relative value of the apartment. The amount of the annual or monthly assessment is determined by the board of directors of the corporation.

■ DIFFERENCES BETWEEN CONDOMINIUMS AND COOPERATIVES

One difference between a cooperative and a condominium is the type of mortgage obtained. In the condominium each unit owner arranges for his or her own mortgage; in the cooperative there is a *blanket mortgage* for the entire building. The blanket mortgage may be more difficult to obtain.

In the cooperative there are restrictions on the ability of the tenants to sell their interest. Generally, the tenant needs the approval of the board of directors for the proposed new tenant. This procedure is a little more stringent than the right of first refusal used in the condominium area. These restrictions on the cooperative go beyond the outright sale and may prevent a tenant from assigning or subletting his or her share of the premises. The purpose behind these restrictions is to ensure that a compatible group of tenants is assembled in the cooperative.

The cooperative form of ownership has advantages for the tenant compared with the usual landlord-tenant situation. The tenant is not subjected to annual rent increases and does not risk having the lease terminated arbitrarily. The cooperative tenant has a long-term lease and participates in any decision to raise the rent.

Like the condominium owner, the cooperative owner or tenant is subject to an extensive set of rules and regulations governing the cooperative. Failure to comply with the terms of the regulations may permit the board of directors to cancel the tenant's lease or to take some other action provided in the rules for redressing the violation.

On the death of the tenant, any successor—an heir under the tenant's will or by law—must clear the screening of the board of directors. There is no automatic right on the part of successors to be able to continue the cooperative lease. This differs from a condominium, where the unit is owned in fee and can freely be passed on to successors.

There are some distinct advantages to fee simple ownership, of which the condominium owner is the beneficiary. The notion of fee ownership itself carries a certain feeling of security and psychological confidence that is not matched by the lease of the cooperative arrangement. Many of these advantages are tangible and specific.

The condominium owner is responsible for his or her own mortgage and is not as vulnerable to default as the cooperative owner, who shares a blanket mortgage with

TABLE 6.1	Contrasting Condominiums and Cooperatives		
Subject-Matter	**Condo**	**Co-op**	
Mortgages	Individual unit	Blanket on building	
Mortgage	Responsible for own only	Vulnerable to others defaulting on blanket mortgage	
Selling Interest	Gives right of first refusal	Needs approval of board	
Selling Interest	To anyone at fair market	To cooperative at stipulated price	
Death of Owner	Owner's designee	Tenant's designee needs board approval	
Ouster of Owner/Tenant	Messy lien foreclosure	Simpler eviction	
Federal Income Tax	Normal homeowner and some business deductions	Limited deductions	

everyone else in the cooperative. If the unit is rented, the condominium owner can directly take advantage of certain tax benefits, such as property tax deduction, interest deductions, casualty loss deductions, and depreciation allowance. Under Section 216 of the Internal Revenue Code, residential cooperatives may be able to take advantage of some federal tax benefits, such as property tax and interest deductions, not available individually to cooperative owners. Under Section 528 of the Internal Revenue Code, however, a condominium owner is permitted to make a tax-free contribution to the association for capital expenses, maintenance, and operating expenses, provided the association meets the requirements of Section 528. Thus, a condominium owner can make a tax-free payment to the association for a new roof or for the pool lifeguard. A payment for similar expenses to a cooperative would not qualify.

On the sale of a condominium unit, the owner can sell at market value and pay the reduced capital gains rate on the gain, subject to postponement and rollover provisions. The cooperative owner generally must sell the stock back to the cooperative at a stipulated price. Often the stipulated price is the original price.

Cooperatives can be troublesome during difficult economic times. Initially, it may be more difficult to get a blanket mortgage loan than to get a mortgage loan on an individual condominium unit. Given the nature of the interdependence created by the blanket mortgage, the default of one or several cooperative owners can cause a default on the mortgage. On default, all cooperative owners stand to lose their investments, even those who can afford to keep up their share of expenses. In a condominium, on the other hand, the default on an individual mortgage does not affect the other condominium owners. Nevertheless, the financial straits that caused the mortgage default are likely to prevent payment of condominium assessments; in this respect, delinquencies can place a financial strain on the other condominium owners.

One advantage the cooperative has over the condominium is that it is relatively easy to get rid of an incompatible tenant. A tenant who refuses to comply with the rules of the cooperative can be evicted in summary proceedings in most instances. Although a condominium owner who is in default on assessments can be ousted through a lien foreclosure, the procedure is likely to be more prolonged and expensive. The differences between condominiums and cooperatives are shown in Table 6.1.

The Levandusky case defines the roles that courts will take in reviewing disputes between owners/tenants and boards of directors. The court provides a useful insight into how condominiums and cooperatives work.

Levandusky v. One Fifth Avenue Apartment Corp.
Court of Appeals of New York
553 N.E.2d 1317 (1990)

Background. Ronald Levandusky lived in an incorporated residential cooperative. Seeking to increase the kitchen area of his apartment, he had renovation plans prepared and presented to the cooperative's board of directors. The board approved the plans, and executed with Levandusky an "Alteration Agreement" that incorporated "Renovation Guidelines." The guidelines provided that special written approval was required for any alteration to the building's heating system, and none was indicated in the initial plan. It later came to the board's attention that Levandusky intended to move the steam pipes. At a later meeting the board reaffirmed its existing policy against relocating vertical steam pipes, and modified Levandusky's plan approval to reflect that limitation. Levandusky hired a contractor and proceeded with the work. The board issued a stop order pursuant to its "Renovation Guidelines." Levandusky sued to have the stop order set aside.

The trial court dismissed Levandusky's petition and ordered him to restore the steam pipes. The intermediate appellate court affirmed in a split decision (3-2). One of the major issues discussed by each of the courts was the role courts should play in reviewing disputes between boards of directors and unit owners/tenants in condominiums and cooperatives.

Decision. The Court of Appeals affirmed the decision of the lower courts.

Judge Kaye. As cooperative and condominium home ownership has grown increasingly popular, courts confronting disputes between tenant-owners and governing boards have fashioned a variety of rules for adjudicating such claims. In the process, several salient characteristics of the governing board/homeowner relationship have been identified as relevant to the judicial inquiry. The cooperative or condominium association is a quasi-government— "a little democratic sub-society of necessity." The proprietary lessees or condominium owners consent to be governed, in certain respects, by the decisions of a board. Like a municipal government, such governing boards are responsible for running the day-to-day affairs of the cooperative and to that end, often have broad powers in areas that range from financial decisionmaking to promulgating regulations regarding pets and parking spaces. Authority to approve or disapprove structural alterations, as in this case, is commonly given to the governing board.

Through the exercise of this authority, to which would-be apartment owners must generally acquiesce, a governing board may significantly restrict the

continued on next page

bundle of rights a property owner normally enjoys. Moreover, as with any authority to govern, the broad powers of a cooperative board hold potential for abuse through arbitrary and malicious decisionmaking, favoritism, discrimination and the like.

On the other hand, agreement to submit to the decisionmaking authority of a cooperative board is voluntary in a sense that submission to government authority is not; there is always the freedom not to purchase the apartment. The stability offered by community control, through a board, has its own economic and social benefits, and the purchase of a cooperative apartment represents a voluntary choice to cede certain of the privileges of single ownership to a governing body, often made up of fellow tenants who volunteer their time, without compensation. The board, in return, takes on the burden of managing the property for the benefit of the proprietary lessees. It is apparent, then, that a standard for judicial review of the actions of a cooperative or condominium governing board must be sensitive to a variety of concerns—sometimes competing concerns. Even when the governing board acts within the scope of its authority, some check on its potential powers to regulate residents' conduct, life-style and property rights is necessary to protect individual residents from abusive exercise, notwithstanding that the residents have, to an extent, consented to be regulated and even selected their representatives. At the same time, the chosen standard of review should not undermine the purposes for which the residential community and its governing structure were formed: protection of the interest of the entire community of residents in an environment managed by the board for the common benefit.

We conclude that these goals are best served by a standard of review that is analogous to the business judgment rule applied by courts to determine challenges to decisions made by corporate directors. A number of courts in this and other states have applied such a standard in reviewing the decisions of cooperative and condominium boards. We agree with those courts that such a test best balances the individual and collective interests at stake.

Developed in the context of commercial enterprises, the business judgment rule prohibits judicial inquiry into actions of corporate directors "taken in good faith and in the exercise of honest judgment in the lawful and legitimate furtherance of corporate purposes." So long as the corporation's directors have not breached their fiduciary obligation to the corporation, "the exercise of [their powers] for the common and general interests of the corporation may not be questioned, although the results show that what they did was unwise or inexpedient."

We emphasize that reference to the business judgment rule is for the purpose of analogy only. Clearly, in light of the doctrine's origins in the quite different world of commerce, the fiduciary principles identified in the existing case law—primarily emphasizing avoidance of self-dealing and financial self-aggrandizement—will of necessity be adapted over time in order to apply to directors of not-for-profit homeowners' cooperative corporations. So long as the board acts for the purposes of the cooperative, within the scope of its authority and in good faith, courts will not substitute their judgment for the board's. Stated somewhat differently, unless a resident challenging the board's action is able to demonstrate a breach of this duty, judicial review is not available.

As this case exemplifies, board decisions concerning what residents may or may not do with their living space may be highly charged and emotional. A cooperative or condominium is by nature a myriad of often competing views regarding personal living space, and decisions taken to benefit the collective interest may be unpalatable to one resident or another, creating the prospect that board decisions will be subjected to undue court involvement and judicial second-guessing. Allowing an owner who is simply dissatisfied with particular board action a second opportunity to reopen the matter completely before a court, which—generally without knowing the property—may or may not agree with the reasonableness of the board's determination, threatens the stability of the common living arrangement.

Levandusky's argument that having once granted its approval, the board was powerless to rescind its decision after he had spent considerable sums on the renovations is without merit. There is no dispute that Levandusky failed to comply with the provisions of the "Alteration Agreement" or "Renovation Guidelines" designed to give the board explicit written notice before it approved a change in the building's heating system. Once made aware of Levandusky's intent, the board promptly consulted its engineer, and notified Levandusky that it would not depart from a policy of refusing to permit the movement of pipes. That he then went ahead and moved the pipe hardly allows him to claim reliance on the board's initial approval of his plans. Indeed, recognition of such an argument would frustrate any systematic effort to enforce uniform policies.

Affirmed.

Suppose the board did not consult an engineer but simply decided that it did not want any pipes "tinkered with"?

■ TIME-SHARES

Time-sharing has become a popular marketing device for resort developments in the United States. **Time-shares** include several very different types of ownership. Some of these forms include ownership of an interest in the real property, and other forms are mere rights of use with no interest in the property itself.

Time-sharing arrangements can be built on several different legal principles. In some instances the arrangement is a variation of the tenancy in common. In others it is a variation of a cooperative. It could also be based on a lease. When it is built on one of these types of legal principles, it always includes a limitation as to the time of use. For example, a tenancy in common is an estate that includes more than one owner, with each co-owner owning an undivided interest. A time-sharing arrangement based on the legal principles of the tenancy in common would introduce the characteristic of time with respect to possession of the property. An ordinary tenant in common has an equal right to possession with the other cotenants. The time-share agreement limits the right to possession to a specific time period each year.

The time-sharing arrangement can also include principles of contract, partnership, license, or corporate law. For example, a time-sharing arrangement based in contract law would include the right to use a specific piece of property at a definite time each year for a certain number of years. At the expiration of that period, the property would be owned by the developer, not the owner of the time-share.

Much of the criticism of time-sharing arrangements is a result of misleading marketing practices. The legal rights associated with time-sharing arrangements can vary significantly from development to development. The variety of legal rights that are being marketed as time-shares coupled with deceptive and misleading information by salespersons has prompted some states to enact legislation dealing specifically with time-shares.

■ REAL ESTATE SECURITIES

■ *Any syndication whereby a person invests money in a common enterprise involving real estate with the expectation of attaining profits from the efforts of a promoter or some other third party.*

A normal transaction for the sale or lease of real property is not a security within the context of federal and state security laws. When a person or promoter offers an interest in the arrangement to the public, however, it may become a security. On other occasions, a person will sell a business, and the assets include real property. In many states, real estate securities and business opportunity sales have separate and distinct control schemes from the usual real estate transactions.

If the transaction constitutes the issuance of a security, unless exempted, the promoter must comply with federal and (probably) state regulations.

CASE EXAMPLE

Fafner offers a group of his friends and neighbors an opportunity to be investors with him in a piece of mountaintop property he is about to acquire. The property has multiple-unit housing on it, and the investors will share in the profits. This purchase is a real estate security and must be registered as described later in this section.

One of the chief federal regulations in the area of securities is the 1933 Securities Act. The language of Section 2 of the act covers any investment contract or profit-sharing arrangement and is therefore broad enough to encompass almost any real estate syndication. The key factors are that transactions be a common enterprise and that there be management of the investment by a third party for the benefit of a passive investor. When an agency or court makes the decision as to whether or not a transaction involves a security, the emphasis is on the substance and economic reality rather than on the form the transaction takes. In defining what a security is, or any other regulation hereinafter discussed, the investor must take care to research the provisions of the state "blue-sky" laws, which regulate security transactions as well.

Condominiums as Securities

The offering of a condominium unit is not normally treated as a security, but as a sale of real estate. Thus, the sale is not subject to the regulation of the Securities and Exchange Commission (SEC) or to similar state laws.

CASE EXAMPLE

Joyce entered a purchase agreement for a condominium unit, which he planned to use for his personal residence. Joyce sued the condominium project owner, contending that his contract was an "investment contract" and subject to federal securities laws. The security had not been registered, nor had Joyce received a prospectus, as required by federal securities law.

The federal district court held that a condominium purchase does not fall within the definition of an investment contract. An investment contract presumes that the investor hopes to realize a profit from the investment due to the activity of a third party. This is not the case where a typical condominium is purchased as a personal residence. *Joyce v. Ritchie Tower Properties*, 417 F. Supp. 53 (D. Ill. 1976).

Nevertheless, several states have extensive regulations of condominiums as securities. It is clear, however, that in any state if condominium advertisements or other documents make any reference to providing rental services for the buyer for the period the buyer is not using the condominium, the purchase will be treated as an **investment contract** and the above-mentioned security regulations will apply. For more detail, SEC Release No. 33-5347 (January 4, 1973) provides guidelines for determining when condominium offerings are securities.

Hocking v. Dubois
United States Court of Appeals, Ninth Circuit
885 F.2d 1449 (1989)

Background. After visiting Hawaii, Gerald Hocking, a resident of Nevada, contacted a Hawaii real estate agent, Marylee Dubois. Hocking asked Dubois to search for a condominium for him to invest in. He indicated that he wanted to buy directly from the developer, to be "a first person buyer." Dubois brought a condominium to Hocking's attention in a resort complex being built by Aetna Life Insurance Co. The particular condominium unit Dubois referred to was owned by the Libermans, but Dubois apparently assured Hocking that he was buying from the developer. She told Hocking that a rental pool arrangement (RPA) would be available if he chose to buy the unit; that units in the complex were renting for an average of $100 a day, or about $2,000 to $3,000 per month. Hocking intended to use the income to make his monthly payments on the unit.

Hocking purchased the condominium unit and joined the RPA, thereby contracting with Hotel Corporation of the Pacific (HCP) to manage his rentals. The contract could be terminated by Hocking on 30 days' written notice, and by HCP if the participation of the number of units in this complex fell below 40 percent. He handled all these matters through Dubois.

Hocking purchased the unit for $115,000, with a $24,000 down payment and installments due thereafter until final payment in June 1982. Subsequently, Hocking "canceled" his investment and refused to make payments because the rental income did not live up to Dubois's predictions. He alleged that his investment was entirely passive; that he relied on

Dubois to select, manage, and protect his investment; and that he relinquished all control over the unit except for two weeks each year. Hocking sued Dubois, contending that she violated the antifraud provisions of the Securities and Exchange Commission Act of 1934. The trial judge ruled for Dubois, granting a summary judgment.

Decision. The U.S. Court of Appeals reversed the trial court's decision and remanded the case for a trial on the issues.

Chief Judge Goodwin. The term "investment contract" has been interpreted to reach "[n]ovel, uncommon, or irregular devices, whatever they appear to be. . . ." "It embodies a flexible rather than a static principle, one that is capable of adaptation to meet the countless and variable schemes devised by those who seek the use of the money of others on the promise of profits." In *Howey* (1946), the Supreme Court found that the combined sale of land and a land service contract, under which the purchaser relinquished all control over the land for a 10-year period, was an investment contract. The Court there put forward the classic definition of an investment contract: [A]n investment contract for purposes of the Securities Act means a contract, transaction or scheme whereby a person invests his money in a common enterprise and is led to expect profits solely from the efforts of the promoter or a third party, it being immaterial whether the shares in

continued on next page

the enterprise are evidenced by formal certificates or by nominal interests in the physical assets employed in the enterprise. *Howey* rejected the suggestion "that an investment contract is necessarily missing . . . where the tangible interest which is sold has intrinsic value independent of the success of the enterprise as a whole."

Subsequent cases have merely refined the three prongs of the *Howey* test. While the first prong, an investment of money, has proved relatively simple, the other two have evolved with time. As discussed below, the second prong's requirement of a "common enterprise" has been construed by this Circuit as demanding either an enterprise common to the investor and the seller, promoter or some third party (vertical commonality) or an enterprise common to a group of investors (horizontal commonality).

While *Howey's* third prong demanded an expectation of profits "solely from the efforts of the promoter or a third party," we have dropped the term "solely" and instead require that "the efforts made by those other than the investor are the undeniably significant ones, those essential managerial efforts which affect the failure or success of the enterprise."

We must therefore determine whether Hocking's purchase of a condominium and rental pool was (1) an investment of money, (2) in a common enterprise, (3) with an expectation of profits produced by the efforts of others.

In *Howey*, as here, the investors purchased real estate and at the same time relinquished much of the right to use or enter the property. In *Howey*, as here, the investors were not obligated to purchase the service contracts, and in fact some decided to purchase the land without a service contract. In Howey, as here, the investors were generally non-residents who lacked the skill, knowledge and equipment necessary to manage the investment.

Hocking, however, did not purchase the condominium in the initial offering from the developer. He purchased in the secondary market from the Libermans. Further, Hocking entered into the rental pool agreement with HCP, and has, defendants argue, failed to demonstrate any link between HCP and the developer. Finally, unlike the investors in *Howey*, Hocking could legally terminate the RPA according to its terms and regain control over the condominium. We must determine therefore whether these differences from *Howey* make Hocking's alleged transaction into an ordinary real estate purchase or whether it nevertheless could prove to be the purchase of a security.

In 1973 the SEC issued a release in order to "alert persons engaged in the business of building and selling condominiums . . . to their responsibilities under the Securities Act and to provide guidelines for a determination of when an offering of condominiums or other units may be viewed as an offering of securities."

The SEC points out that Release 5347 applies to "persons engaged in the business of building and selling condominiums . . . ," and not to brokers in the secondary market.

Given the SEC's position, we do not rely on Release 5347 in determining whether Hocking was offered a security. We instead examine the alleged transaction entirely in terms of the Howey test.

The Howey Test

A. Investment of Money. Defendants attempt to pull apart the package into two separate transactions. They argue that even if Hocking did invest money in the condominium, he did not invest money in the RPA, and it is the RPA that provides the elements necessary to satisfy the *Howey* test's other requirements. Therefore, they claim, Hocking did not satisfy this first requirement. Admittedly, there would be an argument as to whether the "investment of money" requirement had been met if someone who already owned a condominium decided to place the condominium into a rental arrangement, independent of the decision to purchase the condominium. If, however, the condominium and rental agreements were offered as a package, there can be no serious argument that Hocking did not invest money in the package. Since Hocking has created an issue of fact over whether the condominium and RPA were sold as a package, he has met this first requirement of *Howey* for purposes of summary judgment.

B. Common Enterprise. The simple purchase of real estate lacks any horizontal commonality, as no pooling of interests or profits is involved. The purchase of real estate combined with an RPA, however, does evidence horizontal commonality. The participants pool their assets; they give up any claim to profits or losses attributable to their particular investments in return for a pro rata share of the profits of the enterprise; and they make their collective fortunes dependent on the success of a single common enterprise. Because in this case Hocking has raised facts supporting horizontal commonality, we need not consider vertical commonality.

Of course, whether Hocking can prove horizontal commonality at trial will depend on whether he can show that Dubois offered a package which included the RPA. As discussed above, Hocking has raised a genuine issue of fact as to that question.

C. Expectation of Profits Produced by the Efforts of Others. This third prong of *Howey* forms the greatest hurdle for Hocking, assuming he can prove at trial that the condominium and rental agreements were part of one package. He must show an expectation of profits produced by the efforts of others, that the efforts of others are "those essential managerial efforts which affect the failure or success of the enterprise."

The crux of defendants' argument on this point is that the rental agreements allowed Hocking to maintain a high degree of control over his condominium, thus making any managerial efforts of Dubois or HCP nonessential to the success of Hocking's investment.

Hocking was not required to enter into any of the rental agreements as a prerequisite of purchasing the condominium. He elected to delegate control of the condominium to HCP. Further, the rental agreements gave Hocking various termination rights described above, allowing him to regain control over the use and management of his investment.

The record presents a material question of fact: was Hocking dependent on Dubois or HCP, and unable to exercise control over his investment?

Hocking claims to be an unsophisticated, inexperienced investor, lacking any special training or education. He resides thousands of miles away from the location of the investment. He is not in the business of managing condominiums or other real estate. He has raised a genuine issue of fact whether he requested and received an offer of management services.

Further, Hocking observed that the condominium complex was "operated like a hotel from the lobby," and that HCP distributed brochures and advertisements on the mainland. Numerous other condominium owners participated in the RPA, and HCP reserved the right to terminate the RPA if the number of participating units fell below 40 percent of the units in the complex.

Hocking's affidavit and deposition raise a genuine issue of fact whether he intended his investment to be entirely passive, and whether, as alleged, he "relied solely on Dubois to select, manage, and protect" his investment.

In the context of isolated resales, each case requires an analysis of how the condominium was promoted to the investor, including any representations made to the investor, and the nature of the investment and the collateral agreements. The investor's intentions and expectations as communicated to the broker would be relevant in determining what investment package was actually offered.

If the *Howey* analysis is undertaken, the securities laws are found to apply, and the application of the securities laws places undue burdens on developers, real estate brokers, or condominium owners, changes in the law should be sought from Congress or the Securities and Exchange Commission. Howey, on this record, requires this case to proceed beyond summary judgment.

Reversed and Remanded.

Applying the Howey test to the facts given in the case, would you conclude that this was a regulated investment contract?

If the security regulations apply, registration of the entire offering must be made with the SEC. About half the states follow the disclosure rule: the prospect must be fully informed so that an intelligent decision can be made. In the other states, full disclosure as well as minimum standards of "fairness" apply to the condominium offering when treated as an investment contract.

Exemptions

▪ *Transactions that would otherwise meet the definition of a security but that have been statutorily excused from the law's restrictions.*

Exemptions from registration are made in the case of two types of transactions: intrastate sales and private offerings.

Intrastate Offerings. The exemption for **intrastate offerings** is provided in Section 3(a)(11) of the statute and applies to offerings that are made *solely* to residents of the state where the offerer or issuer is a resident and doing business. A key word in this exemption is *solely*. If one sale is made to a single nonresident of the relevant state, or if the issue is not wholly owned by residents up to nine months after the distribution of the issue is complete, the exemption will not apply.

> **CASE EXAMPLE**
>
> Referring back to the earlier example, Fafner, using the intrastate offering exemption, sells a share in his mountaintop venture to Thorsen. It takes six months to sell the full interest in the investment. If Thorsen, prior to completion of the sale, sells her share to her brother-in-law who lives out of state, Fafner's offering would no longer qualify under the intrastate offering exemption.

To use this exemption, therefore, the promoter must have assurances that the purchasers do not intend to resell. The burden of proving this exemption is on the promoter. For a sizable issuance, it is very risky to rely on this exemption in light of its restrictive character. Note that, despite its exemption under the federal statute, the issue may have to comply with the state law regarding securities. An array of remedies is available against an issuer who has relied on the intrastate exemption but who has failed to meet all the requirements of the exemption. Recovery of damages for the price paid for the security, plus interest, is among those remedies. For further clarification of the meaning of this exemption, see SEC Rule 147.

Private Offering. The **private offering** exemption applies to offerings that are made to knowledgeable investors who have adequate information to evaluate fully the risks entailed in the transaction. It is the intent of this exemption that the offering be made to investors who are adequately informed so that they do not need the protective umbrella of the SEC disclosure rules. The purpose behind the exemption is to exclude such issues from expensive and time-consuming regulations.

> **CASE EXAMPLE**
>
> When the SEC challenged an offering made to employees under the private offering exemption by Ralston Purina Company, the Supreme Court adopted a several-fold test in determining the availability of the exemption.

The court stated that these questions should be asked: Were the offerees the type of persons who could fend for themselves? Did the offerees have access to the same type of information that would appear in a registration statement? Were the securities purchased for the investor's own account? *Securities and Exchange Commission v. Ralston Purina Co.*, 346 U.S. 119 (1953).

The determination of whether or not an offering is private is based on numerous factors, including the number of offerees, the sophistication of the offerees, the number of units in the issue and their denomination, and the manner of the offering, that is, personal contact or public advertising. There are no hard and fast rules, but the SEC will weigh the above factors in deciding whether or not the issue is a private one.

The SEC has adopted Regulation D, SEC Release No. 6389 (1982) as a "safe harbor" for those seeking to take advantage of the private offering exemption. If Regulation D is adhered to, the issue is exempt from registration requirements but not the antifraud, civil liability, or other provisions of the SEC Act. The exemption applies only to the original issuer of the security. The requirements of Regulation D are complex and detailed and are not amenable to a brief summary here. The regulation should be followed closely to ensure compliance and the protection of the "safe harbor."

Registration of Securities

■ *The listing of an issuance that meets the definition of a security—and is not otherwise exempted—with the SEC and (perhaps) with state officials.*

Prior to making any offering of a nonexempt security, the promoter must register the issuance with the SEC. No sales can take place before the SEC declares the *registration statement* to be effective. During the period between the filing with the SEC and its approval, the promoter can make oral offers or even written offers by way of a preliminary prospectus, but no investor can be bound and no sale concluded until the registration is declared effective by the SEC.

CASE EXAMPLE

MacLeish has filed a prospectus and supporting documents with the SEC. While awaiting approval, he begins to contact potential investors, providing them with a copy of the preliminary prospectus explaining the benefits of the investment. MacLeish asks for no commitments from these prospects. There would be nothing illegal about MacLeish's conduct.

If the promoter makes any sale prior to SEC approval, all investors have the right to rescind the transaction and get their money back, plus interest.

Prospectus

■ *A written document containing all the information necessary for an investor to make an independent and intelligent decision regarding a securities offering.*

The **prospectus** must be filed with the SEC registration and must be provided to prospective investors. The registration also will include the financial statements for the promoter's operation and the operating statements for the property (for example, statements indicating the income received from the property for the past five years). Any publicity regarding the offering should be avoided prior to filing with the SEC.

The SEC, in examining the proposed registration, compares the annual earnings history with the yearly cash distributions proposed by the issuer. The SEC attempts to see that the information alleged in the prospectus is complete and accurate; it does not pass on the merits of the issue.

For example, the SEC examiner explores the registration documents to determine whether the 6 percent annual return in investment asserted in the prospectus is realistic in light of past performance. The examiner does not comment on the fact that a 6 percent return, given existing market conditions, might be a poor investment.

Under federal law, the offeror is required to give full and fair disclosure and is not permitted to give advice on the wisdom of the investment opportunity. In some states, the state regulatory agency evaluates the merits of the offering as well as determining that the prospectus is accurate.

Forms of Ownership

The modes of ownership or ways of setting up a real estate syndication are varied. A simple vehicle such as concurrent ownership (tenancy in common), discussed in Chapter 5, can be used. Traditional forms of doing business—partnerships, limited partnerships, and corporations—are utilized. Less common techniques such as trusts, particularly the real estate investment trust (REIT), have gained popularity.

Each method of ownership has its intrinsic advantages and disadvantages. Tenants in common retain direct individual control over their investment fates, but the death of a tenant can suddenly propel an heir into the ownership picture as an unwanted tenant. Partners can retain control over decision making, but, as with tenants in common, operational rules must be clearly provided or chaos may ensue. Partners avoid the dual taxation that exists in a corporate form but do not enjoy the limited liability of corporate shareholders. Limited partners enjoy some of the best of both the partnership world and the corporate world because they generally avoid dual taxation and have limited liability. Nevertheless, tax risks exist in the limited partnership technique in the form of income tax recapture penalties that may be imposed on the investor above the loss of the initial investment capital. Because of the additional risks, the limited partnership form has been confined largely to sophisticated investors by choice of both the promoters and the investors.

Each of these techniques is used broadly within and outside the real estate investment area. A complete explanation of them would require an entire textbook; they are usually covered in a separate course of study. It may be useful, however, to discuss in more detail the trust device and the real estate investment trust in particular. It might be helpful to review the general discussion of trusts in Chapter 5 prior to reading about the specialized real estate investment trust.

Real Estate Investment Trust (REIT)

■ *A tax shelter that exempts certain qualified real estate investment syndications from corporate taxes where 95 percent or more of the ordinary income is distributed annually to the beneficiaries or investors.*

The Real Estate Investment Trust Act was passed by Congress in 1960. The rules governing these statutory trusts are very complex and must be strictly adhered to by those attempting to take advantage of the form. The **real estate investment trust** can exist only where it is permissible under state law.

The REIT is a conduit for getting income to certificate holders while avoiding the taxation of the trust as a corporation that would normally occur. For example, a group of friends invest some funds by purchasing certificates in a REIT. The trustee of the REIT, an independent manager, uses their money to purchase an apartment complex for the purpose of attaining a return on that investment through rental income from the units. The net profits from the rentals are distributed to the group of friends (and any fellow investor in the REIT). These profits are taxed as ordinary income to all the investors, but the trust does not pay tax on the distributed portion of the profits.

The major conditions for creating a REIT are as follows:

■ There must be 100 or more certificate holders.

■ A minimum of 95 percent of the gross income of the REIT must be derived from passive investments, such as rents, dividends, and interest.

■ At least 75 percent of the gross income of the REIT must be derived from transactions connected to real estate, such as rents from real estate, mortgage interest, gains on the sale of real property, and the like.

■ The trustees must have centralized authority over the trust.

■ At least 95 percent of the earned income from the trust business must be distributed to the certificate holders.

■ There are additional restrictions on income produced by assets held for less than six months.

There are some distinct advantages to using the REIT form, in addition to the avoidance of dual corporate taxation. Other factors include centralized management, limited liability to the investors, and the availability of real estate experts to do the investing. Nevertheless, the investments are limited to passive ones, and these may not provide the highest return on the investment dollar. Because of the size of the trust distribution (100 or more certificate holders), the trust must generally register with the SEC, which is an expensive procedure. REITs are securities that sell like stocks on the major exchanges. REITs may focus on investing in and owning properties (equity REIT), or invest in mortgages (mortgage REIT), or be a hybrid of the first two.

Due to the complexity of the REIT qualifications, this simplified description of the procedure should not be relied on by anyone interested in forming this type of trust. State laws may provide further restrictions on REITs.

THE CHANGING LANDSCAPE

Condominiums serve two important market segments. Young, educated people who work long hours and have little time to keep up a single-family house often prefer the relatively labor-free condominium form of housing. In contrast to rented housing, singles and newly married couples, by buying a condo as a "starter" house, can see their real estate investment gain in value over time. Likewise, condos provide housing for many senior citizens. Tired or incapable of keeping up with the demands of a single-family house, seniors may prefer a condominium.

The number of seniors is rapidly growing. If you were interested in developing housing for seniors, where would you build it? Would it be in the city, the suburbs, or the exurbs beyond current housing developments? If one looks to see where we have built senior housing to date, we find that large numbers of units are on land zoned for multifamily housing in the suburbs. Support services for seniors, like

the rest of the suburbanites, are usually a car ride away. Going to the doctor, grocery store, pharmacy, or recreational activity generally involves a trip of several miles.

Is our zoning of land for particular uses serving the needs of senior citizens? Should services be provided within walking distance of a seniors' housing development? Would that improve the quality of their lives, increase the economic value of the condominiums, and relieve some stress on the road system? There should be more coordination among town and city planners, highway planners, and seniors' organizations. Perhaps all would benefit from upfront consultation or working as a team. It is not easy making optimal development decisions, but it is probably worth the effort.

Is the market for senior housing likely to be a growth market in the future? As a developer, what would your senior housing project feature?

■ KEY TERMS

common elements 104

condominium 101

condominium
  association 105

cooperative 108

declaration 102

individual unit deed 104

intrastate offering 118

investment contract 115

private offering 118

prospectus 119

real estate investment
  trust 121

real estate securities 114

rules and regulations 103

time-shares 113

■ INTERNET RESOURCES

www.real-estate-law.freeadvice.com/cooperatives_condominiums.htm
(definition of terms of condominiums and cooperatives)

www.timeshares.plus.com
(defines and discusses numerous timeshare issues)

www.tiaa-cref.org/fyi/pa_1018_int.html
(desribes typical real estate security)

www.acerealty.com/reit.asp
(describes REITS)

■ REVIEW AND DISCUSSION QUESTIONS

1. Match the following terms with their correct definitions:

   a. declaration

   b. bylaws

   c. individual unit deed

   (1) Document prepared for each individual condominium unit in the development

   (2) Document, required by state law, that must accompany and be recorded with the master deed for condominium development

   (3) Document outlining the rules governing the internal operation of a condominium development

2. What are the common elements in a condominium arrangement? Distinguish between general common elements and limited common elements.

3. A condominium unit owner surrenders in writing her right to use the swimming pool, one of the common elements. Does that action relieve her of the responsibility of sharing the cost of maintaining the pool?

4. Compare and contrast condominiums with cooperatives.

5. Roberta Geist is undertaking to promote a shopping center construction project. To obtain the necessary capital, Geist is considering offering shares in the venture to 20 business associates and friends.

   a. Geist and all the offerees live in Nebraska. Discuss with Geist the pros and cons of not registering with the SEC and utilizing the intrastate offerings exemption.

   b. All of Geist's proposed offerees are experienced businesspersons. Would you advise her to take advantage of the private offerings exemption? Why?

6. What advantages accrue to investors entering a joint real estate venture who use the real estate investment trust form?

■ CASE PROBLEMS

1. Lynne Voyant inherited $50,000 on the death of her rich uncle. Voyant is exploring investment possibilities and is considering investing in a real estate venture promoted by a friend, Percy Shifter. Shifter has assured Voyant that the investment is

an excellent opportunity to make her money grow because the offering is registered with the SEC. Voyant has a premonition that there is more to consider than this. Clarify the situation for her.

2. Enterprise, Inc., purchased an existing shopping center and converted the commercial rentals into commercial condominium units. Jack Jackson, owner and operator of Jackson's Drug Store, tenant in the shopping center, sued to enjoin the conversion, contending that (1) condominium formulation is illegal for commercial units; (2) the conversion requires the issuance of a prospectus; and (3) it is illegal to deny him a vote because the day-to-day operation of the common elements will be done by the board of directors and not all the members of the condominium association. Was Jackson correct? Why?

3. The original officers and directors of Avila S. Condominium Association contracted with Kappa Corp. to provide the association with recreational facilities. These officers and directors were also officers and directors of Kappa Corp. Other members of the condominium association sued the original officers and directors, contending that they were unjustly enriched as a result of their involvement with the Kappa Corp. Discuss. *Avila S. Condominium Ass'n. v. Kappa Corp.*, 347 So.2d 599 (Fla. 1977).

4. Kellogg owned an individual unit within a condominium. He decided that he wanted to put an additional story onto his unit and to expand the width of the existing story. He got the approval of the town zoning officials but did not get the consent of the other condominium owners. The bylaws of the condominium indicate that unanimous consent of the owners is necessary for a unit owner to make a private use of the common elements. Kellogg claims that he is not using the common elements, but only unused air space. What do you think of Kellogg's argument as to (a) the horizontal expansion? (b) the vertical expansion? *Grey v. Coastal States Holding Co.*, 22 Conn. App. 497, 578 A.2d 1080 (1990).

The Leasehold

■ LEASEHOLD ESTATE

■ *An estate created when the owner of property, known as the* lessor *or* landlord, *conveys a possessory interest in the real property to another, known as the* lessee *or* tenant, *for a specific period of time in exchange for the tenant's payment of rent.*

An unusual aspect of a lease is that it is rooted firmly in two distinct areas of law: contract law and real property law. As a contract, the lease must contain the essential elements of any contract—offer, acceptance, and consideration—to be enforceable. Because it relates to real property, the lease involves a conveyance of an estate in land, or a *leasehold estate*. The landlord surrenders his or her possessory rights to the premises for the duration of the lease. The tenant must pay for that possession during the term of the lease. Because the tenant is getting an estate in land, he or she is required by law to pay the rent even if there is no specific agreement regarding rent. Possession is exchanged for rent.

The granting of a leasehold estate gives to a tenant the *exclusive possession* of the premises for an agreed-on term with a reversion at the end of the term to possession by the landlord. This exclusive right of possession deprives the owner of the premises during the lease. Even where tenants fail to comply with the leasehold bargain, landlords can remove them from the premises only by bringing formal eviction proceedings.

Four different kinds of leasehold estates can be created. They are *term tenancy, periodic tenancy, tenancy at will,* and *tenancy at sufferance.* (See Table 7.1.)

Term Tenancy

■ *An estate for a specified period of time that has a specific beginning date and a specific ending date. When the ending date arrives, the estate is terminated without notice by either party.*

This tenancy, also known as an *estate for years* (it may be for days, months, or years), terminates without any action by either party on expiration of the term stated in the agreement. It should be noted that if a party's lease stipulates notice or other conditions for termination of the tenancy, as written leases often do, then these conditions must be met. In the absence of a statute or an agreement to the contrary, the term tenancy is considered personal property and will pass as such to those entitled to take personal property from the estate of a deceased tenant.

If the parties fail to stipulate the amount of rent due, a *reasonable rent* is required. A reasonable rent is based on prevailing rental rates in the vicinity. Under the common law, however, the rent is not due until the end of the tenancy. By way of contrast, most

TABLE 7.1	Leasehold Estates	
Type of Tenant	**Normal Life Span**	**Normal Notice Required**
Term tenancy	Specific beginning and ending date	None
Periodic tenancy (year or more)	Renewable period to period	Six months
Periodic tenancy (less than year)	Renewable period to period	One period
Tenancy at will	Until a party opts out	None or statutory
Tenancy at sufferance	Option of lessor	None
Holdover tenant	One period up to one year	Same as periodic tenancy

modern leases require that the rent be prepaid because landlords are understandably unwilling to wait until the end of the term to receive payment of rent.

Periodic Tenancy

◼ *An estate from period to period, continuing from period to period until terminated by proper notice from one of the parties.*

The **periodic tenancy** is normally from year to year or month to month but can be for any period up to a year. It can be created in several different ways. One way is by express agreement. If A leases her property to B "from month to month beginning April 1, 2006," a periodic tenancy is created.

This type of estate can also evolve from a term tenancy when the tenant remains, or "holds over," after the expiration of the term tenancy. The holdover tenancy will be discussed in more detail later in this section.

The periodic tenancy can be terminated by either party on giving adequate notice. The parties may contractually agree on what will constitute adequate notice. Absent such an agreement, adequate notice will be one period's notice, up to six months.

CASE EXAMPLE

Karen Kaiser leases Greenacre to Franks "from year to year beginning April 1, 2006." She leases Brownacre to Martin "from month to month beginning April 1, 2006." To terminate the lease to Greenacre, either Kaiser or Franks would have to give six months' notice unless they had an agreement to the contrary. The Brownacre lease could be ended by either party with one month's notice of termination, absent a contrary agreement.

These common-law notice periods have been altered by statutes in many states. For example, the Uniform Residential Landlord and Tenant Act has been adopted in part in several states. This act provides that a week-to-week tenancy requires a written notice of ten days. A month-to-month tenancy requires a notice of at least 60 days. Year-to-year tenancies are not mentioned in the act perhaps because they often apply to agricultural lands and not to residential premises.

Notice given by the terminating party must reach the other party a full period early. The general rule is that the notice must be given one calendar period in advance, although some cases have held to the contrary.

Where there is uncertainty as to the period of the tenancy, a good indicator is the rent payments. If the rent is paid yearly or monthly, it is a good indication that the parties have a year-to-year or month-to-month periodic tenancy. An exception occurs when the yearly rent is stated in the lease but the payment is due monthly. This would be treated as a year-to-year period.

CASE EXAMPLE

The Smits, experienced dairy farmers, entered an oral agreement with the Prescotts to rent their farm. The parties agreed to a lease beginning May 1, for a period of three years, with an annual rental of $14,400 payable in equal monthly installments. The Smits moved onto the land and began paying rent before the written lease was prepared. By the time the written lease was ready, the Smits were having problems with some cows dying and others becoming sick. The problem was apparently a contaminated water supply. The Smits refused to sign the lease, and after several months stopped paying rent and abandoned the farm. The Prescotts sued for nonpayment of rent.

Among other things, the court held that the lease was a term tenancy and that the term was year to year. The court reasoned that it was a year-to-year term because the rent, though payable monthly, was stated in annual terms in their oral agreement. The conclusion was reinforced by the fact that it was a farm lease, and such leases are traditionally entered into on a yearly basis. *Prescott v. Smits*, 505 A.2d 1211 (1985).

Tenancy at Will

■ *A tenancy that exists until either party chooses to terminate it.*

This type of estate may arise by express agreement. For example, a lease may state "to Franks at the will of Kaiser." This wording creates a **tenancy at will.** Despite this restrictive language, tenancies at will can be terminated by either party.

A tenancy at will is more likely to arise by implication.

CASE EXAMPLE

In the Prescott case discussed above, the court had to decide whether the oral lease was an at-will tenancy or a periodic tenancy. In the parties' state, an oral lease for a period longer than one year is unenforceable. Because the three-year term agreed to by the parties was not legally enforceable, the court had to decide what type of tenancy had been created.

As stated above, the court found that the lease was a year-to-year tenancy. If the situation had been altered so that the Smits had not yet moved onto the land, or the amount of the rent was left uncertain, the court probably would have found that a tenancy at will arose by implication.

Under the common law, no notice was required to end a tenancy at will. Many states now have statutes that require a minimum notice period, thereby softening the harshness of the common-law rule. Although the estate exists wholly by permission, all the rights and duties of the landlord-tenant relationship exist. Unlike the previously mentioned leasehold estates, however, a tenancy at will is terminated by the death of either party or by the sale of the property to a third party.

Tenancy at Sufferance

■ *Created when a person is wrongfully in possession of another's land without a valid lease.*

The tenant at sufferance is similar to a trespasser. The major difference is that the tenant at sufferance entered the property legally. Usually he or she is the holdover tenant from a term tenancy. The landlord owes this tenant no duties, and the tenant can be evicted at any time. The classification of a person as a *tenant at sufferance*, not as a trespasser, actually works to the tenant's disadvantage. The tenant is unable to possess the property adversely against the landlord and eventually gain an ownership interest, although a trespasser could.

Holdover Tenant

■ *One who failed to vacate or surrender possession of the premises on the ending date of a term tenancy.*

The term **holdover tenant** is sometimes used in relation to a periodic tenancy, where the tenant stays on despite the landlord's adequate notice to vacate. Under these circumstances, a landlord who permits the tenant to remain and has not started an eviction action, has technically waived the notice and allowed the continuation of the periodic tenancy.

The term tenant who holds over after the expiration date of a lease temporarily becomes a tenant at sufferance. All options shift into the landlord's hands when the tenant holds over. The landlord has the option of evicting the tenant or of holding him or her for another term.

CASE EXAMPLE

Anton leases a house and lot to Glenn and Sarah Williams. The terms of the agreement stipulate that the lease commences on July 1, 2005, and terminates on June 30, 2006. On July 1, 2006, the couple is still living in the house. Anton has the option of beginning eviction proceedings against the Williamses, who are now tenants at sufferance, or of unilaterally extending their lease until June 30, 2007.

Once the landlord exercises the option to hold the tenant for an additional period, the estate becomes a periodic tenancy. The maximum length of the period will be one year, or more accurately year to year, even where the term tenancy was for a longer period. If the original term tenancy was for less than one year, the holdover tenant will be held to a periodic tenancy for that particular period, such as week to week or month to month.

The terms of the holdover tenant's new lease will be the same as those of the original lease except as to length of time, as noted above. One exception arises when the landlord notifies the tenant before the expiration of the lease that he or she is changing the terms (for example, raising the rent). The tenant is usually held to the altered terms.

If the holdover is involuntary and for a short period of time, courts will not hold the tenant for an additional term. For instance, if the holdover is caused by a tornado, a snowstorm, a death in the family, or a one-day delay of the moving van, the court is not likely to hold the tenant for an additional period. The following case involves a less dramatic reason for holding over.

J.M. Beals Enterprises, Inc. v. Industrial Hard Chrome, Ltd.
Appellate Court of Illinois
648 N.E.2d 249 (1995)

Background. Charles Therkildsen, doing business as Industrial Hard Chrome, Ltd. (IHC), leased real property from Beals Enterprises (Beals) commencing in 1985 and expiring December 31, 1992. In July 1992, a dispute arose between the parties over what equipment and materials were part of a 1985 sale of IHC by Beals to Therkildsen. The dispute was settled by agreement on December 10, 1992, and IHC was to perform considerable work on the premises prior to vacating on December 31. IHC was unable to complete the work by the date the lease expired, and was refused an extension by Beals. IHC remained on the premises through January 18, 1993, solely for the purpose of completing the work under the December 10 agreement. Beals filed suit under the state holdover tenant statute that would entitle it to double rent and other fees and costs. After oral argument the trial judge granted a summary judgment to Beals.

Decision. The Illinois Appellate Court reversed the trial court's decision and remanded the case for trial.

Justice Egan. The Holdover Statute, the interpretation of which is the heart of this case, provides as follows:

"If any tenant willfully holds over any lands after the expiration of his or her term or terms, and after demand made in writing, for the possession thereof,

by his or her landlord the person so holding over, shall, for the time the landlord or rightful owner is so kept out of possession, pay to the person so kept out of possession, at the rate of double the yearly value of the land."

The issues as raised by IHC are two-fold: Does the record disclose, as a matter of law, that IHC withheld possession from Beals; and, if so, does the record disclose, as a matter of law, that IHC's holding over was willful within the meaning of the Holdover Statute? One general principle recognized everywhere is that whether a tenant is a holdover and whether the holding-over was willful are questions of fact.

IHC argues that it was not a holdover tenant at all because it did not deprive Beals of possession. We have no doubt that whether IHC was a holdover is, at least, a question of fact, The statute does not define the term "willful," but one of the earliest cases decided under the statute, *Stuart v. Hamilton* (1872) gives us some guidance:

"The courts have held that when the lease had expired according to its terms, the holding over, although intentional, is not within the statute, unless it was knowingly and willfully wrongful; that where the tenant continued to hold under a reasonable belief that he was doing so rightfully, he does not incur the penalty, and yet the language [of the

continued on next page

statute] would embrace such a case as reasonably as if the term had been ended by the landlord by enforcing a forfeiture of the lease."

Although most of the cases which refuse to enforce the double rent statute involved bona fide disputes over the right to possession, we refuse to make such a narrow pronouncement that only a bona fide dispute over the right to possession will excuse a tenant under the statute. We believe the better rule is that where a tenant remains in possession for colorably justifiable reasons, he should not be charged under the statute. In other words, the tenant, to be liable under the statute, must know that his retention of possession is "wrongful." With that understanding we turn to the agreement.

Under the agreement, IHC agreed to leave certain equipment on the premises "in operating condition"; and to remove certain equipment, including a boiler and cooling tower connections and piping, dust collectors and a tank ventilator system, including air duct piping, electrical wiring connections and all other personal property. IHC was also required to "remove or cut off flush with [the] surface, all fasteners, brackets, bolts and attachments in floors, walls and ceilings used to secure or serve equipment removed; [to remove] all depressed concrete pits; [to repair] all roof and/or wall openings resulting from removal performed by IHC pursuant to the

agreement." The agreement further provided that on or before March 1, 1993, IHC was to inspect the premises to determine "compliance" with the agreement; that Beals would provide IHC notice of any claims of Beals "regarding any defaults" by IHC of the settlement terms. IHC would have 30 days after receipt of Beals' default claims to "cure each of the" claims. It is obvious that the parties recognized the possibility that IHC would not complete the removal of equipment by December 31. The agreement also recognized the possibility that IHC would be required to return to the premises after March 1, 1993, to complete work required by Beals.

A reasonable inference may be drawn that IHC was confronted with a formidable task in completing what was required in 21 days. IHC had a Hobson's choice in walking away from the premises on December 31 in compliance with Beals' demand for possession or staying on the premises in an attempt to comply with the agreement. Whether IHC's actions were knowingly wrongful raise at least a question of fact.

Reversed and remanded.

Can Beals hold IHC for another "period" under the common-law holdover tenant rules?

■ LEASE

■ *A contract, either written or oral, that transfers the right of possession of the premises to the lessee or tenant.*

The relationship of lessor and lessee usually arises from an express contract on the part of the parties called a *lease*. As previously stated, the lease is firmly rooted in the law of contracts. The lease or contract, sometimes referred to as a *rental agreement*, normally includes terms giving the lessee the right to possession and entitling the lessor to a certain amount of rent. To this extent these contractual components overlap the possession-rent aspects that arise inherently from the real property notion of a conveyance of an estate in land. The lease contract is likely to specify the terms of the possession and the amount of the rent, as well as many other factors that together compose the essence of the lessor and lessee's agreement.

Essential Elements of the Lease

The purpose of the lease is to detail the rights and duties of each of the parties in the contract. It is incumbent on the parties to take great care in drafting the lease, especially if the terms of the agreement are complex or the duration of the lease is long. To do otherwise is to invite a lawsuit.

A Valid Contract Because a lease is a contract, it must contain the essential elements of a contract. There must be a mutual consent to enter the agreement, and the agreement must be supported by consideration (rent in exchange for possession). The lease agreement will not require the use of any particular prescribed words. Essentially, it must be shown that it was mutually intended for the tenant to have possession and that the landlord retained a *reversionary interest* in the land (that is, the right to have the property back when the lease expired).

The consideration that supports the lease contract is usually the rent. Nevertheless, the periodic payment of rent is not necessary to have a valid contract. The requirement is merely that consideration, or something of value, be given at some time to the landlord.

The other elements of a valid contract, such as the capacity of the parties (both must be sane and of legal age) and legality of purpose, must be met as well.

Statute of Frauds. Prior to 1677, under the common law originally operating in England, leases did not have to be in writing. With the adoption of the **Statute of Frauds**, however, leases for a term in excess of three years had to be in writing to be enforceable beyond those three years. A few states have adopted the English version of the statute of frauds and require written form for leases in excess of three years. In most states, however, the statute of frauds provision necessitates a writing if the lease exceeds one year.

The intent of this requirement is to reduce fraud in the area of leases. It should be made clear that the statutory minimum, usually one year, does not indicate that leases for one year or less should not be in writing. The careful landlord and tenant will benefit if all terms of their agreement are reduced to writing to minimize the opportunity for misunderstanding or outright fraud.

It should be emphasized that an oral lease within the maximum term of the statute of frauds is every bit as valid as a written lease. If a dispute arises over an oral lease, however, the proof may be more difficult to derive. If a dispute arises over a lease that has gone beyond the allowable period under the statute of frauds, the estate is treated as a tenancy at will.

Parties. The lease must identify the parties as *lessor* and *lessee*, and both parties should sign the document. The signature of the lessor, the owner of the property, is normally mandatory. Under the statute of frauds, the signature of the party against whom the lease will be enforced is required.

The spouse of the lessor should sign the lease as well, if he or she has an outstanding interest or potential interest in the property. For example, if a married couple owns the premises jointly, both parties must sign the lease because the spouse is a concurrent owner. The wife should also sign the lease where the state recognizes a dower interest, inasmuch as her potential interest may come into effect during the term of the lease.

Under some contracts, a lessee may have the power to sublease or to assign the property to a third party, in which case the person signing as "lessor" of the property may not be the actual owner of the premises. For this reason, a lessee should make certain that the nonowner lessor has the authority to sublet and convey all or part of the interest to another. Subleasing will be discussed in more detail in the following chapter.

If the lessor is an individual, he or she must have the *capacity* to contract—that is, be mentally competent and of legal age. If the lessor is a fiduciary, entering the lease for another as guardian, executor, or trustee, for example, the lessee must be assured that the authority to lease is within the fiduciary's powers. Similarly, if the lessor is a corporation that is not in the business of leasing real estate, the lessee must verify the authorization of the corporation's board of directors to be assured that the corporation is entitled to lease the premises.

Description of the Premises. To avoid a future dispute, the premises should be described clearly. If the landlord's entire conveyed premises are being leased, then the description as contained in the deed or deeds is satisfactory. A lot number or block number used for assessment purposes may be used if it is complete and accurate. A street number may not be adequate in itself because it relates only to the building and not to the land that is probably part of the leasehold as well.

When the lessor is leasing something less than all that he or she has, the lease should state clearly and exactly what is to be leased. In the absence of an agreement to the contrary, the lease of a building will be construed to include the use of everything reasonably necessary for the enjoyment of the land. It is up to the lessor expressly to exclude a use, or exclusive possession may pass to the lessee.

CASE EXAMPLE

Arthur leases one-half of an apartment house to Melanie, who has three small children. Unless the lease specifically excludes use of the fenced-in backyard, Melanie can use it for ingress and egress and as a play area for the children.

It is also to the lessee's benefit to have the precise nature of his or her use or possession spelled out in the lease, rather than to rely on the uncertain notion that he or she is entitled to certain unstated uses.

Statement of a Lease Term. The term of the lease should be stipulated clearly. Stating the beginning and ending dates as well as the length of the term will reduce doubt as to date of entry and the like. The lease should state, for example, "for one year beginning January 1, 2006, and terminating December 31, 2006." Where the beginning date is not spelled out, some doubt may exist as to whether the tenant began the term on the date the lease was signed, the first of the following month, or some other date. If the beginning date is not stated, the commencement of the lease should be related to some event or ascertainable time so that the beginning of the lease is clear.

CASE EXAMPLE

Sanchez leased to Williams for one year beginning on the surrender of possession by the present tenant or April 1, 2006, whichever comes first.

The courts do not favor leases of unlimited duration. If the time of termination is not fixed, the courts may interpret the agreement to be a tenancy at will, which is probably not what the parties intended. In a periodic tenancy, of course, the time of termination is fixed, although the tenancy is subject to automatic renewal on the existence of certain conditions, such as failure to give notice of termination.

Some courts have been inclined to hold that leases that are too long—for instance, 100 years or more—are barred by statute. The theory behind the term limitation is that when the lease gets to be too long it defies the temporary aspect, or right of reversion, inherent in a leasehold estate. The result of these statutes and judicial rulings has been to popularize the 99-year lease. Similarly, in a few states, there is a restriction on the length of leases for agricultural lands.

There is a correlation between the length of the lease and the care with which the lease must be drawn. If the lease is as long as 75 years, the likelihood increases that the structures will need to be replaced. Some agreement should be reached to cover contingencies of this sort that will occur during the long period of the lease.

■　**Rent.** *The compensation paid by the lessee for the possession of the leased property.*

Normally, **rent** takes the form of a money payment. It could, however, take the form of a percentage of the crops harvested from the land or of relief for the lessor of an obligation owed to the lessee. A statement of the amount of rent is one of the essential terms of a lease; nevertheless, where it has been omitted, courts have declared that the landlord is entitled to a "reasonable rent," based on the area's prevailing rental rates.

The usual practice is to state in the lease that the rent will be paid in advance. If such a statement is lacking, the rent is due at the end of the period. The rationale behind this rule is that the lessee is paying for the possession that he or she has enjoyed, and nothing is due until he or she has had the enjoyment.

In addition to how much and when, the lease should indicate where the rent is to be paid. Absent such an indication, it is payable at the leasehold premises.

Unless stipulated to the contrary, the total rent is due on the date set for payment. The usual practice is to require in the lease monthly, quarterly, or annual payments.

CASE EXAMPLE

Karen leases Greenacre to Frank for a rent of $2,400 annually, payable in advance and on the first of each month in installments of "$200, and presented at the residence of the lessor."

This wording covers each of the above considerations.

For short-term residential leases, it is most common to have a straight rental fee, such as $200 per month. In commercial leases, however, a variety of methods are used for determining the rent. The net lease, percentage lease, and ground lease will be discussed later. Another technique is to assess rent on a *graduated* basis. A lease might stipulate a rent of $2,400 the first year, $3,600 per year for the following two years, and $4,800 per year for the last two years. If the lessee is operating a new business, under the graduated rental the amount of rent is smallest in the start-up period and increases as the business (theoretically) grows.

Other techniques include basing the rent on the consumer price index or on some other criterion that is particularly relevant to the parties, to the business, or to the lease itself. In short, the days of the straight or flat rental fee as the sole method for calculating rent, especially in business leases, have long since passed.

Legal Use of the Premises

If the lease gives no indication as to the uses that can be made of the premises, the general rule is that the lessee can make any legal use of the land he or she wants. Some courts, however, would limit the lessee to "reasonable uses" where the agreement is silent on the matter. The question of reasonable use is a factual question that the court will examine in light of the type of premises involved and the prior uses of the property. If the building was constructed and has been used as a residence from its inception, for example, it would be unreasonable to use it now as a cheese factory.

Although it is appropriate for the lessor to limit the lessee's use by the agreement, careful drafting is warranted. If the lessor limits the use to a clearly designated purpose, courts will uphold that limitation. If the lessor indicates a specific purpose to which the premises can be put—for example, ". . . can be used for a beauty shop"—and nothing more, however, this wording will not prohibit the lessee from making use of the land as other than a beauty shop. The rationale behind these rules is that the law favors unrestricted use of the land conveyed. In short, ambiguities will be construed against the lessor and toward maximizing the lessee's use. If the lessor's limitations on permitted uses are not designated clearly, the lease will be construed to favor the lessee. If the lessor, by permitting use as a beauty shop, has not clearly shown an intent to limit use to that purpose alone, the lessee will be able to make any other use as well. The careful drafter would have stated, ". . . for use as a beauty shop only."

CASE EXAMPLE

In 1974, Waffle House leased property in Biloxi from the Burnetts for the purpose of constructing a business building. The lease was for a 15-year term renewable for seven terms of five years. The lease referred to the building as being a "standard Waffle House." A standard Waffle House in 1974 had 33 seats. Waffle House constructed a 33-seat restaurant, but over time has expanded the restaurant to 51 seats. In 1989, Waffle House attempted to exercise its option to renew the lease, but the Bennetts refused to accept the agreed-on rent. The Bennetts contended that the agreement was violated because the building was no longer a 33-seat "standard Waffle House" as agreed on.

The court decided for Waffle House, holding that the phrase "standard Waffle House" did not clearly and specifically indicate that it was a limitation on the number of seats allowed. The law requires that such restrictions be unambiguous in their intent to limit a lessee's use under the lease. Ambiguous restrictions are construed against the landlord. *Bennett v. Waffle House*, 771 So. 2d 370 (2000).

Where the lessee's use of the property has been made illegal by a change in the law, the lease is not usually invalidated. If the lease permits other legal uses, the lessee can change the type of use. If, however, the lease limits the lessee to the now illegal use, the change in the law will invalidate the lease. The fact that the lessee's business has become unprofitable or that the property no longer suits him or her for a residence will not excuse performance under the lease contract.

A tenant who leases only part of a building for commercial purposes should be careful to reach some agreement with the lessor regarding the leasing of other parts of the building to competitors and use by the lessor as a competitor with the lessee. Without such an agreement, the lessor is free to put the remainder of the property to a competitive use.

Besides the terms of the lease, the tenant should also be careful to check the public regulation restrictions on his or her use. The zoning code may well prohibit uses that the lessor has not prohibited.

Right of Possession

■   *In all jurisdictions the right of possession implicitly resides in the tenant; that is, no one will have possessory rights inconsistent with those granted to the tenant.*

In a majority of jurisdictions, the landlord covenants to give the *right* of possession and nothing more. If there is a wrongdoer in possession at the time the tenant's lease commences, the landlord has not violated his or her implied promise of giving the *right to possession*. The fact that the tenant may have to bring a lawsuit to obtain possession is an excellent reason why the tenant should be careful to see to it that the lease contains a provision ensuring that the landlord will give *actual possession* of the premises, not merely the right to possession. The possibility of the landlord's being unable to deliver actual possession is not terribly remote. Holding over by former tenants is not a rare incident.

In some jurisdictions the landlord implicitly covenants to deliver the possession of the premises. The onus then falls on the landlord to take necessary action (for example, eviction proceedings) to recover possession for the tenant.

It should be remembered that normally the tenant's possession is exclusive. Even the landlord, who may be the owner of the premises in fee simple, is not permitted to invade that exclusive possession without authorization. The landlord would be a trespasser, and the tenant could bring the appropriate legal action against him or her.

Recording the Lease

The practice of recording leases is permitted in most states because a lease is a conveyance of an interest in land. It is uncommon to record residential and other short-term leases, however, because actual possession by the tenant is notice to everyone of the tenant's interest in the land. On finding a tenant in possession, a potential taker of an interest in the land would have actual notice of the possession and would have the duty to inquire as to the possessor's right to be there. Failing to inspect the premises, he or she would still have constructive notice of the possession.

There is, however, more of an inclination to record leases that are for a longer period (three years or more). In about one-third of the states, the rule holding that possession is constructive notice has been abolished where the lease exceeds a given period of time (usually either one year or three years). In these states it is very important that the tenant record the lease for his or her own protection.

Types of Leases

It was indicated earlier that several types of leases exist. Four of these will be discussed in more detail here. Most are used primarily in commercial applications.

■   **Gross Lease.** *A lease in which a flat or fixed amount of rent is paid by the tenant.*

Generally, under a **gross lease** the tenant pays the rent and the landlord is responsible for expenses incurred in operating the premises. The landlord pays the taxes, insurance, special assessments, and the like. Responsibility for ordinary repairs may be bargained for separately. In residential leases the gross rental fee may or may not include heat and other utilities. It would seem to be to the benefit of both parties, and society as a whole, to exclude heat and utilities from the fixed rent to encourage the tenant to minimize the costs by reducing the consumption of energy and water.

Where long-term leases are desired, gross leases have gradually fallen from favor because of inflation and the fluctuation in the value of the dollar. Unless there is some provision in the lease to compensate the lessor for the gradually diminishing value of the periodic rent check, rental property becomes a questionable investment.

■   **Net Lease.** *As contrasted with the gross lease, a type of lease in which the tenant agrees to pay the taxes, insurance, repairs, and other operating expenses of the premises. This is usually on a pro-rata basis if multiple tenants are involved.*

This type of lease assures the lessor of a steady income from the property and relieves him or her of the responsibility of overseeing the operations on the property. In short, the lessor has a real estate investment without most of the problems that usually accompany this type of investment.

As things have evolved, the term **net lease** is a generic one. A "double net lease" is one in which the lessee pays the rent, taxes, and insurance. The lessor assumes the expenses for maintenance of the premises. In a **triple net lease** (nnn) the lessee pays the rent, taxes, insurance, and maintenance costs. Though the lessor remains the owner of the property, the bulk of its traditional responsibilities shift to the lessee. The lessor becomes a kind of silent partner. The triple net lease is commonly used for shopping malls and apartment buildings.

CASE EXAMPLE

Mastracci enters into an agreement with Abend, the owner of a 12-unit apartment building, for a triple net lease. Mastracci will assume all responsibility for the building, including leasing the units, collecting rents, providing building maintenance, and paying all other expenses. Mastracci agrees to pay rent to Abend in an amount somewhat less than Abend was currently collecting from the tenants. Abend is willing to sacrifice some income in exchange for fewer responsibilities.

Normally, selling business properties at a profit involves paying capital gains taxes. If Abend decides to sell the apartment building to Mastracci, she may seek to defer capital gains taxes by making a **1031 exchange**. A 1031 exchange, referring to Section 1031 in the Internal Revenue Code, defers taxes on the sale of investment, business, or rental properties when the net proceeds are reinvested in other business real estate.

Some of the prerequisites for a 1031 exchange are that the seller must make the exchange within 180 days of the original sale. Within 45 days the seller must identify to the IRS the candidate properties for purchase. The seller may target up to three properties, regardless of value, or a group of properties that do not exceed 200 percent of the value of the initial property sold. A 1031 exchange is highly technical and requires expert legal and financial consultation.

Like the gross lease, the net lease does not necessarily take into account the loss of purchasing power due to inflation. Net leases can be drawn up that tie the amount of periodic rent that is payable to some recognized indicator, such as the consumer price index. In this way the lessor will have the same purchasing power at the end of a long-term lease that existed at the beginning.

■ **Ground Lease.** *A specialized type of net lease in which the lessor leases a piece of vacant land to the lessee, usually with the stipulation that the lessee at his or her own expense will construct a building thereon.*

The **ground lease** is a type of net lease in that the lessee agrees to assume the operating expense of the property. Once the building is constructed, it becomes part of the realty and title passes to the lessor. Therefore, several elements are common to the lease agreements in ground-lease situations. The term of the lease is either for the life expectancy of the building or, at least, for a long period. When the term of the lease is not tied to the building's life expectancy, provisions must be made for the building at the expiration of the lease. The parties may agree that the lessor will have to pay the lessee the appraised value of the building at the time the lease expires. Of course the parties can write any agreement that suits them on this matter.

The rent agreement can be for a fixed rate but is often tied to the appraised value of the land. In this way the lessor retains the benefit of the land's appreciating value.

In most such leases the lessee needs financing to construct the building. If this is the case, provisions must be made to accommodate the mortgagee as well as the parties to the lease. The lessor will have to agree to permit the building to be mortgaged while excluding himself or herself from liability on that mortgage. Likewise, the mortgagee will insist on the untrammeled right to sell the property in the case of a foreclosure. In addition, the mortgagee will usually insist that the term of the ground lease extend significantly beyond the duration of the mortgage so that the tenant does not lose the incentive to make mortgage payments during the latter years of the obligation.

■ **Percentage Lease.** *A lease whose rental is based in part on the gross sales made by the tenant on the premises.*

The lessee in a **percentage lease** is required to pay a fixed periodic rental, the amount of the rent to be less than the property's full rental value. In addition, the lessor is entitled to a percentage of the gross sales made by the lessee.

A common practice is to charge a flat minimum rent (perhaps $500 per month) plus a percentage of the gross sales over a stipulated figure (for example, $500 per month plus 2 percent of the gross sales over $30,000). If the lease has a long term, the percentage lease provides some hedge against inflation. As inflation grows, theoretically so do gross sales; once sales exceed $30,000, the rent increases proportionately. Because the flat minimum rent is usually lower than the maximum amount the landlord would expect, the percentage lease is a hedge for the commercial lessee against bad times.

Percentage leases have become very popular in the leasing of commercial property. The percentage may be very low (1 or 2 percent) in the case of a supermarket or very high (70 to 80 percent) where a parking lot is involved. Regardless of the type of business or the percentage agreed on, it is critical that the parties carefully draft their agreement. The lease should make clear exactly what is encompassed within the term *gross sales* and should establish the right of the lessor to examine records of the business. From the lessor's perspective, in addition to the protection of a carefully drafted lease, the lessee should be selected carefully to ensure a sound credit rating and good business history.

The *Papa Gino's* case deals with a percentage lease and shows a court struggling with the meaning of the term *gross sales* as used in the lease. The case speaks loudly for the premise that parties to a lease should be as precise as possible in drafting its terms.

Papa Gino's of America, Inc. v. Broadmanor Associates, Ltd.
Appellate Court of Connecticut
500 A.2d 1341 (1985)

Background. In 1978, Papa Gino's entered into a written lease for the rental of commercial premises at the Manchester Shopping Parkade with Broadmanor Associates' predecessor in title. The lease was for a 10-year term with options to renew. The lease provided a fixed, monthly, minimum rental payment and additional rent equal to 5 percent of Papa Gino's "annual gross sales in excess of $285,000." Papa Gino's had a practice of providing meals free of charge or at a discount to employees and making discount coupons available to the public. When a discount coupon was presented by a purchaser, the face value of each coupon was deducted from the price of the food.

Broadmanor Associates purchased the Parkade in 1981 and in 1982 notified Papa Gino's that it was deficient in its rental payments because under the percentage of gross sales provision, it had not included the value of the free and discounted meals

to employees or the face value of the discount coupons. Papa Gino's paid the amount demanded under protest and sued Broadmanor Associates, seeking a declaration by the court that it was not deficient in the payment of its rent. The trial court held that the term *gross sales* in the lease included the face value of the discount coupons, but not the contested meals to employees. Papa Gino's appealed the ruling on the discount coupons.

Decision. The Appellate Court of Connecticut reversed the ruling of the trial court on the issue of the discount coupons.

Judge Daly. The plaintiff has raised the following issues on appeal: (1) whether the trial court erred in failing to declare that the term "gross sales" in the lease does not include the face value of the discount coupons made available to the public, because the plaintiff receives no monetary compensation for the amount discounted in sales to coupon holders; and (2) whether the trial court erred in denying the return of the escrow fund to the plaintiff. We find that the trial court was in error on both points.

A lease is a contract. In its construction, three elementary principles must be kept constantly in mind: (1) the intention of the parties is controlling and must be gathered from the language of the lease in the light of the circumstances surrounding the parties at the execution of the instrument; (2) the language must be given its ordinary meaning unless a technical or special meaning is clearly intended; and (3) the lease must be construed as a whole and in such a manner as to give effect to every provision, if reasonably possible.

A lease which provides for a percentage rent added to a fixed rent is a common arrangement for the rental of commercial premises. The percentage lease gears the landlord's return to the productivity of his location, such productivity being measured by the tenant's gross dollar volume in sales. In addition to a percentage lease arrangement, the lease in question defined "gross sales" to mean "the entire gross income from the use or occupancy of the leased premises (including advertising and demonstrations) and of all business thereat. These terms shall also include the full price of all sales made and services rendered at the lease premises. . . . There shall also be deducted, to the extent to which they shall be included in the sales price, the amount of sales or other taxes which may be imposed by law on the purchaser."

The definition of the term "gross sales" has no definitive judicial meaning, is imprecise, and depends principally on the wording established by the parties in particular contract. The term "sale," as ordinarily defined and popularly understood, means the transfer of property for money paid or to be paid; this is the usage of the term in the lease with which we are here concerned. The term "receipts" indicates money received from a sale. Further, under the Connecticut sales tax laws, cash discounts are not included as taxable income and not considered as "gross receipts." In the hotel business, total gross revenues from room rentals do not include credit card discounts. It would appear, then, that "gross sales" and "receipts" indicate money or cash that is actually received, and therefore would not apply to the discount coupons.

"The courts do not favor constructions in derogation of the course of conduct of the parties." The purpose of the coupons, presumably, is to lure customers into the plaintiff's restaurant with the expectation that they will purchase other items as well. By this method, the landlord receives a benefit from the gross sales. To give the landlord that value of the inducement as well (the coupon) would be to construe the lease as allowing the landlord an additional, uncontemplated kind of "double recovery." We conclude that this is unwarranted under the circumstances and, therefore, that the trial court incorrectly included the face value of the discount coupons offered to the restaurant patrons in the calculation of gross sales generated by the plaintiff's business.

The judgment is set aside and the case in remanded with direction to render judgment that the term "gross sales" shall not include the value of the subject discount coupons, and the amounts held in escrow shall be awarded to the plaintiff.

Reversed.

If you were Broadmoor Associates, how would you write your next lease to avoid this conflict?

Is someone like Papa Gino's likely to sign your contract?

Other Types of Leases. Leases are as variable as the parties are creative. Some types of leases, such as the variety that relates rent to the consumer price index or some other index, may come into vogue temporarily as a reaction to unstable economic conditions. Others, such as the graduated lease, are tailored to meet the needs of a new business. Here the rent rises over time as the anticipated growth of the business takes place. Still others, such as the sale-and-leaseback arrangement, are attractive for large firms, which sell their real estate and lease it back from the new owner to release investment capital for future expansion. Partners under this type of lease are investors who have capital to invest in order to ensure an agreeable rate of return from the rents on the leased-back property. These examples represent only a few types of leases that have been adapted to the special needs of the parties.

Lease Renewal

Depending on the type of leasehold estate that was conveyed by the landlord or on the terms of the parties' agreement, the lease will terminate on its own or on appropriate notice by either party. It is not unusual, however, to include in the lease a term that provides for the renewal of the lease. The renewal provision may be one that requires the tenant to give notice of renewal by a specified period of time prior to the termination of the lease. Alternatively, the renewal may be automatic, absent notice of nonrenewal by either party.

A renewal is a new lease. Unless otherwise stated, the renewal is under the same terms and conditions as the original lease. The parties may agree that the rent will be altered to reflect the present value of the land. For instance, each renewal may require a reappraisal of the land and a rent adjustment to reflect a specified percentage of the appraised value. Except where the agreement is for an automatic renewal of the lease, the parties should indicate whether the renewal clause will be operative in the second lease and in succeeding renewed leases.

Another method of renewal is by holding over. The legal implications for the holdover tenant were discussed in a preceding section.

THE CHANGING LANDSCAPE

Although zoning is not discussed in detail until Chapter 25, most of us are familiar with the concept of creating zones for specific uses. A community draws up a plan and then assigns specific use zones to the various areas of the community. Single-family houses here, commercial structures there, multifamily housing over here, and farms over there. The one constant in zoning is that each use zone must be separate from other use zones so the use designed for one zone will not interfere with the uses designated for others. Is there a downside to this use separation?

We are all familiar with the saying "You are what you eat." Perhaps we are less familiar with the notion that your lifestyle is determined by what you build. If housing zones are separated by several miles or more from services such as shopping, doctors' offices, and hair salons, we have made several lifestyle decisions. Residents will need a car or public transportation to get almost anywhere. In many areas, a car is the only choice. Cars require significant investment, are expensive to operate, pollute the air, and are very consumptive of land resources.

Think about the land dedicated to cars—roads, parking lots, driveways, garages, gas stations, and so on. Cars require massive amounts of gasoline, much of its imported from abroad. Oil imports create balance of payment problems, military forces strategically stationed to protect supplies, and even wars over oil fields.

So what does all this have to do with leaseholds? Maybe twentieth century style zoning does not make sense anymore. Would mixed-use development—integrating apartments, occupier-owned houses, stores, and schools—make apartment living more attractive? It might improve the lifestyle of those who cannot afford to buy housing, the elderly, and young adults. It would reduce the necessity for as many miles driven, and so on. It might enhance our closeness and sense of community. Stores might be attracted through artfully drawn commercial leases. How do you see it? What are the pros and cons of more apartment living with services within walking distance? How would it change our lifestyles?

■ KEY TERMS

■ INTERNET RESOURCES

www.uslegalforms.com/landlordtenant/General.htm
(Legal forms needed for the laws relating to leaseholds in the United States, plus summaries of important aspects of landlord-tenant relationships)

www.Tenantsunion.org
(Information on tenants' rights in Washington State but many conclusions applicable to other states)

www.intellibiz.com/realty/trip_net.html
(illustrates triple net leases)

http://smallbusiness.findlaw.com/business_operations/commercial_real_estate_lease_types.htm
(outlines various types of commercial leases)

■ REVIEW AND DISCUSSION QUESTIONS

1. Match the following:

   a. Tenancy at sufferance

   b. Term tenancy

   c. Tenancy at will

   d. Periodic tenancy

   (1) Has a specific beginning and ending date.

   (2) Exists as long as neither party chooses to terminate it.

   (3) Continues from period to period until terminated by one of the parties giving proper notice.

   (4) Exists when a person is wrongfully in possession of another's land without a valid lease.

2. Name two ways in which a periodic tenancy can be created.

3. Define the term *holdover tenant*.

4. List and briefly describe four terms that should be specified in a lease contract.

5. What risks are involved in entering an oral lease?

6. Distinguish between "the landlord gives possession of the premises" and "the landlord gives the right of possession of the premises."

7. Match the following:

   a. Net lease

   b. Gross lease

   c. Percentage lease

   d. Ground lease

   (1) The rent is based in part on the gross sales made by the lessee.

   (2) The lessor leases a piece of vacant land to the lessee, usually with the stipulation that the lessee at his or her own expense will construct a building.

   (3) The tenant agrees to pay taxes, insurance, repairs, and other operating expenses of the premises.

   (4) The rent is a fixed or flat amount.

8. Describe and discuss those rules of landlord-tenant law that no longer seem appropriate given present-day expectations of lay parties.

■ CASE PROBLEMS

1. China Doll Restaurant, Inc., leased premises from Schweiger. China Doll agreed to pay a base rent of $600 per month and an amount equal to 5 percent of the restaurant's first $288,000 of gross sales. The owners of China Doll had considerable experience in operating a Chinese restaurant.

    The lease also contained a provision in which lessee agreed to use the premises "for conducting and operating a restaurant business." Before the expiration of the lease, China Doll moved to new and larger premises. At this time they stated that they intended to open a Mexican restaurant at the former China Doll location. Little was done to accomplish this, but they continued to pay the base rent of $600 per month. During this period the premises were unoccupied. Has China Doll violated the terms of the lease? *China Doll Restaurant, Inc. v. Schweiger*, 19 Ariz. 315, 580 P.2d 776 (1978).

2. Chapman rented farmland to Walker on a year-to-year basis beginning each year on January 1. Chapman sold the property to Gregory with a stipulation that Gregory was to have possession as of January 1, 1963. On July 1, 1962, Chapman gave Walker notice to vacate at the end of the year. Is this notice sufficient in a state following the traditional common-law rule? *Gregory v. Walker*, 239 Ark. 415, 389 S.W.2d 892 (1965).

3. Regency Inn leased a rental office in the lobby of its hotel to Americar, a car rental agency. Wagner rented a car from Americar, and while walking through the hotel parking lot to reach her rental car, she was robbed and raped. Wagner sued Regency Inn for damages, alleging that they maintained a public nuisance. A clause in the lease held that Americar was responsible to indemnify Regency Inn for any damages suffered due to the operation of the car rental agency. At the time of assault on Wagner, Americar was a holdover tenant. Can Regency Inn claim indemnification under these conditions? *Wagner v. Regency Inn Corp.*, 463 N.W.2d 450 (1990).

4. Doyle owed Byrne $5,000 for services performed in rewiring Doyle's house. After six months, Doyle had paid nothing on the $5,000 bill and, on being confronted by Byrne, admitted that it was unlikely that he could pay the bill in the near future. Byrne suggested that he would take a lease for a year on Doyle's camp on the lake. Doyle said "fine," and the conversation ended. In the spring, Byrne moved into Doyle's camp and occupied it without incident until mid-July. At that time, Doyle arrived at the camp and ordered Byrne to evacuate. Byrne refused, claiming that he had a one-year lease. Doyle retorted that there was nothing in writing, that no rent was stipulated, and that the services for electrical work could not be used in lieu of cash payments for rent. Discuss the validity of Doyle's arguments.

8

The Landlord-Tenant Relationship

The signing of a lease creates obligations on the part of both the lessor and the lessee. Failure by either party to comply with obligations imposed either by contract or by law gives rise to the availability of certain legal remedies. The remedies available depend on the nature of the obligation breached and on the present circumstances of the parties. For example, did the lessee remain in possession, or were the premises abandoned? Some problems result from actions taken by one of the parties to the transaction—the lessee may have sublet the premises, for example—or from actions involving not the parties but other persons, as when a visitor falls down the stairs of the leased premises. These occurrences lead to legal responsibilities on the part of the parties to the lease. Obligations imposed by the lease contract, by the relationship itself, and by the law are the topics of this chapter. As a broad generalization about modern landlord-tenant law, states have become very protective of residential tenants, but much less protective of commercial tenants.

■ LESSOR'S SECURITY

Several forms of protection have evolved over time to protect landlords from tenants who mistreat the leased premises.

Rent Paid in Advance

■ *A normal requirement for modern leases is that rent payments are due prior to the beginning of the lease period.*

Under common law, where it is not otherwise specified, rent is due at the end of the rental period. The modern practice of requiring advance payment of the rent in the lease gives the landlord some additional assurance of stability. Where the rent is not forthcoming from the tenant by the first day of the rental period, the landlord is given some lead time in pursuing remedies for nonpayment. If the rent were not due until the end of the rental period, the landlord would lose additional time pursuing the remedies.

Security Deposit

■ *Money deposited by the tenant for the security of the landlord, usually at the inception of the lease, over and above the advance payment of rent.*

The **security deposit** is usually equivalent to one month's rent or more. Its purpose is to secure the landlord against damage done to the premises by the tenant or to clean or repair the premises, over and above normal wear and tear, when the tenant vacates.

It may also provide a wider margin of security against a tenant who wrongfully abandons the premises. It has the practical effect of inducing the tenant who wants the security deposit returned to maintain the premises carefully during occupancy and to clean the premises thoroughly on leaving. In some states, there is a limit on the amount the landlord can demand as a security deposit.

The security deposit is held by the landlord in trust for the tenant. The parties may agree that interest will be paid on this money. In some states, it is mandatory that the landlord of multiple-unit housing pay interest on any security deposit.

Because the security deposit is not a form of liquidated damages, the landlord can retain only as much as is necessary to pay for any damage done by the tenant. If the payment is a security deposit and not an advance rental, the tenant cannot use it in lieu of payment of rent for the last month. Whichever it is should be stipulated clearly by the parties.

Some states have adopted parts of the Uniform Residential Landlord and Tenant Act, which is geared toward promoting uniformity in landlord-tenant law. The act provides strict regulation of the security deposit. It would limit the amount deposited to one or two month's rent, require a written explanation of the purpose for and handling of the funds as well as an indication of the reasons for retaining any of the deposit, and provide for the return of any unneeded funds to the tenant within 14 days after the termination of the lease. It also provides for penalties in case the landlord mishandles any of the security deposit funds. Most states have tailored these provisions to fit their needs.

Third-Person Guaranty of Rent

■ *The landlord who has doubts about the capacity or reliability of the tenant in meeting the conditions of the lease may require a third person to guarantee performance.*

In a commercial or industrial lease where the tenant is thinly capitalized, a personal guaranty by the individuals actually running the business under the corporate veil may be required. Also, where the tenant has a poor credit rating, the landlord may insist on the assurance of a more reliable third person. The guaranty would have to be in writing and signed by the guarantor. The guaranty agreement may be a part of the lease or a separate agreement usually appended to the lease.

■ LESSOR'S OBLIGATIONS

The landlord is bound by any promises made to the tenant in the lease. In addition, certain obligations have been imposed on the landlord by the law over and above the contractual understanding. The following covenants and warrants are the major ones with which the parties must be concerned.

Covenant of Quiet Enjoyment

■ *A warrant by the landlord that the tenant will have the premises free from interference by the landlord or anyone claiming better right to the premises than the landlord.*

There is no general guarantee by the landlord against wrongful intrusion by third persons. Should such an intrusion take place, the tenant will have satisfactory legal avenues through which to redress the interference. For centuries, however, the general common-law rule has been that the tenant is protected from a wrongful intrusion by the landlord or someone claiming better rights than the landlord or tenant.

The **covenant of quiet enjoyment** is breached only on eviction by the landlord or by a third person, either actual or constructive. *Actual eviction* consists of a physical removal of the tenant from the premises. *Constructive eviction* could occur when there is a substantial interference with the tenant's enjoyment of the premises.

CASE EXAMPLE

HTM leased commercial property from Goldman, Sachs and Company. Goldman failed to pay the mortgage, resulting in the mortgagee foreclosing on the property and ousting HTM from its lease. HTM sued for breach of implied covenant of quiet enjoyment.

The court noted that in every lease of land there is, absent an agreement to the contrary, an implied covenant of quiet, peaceful enjoyment of the premises. Unfortunately for HTM, a clause in its lease stated that it accepted the premises subject to all mortgages. The mortgage preceded the HTM lease so that HTM had waived its implied covenant of quiet enjoyment by "agreeing to the contrary." *HTM Restaurants, Inc. v. Goldman, Sachs and Company*, 797 S.W.2d 326 (Texas, 1990).

Generally, in the case of either an actual or a constructive eviction the tenant must have vacated the premises before asserting a breach of the covenant of quiet enjoyment.

Covenant to Deliver Possession

■ *The landlord promises to deliver the right of possession to the tenant at the time the lease is scheduled to start.*

This covenant is quite limited. It does not warrant against a wrongdoer being in possession of the premises at the time the lease commences, but only that the tenant will have the *right to possession*.

Should a wrongdoer be in possession, the tenant has the obligation to evict him or her. A few jurisdictions have adopted the so-called English Rule, which requires the landlord to deliver *possession*, not merely the *right* to it. This interpretation is consistent with the usual expectancy of the parties on entering the contract.

One aspect of this covenant that is sometimes misunderstood by residential landlords is that the tenant's right to possession is *exclusive*. This excludes the landlord as well as others.

Covenant of Fitness of the Premises

■ *An assurance that the premises are fit for habitation.*

The common-law rule is that the landlord does not implicitly warrant that the premises are fit for habitation. Some jurisdictions still follow the dictate of this rule, but even in these a few exceptions have been created. Where the lease is for a furnished apartment or is intended for a short duration (a few days, weeks, or months), there is an implied warranty that the premises are habitable on entry. Similarly, when the landlord knew of latent defects—defects that were unknown and not reasonably discoverable by the tenant—there is a breach of an implied covenant of fitness.

The general rule makes sense when placed in the context of the time of its creation. It arose during a period in which land was the predominant concern in a lease, and the tenant could readily discover what he or she needed to know about the land. In modern times the building is usually the chief concern of the parties, and often the building is to be used as a residence. The notion of *caveat emptor*—"let the buyer beware"—seems ill-suited to a situation where the landlord is in a far superior position to know the condition of the premises and understands that the tenant wants to use it as a residence.

Implied Warranty of Habitability

■ *A warranty imposed by law on the landlord by which he or she warrants that a* residential property *is safe and sanitary and fit for living at the time the tenant enters and during the period of tenancy.*

In an effort to bring landlord-tenant law into modern times, many courts and legislatures have imposed an **implied warranty of habitability.** The reason usually cited for changing the law is the inequality of bargaining position between the landlord and the tenant. Normally, the landlord drafts the terms of the lease and the tenant can accept them or look elsewhere for living accommodations. In addition, legislative action by state and municipal governments that created housing codes exhibited a concern for protecting tenants; these actions stiffened the backbone of the courts in imposing the warranty of habitability.

Apparently, the determination of what constitutes a breach of this warranty will be a question of fact. Courts have noted that what constitutes a breach depends on the nature of the deficiency, its effect on habitability, the length of time it persisted, the age of the structure, the amount of the rent, the area in which the premises are located, and whether the tenant waived the defects or caused them through abnormal use of the premises. An apartment leased for an amount substantially below local standards, for instance, may not have to be in as good a condition as other leased properties in the area. At least, rent will be one factor considered by the court in deciding whether the warranty of habitability has been breached.

In effect, this warranty imposes a duty on the landlord to keep the premises in repair during the lease period. This would be true despite his or her failure to agree to perform repairs and contrary to the long-standing common-law rule freeing either party of the duty to repair unless agreed to.

A majority of the states have adopted the theory of *implied* warranty of habitability for residential tenancies. However, the theory has rarely been applied to nonresidential situations. The Uniform Residential Landlord and Tenant Act makes void any provision in the lease waiving or otherwise negating the warranty of habitability. Notice the contrast in the positions of the courts in the following case examples.

CASE EXAMPLE

In a case between Teller and Hager, tenants, and McCoy, landlord, there was an express waiver of the warranty of habitability in the lease. The West Virginia Supreme Court held that such a waiver violated public policy. "Given the proliferation of 'form leases' and the current scarcity of habitable dwellings, there exists a distinct danger that such waivers would become routine. If tenants seeking scarce available shelter are compelled to waive their rights and accept uninhabitable dwellings, then the protection accorded by the implied warranty. . . could become meaningless." *Teller and Hager v. McCoy*, 253 SE 2d 114 (1978).

CASE EXAMPLE

In a similar case Oliver, tenant, had refused to pay rent due to the deteriorated condition of the premises. P. H. Investment, landlord, sued for unpaid rent based on a lease that waived the warranty of habitability. The Utah Supreme Court acknowledged that the majority of courts follow the rule prohibiting such a waiver. It ruled, however, that such waivers were not categorically illegal, because of the need to protect the expectations of the parties and their freedom to contract. If such a waiver is to be valid, it must be expressed, and the express waiver is only effective as to specific defects listed in the waiver in the lease. *P. H. Investment v. Oliver*, 818 P2d 1018 (1991).

Duty to Repair

■ *Absent the existence of an implied warranty of habitability in a state, the landlord has no duty to repair the premises.*

In addition to not covenanting that the premises are habitable on entry, the common-law rule does not require that the landlord repair during the habitation. However, where the landlord retains control over parts of the premises, he or she will be responsible for repairing those areas.

CASE EXAMPLE

Derman Rug Company leased the first floor and basement of a building from Ruderman. The lease contained a provision requiring that the tenant keep the premises in as good order and repair as they were at the beginning of the lease. A steam pipe embedded in the basement floor leaked and was repaired by the landlord, who sued the tenant for the cost of repairs.

The landlord's claim was rejected by the court. Two reasons were given for rejecting this suit. First, the court determined that pipes embedded in floors are within the landlord's exclusive control and as such are the landlord's sole responsibility. Second, the court was convinced that the tenant's duty to repair did not extend to the basement in a building in which upper floors were leased to other tenants, because the land under the building is not part of the leased premises. *Derman Rug Co. Inc. v. Ruderman*, 4 Mass. App. Ct. 437, 350 N.E.2d 727 (1976).

Because of the uncertainty created by the adoption of the warranty of habitability, the parties to a lease should be cautious and thorough in declaring their respective rights in relation to repairs.

In a significant number of states, statutes have been passed imposing a duty on the landlord to perform repairs. The parties should be careful, given the variability of the rules regarding repairs, to make the terms of their agreement clear. When the landlord has the duty to repair and fails to do so, the tenant may sue the landlord for damages or make the needed repairs and deduct the cost from the rent.

If the landlord agrees in the lease to perform repairs, there is a split of authority over the responsibility for rebuilding a structure destroyed by a fire or other catastrophe. Some courts hold that the obligation to repair includes rebuilding; others claim that "repairing" is narrower than "rebuilding." Under the latter rule, once the building is substantially destroyed, it would not be encompassed within the obligation to repair.

If the landlord has agreed to rebuild, whether expressly or by implication in consenting to repair, the failure to rebuild would terminate the tenant's obligation to pay rent, at least where the building is the major concern of the lease.

Duty to Pay Taxes

■   *Absent a contrary agreement, the landlord has the duty to pay the property taxes.*

As the owner of the fee interest in the premises, the landlord is responsible for paying the taxes. If the property is sold at a tax sale for nonpayment, the sale is subject to the existing lease. Where the tenant makes improvements to the property that cause the taxes to rise, the tenant will probably be liable to pay for the increase.

Building Code Compliance

■   *Most cities have adopted building codes for the purpose of protecting the public health, safety, and welfare by regulating building and construction standards.*

Through the requirement of obtaining a building permit or a certificate of occupancy for new construction or substantial alteration of an existing structure, city officials inspect structures for violations of the building code. The code is usually divided into special areas, such as plumbing code, electrical code, and fire code. As a result of the division, there may be several inspectors and a multitude of permits. Failure to comply with the building code may result in the landlord's being fined.

The codes are applicable to existing buildings as well, and the code process usually comes into play when there is a tenant complaint about a violation. Often the result of these complaints is that the tenant receives a notice to vacate the premises at the earliest legal opportunity. Naturally, this discourages tenant complaints. Owing to this landlord reaction, some jurisdictions have created the affirmative defense of retaliatory eviction. Under this defense a tenant cannot be evicted for complaining, at least until a legislated period (sometimes 90 days) has lapsed after the complaint has been remedied. This provides only temporary protection to the tenant, and the landlord is free to terminate the tenancy after the time stated in the statute.

■ LESSOR'S REMEDIES

If one of the parties does not comply with the lease agreement, the other party will have an array of potential remedies. The chief remedies of the landlord will be discussed here.

Eviction

■ *The term usually associated with the legal procedure by which a landlord has the tenant removed from the premises because the tenant has breached the lease agreement.*

Under the common law, the covenants of a lease were mutually exclusive, and therefore the breach of a covenant by the tenant would not entitle the landlord to dispossess the tenant. The landlord would have a cause of action for damages resulting from the breach.

In the modern landlord-tenant situation, generally there is a provision in the lease, or the right may be provided by state statute, that the landlord can sue to regain possession of the premises in case of the tenant's failure to comply with the covenants in the lease. Though the agreement or the statute may not provide for dispossession in the case of *any* breach of a covenant, it normally applies to the failure to pay rent, the violation of the use provisions of the lease, the unlawful use of the premises, or the violation of state and local health codes.

The **eviction** process will be used to dispossess a tenant who has received legal notice to vacate the premises and has failed to do so. Where the basis for the eviction is nonpayment of rent, the landlord will be required to notify the tenant of the possibility of eviction and make a demand for the rent prior to beginning the eviction proceedings.

The eviction of the tenant terminates the obligation to pay future rents. However, many business leases contain "survival clauses" under which the obligation to pay rent continues despite the eviction of the wrongdoing tenant. When it is a long-term lease, however, the right to sue accrues only at the termination of the lease, unless a clause in the lease indicates otherwise. It may be impractical to delay the suit for ten or more years until the lease period ends.

The term *eviction* is used to describe the wrongful dispossession of the tenant by the landlord as well as the legal action of the landlord described above. Wrongful eviction will be discussed under the lessee's remedies below.

Wrongful Abandonment

■ *The tenant's vacating of the premises without justification and with the intention of no longer performing under the terms of the lease.*

When the tenant wrongfully abandons the premises, the landlord has two options: either to do nothing until the lease period ends and then to bring an action for nonpayment of rent or to reenter the premises and reassert possessory rights.

The common-law rule is that the landlord is free to do nothing and recover the full amount of unpaid rent at the termination of the lease. In some states, however, a duty arises to mitigate damages, thereby compelling the landlord to reenter and attempt to relet the premises. In all states, the landlord can secure the right of reentry by including in the lease a survival clause permitting the entry but reserving the right to collect rent from the tenant. With this clause the landlord can minimize the damages by reletting the property while continuing to have the original tenant as a hedge against any losses caused by the **wrongful abandonment.**

When the landlord reenters after a wrongful abandonment and without the protection of a survival clause, he or she is said to *accept the surrender of the premises*. On acceptance of the surrender, the tenant's obligation to pay rent ends. In essence, by the force of the landlord's action of reentry, he or she has implicitly acquiesced to the abandonment of the tenant.

O'Brien v. Black
Supreme Court of Vermont
648 A.2d 1374 (1994)

Background. Pickwick and Perkins, Ltd. (Pickwick), the tenant, entered into a five-year term lease with Burlington Square Mall (Burlington). The lease was to end on November 1, 1991, but Pickwick abandoned the premises and ceased paying rent in January 1990. Burlington requested that Pickwick cure its default, and that if it did not, Burlington could exercise its option to terminate the lease. Burlington terminated the lease in August 1990, when it rented the space to a new tenant. Burlington then sued Pickwick for unpaid rent for the intervening months. Pickwick's defense is that the landlord did not make reasonable efforts to mitigate damages. The basis for the defense is that Ms. Ginsberg, another tenant in the mall, approached the landlord in February 1990 about renting the larger Pickwick space. The landlord refused to discuss the matter, telling her that the space had already been rented. In fact, it was not leased until August to a new tenant at a substantial increase in rent. The trial judge decided for the tenant.

Decision. The Supreme Court of Vermont affirmed the decision in favor of the tenant, Pickwick.

Justice Johnson. Landlord argues that, when a lessee abandons the leased premises, a commercial lessor does not have an affirmative duty to mitigate damages until the lease is formally terminated. Absent formal termination, which is within its control, landlord argues it can allow its damages to accrue until the end of the lease period.

Those jurisdictions that follow the traditional rule that a landlord has no duty to mitigate damages on a tenant's abandonment "proceed from the theory that a lease creates an estate in land and the lessee thus becomes the owner of the premises for the term of the lease. Under this theory the lessor need not concern himself with the lessee's abandonment of the lessee's own property." Thus, under this view, on the lessee's abandonment of the property, the lessor may elect either to: (1) accept the lessee's surrender of the premises, thus terminating the lease, or (2) decline to accept the surrender and continue to hold the lessee liable for rent as it becomes due. Only if the lessor elects to terminate the lease is it obligated to mitigate its damages because then the action is one for breach of lease, in which case basic contract principles apply.

The modern trend, however, is to recognize a landlord's duty to mitigate damages. "In recent years, almost all courts which have faced the question have refused to allow landlords to recover money from a defaulting tenant in damages when the landlord could have avoided those damages by leasing the premises to another with no greater risks to the landlord than he assumed under the original lease." These courts reason that a modern lease is far more than a conveyance of an estate in land and treat a lease as both a conveyance and a contract.

We conclude that the principles underlying the duty-to-mitigate rule in general contract law sound with equal force in the landlord-tenant context. Under the traditional no-duty-to-mitigate rule espoused by landlord, when a tenant abandons the premises, a landlord can delay termination and "unreasonably sit idly by and allow damages to accumulate." We find that it would be palpably unreasonable to provide landlords with what, in essence, would be the power to decide when their duty to mitigate damages arises. Rather, the law should be such as to deter "a landlord from passively suffering preventable economic loss, to encourage the productive use of land, and to decrease the likelihood of physical damage to property."

Moreover, in the context of residential landlord-tenant law, this Court already has discarded the antiquated concepts that defined the landlord-tenant relationship solely in terms of property law and recognized "that a lease is essentially a contract between the landlord and the tenant." In light of the foregoing considerations, we now expressly discard those same notions in the context of commercial landlord-tenant law and recognize that a commercial landlord has a duty to mitigate its damages when a tenant abandons the leased premises.

The duty to mitigate damages does nothing to affect a tenant's existing obligation under the lease to pay rent because our holding does not require landlord to accept a tenant's surrender. By imposing a duty to mitigate damages on commercial landlords, the Court merely seeks to insure that those landlords respond reasonably to their tenants' abandonment. In fact, "[t]he duty to mitigate damages [does] not require [a commercial landlord] to sacrifice any substantial right of its own; or to exalt the interests of the tenant above its own."

Affirmed.

Does the rule in the case free tenants to cavalierly ignore their obligations under a lease?

Action for Rent or Damages

■ *The landlord may permit, or be required to permit, the wrongdoing tenant to retain possession of the property and seek money damages for the landlord's injury.*

The usual action by the landlord for damages involves the recovery of unpaid rent. If no agreement exists to the contrary, the landlord will have to wait until the end of the lease to begin action for unpaid rent. However, most leases provide terms permitting an action for rent prior to termination, though these generally include the right to evict and are discussed above.

Should the tenant cause damage to the premises or otherwise violate the covenants of the lease over and above the value of the rent, the landlord has the right to sue for damages.

■ LESSEE'S OBLIGATIONS

Obligations arise both from the lease contract and from modern real estate law.

Duty to Repair

■ *The tenant's obligation to use the premises in a reasonable fashion and to deliver possession at the end of the lease in about the same condition as when received, reasonable wear and tear excluded.*

Absent an agreement to the contrary, the tenant has no law-imposed duty to make substantial repairs to the premises. However, the tenant is obligated to maintain the property so as to protect it from the weather. This obligation is referred to as the *tenant's responsibility to avoid waste*.

Waste

■ *Damage caused by the tenant including failure to protect the premises from decay and ruin caused by the natural elements.*

The notion of **waste** can take two different forms. *Voluntary waste* results from the positive actions of the tenant, such as willfully breaking the windows or destroying the landscaping. *Permissive waste* results from an act of omission, such as the failure to repair an accidentally broken window, thereby permitting injury to the premises from the weather.

The tenant may agree to perform repairs, just as the landlord might. Similarly, as previously noted under the landlord's obligations, there is a difference of opinion among jurisdictions as to whether the tenant is liable to rebuild the premises in the case of fire or other catastrophe where that tenant has agreed to repair. Because the parties would not normally intend the requirement of repairing to encompass rebuilding, they should expressly exclude this contingency from their agreement.

Whether or not the tenant agrees to repair, he or she will be liable in damages to the landlord for any injury, beyond normal wear and tear, caused to the premises.

Duty to Insure

Neither the tenant nor the landlord has an obligation to each other to insure the premises against loss. However, the failure of the tenant to insure his or her interest may result in a continuing obligation to pay rent without enjoying the benefit of the property whose improvements have been destroyed by fire. Where the tenant leases both land and improvements, he or she is not relieved of the duty to pay rent despite the destruction of the premises. If the tenant leases only the improvements (such as an apartment in a multiple-family building), the obligation to pay rent will terminate when the improvements are substantially destroyed. If the destruction is only partial and the premises are still tenable, however, the tenant must continue to pay rent.

Where the tenant rents both land and buildings, the common-law rule requiring the payment of rent after the buildings' destruction seems unduly harsh. In a few states the rule has been altered to provide for termination of the obligation to pay rent where the improvements have been substantially destroyed or become untenable through no fault of the tenant. The change in the rule seems equitable, given the fact that buildings are often the critical concern in modern leases.

Fixtures

▪ *Any personal property permanently affixed to the realty by the tenant become the property of the landlord at the termination of the lease.*

The tenant can provide in the lease for removal of fixtures at the culmination of the tenancy; absent such an agreement, however, he or she will lose the right to those items attached to the realty that would otherwise be classified as fixtures. The common law created a harsh situation for the tenant.

This doctrine has been altered in some measure. To the extent that the tenant attaches items to the realty that enable him or her to carry on a commercial enterprise, for example, the doctrine of trade fixtures provides that the tenant will be able to remove the items up to the termination date of the lease.

> **CASE EXAMPLE**
> Lubin leases commercial shop space to Murphy. To sell her cards and gifts, Murphy installs shelves that are attached to brackets, and the brackets are affixed to the wall. Prior to the end of the lease Murphy can remove the shelves and brackets as long as the removal does not significantly or materially injure the shop.

The exception to the general rule is based on the idea that it was the presumed intent of the parties to permit removal, and public policy supports rules that will encourage trade through flexibility.

Several things should be noted about trade fixtures. First, the question of whether an item is a trade fixture may be treated as one of fact and left up to the trier of fact (the jury). More certainty can be obtained by stipulating in the lease how these fixtures will be handled. Second, removal can be executed only where serious injury will not result to the premises. Third, if the tenant leaves the trade fixtures at the lease termination and the landlord does not want them, the landlord can have them removed at the tenant's expense. Finally, removal is not permitted after the termination of the lease. On termination of the lease, trade fixtures become the permanent property of the landlord. Obligations of the lessor and the lessee are summarized in Table 8.1.

TABLE 8.1	Summary of Obligations	
Lessor Provides		**Lessee Provides**
Quiet enjoyment		Maintenance of property
Possession		Insurance (for self-protection)
Habitability		Removal of fixtures at termination
Property tax payments		
Building code compliance (some jurisdictions)		

■ LESSEE'S REMEDIES

The lessee has several remedies available when the lessor violates the conditions of the lease.

Wrongful Eviction

■ *An act that occurs when the landlord without justification deprives the tenant of possession of the premises.*

A tenant who has been wrongfully evicted (also referred to as an *actual eviction*) can sue for recovery of possession of the premises or for damages caused by the breach of the covenant of quiet enjoyment. In a somewhat punitive aspect of this area of law, if the landlord wrongfully evicts the tenant from only part of the premises, the tenant may retain the remainder of the property but will have no obligation to pay any rent until the partial wrongful eviction ceases.

A wrongful eviction and breach of the covenant of quiet enjoyment will exist also where the tenant is ousted because a third person has proved rights superior to those of the landlord. In such a case the tenant will have an action for money damages.

Constructive Eviction

■ *An occurrence that results when the actions of the landlord so materially interfere with the tenant's enjoyment as to make the premises untenable.*

Theoretically at least, the right to assert a **constructive eviction** occurs when the tenant is forced by the condition of the premises to vacate. The tenant must notify the landlord of the conditions, where appropriate, and give the landlord a reasonable time to remedy the situation. Finally, the tenant must actually vacate the premises to be able to allege constructive eviction.

Blackett v. Olanoff
Supreme Judicial Court of Massachusetts
358 N.E.2d 817 (1977)

Background. Jerrold Olanoff leased residential premises to Arthur Blackett. Olanoff leased other residential premises in the vicinity and also leased commercial premises to another for use as a bar and cocktail lounge. The noise emanating from the lounge in the late evening and early morning hours was substantial. Blackett complained about the noise to his landlord, who attempted unsuccessfully to control the noise from the lounge. After a reasonable time, Blackett vacated the premises contending that the noise made the premises untenable, thereby breaching his implied warranty of quiet enjoyment.

Olanoff brought this action against Blackett to recover unpaid rent. Blackett offered the defense of constructive eviction. Olanoff contended that he was not responsible for the noise created by the proprietors, employees, and patrons of the lounge. Olanoff did not contend that the noise was not loud enough to cause a constructive eviction. The trial judge concluded that Blackett was constructively evicted.

Decision. The Supreme Judicial Court of Massachusetts affirmed the trial court's decision.

Justice Wilkins. Our opinions concerning a constructive eviction by an alleged breach of an implied covenant of quiet enjoyment sometimes have stated that the landlord must perform some act with the intent of depriving the tenant of the enjoyment and occupation of the whole or part of the leased premises. There are occasions, however, where a landlord has not intended to violate a tenant's rights, but there was nevertheless a breach of the landlord's covenant of quiet enjoyment which flowed as the natural and probable consequence of what the landlord did, what he failed to do, or what he permitted to be done. Although some of our opinions have spoken of particular action or inaction by a landlord as showing a presumed intention to evict, the landlord's conduct, and not his intentions, is controlling.

The judge was warranted in ruling that the landlords had it within their control to correct the condition which caused the tenants to vacate their apartments. The landlords introduced a commercial activity where they leased premises for residential purpose. The lease for the lounge expressly provided that entertainment in the lounge had to be conducted so that it could not be heard outside the building and would not disturb the residents of the leased apartments. The potential threat to the occupants of the nearby apartments was apparent in the circumstances. The landlords complained to the tenants of the lounge after receiving numerous objections from residential tenants. From time to time, the pervading noise would abate in response to the landlord's complaints. We conclude that, as matter of law, the landlords had a right to control the objectionable noise coming from the lounge and that the judge was warranted in finding as a fact that the landlords could control the objectionable conditions.

This situation is different from the usual annoyance of one residential tenant by another, where traditionally the landlord has not been chargeable with the annoyance. Here, although the clash of tenants' interests was only a known potentiality initially, experience demonstrated that a decibel level for the entertainment at the lounge, acoustically acceptable to its patrons and hence commercially desirable to its proprietors, was intolerable for the residential tenants.

Because the disturbing condition was the natural and probable consequence of the landlords' permitting the lounge to operate where it did and because the landlords could control the actions at the lounge, they should not be entitled to collect rent for residential premises which were not reasonably habitable. Tenants such as these should not be left

continued on next page

only with a claim against the proprietors of the noisome lounge. To the extent that our opinions suggest a distinction between nonfeasance by the landlord, which has been said to create no liability, and malfeasance by the landlord, we decline to perpetuate that distinction where the landlord creates a situation and has the right to control the objectionable conditions.

Judgments affirmed.

Suppose there was no clause in the lease with the lounge tenant that expressly authorized the landlord to control the noise level in the lounge. Would the outcome have differed?

Damages, Reformation, and Rescission

■   *Actions a tenant may bring where an implied warranty of habitability exists and the landlord has failed to maintain the premises in a tenable condition.*

The remedies made available to the tenant when the implied warranty of habitability is breached are of a complementary nature. That is, the tenant is afforded relief short of vacating the premises or withholding rent, both of which may be risky remedies.

The tenant may sue for damages measured by expenses incurred as a result of the landlord's refusal to perform the covenants in the lease. The tenant may seek **reformation** of the contract due to the conduct of the landlord in refusing to perform repairs. The reformation could take the form of reducing the amount of rent due to conform to the lessened value of the unrepaired premises. If the breach of covenant has reduced the value of the lease to the tenant significantly, prior to the tenant's entry he or she may seek **rescission**, that is, to have a court rescind or negate the entire agreement.

Rent Withholding

■   *The practice, allowed in some states under limited circumstances, in which the tenant withholds rent as an inducement to force the landlord to perform repairs.*

It should be remembered that at common law the obligation to pay rent arises from the possession of the land and from the covenant to pay in the lease. Each covenant in the lease is independent. Therefore, the tenant normally has the duty to pay the rent despite the landlord's failure to perform some aspect of his or her obligation.

In some states, including New York, Illinois, Connecticut, Vermont, and Michigan, tenants are legislatively authorized to withhold rent in cases where the landlord has failed to obtain a certificate of occupancy as required by the municipal housing code. Similarly, welfare agencies are authorized to withhold rent payments that they normally make directly to the landlord for the welfare tenant. A statute establishes the conditions for rent withholding and the procedures for utilizing the right. It affords protection to the tenant from being evicted. Often, rent may be paid to the court in the event of a dispute.

It should be noted that rent withholding is not a broadly applicable remedy, and local and state law will have to be checked carefully to determine whether the right exists and to what extent. Remedies available to lessors and lessees are summarized in Table 8.2.

TABLE 8.2	Available Remedies	
Lessor	**Lessee**
Eviction	Wrongful eviction
Wrongful abandonment	Constructive eviction
Action for rent	Damages, reformation, rescission
Action for damages	Rent withholding

■ THIRD-PARTY-RELATED TRANSACTIONS

On occasion a person other than the landlord or tenant becomes involved with the leasehold agreement. Because of a job change, for example, a tenant may seek a substitute to complete the tenancy. Or a person visiting the tenant may fall down the hall stairway in the apartment due to poor lighting or a faulty railing. These and other third-party incidents affecting the lease are discussed next.

Sublease

■ *A transfer of part of the leasehold interest of the tenant, with the tenant retaining a reversionary interest.*

CASE EXAMPLE
Granville leases Hilltop Acres to Tomas under a term lease beginning January 1 and ending December 31 of the same year. On March 1, Tomas transfers her interest in Hilltop Acres to Nantes until November 30. This agreement is a sublease, since Tomas has retained a one-month reversionary interest.

Impact of a Sublease. When the tenant creates a **sublease** by conveying less than the entire interest in the land to a sublessee, there is no privity of estate or contract between the landlord and the sublessee. In short, the sublease does not alter in any respect the original landlord-tenant agreement. The sublessee will have an obligation to pay rent to the tenant, and the tenant will continue to have the obligation to pay rent to the landlord. Likewise, any restriction or limitations included in the original landlord-tenant agreement will pertain to the tenant-sublessee contract as well, because the tenant cannot give greater rights than he or she has. The tenant, despite not being in possession, will still have all the obligations arising from the initial landlord-tenant contract.

Assignment

■ *A transfer in which the tenant gives the entire interest in the leasehold estate without retaining a reversionary interest.*

Using the example above, if Tomas had transferred her interest until December 31, the agreement would have been an **assignment**; Tomas transferred her entire interest in the land. Unless otherwise agreed, the tenant is free either to sublet or to assign the premises. Often, however, the lease agreement includes wording that limits the tenant's right to sublet or assign. The permission of the landlord is the normal precondition to the transfer.

It is possible for a tenant to assign only *part of the premises*. The tenant can assign the second floor to an assignee, for example, retaining the first floor. This transfer would be treated as an assignment, as long as the tenant gave the entire interest in the second floor to the assignee.

The distinction between assignment and sublease is not always simple. If the tenant transfers all that he or she has but retains the right to reenter the property in the case of nonpayment of the rent, the majority of courts hold that an assignment still exists. Several states, however, disagree. Courts in these states contend that the reservation of a right of reentry constitutes a reversion in the tenant/assignor, thereby making the transaction a sublease.

To create the proper interpretive environment, it should be noted that courts do not favor restrictions on a party's right to transfer real property. The landlord must be careful in drafting the limitation in the lease on the tenant's right to sublease or assign, or a court may undermine it. The courts' attitude is framed by their general objection to any restraint on the freedom to alienate or transfer property. This attitude has resulted in decisions that a landlord's prohibition against subleasing did not prohibit the tenant from assigning. Similarly, once the landlord consents to an assignment despite a prohibition in the lease, the leasehold is freely assignable thereafter. Even so, a single waiver of the limitation on subleasing does not allow the tenant to sublease later without the landlord's approval.

Impact of an Assignment. At the beginning of the preceding chapter, some care was taken to describe a lease as a conveyance of an estate in land as well as a contractual obligation. In the area of assignment, the dichotomy is important. On taking a transfer by lease, the tenant enters into a dual relationship. Under the estate-in-land aspect of the agreement, the landlord and the tenant are said to have *privity of estate*. Under the contractual side of the agreement, the parties have created *privity of contract*. As explained earlier, *privity* connotes the mutuality that binds parties to their agreement.

A tenant who assigns the lease to a third person surrenders possession and transfers the *privity of estate* to the assignee. The assignee literally stands in the legal shoes of the tenant, because he or she received all that the tenant has, and privity of estate now exists between the landlord and the assignee. The assignee's right to possession makes him or her liable directly to the landlord for payment of rent. Possession automatically gives rise to the obligation to pay rent.

By way of contrast, there is no *privity of contract* between the landlord and the assignee. There is no contract, or mutual agreement to be bound, created by the assignment. An outgrowth of this is that the tenant/assignor continues to be bound by the terms of the lease contract to the landlord.

As the result of privity of estate existing between the landlord and the assignee, the landlord can sue the assignee for nonpayment of rent. If, when the assignment takes place, the assignee agrees to assume the obligations of the lease and to be bound to the lessor for rent, he or she will have privity of contract with the lessor as well as the privity of estate previously discussed.

Sale of the Leased Premises

The landlord is free to convey the leased premises at any time. The buyer takes *subject to* the leasehold interest of the tenant. The buyer has the right to collect all subsequent rents once the tenant has been notified of the sale.

The buyer is the successor in title to the lessor's land; the tenant has an obligation, arising out of the notion of a conveyance of real property, to pay the rent to the new owner. It would not, therefore, be *necessary* to have an assignment of the lease, or the lessor's contract rights to the buyer, in order to collect the rent. However, unless the lease or contract provides otherwise, the lessor would continue to be liable for covenants he or she made to the lessee in the lease.

Tort Liability

■ *In general, the person who has possession and control of the premises owes a civil duty to third parties to maintain the premises in a reasonably safe condition.*

The leased premises are normally in the possession and under the control of the tenant, and the tenant must use reasonable care in maintaining those premises in a safe condition. Failure to do so is a civil wrong, or *tort*. As a consequence of this rule and the rule that does not require the landlord to repair or make the property habitable, generally the landlord owes no duty to the tenant or to third parties when they are injured as the result of a defective condition of the premises. However, the general rule is under siege where jurisdictions have adopted a warranty of habitability. It should be kept in mind, however, that technically, warranty is a contract theory, and the extent of damages recoverable in case of a breach may be limited to contract damages (the cost of repair, not personal injury).

Even without the modern trend to apply a warranty of habitability, there are exceptions to the rule holding that the landlord owes no duty in tort. When the landlord retains control over portions of the premises, such as stairways and halls, he or she will owe a duty to use reasonable care to maintain safe conditions. This is consistent with the general rule because the landlord retains control of these areas.

In addition, where the landlord is aware of latent defects on the premises and fails to notify the unknowing tenant, he or she will owe a duty to the tenant and other third parties. Also, where the lease is for a furnished apartment and the tenant has no opportunity to inspect, the landlord will be liable in tort. Likewise, the landlord will be liable where he or she carelessly performs repairs.

Young v. Garwacki
Supreme Judicial Court of Massachusetts
402 N.E.2d 1045 (1980)

Background. Garwacki and Mastello leased a second-story apartment from LaFreniere as tenants at will. In 1977, Mastello invited a friend, Young, to dinner. Young was helping in the meal preparation. When Mastello left the apartment to pick up another dinner guest, Young went onto the second story porch to yell down to him to bring back certain groceries. As she leaned on the porch railing with her hands, it gave way and she fell to the ground below. Young was injured.

The landlord was aware that the railing was dangerous. He had informed the tenants in 1976 that the railing was faulty, and he had purchased materials to fix it but had not performed the repairs. Young sued the landlord and tenants to recover damages for her personal injuries suffered in the fall. She argued that the railing was negligently maintained. At the trial court, a judgment was entered against the tenants, but not the landlord. Young appealed the decision as to the landlord.

Decision. The Supreme Judicial Court of Massachusetts reversed the lower court finding for the plaintiff against the landlord.

Justice Liacos. In the absence of the landlord's express agreement to keep the rented premises in repair, is he liable to his tenant's guest for injuries resulting from his negligent failure to maintain the safety of the premises? Common law rules defining a landowner's liability in negligence to people coming onto the land reflected the needs of an agrarian society. The landowner was a petty sovereign within his boundaries. The character of his duty to an injured party varied with the party's relationship with the sovereign. Thus, the common law distinguished several classes of tort plaintiffs; among them, trespassers, licensees, invitees, and tenants.

The traditional approach to tenants turned on the concept of a lease as a conveyance of property.

The tenant "bought" the leasehold at his peril, so he could not expect the landlord to have repaired preexisting defects, and at the time of the letting, the landlord ceded to the tenant his dominion over the rented premises. Under this ancient view, the axiom was "there is no law against letting a tumbledown house." The landlord might have been liable for negligent maintenance of common areas, but was not generally liable for the negligent maintenance of the premises themselves.

The landlord "was under a separate and limited duty toward each tenant and that tenant's visitors to exercise reasonable care to maintain the common areas in a condition not less safe than they were, or appeared to be in, at the time of the letting to the particular tenant." As to the demised premises, *caveat emptor* reigned. The tenant took the premises as he found them. "The general rule is that the landlord is not liable to the tenant for defects in the premises existing at the time of the letting unless they are hidden defects of which he is aware and does not warn the tenant."

The ordinary agreement for consideration by which a landlord is to make repairs is construed as an agreement to repair on notice. Failure to repair under such an agreement gives rise only to a contract action for the cost of the repair. Tort liability will exist, however, for negligently made repairs. In the absence of such a specific agreement to repair, no agreement will be implied from the mere letting of the premises, and any repairs made will be treated as gratuitous.

After seven years of reconsideration and reform, little remains of this obsolete machinery of the common law. "Recent decisions of this court clearly reflect . . . a shift in philosophy with regard to status distinctions in tort standards of care. We did away with the legal significance in tort of categories of licensee and invitee and held that a landowner owes a duty of reasonable care to all lawful visitors.

We said: 'The problem of allocating the costs and risks of human injury is far too complex to be decided solely by the status of the entrant, especially where the status question often prevents the jury from ever determining the fundamental question whether the defendant has acted reasonably in light of all the circumstances in the particular case.'"

In the landlord-tenant field, we have held that a landlord is liable to a tenant's guest for failing to exercise due care in maintaining common passageways under the landlord's control without regard to their condition at the time of the letting. We extended the landlord's general and continuing duty to exercise reasonable care as to the safety of common passageways to include tenants as well as their visitors.

We have also attacked the theory on which the tenant's status classification depends. In the line of cases creating and applying the implied warranty of habitability, we have overthrown the doctrine of caveat emptor and the notion that a lease is a conveyance of property. Moreover, we have invoked the doctrine of warranty to afford a tenant compensation not only for economic loss, but for personal injury. Thus, at least to the extent required by the relevant housing and building codes, a landlord may be liable to his tenant for failing to maintain areas not under the landlord's control.

Today, we do away with the ancient law that bars a tenant's guest from recovering compensation from a landlord for injuries caused by negligent maintenance of areas rented to the tenant. Like the other rules based on status, this rule has prevented a whole class of people from raising the overriding issue: whether the landlord acted reasonably under the circumstances. The practical result of this archaic rule has been to discourage repairs of rented premises. In cases like the one before us, a landlord with knowledge of a defect has less incentive to repair it. And the tenant, who often has a short-term lease, limited funds, and limited experience dealing with such defects, will not be inclined to pay for expensive work on a place he will soon be leaving. Thus, the defect may go unrepaired until an unsuspecting plaintiff finds herself with a lawsuit that care could have prevented.

Henceforth, landlords as other persons must exercise reasonable care not to subject others to an unreasonable risk of harm. A landlord must act as a reasonable person under all of the circumstances including the likelihood of injury to others, the probable seriousness of such injuries, and the burden of reducing or avoiding the risk. We think this basic principle of responsibility for landlords as for others "best expresses the principles of justice and reasonableness on which our law of torts is founded."

The former rule was not without its reasons. When a landlord rents an apartment to a tenant, he gives up his right to enter. Matters of control, like matters of status, can be components of familiar negligence analysis; they can affect such questions as reasonableness and foreseeability. So, too, may matters of intervening negligence by the tenant or others be so treated. In particular, a landlord should not be liable in negligence unless he knew or reasonably should have known of the defect and had a reasonable opportunity to repair it.

If a landlord fails to correct the condition within a reasonable time, the tenant or any person rightfully on the premises has a tort action against the landlord for injuries sustained.

Reversed.

Specifically, how soon after the discovery of the faulty railing must the landlord repair it?

Suppose the tenant's conduct had worsened the condition of the railing?

Contrast the *Young* case with the *Camerlin* case that follows.

Camerlin v. Marshall
Supreme Judicial Court of Massachusetts
582 N.E. 2d 539 (1991)

Background. Since May 1981, Johnson Rents, Inc. (Johnson), has leased from the defendant the first floor and one-half of the second floor of a building. In August 1982, the plaintiff, a regional director for Johnson, a medical safety firm, tripped and fell on entering the building. The evidence indicated that the plaintiff either tripped on a tear in the rug or a hole in the tarvia in front of the door. Evidence also showed that there was a tear in the rug and a pot-hole in the tarvia in the parking lot outside the door. The plaintiff had complained several times about the carpeting, and the landlord was aware of the tear in the rug and the hole in the tarvia. Johnson had agreed to provide liability insurance in the lease, to maintain the premises, plow the parking lot, and pay for minor repairs. The plaintiff sued the landlord for damages caused by defendant's negligence. The jury found that the area where plaintiff fell was not under the defendant's control, and that the defendant exercised due care.

Decision. The Supreme Court affirmed the jury's decision in favor of the landlord-defendant.

Justice Lynch. In *Young v. Garwacki*, we ruled that a residential landlord is liable for a defect of which he had notice and had a reasonable opportunity to repair, even though the defect existed on the rented premises. The plaintiff argues that this rule should be extended to this situation and that the judge's failure to do so is reversible error.

In *Young* we specifically reserved the question of its application to leased commercial property. We perceive no circumstances here that warrant an extension of the *Young* rule. Johnson is a national company, headquartered in Pennsylvania, that leased other property in Massachusetts. As a tenant not unsophisticated in such matters, Johnson assumed responsibility for maintaining the premises, plowing the parking lot, and making or paying for minor repairs. In sum, this case does not involve the kind of inexperienced, financially-constrained, short-term tenancy to which the *Young* ruling was addressed. Accordingly, the trial judge properly refused to instruct in accordance with *Young*.

Affirmed.

Under what circumstances might a commercial landlord be held liable for this type of injury?

Measure of Damages

■ *Because the duty of the landlord to perform repairs grows out of the contractual understanding (the lease) or from a law-imposed contractual theory of warranty of habitability, the measure of damages owed is the cost of the repair; however, there is a trend to permit recovery for personal injury and property damages as well.*

To hold that the injured tenant or third party can recover only for the cost of repairing the premises seems a bit conservative in this day and age. Nevertheless, the conclusion is consistent with the contract principle of permitting recovery to the extent of mending the breach but not for the ensuing personal injury. Much of the area of land-lord-tenant law is in flux, and this measure of damages is no exception.

Some courts speak of warranty as being a *tort remedy* as well as a *contract action*. Other courts reject the utility of the concept of privity (one must be a party to a contract to allow recovery against the landlord) in a modern world of broader expectations. It is no surprise then that there is a distinct trend toward permitting the recovery of tort damages when the landlord fails to repair the premises. Under tort damages, the tenant or third party can recover for the personal injury and property damage resulting from the landlord's wrongful conduct, along with the cost of repairing the premises. This trend is consistent with the broader movement toward protection of the tenant, especially residential tenants.

Exculpatory Clauses

A lease clause by which the landlord attempts to excuse himself or herself from liability for negligence in maintaining the leasehold premises.

Under the premise that the parties can reach any agreement they choose, landlords often include an *exculpatory clause* relieving themselves of liability for their negligence. At the present time, there is a sharp split among the courts as to the enforceability of these clauses. Some courts permit the enforcement of the clause because of the notion that the parties have the right to contract freely. The incongruity in this conclusion is the erroneous assumption that the usual leasehold agreement involves equality of bargaining position. At least in residential leasing, the tenant seldom has the freedom to negotiate the terms of the lease.

Conversely, other courts have held that the position of the landlord in exculpating himself or herself from liability for negligence in a typically unbargained-for lease defies sound public policy. Sanctioning these clauses would also lead to the demise of the warranty of habitability, because all form leases would incorporate a waiver clause. The trend in the courts is to prohibit the landlord from exculpating himself or herself from responsibility.

Everyone wants to reduce the amount of energy consumed by our activities because it costs money and usually uses up nonrenewable natural resources. As mentioned in an earlier chapter, there are large indirect costs caused by having to protect U.S. interests in foreign oil lands. The United States currently imports 60 percent of the 20 million barrels of oil it uses every day. In buildings, oil is used for heating and air-conditioning; to generate electricity to power computers, machinery, and lighting; and for many other activities.

Unfortunately, in the landlord-tenant situation, whether commercial or residential real estate, we have a dilemma when our goal is to conserve energy. If achieving savings requires additional investment capital, why would an owner/landlord include energy-saving measures in a building? The capital costs are borne by the landlord, but the energy savings usually accrue to the tenant who pays the utility bills. Theoretically, the landlord can set a higher rent than less energy-efficient competitors can because the

tenant will save money every month on utility bills. There is some risk for the landlord, however, because the higher rental fee may overshadow potential savings that may accrue somewhere down the line. The tenant may choose the less energy-efficient, otherwise comparable building because the lower rent is a higher profile consideration for the tenant.

What can be done to make both landlord and tenant realize that saving energy is to their mutual economic and social interest? Should we give buildings efficiency labels like we give appliances? Perhaps we require that landlords provide prospective tenants with copies of past energy bills. Can we encourage real estate brokers to develop an expertise so that they can offer their services to minimize "occupancy costs"? What would you suggest as a solution? Remember, there is a lot at stake; for example, a lower federal budget (military costs), reduction in the cost of doing business, and a lower monthly cost of living for all of us

■ KEY TERMS

■ INTERNET RESOURCES

http://library.lp.findlaw.com
(Under "Library Search" type "security deposit concerns," then click on the article titled "Security Deposit Concerns for the Thoughtful Tenant

http://library.lp.findlaw.com/scripts/
(type "landlord tenant" in search box, landlord-tenant relationship discussed in several articles)

www.legalmatch.com/law-library/article/implied-warrant-of-habitability.html
(elaborates on implied warranty of habitability)

■ REVIEW AND DISCUSSION QUESTIONS

1. List and briefly describe four remedies aimed at protecting landlords from tenants who mistreat leased premises.

2. The covenant of quiet enjoyment is breached on actual eviction or constructive eviction by the landlord. Define the terms *actual eviction* and *constructive eviction*.

3. (a) What is the *warranty of habitability*? (b) What environmental change has caused this warranty to come into vogue?

4. List and briefly describe three tenant's obligations arising either from his or her lease contract or by law.

5. When a lease agreement is not fulfilled by either of the parties, the injured party can seek several remedies. List the remedies that can be sought by (a) the landlord and (b) the tenant. Explain the situations that would prescribe the use of these various legal remedies.

6. Discuss the reasons why restricting an injured third person to contract damages may be impractical.

7. "The parties should be left to the bargain they made." Discuss the appropriateness of this position in lease situations.

8. As they relate to the area of assignment of leases, define *privity of estate* and *privity of contract*.

■ CASE PROBLEMS

1. Keown leased a house from Housh. During the term of the lease, Swanson, Keown's girlfriend, moved in with the tenant. The house had a second-story deck on which Keown and Swanson sunned themselves. The deck had no railing and had a tangle of television antenna wire connected to an unused antenna on the roof above. One night Keown and Swanson heard a noise and went to the deck to check for possible burglars. Swanson became tangled in the antenna wire and fell to the ground below. She sued Housh for injuries, claiming that he was responsible for the "latent defect" created by the antenna wire. The house was rented unfurnished. Will Swanson recover? *Housh v. Swanson*, 203 Ill. App. 3d 377, 561 N.E. 2d 321 (1990).

2. Stefanik fails to vacate premises at the end of a term lease, holding over into a subsequent month. The owner has leased the property to Nunez. In the majority of American jurisdictions, would the owner or Nunez be obligated to remove Stefanik? Discuss.

3. Lubin owns an apartment in a college town. Many units in the building are rented to college students. Lubin retains keys to these apartments. From time to time she visits the tenants. Although she always phones first, if the tenants are not available she will use her duplicate key to enter. The main purpose of Lubin's visit is to ensure that the utilities, appliances, and plumbing are functioning properly. If she does not interfere with the tenants' occupancy, is Lubin's conduct legally proper? Discuss.

4. Addison leased a unit in an apartment building from Seikely. He tripped over a loose board on an exterior stairway and was injured. He sued Seikely, claiming negligent maintenance of the common stairway. Seikely offers as a defense that a clause in the lease excuses him from liability for any injury incurred on the premises. Discuss the validity of Seikely's defense.

5. Gokey rented a mobile home (part of the realty) to the Bessettes at a monthly rent of $400. During the tenancy, the Bessettes complained of numerous problems, including a leak in the roof, a broken furnace, and a break in the sewer line. The Bessettes complained to code enforcement officials about the sewer line because noxious liquids lay under the trailer for up to four months, causing foul odors to fill their home. Should the Bessettes move out? Should they stop paying rent? Explain. *Gokey v. Bessette*, 580 A.2d 488 (1990).

Easements and Other Nonpossessory Rights

■ EASEMENT

■ *A nonpossessory interest in real property; the right to use another's real estate for a limited purpose.*

Most of the ownership interests considered in prior chapters provide the holder with a current or future right of possession. In these forms of ownership, the owner enjoys now or in the future the right to proceeds from the property and/or the right to occupy it to the exclusion of all others.

Some people have interests in real estate that are limited to use, not possession. These are referred to as *nonpossessory rights*. One important nonpossessory right is the easement. **Easements** are used extensively in real estate. For example, they are essential to the operation of utilities. They also provide a legal basis for condominium ownership, scenic and open-space protection, and preservation of historic buildings. Indeed, few land developments would be successful without the extensive use of easements. Although easements are interests in real estate, the person who has an easement is never entitled to possession of the land itself—only its use.

The holder of an easement has a right to use another's land or buildings for a specified purpose. That purpose might be as simple as crossing the land to reach a beach or as complicated as using a portion of a neighbor's building to support one's own.

The person who owns an easement has neither title nor estate in the land burdened by it. The easement holder's limited interest is, however, protected against interference by third parties, and the easement cannot be terminated at the will of the owner of the land that it burdens.

Frequently, easements authorize a person to perform a particular act. An example would be a right to use a neighbor's driveway to reach the back portion of a lot. These authorizing easements are called *affirmative easements*. Others, called *negative easements*, prohibit the owner of the land from doing something that an owner ordinarily would be entitled to do. Easements of this nature are not as common. A negative easement might prohibit a landowner from constructing a building taller than a designated height in order to provide adjoining land with an unobstructed view; owners of lots in a development might be restricted from painting their houses a particular color or erecting a structure that would block solar usage.

Easements are also classified as *appurtenant* or *in gross*. Each will be discussed.

Easement Appurtenant

■ *The right of an owner of a parcel of land to benefit from the use of another's land.*

> **CASE EXAMPLE**
> Stump and Levit own adjoining parcels of land at Lake Feather. Stump's property borders the lakefront; Levit's does not. Stump has granted to Levit an easement, by deed delivered and accepted, across his lakefront property to the beach. Stump has created an *easement appurtenant.*

An **easement appurtenant** involves two parcels of land, usually, but not necessarily, adjoining. The easement allows the possessor of one parcel to benefit by using the other parcel of land. The parcel that benefits is referred to as the **dominant estate** or *dominant tenement.* The owner of such easement is called the *dominant tenant.* The property that is subject to the easement is known as the **servient estate**. Stump's property in the example above is the servient estate while Levit's is the dominant estate. (See Figure 9.1.) An easement appurtenant cannot exist without a dominant estate.

When an easement is appurtenant, any conveyance of the dominant estate automatically includes the easement, even if the easement is not specified in the deed. The easement is said to *run with the land.* When Levit sells her Lake Feather property to Bach, for example, Bach automatically acquires the right to cross Stump's property to get to the beach.

While the easement is automatically transferred with the dominant estate, it cannot be separated and conveyed independently. In the above examples, Levit cannot simply sell or convey to some neighboring landowner the right to cross Stump's property.

| **FIGURE 9.1** | Easement Appurtenant |

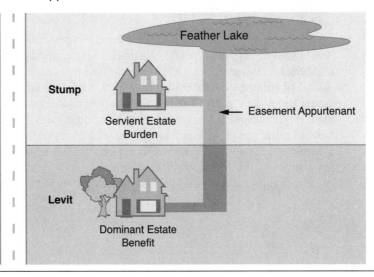

Sometimes the dominant tenement is divided into two or more parcels. In such cases, provided that there are not an unreasonable number of new parcels, the courts have held that the existing easement runs with all of the newly created parcels. For example, if, instead of conveying her entire Lake Feather property, Levit had divided the parcel into two lots and sold one of them to Bach, both Bach's land and Levit's land would have the same easement appurtenant across Stump's property. Suppose, however, that Levit had substantially increased the burden on the servient estate by dividing the parcel into six or seven lots. In that case Stump should be able to obtain a court order preventing the increased use. In some states, courts have even held that substantially increased use terminates an easement.

In addition to running with the land, an easement appurtenant is irrevocable. It cannot be canceled by the servient owner or terminated by a conveyance of the servient tenement. When the servient tenement is sold or otherwise conveyed, the property remains subject to the existing easement. Questions arise, however, as to whether an easement may be unilaterally moved by the property owner. The next case resolves that question.

Lewis v. Young
New York Court of Appeals
705 N.E.2d 649 (N.Y. 1998)

Background. Roger Lewis and Neda Young own adjoining parcels of land in the town of Southampton. Both parcels were formerly owned by the Browns, who divided their land into several parcels and retained the largest tract (four acres). The other two adjacent tracts were sold and one of those was ultimately vested in Roger Lewis. The Lewis deed granted an easement across the Browns' main driveway. It read:

> The perpetual use, in common with others, of the [Browns'] main driveway running in a generally southwesterly direction between South Ferry Road and the [Browns'] residence premises.

Neda Young and her husband purchased the Browns' four-acre tract. The Youngs desired to improve their property by demolishing the small cottage on the property and erecting a new residence with an in-ground pool and tennis court. This required relocation of the existing driveway that was the subject of the easement. The location of the easement had been fixed for 37 years, and Roger Lewis, the owner of the adjacent tract, objected to the change.

But the Youngs went ahead with their plans anyway.

Plaintiff Roger Lewis sued, seeking a declaration of the parties' rights and a permanent injunction compelling the defendant to remove the tennis court and return the driveway to its original location. The trial court found in favor of the plaintiff and ordered that the defendant, Neda Young, restore the driveway or allow plaintiff to do so at defendant's expense. The Appellate Division affirmed.

Decision. The Court of Appeals reversed the Appellate Division.

Chief Judge Kaye. This battle between Southampton neighbors centers on an open question in New York law: can a landowner, without consent, relocate an easement holder's right of way over the burdened premises? We conclude that, under the particular circumstances presented, the landowner can move the right of way, so long as the easement holder's right of access and ingress is not impaired.

* * *

continued on next page

[E]xpress easements are defined by the intent, or object, of the parties.

As a rule, where the intention in granting an easement is to afford only a right of ingress and egress, it is the right of passage, and not any right in a physical passageway itself, that is granted to the easement holder. . . . As this Court observed more than a century ago,

> A right of way along a private road belonging to another person does not give the [easement holder] a right that the road shall be in no respect altered or the width decreased, for his right . . . is merely a right to pass with the convenience to which he has been accustomed.

Thus, in the absence of a demonstrated intent to provide otherwise, a landowner burdened by an express easement of ingress and egress may narrow it, cover it over, gate it or fence it off, so long as the easement holder's right of passage is not impaired . . . . As a matter of policy, affording the landowner the unilateral, but limited, authority to alter a right of way strikes a balance between the landowner's right to use and enjoy the property and the easement holder's right of ingress and egress.

While enjoying a limited right to narrow, cover, gate, and fence off such easements, can a landowner similarly relocate a right of way without the easement holder's consent? Other jurisdictions have broadly required consent to the relocation of easements. . . .

[O]ur prior relocation cases have not concerned rights of way. Rather, the easement holder in those cases was given the right to build a structure—a dock in one instance, a pipeline in the other—on the landowner's property. Unlike the right of way now at issue, those easements could not be enjoyed unless and until their locations were fixed on the landowner's property. . . . By contrast, enjoyment of an undefined right of ingress and egress over the land of another does not require any fixed occupancy of the landowner's premises.

The second category of cases to reach this Court involved relocation attempts by the easement

holder, not—as in the present case—by the landowner. That, too, is a significant distinction.

* * *

Recognition of a relocation right in landowners raises its own policy concerns: that landowners (whose purchase price reflected the existence of the easement) will receive a windfall, that easement holders may be rendered vulnerable to harassment by the landowner and that the settled expectations of the easement holder will be disrupted. . . . We conclude, however, that these concerns are adequately addressed by the limitation that a landowner may not unilaterally change a right of way if that change impairs enjoyment of the easement holder's rights.

Thus, based on our precedents and their underlying policy considerations, we conclude that—as in the easement alteration cases—a balancing test is also appropriate as to relocation of an undefined right of way. In the absence of a demonstrated intent to provide otherwise, a landowner, consonant with the beneficial use and development of its property, can move that right of way, so long as the landowner bears the expense of the relocation, and so long as the change does not frustrate the parties' intent or object in creating the right of way, does not increase the burden on the easement holder, and does not significantly lessen the utility of the right of way.

* * *

The search for the parties' intent begins with the words they used in creating the easement. Here, the deed conveyed . . . a right to "the perpetual use, in common with others, of [Mr. Brown's] main driveway, running in a generally southwesterly direction between South Ferry Road and [Mr. Brown's] residence premises." . . .

The deed, however, does not reflect an intent to deny Mr. Brown the right ever to relocate the "main driveway" to his house in order to accommodate the grantees' right of ingress and egress to their adjoining premises. Indeed, the indefinite description of the right of way suggests the opposite—namely that the parties intended to allow for relocation by the landowner. Notably, the parties themselves in the same deed described two additional easements by explicit reference to metes and bounds. Had they intended the right of way to be forever fixed in its location, presumably they would have delineated it in similar fashion. . . .

Reversed and Remanded.

Alter the facts so that the property owner would not be permitted to change the site of the easement.

The owner of a dominant estate has the sole duty to maintain the easement (unless there is a written agreement to the contrary), and may make reasonable improvements to the easement as long as it does not unreasonably burden the servient estate. However, no use can be made of the easement that is different from that established at the time of its creation and that imposes an additional burden on the servient estate.

CASE EXAMPLE

Hayes owns property that provides an easement for access to marina property owned by Aquia Marina, Inc. The easement is 1,120 feet long and 15 feet wide. The marina is approved for expansion from 84 boat slips to 280. Hayes maintains that this expansion would unreasonably burden the easement. The Marina desires to pave the easement. Hayes objects. The trial court found that the proposed expansion of the marina was a reasonable use of the dominant estate and that the increase in traffic over the easement would not change the type of use and would not overburden the easement. It also held that paving the easement was proper maintenance. The Supreme Court of Virginia affirmed the trial court. *Hayes v. Aquia Marina, Inc.*, 243 Va. 255 (1992).

Party Wall

■ *A single wall located on the boundary of neighboring properties; it simultaneously serves as a common support for buildings on each of the two parcels.*

In many metropolitan areas, adjacent buildings often share a single wall to save space and expense. Walls of this type are referred to as *party walls*. Generally, a party wall is constructed on the boundary line between two parcels of real estate, with half of the wall on one side of the line and half on the other. In the United States, the courts uniformly have held that each landowner owns that portion of the wall on his or her land and holds an easement appurtenant for support in the other half. If the party wall is entirely on the property of one landowner, the wall belongs to that owner; the other landowner normally has an easement in the wall.

Party walls are commonly constructed as the result of agreement, with each party contributing half of the cost. Because party walls have created many legal problems, these agreements must be drawn carefully. Related problems often involve use of the wall for advertising or purposes other than support.

CASE EXAMPLE

Berk and Ershowsky owned adjoining buildings supported by a party wall. The building on Ershowsky's property was much taller than the building on Berk's, and Ershowsky painted a large advertising sign on that portion of the wall above the top of Berk's building. Berk sued to enjoin use of the wall for that purpose. The injunction was granted, and damages were awarded. The court stated that defendant's use of the wall was improper because it prevented plaintiff from using it for a similar purpose. *Berk-Fink Realty Co. v. Ershowsky*, 116 N.Y.S.2d 529 (1952).

Contributions for repairs to party walls can generally be compelled even if the agreement does not cover that issue. The cost of improvements, however, must be borne by the owner who authorizes them. Neither owner may ordinarily remove the wall, but each may remove the remainder of the building without liability if reasonable care is taken.

Easement in Gross

◼   *An easement that exists as a personal right apart from a dominant estate.*

An **easement in gross** is not tied to another parcel of land, as is the easement appurtenant. Thus, an easement in gross exists without a dominant estate. (See Figure 9.2.) Although a servient estate does exist, the privileges given by the easement belong to a person, which may be an artificial "person" such as a corporation. Stump, for example, might give the telephone company an easement to bury its line along the road bordering his Lake Feather property. This would be an example of an easement in gross.

Easements in gross granted to an individual for a *noncommercial purpose* are considered a personal right or privilege. Only the person to whom the easement is given may use it. The easement cannot be sold, assigned, or otherwise transferred, and it ter-

---

FIGURE 9.2   Examples of Easements in Gross

Utility   Billboards   People Picking Fruit

Telecommunications   People Taking Shortcuts

minates on the death of its holder. For this reason, if the parties wish to have the easement continue or to have any value, they must tie it to a dominant estate. If this is done, it would be appurtenant and would run with the land.

Traditionally, the courts have treated easements in gross granted for commercial purposes differently. Because of their importance to the public, they are considered freely transferable. For example, a utility easement may be sold or assigned by one utility company to another. Although transferable, an easement given for a specific purpose, such as a sewer, cannot be used for another purpose, such as an electric line. However, an easement in cable used for telephone transmission may ordinarily be assigned to a cable company for use in television transmission. Here, the character of the easement has not substantially changed.

Inasmuch as the easement in gross is not intended to benefit a parcel of land, it is considered a personal right in another's property, although assignable when deemed a commercial easement.

■ CREATION OF EASEMENTS

An easement is generally created in one of three ways: by expression or contract, by implication, or by prescription. (See Table 9.1.)

Creation of an Easement by Expression

The most common method of creating an easement by expression is by deed. Among other things, a deed describes the land and, in the case of an easement, describes the location of the easement. (Deeds are discussed in Chapter 16.) Most courts are reluctant to accept the idea that an easement may be created orally. The reason is that an easement is an interest in real estate, and statutes in all states require that an interest in real estate may be created only by a written instrument.

TABLE 9.1 | Methods of Creating Easements

Easement by	Created by
Expression	Express Grant
	Express Reservation
Implication	From Prior Use
	From Necessity
	From Plats and Maps
	From Dedication
Prescription	Adverse Use

CASE EXAMPLE

Paul Brangs owned a lot at Lake Feather next to his home. Paul wished to sell the lot but was having difficulty because it was narrow. Paul's driveway bordered the lot. To induce Nan Crampton, a prospective purchaser, to buy, Paul agreed to grant her an easement over his driveway to reach the back portion of the property. At the closing, Paul delivered a deed passing title to the lot and a separate deed conveying an easement over his driveway to Crampton.

The granting of an easement may be an independent transaction. Utility companies often seek easements when they need to run their lines over another's property. In many states, the law gives these companies the right of eminent domain if the landowner refuses to grant the requested easement. Gas pipelines, sewers, and roads are based on easements from property owners.

Deeds creating easements may do so by **express grant** or **express reservation**.

■ **Express Grant.** *An easement created by an owner expressly granting in a deed or other instrument a specific right to another to use the property.*

CASE EXAMPLE

Morgan owns two adjoining lots at Lake Feather. She sells one to Betterman. Morgan's lot includes a private alley, and Morgan's deed to Betterman *expressly grants* by deed to Betterman the use of this alley.

An easement may also be created by a contract between the parties. This is not a preferred method, but if the courts will enforce by specific performance or injunction an agreement in which one party promises to allow another to use land for a limited purpose, an easement has been created. A few courts have even enforced oral contracts that create a limited interest in land. Usually, these involve something like a common driveway or access road.

■ **Express Reservation**. *An easement created when an owner of property conveys title to another by deed while specifically reserving an easement in his or her favor.*

CASE EXAMPLE

Morgan sells Betterman the lot with the alley and keeps the other lot for herself. Morgan's deed includes a clause that *expressly reserves* her right to use the alley.

Provisions expressly reserving an easement are usually found in a deed or sometimes are contactual; also some easements are created by will or trust, but such easements may also be included in a mortgage or lease.

Creation of an Easement by Implication

Courts sometimes presume that the parties intend to create an easement because certain facts exist when real estate is conveyed. The easement supposedly reflects the intention of the parties and is called an **easement by implication**. Support for the creation of easements by implication is found in the idea that a sale of real estate includes that which is necessary to use the property beneficially. Implied easements may be created by prior use, necessity, plats and maps, and by dedication.

Prior Use. When a property owner visibly and continuously has used one part of land for the benefit of another, and this use is reasonably necessary for the fair enjoyment of the other, an easement is actually created when either part is sold separately. This is true even when neither party expressly makes any commitment creating the easement.

> **CASE EXAMPLE**
>
> Hector Rodriquez and his wife, Sylvia, partitioned Blueacre, a ten acre lot they had owned for 20 years, into two five-acre tracts. They sold the front five acres to the Hardings and the back five acres to the Howards. Their residential house was situated on the back five acres. The easterly one emptied onto State Route 62, while the westerly exit emptied onto a gravel back road that took 30 minutes to get to Route 62. The Howards have an easement implied from prior use across the Hardings' front acreage, because there was consistent prior use, and it is reasonably necessary for the enjoyment of the Howards' back acreage.

■ **Necessity.** *An easement permitting the owner of a landlocked parcel to cross a portion of land of which the easement formerly was a part.*

Most courts consider the easement by necessity a form of implied easement. The reasonable assumption is that the parties intended that the grantee of a landlocked parcel have a means of access to the land. Without a right to cross the lands of the grantor, the grantee would derive no benefit from the conveyed property. A few courts have taken the position that presumed intent is not necessary. These courts feel that sound public policy dictates that no land should be inaccessible.

> **CASE EXAMPLE**
>
> O'Mally purchased from Flynn a lot that was part of a larger parcel that abutted Lake Feather. O'Mally did not think to get an easement to reach the lake across Flynn's remaining land. As a result, he had to drive more than five miles to use Lake Feather. If he sued to establish an easement by necessity, a court probably would reject his suit on the grounds that no absolute necessity existed.

Plats and Maps. Courts sometimes recognize an implied easement that arises when a document such as a deed refers to a plat or map with designated streets or areas.

> **CASE EXAMPLE**
>
> Keene purchased several acres on the north side of Lake Feather. He subdivided the property and had prepared a map designating streets, parks, and a beach area. Several of the lots were sold and described by reference to the map. Controversy arose between Keene and a number of the lot owners. Keene, as a result, attempted to restrict their use of the beach.

Courts in most states would rule that the lot owners had acquired easements, even if no easements were mentioned in their deeds. When a person buys property described by lot number on a particular map, that person acquires the right to use all common areas designated on the map. A similar rule applies when a deed describes a tract as bounded by a particular street. The purchaser acquires an easement in the street. A majority of states extend the purchaser's interest to include easements in all streets reasonably necessary for access and reasonably beneficial to the lot owner. A few states limit the easement to abutting streets.

■ **Dedication.** *The granting of real property such as a private street to a government unit for public use.*

Litigation involving public easements in streets and other parcels of land is often complicated. Almost all states have laws dealing with dedication of land designated on plats and maps for public use. When a plat is recorded, land indicated as set aside for public use becomes public property. In many states the local government automatically acquires an easement in the land. In other states the government acquires title to the designated areas.

A completed dedication solves numerous problems for landowners because the street or area becomes public and open to all users. Usage issues arise when the property is abandoned by the state. Does it revert back to the former owner, or do those whose interests may be injured now have implied private easements in the designated parcel? A majority of courts take the position that interest-holders for whom the easement was created continue to have a right to use the street.

Creation of an Easement by Prescription

Prescription is the term used to describe the acquisition of an intangible property right such as an easement through wrongful use of another's land for a period of time. The period of time is usually specified by statute and differs markedly from state to state. Although a 20-year period exists in some states, in numerous other states prescriptive rights can be obtained in ten or fewer years. Several states apply a 15-year period. Basic to the creation of the **easement by prescription** is the idea that an owner who does not take some legal action against wrongful use of his or her property within a certain period of time is *estopped*, or legally prohibited, from asserting whatever rights he or she had. *Adverse possession*, a similar doctrine that allows actual acquisition of the real estate and all ownership rights, is discussed in Chapter 18.

At one time, the easement by prescription was justified on the presumption of a lost written document. Modern courts reject this presumption, but they continue to approve the prescriptive easement. Most courts apparently feel that land use will be stabilized and controversy reduced if the easement by prescription is recognized.

In addition to use for the designated period, two additional requirements must be met before a prescriptive easement is recognized. The use must be *adverse* to the owner's interest as well as *continuous* and *uninterrupted*. Over the years, both of these requirements have been the source of substantial litigation.

A use that is adverse to the owner's interest must be *open* and *notorious*. It must be obvious enough that an owner reasonably concerned with protecting his or her property rights could readily discover it. A use is not adverse if the user has the owner's permission; no matter how long it continues, it will not ripen into an easement. If, however, the owner who has given permission revokes it, later use becomes adverse. Likewise, if the use made of the land differs from the permitted use, the use becomes adverse.

A difference of opinion exists as to the extent to which the use must be hostile to be considered adverse. In this case *hostile* refers not to ill will but to the wrongdoer actually claiming the right to use another's property. Many courts take the position that whenever an easement has been used for the prescribed period, the user did so under a claim of right. Under these circumstances, adverse use will be presumed unless the owner introduces sufficient evidence to overcome the presumption. Adverse use has thus been found in cases where the user actually believed that he or she owned the property. A use under these circumstances is clearly hostile to the owner's interest.

In a number of situations, however, use is not presumed to be adverse. These include use by a relative, use of land that is open and unfenced, and use by many people, none of whom claims an exclusive right.

Creation of an easement by prescription also requires that the use by the person claiming the easement be *continuous* and *uninterrupted.*

CASE EXAMPLE

Dryer and Thurston owned adjoining summer properties near Lake Feather. For some time beyond the prescription period, Thurston had used a path across the Dryer property to reach the lake. In 1997, Dryer constructed a fence across his property, blocking the path. When Thurston claimed an easement, Dryer argued that, as the path was used only in the summer, its use was not continuous. The court rejected this argument.

Continuous use does not mean *constant use.* Use is continuous when a person uses the easement as the occasion may demand. A critical factor is that the person claiming the right does not recognize a superior claim or abandon the use during the prescriptive period. In addition, the use does not have to be a continuous use by the same person. Most states allow *tacking*—the process of adding together periods of prescriptive use by a latter user who has succeeded to the interest of earlier users.

CASE EXAMPLE

Hunkel asserted an interest over Svetlana's adjacent property by walking across a path that transversed Svetlana's back yard. He did this for five years. Hunkel died and his son Nanor inherited the property. Svetlana sold her property to Nicor. Nanor continued to use the walking path as a shortcut continuously for seven years, and then sold his property to Lena, who regularly utilized the "walking path" now on Nicor's property. In a state where prescriptive easements are gained after 12 years, a prescriptive easement through tacking now exists for the benefit of the property.

Uninterrupted refers to the failure of the owner of the land to act. For a use to be uninterrupted, the owner must not succeed in causing a discontinuance of the use. The running of the prescriptive period is stopped when an interruption occurs, for example, by a lawsuit or by otherwise successfully blocking the usage.

Prescription Easements for Light and Air. Energy consciousness continues to spur interest in easements. Owners considering installation of solar heating units in buildings need assurance of enough sunlight to operate the units effectively. Operation of these units could be hindered if the owner of the adjoining parcel were to build a structure that would block much of the incoming light. Easements for light and air over a neighbor's land are a means of dealing with this problem, but the vast majority of

American jurisdictions do not recognize this type of easement except where the parties have entered into an express agreement creating it. English courts have recognized a doctrine of "ancient lights." This doctrine allows an easement for light after a prescriptive period of 27 years, but the "ancient lights" concept has been rejected consistently by U.S. courts.

U.S. courts have also refused to apply the concepts of implied easement or easement by necessity to create easements for light and air. The following case well illustrates this principle.

A few courts recognize a cause of action in nuisance against a person who unreasonably blocks a homeowner's solar access. In those cases the court balances the gravity of the harm to the homeowner versus the utility of the obstructer's conduct to arrive at a determination as to whether such conduct constitutes a nuisance.

The potential user of solar energy faces a substantial cost to ensure the required sunlight to operate his or her unit. The prospective user of solar energy must bargain

Fountainbleau Hotel Corp. v. Forty-Five Twenty-Five Florida
Florida District Court of Appeal
114 So. 2d 357 (1959)

Background. Forty-Five Twenty-Five owns the Eden Roc Hotel, which was built about one year after the Fountainbleau Hotel. They are adjacent to each other. Both are luxurious hotels facing the Atlantic Ocean. The Fountainbleau contracted for a 14-story tower addition to its existing structure. During the winter months, from around 2:00 P.M. through the remainder of the day, the shadow of the addition will extend over the cabana, swimming pool, and sunbathing areas of the Eden Roc.

The Eden Roc sought to enjoin the construction. The trial court granted a temporary injunction.

Decision. The appellate court reversed.

By the Court. No American decision has been cited and independent research has revealed none, in which it has been held that—in the absence of some contractual or statutory obligation—a landowner has a legal right in the free flow of light and air across the adjoining land of his neighbor. Even at common law, the landowner had no legal right, in the absence of an easement or uninterrupted use and enjoyment for a period of 20 years, to unobstructed light and air

from the adjoining land. And the English doctrine of "ancient lights" has been unanimously repudiated in this country.

There being, then, no legal right to the free flow of light and air from the adjoining land, it is universally held that where a structure serves a useful and beneficial purpose, it does not give rise to a cause of action, either for damages or for an injunction . . . even though it causes injury to another by cutting off the light and air and interfering with the view that would otherwise be available over adjoining land in its natural state, regardless of the fact that the structure may have been erected partly for spite.

We see no reason for departing from this universal rule. If, as contended on behalf of the plaintiff, public policy demands that a landowner in the Miami Beach area refrain from constructing buildings on his premises that will cast a shadow on the adjoining premises, an amendment of its comprehensive planning and zoning ordinance, applicable to the public as a whole, is the means by which such purpose should be achieved. But to change the universal rule—and the custom followed in this state since its inception—that adjoining landowners have an equal right under the law to build to the line of their respective tracts and to such a height as is desired by them amounts, in our opinion, to judicial legislation.

The record affirmatively shows that no statutory basis for the right sought to be enforced by plaintiff exists. . . . It also affirmatively appears that there is no possible basis for holding that plaintiff has an easement for light and air, either express or implied, across defendants' property, nor any prescriptive right thereto—even if it be assumed . . . that the common-law right of prescription as to "ancient

lights" is in effect in this state. And from what we have said heretofore in this opinion, it is perhaps superfluous to add that we have no desire to dissent from the unanimous holding in this country repudiating the English doctrine of ancient lights.

Reversed.

What statement in the opinion can you point to in order to construct an exception to the rule the court adopts? Explain.

with neighbors to prevent blocking of the necessary light. However, few property owners are willing to enter into agreements restricting the height of buildings on their land because this might markedly decrease the land's value. Consequently, one who desires to use solar energy, necessitating uninterrupted access to the sun's rays, must think seriously about living in a solar community where this is ensured by restrictive covenants contained within the deeds.

■ TERMINATION OF EASEMENTS

Although an easement is actually a nonpossessory interest, in some respects it resembles a possessory one. Like an estate, an easement may be created for a specific period, for life, or for a designated purpose. Stump, who you recall granted an easement across his property to reach Lake Feather in earlier examples, might have limited the easement to a designated number of years or until a road was constructed to the lake. When an easement is created for a period of time or a designated purpose, it terminates when either the time expires or the purpose is accomplished. Easements for life terminate when the measuring life ends. An easement created by necessity terminates once the necessity disappears. Most easements, however, do not expire automatically. Like the fee simple, they have the potential to last forever.

A number of methods exist for terminating easements that do not expire automatically, including release, merger, estoppel, abandonment, prescription, conveyance, and eminent domain. (See Table 9.2.) Each of these methods is discussed next.

Release

The holder of an easement appurtenant or in gross may extinguish it by means of a written agreement to give up the right. This document is referred to as a **release**. An oral release alone is ineffective. Except for automatic termination of easements, extinguishing by release is probably the most common method.

TABLE 9.2	Methods of Terminating Easements						
	Voluntary	Acquisition	Representation and Reliance	Surrender	Adverse Use	Sale to Third-Party Buyer Without Knowledge	Governmental Taking
Release	✓						
Merger		✓					
Estoppel			✓				
Abandonment				✓			
Prescription					✓		
Conveyance						✓	
Eminent Domain							✓

Merger

An easement terminates by **merger** when the holder of either the dominant or the servient estate acquires the other. An easement establishes a right to use land owned by someone else. As a result, a person cannot have an easement in his or her own land. This principle applies whether the easement is in gross or appurtenant. Either expires if ownership changes in this way

Estoppel

■ *A doctrine by which a person is not permitted to deny the consequences of facts that are inconsistent with his or her previous actions or statements.*

An easement is extinguished by estoppel if the holder causes the servient estate owner to believe the easement will no longer be used and the servient owner justifiably relies on this belief and suffers some damage as a result. The belief might be the result of a statement made by the easement holder or might be inferred from that person's conduct.

CASE EXAMPLE

Stump asked Bach to use another path across Stump's property to reach Lake Feather. Bach orally agreed to do so. Stump then built a tennis court that was partially on the original right-of-way. Bach found the new path inconvenient and demanded to be allowed to use the old recorded right-of-way. Bach's easement had been terminated by estoppel.

Abandonment

Nonuse of an easement for a substantial period of time is generally not a sufficient basis on which to terminate an easement by estoppel. Although nonuse alone does not extinguish an easement, it may indicate an intention to abandon it. For an easement to terminate by **abandonment**, the holder's intention to surrender it must be clearly established. This is accomplished when the holder discontinues use, states his or her intention to do so or acts in a manner consistent with discontinued use.

> **CASE EXAMPLE**
> Bach purchases additional land giving him frontage on Lake Feather. He builds a fence along his line abutting Stump's land and clears a path across the newly acquired tract to Lake Feather. Bach's conduct is probably sufficient to constitute abandonment of his easement across Stump's property.

Prescription

An easement by **prescription** may be extinguished after the owner of the servient estate acts in a manner adverse to the easement for the prescriptive period. This use must be open, notorious, and uninterrupted, that is, the servient owner must act in a manner similar to that which occurs when an easement is created by prescription.

> **CASE EXAMPLE**
> Stump builds a garage on his property, blocking Levit's right-of-way to Lake Feather. Levit does nothing about the garage because she has no interest in reaching Lake Feather. The prescriptive period in the state is seven years. Levit's easement will terminate by prescription unless she asserts her right before the end of the period.

Conveyance

An easement by **conveyance** is sometimes terminated when the servient estate is sold to a person who has no knowledge of the easement's existence. When a written easement is not recorded, or when the easement is not visible from indications on the property, the servient estate may become free of the easement. Easements created by necessity and by prescription, however, are not subject to this doctrine.

Eminent Domain

The right of the state to take private property for public use applies to easements. (See Chapter 24.) If the state takes the servient estate for a purpose that is not consistent with the continued use of the easement, the dominant tenant loses his or her right to continue this use. This is true even if the dominant estate itself is not taken. The owner of the dominant estate is entitled to compensation for the loss in value of his or her easement right. Similarly, condemnation of the dominant estate may terminate the easement. This occurs if the condemnation and the new use destroy the usefulness of the easement.

■ PROFIT À PRENDRE

■ *A nonpossessory interest in real property that permits the holder to remove part of the soil or produce of the land.*

Most authorities consider the *profit*, known as the **profit à prendre**, a type of easement. Others distinguish the profit from the easement, as the profit allows the holder to take specified resources from the land, such as soil, produce, wild animals, coal, and timber. A person who has an easement does not have this right. Suppose, for example, that Stump grants the Cazenovia Lumber Company the right to take "any and all standing timber" from his property at Lake Feather. Although the lumber company does not have title to the timber, it has a right to remove it from the land. This is a profit.

Few differences exist between easements and profits. Like other types of easements, a profit is an interest in land, but it is nonpossessory and limited to a particular purpose. The holder of the profit has a right of reasonable ingress and egress to use the right advantageously. In most states, unless specifically limited by the agreement, the owner of land does not lose the right to use the resource that is the subject of the profit. Like easements, profits may be appurtenant or in gross. The usual profit is in gross. This makes it a personal right not related to a dominant estate. Unlike the noncommercial easement in gross, however, the profit à prendre is freely transferable.

■ LICENSE

■ *A personal privilege to enter another's property for a specific purpose.*

CASE EXAMPLE
Able and Baker are neighbors. Baker is having work done on his driveway, and Able gives him permission to park in Able's driveway for two weeks. Baker has a license.

Purchasing tickets to attend the theater or a sporting event and obtaining a camping permit at a state park are other examples of licenses. Although both easements and licenses are intangible, an easement is an interest in land; a license is not. It is a right that is personal to the licensee, the party to whom it was given. Without a license, if Baker had parked in Able's driveway, Baker would be a trespasser.

Licenses may be created orally or may be in writing. A licensor may revoke it at any time. If the license was created by a contract, the revocation is a breach of the contract. Nevertheless, although the licensee may collect damages, he or she cannot require the licensor to honor the agreement by specific performance because the licensee has no interest in the realty. If Baker had paid for permission to park in Able's driveway, Able could revoke the license. Although Able would be responsible for money damages because of the revocation, Baker could not get a court order requiring Able to make space available.

Because licenses are personal, they are usually invalidated by the licensee's death and may not be transferred. An exception exists when the individual's license is coupled with an interest in the real estate. Under these circumstances the license is irrevocable. Suppose that, instead of merely giving Baker permission to park in the driveway, Able sells Baker timber on Able's property. Because of his interest in the timber, Baker has, in addition, an irrevocable privilege to enter and remove it. Baker's license to enter the land is irrevocable because of the interest in the timber. The license is said to be *coupled with an interest.*

CASE EXAMPLE

Durell had an oil and gas lease and was operating wells on property owned by Freese. A former owner had orally given Durell permission to place equipment on the land to aid in pumping oil. Freese threatened to remove this equipment on the grounds that all Durell had was a license that could be revoked at any time. Durell could get an injunction prohibiting Freese from removing the equipment because the license was irrevocable, as it was coupled with the oil and gas lease. See *Durell v. Freese*, 151 Okla. 150, 3 P.2d 175 (1931).

Table 9.3 summarizes the characteristics of the nonpossessory rights discussed in this chapter.

TABLE 9.3 Nonpossessory Rights: Comparison

	Transferable	Intangible	Interest in Land	Oral	Writing	Revocable
License		✓		✓	✓	✓
Non-commercial Easement in Gross		✓	✓		✓	
Profits	✓	✓	✓	✓	✓	✓

THE CHANGING LANDSCAPE

Easements are a practical reality. Nature did not form boundaries to man's perfection, and man has not parceled out property in a way that always separates boundaries perfectly. Easements are created expressly or impliedly to make egress and ingress possible or practical.

In a society where conflicting interests exist, easements often balance those interests. For example, utility companies need access to homes so that they may maintain the towers and cables that service them. People need to be free from unreasonable interference with their property. A utility easement gives access while not transferring ownership interests.

Recently, conservation easements have been adopted to meet society's needs and to accomplish certain personal interests. A conservation easement is a restriction placed by the owner of his or her property to protect the resources associated with that property. The easement may be donated or sold. Conservation easements, for example, may exclude commercial or residential subdivisions and, by such exclusions, may preserve wooded areas and natural sanctuaries for wildlife. An agricultural easement, a form of conservation easement, limits the type of development of the subject property.

Restrictions associated with the conservation easements "run" with the land perpetually.

There are federal, state, and local tax benefits that may accrue for the conservation easement donor. The value of the easement may be considered a charitable contribution deduction for income tax purposes. It may also constitute a deduction for estate taxes, and property taxes may be eliminated or reduced owing to the conservation easement, depending on the law of the locality.

Conservation easements are held by local government agencies, trusts, or other nonprofit organizations. The easement holder is responsible for monitoring and maintenance. More and more state laws contain statutes that are friendly to conservation easements. For more information about conservation easements see *www.landtrust.org*. Click "Protecting Land." Scroll down and click the link to "Conservation Easements."

To the extent that they may be adapted to meet the needs of an expanding diversified society, easements will be a part of the expanding fabric of society. Perhaps you can think of other potential uses of easements that will accomplish the accommodation of conflicting interests.

■ KEY TERMS

■ INTERNET RESOURCES

Discussions of easements and related issues available at

www.lectlaw.com/files/lat06.htm

www.law.uts.edu.au/~peteru/landlaw/f024588.htm

www.farmlandinfo.org/documents/27762/ACE_1-04.pdf

■ REVIEW AND DISCUSSION QUESTIONS

1. Compare and contrast an *easement appurtenant* and an *easement in gross*.
2. Explain the factors that must exist for an easement to be created by prescription.
3. What is a profit? How does it differ from an easement? In what ways is it similar?
4. Is an easement an estate? Support your answer.
5. What is a license? How does it differ from an easement?
6. Name and define seven ways an easement may terminate and give an example of each.

■ CASE PROBLEMS

1. Hamilton and Tucker owned adjoining farms. For more than 40 years, Mrs. Tucker, her predecessors in title, her agents, and her employees reached her farm by a roadway across the Hamilton farm.

   At one time, the two farms had been a single unit, but it had been divided in 1884 by Mrs. Tucker's grandfather. He had given approximately 200 acres to each of his two sons. The Hamiltons purchased their farm in 1972 from the widow of one of the sons.

   On purchasing the farm, the Hamiltons blocked the roadway to the Tucker place. Mrs. Tucker seeks an injunction to restrain this action. Will she succeed? Discuss. *McIlroy v. Hamilton*, 539 S.W.2d 669 (Mo. Ct. App. 1976).

2. Anderson owned and operated a small motel in a resort area. One of the area's principal attractions was a well-known golf course. Although it was difficult to reach the clubhouse by automobile from the motel, the clubhouse was within easy walking distance.

   To provide easy access to the clubhouse for his guests, Anderson acquired an easement over a neighbor's land "for use as a connecting walk by guests of the Anderson Motel." Three years later Anderson sold the motel to a national franchise, which doubled the room capacity. The neighbor attempted to stop motel guests from crossing the land, and the new owner sought an injunction prohibiting interference. Would the new owner be successful? Present arguments for both the neighbor and the new owner.

3. Soergel owned lot A. He granted Smith, who owned lot B directly to the west of lot A, a ten-foot-wide easement for installation of a sewer line. Smith sold lot B to Preston, who owned lot C directly to the west of lot B. Preston began to install a sewer line from his house on lot C across lots B and A. Soergel sought an injunction prohibiting Preston from constructing the sewer line. Diagram the properties. Was Soergel successful? Support your answer. *Soergel v. Preston*, 367 N.W.2d 366 (Mich. Ct. App. 1985).

4. Bivens and Mobley owned tracts of land that they exchanged. The deed from Bivens to Mobley "reserved an easement, fifteen feet wide, along the east side of what became Mobley's property. . . ." The easement read:

    There is also conveyed an easement to run with the above described land for ingress and egress to and from . . . Patrick Road . . . to the . . . described land. . . .

    Mobley built a house a few feet from the east side easement (which was not being used) and actually incorporated part of the easement into his yard. No one complained for 15 years, and relations between the neighbors were good.

    Bivens and Mobley shared a common water line on the west side of the properties, but the water association informed Bivens that there could only be one dwelling per water meter. Therefore, Bivens sought to run a water line through the east side easement. Mobley objected. What are Mobley's arguments against the pipeline? What are Bivens's arguments in favor of the pipeline? *Bivens v. Mobley*, 724 So. 2d 458 (Miss. App. 1998).

5. Devlin leased a restaurant in a shopping center. The owner of the shopping center did not object when Devlin erected a sign in the parking lot advertising the restaurant. When the shopping center was sold, the new owner demanded that the sign be removed. (a) If Devlin refused to remove it, could the new owner do so legally? (b) Would the result be the same if Devlin had permission from the former owner to erect the sign? Discuss. *Devlin v. The Phoenix, Inc.*, 471 So. 2d 93 (Fla. Dist. Ct. App. 1985).

6. Todd operated a business that provided laundry machines for use in apartments. In 1979, Todd entered into an agreement with Lake Feather Realty giving him the exclusive right to install and maintain laundry equipment in an apartment building owned by Lake Feather Realty. The contract was for a ten-year period and purported to be binding "on the heirs, successors, and assigns" of the parties.

    When the apartment building was sold in 1981, the new owner demanded that Todd remove the machines. Todd sought a permanent injunction to prevent the removal of the machines, arguing that the contract gave him an easement to maintain them. What do you think should be the result? Why?

7. Elaine Owens owned property in Lake Feather Village. For 25 to 30 years, during the summer, people had used the property as a shortcut to reach the beach. In the spring and fall, the property was used by children as a baseball diamond or a football field.

When Owens built a fence around the property, Fink, an abutting owner, sued to prevent the area from being blocked. Would Fink be successful? Support your answer.

8. Ted Cash and Mary Craver own adjoining tracts of land. Both tracts had been part of a larger tract of land owned by W. J. Roberts. In 1917, the 170-acre Craver tract was severed from the whole by deed in 1942. Roberts School Road ran across the Cash and Craver tracts before the severance. The road had always been used by Craver, Cash, and others as a school way and farm-to-market road, as well as a general means of ingress and egress to interior lands for farming and transfer to major highways abutting the tracts.

    Cash sued for an injunction preventing Craver and others from using the portion of Roberts School Road that crosses Cash's property. What should the outcome be and why? *Cash v. Craver*, 302 S.E.2d 819 (N.C. Ct. App. 1983).

9. Glenn Prah owns a residence which has a solar system that includes collectors on the roof to supply energy for heat and hot water. After Prah built his solar-heated house, Richard Maretti purchased an adjacent lot and began constructing a home. Prah immediately advised Maretti that if he built his house on the proposed location, it would adversely affect Prah's solar system. Nevertheless, Maretti ignored the warning and began construction. Prah sues Maretti seeking to stop the construction and the interference to his solar system. Will he be successful? Why or why not? *Prah v. Maretti*, 321 NW 2d 182 (Wis. 1982).

 Go to the Student Study Guide CD-ROM and work through Case 2.

PART THREE

Purchase
Agreements

10 Basic Contract Law

■ CONTRACT

■ *An agreement between two or more parties containing certain essential elements.*

Contracts are the essential fabric of commercial transactions. Most people enter into contracts on a daily basis, by asking for fuel at a gas station, ordering a sandwich to carry out, or purchasing a paper from a newsstand. Real estate listing and purchase agreements, leasehold agreements, options to buy, and mortgages are more complex forms of contracts. Each of these agreements is governed by contract law. Every state has its own body of contract law, derived from the common law and from statutes. The general body of contract law applies to all commercial agreements, including real estate agreements.

Not every agreement entered into between parties is enforceable. The law enforces agreements arising in a commercial context, assuming that certain other ingredients discussed in this chapter are present. The law will not, however, enforce a purely social arrangement.

CASE EXAMPLE

Sam promises to buy his friend, Amy, a steak if she agrees to meet him for dinner after work. Amy agrees. Sam shows up, but Amy does not. Because this is merely a social arrangement, Amy has incurred no liability as a result of her failure to show. See *Balfour v. Balfour*, 2 K.B. 571 (1919).

Social arrangements normally do not evince the type of expectation and reliance that commercial agreements do. Generally, the economic harm that could result from breaking a social promise is comparatively small. The law deems this type of transaction best left to the conscience of the individual.

Most oral contracts are enforceable. However, some contracts are required by statute to be supported by a writing. Real estate contracts fall within this exception, and the writing requirement will be discussed in Chapter 11.

A contract entitles each party to certain rights, as well as imposing certain duties on them. When a legally binding contract exists, each party is assured that should the other party or parties not perform in accordance with the terms, the court will afford a remedy to the aggrieved party. The remedy may be in the form of money damages or a court order for *specific performance*, that is, for the party to perform according to the terms of the contract. A contract thus provides an incentive for each party to perform.

Preliminary negotiations normally precede an agreement. Obviously, each party desires the best possible bargain. But when negotiations ripen into an agreement, the law ensures its enforceability. The real estate purchase or sale is the largest single transaction into which many people will enter. The parties expend substantial time and expense in preparing for the closing of the real estate transaction. If the parties were not legally committed to each other by a binding contract, either the seller or the purchaser could walk away from the transaction, leaving the other party without remedy. A contract is the best legal protection against such behavior.

This chapter is designed to provide a basic introduction to Chapter 11, "Real Estate Purchase Contract." In the following pages the general principles of contract law are examined. First, each of the elements essential to the formation of a contract—offer, acceptance, capacity, consideration, and lawful purpose—is discussed. Next, the chapter covers contract interpretation, the assignment (transfer) of contracts, breach of contract, and the remedies available to the parties in the event one party breaks the contractual agreement. Finally, this chapter discusses the circumstances under which parties are released from their contractual obligations. For a useful Web guide to the principles of contract law discussed in this chapter, see *www.law.cornell.edu/topics/contracts.html.*

■ ELEMENTS OF CONTRACTS

Certain essential ingredients must be present in any contract (including real estate contracts) for it to be enforceable. Basic to the agreement are the *offer* and *acceptance*. In addition, the parties must possess the requisite *capacity*, or state of mind, to contract. *Consideration*, a bargained-for exchange of value, must be present, and the subject matter of the contract must be *legal*. These elements of contracts are covered in the following sections. (See Table 10.1.)

Offer

■   *A proposal intended to create a contract on acceptance by the person to whom it is made.*

The **offer** is made by an *offeror*—one who communicates a proposal. The offer is made to an *offeree*—one to whom a proposal is communicated. If Mary offers to sell her house to Martin for $70,000, Mary is the offeror and Martin is the offeree. If Martin offers to buy Mary's house for $70,000, Martin is the offeror and Mary is the offeree.

The offer must state with *specificity* what the offeror is willing to do and what is expected in return. Terms of an offer must be certain and clear enough to be interpreted

TABLE 10.1	Elements of a Contract
	• Offer
	• Acceptance
	• Consideration
	• Capacity
	• Legality

by a court. The names of the parties and a clear identification of the subject matter of the contract are essential inclusions within the offer. Indefinite or vague language, such as "a price between $80,000 and $100,000," is not sufficiently definite to constitute a valid offer. However, omission of the date or place of closing or, in some cases, even the price, does not necessarily invalidate the offer. The courts may infer a reasonable place, date, and price and, when necessary, look to the usage and customs within the real estate industry to give effect to the intent of the parties.

CASE EXAMPLE

Mr. and Mrs. Beadle desired to purchase three lots in San Rafael, California, and to build homes on those lots for resale. They contacted Vera Rivers, a California real estate broker. Rivers agreed to represent the Beadles regarding the purchase, without compensation, in return for which the Beadles agreed to build a speculative home on each of the three lots, place the lots on the market for sale as soon as the homes were complete, and give Vera Rivers the exclusive right to sell said houses and pay her a 3 percent commission on the selling price.

After the transaction, the Beadles refused to build homes on the lots and maintained that the agreement was too vague. The court, in awarding $1,800 commission to Ms. Rivers, held that, within the context of the real estate industry, "the term *speculative home* means a home built with expectation of selling it for a profit . . . and that in relation to the area of said lots and the type of homes in said area, the homes, if constructed by the defendants, would have been homes that would sell for approximately $20,000." Hence, in arriving at an $1,800 damage award, the court computed 3 percent of $20,000 for commissions for each of the three houses. *Rivers v. Beadle*, 183 Cal. App. 2d. 691, 7 Cal. Rptr. 170 (1960).

An offer must be *communicated* to be effective. Communication may be actual or constructive. *Actual* communication occurs when an offeree receives and then reads or hears the offer. *Constructive* communication occurs when a reasonably prudent offeree, under the circumstances, should have read the contents of the offer, regardless of whether an actual reading occurred.

An offeror has the power to control the terms of a contract. The offeror may make a reasonable offer or an unreasonable offer. If it is to ripen into a contract, the offeree must accept the terms of the offer.

If unaccepted, an offer may terminate in several ways, including by revocation, rejection, counteroffer, lapse of a reasonable time, destruction of the subject matter, death of the offeror, legal incapacity of the offeror, or illegality of the subject matter of the offer. (See Table 10.2.)

Revocation. Generally, an offeror may withdraw an offer any time before the offeree's acceptance. The revocation becomes effective on actual communication of the revocation to the offeree. If the offeree receives a revocation prior to acceptance, the offer is terminated. Any purported acceptance after receipt of a revocation merely operates as a new offer (counteroffer), which the original offeror may accept or reject. The revocation need not in every instance be communicated by the offeror to the offeree to be effective. A communication to the offeree's agent is normally sufficient.

TABLE 10.2	Methods of Terminating Offer

- Revocation
- Rejection
- Counteroffer
- Lapse of Time
- Destruction of Subject Matter
- Death of Offeror
- Insanity of Offeror
- Illegality

CASE EXAMPLE

Behee made a written offer to the Smiths to purchase their real estate for $42,500 plus $250 for a dinner bell and flower pots. The offer was mailed on March 3. The Smiths signed the proposed agreement. Before Behee was notified of the acceptance, he withdrew the offer by notifying the Smiths' real estate agent.

The Missouri Court of Appeals held that the withdrawal was an effective revocation of his offer, because "an offeror may withdraw his offer at any time before acceptance and communication of that fact to him. . . . Notice to the agent, within the scope of the agent's authority, is notice to the principal. . . ." *Hendricks v. Behee*, 786 S.W.2d 610 (Mo. Ct. App. 1990).

Sometimes a revocation is implied. An *implied revocation* occurs when the offeree learns from a reliable source that the offeror has acted in a manner incompatible with the outstanding offer.

CASE EXAMPLE

Frank makes a valid offer in writing to Dale to sell his residence to Dale. Before Dale accepts, Dale learns from Jackie, Frank's agent, that Perry purchased Frank's property. The communication of such information to Dale results in an implied revocation of Frank's offer. See *Dickinson v. Dodds*, 2 Ch. D. 463 (1876).

Rejection. An offeree may simply reject an offer by communicating to the offeror a refusal to accept the offer. A counteroffer—where an offeree alters the terms of the offer and thus makes a proposal with new terms—amounts to a rejection of the offer. An offeree who communicates a rejection of an offer and then decides to accept the offer has actually rejected the offer. The purported acceptance merely results in a counteroffer, which the original offeror is free to accept or reject.

CASE EXAMPLE

Mr. and Mrs. Leavey owned the Hereford Ranch in Wyoming. They desired to sell the ranch. Edward Murray, a real estate broker, learned the ranch was for sale and actively looked for buyers. Verne Woods and A. Trautwein were interested in purchasing the property for $2,300,000. After negotiations, the Leaveys made an offer that was communicated by Murray to Woods and Trautwein. Woods and Trautwein signed the agreement but attached three material amendments to the instrument. The Leaveys refused to accept the agreement with the amendments because "they changed the whole deal." After learning of the Leaveys' refusal to accept the amendments, Trautwein advised Mr. Leavey that the amendments were removed and the original offer acceptable. The Leaveys refused to sell the property to Woods and Trautwein, who sued for breach of contract. The court held that the Woods-Trautwein amendments constituted a rejection of the Leaveys' offer, which terminated the offer. Consequently, the subsequent assent to remove the amendments did not result in a contract. *Trautwein v. Leavey*, 472 P.2d 776 (Wyo. 1970).

Lapse of Reasonable Time. An offeror may specify an expiration date for an offer. A purported acceptance after the specified date is ineffective. If no date is specified, then the offer lapses after a reasonable period of time. What is considered reasonable varies from case to case, depending on the circumstances. In general, however, an offer to purchase realty will not expire as rapidly as, for example, an offer to purchase shares of stock because the price of stock normally fluctuates more rapidly than that of realty.

Destruction of the Subject Matter. Destruction of the subject matter of the offer before acceptance results in a termination of the offer. If a seller offers to sell land and the house on it to a prospective purchaser, the offer will automatically terminate, before acceptance, on the destruction of the house. This would be true even if the prospective purchaser were unaware of the destruction. (Nevertheless, a contract, as distinguished from an offer, does not necessarily terminate because of the destruction of the subject matter.) Normally, the contract specifies who bears the loss in the event the property is destroyed by accident. Obviously, one who willfully destroys the subject matter of the contract will not be excused from performance but will be liable for damages.

Death of the Offeror. Death of the offeror results in a termination of the offer, whether the offeree knows of the death or not. If the offeree accepts the offer and then the offeror dies, a contract exists. Death will normally not excuse performance of one's contractual obligation unless the performance involves personal services. If a seller who was bound under a purchase contract to sell realty dies, the seller's representative will be required to execute a good deed conveying the property to the buyer. If the buyer dies, the purchase price will be paid out of the estate proceeds, and the seller will convey the deed directly to the buyer's estate, heirs, or next of kin, as the law provides.

Insanity of the Offeror. An offer terminates before acceptance in the event the offeror becomes incapacitated by insanity. Otherwise, the offeror would be at a disadvantage because a legally incapacitated person (not unlike a deceased person) does not possess the faculties necessary to decide to revoke an offer. A contract for the sale of realty, however, is not affected should a party become legally incapacitated after entering the contract; the guardian or other representative of the incapacitated person is required to perform.

Illegality of the Subject Matter. A change in the law may cause an offer that was legal when made to become illegal. Such a change causes an offer to terminate. Assume, for example, that a corporation offers to spray fruit groves. Thereafter, a law is passed that prohibits the particular "spray" that is required under the contract. The offer would automatically terminate due to illegality. Similarly, a valid contract that later becomes illegal due to a change in law is generally unenforceable.

Acceptance

■ *Assent to the terms of an offer.*

Acceptance is the second component of the agreement. The offeree has the power to create a contract merely by communicating an acceptance. The offeree does not have the authority to modify the terms of a proposal. As mentioned earlier, should the offeree change the terms of the offer, the variation creates a *counteroffer*, which actually constitutes a rejection of the original offer. The original offeror may then reject or accept the counteroffer.

At times, an offeree appears to add terms to an offer when in fact the new terms were implied within the original offer. In such a case, the purported terms will not defeat the acceptance.

> **CASE EXAMPLE**
> Allen offers to sell Solid Rock to Baldoro for $170,000. Baldoro responds by saying, "I accept, provided the title is good." Because the law implies in Allen's offer that Allen will tender good title, Baldoro has added no new terms and the acceptance is valid.

The offer and the acceptance constitute the agreement. It may not always be feasible or possible to determine which party made the offer and which party accepted. In many instances, after final negotiations, the entire agreement is reduced to writing. Both parties then sign the agreement. It is only academic in such a case to break the agreement down to the offer and acceptance components. However, the party who signed first could be considered the offeror and the second signer the offeree. In reality this is not always true, because a contract may arise prior to the signing of the agreement. In such a case, the signing merely evidences the oral agreement.

Manifest Intent. Courts often articulate that no agreement exists without a "meeting of the minds." This subjective test requires an examination of the inner psyche of each of the parties, which is, of course, impractical and usually impossible. The more acceptable approach is the objective test, one that is designed to determine whether the parties manifested an intent to be bound. Regardless of the mind of the offeror, if a reasonable offeree believes an offer to have been communicated seriously, then acceptance of the offer ripens into a contract. This is true even when the offer was made in excitement or jest, as contended in the following case.

Lucy v. Zehmer
Supreme Court of Virginia
196 Va. 493, 84 S.E.2d 516 (1954)

Background. Mr. Lucy sought to purchase the Ferguson Farm from its owners, the Zehmers. He made contact with them at a restaurant Mr. Zehmer operated. Lucy said, "I bet you wouldn't take $50,000 for [the farm]." Zehmer replied, "Yes, I would too; you wouldn't give 50." Lucy asked Zehmer to write up the agreement. On the back of a restaurant check Zehmer wrote, "We do hereby agree to sell to W. O. Lucy the Ferguson Farm for $50,000 complete." It was signed by Mr. and Mrs. Zehmer. Both Lucy and Zehmer had been drinking.

The Zehmers attempted to back out of the transaction, contending that the agreement was signed in jest. W. O. Lucy and J. C. Lucy, husband and wife, sued A. H. Zehmer and Ida S. Zehmer for specific performance of the contract. The trial court found in favor of the defendants, the Zehmers.

Decision. The Supreme Court of Virginia reversed and remanded the case to the trial court, ordering specific performance of the contract in favor of the plaintiffs, the Lucys.

Justice Buchanan. In his testimony Zehmer claimed that he "was high as a Georgia pine," and that the transaction "was just a bunch of two doggoned drunks bluffing to see who could talk the biggest and say the most." . . . [This] is contradicted by other evidence as to the condition of both parties, and rendered of no weight by the testimony of his wife that when Lucy left the restaurant she suggested that Zehmer drive him home. The record is convincing that Zehmer was not intoxicated to the extent of being unable to comprehend the nature and consequences of the instrument he executed, and hence that instrument is not to be invalidated on that ground.

* * *

The appearance of the contract, the fact that it was under discussion for forty minutes or more before it was signed; Lucy's objection to the first draft because it was written in the singular, and he wanted Mrs. Zehmer to sign it also; the rewriting to meet that objection and the signing by Mrs. Zehmer; the discussion of what was to be included in the sale; the provision for the examination of the title; the completeness of the instrument that was executed; the taking possession of it by Lucy with no request or suggestion by either of the defendants that he give it back, are facts which furnish persuasive evidence that the execution of the contract was a serious business transaction rather than a casual, jesting matter as defendants now contend.

If it be assumed, contrary to what we think the evidence shows, that Zehmer was jesting about selling his farm to Lucy and that the transaction was intended by him to be a joke, nevertheless the evidence shows that Lucy did not so understand it but considered it to be a serious business transaction and the contract to be binding on the Zehmers as well as on himself. The very next day he arranged with his brother to put up half the money and take a half interest in the land. The day after that he employed an attorney to examine the title. The next night . . . he was back at Zehmer's place and there Zehmer told him for the first time, Lucy said, that he wasn't going to sell and he told Zehmer, "You know you sold that place fair and square."

In the field of contracts, as generally elsewhere, "We must look to the outward expression of a person as manifesting his intention rather than to his secret and unexpressed intention. 'The law imputes to a person an intention corresponding to the reasonable meaning of his words and acts.'"

At no time prior to the execution of the contract had Zehmer indicated to Lucy by word or act that he was not in earnest about selling the farm. They had argued about it and discussed its terms, as Zehmer admitted, for a long time. . . . In any event there had been what appeared to be a good faith offer and a good faith acceptance, followed by the execution and the apparent delivery of a written contract. Both said that Lucy put the writing in his pocket and then offered Zehmer $5 to seal the bargain. Not until then, even under the defendant's evidence, was anything done or said to indicate that the manner was a joke. Both of the Zehmers testified that when Zehmer asked his wife to sign he whispered that it was a joke so Lucy wouldn't hear and that it was not intended that he should hear.

An agreement or mutual assent is of course essential to a valid contract but the law imputes to a person an intention corresponding to the reasonable meaning of his words and acts. If his words and acts, judged by a reasonable standard, manifest an intention to agree, it is immaterial what may be the real but unexpressed state of his mind.

continued on next page

So a person cannot set up that he was merely jesting when his conduct and words would warrant a reasonable person in believing that he intended a real agreement.

Reversed and Remanded.

Do you think there would be a different result if the price was $5,000 for the property? Why?

Transmittal of Acceptances and Revocations. An acceptance is effective on actual communication to the offeror or the offeror's agent. The offeror may expressly name an agent, or one may be implied. The law deems that an offeror impliedly invites acceptance from the offeree by the same mode of communication the offeror used to communicate the offer. This is known as the *implied agency rule* or the *mailbox rule*. If an offeror communicates an offer by mail, then the mailboxes would be the offeror's implied agents. Under that circumstance the deposit of an acceptance in the mail results in a valid acceptance at the time of deposit. The offeror assumes the risk of nondelivery of the acceptance in such a case, so that even if the offeror never receives the acceptance, it is nonetheless effective at the moment of delivery to the mailbox. Of course, the offeror may eliminate this risk by expressly stating as a term of the offer that acceptance is effective only on actual receipt by the offeror. Many jurisdictions have expanded the implied agency rule to apply to any reasonable mode of communication utilized by the offeree.

An offer may be revoked any time before it is deemed accepted. Revocation is effective on actual receipt by the offeree or the offeree's express agent. The implied agency rule does not operate for revocations, only for acceptances.

CASE EXAMPLE

Jan. 3   *A* offers by mail to sell Landacre to *B* for $5,000 an acre.

Jan. 4   *B* mails an acceptance.

Jan. 5   *A* mails a letter to *B* revoking her previous offer.

Jan. 6   *B* receives the letter of revocation.

Jan. 7   *A* receives the acceptance.

A contract exists on January 4 because an effective acceptance was delivered to *A*'s implied agent prior to actual receipt by *B* of *A*'s letter of revocation.

The law of transmittal of acceptances and revocations is based on fairness and establishes firm rules that a businessperson may rely on in decision making.

Reality of Assent. There must be reality of assent to an agreement between the parties; the appearance of assent is not sufficient. Any nonassenting party may avoid the contract. Causes that may intervene to negate a party's assent include fraud, innocent misrepresentation, mistake, duress, and undue influence. (See Table 10.3.)

Fraud is an intentional misrepresentation of a material fact that induces justifiable reliance, to the detriment of a party. Fraud is examined in detail in Chapter 13. The defrauded party not only may seek cancellation (rescission) of the contract, but also may have an action in tort to recover damages against the defrauder, including punitive dam-

TABLE 10.3	Acts that Negate a Party's Assent	
Fraud		Intentional misrepresentation
Innocent misrepresentation		Unintentional misrepresentation
Mistake		Error
Duress		Coercion
Undue influence		Exertion of dominion

ages, when appropriate. *Innocent misrepresentation* is an unintentional misrepresentation of a material fact that induces justifiable reliance, to the detriment of a party. Because the misrepresenter does not do so intentionally, most courts permit the party relying on the material fact to rescind the contract but deny recovery for damages.

Mistake is an unintentional error. When both parties enter into a contract under a mistaken belief as to a material matter related to the contract, either party may rescind the contract. If, for example, a seller and buyer of Redacre enter into a real estate sales contract under the misimpression that the property is a historical landmark when, in fact, it is not, rescission is available to either party. If only one party is mistaken concerning a material fact, rescission is not generally an available remedy.

Duress is coercion that overcomes a party's will. Duress results when one is induced to enter into an agreement by force or threat of force. The threat must be of such a nature as to place a reasonable person in fear, such as the threat of bodily harm. When present, rescission is available.

Undue influence is the exertion of dominion over another person that destroys that person's ability to exercise independent judgment. Undue influence cases giving rise to a right of rescission involve situations where one party has developed a total trust or dependency on another. For example, an elderly aunt may be so mentally overpowered by her nephew that she conveys her land to him at his insistence. Or, a sick patient may develop such a trust in a nurse that he loses his power to resist the nurse's plea to convey his property to her.

Consideration

■ *A promise, act, or forbearance bargained for and given over in exchange for a promise, act, or forbearance.*

Consideration is a necessary element of a contract. Generally, if a defendant's promise is not supported by consideration, it is unenforceable. For a promise to be supported by consideration, it must result in a detriment to the promisee (the one to whom a promise is made). The detriment may be in the form of a return promise, an act, or a forbearance.

A return promise to do something that one was not otherwise obligated to do is sufficient consideration. Most real estate contracts take the form of a promise for a promise. This type of contract is designated as *bilateral*.

CASE EXAMPLE

Burnside promises to pay Yerkes $25,000 for Needleacre, and Yerkes promises to sell Needleacre to Burnside for $25,000. All the material details of the contract are reduced to writing. Because there is a promise for a promise, a bilateral contract exists. Each promise is supported by consideration supplied by the other's promise.

An *act* may constitute good consideration for a promise. If the promisor is bargaining for the act, the performance of the act usually constitutes a legal detriment to the promisee. Such a contract is termed *unilateral* because there is only one promisor.

CASE EXAMPLE

Burnside promises to convey Needleacre to Johannes if Johannes cares for Burnside's mother for her life. Johannes cares for Burnside's mother for her life. Because there is a promise for an act, the contract is unilateral. The act is sufficient consideration to support Burnside's promise because it was bargained for and results in a detriment to Johannes.

Consideration also may take the form of a *forbearance*. Such a contract is also unilateral, because there is only one promise.

CASE EXAMPLE

Burnside promises to convey Needleacre to Lasser if Lasser refrains from smoking for ten years. Lasser refrains. Since there is a promise for a forbearance, the contract is unilateral. The forbearance is sufficient consideration to support the promise because it was bargained for and results in a detriment to Lasser. See *Hamer v. Sidway*, 124 N.Y. 538, 27 N.E. 256 (1891).

Promissory Estoppel. *Promissory estoppel* is a doctrine that prevents a party from denying that a promise is supported by consideration. The doctrine of promissory estoppel is applicable when no consideration exists, but it is necessary to enforce a promise to prevent an injustice. The following elements must also be present: (1) a promise (2) calculated to induce reliance, (3) actual justified reliance by the promisee, and (4) injury. (See Table 10.4.)

CASE EXAMPLE

Montrasor is in arrears on her mortgage payments and requests additional time from the mortgagee to permit her to pay the arrearage. The mortgagee extends the time by 90 days. There is no consideration to support the promise to extend. Thirty days thereafter, Montrasor makes substantial improvements to the property in reliance on the mortgagee's promise. The mortgagee files an action in foreclosure prior to the expiration of the 90 days. Because each of the ingredients of promissory estoppel is present, the mortgagee's promise not to foreclose for 90 days is enforceable.

Capacity

■   *A legal qualification that determines one's ability to enter into a binding contract.*

For a legally binding agreement to exist, both parties must have the **capacity** to enter into the contract. Some persons have no capacity to contract; their contracts are

TABLE 10.4	Promissory Estoppel Elements

- Promise
- Calculated to Induce Reliance
- Justifiable Reliance
- Injury

TABLE 10.5	Contract Status for Incapacitated Persons

Incapacity	Status of Contract
Adjudicated insane	Void
Actually insane	Voidable
Minors	Voidable
Drugged persons	Voidable

designated as *void*. Other persons possess limited capacity to enter into contracts; their contracts are classified as *voidable*. (See Table 10.5.) Examples of both categories are discussed below.

Insane Persons. An insane person, under the law, is one who lacks the requisite reason to comprehend the nature and consequences of transactions. Any contract entered into by a person who has been determined to be insane by a court—that is, one who has been *adjudicated insane*—is automatically void. Since such information is a matter of public record, all are deemed to be on notice that the person cannot enter into a valid contract and may not be held liable because the court has determined that person to be insane. A person who is *actually insane* but has not been adjudicated insane by a court is deemed to possess limited capacity to enter into contracts. Those contracts are classified as voidable. A *voidable contract* is one that may be voided or validated at the option of the party who possesses limited capacity. During the course of the insanity and up to a reasonable time after being restored to sanity, a person who is actually insane (or his or her legal representative) may elect to *disavow* the contract and treat it as void. In such a case, the insane person must tender back the property received and is then entitled to a return of the property he or she previously conveyed. Or, after being restored to sanity, that person may *ratify* the contract and treat it as valid.

Minors. The law seeks to protect the immature as well as the insane. For that reason, the law discourages adults from contracting with minors. In most states, those under the age of 18 are considered minors. Generally, a contract entered into with a minor is *voidable* by the minor. That means that the minor may choose to disaffirm the contract any time during minority and up to a reasonable time after attaining majority. If the contract is *executory* (unperformed), then that disaffirmance releases the minor from the obligation to perform the contract. If the contract is *executed* (performed), then the disaffirming minor need give back to the other party only that which remains of what the minor received from the adult. Then the minor would be entitled to a full return of the money or property originally conveyed to the other party. In most states, however, when the transaction involves a completed sale of the minor's realty, the minor is obliged to await the age of majority before disaffirming the transaction. In these states, the minor must disaffirm within a reasonable period of time after attaining majority, with six months being a "rule of thumb."

CASE EXAMPLE

Clifford Spencer and his sister owned land. Clifford was a minor and did not attain majority until April 5, 1919. On November 30, 1918, MacCloon purchased the property from Clifford and his sister. MacCloon later conveyed the property to Lyman Falls Power Company and Hutchins. Thereafter, Lyman Falls conveyed its interest in the property to the Public Service Company of New Hampshire. On September 8, 1936, Clifford sued to disaffirm the contract and sought to have the property reconveyed to him. The court held that, although Clifford could disaffirm on attaining majority, "a delay of 17 years and 5 months after the plaintiff attained his majority until the bringing of this suit . . . was unreasonable." Consequently, Clifford's attempt to disaffirm was unsuccessful. *Spencer v. Lyman Falls Power Co.*, 109 Vt. 294, 196 A. 276 (1938).

Minors are obligated to pay for the necessities of life for which they contract and receive. Although minors may still disaffirm contracts for necessities, they will nonetheless be required to pay the reasonable value of the property or services received. Normally, real estate that provides housing is not deemed to be a necessity for a minor because the minor can live with his or her parent(s). However, for a minor who has been emancipated—set free by his or her parents—housing may be a necessity. In fact, emancipated minors are generally treated as adults for purposes of contracting.

Drugged Persons. Contracts entered into by a person who is intoxicated or under the influence of drugs are voidable if the drug renders such a person unable to appreciate the nature and consequences of his or her acts. Most courts are less sympathetic to this classification of persons than to minors and will permit disaffirmance of a completed contract only if the person contracting with the drugged person can be restored to the original position without suffering loss.

Lawful Purpose

A contract must have a legal purpose. For example, a landlord-tenant lease that states that the purpose is for gambling would be unlawful. Any contract that runs afoul of a statute or public policy is illegal and hence void.

A party to an illegal bargain will not normally be assisted by the courts. Simply, the courts will leave the parties in the same position in which they are found. There are, however, some exceptions to this rule.

Sometimes the parties to the contract are not deemed to be *in pari delicto*—that is, not at equal fault. A landlord who lets property to a tenant who uses the property to traffic drugs may be innocent of the illegal purpose for which the property was intended. In that instance, the courts aid the innocent party in the collection of the rents. An elderly man who is tricked out of his real estate or other property will be protected in many jurisdictions, regardless of the fact that he was a willing participant in an unscrupulous scheme.

When a contract involves an illegal provision, the courts may excise that portion and enforce the remainder of the contract. However, if the illegal provision is so interconnected with the whole as to render it nonseverable, the entire contract will be rendered void.

A number of states have passed civil forfeiture statutes that authorize the government to confiscate property that has facilitated the commission of a crime. The following case decided by the United States Supreme Court considers the constitutionality of such statutes.

Austin v. United States
Supreme Court of the United States
509 U.S. 602 (1993)

Background. After a state court sentenced Austin on his guilty plea to one count of possessing cocaine with intent to distribute in violation of South Dakota law, the United States filed an action in Federal District Court against his mobile home and auto body shop under a statute that provides for the forfeiture of real property used, or intended to be used, to facilitate the commission of certain drug-related crimes. The court rejected Austin's argument that forfeiture of his properties would violate the Eighth Amendment's Excessive Fines Clause. The Court of Appeals affirmed, agreeing with the government that the Eighth Amendment is inapplicable to civil forfeitures.

Decision. The U.S. Supreme Court reversed and remanded.

Justice Blackmun. In this case we are asked to decide whether the Excessive Fines Clause of the Eighth Amendment applies to forfeitures of property [under a particular federal statute]. We hold that it does and therefore remand the case for consideration of the question whether the forfeiture at issue here was excessive.

Austin contends that the Eighth Amendment's Excessive Fines Clause applies in civil forfeiture proceedings. We have had occasion to consider this

Clause only once before. [In that previous case] we held that the Excessive Fines Clause does not limit the award of punitive damages to a private party in a civil suit when the government neither has prosecuted the action nor has any right to receive a share of the damages. The court concluded that both the Eighth Amendment and . . . the English Bill of Rights . . . from which it derives, were intended to prevent the government from abusing its power to punish; and therefore "that the Excessive Fines Clause was intended to limit only those fines directly imposed by, and payable to, the government."

We found it unnecessary to decide . . . whether the Excessive Fines Clause applies only to criminal cases. The United States now argues that "any claim that the government's conduct in a civil proceeding is limited by the Eighth Amendment generally, or by the Excessive Fines Clause in particular, must fail unless the challenged governmental action, despite its label, would have been recognized as a criminal punishment at the time the Eighth Amendment was adopted." It further suggests that the Eighth Amendment cannot apply to a civil proceeding unless that proceeding is so punitive that it must be considered criminal. . . . We disagree.

Some provisions of the Bill of Rights are expressly limited to criminal cases. The Fifth

continued on next page

Amendment's Self-Incrimination Clause, for example, provides: "No person . . . shall be compelled in any criminal case to be a witness against himself."

The purpose of the Eighth Amendment . . . was to limit the government's power to punish . . . thus, the question is not, as the United States would have it, whether forfeiture . . . is civil or criminal, but rather whether it is punishment.

In considering this question, we are mindful of the fact that sanctions frequently serve more than one purpose. We need not exclude the possibility that a forfeiture serves remedial purposes to conclude that it is subject to the limitations of the Excessive Fines Clause. We, however, must determine that it can only be explained as serving in part to punish. . . . We turn, then, to consider whether, at the time the Eighth Amendment was ratified, forfeiture was understood, at least in part, as punishment, and whether forfeiture . . . should be so understood today.

[The court went on to find that historically forfeiture was considered a punishment.]

Furthermore, Congress has chosen to tie forfeiture directly to the commission of drug offenses. . . . Under [the statute in question] real property is forfeitable if it is used or intended for use to facilitate the commission of a drug-related crime punishable by more than one year's imprisonment.

Austin asks that we establish a multifactor test for determining whether a forfeiture is constitutionally "excessive." We decline that invitation. Although the Court of Appeals opined "that the government is exacting too high a penalty in relation to the offense committed," it had no occasion to consider what factors should inform such a decision because it thought it was foreclosed from engaging in the inquiry. Prudence dictates that we allow the lower courts to consider that question in the first instance.

Reversed and remanded.

What factors do you think would be appropriate for determining whether a particular forfeiture is an "Excessive Fine"?

■ CONTRACT INTERPRETATION

All the essential terms of an agreement must be definite and certain for an enforceable contract to exist. Courts will not normally construct terms or fill in gaps where the instrument is deficient. It is the duty of the courts to interpret language within a contract and to give effect to the intent of the parties. If the language is ambiguous and the court cannot arrive at the intent of the parties, the court will not enforce the instrument. In a real estate purchase contract, the parties and property must be identified. Essential terms left open for future negotiation may invalidate the contract.

Courts use various rules for interpreting contractual provisions, each designed to ascertain the intent of the parties. Words are assigned their plain meaning and are read in the context of the entire contract. Technical language often pervades real estate contracts. Terms such as escrow, balloon payment, wraparound mortgage, land contract, and others must be interpreted. Courts are prone to look to the real estate industry to assign meaning to these technical terms.

Sometimes there is a conflict between provisions in the contract. To resolve the conflict, specific provisions will control over general provisions. In addition, handwritten provisions will take precedence over typewritten provisions, and typewritten provisions will prevail over printed-form provisions. Addendums will control over the body of the contract when portions are in conflict. Once again, these rules are intended to effectuate the intent of the parties. (See Figure 10.1.)

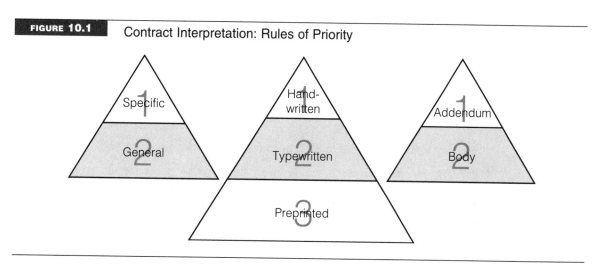

FIGURE 10.1 Contract Interpretation: Rules of Priority

■ ASSIGNMENT

■ *The present transfer of a property right from one person (the assignor) to another (the assignee).*

Rights to a contract may be transferred to a third party unless the contract prohibits assignment. A party who transfers this right is called an *assignor*. The third party who receives the right to title is called an *assignee*. An assignee succeeds to the rights that were previously vested in the assignor. The assignee of a right to receive a deed may ordinarily enforce that right against the seller.

CASE EXAMPLE
Walter and Thelma Terry entered into a contract to sell real property to William and Shirley Born, husband and wife. The Borns agreed to pay the purchase price in monthly installments over a specified period of years. A provision within the contract stated that the contract was "not assignable nor [could] the buyer convey the property without the seller's written consent." The Borns subsequently contracted to assign the contract to Rollins without the Terrys' consent. The Terrys commenced an action against the Borns seeking forfeiture of the contract. The appellate court held that the provisions prohibiting assignment were unreasonable restraints on trade unless necessary to protect the sellers' security. The case was returned to the trial court to determine whether the Terrys' security would be impaired by the Borns' conveyance to Rollins. *Terry v. Born*, 24 Wash. App. 652, 604 P.2d 504 (1979).

An assignee is bound to perform the obligations the assignor promised the seller, including payment of the purchase price. Failure to perform on the part of the assignee constitutes a breach of the agreement and results in liability for damages. An assignment does not ordinarily relieve the assignor from obligations under the contract. In the event that the assignee does not perform, the seller may hold the original purchaser (assignor) responsible to perform in accordance with the agreement.

The seller, as a party to an executory contract, has a right to receive the purchase price in accordance with the terms of the contract. The seller may assign the right to receive this purchase price. The same rules that apply to the assignment of a purchaser's rights apply to the assignment of a seller's rights.

■ BREACH OF CONTRACT

■ *The unexcused failure to perform an obligation under a contract.*

The failure of a purchaser to tender the purchase price for the property at the appointed time is one example of a **breach of contract.** Another example is the seller's failure to tender title to the purchaser at the appointed time. Any nonperformance of a term within the contract may give rise to a breach of that contract. The law provides remedies in the event of breach. This serves as an incentive to both parties to live up to the terms of the agreement.

Anticipatory Breach

■ *A breach of contract that occurs as a result of repudiating a contract before the due date for performance.*

It is not always necessary to await the day designated for performance to determine that a party is in breach. Sometimes an *anticipatory breach* occurs. To constitute an anticipatory breach, the nonperforming party must clearly communicate to the other party an intention not to perform. Or, an intention not to perform may be clearly determined from a party's behavior.

> **CASE EXAMPLE**
> R. Brower, a contractor, agreed to paint John Dooley's home for $2,500. Pursuant to the contract, the work was to begin August 1. Thereafter Brower informed Dooley that he was going out of business and asked him to find someone else to do the work. On July 15, Dooley learned from a reliable source that Brower went out of business, sold all of his equipment, and dishonored all of his existing contracts. Under such a circumstance, Dooley may treat Brower as in anticipatory breach of contract and immediately sue for damages.

Substantial Performance

■ *The degree of compliance under the terms of a contract that discharges a party from further obligation.*

The law recognizes that humans, frail as they are, cannot always perform certain contracts according to the exact specifications. In the area of building contracts, a contractor who builds a home and incurs minor deviations from the specifications may nonetheless have substantially complied with the contractual provisions. In such a case, the contractor will be entitled to the contract price less the cost to remedy the deviations to the property. If, for example, a contractor complies with all the specifications under a $60,000 building contract but fails to paint three out of 14 window panels, the contractor is entitled to $60,000 less the cost of having the window panels painted.

CASE EXAMPLE

Thomas Haverty Company entered into a contract with Jones whereby Haverty agreed to build and install plumbing, heating, and ventilation equipment in Jones's building for $27,332. The total cost of the building was $186,000. After completion, Jones refused to pay a balance of $10,123 to Haverty Company. Jones maintained that Haverty's performance was not in accord with the contract. The company sued Jones for the balance. The trial court held that Haverty's performance deviated from the contract specifications in 12 respects, that nine could be resolved at a cost of $99, that the remaining three defects could not be remedied without a greater expenditure than was justified, and that the damage to the building as a result of the three deviations amounted to $2,180. The court found that the deviations were made as a result of mistakes and misinterpretations. Finding that the contract had been substantially performed, the court awarded $7,844 ($10,123 minus $99 and $2,180) to Haverty Company. The appellate court affirmed the decision. *Thomas Haverty Co. v. Jones*, 185 Cal. 285, 197 P. 105 (1921).

There is no substantial performance if the utility of the property or its purpose is significantly thwarted by the contractor's deviation. If the specifications in the contract called for gas heating and the contractor installed oil heating instead, the deviation would amount to a breach, and the contractor would not ordinarily be entitled to any compensation. Some courts do, however, permit the contractor to recover the reasonable value of the services rendered and goods supplied where a substantial deviation is not willful. (See Table 10.6.)

Remedies for Breach of Contract

To be entitled to a remedy, a party must first show a readiness, willingness, and ability to perform the obligations under the contract. A seller must tender (offer) the deed and a buyer must tender the purchase price, unless it is clear from the circumstances that the tender would be fruitless. The common remedies enjoyed by each party in the event the other breaches the contract are specific performance, rescission, damages, and foreclosure. (See Table 10.7.)

■ **Specific Performance.** *A court decree mandating a party to perform according to the contract.*

Specific performance is ordinarily applicable to contracts involving a unique subject matter. Every parcel of real estate is considered unique and irreplaceable. Therefore, should the seller refuse performance, a court may award specific performance, requiring the seller to execute a deed in favor of the buyer. Refusal by the seller to comply with the decree may result in contempt of court and punishment. The court may also execute a deed in the buyer's favor, or, in the event of the seller's refusal to perform in accordance with the decree, the very court decree may be deemed to pass title to the

TABLE 10.6	Building Contractor's Recovery for Breach of Contract: Majority View		
Substantial Performance	Intentional deviation	No recovery
	Unintentional deviation	Contract price minus cost to remedy
Insubstantial Performance	Intentional deviation	No recovery
	Unintentional deviation	No recovery

TABLE 10.7	Remedies for Breach
	Specific Performance
	Rescission
	Compensatory Damages
	Liquidated Damages
	Foreclosure

buyer. In many jurisdictions, specific performance is also available to a seller against a defaulting buyer. A decree of specific performance in such a case compels the purchaser to pay the purchase price and accept title to the property.

A court will grant specific performance only if the party seeking it has "clean hands." When one of the parties has taken advantage of the other's unsound condition, for example, or has been guilty of fraud, the court will deny this equitable relief.

■ **Rescission.** *Cancellation of a contract that results in the parties being restored to the position they were in before the contract was made.*

A buyer, on a seller's default, may elect to *rescind* the contract. Under such a remedy, the seller must return to the buyer all payments received. The remedy is especially desirable for the buyer when the real estate has depreciated in value below the contract price. In the event the buyer is in breach of the contract, the seller may elect the remedy of **rescission**, thus restoring the parties to their original position.

Either party may seek rescission on grounds of fraud, innocent misrepresentation, mistake, duress, or undue influence. In addition, a contract may be rescinded by mutual consent of the parties.

■ **Damages.** *Money recoverable by one suffering a loss or injury due to breach of the contract.*

A buyer may, for example, incur actual **damages** when the seller breaches the obligation to tender the deed. The damages may be in the nature of the loss of the bargain. Translated into monetary terms, loss of the bargain is the difference between the market value of the property at the date set for closing and the contract price. That difference represents the value of damages to which the purchaser is entitled, assuming that the market value of the property at the time of breach is greater than the contract price. In addition, damages may include the deposit made by the purchaser and actual costs incurred incidental to the contract. Incidental expenses include attorney fees for handling the purchase transaction as well as the expense related to a title search.

CASE EXAMPLE

Joe Deal, seller, refused to tender his deed to John Tiehl, purchaser, on March 13, the date set for closing. The purchase price was $85,000. Tiehl additionally expended $500 for a title search of the property. The market value of the property was $90,000 on March 13. In an action by Tiehl against Deal for damages, Tiehl will be entitled to $5,500, computed as follows: $90,000 (market value) – $85,000 (contract price) = $5,000 + $500 (title search).

When the buyer breaches the contract, the seller is entitled to retain any deposit the buyer made and retain the real property. In the event the market value of the property falls in an amount greater than the deposit forfeited, the seller may also sue for damages. Damages in such a case are computed by deducting the market price from the purchase price minus any earnest money payment forfeited to the seller.

A court judgment for damages becomes a general lien on all real property a party owns (in the country where the judgment is recorded) until the judgment is satisfied. (This is discussed in greater detail in Chapter 15.) A judgment creditor may foreclose on the real property to satisfy the judgment. Other means of satisfying a judgment may include the attachment and sale of the debtor's personal property and garnishment of wages or monies in a bank account.

■ **Liquidated Damages.** *An amount of money stipulated in a contract that will be awarded in the case of a breach, which amounts are reasonably calculated to approximate the actual damages.*

Some real estate purchase contracts contain a **liquidated damages** clause that will state, for example, the per diem dollar award in the event of breach. The amount must be reasonably calculated to approximate the actual damages in the event of breach. It cannot be a penalty. For example, a buyer may be planning on moving out of an apartment on the day of the closing of a purchased house. In the event that the house does not close due to the breach by the seller, the buyer may have additional expenses, including storage and additional rentals. Hence, a liquidated damages clause might state that "in the event that the buyer may not be able to move into the house on the date of the closing due to the seller's breach, the seller shall be assessed an amount of $75 per day for every day after the closing date that the buyer is unable to move into the house." The clause will be upheld as long as the per diem amount is reasonably calculated to compensate for actual loss due to storage, rentals, and other losses. Otherwise it would be considered a penalty and not enforceable.

■ **Foreclosure.** *A legal process where a nonbreaching party can obtain possession of the real property and sell it to recover an amount due.*

The buyer of real property has equitable title to the property—the right to obtain ownership on payment of the purchase price. This right gives the buyer an equitable lien on the property securing the amount of money paid. Consequently, the buyer may foreclose on the property to recover the purchase payments in the event the seller breaches the contract. (Foreclosure is discussed in greater detail in Chapter 21.)

The seller possesses a lien for the unpaid purchase price on property that has passed to the buyer. The seller may foreclose on the property to satisfy this lien in the event the buyer fails to make timely payment.

■ DISCHARGE

■   *The release of contractual obligations.*

Parties who complete their obligations under a contract are discharged from any further performance. Normally, total performance is required before **discharge** occurs. Discharge may occur, however, after substantial performance (discussed earlier in this chapter). In addition, under certain circumstances parties may be discharged from their obligation to perform by operation of the parties or by operation of law. (See Table 10.8.)

Operation of the Parties

Parties to a contract may mutually agree to cancel a contract. Such an agreement results in a discharge. Or, the parties may agree to substitute another person's obligation to perform. This agreement to substitute indebtedness is called a *novation,* and it relieves the original obligor of any liability.

> **CASE EXAMPLE**
> Kerry is indebted to Ponce in the amount of $5,000. Ponce is indebted to Darin in the amount of $5,000. Kerry, Ponce, and Darin may agree that Ponce will release Kerry of the debt, Darin will release Ponce, and Kerry will pay $5,000 directly to Darin. (See Figure 10.2.)

Additionally, parties may agree to substitute a kind of performance that is different from that originally required under the contract. This agreement is called an *accord*, and the performance of the agreement is referred to as a *satisfaction*. An accord and satisfaction discharge a party from the original obligation.

TABLE 10.8	Discharge	
By Operation of the Parties	**By Operation of Law**	
Novation	Destruction of Subject Matter	
Accord and Satisfaction	Death of Party	
	Insanity	
	Intervening Illegality	
	Commercial Impracticality	

FIGURE 10.2	Novation

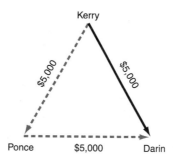

CASE EXAMPLE

Castor Andora was indebted to Andrea Hammer, a former employer, in the amount of $2,000. Hammer made a demand for the amount. Andora was out of work and did not have the money. He offered, however, to paint Hammer's house in lieu of the $2,000. Hammer agreed, and Andora, pursuant to the agreement, painted Hammer's house. This constitutes an accord and satisfaction. Andora is discharged of any further obligation to pay Hammer $2,000.

Operation of Law

Circumstances may occur that make it impossible or impractical for a party to fulfill obligations under a contract. Under these circumstances, the law will excuse the party from performance. Assume, for example, that Dante and Raymond enter into an agreement whereby Dante is to purchase Hellacre. Before closing, the house on Hellacre burns down. In most jurisdictions, in absence of a provision in the contract covering this event, the parties would be excused from performance because the *subject of the contract has been destroyed.*

Death of a party is not ordinarily an excuse for nonperformance of a contract. In the event a party dies, the representative of the estate will be required to complete performance. However, if the contract involves personal services, the rule is different. Assume, for example, that a carpenter agrees to build a tree house. Death of the carpenter will result in a discharge of obligations under the contract because of the personal nature of carpentry services. The same rule holds regarding *insanity of a party*. A party to a contract who is unable to complete a personal service contract due to insanity is excused from performance.

When a contract that was legal when entered into *becomes illegal*, the parties are discharged from performance. Suppose, for example, that a contractor enters into a contract with a shipper to transport specified building materials from a foreign country. Should the U.S. government issue an embargo forbidding the transport of goods from that foreign country, the parties will be discharged from their contractual obligations.

Finally, the law has evolved to recognize that certain contracts cannot be performed because it is *commercially impracticable* to do so. Some courts have discharged parties from their obligations in these types of cases. The impetus for this rule emanates from Section 2-615 of the Uniform Commercial Code, which reads in part:

> Delay in delivery or non-delivery in whole or in part by a seller . . . is not a breach of his duty under a contract for sale if performance as agreed has been made impracticable by the occurrence of a contingency the non-occurrence of which was a basic assumption on which the contract was made. . . .

Courts have not limited this doctrine to the traditional cases involving sale of goods, but have extended it to other cases as well.

CASE EXAMPLE

Northern Corporation entered into a contract with Chugach Electric Association. Under the contract, Northern was to install protective riprap on a dam located on Cooper Lake, Alaska, owned by Chugach. The work required that Northern transport rock and install it on the face of the dam.

The contract was silent as to the method for transporting the rock to the dam site. Apparently the parties contemplated that it would be transported across the frozen lake during the coming winter.

Attempts to haul the rock across the ice were frustrated by the unsafe condition of the ice. On one occasion two trucks broke through the ice, resulting in the drivers' deaths.

Northern ceased performance and sought a ruling discharging it from any further obligations under the contract. Chugach countersued, seeking damages for breach of contract. In upholding the trial court's ruling in favor of Northern, the Supreme Court of Alaska said:

> Under [the doctrine of commercial impracticality], a party is discharged from his contractual obligations, even if it is technically possible to perform them, if the cost of performance would be so disproportionate to that reasonably contemplated by the parties as to make the contract totally impractical in a commercial sense. . . .
>
> [The concept of commercial impracticality]—which finds expression both in case law and in other authorities—is predicated on the assumption that in legal contemplation something is impractical when it can only be done at an excessive and unreasonable cost. . . .
>
> There is ample evidence to support [the findings that] "the ice haul method of transporting riprap was within the contemplation of the parties and was part of the basis of the agreement which ultimately resulted in the contract amendment," and that that method was not commercially feasible within the financial parameters of the contract. . . .

Northern Corporation v. Chugach Electric Association, 518 P.2d 76 (Alaska 1974).

THE CHANGING LANDSCAPE

The ancient law of contracts required that parties to a contract enter into an agreement supported by essentially equal consideration. The courts would actually scrutinize the contract to determine whether there was adequate consideration—mutual promises of equal value. The courts were paternalistic and would protect a party who did not get a fair bargain.

In this country at the outset of the Industrial Revolution, U.S. courts were prone to give parties the freedom to contract without the judicial scrutiny of the past. Influenced by the need to permit industry to grow and recoup its sunken costs, they shifted to a buyer-beware mode. No longer did the courts require adequate consideration. They demanded only sufficient consideration, defined as some detriment to the promisee.

Sometime during the twentieth century, the tide began to change and once again the courts started scrutinizing contracts, although not so much in the area of adequacy of consideration. The focus was on the equality of bargaining position, not solely the disparity of the values of the respective bargains. Following the lead of the unconscionability provisions in the Uniform Commercial Code (UCC), common-law decisions struck down contracts based on this doctrine of unconscionability. One author was inclined to declare contract law (as we knew it) dead, because freedom of contract was no longer the rule of the day but, instead, had been replaced by a "fairness doctrine." Also, consumer statutes and regulations were passed at the state and federal levels to equalize the bargaining position of consumers.

As we proceed into the twenty-first century, it will be interesting to see whether contract law application reflects a return to "freedom of contract" or continues in a more consumer-oriented fashion—or whether it takes an entirely different turn. As you look at the economy and the signs of the times, what is your best guess—freedom of contract or greater scrutiny to ensure fairness or some other trend? Explain.

■ KEY TERMS

■ INTERNET RESOURCES

Good indexes of contract law and commercial law are found at:

http://profs.lp.findlaw.com/contracts/index.html

www.hg.org/commerc.html

■ REVIEW AND DISCUSSION QUESTIONS

1. (a) Which agreements will a court enforce? (b) Which agreements will a court not enforce? (c) Why?

2. Name five elements of a contract and define each.

3. Explain the rationale behind the objective test of contract formation.

4. Give an example of when the doctrine of promissory estoppel will be applied.

5. When does a breach of contract occur?

6. (a) Explain the remedies available to a buyer when the seller breaches the contract for the sale of real property. (b) Explain the remedies available to the seller in the event of the buyer's breach.

7. What are the ways in which parties to a contract may be discharged from their obligation to perform by operation of the parties? By operation of law?

■ CASE PROBLEMS

1. Burns and Pugmire entered into a contract for the sale and purchase of real estate. The contract stated that the purchase price was $79,500, to be paid in installments of $675 per month, including taxes and insurance for the contract "period remaining, or until buyer elects to refinance." The contract was silent as to the closing date, which party was to pay closing costs, and when transfer of title and delivery of a deed would take place. Is this agreement sufficiently definite and certain? Explain. *Burns v. Pugmire*, 194 Ga. App. 898, 392 S.E.2d 62 (1990).

2. The Bakers made a written offer to purchase Nelson's home. Nelson was unhappy with the downpayment provision and formulated an addendum that was added to the Bakers' original offer and returned to them. The Bakers signed it. Nelson then purported to accept the Bakers' offer by sending a mailgram to the Bakers that included financing terms that varied from those found in the original offer and also introduced additional terms relating to the fixtures and appliances. After receipt, the Bakers withdrew from the transaction in writing. Nelson maintains that there is a contract. Do you agree? Explain. *Nelson v. Baker*, 776 S.W.2d 52 (Mo. Ct. App. 1990).

3. On November 27, 1937, Morrison, seeking to purchase a tract of land from Thoelke, executed and mailed Thoelke a contract for the sale of the property. On the same day, Thoelke signed the contract and placed it in the mail, addressed to Morrison's agent. After mailing the contract, but before Morrison's agent received it, Thoelke called the agent and repudiated the contract for the sale of the land. (a) Was Thoelke's call an effective rejection of Morrison's offer? See *Morrison v. Thoelke*, 155 So. 2d 889 (Fla. Dist. Ct. App. 1963). (b) What would be the result if Thoelke died after mailing his acceptance and his executor (representative of the estate) refused to honor the agreement? (c) What if Morrison died after mailing the offer and Thoelke accepted the offer before learning of Morrison's death?

4. Hazel Miller listed her real estate for sale with a local real estate agent. Michael Normile and Wawie Kurniawan signed a written offer to purchase the property. The offer stated that "this offer must be accepted on or before 5:00 P.M. August 5, 1980." Miller signed and returned the offer with several changes, including an increase in the deposit from $100 to $500 and an increase in the downpayment from $875 to $1,000. Normile and Kurniawan neither accepted nor rejected the new terms. At 12:30 A.M. on August 5, Segal signed an offer to purchase the property, which was accepted the same day at 2:00 P.M. The agent then informed Normile that Miller had revoked her counteroffer. Before 5:00 P.M. on the same day, Normile and Kurniawan accepted the counteroffer. Who owns the property and why? *Normile v. Miller*, 326 S.E.2d 11 (N.C. 1985).

5. Miss Roland, owner of a parcel of land, leased it to Mr. Kent for a term of five years. A second agreement between the parties granted Kent an option to extend the lease for another four years if Kent undertook to make about $10,000 of improvements to the property. Kent engaged and paid an architect to study the property and suggest possible improvements. Roland died after the architect completed his sketches but before the construction of any of the contemplated improvements. Roland's executor sought to set aside the option contract on the grounds that it was a mere offer unsupported by consideration and was therefore revoked by the death of Roland. (a) Does the payment of the architect's fee qualify as good consideration? Discuss. See *Bard v. Kent*, 19 Cal. 2d 449, 122 P.2d 8 (1942). (b) Assuming that there is no consideration, what doctrine may aid Kent? Explain.

6. In 1991, the Neuhoffs purchased and installed 60 windows manufactured by Marvin. Three years later, the Neuhoffs noticed that many of the windows were decaying and notified the contractor who had installed the windows of the decay. In March 1998, Marvin sent the Neuhoffs a letter offering to replace 33 of the windows for free. Several weeks later, Marvin's agent orally informed the Neuhoffs that the remaining windows would also be replaced gratis. Marvin did replace 33 windows for free, but refused to replace the remainder of the decaying windows. The Neuhoffs sued him for breach of contract. Marvin argues that no contract to replace the windows was ever formed because the Neuhoffs never provided any consideration to support his promise; the Neuhoffs maintained they did. Who is correct? Explain. See *Neuhoff v. Marvin Lumber & Cedar Co.*, 370 F.3d 197 (1st Cir. 2004).

7. Plaintiff entered into an agreement with defendant whereby plaintiff agreed to construct a country house for defendant, who in return agreed to pay plaintiff for his work. A proviso of the agreement stated that Reading pipe was to be used in the plumbing system of the house. Plaintiff completed the house, yet through inattention installed Cohoes pipe, a different brand of pipe though one of substantially similar quality to Reading pipe. Defendant now refuses to pay plaintiff the balance of the contract price unless he replaces all the Cohoes pipe in the house with Reading. Defendant's demand would involve the demolition and reconstruction of a major portion of the house. (a) What doctrine, if any, may plaintiff rely on to force defendant to pay for the work "as is"? (b) Would the result be different if Reading pipe were found to be of significantly higher quality than the Cohoes pipe? Explain. See *Jacob & Youngs, Inc. v. Kent*, 230 N.Y. 239, 129 N.E. 889 (1921).

8. Carmen Ruggerio contracted to sell 10.24 acres of industrial land for $38,912 to Tanners Realty. The sale was conditioned on Tanners' ability to obtain financing. The agreement provided that Ruggerio would convey good marketable title to said premises, except for utility easements. In addition to utility easements, a search of the title revealed a railroad easement on the property. (a) What remedies are available to Tanners Realty? (b) What would it have to prove in order to prevail? *Tanners Realty Corporation v. Ruggerio*, 490 N.Y.S.2d 73 (App. Div. 1985).

9. Taylor and Caldwell entered into an agreement whereby Taylor was to receive the use of Caldwell's concert hall for four days. Before Taylor had an opportunity to use the hall, it was completely destroyed by fire, rendering its use impossible. (a) Can Taylor recover against Caldwell for damages sustained as a result of being deprived of the use of the concert hall? Explain. See *Taylor v. Caldwell*, 122 Eng. Rep. 309 (1863). (b) Would the result be different if Caldwell owned two halls and only one were destroyed? Explain.

Real Estate
Purchase Contract

■ REAL ESTATE PURCHASE CONTRACT

■ *An agreement whereby a seller promises to sell an interest in realty by conveying a deed to the designated estate for which a buyer promises to pay a specified purchase price.*

Generally, contracts need not be in writing to be enforceable. **Real estate purchase contracts**, however, fall within a unique class of contracts that necessitate a writing. They are governed by the Statute of Frauds.

Statute of Frauds

■ *A statute that necessitates that certain contracts, to be enforceable, must be supported by a written memorandum signed by the party against whom enforcement is sought.*

The British Parliament enacted the Statute for Prevention of Frauds and Perjuries in 1677. This statute modified the common law that enforced oral contracts for the sale of real estate. The **Statute of Frauds** was intended to protect against fraud and perjury. Prior to passage of the Statute of Frauds, it was not uncommon for a person to pay witnesses to fabricate testimony to support a nonexistent oral contract for the sale of realty. Section 4 of the Statute required that a contract for the sale of an interest in land be in writing, or supported by a written memorandum, and signed by the party against whom enforcement was sought. Nearly every state has modeled its version of a statute of frauds after the English statute. The Ohio statute, for example, reads, in part:

> No lease, estate, or interest, either of freehold or term of years, in lands . . . shall be assigned or granted except by deed, or note in writing, signed by the party assigning or granting it, or his agent thereto lawfully authorized. . . .

CASE EXAMPLE
Wayne Gibbens and Mark Hardin entered into a joint effort to purchase three parcels of real estate. A purchase offer of $2.4 million for the property was accepted. Gibbens claimed that there was an oral agreement that required that Hardin make a 3.075-acre boundary adjustment to the property in favor of Gibbens. Gibbens would receive the two houses located on Parcel #3 and an easement of access to one of the houses. Hardin denied this. The Supreme Court of Virginia found "[t]he alleged oral boundary agreement . . . unenforceable because it fails to comply with Virginia's statute of frauds." *Gibbens v. Hardin*, 389 S.E.2d 478 (Va. 1990).

■ **Memorandum.** *A writing that contains essential terms in satisfaction of the statute of frauds.*

Normally, the entire agreement of the parties—the real estate purchase contract—is reduced to writing. This writing will, of course, satisfy the **memorandum** requirement of the Statute of Frauds. The entire agreement of the parties need not be in writing, however, to satisfy the Statute of Frauds. The Statute requires only a written memorandum, which must ordinarily contain:

■ the names of the parties to the contract,

■ a description of the property,

■ the purchase price,

■ other essential terms and conditions of the sale, and

■ the signature of the party against whom enforcement is sought. (A few states also require the signature of the party seeking to enforce the transaction.)

The memorandum may be prepared anytime before suit on the contract is commenced. Loss or destruction of the memorandum does not render the contract unenforceable. In such a case, the existence of the memorandum may be proved by witnesses or other documents. The memorandum need not be contained within one instrument. It may be gleaned from a series of related writings, such as letters or faxes. The next case illustrates that an ordinary check may satisfy the statute.

Clark v. Larkin
Supreme Court of Kansas
172 Kan. 284, 239 P.2d 970 (1952)

Background. Plaintiffs, Clark and Musser, are residents of Hutchinson and Kansas City, Missouri, respectively. Defendant is a resident of Wichita. Plaintiffs were the owners of and were in possession of six lots, known as 405 East A, in the city of Hutchinson. The property was a well-improved tract on a corner of the intersection of Avenue A and Elm Street. Plaintiffs advertised the property for sale and had placed it in the hands of Scott Clark, husband of one of the plaintiffs, with oral authority to sell. Defendant came to Hutchinson for the express purpose of purchasing a residence property, and, through a mutual acquaintance, contacted Scott Clark. Clark and defendant then went to the property, at which time defendant made a careful inspection, including the improvements. They agreed on a purchase price of $17,000—$1,000 to be paid down, $7,000 to be paid on approval of abstract of title, and the balance of $9,000 to be paid in five years with interest at the rate of 5 percent per annum. At the suggestion of defendant, he and Clark then went to the latter's office for the purpose of consummating the agreement of purchase and sale. Defendant produced his checkbook on The Security Bank of Blackwell, Oklahoma, and requested that Clark make out a check for the downpayment. Clark did as requested, and defendant signed the check and delivered it to Clark. This check, including notations on it, a copy of which was attached to the amended petition as an exhibit, is as follows:

No, 45

Blackwell, Oklahoma, Mar. 31, 1950

Pay to the Order of Opal F. Clark $1,000

One Thousand & no/100 DOLLARS

To apply on 405 East 'A' at $ 17,000.00 . . .

$7,000.00 to be paid on approval of abstract &

$9,000.00 to be paid in 5 years at 5%.

Jon. P. Larkin

To The Security Bank

Blackwell, Oklahoma

Plaintiffs, in due course of business, deposited the check, properly endorsed, with a bank in Hutchinson. In the meantime defendant caused payment of the check by the Blackwell bank to be stopped. On inquiry as to the reason therefor he advised plaintiffs that due to his wife's request and insistence he was refusing to go through with the deal.

Plaintiff sued. The trial court denied defendant's motion to dismiss for failure to comply with the statute of frauds.

Decision. The Kansas Supreme Court affirmed.

Justice Price. In this court defendant contends, as he did in the court below, that the memorandum [check] is too indefinite and uncertain to take the alleged oral agreement for the sale of the property out of the statute of frauds[,] the pertinent portions of which read as follows:

"No action shall be brought whereby to charge a party on . . . any contract for the sale of lands, tenements, or hereditaments, or any interest in or concerning them . . . unless the agreement on which such action shall be brought, or some memorandum or note thereof, shall be in writing and signed by the party to be charged therewith... ."

The general rule as to the sufficiency of a written memorandum to meet the requirement of the statute is as follows:

"Generally speaking, a memorandum in writing meets the requirements of the statute of frauds that certain contracts shall be evidenced by writing if it contains the names of the parties, the terms and conditions of the contract, and a description of the property sufficient to render it capable of identification."

On the question whether a check may constitute a sufficient memorandum under the statute . . . a check, given in connection with the sale of lands, bearing notations or references to papers or matters which, by the rules of contract and evidence, may properly be deemed a part thereof, and which contains the essential terms of the contract of sale, is sufficient.

In the nature of things and in the light of common, everyday business dealings, the check and notations on it clearly indicate that defendant, as maker, was purchasing from payee, as owner, certain real estate described as "405 East 'A'," for the sum of $17,000; that the amount of the check ($1,000) was a down payment; that the sum of $7,000 was to be paid on approval of the abstract of title; and that the balance of $9,000 was to be paid in five years with interest on such latter sum at the rate of 5 percent. The names of the parties, as payee and maker of the check, are thus designated as seller and purchaser, respectively, with no uncertainty. There is nothing left to conjecture or speculation with respect to the purchase price, the amount being paid down, or as to when the balance of $16,000 was to be paid. To place any other construction on the instrument would do violence to the plain and ordinary meaning of the very language used.

Defendant strenuously argues that the location and identity of the property are not given with reasonable certainty, and that on account of the check being given on a Blackwell, Oklahoma, bank it is logical to assume the property is located in that city. It is true that nowhere on the check and its notation is the location of the property, as to city, county or state, listed.

On the other hand, it is to be remembered that by the allegations of the amended petition the

continued on next page

property is specifically described as being located on a corner of the intersection of Avenue A and Elm Street in the city of Hutchinson, known as 405 East A. It is further alleged that it was the only real estate owned by plaintiffs known and described as 405 East A; that it was the only tract with that description placed for sale with Scott Clark, and that defendant personally inspected the same.

We think that under the above rules there can be no question but that the description of the property as "405 East A" is sufficient to satisfy the statute. It cannot be said defendant is being in any way misled by the use of that description. He knew exactly the property for which he was bargaining, and that it was the property described by its street address on the check. The statute of frauds was enacted to prevent fraud and injustice, not to foster or encourage it, and courts will, so far as possible, refuse to allow it to be used as a shield to protect fraud and as a means to enable one to take advantage of his own wrong.

Holding as we do, that the memorandum in question is a sufficient compliance with the statute of frauds, the court did not err in [failing to dismiss the plaintiff's Complaint] and its ruling is therefore . . .

Affirmed.

Would there be a different result if the seller owned other real estate in a different city? Explain.

The best way to ensure compliance with the Statute of Frauds is to require that all parties sign the real estate purchase contract. Although the entire agreement of the parties need not be reduced to writing, as a practical matter it is best to do so. This prevents uncertainty and provides a controlling document to resolve disputes.

Part Performance. There are certain exceptions to compliance with the Statute of Frauds. The most notable exception is the doctrine of *part performance.* There are various views as to what constitutes an act of part performance sufficient to remove a contract from the Statute of Frauds so that a writing will not be required. Some courts take the position that part performance is satisfied if a purchaser takes possession of the property pursuant to an oral contract. Other courts require both possession and payment of the purchase price to prevent the seller from successfully raising the defense of the statute. Still others require that possession be accompanied by a substantial improvement to the property. Finally, other jurisdictions limit the scope of the doctrine of part performance by requiring payment of the purchase price, the purchaser's possession, and a change of position in reliance on the contract that would result in irreparable harm unless the contract were enforced.

CASE EXAMPLE

Brown entered into an oral contract to purchase a farm from Burnside. Brown took possession of the farm, made several improvements, tore down an old farmhouse, paid taxes, and made payments on the purchase price. Burnside thereafter refused to deed the farm to Brown. Brown sought specific performance of the contract. The court held for Brown on the theory that the Statute of Frauds does not apply when there has been partial or complete performance, as there was under these circumstances. *Brown v. Burnside*, 94 Idaho 363, 487 P.2d 957 (1972).

Parol Evidence

■ *Oral or other evidence extraneous to the written instrument.*

Parol evidence is not admissible for the purpose of varying or contradicting the terms of a contract. However, parol evidence is permissible if

■ it is consistent with the writings of the parties;

■ its purpose is to clarify ambiguous terms in the contract or prove that the writing was induced by fraud, illegality, duress, undue influence, or mistake;

■ it is a subsequent agreement that alters the previous writings.

CASE EXAMPLE
Jim Hutchins and Jerry Bolen enter into a real estate contract for the sale of Hutchins's property. Afterward, they enter into a contract canceling the prior real estate contract. The introduction into evidence of the new contract containing the cancellation does not violate the parol evidence rule because it was entered into after the purchase contract.

Brokers' Authority

Many localities use preprinted purchase contract forms that have been approved by the local bar association and/or association of real estate brokers. The provisions within these form contracts are designed to reflect the practices within the locality. Normally, the broker assists the parties in filling in the blanks in such a contract, including the names of the parties, a description of the property, the price, and other terms. A standard real estate purchase contract is shown in Figure 11.1. Sometimes, it is necessary to delete certain inapplicable provisions from the form. Often, lengthy additions are necessitated by the particular nature of the transaction. To what extent a broker may prepare a purchase contract without engaging in the offense of unauthorized practice of law differs from state to state. Some states prevent a broker from drafting a purchase contract because that act constitutes the practice of law. Other states permit such brokerage activity on the theory that it is normally incident to the practice of a broker's profession. Although most states permit brokers to fill in the blanks, there is often a thin line between filling in the blanks and unlawful drafting.

Cultum v. Heritage House Realtors, Inc.
Supreme Court of Washington
694 P.2d 630 (Wash. 1985)

Background. Yvonne Ramey, a real estate agent for Heritage House Realtors, Inc. (Heritage), prepared a real estate purchase contract (earnest money agreement), setting forth Cultum's offer to purchase Smith's home. The agreement was prepared on standard forms drafted by attorneys. Ramey filled in the blanks and also prepared an

continued on next page

addendum, which stated: "This offer is contingent on a Satisfactory Structural Inspection, to be completed by Aug. 20. . . . " The Smiths accepted the offer. Based on the inspection report, Cultum found the condition of the house unsatisfactory. He demanded return of a $3,000 deposit. Heritage refunded the money and Cultum sued Heritage for loss of use of the money during the period Heritage held it, and sought a permanent injunction restraining Heritage from engaging in the practice of law.

Decision. The trial court found in favor of Cultum, holding that Heritage engaged in the unauthorized practice of law and it granted damages and permanently enjoined Heritage from "completing, filling in the blanks, or otherwise preparing any clause with respect to any real estate purchase or sale agreement. . . ." The Supreme Court of Washington affirmed the damage award but found that Heritage was not engaged in the unauthorized practice of law.

Justice Pearson. At issue in this appeal is whether the completion by a real estate salesperson of a form earnest money agreement containing a contingency clause constitutes the unauthorized practice of law. . . .

* * *

A]lthough the completion of form earnest money agreements might be commonly understood as the practice of law, we believe it is in the public interest to permit licensed real estate brokers and salespersons to complete such lawyer prepared standard form agreements; provided, that in doing so they comply with the standard of care demanded of an attorney.

For a long time suppression of the practice of law by nonlawyers has been proclaimed to be in the public interest, a necessary protection against incompetence, divided loyalties, and other evils. It is now clear, however, as several other courts have concluded, that there are other important interests involved. These interests include:

(1) The ready availability of legal services.

(2) Using the full range of services that other professions and businesses can provide.
(3) Limiting costs.
(4) Public convenience.
(5) Allowing licensed brokers and salespersons to participate in an activity in which they have special training and expertise.
(6) The interest of brokers and salespersons in drafting form earnest money agreements which are incidental and necessary to the main business of brokers and salespersons.

We no longer believe that the supposed benefit to the public from the lawyers' monopoly on performing legal services justifies limiting the public's freedom of choice. The public has the right to use the full range of services that brokers and salespersons can provide. The fact that brokers will complete these forms at no extra charge, whereas attorneys would charge an additional fee, weighs heavily toward allowing this choice.

Another important consideration is the fact that the drafting of form earnest money agreements is incidental to the main business of real estate brokers and salespersons. These individuals are specially trained to provide buyers and sellers with competent and efficient assistance in purchasing or selling a home. Because the selection and filling in of standard simple forms by brokers and salespersons is an incidental service, it normally must be rendered before such individuals can receive their commissions. Clearly the advantages, if any, to be derived by enjoining brokers and salespersons from completing earnest money agreements are outweighed by the fact that such conveyances are part of the everyday business of the realtor and necessary to the effective completion of such business.

The interest of protecting the public must also be balanced against the inconveniences caused by enjoining licensed brokers and salespersons from completing form earnest money agreements. Although lawyers are also competent to handle these transactions, lawyers may not always be available at the odd hours that these transactions tend to take place. . . .

In a few instances earnest money agreements may be complicated and one or both parties may realize the need for a lawyer to prepare the contract rather than use a standardized form. In fact, if a broker or salesperson believes there may be complicated legal issues involved, he or she should persuade the parties to seek legal advice. More often, however, these transactions are simple enough so that standardized forms will suffice and the parties will wish to avoid further delay or expense by using them.

It should be emphasized that the holding in this case is limited in scope. Our decision provides that a real estate broker or salesperson is permitted to complete simple printed standardized real estate forms . . . approved by a lawyer. . . . These forms shall not be used for other than simple real estate transactions actually handled by such broker . . . or salesperson and then without charge for the simple service of completing the forms.

The trial court awarded Cultum damages . . . representing the interest lost during the time that Heritage retained her earnest money. If a real estate broker fails to exercise reasonable care and skill, the real estate broker is liable to the client for damages resulting from such failure. Based on this rule and our conclusion that Ramey failed to exercise the reasonable care and skill of a practicing attorney, we affirm the trial court's award of damages. . . .

Affirmed in Part and Reversed in Part.

A broker should exercise caution when rendering advice to a party or giving detailed explanation of the terms of the contract; these activities may be deemed the unauthorized practice of law.

Assume that the real estate broker who had a contracts course in college added one new page of terms to the form contract. Do you think that there would be a different result? Explain.

■ PROVISIONS OF THE REAL ESTATE PURCHASE CONTRACT

It is important to note that, in addition to the essential elements of a basic contract—offer, acceptance, consideration, capacity, lawful purpose—there are major provisions peculiar to a real estate purchase contract. (See Table 11.1.) Some of these provisions included within the real estate purchase agreement are there to satisfy the Statute of Frauds. Others are present to clarify the details of the agreement. Common real estate contract provisions include the date, the names of parties, and other elements presented on the following pages. Figure 11.1 is an example of a typical real estate purchase contract, and may be referred to in conjunction with this discussion concerning provisions of the real estate purchase contract.

Date

A purchase contract comes into being when the purchase offer is accepted. The contract should be dated. The date may appear at the beginning or the end of the contract, or in both places. Failure to include the date does not render the contract unenforceable. However, the question of the date of the signing may arise in several situations. The contract may contain provisions that require the happening of events by reference to the date the contract came into existence. For example, a clause within a contract might

TABLE 11.1	Provisions of the Real Estate Purchase Contract

- Date
- Parties
- Property Description
- Price
- Contingency Clause
- Possession
- Evidence of Title
- Form of Deed
- Proration
- Property Inspection
- Home Warranty Plan
- Earnest Money
- Proper Execution

read, "Buyer shall obtain financing within 30 days of the signing of this contract." In some instances, the statute of limitations may begin to run on the date the contract was signed. The statute of limitations is the time period within which one must sue or be barred from recovery. Some states require that a suit for breach of a written contract be commenced within six years of the signing of the contract, while other states permit a longer period of time.

Parties

To satisfy the Statute of Frauds, the names of the parties must be included within the writing. Care should be taken to ensure that the names of the buyer and seller are accurate. An attorney who later draws up the deed may derive the names to insert in the deed from the contract. Accurate spelling prevents problems at a later date when a title search may otherwise uncover discrepancies.

The marital status of the seller should be included; if the seller is married, then the spouse should be named as well. A seller's spouse possesses certain legal rights that must be relinquished by signature for the buyer to be assured a good title. For this reason, the spouse should sign the contract.

There may be more than one seller or buyer. All parties should be named. When there are multiple buyers, it is essential to include a statement of the type and fraction of ownership interest each will receive.

FIGURE 11.1   Real Estate Purchase Contract

This document has been prepared by the Columbus Board of REALTORS® and the Columbus Bar Association and is for the use of their members only.
Columbus Board of REALTORS ® and the Columbus Bar Association © Copyright 2005.

The CBR/CBA purchase contract shall be printed in 11 point Arial font, and all deviations in the standard form must be printed in `12 point or larger courier font in bold.` Use of `courier font in bold` denotes deviation from the standard CBR/CBA purchase contract. All deletions from the standard form are to be noted by "strike-out".

Agent _____

Company _____

Address _____

City _____ State _____ Zip _____

Real Estate Purchase Contract
It is recommended that all parties be represented by a
REALTOR® and an Attorney

Date: _____

The undersigned Buyer agrees to buy and the undersigned Seller agrees to sell, through the Broker referred to below, upon the following terms, the premises located in the State of Ohio, County of _____, tax parcel no. _____ described as:

1. Terms:

1.1 Purchase price shall be $ _____
_____.

1.2 Lender Pre-Approval:

Buyer shall deliver a written lender's pre-approval letter for said premises, to the Seller and/or Seller's Broker, within _____ (not applicable if the number of days is not inserted) calendar days after written acceptance of this contract. The lender's pre-approval letter shall state that the Buyer's credit report has been reviewed and all information provided meets lender's guidelines necessary for approval, subject to an appraisal, standard qualifications and final underwriting approval.

The Buyer's delivery of said lender's pre-approval letter is confirmation that the Buyer has made loan application and that the loan terms are acceptable to the Buyer.

If the Buyer does not deliver a copy of the lender's pre-approval letter to the Seller and/or Seller's Broker within the stated time period, this contract shall terminate and the earnest money deposit shall be returned to the Buyer pursuant to paragraph 10.

1.3 Loan Commitment:

The Buyer's obligations are contingent upon the Buyer obtaining a (write in type of loan: Conventional, FHA, VA) _____ loan commitment within _____ (not applicable if the number of days is not inserted) calendar days after written acceptance of this contract. Within the stated time period, the Buyer shall deliver to the Seller and/or Seller's Broker a written notification from the Buyer's lender that the loan commitment has been obtained. The delivery of the written notification to the Seller and/or Seller's Broker that a loan commitment has been obtained shall satisfy this contingency.

If, at the expiration of the stated time period, the Buyer has not delivered the written notification referenced above, or has not waived this contingency in writing, this contract shall terminate and the earnest money deposit shall be returned to the Buyer pursuant to paragraph 10.

1.4 Additional Terms and Conditions:

FIGURE 11.1	Real Estate Purchase Contract *(cont'd)*

Premises Address:_____ page 2 of 8

2. Taxes and Assessments:

2.1 At closing, Seller shall pay or credit on purchase price: (a) all delinquent taxes, including penalty and interest; (b) all assessments which are a lien on the premises as of the date of the contract; (c) all agricultural use tax recoupments for years prior to the year of closing; (d) all other unpaid real estate taxes and community development charges imposed pursuant to Chapter 349 of the Ohio Revised Code which are a lien for years prior to closing and a portion of such taxes and community development charges for the year of closing shall be prorated through the date of closing, based on a 365 day year and, if undetermined, on the most recent available tax rate and valuation, giving effect to applicable exemptions, recently voted millage, change in valuation, etc., whether or not certified. These adjustments shall be final, except for the following: (none if nothing inserted) _____.

2.2 The community development charge, if any, applicable to the premises was created by a covenant in an instrument recorded at (insert county) _____ , Vol. _____ , Page number _____ or Instrument number_____. **(Note: If the foregoing blanks are not filled in and a community development charge affects the premises, this contract may not be enforceable by the Seller or binding upon the Buyer pursuant to Section 349.07 of the Ohio Revised Code.)**

2.3 Buyer and Seller understand that real estate taxes and assessments are subject to retroactive change by the governmental authority. The real estate taxes for the premises, for the current year, may change as a result of the transfer of the premises or as a result of a change in the tax rate.

2.4 Seller warrants that no improvements or services (site or area) have been installed or furnished, nor notification received from public authority or owner's association of future improvements of which any part of the costs may be assessed against the premises, except the following: (none if nothing inserted)

3. Fixtures and Equipment:

3.1 The consideration shall include any fixtures, including but not limited to: built-in appliances; heating, central air conditioning, and humidifying equipment and their control apparatus; stationary tubs; pumps; water softening equipment (unless leased); roof antennae; attached wall-to-wall carpeting and attached floor coverings; curtain rods and window coverings (excluding draperies and curtains); attached mirrors; all light fixtures; bathroom, lavatory and kitchen fixtures; storm and screen doors and windows, awnings, blinds and window air conditioners, whether now in or on the premises or in storage; garage door openers and controls; attached fireplace equipment; security systems and controls (unless leased); smoke alarms, satellite TV reception system and components; all exterior plants and trees, all landscaping lights and controls; and the following:

3.2 The following shall be excluded: (none if nothing inserted)

4. Inspections And Tests:

4.1 The Broker strongly recommends that the Buyer conduct inspections and/or tests. The Buyer and the Seller understand and agree that the Broker neither warrants nor assumes responsibility for the physical condition of the premises.

Buyer shall be responsible for the repair of any damages caused by the Buyer's inspections and tests; which repairs shall be completed in a timely and workmanlike manner at Buyer's expense.

4.2 Seller shall cooperate in making the premises reasonably available for inspections and/or tests.

FIGURE **11.1**   Real Estate Purchase Contract *(cont'd)*

Premises Address:_____ page 3 of 8

4.3 Specified Inspection Period: Buyer shall have_____ (not applicable if the number of days is not inserted) calendar days after the date of written acceptance of the contract by both parties to have inspections, environmental inspections and/or tests completed. This time period shall be known as the Specified Inspection Period. The number of days for the Specified Inspection Period is a specific time frame agreed upon by the Seller and the Buyer. The number of days cannot be modified or waived except by a written agreement signed by both parties.

All requests to remedy shall be submitted to the Seller or Seller's Broker within the Specified Inspection Period. Time is of the essence in completing any of the inspections, tests and/or reports.

The Buyer, at Buyer's expense, shall have the right to have any and all inspections, tests and/or reports conducted, including but not limited to:

a. Confirmation of the insurability of the premises with an insurance company of the Buyer's choice.
b. Inspection of the premises and all improvements, fixtures and equipment.
c. A pest inspection for termite and wood destroying insects with a report provided on a FHA/VA approved form by a licensed Ohio Certified Pest (Termite) Control Applicator.
d. Inspection of the gas lines on the premises.
e. Inspection of the waste treatment systems and/or well systems by a local health authority or state EPA approved laboratory of the Buyer's choice.
f. Inspection or testing for mold, radon and any other environmental test.
g. A lead-based paint inspection and test.

With respect to housing constructed prior to January 1, 1978, the Buyer must be provided with the pamphlet entitled "Protect Your Family from Lead in Your Home" and the "Lead-Based Paint and Lead-Based Hazard Disclosure Form." Every Buyer of any interest in residential real property on which a residential dwelling was built prior to 1978 is notified that such property may present exposure to lead from lead-based paint that may place young children at risk of developing lead poisoning.

Lead poisoning in young children may produce permanent neurological damage including learning disability, reduced intelligence quotient, behavioral problems and impaired memory. Lead poisoning also poses a particular risk to pregnant women. The Seller of any interest in residential real property is required to provide the Buyer with any information on lead-based paint hazards from risk assessments or inspections in the Seller's possession and notify the Buyer of any known lead-based paint hazards. A risk assessment or inspection for possible lead-based paint hazards is recommended prior to purchase.

4.4 If the Buyer **is not**, in good faith, satisfied with the condition of the premises as disclosed by the Buyer's inspections, tests and/or reports provided for in paragraph 4.3, then the Buyer may elect to proceed under one of the following provisions, 4.4(a) or 4.4(b):

4.4(a) Agreement to Remedy Period: On or before the end of the Specified Inspection Period, the Buyer shall deliver to the Seller or the Seller's Broker, a written request to remedy, signed by the Buyer, stating the unsatisfactory conditions, along with a written copy of the inspections, tests and/or reports, specifying the unsatisfactory conditions.

The Buyer and Seller shall have_____calendar days, **after the end of the Specified Inspection Period**, to reach a written agreement regarding remedying the unsatisfactory conditions. This time period shall be known as the Agreement to Remedy Period. The number of days for the Agreement To Remedy Period is a specific time frame agreed upon by the Seller and the Buyer. The number of days cannot be modified or waived except by a written agreement signed by both parties. In the event the Buyer and Seller do **not** reach a written agreement regarding remedying the unsatisfactory conditions within the Agreement to Remedy Period, and the Buyer and Seller have **not** executed a written extension

FIGURE 11.1   Real Estate Purchase Contract *(cont'd)*

Premises Address:_____ page 4 of 8

of the Agreement to Remedy Period, this contract shall terminate. Upon termination of the contract under this provision, the earnest money deposit shall be returned to the Buyer pursuant to paragraph 10.

OR

Prior to the end of the Agreement to Remedy Period, the Buyer can waive such request to remedy, in writing, and proceed with the contract.

The commencement of the Agreement to Remedy Period does not obligate the Seller to reach an agreement with the Buyer.

The delivery by the Buyer of a written request to remedy any unsatisfactory conditions does not preclude the Buyer from later delivering a notice of termination as contemplated by paragraph 4.4(b) below during the Agreement to Remedy Period, unless the Buyer and Seller have reached a signed agreement regarding the Buyer's written request to remedy.

OR

4.4(b) Notice of Termination: Within the Specified Inspection Period or as provided in paragraph 4.4(a), the Buyer may terminate this contract by delivering written notice of termination to the Seller or Seller's Broker, along with a written copy of the inspections, tests and/or reports, specifying the unsatisfactory conditions. Upon termination, the earnest money deposit shall be returned to the Buyer pursuant to paragraph 10.

IT IS NOT THE INTENTION OF THIS PROVISION TO PERMIT THE BUYER TO TERMINATE THIS AGREEMENT FOR COSMETIC OR NON-MATERIAL CONDITIONS. FAILURE OF THE BUYER TO DELIVER WRITTEN NOTICE PURSUANT TO PARAGRAPHS 4.4(a) OR 4.4(b) CONSTITUTES ACCEPTANCE OF THE CONDITION OF THE PREMISES AND SHALL BE A WAIVER OF THE BUYER'S RIGHT TO TERMINATE PURSUANT TO THIS PROVISION.

5. **Warranties:**

   5.1 Home Maintenance Plan: The Seller, at the Seller's expense not to exceed $ _____, shall provide a home maintenance plan from _____ (not applicable if plan name not inserted). The Broker may receive compensation in connection with the sale of the home maintenance plan.

   5.2 Gas Line Warranty: The Seller at the Seller's expense not to exceed $ _____ (not applicable if the dollar amount is not inserted) shall provide a gas line warranty from a gas line repair company. Seller may obtain the gas line warranty from a vendor of the Seller's choice, unless Buyer specifies a specific vendor hereafter: _____ .

6. **Deed:**

   6.1 The Seller shall convey to the Buyer marketable title in fee simple by transferable and recordable general warranty deed, with release of dower, if any, or fiduciary deed, as appropriate, free and clear of all liens and encumbrances not excepted by this contract, and except the following: (none if nothing inserted.) _____ .

7. **Title Insurance:**

   7.1 The Seller shall furnish and pay for an owner's title insurance commitment and policy in the amount of the purchase price, with a copy of subdivision or condominium plat. The title evidence shall be certified to within thirty (30) calendar days prior to closing with endorsement as of 8:00 AM on the business day prior to the date of closing, all in accordance with the standards of the Columbus Bar Association, and shall show in Seller marketable title, in fee simple, free and clear of all liens and encumbrances except: (a) those created by or assumed by the Buyer; (b) those specifically set forth in this contract; (c) zoning ordinances; (d) legal highways; and (e) covenants, restrictions, conditions and easements of record which do not

FIGURE 11.1   Real Estate Purchase Contract *(cont'd)*

Premises Address:_____ page 5 of 8

unreasonably interfere with present lawful use. At closing, the Seller shall sign an affidavit with respect to off record title matters in accordance with the community custom.

7.2 If title to all or part of the premises is unmarketable, as determined by Ohio law with reference to the Ohio State Bar Association's Standards of Title Examination, or is subject to liens, encumbrances, easements, conditions, restrictions or encroachments, other than those excepted in this contract, the Seller shall, within thirty (30) calendar days after the Seller receives written notice thereof, remedy or remove any such defect, lien, encumbrance, easement, condition, restriction or encroachment or obtain title insurance without exception therefor.

7.3 If required by the Buyer's lender, the Buyer shall pay any expense incurred in connection with the mortgagee title insurance issued for the protection of the Buyer's lender. If the Buyer or Buyer's lender wants a survey, it will be at the Buyer's expense.

8. Utility Charges, Condominium Charges, Interest, Rentals, and Security Deposits:
8.1 Through the date of possession, the Seller shall pay all accrued utility charges and any other charges that are or may become a lien on the premises.

8.2 Adjustments shall be made through the date of closing for: (a) rentals; (b) interest on any mortgage assumed by the Buyer; and (c) condominium or other association periodic charges.

8.3 Security deposits shall be transferred to the Buyer.

9. Damage or Destruction of Premises:
9.1 Risk of loss to the premises and appurtenances occurring prior to closing shall be borne by the Seller. If any part of the premises covered by this contract shall be substantially damaged or destroyed from the date of written acceptance of this contract through the date and time of closing, the Seller shall give a written notice to the Buyer and/or Buyer's Broker that the damage or destruction has occurred. Such notice must include all pertinent information regarding insurance policies and claims covering the premises that has been damaged or destroyed. The written notice shall be delivered within two (2) calendar days from the date of the discovery of the damage or destruction. The Buyer may (a) proceed with the transaction and be entitled to all insurance money, if any, payable to Seller under all policies covering the premises, or (b) rescind the contract, by giving written notice to Seller and/or Seller's Broker within ten (10) calendar days after the Seller and/or Seller's Broker has delivered written notice to the Buyer and/or Buyer's Broker of such damage or destruction and thereby release all parties from liability, in which event the earnest money deposit shall be returned to the Buyer pursuant to paragraph 10.

9.2 Failure by the Buyer to so notify the Seller and/or Seller's Broker in writing, within the ten (10) calendar days, shall constitute an election by the Buyer to proceed with the transaction.

9.3 Failure by the Seller to provide the required written notice to the Buyer and/or Buyer's Broker shall result in the Buyer, upon discovery of the damage or destruction, having the right to: insurance proceeds; reimbursement for repairs; or rescind this contract, in which case, the earnest money deposit shall be returned to the Buyer pursuant to paragraph 10.

10. Earnest Money Deposit:

Broker acknowledges receipt of the sum of $_____
by cash or check (check #_____) which shall be held, deposited and disbursed pursuant to paragraph 10.

Brokerage _____ , By_____ , Date_____

FIGURE 11.1   Real Estate Purchase Contract *(cont'd)*

Premises Address:_____ page 6 of 8

10.1 The Buyer has deposited with a Broker the sum receipted for in the Earnest Money Deposit box in paragraph 10.

10.2 If no contract shall have been entered into, then upon the Buyer's written request, the earnest money deposit shall be returned to the Buyer.

10.3 Upon acceptance of this contract by both parties in writing, the Broker shall deposit the earnest money deposit in its trust account. Subject to collection by the Broker's depository, the earnest money deposit is to be disbursed as follows:

    a.   The earnest money deposit shall be applied on the purchase price or returned to the Buyer when the transaction is closed.

    b.   If any written contingency is not satisfied or waived, or if the Seller fails or refuses to perform or if the Buyer rescinds this contract pursuant to paragraph 9.1(b), the earnest money deposit shall be returned to the Buyer. If the Buyer fails or refuses to perform, the earnest money deposit shall be paid to the Seller. In any event the following will apply:

        The party requesting the return or payment of the earnest money deposit shall submit a written request, specifying the contingency that has not been satisfied or waived or the reason for the request, to the Broker holding the earnest money deposit. Within two (2) calendar days (excluding weekends and legal holidays) after receiving the request to return or pay the earnest money deposit, the Broker shall advise the other party and/or Broker in writing that the earnest money deposit shall be returned or paid in accordance with the request, unless the other party delivers written objection to the Broker within ten (10) calendar days after delivery of the written notice by the Broker.

        If the Broker **does not** receive any written objection from the other party within the ten (10) calendar day period, then the Broker shall return or pay the earnest money deposit in accordance with the terms of the request.

        If the Broker **does** receive a written objection from the other party within the ten (10) calendar day period, then the Broker is required to and shall retain the earnest money deposit until (i) Buyer and Seller have settled the dispute in writing, (ii) disposition has been ordered by a final court order, or (iii) Broker deposits the amount with a court pursuant to applicable court procedures.

10.4 The return or payment of the earnest money deposit shall in no way prejudice the rights of the Seller, Buyer or Broker in any action for damages or specific performance.

11. NOTICES TO THE PARTIES:

    11.1 Professional Advice and Assistance: The parties acknowledge and agree that the purchase of real property encompasses many professional disciplines. While the Broker possesses considerable general knowledge, the Broker is not an expert on matters of law, tax, financing, surveying, structural conditions, hazardous materials, environmental conditions, inspections, engineering, etc. The Broker hereby advises the parties, and the parties acknowledge that they should seek professional expert assistance and advice in these and other areas of professional expertise.

In the event the Broker provides to the parties names of companies or sources for such advice and assistance, the parties additionally acknowledge and agree that the Broker does not warrant, guarantee, or endorse the services and/or products of such companies or sources.

    11.2 Ohio Fair Housing Law: It is illegal, pursuant to the Ohio Fair Housing Law, Division (H) of Section 4112.02 of the Revised Code and the Federal Fair Housing Law, 42 U.S.C.A. 3601, to refuse to sell, transfer, assign, rent, lease, sublease, or finance housing accommodations, refuse to negotiate for sale or rental of housing accommodations, or otherwise deny or make unavailable housing accommodations because of race, color, religion, sex, familial status as defined in Section 4112.01 of the Revised Code,

| **FIGURE 11.1** | Real Estate Purchase Contract *(cont'd)* |

Premises Address:_____ page 7 of 8

ancestry, disability as defined in that section, or national origin or to so discriminate in advertising the sale or rental of housing, in the financing of housing, or in the provision of real estate brokerage services.

It is illegal, for profit, to induce or attempt to induce a person to sell or rent a dwelling by representations regarding the entry into the neighborhood of a person or persons belonging to one of the protected classes.

11.3 Residential Property Disclosure Form: With respect to the sale of real property that has from one to four dwelling units, most Sellers will be required to provide the Buyer with a completed Property Disclosure Form complying with the requirements of Ohio law. If such disclosure is required, but is not provided, by the time the Buyer enters into this agreement, the Buyer may be entitled to rescind this agreement by delivering a document of rescission to the Seller or the Seller's Broker, provided such document of rescission is delivered prior to all three of the following dates: (a) The date of closing; (b) 30 days after the Seller accepted the Buyer's offer; and (c) within 3 business days following the receipt by the Buyer or the Buyer's Broker of the Property Disclosure Form or amendment of that form.

11.4 Ohio's Sex Offender Registration and Notification Law: If a sex offender resides in the area, Ohio's Sex Offender Registration and Notification Law requires the local sheriff to provide written notice to certain members of the community. The notice provided by the sheriff is a public record and is open to inspection under Ohio's Public Records Law.

The Buyer acknowledges that any information disclosed may no longer be accurate. The Buyer assumes responsibility to obtain accurate information from the sheriff's office. The Buyer shall rely on the Buyer's own inquiry with the local sheriff's office and shall **not** rely on the Seller or any Broker involved in the transaction.

12. Miscellaneous:

12.1 The Buyer has been given the opportunity to examine the premises and, in making this offer shall rely solely upon the Buyer's inspections and/or tests with reference to the condition, character and size of the premises.

12.2 This contract constitutes the entire agreement and there are no representations, oral or written, which have not been incorporated herein.

12.3 Time is of the essence regarding all provisions of this contract. Whether or not so stated elsewhere in this contract, no deadline or time period under this contract can be modified or waived except by written agreement signed by both parties. Repetition of this provision in any given paragraph of this contract is intended for emphasis only, and shall not reduce the effect of this paragraph as to any other provision of this contract.

12.4 All representations, covenants and warranties of the parties, contained in this contract, shall survive the closing.

12.5 Term Definition: The term "Broker" shall include, without limitation, Broker and/or Broker's agents and shall include collectively, except where the context clearly indicates otherwise, both the Seller's Broker and the Buyer's Broker, if different.

12.6 Signatures: Only original manual signatures or facsimile signatures (which includes faxes, PDF and scanned documents sent by e-mail) shall be valid for purposes of this contract and any amendments or any notices to be delivered in connection with this contract. Only original, manually signed documents shall be valid for deeds or other documents to be delivered at closing. This paragraph cannot be waived except by a manually signed agreement of the parties.

13. Closing and Possession:

13.1 Closing: This contract shall be performed and this transaction closed on or before _____ unless the parties agree in writing to an extension.

FIGURE 11.1	Real Estate Purchase Contract *(cont'd)*

Premises Address: _____ page 8 of 8

13.2 Possession: Seller is entitled to possession through _____ .
At the time the Seller delivers possession, the premises will be in the same condition as the date of acceptance of this contract, except as provided in paragraph 9, and normal wear and tear excepted.

13.3 Debris and Personal Property: The Seller shall remove all debris and personal property not included in this contract by the date and time of the Buyer's possession.

14. Duration of Offer:
This offer shall be open for acceptance through: _____ .

The undersigned Buyer agrees to the terms and acknowledges the receipt hereof:

Signature: _____

Print Name: _____

Date Signed: _____

Signature: _____

Print Name: _____

Date Signed: _____

Address: _____

_____

Phone #: _____

Deed to: _____

Attorney: _____

Ofc. # _____ Fax #: _____

Broker: _____

Broker Number: _____

Ofc. #: _____ Fax #: _____

Address: _____

_____

Agent: _____

Agent File Number: _____

Home #: _____ Fax #: _____

The undersigned Seller agrees to the terms and acknowledges the receipt hereof:

Signature: _____

Print Name: _____

Date Signed: _____

Signature: _____

Print Name: _____

Date Signed: _____

Address: _____

_____

Phone #: _____

Attorney: _____

Ofc. # _____ Fax #: _____

Broker: _____

Broker Number: _____

Ofc. #: _____ Fax #: _____

Address: _____

_____

Agent: _____

Agent File Number: _____

Home #: _____ Fax #: _____

REV 1/05

Property Description

Property descriptions contained in the contract must sufficiently identify the property. Courts are rather liberal in upholding descriptions of real property contained within the contract. Consequently, a contract for the purchase of "all my lands" has been held sufficient to identify the subject of the sale and to comply with the statute of frauds. Even where the quantity of the lands to be sold is not accurate, it is enough if the terms within the description are sufficient to identify the subject property accurately.

CASE EXAMPLE

Vander Graff contracted to sell "all my lands lying on the Miami River, in the State of Ohio, 1,533 acres . . . in my name." Should the actual quantity be greater than the acreage mentioned, the sale would include the excess of the quantity stated in the contract.

Parol evidence is admissible to clarify specific lands. However, parol evidence will not be admitted to reform a description to include lands not specifically referred to by the description.

CASE EXAMPLE

"December 13, 1950, received of P. H. Pilgreen ten dollars ($10) as binder on 20 acres of land and timber; price to be $200 for land and timber. Deed to be made later." Parol evidence will not be admitted in this particular case because the description as written does not allude to a definite parcel of property.

It is best to include in the real estate purchase contract a complete and accurate legal description of the property (for example, metes and bounds or government survey discussed in Chapter 17) so that there is no room for any alternative interpretations. In many jurisdictions, however, it is customary to include only the street address for sales of residential property.

Price

To satisfy the statute of frauds, the amount of the purchase price must be clearly ascertainable. Consider this example:

The total purchase price shall be $250,000 payable as follows:

- $2,500 on the signing of the contract,
- $13,500 in cash or the equivalent to be paid at closing on delivery of the deed, and
- the balance to be paid by assuming the existing mortgage on said property in the amount of $234,000 held by Citizens Savings & Loan Company.

In the event the purchase price is not specified, it must be subject to ascertainment by computation. For example:

The acreage of the property is to be determined by survey, and the price is to be computed by multiplying the number of acres and any fraction thereof by $5,000.

The usual and safest form of payment is a cashier's or certified check or the equivalent. These forms of payment reduce the risk that the buyer will be able to stop payment after tender, which could easily occur if a personal check were issued.

Contingency Clause

■ *A provision within a contract that makes performance under the contract conditional on the occurrence of a stated event.*

A **contingency clause** may be inserted within a contract to benefit a purchaser or a seller. A common contingency within a purchase contract conditions performance "upon the buyer's obtaining financing." The details of the acceptable financing are normally specified; for example:

> The within obligations of the buyer are conditional on buyer obtaining a 25-year loan from a financial institution in the amount of 80 percent of the purchase price at 18 percent interest; otherwise, this contract to become null and void.

This contingency is for the benefit of the purchaser. The purchaser who cannot obtain terms as favorable may elect to waive the contingency and proceed with the purchase. Other contingencies that benefit a buyer may be contained within a purchase contract; for example, making the contract conditional on the sale of buyer's house or on the change of a zoning regulation.

Contingencies may also be included within a contract for the seller's benefit. The seller may desire to make performance under the contract conditional on confirmation of a job transfer by a present employer. Also, there may be other circumstances which make it desirable for the seller to include other contingencies within the contract.

CASE EXAMPLE
Pete Perry owns a home in Tulsa, Oklahoma, and he is interested in selling that home and moving to Seattle, Washington. Perry enters into a valid purchase contract with Sam Sells whereby Perry is to buy Sells's residence for a stated sum. After signing the contract, Perry is not able to sell his residence in Tulsa and consequently is unable to accumulate the funds necessary to close on the Seattle property. Nonetheless, Perry is obligated to perform. A contingency clause as follows would have adequately protected Perry against such a misfortune: "The purchase of Sells's residence is contingent on Perry selling his residence in Tulsa at market price within at least 30 days prior to the date set for closing."

Contingency clauses are often cunningly drafted in an attempt to permit a party to be relieved of obligations at the party's whim, for example, "subject to the buyer's satisfaction after inspections." Courts will often construe such clauses in such a way as to require good faith and honesty on the part of the party the contingency benefits.

CASE EXAMPLE
Brenda Rodgers enters into a purchase contract to buy Hedgeacre. A contingency clause within the contract reads, "Said contract contingent on buyer obtaining a 6½ percent loan for 80 percent of the sales price." Brenda had a change of mind about Hedgeacre and refused to attempt to obtain financing. Brenda's refusal would be considered a lack of good faith and would constitute a breach of contract.

Possession

The date (or the recording of the deed) the seller is required to surrender possession to the buyer is usually negotiable. In many contracts, the date on which the purchaser is entitled to possession coincides with the closing. Ordinarily, in the absence of a possession provision, the buyer is entitled to possession upon payment in full. This often occurs at the closing. The parties may always agree to a different date of possession. For example the parties may agree that the buyer take possession on the signing of the contract, especially if the property is otherwise vacant. Sometimes a purchaser is impliedly entitled to immediate possession; for example, this may occur when the contract requires that the purchaser maintain the premises from the date the contract is signed.

There are dangers to the seller associated with the purchaser's possession before payment. The purchaser in possession may commit waste to the property and then fail to make payment to the seller pursuant to the contract. Or, the purchaser might remain on the property and refuse to close the transaction. When this occurs, the seller may have to engage in a lengthy suit before possession is legally returned to the seller or some other favorable remedy is achieved. From the seller's viewpoint, it would be much better for the buyer who takes possession before payment of the purchase price to be characterized as a tenant until payment. In this event, the seller would be in a position to evict the purchaser/tenant, an action that would normally result in a quick return of possession to the seller.

Sometimes in residential sales, the contract allows the seller to maintain possession rent-free for a period of time after closing, such as 30 or 60 days. In such a case, a danger exists that the seller will hold over or commit waste to the premises. For protection against this possibility, the purchaser may require a security deposit, returnable to the seller if the premises are vacated in the condition they were in at the time of contract, reasonable wear and tear excepted.

Evidence of Title

■ *A document, such as title insurance, which verifies ownership of property.*

The seller is not under any affirmative obligation to prove that title to the realty is marketable, that is, free of liens or other encumbrances. When a general warranty deed is used, the seller personally warrants that the property is free and clear of encumbrances other than those specifically excluded and that the seller will warrant and defend the title against the lawful claims and demands of all persons. A purchaser may maintain an action for damages against the seller under the general warranty in the event of a breach of the warranty against encumbrances. However, the warranty is only as good as the seller's net worth.

When making an investment in realty, the purchaser should take extreme precaution. Toward that end, the purchaser may hire an attorney to do a title search and render an opinion as to the marketability of the title. Alternatively, the purchaser may purchase title insurance from a reputable company. (Title search and title insurance are discussed in Chapter 19.) Still better, the purchaser may insist on a clause in the contract that stipulates that the seller provide evidence of title in the form of an owner's title insurance policy. The prevailing custom within the real estate industry in many localities is for the seller to provide such proof of title; however, in some jurisdictions there is no such prevailing custom and it behooves the buyer to purchase a title insurance policy. The standardized real estate purchase contract within the locality normally reflects the common and approved practice within the area.

Form of Deed

The type of deed to be conveyed by the seller may be controlled by the terms of the contract. It is most desirable for the contract to specify the type of deed, whether it be a general warranty deed, special warranty deed, bargain and sale deed, or quitclaim deed. The various types of deeds are fully treated in Chapter 16. In the absence of agreement, the law within the jurisdiction governs the type of deed the seller is required to convey. Under this circumstance, some jurisdictions obligate the seller to convey a general warranty deed, whereas other jurisdictions require only a bargain and sale deed.

Proration

Certain expenses or income associated with the realty at the time of closing may be due but unpaid. Other expenses or income may have been prepaid. Because these expenses and income are related to the use of the premises, in part by the seller and in part by the buyer, apportionment is necessary. A clause within the contract may read as follows:

> Taxes, insurance, utilities, assessments, and rental income shall be apportioned pro rata as the interests of the parties may appear at closing.

Taxes on real property, for example, may be payable annually, semiannually, or otherwise. The fiscal year may not correspond to the calendar year; the tax assessment period may be, for example, July 1 to June 30 of the next year. To complicate matters, some local jurisdictions run six months to a year behind in their billing, so the owner is always paying taxes due in the past. Fairness demands that an adjustment be made so that the seller is charged with accrued but unpaid taxes.

CASE EXAMPLE

Olivieri pays $520 a year for real estate property taxes on her home. The fiscal period for tax purposes is July 1 to June 30. Olivieri is billed $260 twice a year, in December and June. Each installment of $260 covers the previous six months. On March 31, 2002, Olivieri appears at a closing on her house. The contract provides for apportionment of taxes as of the date of closing. Olivieri is current in her payments of taxes and presents a paid receipt for the December installment. Olivieri will owe $130 for accrued and unpaid taxes for the period covering January 1 to March 31, which amount will be credited to the buyer against the selling price.

Hazard insurance policies may be transferred from the seller to the buyer. However, the transfer may necessitate an apportionment. Insurance is often payable in advance, and the unaccrued portion that was paid by the seller for a period during which the purchaser has the use of the premises must be reflected in the apportionment. Sometimes it is possible to notify the insurance carrier to refund the unaccrued portion to the seller and bill the purchaser for the applicable amount. A more frequently used method is for the seller to cancel the insurance policy and receive a rebate for the unused premium and for the buyer to purchase another policy.

Other expenses, such as fuel, electricity, water, and other assessments, are often prorated. Usage of these utilities is not always the subject of exact computation. The parties may notify the respective companies to read the utility meters as of the date of closing and divide the bill accordingly.

Income from rentals is often apportioned as of the date of closing. Normally, rentals are paid in advance. When the closing occurs in the middle of a rental payment period, an adjustment is required because the seller in such an event receives from the tenant a rental payment covering a portion of the time after ownership has passed to the buyer.

CASE EXAMPLE

Jerry Rogers, seller, and Ronald Dodge, buyer, are to close July 15 on commercial property owned by Rogers. A tenant is under a leasehold agreement for such property and pays $350 per month on the first of each month. A clause within the real estate purchase contract requires apportionment of rentals as of the date of closing. On July 15, the buyer would be entitled to $175, which represents the unused portion of the rental.

Prorations are also covered in Chapter 20.

Property Inspection

The condition of the property may be the subject of dispute at closing or thereafter. To reduce the possibility of such a dispute, the contract may contain an inspection clause. Inspection clauses may permit the buyer to have the premises inspected within a specified number of days from the signing of the contract, or may require that the seller produce certificates evidencing the results of an inspection. Types of inspection include termite, gas line, radon, electrical, plumbing, mold, and structural.

In the event that the inspection shows a defect, the contract governs as to the responsibilities of the parties. The following is an example of a contractual provision:

> Seller shall make all repairs to the property not to exceed 5 percent of the purchase price. In the event Seller fails to make said repairs, Buyer may make the repairs and deduct the amount from the purchase price at closing. In the event the cost of repairs exceeds 5 percent of the purchase price and Seller agrees to make the repairs, the Buyer may (1) close the sale with the completed repairs or (2) terminate the contract.

Under such a provision, assume that the purchase price of a home is $200,000. A termite inspection reveals termite infestation and structural damage. The cost of repair is $8,000. The seller must make the necessary repairs. If, however, the cost of repairs is over $10,000 (over 5 percent), the seller does not have to make the repairs. In such a case the contract terminates. In the event that the seller agrees to make the repairs, the buyer may accept the repairs or refuse the repairs and terminate the contract. In practice, the inspection clause often provides the buyer with an opportunity to renegotiate the purchase price when defects in the property are such, that the buyer has the right to otherwise terminate the contract.

Home Warranty Plan

Many contracts contain protection for the buyer through **home warranty plans**. Various private companies, for a fee, will contract to repair major systems and appliances for a period of time, normally one year. The cost may range from $250 to $500, depending on the location and terms of the plan, and there may be a small deductible. In the event that a home maintenance provision is not included within the purchase contract, the option is usually open for the buyer to pay for, and obtain, coverage.

Earnest Money

A real estate purchase contract normally calls for the purchaser to deposit **earnest money**. Contrary to popular belief, this deposit is not necessary to validate the contract. Sufficient consideration exists in the form of mutual promises contained within the agreement.

Earnest money may be a nominal sum, such as $100, or it may be as substantial as 10 percent of the purchase price or more. Normally, the real estate broker holds the deposit in an escrow account pending closing. At closing, the earnest money may be returned to the purchaser, applied to the broker's commission, or credited against the amount due to the seller.

Signing

A contract for the sale of real estate should be signed by all parties. A writing not executed by all parties is arguably not the agreement of any party who has failed to sign. Today, with high-speed communication, it is possible to send e-mails and faxes almost instantaneously. The question arises as to whether a signature on a fax (though not original) or a name on an e-mail is sufficient to satisfy the "signature" requirement of a contract. Although not every state is settled on this issue, the trend is to recognize fax and electronic "signatures."

Sometimes a party to the sale (seller or buyer) designates an agent to negotiate and/or sign the contract. This practice should be reserved for extreme cases where it is not feasible for the actual party to act. When a party designates an agent, known as an attorney, such appointment should be evidenced by a written power of attorney. A power of attorney must be notarized to be valid. A copy of the power of attorney should be attached to the contract and, in some states, recorded. Even here, in fact, problems may occur because no one can be absolutely sure that the power of attorney has not been revoked by a subsequent act or event, such as the death of the authorizing party.

CASE EXAMPLE

Howard Moore, owner of a tract of land that is for sale, is planning a visit to Australia. To prevent his absence from the country from impeding the sale, he executes a power of attorney, giving his real estate broker power to negotiate, contract, and sign the deed of conveyance. Hugh Fine, a farmer, enters into a contract for the sale of Moore's land. The broker appears at the closing and executes a deed on behalf of Moore. Fine takes possession and learns later that before the date of closing Moore was killed in Australia in a hunting accident. Because death revokes a power of attorney, Fine's title is seriously impaired.

Attestation and Acknowledgment

In most jurisdictions, a contract for the sale of realty need not be witnessed (attested). The parties who sign the writing need not acknowledge their signatures as genuine before a notary public. Neither does the contract have to be recorded to be considered binding between the parties. (Some jurisdictions require that the land installment contract, discussed in Chapter 22, be recorded.)

Closing

The contract normally states the date and place of **closing**. (The closing is discussed in detail in Chapters 14 and 20.) At closing, the buyer makes payment to the seller and the seller passes title by signing and conveying the deed in accordance with the terms of the contract. In the event that the time and place of closing are not specified within the contract, the law presumes that the parties intended that the closing take place within a reasonable time at a reasonable location.

Normally, time is not of the essence in real estate closings. Hence, even if a date is specified, failure to close on that date is not considered critical, as long as the noncomplying party has acted in good faith and is able to close within a reasonable time thereafter. The parties, of course, may agree within the contract that time is of the essence, and under such a clause, even a day's delay on the part of a party would be deemed a breach of contract.

Under certain circumstances, time is of the essence even in absence of express language in the contract to that effect. Time is of the essence when parties are dealing in highly speculative land transactions that are subject to rapid fluctuations in value. In addition, when one party is made aware of particular circumstances that make the timing of the closing date critical (such as the necessity for the buyer to vacate an apartment the day of closing), time is deemed an essential element to the contract.

A buyer who appears at a closing that is unattended by the seller must be ready, willing, and able to perform. The buyer must tender the purchase price by depositing it in escrow or through a show of the money to witnesses in attendance. Conversely, a seller makes tender by showing a readiness, a willingness, and an ability to deliver marketable title to the buyer.

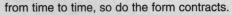

THE CHANGING LANDSCAPE

Our real estate law originated from the land laws in England starting in 1066, when King William conquered England and usurped authority and ownership over all the land in the English realm. That is where we derive the old semantics that are so much a part of real estate today.

The real estate contract is a more modern innovation, although it too has some derivatives from old English law. The states' Statutes of Frauds, for example, are based on a Parliamentary Act from 1677, the Statute for Prevention of Frauds and Perjuries. The Statute of Frauds requires that a contract for the sale of real property be supported by a written memorandum, with some judicially created exceptions.

The contents of the real estate contract are dictated by a combination of law, custom, and experience. Many localities, through their bar associations and/or Boards of REALTORS®, have adopted a standard form contract for suggested use among brokers and attorneys involved in real estate purchase contracts. Of course, these forms may be appropriately modified to fit the particular needs and circumstances surrounding the specific transaction. The form contracts are, in part, a reaction to local practitioners' experience and seek to conform to the reality of local practice. Because the practices change from time to time, so do the form contracts.

One provision that is found more and more in contracts is the "arbitration clause." This requires that the parties in a dispute arbitrate rather than litigate, at least as an initial attempt to resolve the conflict. In addition, there appears to be a trend where REALTOR® associations and others, such as the Better Business Bureau and Builders Industry Association, offer alternative dispute resolution (ADR) services. This trend toward more ADR services will undoubtedly find itself woven into the real estate purchase contracts in the days ahead. In a faster-paced, more decentralized world, there is a need to formulate contracts by e-mail. We already see the trend in the law to accept e-mail and facsimile signatures.

Another concern that may well find itself addressed in the purchase contract is "toxic mold." In some parts of the country, there is an outbreak of toxic mold requiring very expensive remediation. Many insurance policies do not cover toxic mold damages and resulting personal injury. The real estate purchase contract may have to address this. What other clauses will find themselves within those contracts will be known only as trends in society emerge. What do you see coming that will have to be addressed in the contract?

■ KEY TERMS

■ INTERNET RESOURCES

For real estate offers, forms, and practical issues see

www.nolo.com/index.cfm
(click on "Property of Money," then click on "Real Estate" under Main Topics)

For an overview of real estate transactions see

www.law.cornell.edu/topics/real_estate.html

■ REVIEW AND DISCUSSION QUESTIONS

1. What are the elements necessary to satisfy the statute of frauds?

2. (a) What is the purpose of applying the statute of frauds to sales of interests in real estate? (b) Give an example of a case involving a real estate transfer that is excepted from the statute of frauds.

3. What is the purpose of the parol evidence rule?

4. What limitation may a broker confront when preparing real estate purchase contracts?

5. Describe five major provisions contained within the real estate purchase contract.

6. (a) What is a contingency clause? (b) What purpose does it serve? (c) Whom does it benefit?

7. When does the closing occur? Explain.

■ CASE PROBLEMS

1. A trustee of real property held a public auction to sell the property. Charles McCabe was the highest bidder. There was no written contract or memorandum of sale. The next day, when the trustee of the property submitted a deed for delivery, McCabe refused to pay the price. The trustee sued for specific performance. Who wins and why? *Watson v. McCabe*, 527 F.2d 286 (6th Cir. 1975).

2. The Roths entered into a contract to purchase real property from Loye Ashton and his co-owners. There was no writing evidencing the sale. The Roths paid most of the purchase price for the property and constructed a building on the property in which they were operating a business. Is it possible for Ashton to rescind the agreement? Explain. See *Williston Co-op Credit Union v. Fossum*, 459 N.W.2d 548 (N.D. 1990).

3. The Whites entered into an agreement with the Rehns to purchase "all land west of road running south to the Rehn farmstead containing 960 acres." Nothing within the description pinpointed exactly which 960 acres was to be transferred. Immediately before the purchase agreement was to be signed, the extent of the specific parcel was explained orally to Mr. White. (a) Should the Rehns desire to back out of the sale, what argument could they make? (b) How should the Whites respond? *White v. Rehn*, 103 Idaho 1, 644 P.2d 323 (1982).

4. River Birch Associates, a developer, entered into a plan to develop a 144-unit town home project on 19.6 acres. River Birch agreed to convey fee simple title to the "common area" to the Homeowner's Association of the project. The specific identity of the common area was not designated in the contract. Can the Homeowner's Association resort to extrinsic evidence to clarify the quantity and the specific identity of the common areas? Explain. What extrinsic evidence may be helpful? *River Birch Associates v. City of Raleigh*, 326 N.C. 100, 388 S.E.2d 538 (1990).

5. A contract of sale required the Laddons, the buyers, to pay, as part of the purchase price, a $1,000 deposit to be held by Rhett Realty, the broker, "in escrow on behalf of seller until settlement." The contract further provided that the deposit would be forfeited to the sellers in the event the Laddons breached the contract. In such a case, under the terms of the contract, Rhett Realty would be entitled to 50 percent of the amount forfeited. The contract was contingent on the buyers obtaining financing, which they were unable to do. Who is entitled to the earnest money? Explain. *Laddon v. Rhett Realty, Inc.*, 63 Md. App. 562, 493 A.2d 379 (1985).

6. Hillary Nidor, purchaser, and William Nolan, seller, signed a real estate contract that required the closing occur "within 30 days of the signing of the agreement. Time is of the essence." Nidor submitted all of the documentation that the bank desired, but due to some last minute mortgage rate changes, the intervention of holidays, and some scheduling conflicts, ABC Title was not able to be ready within the 30 days to close. It sought to have the parties agree that the closing be extended for two (2) days. Nolan agreed. Nidor, who was looking to escape from what she now believed was a bad deal, refused to consent to any delay. The 30 days came and went without a closing through no fault of Nidor or Nolan. Nolan filed suit against Nidor for breach of contract contending that she acted in bad faith. How should the court rule? Explain.

7. 805 Third Avenue Co. (Third Avenue) and M.W. Realty Associates entered into a contract whereby Third Avenue was to purchase M.W. Realty's air rights. Third Avenue needed the air rights to construct an office building. Third Avenue obtained a city permit authorizing it to commence construction, and it began to excavate and enter into contracts for the erection of the structure. M.W. Realty refused to complete its obligations under the purchase contract, insisting on a modification of the contract on terms less favorable to Third Avenue. Knowing that any delay would result in serious injury, Third Avenue agreed to the unfavorable terms. (a) What remedy is now available to Third Avenue? (b) What is the legal justification for the remedy? Explain. *805 Third Avenue Co. v. M.W. Realty Assoc.*, 58 N.Y.2d 447, 461 N.Y.S.2d 778 (1983).

12 Agency and Brokerage

■ AGENCY

■ *A legal relationship in which one party, called the* principal, *authorizes another, called the* agent, *to act in the principal's behalf in dealing with third parties.*

Agency is a useful legal relationship in business and personal transactions. A substantial amount of business in the United States is done through agents, both by corporations and partnerships that are unable to act for themselves and by individuals, who find acting through agents convenient and efficient in their business and private affairs.

Agency and Real Estate Transactions

The agency relationship is used extensively in many phases of the real estate business. It is especially prevalent in selling and leasing residential and commercial property. Owners of these types of properties often retain agents to help them find buyers or tenants, as agents usually have extensive knowledge of the market as well as contacts with potential occupants.

Agencies created to bring about the sale or lease of real estate differ in two significant ways from agencies in many other businesses. One difference is that in all states an agent appointed to sell or buy real estate must be licensed. License requirements for real estate agents will be discussed later in the chapter.

A second difference between the real estate agent and other agents is the extent to which the real estate agent has the power to contract on behalf of the principal. In many, if not most, business agencies, the agent has this power. For example, if the president of a corporation that is developing land for a shopping mall signs a contract to have the land cleared, the contract is binding on the corporation. However, in most transactions that involve the sale or lease of real estate, the agent does not have the power to contract for the principal. If the owner wishes the agent to have this authority, the owner must execute a written document called a *power of attorney*. The power of attorney grants the agent, usually referred to as an *attorney-in-fact*, the authority to contract for the owner.

Creation of Agency

The usual method of creating an agency is by agreement. The principal authorizes the agent to act in the principal's behalf, and the agent agrees to do so. As a general rule, no particular formality is required to create an agency; the agreement may be oral or in writing. This rule ordinarily does not apply to transactions involving the sale or lease of real estate. To be valid, a power of attorney must be in writing. In addition, almost half the states by statute require that the appointment of an agent to procure a buyer or tenant for real estate be in writing.

■ BROKER

■ *An agent who for a commission or fee brings parties together to negotiate or conducts negotiations to complete a transaction, usually involving the sale or exchange of property or the acquisition of contract rights.*

A **broker** is an intermediary or go-between whose primary function is to facilitate a transaction. In many fields, brokers play important roles in bringing business dealings to fruition. Although stockbrokers and real estate brokers are common examples, the long list of brokers includes those who arrange the sale of yachts, produce, hides and furs, and in some societies, even marriage. What brokers do and the authority they enjoy differ from one business to another, but brokers almost always represent buyers or sellers in some capacity.

Most states have statutory provisions that define real estate brokers and sales personnel for the purpose of licensing and regulation. These statutes frequently designate brokers in terms of activities relative to real estate transactions. When people engage in these activities for others and for a commission or fee, they are brokers or salespersons for regulatory purposes and must be licensed. Most state regulatory agencies require a broker to be appointed as a principal broker of a firm to be responsible for the activities of all licensees.

The statutes contain words such as *auctions, sells, offers for sale, buys, solicits prospective sellers or buyers, negotiates the sale,* and *exchanges.* Similar broad terminology is used to describe activities relative to rental of real property. In some statutes, activities such as finding borrowers or lenders, negotiating or collecting loans, and arranging investments secured by real estate also are included in the statutory definition of broker.

A corporation or a partnership may be a real estate broker. In most states, members of the firm who actively engage in the brokerage business must be licensed. A few states require that anyone actively engaged in management be licensed as well. In some states one member of the firm may be designated on the license as a *broker* and others as *associate brokers* or *sales personnel.* License requirements will be discussed more fully later in this chapter.

Independent Contractor

■ *A person who is retained to do a job and uses his or her own judgment as to how the work will be done.*

The broker is, in a technical sense, retained by the seller as an agent. Nevertheless, the agency agreement establishes only the broker's authority to act, not the manner in which the broker is to accomplish the result. The broker controls the hours, methods, and details of the job. As the broker's actions are not controlled by the seller, the seller is not liable for negligent harm caused by the broker unless the act causing harm was authorized or within the broker's inherent powers. In addition, as the broker is not an employee but an **independent contractor**, the seller does not have to withhold federal or state income taxes or make contributions to the Social Security or unemployment compensation funds on the broker's behalf.

Listing

■ *A contract between a seller of real estate and a broker authorizing the broker to secure a buyer for the property on specified terms in return for a fee if the broker is successful.*

The listing creates the agency relationship between the seller and the broker. A number of states require by statute that a listing be in writing. In these states, if there is no written listing, the broker is not entitled to a fee. In the absence of a statute requiring a writing, an oral listing is enforceable. This question should not come up, however, because both the prudent seller and the broker would insist on a written contract clearly spelling out the rights and obligations of the parties. An appreciable portion of the litigation that centers around suits for brokers' commissions could be prevented by carefully drawn brokerage agreements. This problem as well as some others that can be alleviated by a writing will be discussed later.

In those states that recognize the oral listing, a broker may establish employment by implications arising from a property owner's actions.

CASE EXAMPLE

Frewert owned a home that he had been trying to sell. Carlson, a real estate salesperson, obtained permission to show the home to the Coopers. Carlson obtained an offer, which she presented to Frewert. In discussing the transaction, she told Frewert that she was representing him. Frewert then quoted a minimum net price that he wanted for the property and discussed possession with her. Carlson obtained a second offer from the Coopers that was slightly less than Frewert's minimum net price. Frewert rejected this offer. Two days later, he signed a contract directly with the Coopers and refused to pay a commission.

In a successful suit against Frewert for a commission, the court stated, "[W]hile a contract of employment is necessary to create an agency relationship . . . no particular form is required. Ordinarily, all that is necessary is that the broker act with consent of his principal either by written instrument, orally, or by implication from the conduct of the parties." *Dickerson Realtors, Inc. v. Frewert*, 16 Ill. App. 3d 1060, 307 N.E. 3d 445 (1974).

The listing agreement should contain all the important elements of any contract: the amount of compensation, duration of the listing, point at which the commission is earned, and the like. The contract should also outline defects and encumbrances to which the title is subject, terms on which the owner will sell, and details as to possession. The listing should also indicate whether it is a nonexclusive, or open, listing or an exclusive one. (See Table 12.1.)

TABLE **12.1**	Listing Contracts	
	Type	**Who Can Sell**
	Exclusive agency	Contracting broker
		Seller
	Exclusive Right to Sell	Contracting broker
	Open Listing	Multiple contracting brokers
		Seller

■   **Exclusive Agency.** *A listing in which the seller gives one broker authority to pro-cure a buyer for property but retains the right to procure a buyer for the property himself or herself.*

The **exclusive agency** is one of the two types of exclusive listings common in the United States. In this type of exclusive listing, if the seller procures the buyer the broker is not entitled to a commission.

■   **Exclusive Right to Sell.** *A listing in which the seller gives one broker authority to procure a buyer for property. The broker is entitled to a commission even if the buyer is procured by the seller.*

The **exclusive right to sell** differs from the *exclusive agency* in that the exclusive right to sell entitles the broker to a commission even if the seller procures the buyer without the broker's assistance. Courts in most states require unequivocal language in a listing before accepting it as an exclusive right to sell. These courts reason that the ordinary seller should be clearly informed that even if he or she makes the sale alone, the commission must be paid.

Both types of exclusive listings protect the broker against appointment by the seller of any other broker. Brokers prefer these types of listings because they provide added assurance that time and money spent procuring a buyer will be rewarded. The broker does not have to fear loss of a commission if another broker arranges a prior sale of the property.

Most exclusive listings are given for a specified period of time. They terminate automatically at the end of that period unless renewed. For a broker to take an exclusive listing for an indefinite period is generally considered poor practice, and in many states an indefinite exclusive listing is illegal. This protects sellers who, unaware that the exclusive listing is still in effect, list with another broker and thus find themselves liable for two commissions. If an exclusive listing is open-ended, it is subject to cancellation on notice. A few states allow the broker a reasonable period of time to arrange the desired transaction. In any case, most courts agree that a seller may not terminate a listing where the only objective is to bypass the broker and sell to a buyer with whom the broker has been negotiating.

■ **Open Listing.** *A listing that entitles the broker to compensation only if his or her activities bring about the desired result.*

The **open** or nonexclusive **listing** is common in some states. Unless the agreement clearly indicates otherwise, courts presume that a listing is open. A seller who enters into an open listing agreement may list the property with any number of brokers. The broker who brings about the sale is entitled to the commission. Authority of all of the brokers is automatically revoked without notice if and when the seller enters into a contract to sell the property.

In an open listing, the seller retains the right to negotiate a sale on his or her own. If the sale is effected by the seller without the aid of a broker, no commissions are due and all listings are automatically terminated. Ordinarily, an open seller listing has no time limit and the seller can withdraw at any time. The seller has no commitment until the broker has procured a buyer ready, willing, and able to buy. To escape paying a commission, a dishonest seller, suspecting that a broker is about to submit an offer, might revoke the broker's authority and attempt to deal directly with the potential buyer. A seller who revokes in bad faith under these circumstances is subject to liability if the property is sold to a buyer located by the broker. Some open listings contain provisions entitling the broker to a commission after the expiration of the listing if the property is purchased by one to whom it has been shown by the broker.

■ **Multiple-Listing Service.** *An organization in which brokers have contracted with each other to share their exclusive listing contracts.*

The **multiple-listing service** is a marketing strategy that brokers have developed among themselves to increase their effectiveness in brokering real estate. Brokers participating in the service have agreed to pool their exclusive listings and to divide the commission received for negotiating a sale. Multiple-listing services are common in most areas of the United States.

In a transaction involving broker members of a multiple-listing service, the selling broker was traditionally considered to be a subagent of the listing broker. The subagent relationship is no longer required in many jurisdictions. A selling broker may choose to represent the buyer in the transaction rather than be a subagent of the seller. Each of the brokers involved receives a percentage of the commission that had been negotiated by the listing broker with the seller. The split of that percentage that each broker receives is determined by them. Some multiple-listing services allow their members to withhold certain real estate from multiple listing; others require that all listings be submitted. Some multiple-listing services will allow the listing broker a period of time to attempt to sell the property before registering it with the organization. Because brokers have limited rights to delegate their authority, the members of a multiple-listing service should be sure that their contracts with the owners permit them to submit property to multiple listing.

Authority

■ *Term used in the law of agency denoting the agent's power to perform acts author-ized by the principal.*

The broker is a special agent with limited authority, usually restricted to a single transaction. In addition, although many people in real estate—and often the courts—refer to a broker's authority to sell, most listings merely authorize the broker to find a buyer, not to enter into a contract on behalf of the principal.

The broker does not bargain as to terms but assists the parties in arranging terms on which agreement can be reached. Although the seller may give the broker authority to execute a contract of sale, this authority must be clearly spelled out in the listing. Because brokers usually do not have the power to contract for a seller, a buyer should demand evidence of the broker's authority to do so if the broker signs on the seller's behalf. Brokers who are employed as property managers or rental agents often have the authority to contract for their principal.

■ **Express Authority.** *Authority a principal confers on an agent explicitly and distinctly; may be conferred orally or in writing.*

An agency authorization in the listing contract between the broker/agent and the owner/principal is the foundation on which the broker's authority rests. Such authori-zation establishes certain tasks the broker is given the power to accomplish.

Implied Authority

■ *An agent's authority to do those things necessary and proper to accomplish the express terms of the agency.*

Implied authority includes activities such as advertising, showing the property, and transmitting proposals relating to the sale between buyer and seller. The broker has the implied authority to do these things as they are necessary to achieve the result sought by his or her **express authority**, that is, to find a ready, willing, and able buyer.

The broker also has the implied authority to make certain representations about the property. A real estate broker, however, is a special agent. This means that the broker's implied authority is confined strictly to the terms of the agency, and the broker is bound by his or her obligation as an agent to obey the directions of the principal.

CASE EXAMPLE

Mustafa Ali owned a profitable bakery that he desired to sell. He listed the business and property with Dave Gould Realty, Inc., for $150,000.

Gould obtained an offer for the property, which Ali accepted; a $1,500 deposit to be held by Gould accompanied the offer. The contract provided that the deposit on the purchase price would be paid to the seller if the buyer defaulted. The buyer refused to close the sale because of alleged defects in the title. Without contacting Ali, Gould returned the $1,500.

Because the contract did not close as scheduled, Ali sold the property to another. If Gould sued for a commission, the court would rule against him because he had no implied authority to modify the contract by returning the deposit to the buyer.

The extent of the broker's authority is a critical issue in determining the seller's responsibility for representations made by the broker about the property. In a majority of jurisdictions, these statements are binding on the seller. If the statement is material and untrue, the buyer may rescind the contract and in some cases collect damages. These results follow even if the broker thought the statement was true or if the seller was unaware that the statement was being made. As a general rule, courts consider statements made by a broker within the scope of the broker's implied authority. Any loss occasioned by these statements should be borne by the seller, who selected the broker, and not by the buyer, who was misled by the false statement. However, some states have modified these general rules through statutes.

Brokers generally are chosen for their knowledge, skill, and judgment. The relationship between the broker, or the brokerage firm, and the seller is personal, and generally the broker has no authority to delegate to another the tasks that he or she has been hired to perform. This rule applies, however, only to broker's actions that are discretionary, such as determining the terms of the sale.

A broker may delegate to another the authority to perform acts that are ministerial or mechanical in nature. Thus the broker may assign to a salesperson the task of showing the property or finding a buyer, inasmuch as these acts do not involve the broker's discretion. When a ministerial task is accomplished by a broker through a subagent, the broker is entitled to collect a commission even if the subagent's relationship to the broker was unknown to the seller.

CASE EXAMPLE

Dave Gould Realty, Inc., was authorized to sell property that belonged to Edna Philbrick. Gould mentioned this to Arthur Clairmont, a fellow broker. Several days later, Clairmont obtained Gould's permission to show the property to one of Clairmont's customers. Clairmont described the property and terms to this buyer. The buyer on his own examined the property and entered into an agreement with Philbrick, who refused to pay Gould a promised commission. Philbrick argued that she had not authorized Clairmont to procure a buyer.

Courts would ordinarily find for Gould in this situation, as Clairmont's verbal description and transmittal of terms represented a mechanical act.

Broker's Duties to Seller

A real estate broker owes his or her principal, the seller, essentially the same duties that any agent owes to a principal. Like other agents, the broker is a fiduciary. A *fiduciary* is a person who acts primarily for the benefit of another in a relationship founded on trust and confidence. In selecting the broker as agent, the seller has relied on the broker's integrity, fidelity, and ability. (See Table 12.2.) This relationship of confidence and trust requires high standards of conduct, and the broker must exercise good faith and

TABLE **12.2**	Broker's Legal Duties	
To Seller (Client)		**To Buyer (Customer)**
Fully disclose relevant matter		Avoid misrepresentation of material facts
Obey legal instructions		Refrain from concealing defects
Account for proceeds handled		Disclose material facts (some states)
Act reasonably and carefully		Act honestly

loyalty in all matters relating to the agency. Some states have modified the common law rules on real estate via statutes.

Good Faith and Loyalty. Good faith and loyalty require that the broker advance the principal's interest even at the expense of his or her own. A broker may not purchase the seller's property unless the seller has complete knowledge of all the facts and freely consents to the sale. This prohibition applies even if the broker can show that the transaction is beneficial to the seller and the seller is not injured in any way.

The duty of good faith and loyalty controls situations in which the broker can represent both parties. If a broker has the authority *to enter into a contract for either buyer or seller*, the broker violates the fiduciary duty if he or she accepts compensation from both. Courts reason that it is impossible for a broker under these circumstances to satisfy the diametrically opposed interest of both parties.

In the common brokerage agreement, however, the broker is employed merely to bring the parties together. In this situation the broker may act as a dual agent and receive a commission from each, as long as this dual capacity has been fully disclosed and is agreed to in writing by both buyer and seller. In the effort to bring the parties together, the broker who is to receive compensation from buyer and seller must be certain to act impartially.

Abstract terms such as *trust*, *good faith*, and *loyalty* indicate the general scope of the broker's responsibility to his or her principal. In reality a broker must take at least three positive actions to meet these general requirements:

1. The broker must fully disclose to the principal all matters relating to the agency.
2. The broker must obey the principal's lawful instructions.
3. The broker must account to the principal for any proceeds of the agency coming in to his or her hands.

Full disclosure requires that the principal be informed of all offers, the identity of purchasers, commission-splitting arrangements with other brokers, relationships between buyer and broker, financial limitations of the purchaser, and the selling price of comparable property.

CASE EXAMPLE

Neibert listed property with Alfred C. Moore, a broker. One of Moore's salespeople obtained a purchase offer for the property. The offer acknowledged receipt of $3,000 from the buyer and provided that the deposit should be "forfeited as liquidated damages" if buyer failed to close.

Unknown to Moore, the deposit was in the form of a promissory note, not cash. Moore discovered this later but failed to inform Neibert, because the buyer assured Moore that the note would be honored. When the sale did not close, Neibert demanded the deposit to cover losses incurred. The buyer refused to pay the note.

In an action affirming the real estate commission's 60-day suspension of Moore's license, the court recognized that the temptation to withhold information is "especially strong when it is only a matter of disclosing bad news which may improve." The court added that "it is an agent's duty to give his principal timely notice of every fact or circumstance which may make it necessary for him to take measures for his security." *Moore v. State Real Estate Commission*, 9 Pa. Common. Ct. 506, 309 A.2d 77 (1973).

Skill and Care. In addition to meeting the high standards of conduct of a fiduciary, the broker must not be negligent in carrying out the duties of the agency. A broker is negligent if he or she acts in an unreasonable or careless manner and this action is the proximate cause of loss to the principal.

CASE EXAMPLE

Ponia Towski, who could neither read nor write English, owned a house in Camden, New Jersey. There was a vacant lot on each side of the house. Between the lot on the east and the house was an alley. Towski's house was on the boundary of the west lot. Because of this, Towski wished to purchase that lot and erect a dwelling, using his west wall as a party wall.

All of this was explained to Joshua Griffiths, a real estate broker. Through Griffiths, Towski purchased what he thought was the lot on the west and built an adjoining structure with a party wall. Unfortunately, Griffiths had negotiated a sale with the owner of the eastern lot. Because Towski did not own the property on which the adjoining building was located, his tenants were forced to vacate the premises. Towski then brought a successful damage action against Griffiths. *Towski v. Griffiths*, 91 N.J.L. 663, 103 A.192 (1918).

Although the facts of this case are unusual, in finding for Ponia Towski the court applied a test that is relatively common. It held the defendant liable because he had not used the degree of care and skill ordinarily employed by people engaged in the brokerage business.

Liability for negligence depends on factors that vary from one case to another. As a result, it is impossible to say that a broker is negligent because of acting in a particular manner. A slight variation in the circumstances might cause a court or jury to consider a particular act careless in one instance and not in another. There are, however, a number of relatively common situations in which principals have brought successful negligence actions against their brokers or have used the broker's conduct as a defense in an action brought for commissions. Cases exist in which brokers have been found negligent because they did not use ordinary care and skill in securing an adequate purchase price, investigating encumbrances, preparing papers relative to the sale, collecting payments due the principal, and filing discharges for mortgages and liens.

It has been held that a broker who fails to make a determined effort to sell, especially a broker with an exclusive agency, is liable to the principal. Other cases have held that a broker charged with renting property is liable for failure to properly investigate prospective tenants who later damage the property.

Numerous remedies are available to the principal when the broker violates these duties. The principal may

- sue for breach of contract,
- bring a tort action for negligence,
- withhold the commission requiring the broker to bring a suit against the principal,
- discharge the broker without compensation,
- force the broker to account, or
- recover for loss and misuse of the principal's property.

Broker's Duty to Buyer

Business relationships between buyers and brokers arise in one of two ways. In the traditional real estate sale, the seller lists his or her property with the broker. The listing authorizes the broker to act as the seller's agent in procuring a buyer for the property. The buyer is a third party (customer). In negotiations with third parties (buyers), the broker is acting in the seller's behalf and, like the seller, deals at arm's length with the buyer. In an arm's-length transaction each party acts in his or her own interest. In the past, courts have applied the principle of caveat emptor, that is, let the buyer beware, to the relationship between the seller's broker and the buyer.

Seller's brokers are liable to buyers in some situations. Traditionally, to recover against a broker representing the seller, the buyer needed to rely on some tort theory, not on any duty the broker owed to the buyer arising out of the relationship between them. Sellers' brokers are liable to buyers for misrepresentation of material facts about the property or for actively concealing any defects. If the misrepresentation is intentional, the broker is liable for fraud; if the misrepresentation is made innocently, the broker is liable, but the buyer's remedies may be limited. Fraud and misrepresentation are discussed in Chapter 13.

The liability of the seller's broker to the buyer for fraud or misrepresentation has been expanded in a number of states in recent decades. Many courts have held sellers' brokers liable to buyers for failing to disclose material facts about the property. For example, buyers have recovered against sellers' brokers who have not disclosed a termite problem, a defective sewer, a leaky basement, or personal interest in the property. More problematic are cases involving "stigmatized property," where houses are reputedly haunted, or were the site of a murder, or are in a neighborhood where a pedophile lives. There is no uniformity regarding the obligation of a broker to disclose facts regarding a stigmatized property. Some states have statutes requiring notification; many do not. A broker needs to check with a professional to determine the status of the law in an individual state.

Courts holding that sellers' brokers have a duty to disclose material facts to buyers justify this stance in several ways. Some have applied a theory of negligence or negligent misrepresentation. To establish a claim of negligence, the buyer must show that the broker owed the buyer a duty to conform to a certain standard. In a number of cases, to establish this standard, courts have referred to standards in ethical codes promulgated by state real estate commissions and/or the Code of Ethics of the National Association of REALTORS®. These codes impose on the broker a duty to treat all parties honestly. In other cases, courts have held sellers' brokers to a high standard of care in relations with buyers on grounds that state legislation licensing real estate brokers must be interpreted in the light of its obvious purpose of protecting the public. A broker does not stand in the same shoes as a seller. Brokers owe the buyer the same duties of integrity owed the public at large. They must be answerable at law for breaches of statutory duty to the public. In addition, courts have stated that the broker's license is a privilege conferred by the state in return for which the broker must act in the public interest.

Hoffman v. Connall
Supreme Court of Washington
736 P. 2d 242 (1987)

Background. In January 1983, Bryan and Connie Connall signed a listing agreement with Cardinal Realty, Inc., to sell five acres of land. Shortly thereafter a Cardinal broker went to the site with one of the sellers. The seller pointed to a stake that marked the southeast corner, and the broker noted that the stake lined up with a fence line to form the west boundary. The seller had built a corral and horse barn six inches inside the fence line, and assured the broker that the fence and other improvements were inside the property line. The seller pointed out that the southwest corner stake lined up with a row of poplar trees to form the west boundary. The seller also located the approximate location of the northwest corner.

James and Verna Hoffman saw an advertisement for the property and contacted the broker, who took them to the site. The broker pointed out the corner stakes and other locational information given him by the seller. The Hoffmans owned a horse, so the fence, corral, and horse barn were important to them. The Hoffmans bought the property in February, and in May were notified by a neighbor that according to his recent survey, the fence and part of the corral and horse barn encroached on his property by 18 to 21 feet. The buyers determined that the cost of moving the improvements was about $6,000. The buyers sued the sellers and the broker for misrepresenting the true property line. The trial court held that the broker did not breach the duty of acting like a reasonably prudent real estate broker. The Court of Appeals reversed, holding that a broker is liable for innocent misrepresentations to the buyer.

Decision. The Washington Supreme Court reversed the Court of Appeals affirming the trial court's decision in favor of the broker.

Justice Andersen. A real estate broker is held to a standard of reasonable care and is liable for making "negligent," though not "innocent," misrepresentations concerning boundaries to a buyer. The Restatement (Second) of Torts defines the tort of innocent misrepresentation as follows:

One who, in a sale, rental, or exchange transaction with another, makes a misrepresentation of a material fact for the purpose of inducing the other to act or to refrain from acting in reliance on it, is subject to liability to the other for pecuniary loss caused to him by his justifiable reliance on the misrepresentation, even though it is not made fraudulently or negligently. The Restatement, however, leaves open the question of whether such a cause of action lies against real estate brokers.

We recognize that some other jurisdictions have agreed with the viewpoint of the Court of Appeals in this case and have held real estate

continued on next page

brokers liable for making innocent misrepresentations on which buyers justifiably rely. Courts that so hold do so because of their belief that the innocent buyer's reliance tips the balance of equity in favor of the buyer's protection. The courts justify placing the loss on the innocent broker on the basis that the broker is in a better position to determine the truth of his or her representations.

This approach has been criticized for imposing a standard of strict liability for all misrepresentations that a broker might make or communicate, however innocent, in a real estate transaction. Another commentator observes the obvious—that there is a problem with subjecting brokers to liability for innocent misrepresentations without imposing a corresponding duty of inspection for defects, and that without such a duty, a broker may be tempted to provide less information to a buyer, fearing that his or her chances of exposure to liability for innocent misrepresentations will multiply with the quantity of information provided.

At the other end of the spectrum from liability for innocent misrepresentation is the view that a real estate broker is an agent of the seller, not of the buyer, and is protected from liability under agency law. Thus, an agent would be permitted to repeat misinformation from his principal without fear of liability unless the agent knows or has reason to know of its falsity. This principle has been upheld by approximately half the jurisdictions that have addressed the issue of broker liability for innocent misrepresentations. The Supreme Court of Vermont recently reaffirmed this rule, holding that "[r]eal estate brokers and agents are marketing agents, not structural engineers or contractors. They have no duty to verify independently representations made by a seller unless they are aware of facts that tend to indicate that such representation[s are] false."

A recent decision of our Court of Appeals declared a middle ground that we find persuasive. At issue in *Tennant v. Lawton*, was a broker's liability for misrepresenting that a parcel of land could support a sewage system and thus was "buildable." The *Tennant* court echoed the Vermont court in holding that a broker is negligent if he or she repeats material representations made by the seller and knows, or reasonably should know, of their falsity. The court went on, however, to hold that a broker has a limited duty toward a purchaser of real property.

The underlying rationale of [a broker's] duty to a buyer who is not his client is that he is a professional who is in a unique position to verify critical information given him by the seller. His duty is to take reasonable steps to avoid disseminating to the buyer false information. The broker is required to employ a reasonable degree of effort and professional expertise to confirm or refute information from the seller which he knows, or should know, is pivotal to the transaction from the buyer's perspective.

We perceive no persuasive reason to hold real estate brokers to a higher standard of care than other professionals must satisfy. We have held that lawyers must demonstrate "that degree of care, skill, diligence and knowledge commonly possessed and exercised by a reasonable, careful and prudent lawyer in the practice of law in this jurisdiction."

Of relevance in this connection is RCW 18.85.230(5), which provides that a real estate license may be suspended or revoked if the holder is found guilty of [k]nowingly committing, or being a party to, any material fraud, misrepresentation, concealment, conspiracy, collusion, trick, scheme or device whereby any other person lawfully relies on the word, representation or conduct of the licensee. . . . Under this statute, a broker is only guilty of knowingly committing a misrepresentation.

Absent a legislative directive to the contrary, we do not consider it appropriate to impose liability on a real estate broker without a similar requirement of knowledge. Knowledge, or any reasonable notice, that the boundaries pointed out by the seller were incorrect is absent in this case, as the trial court found in its findings of fact.

There was no evidence on the property which suggested to [the broker] he should investigate the boundary lines further. There was nothing in the surrounding circumstances that would have put [the broker] . . . on notice that there may have been something wrong with the property lines.

In short, a real estate broker must act as a professional, and will be held to a standard of reasonable care. If a broker willfully or negligently conveys false information about real estate to a buyer, the broker is liable therefor. We decline, however, to turn this professional into a guarantor. Real estate agents and brokers are not liable for innocently and nonnegligently conveying a seller's misrepresentations to a buyer.

The broker did not breach the standard of care of a reasonable prudent broker.

The improvements on the property were important to the buyers because they wanted to raise and ride horses. The broker saw markers for some of the boundaries when he walked the property with the seller, but could not locate all of the boundaries with certainty. Trees and other physical features on the land supported the seller's representations regarding the boundaries, however, and the broker testified that the seller assured him that the improvements were inside the property line.

The trial court is sustainable in its view that the broker in this case had no notice that anything was wrong with the boundaries as represented by the sellers. While hindsight suggests that the broker would have done well to check on the alleged survey, there was no testimony that such a check was the prevailing practice in the real estate business. Moreover, natural and man-made boundaries reinforced the seller's representations concerning the legal boundaries. Accordingly, the trial court did not err in finding and concluding that the broker in this case was not negligent.

Reversed.

Despite the notion that the broker is the seller's agent, traditionally buyers have relied heavily on the agent. Does this holding make the buyer's reliance even more precarious?

Does this force the buyer to hire his or her own broker to feel fairly represented?

Does this add unnecessarily to the expense of a real estate transaction?

Prior to the purchase, how can the prospective buyer protect himself or herself from the unfortunate outcome of this case?

In most states that recognize a duty on the part of the seller's broker to disclose all material facts to the buyer, the duty is limited to facts the broker actually knew or should have known. In addition, most of these states hold the broker liable only if the buyer has no reasonable opportunity to discover the information himself or herself. One intermediate appellate court in California, in *Easton v. Strassburger* (1984), however, has held in a case involving residential property that the broker has not only a duty to disclose material facts but also an affirmative duty to conduct a reasonable inspection to discover all facts materially affecting the value or desirability of the property.

Though no other state court has gone as far as the *Easton* court, the decision triggered a flurry of new legislation. Apparently promoted by the National Association of REALTORS® and beginning in California, a significant number of state legislatures have enacted disclosure laws. Though there are wide variations among the new laws, generally they require that a buyer be provided with a disclosure form completed by the seller containing specified information about the property to the extent known by the seller. Some statutes prescribe use of a specific form; others are quite vague on the disclosure requirement. It should be recognized that the early submission of the disclosure forms to the buyer is very important. A few state statutes use the disclosure forms in lieu of the buyer's common-law agency protections discussed in this chapter. Despite the disclosure form, the buyer must undertake an inspection of the premises as a protection against overpayment and to establish reasonable reliance for a possible fraud claim.

■ **Buyer's Broker.** *A broker who has contracted to locate real estate for a buyer.*

In most real estate transactions, the seller hires a broker to procure a buyer for the property. However, in some transactions the agency relationship is created by a buyer who authorizes a **buyer's broker** to negotiate for the purchase of real estate suitable for the buyer's needs. In these transactions, the broker's fiduciary duties are owed to the buyer.

Salahutdin v. Valley of California, Inc.
California Court of Appeal
29 Cal. Rptr.2d 463 (1994)

Background. Shaucat Salahutdin and his wife, Jeannie, immigrants from Korea, engaged David Seigal, a Coldwell Banker broker, to find property that they could purchase in Hillsborough. They informed him that it was essential that the property could be subdivided so that they could leave one-half to their daughter. Seigal informed the Salahutdins that a parcel had to be larger than one acre in Hillsborough for them to be able to subdivide. The Salahutdins agreed to wait as long as necessary to find a parcel large enough to subdivide. Later, Seigal found a parcel listed by another Coldwell Banker broker (the name under which Valley of California, Inc., did business) called the Black Mountain property that was shown as larger than one acre on the multiple listing information sheet. Seigal notified the Salahutdins of the Black Mountain property, and on their inquiry, assured them that it could be subdivided. Seigal relied solely on the multiple-listing information sheet and on an "eyeball" examination of the property for giving the assurance. The Salahutdins purchased the property. Actually the property was less than one acre, unbeknownst to Seigal, and the Salahutdins could not subdivide it. The Salahutdins sued Coldwell Banker

for money damages claiming that Seigal breached his fiduciary duty of care and committed constructive fraud by making false representations. The trial court awarded the Salahutdins $175,000 in damages plus costs against Coldwell Banker.

Decision. The California Court of Appeal affirmed the decision.

Justice Kline. In a cause of action entitled "negligent misrepresentation," plaintiffs alleged that Coldwell Banker made false representations about the size of the property and concealed its failure to adequately investigate or disclose the true facts.

Experts for the parties testified that in 1979 if a real estate broker represented that a property could be subdivided, he or she had an obligation to investigate and determine if the property could in fact be subdivided; a broker who was aware that his client wanted to subdivide property and who did nothing more than "eyeball" the property to investigate the accuracy of the seller's representation that the lot size was sufficient to subdivide had not satisfied his duty of care to his client; a broker should not have confirmed the location of the boundary lines without the assistance of someone such as a surveyor, competent to do so; a broker was required to advise his or her client whether the boundary line location had been verified by a surveyor; and if a broker knew the subdividability of the property was a material fact, and also knew the seller's representation that the property was more than one acre was merely the seller's belief, the agent had a duty to investigate to determine the accuracy of that representation.

The record amply supports the finding that David Seigal breached his fiduciary duty to plaintiffs and committed constructive fraud. He knew the size of the property and its ability to be subdivided was critical to plaintiffs' decision to purchase it, yet misrepresented to plaintiffs that the property was more than one acre in size and that it could therefore be subdivided, confirmed that the south boundary of the property was marked by the fence, and failed to disclose that he had done nothing to independently confirm the accuracy of this information.

In addition to the traditional liability for intentional or actual fraud, a fiduciary is liable to his principal for constructive fraud even though his conduct is not actually fraudulent. As a general principle, constructive fraud comprises any act, omission or concealment involving a breach of legal or equitable duty, trust or confidence which results in damage to another even though the conduct is not otherwise fraudulent. Most acts by an agent in breach of his fiduciary duties constitute constructive fraud. The failure of the fiduciary to disclose a material fact to his principal which might affect the fiduciary's motives or the principal's decision, which is known (or should be known) to the fiduciary, may constitute constructive fraud. Also, a careless misstatement may constitute constructive fraud even though there is no fraudulent intent. A broker who is merely an innocent conduit of the seller's fraud may be innocent of actual fraud but in this situation the broker may be liable for negligence on a constructive fraud

theory if he or she passes on the misstatements as true without personally investigating them.

The broker has a fiduciary duty to investigate the material facts of the transaction, and he cannot accept information received from others as being true, and transmit it to the principal, without either verifying the information or disclosing to the principal that the information has not been verified. Because of the fiduciary obligations of the broker, the principal has a right to rely on the statements of the broker, and if the information is transmitted by the broker without verification and without qualification, the broker is liable to the principal for negligent misrepresentation.

As a fiduciary, Seigal had a duty to his clients to refrain from advising them that the parcel was more than an acre, that it could therefore be subdivided, and that the fence represented the southern boundary of the property where he did not know that to be the case and where he knew these facts were material to plaintiffs' decision to purchase the property. While he was not required to investigate the sellers' representations or the truth of the description contained in the multiple listing service sheet before showing the property to plaintiffs, Seigal was at least required to tell plaintiffs that he had not verified the information he was passing on to them; that he was simply relying on the description provided by the sellers.

There is no clear line establishing when a fiduciary's breach of the duty of care will be merely negligent and when it may be characterized as constructive fraud. However, a breach of a fiduciary duty usually constitutes constructive fraud.

Affirmed.

Why was the broker held liable here but not in the Hoffman case (page 263)?

Until the 1980s the buyer-broker relationship was not common in residential transactions. On the other hand, buyers often hired brokers to locate commercial property. In commercial transactions the buyer usually compensated the broker. As buyer brokerage became popular in residential transactions, the broker often received compensation from the seller. If the buyer's broker receives compensation from the seller, the buyer must be informed and consent, or the broker will have violated his or her fiduciary duty. At the initial conversation, the broker must inform the seller of the existence of the agency relationship with the buyer.

In the past, multiple-listing service rules presume that a broker member of a multiple-listing service attempting to negotiate a sale is a subagent of the listing broker. If the broker is representing the buyer, the broker must reject the offer of subagency by notifying the listing broker at the initial contact between them. If the buyer broker does not do so, a dual agency has been created. Most multiple-listing service rules have been changed to indicate that the selling agent is not necessarily a subagent. This has facilitated the growth of buyers' brokers. Buyers' brokers must specify that they represent the buyer.

■ **Dual Agency.** *A transaction in which an agent represents both principals.*

In a real estate transaction, a **dual agency** would exist if a broker were to represent both buyer and seller or owner and tenant. Undisclosed dual agency is generally considered to be illegal. Courts reason that an agent cannot adequately fulfill his or her fiduciary duty of loyalty to both principals. If representing the seller, the broker is obligated to obtain the best price for the seller's property. If representing the buyer, the broker's obligation is to obtain the property for the lowest possible price.

There are conditions, however, under which dual agency is permissible. The key seems to be for the broker to obtain the consent of both parties. The two principals must clearly understand that the agent is representing both of them, and the broker must obtain their consent in writing. In a dual agency situation, the broker cannot disclose to either party confidential information the broker possesses. The broker should confine disclosures to matters concerning the property itself. In some states it is illegal for the broker to collect a fee from both principals, even though both have agreed.

Cashion v. Ahmadi et al.
Supreme Court of Alabama
345 So.2d 268 (1977)

Background. Phillip and Donna Cashion (plaintiffs, appellants) purchased a home from Timothy and Nettie Ahmadi (defendants, appellees) through the realty firms of Pope and Quint (defendants, appellees) and Vergos Realty Company (defendant, appellee). After the purchase, the Cashions discovered a serious water seepage problem in the basement. They tried, unsuccessfully, to have this stopped, and then moved out. The Cashions then sued the former owners and the realty companies. The defendants moved for summary judgment. The trial court dismissed the case and plaintiffs appealed. Additional facts are in the opinion.

Decision. The appellate court affirmed in part; reversed in part; and remanded.

Justice Almon. Marge Mills, realtor for Pope and Quint, was initially contacted by Mrs. Cashion because of a newspaper advertisement either about the house in question or another house. The house in question had been previously listed by Pope and Quint, but at the time Marge showed it to Mrs. Cashion, it was listed under an exclusive contract with Vergos Realty and Bauer Realty (not a party to this suit). At no time did the Cashions converse directly with Gus Vergos or the Ahmadis.

The Cashions sued the appellees alleging a confidential relationship existed between themselves and the Ahmadis, Pope and Quint, and/or Vergos Realty, and because of the confidential relationship, any one or all of the appellees had a duty to disclose that the house had a water problem which the appellees knew about. The trial judge dismissed the counts based on confidential relationship, apparently on the basis that the facts alleged did not show such a relationship.

By amendment, the Cashions alleged further (1) that they employed Pope and Quint to find them a residence to purchase, that they reposed trust and confidence in Pope and Quint, that Pope and Quint knew about the water problem, and that Pope and Quint breached their obligation arising out of their confidential relationship in failing to inform the Cashions about it, and (2) that Vergos Realty, as agent for the Ahmadis, negligently failed to disclose the water problem.

The Cashions contend they should have been allowed to prove that Pope and Quint was their agent, or, alternatively, that a confidential relationship existed because of the "particular circumstances" associated with this case.

A real estate broker may be hired to find a buyer or to find a seller. In either case the broker owes a duty of faithfulness to his principal.

A broker is a fiduciary and holds a position of trust and confidence. He is required to exercise fidelity and good faith toward his principal in all mat-

ters within the scope of his employment, and to account for all funds or property rightfully belonging to his principal. He cannot put himself in a position antagonistic to his principal's interest, by fraudulent conduct, acting adversely to his client's interests, or by failing to communicate information he may possess or acquire which is or may be material to his employer's advantage, or otherwise.

The more common situation appears to be where the broker is hired by the seller to find a buyer for a percentage of the sale price, to be paid by the seller. From there, the house may be placed on a multiple listing, whereupon any number of realty firms may partake in the commission by finding a buyer.

In the instant case the house was listed under an exclusive contract with Vergos and Bauer Realties. However, Pope and Quint was allowed 50 percent of the commission for finding a buyer. In essence, the sale was treated as if it were a multiple listing.

The question raised by the Cashions is where did Pope and Quint's duty of faithfulness lie in this sale, with the sellers, the Ahmadis, or the buyers, the Cashions? Interestingly, Marge Mills, Frank Hicks (ex-broker for Pope and Quint), and Gus Vergos all acknowledged that if they were aware of a material defect in a residence they were selling, they should and would inform the buyer of the defect.

The Cashions contend that Pope and Quint was their agent and that it violated its duty of faithfulness to them in not disclosing the water problem. A broker, as well as any agent, may be an agent for both parties in a sale transaction; however, he opens himself to possible liability when he does so without full disclosure to both parties. Any broker, though especially a broker working with a multiple listing in which he has to work through another broker who deals directly with the seller, often finds himself in the precarious situation of seeking the trust and confidence of the prospective buyer while still claiming faithfulness to the seller. He cannot have it both ways.

Whether one is an agent of another is normally a question of fact to be determined by a jury. We believe that whether the total circumstances of this

continued on next page

case require the conclusion that Pope and Quint, via their agent, Marge Mills, was an agent of Cashions, regardless of whether it may have been also an agent of the sellers, the Ahmadis, is a question for the jury under our scintilla evidence rule.

As to the question of whether Pope and Quint knew about the water problem, we note that while Marge Mills, Frank Hicks (ex-real estate agent for Pope and Quint) and Arthur Pope deny such knowledge, Dr. Ahmadi was sure that he had informed Hicks about the problem, though what seepage problem existed while he owned the house had been remedied several years prior to the sale to the Cashions. Dr. Ahmadi also stated that dampness in the basement was the reason the price of the house was reduced, though such is denied by the realtors.

The judgment in this cause is affirmed as to the Ahmadis and Vergos Realty Company and reversed as to Pope and Quint, Inc.

Affirmed in Part; Reversed in Part; and Remanded.

Suppose the Ahmadis had not told any of the brokers about the water problem. Would Pope and Quint be liable?

During the 1980s the unintentional dual agency problem was of major concern to the real estate industry. Many consumer protection groups and regulatory agencies sought a solution to it that would protect both buyers and the reputation of the real estate industry. As a result, a number of state legislatures and administrative agencies charged with regulating real estate sales personnel mandated that the agency relationship be disclosed in every transaction in which a broker is involved.

The rules and regulations that evolved require that the broker disclose to the parties the party he or she represents. The disclosure must be in writing, usually on a standard form that has been prescribed by the state's real estate regulatory body. (See Figure 12.1.) Additionally, disclosure must occur before the submission of an offer to purchase. Dual agency is not prohibited as long as the parties agree and proper disclosure is made.

Transaction Brokers. With some recent success, brokers have been lobbying for independent contractor status. Under the **transaction broker** approach, brokers act as finders, putting sellers and buyers in contact with one another, thereby facilitating the progress of the deal. The broker's only responsibility, in order to be paid, is to conclude the deal. The broker is not within the control of either party. The good news for the seller and buyer is that neither would be liable for the illegal acts of the transaction broker. The bad news is that many of the remedies provided by agency law to the seller and buyer may be eliminated. Most state statutes that permit the transaction broker, or independent contractor, status do require that the broker act reasonably and in good faith.

One of the fears concerning the transaction broker is that it will only add to the existing confusion over the primary loyalties of the broker. Sellers and buyers who pay brokers' commissions expect loyalty from that broker. Whatever the outcome, the existence of transaction brokers is increasing.

FIGURE 12.1 Notice to Prospective Real Estate Purchasers/Tenants

In Ohio, real estate licensees are required to disclose which party they represent in a real estate transaction. Under Ohio law, a real estate licensee is considered to be an agent of the owner of real estate unless there is an agreement to the contrary and that agreement is disclosed to all parties.

Some duties of the licensee, as the agent of the owner, are to:

- treat all parties to a transaction honestly;

- offer the property without regard to race, color, religion, sex, ancestry, national origin, familial status, or handicap;

- promote the best interest of the owner;

- obtain the best price for the owner;

- fully disclose to the owner all facts which might affect or influence a decision; and

- present all offers to the owner.

As a buyer, if you choose to have a real estate broker represent you as your agent, you should enter into a written contract that clearly establishes the obligations of both you and your agent and specifies how your agent will be compensated.

Under Ohio law, the disclosure statement below must be submitted to the prospective purchaser/tenant in each transaction. This form has been approved by the Ohio Real Estate Commission for use by Ohio real estate licensees. Please sign below.

AGENCY DISCLOSURE STATEMENT

The listing broker and all agents associated with the listing broker represent the owner. The
_____ (Selling Broker) and _____ (Selling Agent) represent (please check one): the purchaser/tenant _____; the owner _____.

If a broker/agent is representing both the purchaser/tenant and the owner as a dual agent, he/she must attach a copy of the agreement signed by the purchaser/tenant and owner acknowledging their agreement to this arrangement.

By signing below, the parties confirm that they have received, read and understood the information in this Agency Disclosure Form and that this form was provided to them before signing a contract to purchase/lease real estate.

_____   _____

Purchaser/Tenant Date   Owner   Date

_____   _____

Purchaser/Tenant Date   Owner   Date

Any questions regarding the role or responsibilities of real estate brokers or agents in Ohio can be directed to an attorney or to:

State of Ohio

Department of Commerce

Division of Real Estate

Telephone: In Ohio 1-800-344-4100 or in Columbus 614/466-4100

The Broker's Commission

Disputes sometimes arise between broker and seller over whether the broker has earned a commission. One reason may be that terms of the parties' agreement are vague, without clear provisions as to matters that later become subjects of disputes. In addition, legal misunderstandings may arise. The seller makes the agreement believing that no commission is due until the property has been paid for and plans to pay the commission out of the purchase price. On the other hand, the broker expects compensation for finding a purchaser whose offer is accepted even if title never passes. Potential problems involving payment also occur because payment is not a primary concern of the parties when the broker is hired.

When there is a problem concerning the commission, some brokers as a matter of policy refuse to litigate. They believe that a lawsuit can damage their reputation. They reason that adverse community reaction to litigation outweighs any monetary gain resulting from a successful suit. It is true that litigation is unpleasant and should be avoided, but civil suits are not publicized extensively. In fact, the word-of-mouth injury to the broker's reputation caused by a quarrel over commissions with a dissatisfied seller probably occurs even if the broker does not sue. A broker should not avoid litigation to collect a commission that has been earned, although all other solutions to the problem should be exhausted first.

Commission disputes generally involve two questions. Although they are frequently interrelated, either question may be the subject of the dispute. One common question is, Has the broker done the job he or she was hired to do? The other is, When has the broker's job been accomplished so as to entitle him or her to a commission?

In one typical scenario, the broker locates a buyer willing to purchase the property on terms agreeable to the seller. When presented with an offer, the seller refuses to accept for one reason or another, although he or she previously indicated that the terms were acceptable. In another common situation, the broker negotiates a contract between buyer and seller, but the seller cannot perform because the title is defective. Or perhaps the owner just decides not to sell and refuses to honor the agreement. The broker cannot compel performance of the contract, and the buyer, reluctant to sue, looks for property elsewhere. The broker, feeling that he or she has performed, now seeks to recover a commission.

For the broker to be entitled to a commission, a number of threads must come together. Initially, the court needs to determine what the broker was hired to do. The broker may have been hired to sell or lease property on specific and detailed terms. If so, the broker's sole responsibility is to find a ready, willing, and able buyer on these terms. Once this has been accomplished, the broker is entitled to the fee, even if the parties never enter into a contract. When there is a variance between the terms authorized by the seller in the listing agreement and those tendered by the prospective buyer, the broker is not entitled to a commission if the seller refuses to contract.

CASE EXAMPLE

Corbin listed property with Rucker, a real estate broker. The listing described the property as 120 acres more or less and specified a price of $3,500 an acre. Rucker brought Corbin an offer, which was for $3,500 per acre. Corbin rejected the offer because of two provisions in the proposal. The first read "exact acreage to be determined by current survey which is to be provided by the purchaser at time of closing." The other stipulated that "[t]he rights of purchaser hereunder may be assigned without consent of the seller." Rucker sued for a commission. The lower court dismissed and the appellate court affirmed. The appellate court stated that the two terms constituted variances from the listing. As a result, Rucker was not entitled to recover. *Rucker v. Corbin*, 372 S.E.2d 512 (Ga. App. 1988).

In a few states, sellers have successfully avoided paying commissions by overpricing the property when listing it, rejecting initial offers below that price and negotiating a subsequent sale at less than the listing price. When the broker demands a commission, the seller defends on grounds that the offer submitted did not meet the terms specified. If a seller accepts an offer lower than the asking price from a purchaser found by the broker, most courts protect the broker by holding that he or she is entitled to a commission. The broker, however, must remain active in the negotiations unless deliberately excluded by the seller.

In some listing agreements, the broker is merely informed in general terms what the seller would like to get for the property. Although a price is usually mentioned, specific terms are left for future determination. In this type of contract, the broker is not entitled to a commission until the buyer and the seller execute a binding contract.

Procuring Cause. A broker must be the procuring cause in bringing about a "meeting of the minds" between buyer and seller. A broker is the procuring cause of a sale if he or she initiates a series of continuous, related, and unbroken events that result in a sale on the seller's terms. Merely introducing buyer and seller will be enough if the seller takes over the negotiations and completes the transaction. If the broker is unable to obtain an offer and abandons his or her efforts, the seller is not liable for a commission if the sale is completed without the broker's aid.

Sometimes two brokers contribute to the sale. Problems may arise if the seller pays the full commission to one of the brokers, knowing that broker is under a duty to share the commission with the other. The seller would be liable for the half of the commission unpaid to the broker if the broker who has been paid the full commission refuses to share.

The best solution to this problem is to have the brokers agree as to the manner in which the commission will be divided. If no agreement was reached or if the seller did not realize that two brokers were involved, some courts insist that the full commission go to the broker who was the "primary, proximate and procuring cause of the sale." Which broker fits this definition is determined in court on the basis of whose efforts tipped the scale and induced sellers and purchasers to come to terms.

▦ **Ready, Willing, and Able.** *Capable of present performance.*

To be entitled to a commission, the broker must procure a **ready, willing, and able buyer** to complete the transaction. The test of whether the buyer is ready and willing is his or her intention at the time the contract is made. Intent at the time the contract is to be consummated (closed) is not material. Most courts infer readiness and willingness if the buyer submits an offer on terms stipulated by the owner.

A buyer is said to be *able* if he or she has the financial ability to complete the transaction.

Chester Winkelman, a real estate broker, brought suit against J. R. Allen to recover a commission. The basis of Winkelman's action was that he had procured a ready, willing, and able buyer. The evidence indicated that Allen had listed his ranch with Winkelman at $350,000. The listing was open. Winkelman showed the ranch to Russell Bird and his father, Randall. Randall Bird was a prosperous rancher. Russell, age 22, had appreciable ranching experience but little capital.

The Birds and Allen discussed the sale on several occasions. On one of these, Allen was informed that only Russell, the son, was to sign the contract. After apparent agreement was reached on terms satisfactory to Allen, a written offer signed by Russell and a $1,000 deposit were submitted. Allen held the offer for several days and then sold the property to another.

After a lower court found in Winkelman's favor, an appellate court reversed and ordered judgment for Allen. The court stated, "[W]here the only available source from which the money is to come is . . . admittedly in the possession of a third person . . . who is in no way bound . . . such a purchaser cannot be considered able to buy. . . ." *Winkelman v. Allen*, 214 Kan. 22, 519 P.2d 1377 (1974).

In the *Winkelman* case the broker did not produce a ready, willing, and able buyer. No commission was due. A buyer is considered financially ready and able to buy under any of three conditions:

1. The buyer has cash on hand to complete the sale.
2. The buyer has sufficient personal assets and a strong credit rating that ensures with reasonable certainty that he or she can complete the sale.
3. The buyer has a binding commitment for a loan with which to finance the sale.

When Commission Is Earned. In most states, the broker has procured a buyer when the broker submits a binding, enforceable offer from a buyer on the seller's terms. The result is that, as long as the buyer is financially able, the broker has earned the commission at that time. The broker and seller may, and frequently do, agree that the commission will be earned on conditions other than submission of a binding offer. Their contract may state that the commission is due on closing of title or out of the proceeds of the sale. If this is the case, the broker's commission has not been earned until that condition is met. As a general rule, if the broker procures a counteroffer that deviates in price or otherwise from the specified terms, the seller may accept or decline. If the seller accepts, the commission is due the broker for services rendered.

Recent case law in some states modifies the traditional general rule as to when the commission is earned. Courts in these states hold that the broker is not entitled to a commission if the buyer defaults on the contract. As a result, the broker does not earn the commission until the transaction closes.

Several reasons exist for this change. For one, most sellers listing property with a broker anticipate paying the broker's commission out of the proceeds of the sale. If the sale fails to close through no fault of theirs, sellers feel that they should not be responsible for a commission. A second reason is that the rule obligating the seller to pay a commission on contracting places on the seller the burden of determining the buyer's financial ability. But the seller is the wrong person to make this decision. Determining the prospect's financial status and willingness should rest with the broker, who ordinarily has had closer contacts with the buyer and is better able to measure financial capacity and willingness. From the point of view of paying a commission, the time when financial ability and willingness are important is not when the agreement is signed but at the time of closing. If the buyer refuses or is unable financially to perform at that time, the broker has not really done the job. If, however, failure to complete the transaction results from the seller's wrongful act or refusal, the broker has a valid claim for the commission.

Traditionally, the broker's compensation has been based on a percentage of the selling price. Most brokers in the same market customarily charge a similar commission, although even informal agreement among brokers to do so is illegal. In the late 1970s and early 1980s, as competition in the real estate industry increased, some brokers adopted alternative methods for determining fees. An obvious competitive strategy was to reduce the percentage charged to below that being charged by other brokers in the market. Another approach was to charge a flat fee instead of a percentage of the selling price. A third approach was to separate or "unbundle" the services provided a client and charge for each on an individual basis. For example, a broker might determine separate fees for appraising the property and suggesting a selling price, for advertising and showing the home, for conducting negotiations, and for assisting at the closing. Clients could select the services desired and be billed only for these. Although discounting, flat fees, and unbundling have been resisted in the industry, they probably will be used more frequently as real estate brokerage becomes more competitive.

Termination of Agency

The agency relationship is based on a "personal service" concept and may be terminated in numerous ways. Probably most agencies terminate on accomplishment of the purpose for which the agency was created or on expiration of the time agreed on for performance. The latter is important in real estate, as many exclusive listings contain a date on which the listing will end. In fact, regulations in many states require that a listing include a specific termination date. Of course, the agency will continue if the parties renew the agency at that time.

By Acts of the Parties. As agency is a consensual relationship, either party has the power to end it at any time. However, the fact that one has the power to terminate the agency does not necessarily mean that he or she has the right to do so. For example, if a seller gives a broker an exclusive-right-to-sell listing for 90 days, the seller has the power to revoke the broker's authority before 90 days have passed, but if the seller revokes without justification, the broker can sue for damages.

> **CASE EXAMPLE**
> Hague owned 240 acres of farmland. He listed 80 acres with Hilgendorf, a licensed broker. Before the listing expired, Hague terminated it, as he had encountered financial problems and decided to sell the entire farm. The farm was not listed with Hilgendorf.

Hilgendorf found a ready, willing, and able buyer for the 80 acres. When Hague refused to accept the buyer's offer, Hilgendorf sued for his commission. Hague argued that Hilgendorf's duty of loyalty required him to give up the listing. Both the trial and appellate courts rejected this argument. The appellate court stated that "[i]n performing agency functions an agent does indeed occupy a fiduciary position, and his duty requires him to place the principal's interests first. But in the contract of agency . . . neither of the parties is acting for the other; each is acting for himself."

On this basis the appellate court rejected Hague's argument and awarded damages to Hilgendorf. The court stated that, although the principal has the power to terminate an unexpired agency, the principal subjects himself to damages for doing so. *Hilgendorf v. Hague*, 293 N.W.2d 272 (Iowa 1980).

By Operation of Law. In addition to termination by the acts of the parties, the agency relationship terminates automatically by operation of law if any of the following events occur:

- Death, incompetency, or bankruptcy of principal or agent
- Destruction of the subject matter
- Change in law, making the agent's duties illegal
- Loss of license required by either principal or agent
- Conflict of interest

Although termination for any of the above reasons is easy to understand, a difficult termination problem arises when an unusual change in conditions related to the agency takes place. For example, if a broker is authorized to sell land at a specified price and the value of the land suddenly increases substantially, has the original authority terminated? Most courts would say so.

■ **Agency Coupled with an Interest.** *An agency that cannot be revoked by the principal.*

Although ordinarily an agency can be terminated at the will of either party, an agency coupled with an interest is irrevocable. In this type of agency, the principal has given the agent certain powers and coupled these with a financial or security interest in the subject matter of the agency. As a result, the principal does not have the right to revoke the agent's power. In addition, when an agent has authority coupled with an interest, the death, incompetency, or bankruptcy of the principal does not terminate the agency.

One common example of the agency coupled with an interest is a mortgage in which the borrower gives the lender the power to have the security sold if the mortgage debt is in default (see Chapter 21 and discussion of power of sale foreclosure). A less common example would be a business arrangement in which a broker advances funds to a contractor to complete a home on speculation. In addition to agreeing to repay the loan, the contractor gives the broker an exclusive right to sell the property when the home is completed.

Real Estate Sales Associate

■ *A person employed by a real estate broker who, under the broker's direction, lists and sells real estate.*

In many real estate transactions, much of the work is done by sales personnel who are not licensed brokers. Although many state licensing statutes use the designation *salesman* for both male and female sales personnel, the term *associate* is becoming more common. That word will be used in this chapter.

All states require that **real estate sales associates** be licensed. The procedures that are followed to license sales associates are similar to those for licensing brokers; however, the requirements for obtaining a sales associate's license are less demanding. For example, to obtain a broker's license a person is usually required to have experience in selling real estate, but experience is not necessary to obtain a sales associate's license. If a competency examination is required to obtain a sales associate's license, it is almost always less comprehensive than the licensing examination for brokers.

In large firms, sales associates do much of the legwork for the business. A sales associate prospects for buyers and sellers, assists the seller in determining price, and completes listings and sales contracts. Sometimes the sales associate helps to arrange financing and may provide assistance to lenders and attorneys with regard to title evidence and documents necessary to complete the sale of real property.

A sales associate is required by law to be associated with a broker. The broker holds the sales associate's license and directs and supervises his or her work. Commissions on each sale are collected by the broker. The sales associate receives as compensation a previously agreed-on percentage of the commission. There is some judicial disagreement as to the relationship between broker and sales associate. A majority of courts conclude that the sales associate is an independent contractor, not an employee. Under this view, the broker is not responsible for workers' compensation, unemployment insurance premiums, or withholding taxes. Some recent cases, however, tend to view the relationship between broker and sales associate as that of employer-employee. Where this view is taken, the broker has the same legal responsibility to the sales associate that all employers have to their employees. Actually, whether an employer-employee or independent contractor relationship exists depends on the facts of the particular relationship.

CASE EXAMPLE

McGinnis worked exclusively for Berens on a commission basis. He was hired to obtain listings of property suitable for sale to commercial developers. McGinnis was required (a) to clear all listings with Berens, (b) to attend sales meetings, (c) to report all transactions before they were finalized, and (d) to comply with requirements, standards, and methods of doing business established by Berens. Berens also provided office support, advances on expenses, hospitalization, and life insurance.

McGinnis was injured because of the negligence of another Berens sales associate who was driving the two in a company car to inspect real property listed by Berens. When McGinnis sued to collect damages for the injury, Berens argued that he was not liable, as McGinnis was an independent contractor, not an employee. The court disagreed. It held

McGinnis an employee because Berens exercised "control" over the manner in which McGinnis did his job. As the injury was caused by the negligence of another Berens employee, Berens was liable. *McGinnis v. Frederick W. Berens Sales, Inc.*, 308 A.2d 765 (D.C.1973).

Other cases have also held the real estate sales associate an employee, even though the parties themselves have agreed that the sales associate was an independent contractor. These courts looked beyond the parties' understanding of their relationship to the degree of control exercised by the broker. A sales associate can work only for a single broker who holds his or her license; state regulatory statutes require the broker to exercise supervision of the sales associate's activity; therefore, control is usually relatively simple to establish.

Licensing Laws

■ *State laws that require a person to obtain a license to act as a real estate broker or sales associate and regulate the conduct of those who act as brokers or sales associates in real estate transactions.*

Real estate licensing laws are an exercise of the police power by the state. Based on this power, each state as sovereign may legislate to protect the general welfare of its citizens. In 1917, California became the first state to adopt a comprehensive, statewide licensing statute. Since then, all states have passed some type of legislation regulating the activities of real estate brokers and sales associates. The core of this legislation is a licensing requirement. A major goal of these laws is to ensure that only people who are honest and competent operate as brokers and sales personnel.

Most state statutes define broker broadly, using as a basis typical activities involved in the sale and rental of real estate. Usually these statutes exempt lawyers and others acting in special relationships under court supervision. These would include administrators, executors, trustees, and receivers. All states allow an individual owner to sell his or her own property without a real estate license, although some questions arise when the owner is a corporation. The general rule appears to be that a corporation selling its own land is not required to be licensed if it operates through regular employees who have actual authority to exercise the general powers of the corporation. Ordinarily, the board of directors and corporate officers such as the president and secretary have this power. However, when a corporation hires sales personnel solely to attempt to sell corporate land, these people must be licensed.

A number of sanctions exist for engaging in brokerage activity without a license. Most states merely deny the unlicensed broker the right to collect a commission or other fee. In a few states, acting as a broker or sales associate without a license is a misdemeanor, punishable by fine and/or imprisonment. Some states allow any person who suffers a monetary loss because of the acts of an unlicensed broker or sales associate to sue for damages.

Although the license laws of the states have many differences, some relatively common elements do exist. One reason for this is that many state laws are based on a pattern of law recommended by the National Association of REALTORS®.

Licensing statutes are usually administered by an appointed real estate commission or board. The commissioners are usually highly regarded people active in the real estate business. The commission has the power to make rules and regulations of its own to carry out the directives of the legislature. In addition to the commission, a full-time executive director is hired by the state to perform the administrative duties of the commission. Although the primary function of the commission is to administer licensing laws, most real estate commissions have other responsibilities. These commonly include the establishment and promulgation of educational and ethical standards.

In most states the competency of applicants for brokers' and sales associates' licenses is established by written examination. Many states have added minimal educational requirements, which must be met before a person is eligible to take a broker's or sales associate's license examination. Usually, to be eligible for the broker's examination, an individual must have had some experience as a sales associate or meet certain educational criteria. The examination for a broker's license is ordinarily more comprehensive than that for a license to sell. A number of states have adopted legislation requiring continuing education for brokers and sales associates. In Ohio, for example, they must complete 30 classroom hours of real estate education every three years to retain their licenses.

The principal sanction available against a broker or sales associate is the revocation of his or her license. Numerous actions serve as the basis for revocation or suspension. Frequently these actions are indicated by statute, but in some states the real estate commission has authority to promulgate its own rules and regulations. Misconduct punishable under statute by suspension or revocation need not involve real estate transactions or dealings with the licensee as a broker, and a broker may be punished for misconduct even when no one actually suffers a monetary loss.

Unauthorized Practice of Law

In attempting to bring buyer and seller together to complete a sale, one of the perennial problems faced by brokers is the extent to which they can give legal advice, draft legal instruments, or fill in blanks on printed forms without practicing law illegally. Little agreement exists in the United States as to what the broker can do without being involved in the unauthorized practice of law. Some states allow conduct clearly prohibited in others. Nevertheless, two principles do seem commonly accepted. First, permitted activities must be incidental to a transaction in which the broker is involved. A number of states, for example, allow brokers to fill in blanks on printed forms drafted by lawyers. In any state, however, a broker who did this for someone not a client or a prospective purchaser of real estate listed with the broker would be guilty of unauthorized practice of law. Second, a broker is not entitled to charge a separate fee for any legal work that is permitted.

Some states have attempted to clarify by statute what constitutes unauthorized practice. These statutes generally prohibit someone who is not a lawyer from giving legal advice and from drafting legal instruments. A few of these states exempt real estate brokers and title insurance companies from prosecution for drafting certain types of legal instruments related to real estate. At least one state, Arizona, by a constitutional amendment adopted in 1970, specifically gives real estate brokers the right to prepare legal documents incident to their trade.

In a majority of states, by judicial decision interpreting unauthorized practice statutes, it is clear that a broker may neither give legal advice nor draft instruments relating to real estate. For the broker to do so constitutes the unauthorized practice of law. This is true even if the broker does these things only for his or her own clients, only occasionally, and receives no compensation for such work. A few states do permit a broker to draft simple deeds or other real estate instruments if this is done on isolated occasions and without compensation.

Brokers in most states are permitted to fill in blanks on certain printed forms that have been prepared by attorneys. In a majority of states the forms are restricted to the contract offer, and acceptance. The rationale for this position is that these are the only forms that are incidental to the broker's business. Other states allow the broker to complete blanks on lawyer-approved instruments such as a deed or mortgage.

The reality of the marketplace is that many residential sales, from signing of the purchase agreement to the transfer of the title at the closing, take place without the presence or advice of a lawyer. In these situations, brokers are hard pressed not to explain legal terms and their effect. Most states, however, make it clear that such advice is an illegal practice of law. One interesting twist is that the New Jersey Supreme Court concluded that brokers conducting these transactions were engaged in the practice of law, but not the "unauthorized" practice of law. It stated that the parties in these situations did not suffer damages and the public interest was served by handling real estate transactions in this fashion. So far, other states have not followed the New Jersey lead.

Penalties for practicing law without a license are harsh. In most states the unauthorized practice of law is a crime. The person convicted is subject to both a fine and imprisonment. A real estate broker who engages in unauthorized legal practice can have his or her license suspended or revoked. In addition, a person who suffers a monetary loss because of a broker's erroneous legal advice can collect from the broker in a suit for malpractice.

■ KEY TERMS

agency 253	express authority 258	open listing 257
broker 254	implied authority 258	ready, willing, and
buyer's broker 266	independent	able buyer 273
dual agency 268	contractor 255	real estate sales
exclusive agency 256	multiple-listing	associate 277
exclusive right to sell 256	service 257	transaction brokers 270

THE CHANGING LANDSCAPE

Real estate brokers and other professionals are primarily engaged in the business of selling. Any salesman knows that it is easier to sell a new, exciting product than one that is seen as mundane or run of the mill. Assuming you are a broker, does the product described below excite you?

In surfing the Web we came across *www.civano.com.* Civano is the name of a residential development in the Sonoran Desert in Tucson, Arizona, begun in 1999. The home page refers to the development as "(A) community with a commitment to sustainable living, and neighbors who celebrate their vibrant, special lifestyle." In an era when there is broad concern about environmental damage being done by development and about the loss of a sense of community is our lives, Civano sounds good; but most promotional pieces do.

Though we have no firsthand knowledge of the development, it takes a very professional, businesslike approach. It has a mission statement that states in part that it wants to "(c)reate a sense of place that invites community and connects people to each other and their natural surroundings."

Among other things it has narrow, winding streets, front porches, a mixture of big houses and small houses, and integrated uses, including retail and restaurants. One of its goals is to follow IMPACT standards that seek a balance between growth, affordability ($90,000 to $200,000 for 1,150 to 2,200 square feet), and greater integration with the environment. Another goal is to reduce energy consumption by 50 percent compared with a comparable home. This will be achieved through a mix of new and old technologies; for example, thermally efficient, thick adobe walls and double pane, specially coated windows. Several other "technologies" are mentioned, but you get the idea.

Would you like to be selling these houses? Would there be a market beyond the dedicated environmentalists? Would you like to live there? Do you think the approach is geographically transferable; for example, to the East, Midwest, and other areas of the U.S.? Do you see any downside to this type of development?

■ INTERNET RESOURCES

www.trel.com/using.html
(Using a broker to sell property—things one should know about the agency relationship)

www.lectlaw.com/files/lws46.html
(Creation of an agency relationship)

www.mass.gov/dpl/consumer/fspagere.htm
(Discusses real estate brokerage for consumers)

■ REVIEW AND DISCUSSION QUESTIONS

1. What are the two types of exclusive listings? Explain how they differ.

2. Compare and contrast express authority and implied authority. Provide some examples of implied authority.

3. Although appreciable differences exist in the United States as to what constitutes unauthorized practice of law, two principles are commonly accepted. State these principles.

■ CASE PROBLEMS

1. Ed Kelly gave Dave Gould Realty an exclusive listing on property owned by Kelly. Gould showed the property to Nadine McNicols, a real estate developer. McNicols had numerous questions relating to zoning, and Gould referred her to Kelly's attorney, who answered her questions and supplied her with additional information.

   When McNicols learned that Gould was showing the property to other prospective buyers, she made an offer directly to Kelly. Kelly accepted the offer but refused to pay Gould a commission. (a) What argument could be made for Kelly? (b) For Gould? (c) Who would win if Gould sued? Why?

2. Sam Guidi, a real estate broker, learned from a friend that Arro, Inc., was interested in buying vacant land for a warehouse. Knowing that Byron Lane owned land that he was trying to sell, Guidi phoned Lane, who quoted him a price of $35,000 for the parcel. Lane knew that Guidi was a broker, but no commission or other arrangements were discussed. Guidi obtained an offer of $28,000 from Arro, which Lane rejected. Shortly thereafter Lane contacted Arro directly and entered into a contract at $33,000. In a suit by Guidi against Lane for a commission, what resulted? Why?

3. Caldwell listed property with Burnette, a broker, at $3,000 per acre. The listing was open. Burnette showed the property to Donaldson, who stated that the price was too high. He requested Burnette to persuade Caldwell to reduce it. Burnette submitted an offer of $2,750 to Caldwell, but Caldwell would not accept the lower price.

   Several months later, Caldwell listed the property with Crutchfield at $2,500. Crutchfield showed the property to several prospective purchasers, including Donaldson. Donaldson offered $2,750 and the property was sold to him at that price. When Burnette heard of this, he demanded a commission. When Caldwell refused, Burnette sued. Would Burnette be successful? Support your answer. *Leon Realty, Inc. v. Hough*, 310 So.2d 767 (Fla. Dist. Ct. 1973).

4. Lewis, a licensed real estate sales associate, listed residential property owned by Flavin. Flavin informed Lewis that the property was in the South West School District. Actually the property was in the Columbus School District. Flavin, however, did not know this because he had no children and had frequently received mailings from the South West schools. In addition, children who lived next door attended schools in the South West District.

   Katz and her husband were looking for a home, but they did not want to buy property in the Columbus district because children were bused substantial distances to achieve racial balance. The Katz family was interested in Flavin's home and agreed to buy it after Lewis assured them that it was in the South West District. Would the erroneous statement made by Lewis be a basis for Katz to recover damages? Discuss.

13 Fraud

Generally, in commercial transactions, the applicable rule is *caveat emptor,* or "let the buyer beware." The risk of loss due to "defects" in such cases, falls on the buyer. However, as you will see in this chapter, residential real estate transactions are subject to different rules, often requiring something more than the "morals of the marketplace."

■ FRAUD

■ *A deceptive act or statement deliberately made by one person in an attempt to gain an unfair advantage over another.*

No evidence exists that misrepresentation and fraud are more prevalent in real estate than they are in other sectors of the economy. However, deceptive acts that occur in real estate transactions probably have a greater impact than they do in other areas for several reasons. First, most real estate transactions involve relatively large sums of money; as a result, people who feel deceived are more apt to complain or take legal action to assert their rights. A second reason is that licensing laws in every state have placed substantial supervisory responsibility on brokers for the conduct of their sales associates, as was detailed in Chapter 12. Unauthorized and even unintentional misrepresentation by the sales associate may subject the broker to liability, including loss of license. Finally, in many transactions little direct contact takes place between buyer and seller. Inasmuch as information is often transmitted through a third party, misunderstanding and error may result in the buyer, seller, or both feeling that they have been deceived.

Fraud may be classified into two major categories, based on the intent of the one who practices it. *Actual fraud*, or misrepresentation, is based on intentional deception and is usually accomplished by misstating or concealing a material fact. Actual fraud is often called *deceit*, and the two terms are used synonymously in this chapter. *Constructive fraud*, on the other hand, is not based on *intentional* deception. Constructive fraud often consists of a breach of duty arising out of the fiduciary relationship discussed in previous chapters. Liability for constructive fraud may be based on a negligent or even an innocent misrepresentation. The law imputes fraud here because of its tendency to deceive another or to injure the public interest.

Those who enter into an agreement because they have been the victim of fraud, actual or constructive, are entitled to some form of remedy for injury suffered as a result. The remedy available often depends on the extent to which the person making the misrepresentation intended to deceive. Remedies will be discussed more fully later in the chapter.

Various parties involved in a real estate transaction are potentially liable for fraud or deceit: buyer, seller, broker, sales associate, or attorney. A defendant is liable for fraud if plaintiff can establish that defendant *intentionally misstated a material fact* on which plaintiff *justifiably relied*. Additionally, the plaintiff must be able to prove *damages*.

Intentional. An intentional, conscious misrepresentation is an essential element of actionable fraud. Courts usually refer to this as an *intention to deceive*. The technical term *scienter* is also used. Scienter exists if a person knowingly makes a false statement or asserts that something is true or false without actual knowledge of whether this is the case. An evil intention is not necessary, nor is it required that the speaker intend to injure the other party.

Early cases found the requisite intent only in those situations in which the speaker had actual knowledge of the falsity of the representation; the courts equated intent to deceive with knowledge of falsity. This restrictive interpretation did not long survive. Today all American jurisdictions find scienter not only when the speaker knew the representation to be false but also when the representation was made either without belief in the statement's truth or with reckless disregard of its truth or falsity. Included are statements made when the speaker does not have sufficient basis or information to justify them.

CASE EXAMPLE

Gertrude Hall contracted to exchange her home for one being built by Haskin. The agreement was conditioned on rezoning her property from residential to commercial use. After the property was rezoned, Haskin asked her to sign a blank deed. Mrs. Hall questioned this and inquired of Wright, her attorney, about the title to Haskin's property. Although Wright had never examined the title, he told her to sign the deed and that he would see that she got an abstract showing clear title.

Hall moved into the Haskin property. Some time later, Wright discovered that it was heavily mortgaged. Hall refused to make the mortgage payments, and she was ousted from possession. She then sued Wright for fraud. Wright defended on the grounds that he had not intended to deceive her. This defense was unacceptable to the court on the grounds that Wright spoke without knowledge. See *Hall v. Wright*, 261 Iowa 758, 156 N.W.2d 661 (1968).

A majority of courts in the United States will not award damages for fraud if the speaker honestly believes, on the basis of credible evidence, that the representation is true. A substantial and growing minority do not accept this limitation when the innocent misrepresentation is made in a transaction involving the sale, rental, or exchange of real estate. In these transactions the courts allow damages but limit them to the difference in value between what was paid and the value of what has been received and retained.

CASE EXAMPLE

Glenn, a father of two preschool children, leased a house from Takio on a five-year term. The rental was $600 per month. Takio had innocently represented to Glenn that a new school was to be built in the neighborhood. Takio did not know that the plans had been canceled. When Glenn discovered the cancellation, he sued Takio for damages, claiming deceit. Glenn was able to prove that the rental value of the property without the new school was $450. The court awarded damages to compensate him for the reduced rental value of the property.

Misstatement of a Past or Present Fact. An important premise of American contract law is that adults are competent and have the ability to make rational decisions. As a result, courts do not aid those who rely on statements not worthy of belief. Judges reason that the rational person discounts statements that are not factual.

CASE EXAMPLE

Elfrieda A. Scantlin contracted to purchase a house being constructed by Superior Homes (Superior). In the course of the negotiations leading to the sale, an agent for Manning Real Estate, the builder's broker, stated that Superior was "a good builder and constructed excellent homes." After Scantlin took title, she found several things wrong with the building. When Superior did not repair these defects satisfactorily, she sued both Superior and Manning Real Estate. Scantlin claimed that the statement made by the agent was fraudulent. Scantlin's case against Manning was dismissed as the court held the agent's statement was merely his opinion. *Scantlin v. Superior Homes*, 627 P.2d 825 (Kan. Ct. App. 1981).

Although the rule that only factual statements that are misrepresented may be the basis for fraud is clear, often it is difficult to determine what statements are factual. A fact is something that is knowable: a physical object that actually exists or existed or an event that is underway or has taken place. Understanding what the law means by a statement of fact is often clarified by examining statements that courts generally consider as not factual. These include opinions and estimates (as illustrated by the previous case example), predictions, guesses, and promises.

Promises require a special word of caution. As discussed in Chapter 10, one who breaks a promise may be liable for breach of contract. One who makes fraudulent statements may have committed a tort. Whether a party has been injured by a breach of contract due to a failure to perform on a promise or by a fraudulent representation makes a difference. For example, in a breach of contract action, the successful plaintiff may recover for compensatory damages. If successful in a suit based on fraud, however, the plaintiff may collect punitive damages as well.

Puffing. Sellers have a natural tendency to commend the item they are selling. Such expressions as "I built it with the best," "It's the best building in town," and "You have nothing to worry about; it's a good well" are examples. Statements of opinion like this, made by a seller to induce the purchaser to buy, are often referred to as **puffing** or *dealer's talk*. Such statements are not actionable as fraud, even when false, because courts treat them as expressions of opinion or an exaggeration. (See Table 13.1.) A leading American jurist, Judge Learned Hand, explained why in the following language.

> There are some kinds of talk which no sensible man takes seriously, and if he does he suffers from his credulity. If we were all scrupulously honest, it would not be so; but, as it is, neither party usually believes what the seller says about his opinions, and each knows it. Such statements, like the claims of campaign managers before election, are rather designed to allay the suspicion which would attend their absence than to be understood as having any relation to objective truth. *Vulcan Metals Co. v. Simmons Mfg.* Co., 248 F. 853, 856 (2d Cir. 1918).

TABLE 13.1	Fact and Puffing: A Contrast	

Statements of Fact	Puffing
"This house was constructed in 1999."	"This house is like new!"
"This building is constructed with steel support beams."	"This is a solid building."
"A king lived in this house."	"This house is for kings."
"This house is scheduled to be annexed by the city."	"This is the best house in the city."

Opinion. Although generally the law does not protect the naive buyer who relies on the seller's opinion, a number of situations exist in which courts allow recovery for fraud based on nonfactual statements. Opinions expressed by (1) a person who enjoys a relationship of trust and confidence or has superior knowledge, (2) an expert hired to give advice, or (3) a person who actually does not have this opinion are all actionable.

In the following examples, assertions that ordinarily would have been treated as opinion became the basis for fraud. In each case the court determined that the other party had a right to rely on the representation. Courts often rule this way when a pattern of deceptive conduct exists, or when the speaker has concealed something that fairness dictated should be revealed.

CASE EXAMPLE

Mel Erickson, a licensed real estate broker, specialized in investment properties. Tillitz, a wealthy rancher, wished to invest in a multifamily dwelling. Erickson showed Tillitz several properties. After inspecting one large unit, Erickson stated, "That's a fine building, and the return on your investment would be substantial." At the time, Erickson had never inspected the records and was unaware of some major problems with the heating units.

Tillitz purchased the building, lost money, and sued Erickson for fraud. Because of Erickson's superior knowledge, many courts would consider the statement a basis for fraud.

In the case that follows, a statement is clearly opinion, but the speaker is asserting an opinion that she does not actually share.

CASE EXAMPLE

Grover and his wife owned a house on a bluff overlooking Lake Michigan. For a number of years, the Grovers and their neighbors had been concerned with erosion along the shore and the safety of their homes. In fact, a group of people from the area, including the Grovers, had met with the Army Corps of Engineers to work out a solution to the erosion problem.

A prospective buyer of the Grover property expressed concern as to the safety of the house. Mrs. Grover responded, "The house is perfectly safe. We are living here, aren't we?" In an action to rescind the contract of sale, the Grovers defended on the grounds that the statement was merely an expression of her opinion. This defense would not be successful, inasmuch as the Grovers did not actually have this opinion. See *Groening v. Opsota*, 67 Mich. 244, 34 N.W.2d 560 (1948).

Law. During the past 50 or 60 years, the trend has been to expand the type of statement that may serve as the basis for fraud. Courts look beyond the form of the statement and consider the circumstances in which it was made when attempting to determine whether there was deceit. One example is the manner in which most state courts treat statements of law made by a layperson. Courts traditionally considered these statements of opinion. They arbitrarily reasoned that all laypeople had comparable knowledge of the law; as a result, the person to whom that statement was made had no right to rely on it. Today, the law in most states differs. Courts generally examine the context in which such statements are made. In many instances, they conclude that the circumstances are such that a reasonable person has the right to rely on the layperson's representation concerning the law.

Silence. Both buyers and sellers of real estate have been successful in actions for fraud, even when specific words concerning particular facts were never spoken. Most actions for fraud are based on oral or written statements, but numerous other methods are used to deceive. Actions, failure to act, concealment, and silence may all be employed to mislead another.

> **CASE EXAMPLE**
>
> Lawson purchased land in a development called Vanderbilt Hills. He had a house constructed on this property. After a few months, the house began to sink. On investigation, Lawson discovered that the developer had filled a large gully with logs, stumps, and other types of debris and covered this with clay. The land apparently was level, and enough clay had been dumped into the gully so that excavation for the foundation did not disclose the fill. Lawson was successful in a suit against the developer for fraud, inasmuch as the court held that the seller had a duty to disclose what he had done because the purchaser could not discover this through a reasonable inspection. *Lawson v. Citizens So. Nat'l Bank of South Carolina*, 259 S.C. 477, 193 S.E.2d 124 (1972).

The most difficult legal questions arise in cases in which a buyer has suffered a loss because of the seller's failure to speak. In some instances, the seller simply fails to disclose an element important in the transaction. In others, the seller employs some trick or scheme to conceal a condition or fact that is material to the transaction.

The cases that involve concealment are much easier to decide than those that merely involve silence, absent concealment. Active effort to hide something usually overcomes any reluctance courts have to refuse relief on the grounds of *caveat emptor.*

As a general rule, a party's silence—even silence concerning a critical factor—is not actionable as a misrepresentation. U.S. contract law does not ordinarily require that an individual voluntarily disclose even material facts detrimental to the other party to the transaction. However, there is a positive obligation to disclose defects that are material, and which are not ordinarily discoverable by a reasonably prudent person. Courts call this a duty to speak. Such is the following case involving a "stigmatized house" in which a seller failed to disclose certain facts about the property.

Reed v. King
Court of Appeals of California
145 Cal. App. 3d 261 (1983)

Background. Dorris Reed purchased a house from Robert King. Neither King nor his real estate agent told Reed that a woman and her four children had been murdered in the house ten years earlier. Reed learned of the gruesome episode from a neighbor after the sale. Reed sued King and his agent seeking rescission and damages. The trial court dismissed the case on defendant's motion that the plaintiff's complaint failed to state a cause of action. Reed appealed.

Decision. The Court of Appeals reversed the trial court decision.

Judge Blease. King and his real estate agent knew about the murders and knew the event materially affected the market value of the house when they listed it for sale. They represented to Reed the premises were in good condition and fit for an "elderly lady" living alone. They did not disclose the fact of the murders. At some point King asked a neighbor not to inform Reed of that event. Nonetheless, after Reed moved in neighbors informed her no one was interested in purchasing the house because of the stigma.

* * *

"The elements of fraud . . . may be stated as follows: There must be (1) a false representation or concealment of a material fact . . . susceptible of knowledge, (2) made with knowledge of its falsity or without sufficient knowledge on the subject to warrant a representation, (3) with the intent to induce the person to whom it is made to act on it; and such person must (4) act in reliance on the representation (5) to his damage."

* * *

Concealment is a term of art which includes mere nondisclosure when a party has a duty to disclose. Accordingly, the critical question is: does the seller have a duty to disclose here? Resolution of this question depends on the materiality of the fact of the murders.

In general, a seller of real property has a duty to disclose:

Where the seller knows of facts materially affecting the value or desirability of the property which are known or accessible only to him and also knows that such facts are not known to, or within the reach of the diligent attention and observation of the buyer. . . . This broad statement of duty has led one commentator to conclude: The ancient maxim caveat emptor (let the buyer beware) has little or no application to California real estate transactions.

Numerous cases have found nondisclosure of physical defects and legal impediments to use of real property are material. However, to our knowledge, no prior real estate sale case has faced an issue of nondisclosure of the kind presented here. Should this variety of ill-repute be required to be disclosed? Is this a circumstance where "non-disclosure of the fact amounts to a failure to act in good faith and in accordance with reasonable standards of fair dealing[?]"

The paramount argument against an affirmative conclusion is it permits the camel's nose of unrestrained irrationality admission to the tent. If such an "irrational" consideration is permitted as a basis of rescission the stability of all conveyances will be seriously undermined. Any fact that might disquiet the enjoyment of some segment of the buying public may be seized on by a disgruntled purchaser to void a bargain. In our view, keeping this genie in the bottle is not as difficult a task as these arguments assume.

* * *

Murder is not such a common occurrence that buyers should be charged with anticipating and discovering this disquieting possibility. Accordingly, the fact is not one for which a duty of inquiry and discovery can sensibly be imposed on the buyer.

Reed alleges the fact of the murders has a quantifiable effect on the market value of the premises. We cannot say this allegation is inherently wrong and, in the pleading posture of the case, we assume it to be true. If information known or accessible only to the seller has a significant and measurable effect, we see no principled basis for making the duty to disclose turn on the character of the information. Physical usefulness is not and never has been the sole criterion of valuation. . . .

Reputation and history can have a significant effect on the value of realty. "George Washington slept here" is worth something, however physically inconsequential that consideration may be. Ill-repute, or "bad will," conversely may depress the value of property. Failure to disclose such a negative fact where it will have a foreseeably depressing effect on income expected to be generated by a business is tortious. Some cases have held that unreasonable fears of the potential buying public that a gas or oil pipeline may rupture may depress the market value of the land. . . .

Whether Reed will be able to prove her allegation that the decade-old multiple murder has a significant effect on market value we cannot determine. If she is able to do so by competent evidence she is entitled to a favorable ruling on the issues of materiality and duty to disclose. Her demonstration of objective tangible harm would still the concern that permitting her to go forward will open the floodgates to rescission on subjective and idiosyncratic grounds.

The judgment is reversed.

What about a "haunted house"? Should that be subject to the same consideration as a "murder in a house"? What about a "registered sex offender" in the neighborhood? Should that require disclosure? Some states do not require sellers or real estate licensees to disclose stigmatizing facts to the buyer.

In the following situations, courts in most states have ruled with consistency that a person must speak out about relevant circumstances and facts known to him or her:

- A hidden defect exists that is likely to result in personal harm to persons using the property.
- A hidden defect exists that is likely to limit a use the seller knows the buyer intends to make of the property.
- The seller enjoys a confidential relationship with the buyer.
- The buyer has asked a question that the seller has answered truthfully, but the situation changes and the answer is now false.

Another troublesome problem exists where the seller has made an oral or written representation that is only partially true. Like silence and concealment, the "half-truth" is a misrepresentation actionable as fraud. In many cases, a half-truth is more misleading than a statement that is completely false. The half-truth can more easily lull the listener into accepting other representations that are made.

CASE EXAMPLE

Franks owned property on the outskirts of town. Although sewer lines had been constructed in the area, Franks's property was not yet connected. A prospective buyer asked Franks if the property was connected to a sewer. Franks replied, "The sewer line is across the street." Later, the buyer discovered that sewage from the house was being piped to the back end of the property. She sued Franks for the cost of having the property hooked to the sewer. Franks argued that his statement was true, but the court awarded damages to the buyer. *McWilliams v. Barnes*, 172 Kan. 701, 242 P.2d 1063 (1952).

Reliance. To be successful in an action for fraud, the injured party must prove that (1) he or she acted in reliance on the false information and (2) the reliance was justified. A person cannot have relied on false information if the information was acquired after the person acted, nor may a person rely on statements that investigation indicates are false.

CASE EXAMPLE

Grace Kiner was interested in purchasing a music store from Helen Little. Kiner's marketing strategy required a large volume of potential customers. Little informed Kiner that on the average 250 people came in daily. Little knew that this was false.

On several occasions, Kiner visited the store, remaining for appreciable periods of time. After Kiner purchased the store, it became apparent that Little's statement was false. As a result, Kiner sued to rescind. Rescission would be denied if the jury determined that Kiner should have relied on her own inspection, rather than Little's statement.

In spite of the previous example, the fact that a purchaser makes an independent investigation does not automatically prove self-reliance. In these situations the courts must weigh the circumstances of the particular case to determine whether continued reliance on the misrepresentation after investigation is justifiable. Critical factors are such elements as the background of the person investigating; amount of time available to investigate; sources of information available; and techniques needed to secure correct information.

Courts use different criteria to determine whether reliance is justifiable. Some states measure the plaintiff's conduct against that of a reasonably prudent person. If a jury decides that a reasonably prudent person, one who uses ordinary care under the circumstances, would not have relied on the statement, the plaintiff's reliance was not justified. Most states, however, have rejected this standard. The test that is applied is tailored to the particular individual to whom the misrepresentation has been made. Courts in these states take the position that the law should not protect positive, intentional fraud practiced on the simpleminded or unwary. At the same time, a person who has special knowledge and competence is not justified in relying on statements that the ordinary person might believe. Similarly, a person whose background and information are those that a normal person might have is not barred from recovery because he or she carelessly accepts a misrepresentation; but if the alleged fact is preposterous, reliance is not justified, and recovery for fraud will be denied.

Material. Not only must the misrepresentation be relied on but it must also be material. A person is not justified in acting on a false statement that is trivial in relation to the entire transaction. Inconsequential information of this nature is not material and thus not grounds for suit. On the other hand, some false statements that in themselves seem to be of no significance are important in particular situations. Consider the following examples, in both of which the representations are false.

CASE EXAMPLE
Rex Todor is purchasing a house in Memphis, Tennessee. The sales associate states, "Elvis Presley's uncle once lived here."

CASE EXAMPLE
Rex Todor is purchasing an inn in Memphis, Tennessee. The sales associate states, "Elvis Presley slept here."

In the first example, the misrepresentation would not be material. A reasonable person would not consider this a significant factor. If, however, the speaker knew that this was important to the buyer, the result would be different. Courts ordinarily will not allow a person knowingly to practice a deception, even though the supposed fact might be unimportant to most people. In the second example, the misrepresentation is material. The fact that Elvis Presley had slept at a particular inn would increase the property's value as an attraction for tourists.

Materiality also has a second dimension, which causes some legal problems. Frequently, a false statement is only one of several reasons that cause the person to act. A difficult factual question exists when the plaintiff has numerous bits of valid information on which a decision could logically be reached but, in addition, has been given some information that is false. Most courts hold that for the false information to be material, it must have contributed substantially to the plaintiff's decision to act. If without this information the injured party would not have contracted, the false information may be the basis of an action for deceit. Whether the information is material is a question for the jury or the trier of the facts.

Remedies Available to the Injured Party. A majority of courts in the United States have taken the position that a party deceived by an innocent misrepresentation is entitled to rescind the contract but not to collect damages. A few courts have held that even an innocent misrepresentation may justify an award of both rescission and damages.

If the misrepresentation is intentional, the injured party may proceed in a number of ways. He or she may

- refuse to perform, using the deceit as a defense if sued for breach of contract;
- affirm the contract and sue for damages; or
- ask a court for a decree rescinding the contract.

In a number of states, courts will not allow the party who rescinds to collect damages. Courts in these states reason that rescission is based on a theory that no contract ever existed. Thus, rescission is inconsistent with an award of damages for breach of contract. The trend in most states, however, is to allow the deceived party who rescinds to collect damages notwithstanding the rescission.

CASE EXAMPLE

Mrs. Slade sold her house to Garrity. At the time that Garrity inspected the property, Slade informed him that the heating unit was new. Actually, the unit had been installed ten years earlier. In a suit for fraud based on the deceit, Garrity would be entitled to damages. These would be related to the cost of installing a new unit. He could also, if he desired, rescind the contract and recover the expenses involved in replacing the old unit.

In an action for fraud, a plaintiff is not entitled to recover damages unless actual monetary loss can be proved. Ordinarily, this requirement is met easily because usually the relationship between the misrepresentation and monetary injury is clear. Few people would sue for misrepresentation unless they believed the deception caused them to lose money. The costs and trauma of litigation make it an expensive way to prove a person a liar if the plaintiff lost nothing.

Punitive damages are those awarded as a punishment to the wrongdoer. To recover punitive damages for the tort of fraud and deceit, the plaintiff must have suffered actual damages. In most states punitive damages will not be awarded unless the action is egregious, oppressive, and committed with ill will. Thus, a person whose misrepresentation was the result of negligence would not be liable for punitives.

The purpose of punitive damages is to deter others from committing similar acts. The award of punitive damages is discretionary with the jury. Punitive damages usually include an amount sufficient to cover an amount the trier of fact considers appropriate to dissuade others. Punitive damages must have some fair relationship to the compensatory damages that have been proved. Punitive damage awards that "shock the conscience" of the court will be abated or reduced. Many states have legislated a "ceiling" on punitive damages.

Negligent Misrepresentation

The rules of negligence apply to a false representation made carelessly in a business transaction. The person supplying false information who fails to exercise reasonable care in obtaining or communicating it (**negligent misrepresentation**) is liable for actual loss suffered by the listener. Because there was no intent to deceive, the speaker's liability is more limited than in a case of intentional misrepresentation. For example, punitive damages are not awarded. (See Table 13.2.) In addition, the defendant may assert defenses, such as plaintiff's contributory negligence, that are not available in an action for deceit.

Waiver

▩ *Intentional surrender of a known right or privilege.*

Under certain circumstances, one who has been induced to enter a contract because of fraud or deceit waives the available remedies. Generally, **waiver** occurs when a person discovers the fraud and then does nothing about it. American courts generally hold that a person learning of deceit must take some action, or the contract based on the deception is considered ratified.

TABLE 13.2	Fraud and Negligent Misrepresentation: Comparison		
		Fraud	**Negligent Misrepresentation**
Intentional		✓	
Misrepresentation		✓	✓
Material		✓	✓
Fact		✓	✓
Reliance		✓	✓
Injury		✓	✓
Compensatory Damages		✓	✓
Punitive Damages		✓	
Rescission		✓	✓

In a majority of U.S. jurisdictions, if the contract is wholly executory—that is, neither party has performed—the defrauded party, on discovery of the fraud, must rescind. Often courts in these jurisdictions do not allow the injured party to recover damages when an executory contract is rescinded. This rule is open to criticism because it denies the injured party the benefit of any bargain that has been made.

When a contract has been substantially performed, the injured party may elect to rescind or affirm the contract and sue for damages. Some action, however, must be taken, and the position of the person defrauded must be made clear to the perpetrator of the fraud. Waiver by the injured party occurs if, after discovery of the fraud, the injured party merely continues to perform. Completion of the contract and a subsequent suit for damages is an available option, but the injured party's position must be established within a reasonable period of time. Otherwise, the injured party is deemed to have "sat on his rights," and, thus, waived any claim of wrongdoing.

Real estate contracts sometimes contain provisions stating that the purchaser has not relied on any representations made by the owner or broker. A modification of this is a statement that the purchaser has personally examined the property and enters the contract relying solely on his or her own inspection. A typical example is a clause such as "buyers agree that they have entered into this contract relying on their own knowledge and not on any representations made by the seller or any other person." Clauses of this type do not waive the injured party's rights to sue for fraudulent representations made by an owner or a broker. The courts reason that to accept such clauses as defenses would provide the seller and the seller's agent with a license to commit fraud. Most buyers would neither recognize the significance of the language nor consider that it applied to outright deception. To allow its enforcement would violate the clear public policy of protecting people who act on the basis of deceptive statements.

THE CHANGING LANDSCAPE

Human nature has not changed over the centuries. Because of greed and the desire for money, people continue to engage in fraud and deceit.

Fraud comes in many varieties when related to real estate. There are as many ways to defraud buyers and sellers as there are people who are willing to do it. Active fraud, passive fraud, and misrepresentation are a few types discussed in this chapter. When the wrong is accompanied by the requisite criminal intent, the wrongdoer may suffer the consequences of fine and imprisonment. To some extent, this acts as a deterrent. Most fraud, however, in this area is confined to the civil arena. A victim must ordinarily sue and seek redress by way of rescission or compensatory damages and punitive damages, when appropriate. Suits are costly, time consuming, and emotionally rending, and although a persevering victim may collect in the long run, winning is not without a heavy toll. This has prompted some reformers to look for fair solutions to this complex problem.

A number of states have a victims' compensation fund available to those who have suffered loss as a result of broker fraud. These recovery programs are funded out of licensing fees. In addition, some states have victims' compensation statutes whereby a victim may seek compensation out of a state fund. These are usually very restrictive and pay only for medical costs and lost wages. Cases of fraud are ordinarily beyond the scope of these statutes. However, there is nothing to prevent a state legislature from implementing legislation that would grant defrauded buyers reasonable compensation for their loss out of a state fund. What would you think of such a law? How would it be funded? Can you suggest a process?

■ KEY TERMS

fraud 285

negligent
  misrepresentation 294

puffing 287

waiver 294

■ INTERNET RESOURCES

For a resource library on fraud see

www.cfenet.com/resources/resources.asp

■ REVIEW AND DISCUSSION QUESTIONS

1. Explain the difference between actual and constructive fraud.
2. What is the meaning of scienter?

3. A limited number of situations exist in which silence may be the basis for a successful action based on fraud. Discuss these situations.

4. Under what circumstances should a court award punitive damages in a case involving fraud?

5. Many courts refuse to award damages for fraud if a contract is wholly executory. Critically evaluate this rule.

■ CASE PROBLEMS

1. Able hired a contractor to repair several cracks in the walls of his home. The cracks were the result of settling, but the contractor never mentioned this fact to Able. Somehow Able got the impression that the cracks were caused by green lumber. When Able later tells Baker, a prospective purchaser, about the cracks, he explains the cause as green lumber. Baker purchases the property. When additional cracks appear and Baker discovers their true cause, he sues Able for fraud. Is Able liable? Discuss.

2. J. B. Williams was an experienced businessman. In 1977, he entered into a written contract to buy realty from Threlkeld and Murray for $1 million. During the negotiations, Van Hersh, who represented the sellers, stated that New York Life had made a commitment to loan $6 million to develop the property. The terms of this loan were never discussed, nor did the parties ever talk about interest rates or any possible conditions. Williams did not check with New York Life. When Williams discovered that the life insurance company had not made a commitment, he attempted to rescind the contract on the grounds of fraud. Would he be successful? Discuss. *Williams v. Van Hersh*, 578 S.W.2d 373 (Tenn. 1978).

3. Kaye was interested in buying a large piece of land from Katzenberry, who lived nearby. Katzenberry did not want to sell the land to a buyer who would use it for commercial purposes; he asked Kaye what he planned to do with the property. Kaye told Katzenberry that he was going to build a house on part of it and probably would use the rest for a garden. This was true, but before the closing Kaye changed his mind and made plans to build a hamburger stand next to his house. Katzenberry learned of this and refused to convey the property. Kaye sued for breach of contract; the defense claimed fraud. Would Kaye be successful? Discuss.

4. Hayes owned a valley home that he wanted to sell. He listed the property with Watkins, a local broker. Hayes knew that the basement of the house was subject to extensive flooding, especially during the spring. He did not inform Watkins of this. Watkins did know that rains and melting snow in the spring often caused a flooding problem for valley property.

    During the fall, Hayes showed the house to Morris, who was from out of state. While the two were examining the basement, Morris expressed concern about obvious water damage. Watkins, who stood nearby, said nothing. Later, while talking to Hayes, Morris asked about basement flooding. Hayes stated that in the spring, water sometimes seeped into the basement. Watkins, who listened to the conversation, again said nothing.

Morris purchased the property. The following spring the basement was damaged by severe flooding. Morris sued both Hayes and Watkins for fraud. What defenses, if any, are available to Hayes and Watkins? Will Morris be successful? Support your answer.

5. In June 1979, Marilyn Kramer decided to buy a house in Manchester, Vermont, for $42,500. Prior to the purchase she signed an agreement with the seller stating that the purchase was contingent on her obtaining a favorable inspection report on the property. Kramer hired Lee Chabot, a builder, to carry out the inspection.

   Chabot gave Kramer a one-page report stating that the house was in good condition. In reliance, Kramer completed the purchase. Later, after the sale, Kramer discovered numerous defects in the house that required substantial repairs, requiring more than $25,000 to put the house into shape. Kramer sued Chabot for breach of professional duty and misrepresentation for the amount she had spent on repairs after buying the house. After the repairs the house was worth in excess of the purchase price plus the repairs. Who should win? How much? *Kramer v. Chabot*, 564 A.2d 292 (Vt. 1989).

6. Hattie Griffin agreed to give a lot to Charles Spence, a self-educated itinerant preacher, and his wife. Mrs. Griffin had befriended the Spences and they had provided her with spiritual comfort on the death of her son. The transfer was conditioned on the Spences building a church on the lot and allowing Mrs. Griffin the right to use the church parking facilities as a parking lot for her restaurant on an adjoining lot. The parties had also agreed that the lot was to revert to Mrs. Griffin if it was not used for a church.

   At the closing, which was hastily arranged, Mrs. Griffin read the deed, but not carefully. Both Spence and his attorney assured her that it was "drawn up like you asked." However, the deed did not contain wording that restored the property to Mrs. Griffin if it was not used for a church. At the trial the attorney testified that he had tried to explain the contents of the deed to Mrs. Griffin, but he felt she did not understand it.

   When problems arose concerning the use of the parking facilities by Mrs. Griffin's customers and financing a building on the lot, Mrs. Griffin sued for rescission on grounds of fraud. Would she be successful? Discuss.

7. Reilley owned a small ranch that he planned to sell. The ranch was in a rural area, and the exact boundaries were not clear. Although a survey of the ranch existed, Reilley felt that it was incorrect. As a result, he hired Gavin, a licensed surveyor, to resurvey the ranch. Reilley placed stakes in the ground where he believed to be one of the corners, and Gavin surveyed with that as the starting point.

   When Reilley placed the property on the market, he used Gavin's survey as the basis for the description of the property. Herman contracted to purchase the ranch on the basis of the Gavin survey. During the negotiations, Herman and Reilley walked what Reilley informed Herman were the boundaries. Reilley did not inform Herman of the questionable boundaries or the existence of the first survey.

After Herman took the title, he discovered that boundaries were questionable and that another survey existed. This survey indicated that the ranch was smaller than the Gavin survey indicated. Herman sued to rescind, arguing fraud in that Reilley had not informed him of the questionable boundaries and the discrepancy between the two surveys. Would Herman be successful? Support your answer.

8. Plaintiff, a resident of New York City, contracted to purchase a house in Nyack, New York. Not being a "local," plaintiff could not readily learn that the home he had contracted to purchase was haunted. Defendant had capitalized on the presence of ghosts and her haunted house to further its reputation. Defendant failed, however, to disclose the presence of ghosts to plaintiff when the contract for the sale was entered into. The court allowed the buyer to seek rescission of the contract of sale and a return of his down payment. Do you agree with the result? Explain. See *Stambovsky v. Ackley,* 169 A.D.2d 254 (N.Y. Sup. Ct. App. Div., 1991).

 Go to the Student Study Guide CD-ROM and work through Case 3.

PART FOUR

Closing the Transaction

14 Escrow Closing

■ REAL ESTATE ESCROW

■ *A deed delivered by a grantor to an escrow agent, who is directed to deliver the deed to a grantee when specified conditions are met.*

In Chapter 20, we will examine a conventional closing, where buyer and seller meet face to face to exchange the deed for the purchase price. The **real estate escrow** closing is a modification of this procedure that is practiced in some localities. (See Table 14.1.) Instead of the buyer and seller meeting face to face, a third party acts as an intermediary. The third party, commonly called an *escrow agent*, is charged with certain responsibilities designed ultimately to invest the seller with the full purchase price and the buyer with good title to the property. Not all localities commonly employ the escrow closing; however, there is no reason why it cannot be employed as the need arises.

The subject of the escrow transaction is a written instrument. The written instrument in the normal real estate escrow transaction involves a deed. Technically, the term *escrow* characterizes the instrument—the deed itself—while it is held by the third party. This strict terminology has been relaxed, however, and it is common to refer to "depositing a deed into escrow." In this regard the escrow is the "receptacle" of the instrument rather than the instrument itself. Courts refer to escrows in both senses, and either reference is acceptable. As you study this chapter you may find the following Web site helpful: *www.escrowhelp.com/articles.html.*

Escrow Closing Distinguished

An escrow closing should not be confused with an escrow account established by a real estate broker to hold funds belonging to others. Nor should it be confused with the escrow *account*. Many mortgages include a clause requiring that the mortgagee set up an escrow account to be used to disburse payments for real estate taxes and/or hazard insurance premiums. The particulars of this escrow account vary from jurisdiction to jurisdiction. Generally, the mortgagor pays into the escrow account monthly an amount equal to one-twelfth of the amount of the yearly property tax and hazard insurance premium. This constitutes an additional amount above the normal mortgage payment. Oftentimes, the purchaser, at closing, will be initially required to deposit up to six months of the tax and insurance premium monies into escrow. The mortgagee then makes payments directly from the escrow account to pay taxes and insurance premiums when they become due. This type of escrow procedure is required for FHA-insured loans and for most conventional loans; it is suggested for VA-guaranteed loans. These escrowed funds are normally placed in non-interest-bearing accounts; depositors are not ordinarily paid for the use of

TABLE 14.1	Conventional Closing vs. Escrow Closing		
		Conventional Closing	**Escrow Closing**
Face-to-Face		Yes	No
Written Contract		Yes	Yes
Escrow Agent		No	Yes
Delivery of Deed		Yes	Yes

the funds. Periodically, usually annually, the escrow needs are re-evaluated and the mortgagor's escrow payments may be adjusted up or down, accordingly.

The Escrow Transaction

In the most elementary real estate escrow transaction, a seller and a buyer enter into a contract for the purchase of specified real property. They agree to close the transaction in escrow, and they appoint a bank or other escrow agent to be responsible for handling the closing. As part of the agreement between the parties, the seller then deposits a fully executed deed with the escrow agent. The escrow agent is instructed to deliver the deed to the purchaser after receipt of the purchase price. When the purchase price is deposited by the purchaser, the escrow agent delivers the deed to the purchaser and the purchase price to the seller. At this point, the escrow closing is complete. (See Figure 14.1.)

Another typical example of the real estate escrow transaction involves conditions relating to title. In this arrangement, the seller deposits the deed, and the purchaser deposits the purchase price, with the escrow agent. When the purchaser's attorney approves the title to the property, the escrow agent is bound by the purchase contract or other agreement to deliver the deed to the purchaser and the money to the seller. The escrow agent may be instructed to record the deed in favor of the purchaser as soon as the purchaser deposits the money, even before the title to the property is approved.

FIGURE 14.1	Escrow Transaction

Then, in the event the title cannot be approved, the purchaser is entitled to a return of the purchase money upon reconveying the deed to the seller. A variation of this procedure requires that the purchaser execute a quitclaim deed in favor of the seller and deposit it with the escrow agent at the time the purchase money is deposited and the deed is recorded in favor of the purchaser. In the event that title cannot be approved, the escrow agent is required to record the quitclaim deed and return the purchase money to the purchaser, thus returning the parties to their previous position.

The real estate escrow device is not confined to money transactions, but may also be used when the seller and purchaser are merely interested in exchanging deeds to real estate.

CASE EXAMPLE

Rocky Hayes owns a five-acre tract of land in Florida and is interested in selling his land and moving to Colorado. Johnny Ruskin owns a five-acre tract of land in Colorado and is interested in moving to Florida. A real estate broker brings the two together, and an even exchange of property is agreed on. Hayes deposits his deed to the Florida property with Jerry Bloom, a third party, on condition that the Florida deed be delivered to Ruskin on receipt of the deed to the Colorado property. When Ruskin deposits the deed to the Colorado property, Bloom will deliver it to Hayes and deliver the deed to the Florida property to Ruskin, thus completing the escrow transaction. See *Morris v. Davis*, 334 Mo. 411, 66 S.W.2d 883 (1933).

■ ADVANTAGES OF ESCROW

The objective of the escrow transaction is to ensure that the buyer is invested with marketable title to the property and the seller receives the purchase price. The use of the escrow device in closing sales of real estate enjoys the advantages of convenience and protection against a party's change of mind.

Convenience

Sometimes it is simply inconvenient for parties to be present at a closing. The escrow method of closing enjoys the advantage of facilitating interstate transactions or other closings where it is not feasible for the parties to appear at the closing.

CASE EXAMPLE

Junior Wells, a resident of California, owns farmland in Kentucky that he desires to sell. Senior Johnson, a resident of Kentucky, desires to buy the farmland. The cost of Junior Wells's appearance at a closing in Kentucky is prohibitive. The parties enter into a purchase contract for the sale of the farmland and agree to close in escrow. Wells mails a fully executed deed for his Kentucky farm to Kentucky Loan & Trust Co., which is instructed to deliver the deed to Johnson on receipt of the purchase price. When Johnson delivers the purchase price, Kentucky Loan & Trust, as previously instructed, delivers the deed to Johnson.

Protection Against a Party's Change of Mind

With the use of the escrow device, the closing is less likely to fail because an independent third party is charged with carrying out mechanical details of the transaction. Both buyer and seller are to some extent protected from the other's change of mind. For example, in a conventional closing, a seller who has "second thoughts" may refuse to appear at the closing and to sign the deed. In an escrow closing, however, even if the seller desires to back out of the transaction, the escrow agent, who is in control of the deed previously deposited, is instruction-bound to deliver it to the purchaser on the happening of a specified condition. This course may not be altered at the seller's whim.

The escrow device, while avoiding face-to-face contact between parties, also often avoids a confrontation of conflicting interests and personalities. The sale and the purchase of a home in many cases is an emotionally charged transaction. As such, it may create a volatile atmosphere for the parties. The slightest innuendo may often trigger a dispute and present unnecessary problems. Because the escrow closing avoids a face-to-face encounter, it prevents this potential problem from arising.

■ REQUIREMENTS OF AN ESCROW

For a valid real estate escrow to exist, the following ingredients are necessary: valid deed, enforceable contract, delivery, escrow agent, escrow agreement, and condition. (See Table 14.2.)

Valid Deed

A deed that is the subject of an escrow must be executed properly, in accordance with the state law that is applicable to the transaction. A deed lacking the essentials of valid execution cannot be the subject of a valid escrow transaction, and the escrow agent holding such a deed is under an obligation to surrender it to the grantor on request.

CASE EXAMPLE
John Hines signs a deed and delivers it into escrow. The deed is not witnessed at the time of delivery. State law requires that the grantor "acknowledge the signing of a deed to be his or her voluntary act before two witnesses." The deposit of the deed will not operate as an escrow because it lacks the appropriate attestation. The deed is subject to recall by Hines. See *Collins v. Kares*, 52 S.D. 143, 216 N.W. 880 (1927).

Omission of the grantee's name in the deed does not invalidate the escrow as long as the grantor authorizes the escrow agent to insert the grantee's name. Likewise, failure to include a legal description of the real estate within the deed does not invalidate the escrow if the grantor authorizes the depositary to insert the designated description.

Enforceable Contract

For an instrument to operate as a real estate escrow, there must be an enforceable contract between the parties concerning the property. In the absence of a valid purchase contract, the deposit of a deed with an escrow agent cannot be the subject of a valid

TABLE 14.2	Escrow Requirements

- Valid Deed
- Enforceable Contract
- Delivery
- Escrow Agent
- Escrow Agreement
- Condition

escrow. Consequently, the deed is subject to recall at the grantor's request. This is true even if the deed is signed properly and is in conformity with all the requirements of execution. Because a contract for the sale of real estate is within the Statute of Frauds, there must be a written memorandum to support the contract. A wholly oral contract to sell real estate cannot be the basis of an escrow.

CASE EXAMPLE

Anna Skibosh entered into a land contract with Auto Acceptance for the sale of her premises. Two days later, Auto Acceptance assigned its interest in the land contract to Interstate. Interstate then executed a quitclaim deed in favor of Joseph Sorce and delivered it to Auto Acceptance with an attached letter stating that the deed would be held in trust by Auto Acceptance until Sorce paid off certain debts owed to Auto Acceptance.

The land contract was fulfilled, and Skibosh conveyed the property to Auto Acceptance, which conveyed it to Interstate. Sorce's creditors claimed that Sorce was the owner of the property. The court disagreed, and stated as part of its rationale that the escrow of a deed to real estate must be accompanied by an agreement that satisfies the Statute of Frauds and that the letter attached to the deed was insufficient for that purpose. *West Federal Savings & Loan Association v. Interstate Investment, Inc.*, 57 Wis. 2d 690, 205 N.W.2d 361 (1973).

The deed itself does not ordinarily satisfy the Statute of Frauds because the essential terms of sale such as price are not normally included in the deed. To insert the required terms in the deed would be a cumbersome departure from acceptable deed drafting. The most common practice is for the seller and the buyer to execute a writing that, independent of the deed itself, satisfies the Statute of Frauds. This is usually the purchase contract.

Delivery

■ *Surrender of possession and control of a document to the third party depositary.*

The deed must be delivered to the escrow agent by the grantor or grantor's agent with the intent to surrender possession of the instrument. This surrender is known as the *first delivery*. The grantor must absolutely relinquish control over the deed. In the event that the deed is subject to recall by the grantor, **delivery** has not been accomplished.

Accordingly, delivery does not occur until the instrument is beyond the legal power of the grantor to retrieve it.

CASE EXAMPLE

Kevin Armstrong, who is afflicted with a serious kidney disorder, deposits a deed with an escrow agent before entering the hospital for surgery. Kevin instructs the depositary to deliver the deed to his sister "in the event I do not survive the operation; otherwise, I will pick it up after I am released from the hospital." Because Kevin did not relinquish total control over the document, there was no legal delivery to the escrow agent. See *Gilmer v. Anderson*, 34 Mich. App. 6, 190 N.W.2d 708 (1971).

Escrow Agent

■ *The third party who is the depositary in an escrow transaction.*

The deed is delivered to an **escrow agent**. The escrow agent, designated as an *escrowee* or *escrow holder*, represents the interests of both the buyer and the seller. In that sense, the escrowee is a dual agent who owes a duty to both parties to act in good faith. The escrow agent has no authority other than that derived by the agreement of the parties and is strictly confined to acting in accordance with that agreement. The escrow agent is a conduit, bound by the terms of the escrow agreement.

Generally, neither the buyer nor the seller should act in the capacity of an escrow agent because the objectivity of either is suspect. Moreover, an escrow held by the grantor violates the principle that control over the instrument must be surrendered. Delivery of an escrow to the grantee raises the question of whether delivery is absolute. As a rule, however, the intention of the grantor governs. If the grantor delivers a deed intended as an escrow to the grantee for purposes of transporting it to a third-party depositary, the grantee is deemed the grantor's special agent for that purpose and delivery to the grantee is incomplete. Nevertheless, it is a dangerous practice to deliver the escrow to the grantee, regardless of any stated preconditions, and should be avoided.

The traditional rule is that attorneys or agents of either party cannot act as escrow agents because to do so could create a conflict of interest. Some states do, however, permit agents of the parties or their attorneys to be escrow agents as long as their capacity as such is not antagonistic to their principal's interest. Although some states expressly permit a real estate broker or salesperson to be an escrow agent, real estate agents customarily avoid this potentially conflicting office.

The escrow agent may not act contrary to the escrow instructions. Deviation from the instructions constitutes a breach of the agreement and relationship of trust. In such a case, the escrow agent would be liable for any resulting damages.

CASE EXAMPLE

Lon Luebel, escrow agent, delivers a deed to Mike Lerman, grantee, prior to the deposit of the $170,000 purchase price, a precondition of the instructed delivery. Lon is liable to Kim Sipe, the grantor, for damages because he acted contrary to the escrow instructions. See *Allen v. Allen Title Co.*, 77 N.M. 796, 427 P.2d 673 (1967).

Sometimes an escrow agent is charged with delivering the deed to the grantee and the purchase price to the grantor when a title search proves that the title is free and unencumbered. If a title search shows that the title is not free and clear, the escrow agent must return the deed and purchase money to the respective parties. In the event that the escrow agent instead tenders the purchase money to the grantor, the escrow agent will be liable to the grantee for the purchase price. However, a deviation that does not cause damages does not result in escrow agent liability.

CASE EXAMPLE

The purchaser failed to provide evidence of fire insurance prior to an escrow closing, contrary to the terms of the escrow agreement. Nonetheless, the escrow agent closed the transaction, delivering the deed to the buyer and the money to the seller. The lender objected to the closing and sought damages. The property did not burn. The California Court of Appeals, finding for the defendant, affirmed language of the trial court, which said: "The court . . . cannot find that the failure to comply with the written instructions . . . [resulted in any] . . . [damages]." See *Claussen v. First American Title Guaranty Co.*, 186 Cal. App. 3d 429, 230 Cal. Rptr. 749 (1986).

In an escrow transaction, property comes into the hands of an escrow agent who is in a relationship of trust to the parties involved in the sale. Should the escrow agent unauthorizedly converts the property to personal use, by most state standards, the escrow agent is guilty of a crime.

An escrow agent should open up an escrow account to receive funds related to the escrow transaction. Commingling escrow funds with personal funds of the escrow agent may result in liability. However, an escrow agent is sometimes authorized to maintain the delivered funds in a personal bank account. In that case, it is extremely important for the escrow agent to keep an account balance at least equal to the amount of the escrow funds. Otherwise, the escrow agent is deemed to have converted the monies to personal use and is guilty of a crime.

When an escrow agent embezzles escrow funds, either the buyer or the seller bears the loss. The rule of law is that the party who was entitled to the funds at the moment of conversion is the one who must bear the loss. If the condition under which the purchase money was to be held in escrow was performed, then the loss falls on the seller because the seller was entitled to the money. Until the happening of the condition, the loss falls on the buyer because the legal right to receive the funds has not passed to the seller.

Of course, an escrow agent who embezzles or otherwise misappropriates funds is liable to the person on whom the loss falls. As a practical matter, however, it is very difficult to collect against an absconding or incarcerated escrow agent, as the parties in the next case learned.

GE Capital Mortgage Services v. Avent
North Carolina Court of Appeals
442 S.E.2d 98 (N.C. App. 1994)

Background. GE Capital performs relocation services for corporate employees. It pays relocating employees a sum equal to their home equity plus it satisfies any outstanding mortgage liens against their properties. In exchange, GE Capital receives the right to market and sell the employees' homes and receive the proceeds.

GE Capital contracted with the Selheims to purchase their Rocky Mount residence for $147,950. GE Capital paid the Selheims about $80,000 and, in accordance with its obligation, satisfied the Selheims' mortgage. It did not, however, have the mortgage (deed of trust) canceled of record.

GE Capital sold the house for $147,500 to the Hendersons and hired Tyson Avent as its closing attorney. Because GE Capital had failed to obtain a release of the mortgage, the net proceeds of the sale, $136,723.74, were placed in escrow with Avent as escrow agent. He was to disburse the proceeds to GE Capital when the outstanding mortgage was canceled. Thereafter GE Capital caused the cancellation of the mortgage. It notified Avent, but he failed to disburse the funds because he had misappropriated them. Plaintiff GE Capital sued the Hendersons for the net proceeds. The court entered summary judgment in favor of the buyers, the Hendersons.

Decision. The North Carolina appellate court upheld the trial court decision.

Judge Martin. Although this is an issue of first impression in this jurisdiction, the parties agree that generally when property in the custody of an escrow holder is lost or embezzled by the holder, as between the buyer and the seller, the loss falls on the party who was entitled to the property at the time of the loss or embezzlement.

* * *

Ordinarily, the determination as to which party is entitled to the escrow property depends on whether the conditions of the escrow were satisfied prior to the loss or embezzlement. For example, if the escrow agent embezzles the purchase price prior to the seller's performance of the escrow condition, the buyer has retained title to the money and must therefore bear the loss. Conversely, if the embezzlement occurs after the seller has performed the escrow condition, then the seller must bear the loss because he was entitled to it at the time of the embezzlement.

There is an exception, however, to this general rule; where the buyer would under no circumstance be entitled to return of the escrow funds, the burden of loss is on the seller whether the embezzlement occurs before or after the performance of the escrow condition.

* * *

This exception to the general rule was . . . recognized in *Stuart v. Clarke*, a case that bears a strong factual resemblance to the present case. In *Stuart*, the plaintiff contracted to sell a parcel of real property to the defendant. At the time of the contract, the seller was aware that there was an unreleased [mortgage] on the property. Prior to closing, the seller was advised that he could not convey clear title to the property without first obtaining a release of the [mortgage]. Despite this knowledge, the seller took no action to obtain a release of the [mortgage] prior to the date of closing. Conversely, the buyers came to the closing prepared to meet their contractual obligations and pay for the property. Due to the seller's inability to convey good title, the parties agreed to escrow a portion of the purchase price until the seller obtained a release of the [mortgage]. *However, the deed to the property was delivered to the buyers at the closing.* The escrow agent thereafter absconded with the escrow funds.

In arriving at its decision to place the loss on the seller, the court recognized the rule which places the loss on the party entitled to receive the funds at the time of their loss. The court then said:

> [T]his case is distinguishable from other, more typical escrow situations because the title to the property has passed to the buyer, and thus the proceeds of the sale—including the amount retained in escrow—have passed to the seller, subject to his performance of a condition subsequent entitling him to release of the escrowed funds. The buyers cannot logically be the owners of both the purchased property and the portion of the money in escrow.

Like the buyers in *Stuart,* the Hendersons came to the scheduled closing prepared to fulfill all of their obligations under their contract . . . . Plaintiff, however, came to the closing knowing that it had not obtained cancellation of the outstanding . . . [mortgage] and that it was unable to convey to the Hendersons the marketable title for which they had bargained. Despite plaintiff's failure to meet its contractual obligations, the Hendersons agreed to proceed with the closing and to the deposit of the net proceeds of the sale due plaintiff in Avent's trust account pending cancellation of the . . . [mortgage]. In return, plaintiff delivered the deed to the property to the Hendersons which they promptly recorded.

Clearly, the purpose of the escrow was to insure that the funds were available to obtain cancellation of the . . . [mortgage] if plaintiff failed to do so; or, if the . . . [mortgage] was otherwise released and cancelled by plaintiff, the funds were to be paid to plaintiff. In either situation, the funds were held by Avent for the benefit of plaintiff; in no event were the funds to be returned to the Hendersons. Having obtained title to the property, the Hendersons no longer held title to the funds in escrow. Thus, . . . plaintiff must bear the loss resulting from Avent's embezzlement of the escrow funds.

. . . [I]t was plaintiff who gave him the opportunity to abscond with the escrow funds by failing to meet its contractual obligations, thereby necessitating the escrow agreement as a means of closing the transaction as scheduled.

Affirmed.

What can the parties do to protect themselves against loss due to an embezzling escrowee?

Escrow Agreement

> ▨ *An agreement that directs the escrow agent regarding terms and conditions under which the deed or other instruments are to be delivered to the parties and the disposition of the deed or other instruments on default.*

The **escrow agreement** need not be reduced to writing. Even so, in retrospect, many buyers and sellers regret their failure to do so. Some lawyers who draft escrow agreements include the terms of the escrow agreement in the purchase contract; others include them in an entirely separate instrument. The escrow agreement should be sufficiently detailed in writing to express the intent of the parties and to cover various contingencies. Some of the terms commonly included within an escrow agreement are:

- names and addresses of seller, buyer, and escrow agent;
- description of the property that is the subject of the escrow;

- obligations of buyer and seller regarding the deposit of instruments and money into escrow;
- directions to escrow agent regarding the recording of the deed and disbursement of the purchase money;
- the specific condition on which title is to pass;
- directions to the escrow agent regarding procedure in the event the condition is not met;
- instructions on payment of escrow brokerage and attorney fees, recording charges, and other costs; and
- signatures of the seller, buyer, and escrow agent.

The escrow agent is bound by the terms of the escrow agreement and may not deviate from it in any respect, unless, of course, it is contrary to law. Where a conflict exists between the terms of the purchase contract and the escrow agreement, the agent is bound to follow the instructions contained in the escrow agreement. The escrow agent may not follow oral instructions that contradict the terms of the written agreement. A typical escrow agreement is shown in Figure 14.2.

When the condition on which title is to pass occurs, the escrow agent must deliver the deed to the grantee. If the condition does not occur, under the terms of the agreement the escrow agent is normally charged with returning the purchase money to the purchaser and redelivering the deed to the grantor.

An escrow agreement is a contract; it is not revocable by any party without the consent of all the parties to the agreement. In the event that one of the parties attempts to revoke the agreement and demands the return of the deposit, the escrow agent must ignore the demand. When conflict or doubt as to interpretation of the agreement arises, a judicial declaration should be sought.

Under the Federal Rules of Civil Procedure, as well as many state laws whose civil rules are patterned after the federal rules, an escrow agent who is faced with conflicting claims of liability or ownership may secure a judicial declaration by interpleading the claimants. The practical result of this procedure is to force the parties to litigate their rival claims in one court action. The escrow agent becomes a stakeholder who holds the contested property pending the outcome of the lawsuit, or who deposits the funds in court. The interpleader device is not available to an escrow agent who is guilty of misconduct in the escrow transaction.

Condition

Before an instrument can be considered an escrow, its deposit with the escrow agent must be coupled with the depositor's intention that it not take effect until the happening of a specified condition. This condition is essential to suspend passage of the instrument to the buyer. If there is no specified condition, then delivery of a fully executed deed to the escrow agent immediately vests title in the purchaser.

The escrow may be used to require any number of conditions to attach before the deed and purchase money pass to the respective parties. Buyers' conditions may

| FIGURE 14.2 | Escrow Agreement |

This agreement is entered into between Rocky Sylvester [hereafter referred to as Seller] and Andora Klimer [hereafter referred to as Buyer]. Whereas the Seller and Buyer have entered into a contract dated May 20, 2006, of which a true copy is attached, for the sale of premises described in Plat Book No. 13, page 33, Parcel 17 of Wilona Township.

Now, therefore, it is mutually agreed:

- That Henry Earnest is hereby appointed escrow agent and empowered to carry said contract and this agreement into effect;

- That the Seller will deposit with said escrow agent a fully executed deed to said premises to the Buyer with general warranty that the title is good and unencumbered except use restrictions and easements of record, if any, and taxes and assessments for the year 2006 and thereafter;

- That the buyer will deposit with said escrow agent the sum of $225,000, being the balance of the purchase price of $237,500;

- That said escrow agent is directed to file said deed for record and make disbursements when the terms of said contract can be complied with, and provided he can furnish to the Buyer a certificate of title showing record title to said premises to be good and unencumbered;

- That the escrow agent shall return any deposit to Buyer if all deposits and requirements necessary to closing are not made within 60 days from this date;

- That Seller shall pay for the preparation of deed, the cost of obtaining a certificate of title, and one-half of the costs of the escrow charges;

- That Buyer will pay the fees for filing the deed and one-half of the cost of the escrow charges;

- That taxes and assessments, prepaid insurance premiums and rents will be prorated as of the date of closing, and no adjustments are to be made by the escrow agent for water or other utilities.

Dated this 20th day of May, 2006

_____
Seller

_____

_____
Buyer

include, for example, conditioning the passage of title on the buyer's obtaining financing, making payment of the purchase price, selling a house, or securing a zoning change. Sellers' conditions may include providing evidence of title, proof that the property is free from wood-destroying insect infestation, or proof that the electrical system in the house is free from defects. Before the grantee is entitled to delivery of the deed, the specified condition must occur. Until such occurrence, the legal title to the deed remains with the seller. In the event the depositary delivers the deed over to a grantee prior to the happening of the condition, no title actually passes since the delivery is unauthorized.

■ TITLE PASSAGE

In a completed escrow transaction, there are two deliveries. The *first delivery* is accomplished when the grantor surrenders control over the deed and delivers it to the escrow agent. The *second delivery* occurs when the escrow agent surrenders the deed to the purchaser after the occurrence of the condition. As soon as the condition occurs on which the escrow is predicated, the grantee is entitled to delivery of the escrow. The trend in authority is that title actually passes to the grantee when, pursuant to the escrow agreement, the grantee is entitled to the delivery.

Relation Back

▓ *A legal doctrine whereby the title acquired by a deed relates back to the moment of the first delivery to an escrow agent.*

In some instances the second delivery of the deed is accounted as taking effect as of the time of the first delivery to the agent. This *doctrine of* **relation back** is applied when an event that would otherwise thwart the intent of the parties or cause a manifest injustice intervenes between the first and second deliveries.

Death and Disability. The doctrine of relation back avoids complications that might normally arise where death or insanity of the grantor intervenes between the first and second deliveries. The death of the grantor whose deed is held in escrow does not invalidate the escrow. On the happening of the escrow condition, the grantee is entitled to delivery. The delivery relates back in time to the original moment of transfer to the escrow agent. Under this doctrine of relation back, title passage is deemed to have occurred while the grantor was living. Similarly, if after the delivery of a deed in escrow the grantee dies, the grantee's representative will be entitled to delivery on the happening of the condition. Under the doctrine of relation back, the passage of title is deemed to have occurred at the time of the first delivery, during the life of the grantee.

> **CASE EXAMPLE**
> Birdie H. Fuqua executed a contract for the sale of a 50-acre tract of property to Selected Lands Corporation (SLC). Shortly thereafter, she signed a deed and placed it in escrow. Under the terms of the agreement, the escrow agent was to deliver the deed to SLC when SLC's attorney approved the closing papers. Before the approval, Birdie died. Thereafter, the attorney approved the papers. The court held that the death of the grantor did not invalidate the instrument and that, on the occurrence of the condition, the grantee was entitled to the deed. Under the doctrine of relation back, title would be deemed to pass as of the date of the first delivery. *Fuqua v. Fuqua*, 528 S.W.2d 896 (Tex. Civ. App. 1975).

The doctrine of relation back is similarly applicable to a case where the grantor becomes insane or otherwise incompetent to effect a transfer after delivering the deed to the escrow agent but before delivery to the purchaser. Under the doctrine, on the happening of the condition, the grantee is entitled to passage of title, which is deemed to have occurred on the date of the first delivery, thus avoiding frustration of the intent of the parties.

Dower. The doctrine of relation back may protect the purchaser from dower claims by the seller's spouse where the spouse of a deceased seller had no dower expectancy at the time the deed was deposited into escrow. This may occur as a result of a marriage by the seller after delivery of the deed into escrow but before the second delivery to the purchaser. In such a case, on the happening of the condition, the title passage relates back to the date of the first delivery; consequently, the seller's spouse has no dower interest.

CASE EXAMPLE

Seth Nathan, unmarried, executes a deed and deposits it in escrow. The escrow agent is directed to deliver the deed to the buyer when the buyer secures financing and deposits the purchase price. Before the deposit of the purchase price, Seth marries; thereafter, the buyer deposits the purchase price. Seth's wife refuses to release dower interests in the property. Regardless, the escrow agent is charged with conveying the deed to the grantee, who takes possession free of spousal interests pursuant to the doctrine of relation back.

Intervening Liens. Application of the doctrine of relation back may avoid problems caused by liens, encumbrances, and judgments that attach to the property between the times of the first and second deliveries. When a seller conveys title by deed to a third party who has knowledge that the deed is the subject of an escrow, the doctrine of relation back normally protects the original purchaser. Under this doctrine, the purchaser is deemed to have taken title at the first delivery; consequently, the seller was without power to convey good title to the third party. If the third party is a bona fide purchaser for value without notice that the instrument is the subject of an escrow, however, the courts are less likely to apply the doctrine to defeat the third party's title. The same rules apply where the grantor creates an encumbrance on the property during escrow. If the lienholder is without knowledge of the escrow, the lienholder has priority. Otherwise, the doctrine of relation back will protect the grantee because the grantor's title is deemed cut off at the time of the first delivery.

Follow the reasoning in the next case involving the application of the doctrine of relation back.

Hartman v. Wood
Supreme Court of South Dakota
436 N.W.2d 854 (S.D. 1989)

Background. The Woods entered into a contract for the sale of a parcel of real property to Garrett Ranch, Inc. (Garrett). The contract required that the Woods deliver fee title to the property when Garrett completed all of the payments called for in the contract for deed. Delivery of the fee title was to be accomplished through an escrow. The Woods executed a warranty deed to the property, naming Garrett as grantee, and deposited the deed with an escrow agent (escrowee). The escrowee was to deliver the deed to Garrett when Garrett made all the payments for the property. Prior to the condition being met, Garrett transferred the contract for deed to a related partnership, which interests were then assigned to Connecticut Mutual Life Insurance

continued on next page

Company as security on a mortgage. Connecticut Mutual foreclosed its mortgage and purchased the contract for deed at a sheriff's sale. Connecticut Mutual assigned its interest in the property to First National Bank of Minneapolis, which assigned its interest to Hartman. Hartman completed all of the payments required under the contract for deed and the Woods accepted the payments. Hartman asked the Woods to convey a new warranty deed to the property, in effect bypassing the original deed that was placed in escrow. The Woods authorized release of the original deed in escrow to Hartman but refused to give a new deed.

Hartman brought an action for specific performance to execute a new deed. The trial court granted summary judgment in favor of the Woods.

Decision. The Supreme Court of South Dakota affirmed.

Justice Miller. The question is whether an assignee of a purchaser under a contract for deed is entitled to a warranty deed from the vendor when the vendor has previously deposited a warranty deed with an escrow for delivery to the purchaser on payment of the purchase price.

Generally, title to property under a deed deposited into escrow transfers when the [escrowee] delivers the deed or when conditions placed on its delivery have been met. There is an exception to this rule holding that transfer of title by deed will be treated as relating back to the deed's original deposit into escrow where resort to this fiction is necessary to give the deed effect. Thus:

> Where the grantee in an escrow deed, after the deposit of the instrument in escrow but before the performance of the condition on which it was to be delivered, makes a conveyance of the land to a third person, the escrow deed relates back to the original deposit, on the performance of the condition, so as to validate the conveyance made by the grantee.

This is precisely the situation confronted in this case. Prior to performance of the conditions for delivery of the escrow deed, Garrett assigned its interest in the property to another party. Successive assignments were made to additional parties until Hartman performed the conditions for delivery of the escrow deed. Applying the above rule, the escrow deed should be treated as having vested title to the property in Garrett at the time the deed was placed in escrow. This would have the effect of validating the "subsequent" conveyances of the property by Garrett and its successors in interest (e.g., the sheriff's deed and the . . . warranty deed to Hartman).

Based on the foregoing discussion, Hartman's action for specific performance against [the] Woods was not an appropriate means of removing some cloud that he may have perceived on his title. Hartman had a deed to the property validated by the escrow deed's vesting of title to the property in Garrett prior to Garrett's conveyance of the property. . . .

We additionally observe that [the] Woods performed all of their obligations under the contract for deed when they deposited the warranty deed into escrow. Specific performance against [the] Woods was, therefore, unavailable because there was nothing left for [the] Woods to specifically perform.

Affirmed.

Provide language in the escrow agreement that would have made this outcome clearer and thus avoided litigation.

■ OTHER USES OF ESCROW

Two other uses of escrow are notable. They are the long-term escrow and the mortgage escrow.

Long-Term Escrow

The **long-term escrow**, sometimes called a deed of trust, is a tool for financing a real estate transaction. In this situation, a deed is conveyed by a seller (trustor) to a trustee which gives the trustee legal title to real property until the grantee (beneficiary) repays the trustor the amount due on the loan. This type of transaction resembles a mortgage, and the deed conveying title to the real property is used as collateral to secure the repayment of the loan. A long-term escrow may range in duration from one year to 30 or more years. It is actually a combination of a land installment contract, the subject of Chapter 22, and the escrow.

A buyer may not be in a position to borrow funds. Nonetheless, a seller may desire to sell the land to such a purchaser by requiring installment payments. To secure the payment of the purchase price, the seller may withhold the deed from the buyer until the final installment is paid. Under such an arrangement, the seller delivers into escrow a fully executed deed with instructions to the escrow agent to deliver the deed to the buyer on full payment of the purchase price.

> **CASE EXAMPLE**
>
> Jake Rubin owns 50 acres of farmland that has been on the market for two years, listed at $100,000. Lance Lane desires to buy the land but is unable to obtain financing from a lending institution. Rubin and Lane enter into a land installment contract whereby Lane pays $10,000 down and agrees to pay the remaining $90,000 over nine years at 9 percent interest. Rubin executes the deed in favor of Lane and deposits it with Fidelity Trust Co., an escrow agent that is directed by the terms of the escrow agreement to deliver the deed to Lane on receiving receipts evidencing that the purchase price has been paid in full. Rubin does not have control over the deed as long as Lane does not default on the terms of the installment contract. After nine years of timely payments, Lane is entitled to the deed. See *Been Corp. v. Shader*, 198 Neb. 677, 255 N.W.2d 247 (1977).

If a purchaser fails to make the timely payments, the escrow agent is normally charged with returning the deed to the seller pursuant to the escrow agreement.

One major disadvantage of the long-term escrow is risk. The buyer takes a chance that the seller will not convey the property by deed to another or mortgage the land in an amount that would interfere with the buyer's equity in the property. Because the seller remains the titleholder of record, a bona fide purchaser for value without notice of the contract may take from the seller and defeat the buyer's interest. However, if the installment buyer is in possession, then the purchaser has constructive notice of the buyer's interest and would not take good title. The installment buyer may also be protected by recording the instrument. This would be sufficient to give notice to subsequent grantees or mortgagees and thus protect the contract buyer.

THE CHANGING LANDSCAPE

The escrow closing practiced in some localities throughout the United States is an alternative to the conventional face-to-face closing. In some respects it is more convenient. The parties do not have to interrupt their schedules to come to the closing. Instead, they may devote time to satisfying the requirements pursuant to the contract. The escrow agent can close the transaction by recording the deed in the buyer's favor and delivering the monies to the seller.

Even in the conventional closing there may be shades of the escrow closing, at least when trouble occurs. Not infrequently, a matter arises that requires that one or both parties to the transaction place monies in escrow to "save" the closing. For example, in the event that the "walk though" discloses a problem or if the water bill has not been paid by the seller, the parties may establish an escrow for the purpose of resolving the issue.

In the twenty-first century, with electronic banking and the Internet, it may be possible to innovate a new and useful kind of closing that will facilitate the closing in a most efficient manner. Online "distant closings" may displace conventional face-to-face and escrow closings. This would enable buyers and sellers to close in the convenience of their homes by using electronic signatures and downloading and uploading documents. Can you think of any downside to this type of closing? Do you have any suggestions as to how this closing would operate? Would an escrow agent be desirable?

Mortgage Escrow

A mortgagee may desire to set up an escrow to be protected. In this event, the money to be lent to the mortgagor is deposited in a **mortgage escrow**, awaiting proof that there are no outstanding liens on the property. On such assurance, the mortgage may be recorded and the funds released to the mortgagor as directed; the mortgagee is secure as a first lienor. The surrender of the money into escrow is deemed to be the creation of a debt, which is necessary for a mortgage to be a valid lien on property.

■ KEY TERMS

delivery 307	long-term escrow 317	real estate escrow 303
escrow agent 308	mortgage escrow 318	relation back 314
escrow agreement 311		

■ INTERNET RESOURCES

For an overview of an escrow closing, see

www.heckofahome.com/buyer/process/escrow/closing.html

For information on choosing an escrow officer or title attorney, see

www.owners.com/tools/library/showarticle.asp?ID=15

■ REVIEW AND DISCUSSION QUESTIONS

1. Name the parties to an escrow transaction and describe the flow of documents.

2. What are the advantages of an escrow transaction?

3. Name the six requirements of an escrow and briefly describe each.

4. What are the responsibilities of an escrow agent?

5. Name some sellers' conditions on which an escrow may be predicated. Buyers' conditions?

6. When does the loss due to embezzlement of funds held by an escrow agent fall on the seller?

7. Describe the doctrine of relation back and give some examples as to how it affects the buyer.

8. What is a long-term escrow and when is it used?

■ CASE PROBLEMS

1. Tillie Ganser entered into a contract with her four children whereby Tillie agreed to convey a specified tract of land to each child on the payment by each child of a specified sum. It was agreed that an escrow would be used to handle the transaction. Tillie deposited four valid deeds with the escrow agent, but before any of the children paid the agent the amount due under the contract, Tillie died. Tillie's executor seeks to set aside the land sales as mere offers revoked by Tillie's death. (a) Will the executor be able to set aside the contracts for the sale of the land? Explain. See *Ganser v. Zimmerman*, 80 N.W.2d 828 (N.D. 1956). (b) Would the following fact pattern present a different result? Tillie deposited four valid deeds, executed in the names of each of her four children, with her attorney, accompanied by instructions to convey the deeds to her children when all contracts for the sale of the property were negotiated. Before any contracts could be negotiated, Tillie died. See *Merry v. County Bd. of Educ.*, 264 Ala. 411, 87 So.2d 821 (1956).

2. Ellen Love deposits a fully executed deed in escrow. Pursuant to a purchase contract and escrow instructions, the deed is to be delivered to Sarah Gibson when the zoning of the property is changed from residential to commercial. After the zoning change occurs, but before the escrow agent delivers the deed to Gibson, a judgment creditor of Gibson seeks to levy on the property. Will the judgment creditor be successful? Explain. See *Sturgill v. Industrial Painting Corp.*, 82 Nev. 61, 410 P.2d 759 (1966).

3. Robert O'Neal agreed to sell a parcel of land to Thomas Ryan. The parties agreed to handle the transfer through an escrow agent. According to the escrow agreement, O'Neal was to deposit a valid deed executed in Ryan's name with the escrow agent. The agent was to deliver the deed to Ryan when Ryan deposited $12,000 with the escrow agent. Before Ryan or O'Neal performed their obligations under the agree-

ment, O'Neal informed the escrow agent that the property was worth much more than $12,000 and that O'Neal would not deliver the deed unless Ryan paid $13,000. (a) Because neither party has performed his contractual duties, can O'Neal alter the terms of the escrow agreement? Why or why not? (b) What if Ryan agrees to the additional amount? Does that change the result? Explain. See *Gelber v. Cappeller*, 161 Cal. App. 2d. 113, 326 P.2d 521 (1958).

4. The Caulfields entered into a contract to purchase property owned by the Freddie Thomas Foundation, Inc., with a condition that the contract was subject to "the necessary Supreme Court approval authorizing this conveyance." The deed and closing papers were held in escrow, pending the Court's approval. The Caulfields took possession of the property on October 1. On October 4, the premises were partially destroyed by fire. Court authorization for the sale was obtained on October 29. Under the purchase agreement the risk of loss was to remain with the seller until the "closing." Whose insurer (the buyer's or the seller's) is responsible for the loss? Explain. *Caulfield v. Improved Risk Mutuals, Inc.,* 486 N.Y.S.2d 531 (Sup. Ct. App. Div. 1985).

5. Maxum and Nelson reached a tentative agreement for the exchange of a parcel of land owned by Nelson for a parcel owned by Maxum. Maxum had not seen the Nelson property, located in a distant state, and so planned to visit the site before consummating the deal. Before leaving, Maxum deposited a valid deed to his property with Wallace. Maxum instructed Wallace that if he found the property suitable he would write to Wallace and direct him to deliver the deed to Nelson. The delivery of Maxum's deed was contingent on Nelson's delivering the deed to his land to Wallace. Nelson delivered his deed to Wallace. Maxum, after examining the property, found it unsatisfactory and promptly wrote to Wallace, instructing him not to deliver the deed to Nelson. Nelson objected to Maxum's action. Nelson claims that a valid escrow agreement was formed and, on the tender of his deed to Wallace, Wallace was bound to deliver the Maxum deed to Nelson. Is Nelson correct? Discuss. See *Nelson v. Davis*, 102 Wash. 313, 172 P. 1178 (1918).

6. A contract of purchase sale provided that "The Seller shall give and the purchaser shall accept a title such as The Security Title and Guaranty Company will approve and insure." At the time of closing the vendors were unable to deliver to the buyers a good and marketable title because a New York Estate Tax against a party in the chain of title had not been fixed and paid. The sellers offered to deposit a sum of money as security for the payment of the estate tax. This offer was rejected by the buyers. Pursuant to the terms of a real estate purchase contract, the buyers left a deposit with Irwin Dickman, the escrow agent, who was also the sellers' attorney. Dickman embezzled the funds. Who assumes the loss? Buyers or sellers? Why? See *Asher v. Herman*, 49 Misc. 2d 475, 267 N.Y.S. 2d 932 (Sup. Ct. App. Div. 1966).

7. James Stuart (the seller) contracted to sell land to Cecil Clarke and Farid Srour (the buyers). However, the land was subject to an unreleased deed of trust which required payment before marketable title could be conveyed. The parties agreed at settlement that the buyers would receive title to the land, the seller would receive most of the purchase price, and the buyers would deposit most of the purchase price,

equal to the amount of the deed of trust ($13,500) in escrow. The seller could then receive that money once he arranged for the release of the deed of trust. At some point later, the escrow agent fled with the money. On which party does the burden of loss fall? Explain. See *Stuart v. Clarke*, 619 A.2d 1199 (D.C. Ct. App. 1993).

8. Mr. Konopka and Mr. Zaremba negotiated a contract for the sale of Konopka's residence to Zaremba. The parties agreed to establish an escrow account with Ms. Wourms, Konopka's real estate agent. The escrow agreement required that Zaremba immediately deposit a down payment of $2,500 with Wourms, which he did. The ultimate sale of the residence was contingent on Zaremba's obtaining a mortgage loan of $20,500. Zaremba obtained the loan, at which time Konopka requested delivery of the down payment from Wourms. Wourms admitted that she was unable to deliver the money because she had used the money to pay her business creditors. Konopka refused to close the deal until Zaremba paid the contract price to him. Zaremba contended that he owed the contract price less the $2,500 he had already paid to Wourms. (a) Who was right? On whom did the loss of the money fall? Why? (b) Is it relevant that Wourms was employed by Konopka to act as his real estate agent? Explain. See *Zaremba v. Konopka*, 94 N.J. Super. 300, 228 A.2d 91 (1967).

Liens Against Title

■ LIEN

■ *A claim against another's property securing either payment of a debt or fulfillment of some other monetary charge or obligation.*

Liens are important in all spheres of commercial law. They take many forms and are subject to extensive variations from state to state. Despite these differences, the underlying concept of all liens is much the same. The purpose is to provide security for a debt, obligation, or duty. A lien cannot exist in the absence of a financial claim against another person. There must be an underlying debt.

CASE EXAMPLE

Revisi, a contractor, obtained a long-term lease on land outside of Utica, New York, for construction of a small warehouse. Wilson Building Supply furnished all materials for the project. When Revisi did not pay his bills, amounting to $275,000, Wilson obtained a material supplier's lien (mechanic's lien) on the building.

Shortly thereafter, the state acquired Wilson's lumberyard as part of a slum clearance project. This left the company without facilities, and it demanded possession of Revisi's building on the basis of the lien.

Although courts sometimes refer to liens as *property*, a lien is not a property right in the thing itself. The lienholder has neither the title nor the rights of a titleholder. The lienholder's only right is to have a monetary obligation satisfied out of proceeds from the sale of the property. A lien thus differs from an estate, which is the right to *possess* realty, or an easement, which is the right to *use* realty. No court would award Wilson Building Supply possession of Revisi's warehouse on the basis of the material supplier's lien, even if the lien exceeded the value of the property. A lien simply does not give the holder of the lien title or the right to possession or use.

Because the fundamental nature of a lien is security, interests in real estate are frequently the subject of liens. Land and buildings provide excellent security. They are valuable, their value is relatively stable, and they are difficult, if not impossible, to move or conceal. Further, in the United States, land is subject to a system of recording that gives constructive notice to the world of the existence of any liens against a parcel of land. For example, Wilson Building Supply, in obtaining its lien, had to follow a procedure designed to notify other creditors of Revisi of its claim against the property.

■ TYPES OF LIENS

Liens are either *voluntary* or *involuntary*. *Voluntary liens* are those the owner agrees to place against his or her land, usually to secure repayment of long-term debt. Funds are advanced to the property owner, who agrees to repay the debt and provide a lien on the property as security for repayment. In many states, a real estate mortgage is regarded as a voluntary lien. Real estate mortgages are discussed extensively in Chapter 21.

A number of involuntary liens are also important to real estate practitioners. *Involuntary liens*, discussed in this chapter, are created by law to protect interests of persons who have valid monetary claims against an owner of real property. (See Table 15.1.) The claim might arise out of a judgment, sale, or furnishing of a service of some kind. Involuntary liens also aid the government in the collection of taxes and special assessments.

Liens may also be classified as *general* or *specific*. *Specific liens* apply to a specific parcel of realty only. The mechanic's lien, treated in this chapter, is an example. Other specific liens considered in the chapter are the vendor's lien and the property tax lien. A *general lien* is a lien against all the realty of a person in a given jurisdiction. Thus, a judgment against Mrs. Jones in a lawsuit in Washington County imposes a lien against *all* of her realty in that county, not just against one or more specific parcels owned by her in Washington County. This type of general lien is known as a judgment lien. The federal tax lien, also discussed in this chapter, is a general lien.

Mechanic's Lien

■ *The right of one who renders services or supplies materials in connection with the improvement of real property to seek a judicial sale of the realty to satisfy unpaid claims.*

By statute in most states, contractors and suppliers who work on real estate or furnish material for such work are entitled to a lien if they are not paid for their services. The lien provides them with a means of compelling payment because it allows the property to be sold to satisfy the claims. Generally, the lien attaches to both buildings and the land, and the work must have been done at the owner's request. The **mechanic's lien**, also known as a *material supplier's lien* or *contractor's lien*, is not the only action an unpaid supplier or contractor may take. By filing the lien, the supplier or contractor does not lose the right to recover on the contract.

TABLE 15.1	Types of Involuntary Liens	
	General	Specific
	Judgment	Mechanic's
	Tax	Vendor's

The mechanic's lien is not proof of the right to collect monies. This must be proved in a lawsuit, which might be in a foreclosure on the lien action, or in a separate action, such as a suit for breach of contract.

> **CASE EXAMPLE**
>
> Eldon Horn and his wife purchased a lot. Shortly thereafter, they contracted with Jamco Builders for the construction of a home on the lot. Jamco subcontracted some of the work to Mid-American Homes. Mid-American, as required by law, notified the Horns of its right to place a lien against the real estate. Jamco did not pay for the subcontracted work, and Mid-American filed a mechanic's lien against the property. This established its right to petition a court to have the property sold and the proceeds applied against the debt.

Valid reasons exist for granting contractors and suppliers a special lien against real property. In collecting for services and materials, they are at a disadvantage when compared with sellers of personal property on credit. When not paid, the seller of personal property, who has a valid security agreement, can usually repossess the item. This remedy does not exist for suppliers whose materials have been incorporated into a structure. Similarly, a contractor or laborer cannot get back time and effort expended on the job. Except for the mechanic's lien, such claimants are limited to suing for the contract price. Litigation such as this is time-consuming and expensive, and the winning plaintiff may have difficulty collecting the judgment. There is also the question of priority of distribution in the event there are a number of creditors. A mechanic's lienor will secure a higher priority than the general judgment lienor.

The lien also has nuisance value in that, until the debt is paid, a purchaser takes title subject to the lien. As a practical matter, buyers will not purchase the property unless there is an assurance that the lien will be satisfied. The mechanic's lien laws thus aid many small entrepreneurs who might be reluctant or financially unable to take judicial action to collect an unpaid claim.

Mechanic's lien laws did not exist at common law. They are the result of 19th-century state legislation that was necessary to protect the contractors, laborers, and suppliers who were crucial to the building of American cities.

Every state in the United States now has some type of mechanic's lien legislation. Because this legislation is often merely the ad hoc response to problems of a particular area and time, it is extremely varied and often complicated. In those jurisdictions that have a basic mechanic's lien statute, political pressures may lead to substantial amendments, which increase variability and add further complications. Any person in real estate working with transactions involving mechanic's lien laws must be particularly concerned with local statutes on the subject. These statutes are usually quite technical, and their requirements must be followed strictly for the lien to be valid.

Claimants. Mechanic's lien statutes generally include several categories of potential claimants. A typical statute might name mechanics, material suppliers, contractors, subcontractors, lessors of equipment, architects, engineers, and surveyors. In addition, a statute usually includes a catchall provision that allows anyone to claim a mechanic's lien who has performed labor on, or supplied materials to improve, property. Courts, too, have interpreted such statutes in a manner that extends the classes of persons who may claim mechanic's liens for making improvements to realty.

CASE EXAMPLE

Reet Development was constructing a large office building. It hired Francis Trucking Company to deliver materials to the site and Payne to serve as watchman. When Francis and Payne were not paid, they filed mechanics' liens. Reet argued that they were not entitled to liens, as their labor did not improve the premises. Although courts in numerous states would disagree, it is reasonable to hold that the services improved the premises, as they were necessary for ultimate completion of the job. These services could thus be the basis for a mechanic's lien.

Ownership Interest. Mechanic's lien laws apply to various ownership interests in real property. Absolute ownership is not required, but the lien ordinarily attaches only to the interest of the party ordering the work. Usually, when the term *owner* is used in a statute, that term has been defined broadly. In addition to persons having fee simple title, other owners include those who have life estates, persons with remainder interests, and tenants under lease. As the following case example illustrates, in some situations an owner's interest may be subject to a mechanic's lien, even though the owner did not contract for the improvements.

CASE EXAMPLE

Balbo purchased property from Sanchez on a land installment contract. In a land installment contract (see Chapter 22), the buyer pays the purchase price on an installment basis. The owner/seller, Sanchez, retains title until the purchase price is paid. The contract was recorded. Balbo commenced to build on the property, serving as his own contractor. Balbo contracted with American Wallboard to put in the walls. American purchased the necessary wallboard from Tri-City Building. Although Balbo paid American, American did not pay Tri-City. When the wallboard was delivered, Tri-City notified Sanchez of delivery, although Sanchez had not ordered the material. Most courts would hold that this notice was sufficient to establish mechanic's lien rights against Sanchez, inasmuch as Sanchez had ownership rights.

In most states, statutes allow a noncontracting owner to block a lien against his or her interest by posting a *notice of nonresponsibility*. The notice must be in some conspicuous place on the land and be posted within a short time after the owner finds out about the work being done. Depending on the state, the time ranges from three to ten days.

Type of Work. The statutes that establish mechanics' liens use various general terms to describe the type of work for which a lien may be obtained. Frequently, the terms are defined in the statutes themselves. When they are not defined by statute, the courts, as a rule, have tended to interpret these general terms broadly.

A number of statutes use the term *improvement(s)*. This term has been defined to include demolition, erection, alterations, or repairs. Some courts have refused to allow mechanics' liens for tearing down a building unless the term *demolition* is included in the statutory definition or is necessary for improvement. Terms such as *building*, *structure*, and *appurtenance* usually have also been defined broadly when included in mechanic's lien laws. Mechanic's lien laws in a number of states use *improvements* as a synonym for *building* or *structure*, not to indicate the type of work for which a lien may be granted.

Consent. For property to be subject to a mechanic's lien, most states require that improvements be made with the consent and knowledge, or at the request, of the owner. A contract is the basis for a mechanic's lien in most states, but a contract between an owner and a person seeking a lien is not required. As a result, numerous circumstances exist in which such a lien may attach even when the owner has not personally entered into a contract with the lienor.

CASE EXAMPLE

Rutgers Roofing contracted with a homeowner, Melaney April, to put on a new roof for $3,500. Rutgers hired Roofing Subcontractors, Inc., (RSI) to actually do the job. RSI completed the work but was not paid by Rutgers, who collected part of the money from April. The mechanic's lien statute in the jurisdiction authorizes the subcontractor to place a lien on property even though there was no contract between the homeowner and the lienor, as long as the lienor complies with the notice of filing requirements of the statute. This RSI did. Consequently, RSI is entitled to its mechanic's lien even though it had not contracted with April.

Consent of the owner may be *express* or *implied*. One example of *implied consent* is when a lease provision requires that a tenant make alterations or specific improvements. If a lease contains this type of provision, the lessor's interest is subject to a lien in most jurisdictions, even if the modifications are made at the tenant's request. On the other hand, a lease that contains the usual covenant that the tenant maintain or repair the premises and nothing more does not establish implied consent. In addition, except in states that have implied consent based on knowledge, mere knowledge by a lessor that improvements are being made is not sufficient to establish a lien against the lessor's interest.

The owner may give consent through an agent. Some states have, by legislation, established classes of persons as statutory agents for the owner. These people have the implied authority to consent in the owner's behalf. The statutory agents are contractors, subcontractors, architects, builders, and any others who are in charge of work. An artisan or material supplier dealing with one of these persons is ordinarily entitled to a lien.

Permanency. The concept underlying most mechanic's lien laws is that work or materials that are subject to a lien to be lienable must result in a *permanent benefit* underlies most mechanic's lien laws. *Permanent* refers to material and labor that become part of the premises. Permanent labor and materials are distinguished from those that are part of the contractor's plant or equipment in the project, which are not lienable.

CASE EXAMPLE

ABC Plumbing had a contract to furnish plumbing fixtures to a developer. The contract required delivery of fixtures to the individual units. To protect its delivery truck and to store fixtures, the company built a small storage shed at the site. When the company was not paid, it filed a notice of lien that included $1,500, the cost of the structure. A court would probably hold that this amount was not included in the lien against the premises since the benefit was not permanent.

Permanent is construed broadly to last as long as the item remains part of the premises. As a result, many improvements of short duration, as well as items detached from the structure, may be the basis for a mechanic's lien. This includes work done to protect a permanent installation or even a structure not intended to be permanent but designed to be removed at a future time. Electrical signs, telephones, and telephone equipment have been the basis for mechanics' liens. Items such as tables and benches have been considered permanent when necessary to the normal use of a structure and furnished for this use. Services such as mowing, trimming, and spraying plants as well as weeding and raking lawns are not permanent improvements.

■ **Perfection of Lien.** *The performance of those steps required by statute to sell real property under mechanic's lien laws.*

The time periods and procedures involved in, and required for, perfecting a mechanic's lien vary appreciably from state to state. They also frequently vary within the same state for different categories of claimants as well as for different types of benefits conferred. For example, in a number of states, the steps that a subcontractor must take to perfect a lien differ from those the prime contractor must follow. Material suppliers usually have to follow procedures different from those required of the artisan supplying labor. Despite these and other differences, two almost universal requirements for perfecting a mechanic's lien are notice to the owner and the filing of a mechanic's lien claim in the county or city land records.

Notice. Statutes generally require that a lien claimant notify the owner before filing a lien. The purpose of this requirement is to warn the owner not to pay a contractor against whom outstanding claims exist in favor of laborers, subcontractors, or material suppliers. Knowing of the existence of these claims, the owner may be protected against paying twice by retaining funds due to the contractor until the lien claimant is paid, or obtaining a lien waiver signed by the claimant. In most states, a defective notice or failure to provide the owner with notice invalidates a lien.

CASE EXAMPLE

Walker Process Equipment served a notice on Advance Mechanical Systems in order to perfect a lien under the Mechanic's Lien Act. However, the notice had been drafted as a notice under the Public Construction Bond Act. The court held that the notice did not meet the particularity requirement of the notice required under the Mechanic's Lien Act. See *Walker Process Equip. v. Advance Mech. Sys.*, 282 Ill. App. 3d 452 (Ill. Ct App. 1996).

Notice to the owner ordinarily includes the following information: the name and address of the lienor, the name of the person with whom the lienor contracted if not the owner, the labor performed or material furnished, dates when the work was started and completed, the balance due, and a description of the property and the owner's interest. Most states require that the notice be in writing; some require an affidavit as to the amounts due. Usually, the statute gives the potential lienor a limited time period of 20, 30, or sometimes 60 days after the work is completed to notify the owner of the claim.

Some categories of claimants are excused by statute from giving a preliminary notice, for example, laborers working for a daily wage. The reason for this exception is to protect these people from losing the lien right because of a technicality of which they might not be aware. In a number of states, preliminary notice is necessary only if the lien claimant did not deal directly with the owner. In jurisdictions following this rule, a prime contractor would not be required to give notice, but a subcontractor would. A few states permit notice to the owner after the lien has been filed.

Filing. A second critical point in perfecting a lien is filing for record. Doing the work or furnishing the materials merely gives the claimant a right to acquire a lien. In some states this right is referred to as an *inchoate lien*. Usually, the statute requires that the claimant file a verified statement of the claim. This statement ordinarily includes a brief explanation of the contract, the balance due, and a description of the property as well as the names and addresses of the parties.

A filed lien, like a recorded deed or mortgage, is part of the public record. The act of recording ensures that third parties dealing with the property will have knowledge of claims against it if they search the record. In a number of jurisdictions, filing is unnecessary if the mechanic sues for the sum owed. These states reason that the suit provides sufficient notice of claims against the property.

Most jurisdictions require that the verified statement, sometimes referred to as the *lien claim* or *affidavit*, be filed within a specified time after work is completed. This period varies, but 30, 60, and 90 days are common.

In a few states, the lien attaches as of the time the original contract was made. In others, the lien attaches from the date materials were first furnished or work commenced at the site.

CASE EXAMPLE

Scarlet and Grey Construction Company contracted to build a stable for Perry. Work began on November 10. On December 5, before the job was completed, Perry executed a mortgage on the property in favor of Betz. The stable was finished on December 12, but a portion of the contract price was not paid. Scarlet and Grey filed a lien against the property on January 3. In many states, this lien would have priority over Betz's mortgage because the lien reverts back to November 10, the day work began.

Termination. Mechanics' liens may be extinguished in numerous ways. Probably the most common is by payment of the obligation on which the lien is based. Other procedures are also widely used.

Ordinarily, discharging a debt terminates the existing liens securing the debt and precludes a future lien based on the same debt. In some jurisdictions, however, mechanic's lien rights of subcontractors and suppliers survive payment to a principal contractor. In these states, the subcontractors may obtain liens for the full value of their respective claims even if the principal contractor has been paid. This practice is known as the *Pennsylvania Rule*. In states following this rule, the subcontractor's lien is considered direct, not a right that derives from the general contractor. These jurisdictions consider the contractor the owner's agent; thus, through an agent, the subcontractor is deemed to have contracted directly with the owner. When a state has a mechanic's lien statute of this type, the owner may be required to pay twice.

CASE EXAMPLE

Randolph Estates contracted with the ABC Pool Company for construction of a $28,000 pool. The pool was to serve residents of an apartment complex being constructed by Randolph Estates. ABC subcontracted excavation and grading to Montefresco Company for $1,500. On completion of the pool, Randolph paid ABC as per the contract. ABC failed to pay Montefresco. When ABC went bankrupt, Montefresco filed a mechanic's lien against the premises. In states following the Pennsylvania Rule, Randolph would have to pay the $1,500 to Montefresco to extinguish the lien.

Probably the majority of states follow what is called the *New York Rule*. In these jurisdictions, a subcontractor's lien is limited to the amount still owed the general contractor at the time the lien is filed. The owner is not compelled to pay more than the contract price, inasmuch as any subcontractor's lien derives from the principal contractor. The result is that the owner may pay the principal contractor as work progresses without fear of a subcontractor's lien for the same work.

Many jurisdictions permit the owner to release an existing lien not only by paying the claim it represents but by giving a bond or paying cash into court to cover potential claims by contractors and/or subcontractors and artisans. If the claim is disputed, this process protects both the owner and the claimant. The owner is protected because the funds are controlled by the court; the claimant is protected because monies are available to pay any valid claim. This procedure is also valuable to the owner because the property is not tied up during litigation by being subject to a filed mechanic's lien.

Liens may also terminate by *waiver*. The waiver may be made before the improvement as part of the contract, as a *no-lien provision*. This provision must be clear and unambiguous. Any doubts will be resolved against the waiver. Some state courts have held that a waiver by a principal contractor is also applicable to subcontractors claiming through the principal. In other states, a subcontractor is bound by this type of provision only if he or she had actual knowledge of, or expressly consented to, the contractor's waiver.

Mechanics' liens are also extinguished by the lienor's *failure to foreclose* within a time period. This period is often short. Six months and a year are common, although in some states a two-year limitation is applicable. A number of jurisdictions shorten the time further by permitting the owner to demand that the lienholder commence an action to foreclose the lien. Failure of the lienor to begin foreclosure proceedings within the allowed time results in forfeiture of the lien. The purpose of these statutory provisions is to eliminate the cloud on the title resulting from a properly filed mechanic's lien claim.

Judgment Lien

■ *A lien that automatically attaches to real property of a defendant when a plaintiff wins a judgment in the jurisdiction in which the property is located.*

CASE EXAMPLE

Justin Lane purchased a lot for $10,000. Lane was the defendant in a tort case, and a judgment was entered against him for $8,500. Lane refused to pay the judgment as he believed it to be unfair. When Lane attempted to sell the lot, the purchaser's attorney refused to certify that the title was marketable because of a judgment lien resulting from the tort case.

Collecting a money judgment in a civil case may be more difficult than winning it. In most instances, the losing defendant does not rush up to the winning plaintiff with check in hand. If the judicial process by which the money judgments are awarded is to be respected, the law must assist plaintiffs in collecting their judgments.

The ultimate method is the forced sale of enough of the defendant's property, real and personal, to cover the judgment. Although some property may be exempt by statute, the nonexempt property of a defendant may be seized and sold to satisfy the judgment. This is known as an *execution* or a *levy of execution*. It is accomplished by a writ from the court. The writ authorizes a court officer, usually the sheriff, to sell the property.

A **judgment lien** is an involuntary lien attaching to real property when a money judgment is obtained against the owner. The lien establishes the claim of the *judgment creditor* against the defendant's real estate in the jurisdiction of the court that awarded the judgment and helps to ensure that the plaintiff will eventually collect the judgment. While the lien exists, a sale or mortgage of the property is subject to the judgment creditor's interest. As a result, the defendant often pays the judgment to free the property from the judgment creditor's lien. If the judgment is not paid, the real estate may be levied against and sold. Some states use a process similar to that used to foreclose a mortgage.

Judgment liens did not exist at common law. They are created by statute, and their existence and operation depend on the statutory provisions establishing them. Not all states have provided the judgment creditor with this method of enforcing a judgment.

A judgment lien is a general lien. It applies to all real estate owned by the defendant in the county where the judgment was rendered. The lien may be made specific by levy of execution. Most states have a simple procedure for extending the lien to other real estate owned by the defendant within the state. This is done by filing a transcript of the judgment in other counties in which the judgment debtor has real property. Federal statutes provide that a judgment of a United States district court sitting in a state having a judgment lien statute is a lien to the same extent as the judgments of a state court of general jurisdiction.

Requirements. The time at which a judgment lien attaches depends on the state statute. This time is important because it may determine the conflicting claims of creditors. In a few states, the lien commences when the judgment is rendered; however, most state statutes require that the judgment be made part of the public record in some manner before the lien is created. This is a reasonable requirement. Official records should be available to third parties dealing with a judgment debtor so that they have a source whereby they can determine potential problems. A common requirement for establishing general notice of the judgment is that it must be filed, docketed (officially listed), and indexed before a lien based on it is effective. Some states require only that the judgment be filed and docketed.

In a few states, legislation provides that when a judgment is indexed, the lien reverts to some earlier date. Sometimes this is the first day of the court term during which the judgment was rendered; more often it is the day the judgment was rendered. This *doctrine of relation back* means that the judgment lien might be superior to interests created before the lien became part of the public record.

Not all judgments rendered create liens. Of course, it is critical that the judgment be rendered validly by a court having jurisdiction. Another basic requirement is that the judgment be final. An *interlocutory judgment* or one that settles some intermediate plea or motion is not final and cannot give rise to a judgment lien. In addition, the judgment must be for a specific sum of money. In most states, liens are based on the judgments of any court of record. Frequently, however, state statutes require judgments of inferior courts to be filed with the statewide court of original jurisdiction before becoming a lien.

Legal Effect. As a general rule, liens and other interests in realty rank in the order in which they are created. This is the principle of "first in time, first in right." As a result of this principle, judgment liens have important consequences for two classes of people: buyers from a judgment debtor and other creditors of the judgment debtor.

If a judgment lien has been perfected before the signing date of a contract for the sale of realty, the buyer takes the real property subject to the lien. Because the real property is subject to a judgment lien, the real property may be sold by the sheriff to satisfy the judgment debt. As the lien existed at the time the buyer obtained his or her interest, the buyer will lose the real property unless the debt is paid off.

Creditors of a judgment debtor are also affected by a judgment lien. A valid judgment lien has priority over the claims of creditors who have not established a security interest in the debtor's real property prior to the judgment. The reason is that the judgment lien was created first.

Termination. In most instances, statutes creating the judgment lien also establish the lien's duration. Usually, the period is short. Periods of three to five years are common. In only a few states are judgment liens enforceable for more than ten years from their commencement.

In many states, the period of time in which a suit on a judgment may be initiated is longer than the period during which a judgment lien may be enforced. If this is the case, the judgment lien terminates, but the judgment remains outstanding. Both the common law and a number of states by statute provide for the revival or renewal of expired judgment liens. To revive a judgment lien, the judgment itself must still be enforceable. Any liens that attach during the period in which the judgment lien was dormant and before its revival take precedence over the revived lien.

■ **Notice of Lis Pendens.** *A recorded document that gives constructive notice that an action has been filed that might affect the title or possession of a specified parcel of real estate.*

At common law, a general principle existed that all persons were bound to take notice of suits affecting title to property. This principle was known as the doctrine of **lis pendens**, or suit pending. A person acquiring an interest in real estate that was the

---

United States v. Bostian
Eleventh Circuit Court of Appeals
59 F.3d 474 (11th Cir. 1995)

Background. Samuel Bostian deeded about 240 acres of land to a Trust, which he and his family controlled. Thereafter, the Internal Revenue Service determined that Bostian had a large income tax deficiency. It filed tax liens and sued to foreclose on those liens. Bostian handled the suit himself. Judgment was entered against him, and the court held that the Trust was really Bostian. It thus ordered that the 240 acres be sold at public auction.

Three days before the auction, Bostian filed a lis pendens against the property, stating that the Trust was the true owner of the property. Bostian's daughter and a male companion attended an open house viewing of the property one day before the auction. She began handing out the lis pendens notices to prospective buyers. Bostian himself posted a large notice of the lis pendens on the top of one of the signs advertising the auction. Bostian was arrested and charged with corruptly obstructing and impeding and endeavoring to impede the administration of the IRS by interfering with the auction. The jury convicted Bostian and he was sentenced to five years' proba-

tion and ordered to pay a fine of $3,000. He appealed the conviction.

Decision. The conviction was upheld.

Judge Lively. [A] defendant violates [the statute] by either 1) "corruptly" or "by force or threats of force" endeavoring to "intimidate or impede"; or by 2) "in any other way corruptly or by force or threats of force" impeding administration of the tax laws. . . . Resolution of the case hinges on the meaning of the key words "corruptly" and "impede," and whether Bostian's actions fall within these defined terms.

Bostian contends that the filing and dissemination of the lis pendens did not constitute a "corrupt" obstruction and impediment of [the statute]. Instead, these actions only created additional work for the government. . . . He also asserts that he did not act corruptly, since he did not act, as the jury instructions required, "with the intent to secure an unlawful benefit either to [himself] or for another." Frightening

continued on next page

away auction bidders would have been to his detriment, he claims. . . . We disagree.

[Bostian] acted corruptly by filing the lis pendens and attempting to interfere with the sale by affixing an enlarged copy of that document to a sign advertising the auction. By these actions he did intend to "secure an unlawful benefit" to himself—prevention of the sale of the property. His argument that he would suffer from, rather than benefit from actions that reduced the sale price misses the point. His purpose was not to obtain the highest price from the sale; rather, it was to prevent the sale altogether by creating a cloud on the title with his spurious claim that the trust owned the property.

Bostian also contends his actions were not unlawful. . . . Even assuming that his posting of the enlarged copy of the lis pendens and the distribution of copies of the document violated no law, these actions clearly were intended to impede the government's efforts to sell the seized property at auction. Bostian's argument that the sale took place, and thus his actions did not impede the government's efforts to sell the seized property at auction, is meritless. . . Only intent to impede, not successful impediment, is necessary for [the statute] to be violated.

There was no failure of proof in this case. The evidence of Bostian's activities was sufficient to support the jury's finding beyond a reasonable doubt.

Affirmed.

What actions particularly moved the court against Bostian? Can you suggest any alternative for Bostian?

---

subject of litigation, such as a suit to foreclose a mortgage, enforce a lien, or set aside a deed, took the interest subject to any judgment that might later be rendered in the lawsuit. This doctrine was harsh because it was often difficult to determine if the property was the subject of litigation.

Because of the harshness of the common-law doctrine, most states by statute provide for the filing of a notice of lis pendens in the county in which the property that is the subject of litigation is located. If the plaintiff does not file this notice, a person acquiring an interest in the real estate who has no actual knowledge of the litigation will not be subject to any judgment that might be awarded as a result of the lawsuit.

A notice of lis pendens is not a lien, but in many ways it has the effect of a lien, for once such a notice has been filed, the title to the real estate is encumbered. As a result, the title is unmarketable until litigation is settled or the notice of lis pendens vacated. One must, however, be careful when filing a lis pendens that it is done in good faith, and only after litigation has commenced. Otherwise, a person may be guilty of slander on the title, a tort, or even, as the *Bostonian* case illustrates, a criminal wrong.

■   **Attachment.** *The act of seizing a defendant's property by legal process, to be held by the court to ensure satisfaction of any judgment that might be awarded.*

In some cases, after winning a judgment, the plaintiff discovers that the defendant has disposed of all assets that might be used to satisfy the judgment debt. To prevent the defendant from doing this, statutes in many states allow **attachment**; that is, they allow a plaintiff to seize property of the defendant by judicial order at the commencement of litigation. The property is held in the custody of the court as security for any judgment that the plaintiff might win.

The circumstances under which a plaintiff is entitled to attach defendant's property are regulated in detail by the various state statutes. Requirements for obtaining an attachment order usually are strict. In general, the statutes allow attachment only if the plaintiff is seeking money damages. In a number of states, the monetary amount of the plaintiff's claim must be fixed or undisputed and only its validity contested.

A minority of states have unlimited attachment statutes. In these states, the plaintiff is permitted to attach the defendant's property in actions for money damages without showing special circumstances. Most states, however, require that the plaintiff show that some special reason exists to attach the defendant's property. Permissible reasons are indicated by the state statute establishing the attachment remedy.

Typical state statutes allow attachment of the property of nonresident defendants. They also allow attachment of property that might easily be concealed or where facts indicate that the defendant might leave the jurisdiction. Ordinary business or pleasure trips outside of the state, openly made, are not within the contemplation of the statute as grounds for attachment. In many jurisdictions, the fact that a defendant cannot be found is sufficient for the issuance of a writ of attachment. In almost all cases, a defendant may obtain the release of attached property by posting sufficient bond.

Vendor's Lien

▨ *In some states, a right of a seller to a lien against land conveyed for any unpaid or unsecured portion of the purchase price.*

CASE EXAMPLE
Dwayne and Beulah Blankenship contracted to exchange their ranch in Bonner's Ferry, Idaho, for one owned by Roy C. Myers and his son Ron. In addition, Roy Myers agreed to pay them $105,000 in contracts and cash.

Myers delivered the contracts and cash to his agent, Patrick, who converted $50,000 of these assets to his own use. A short time later, Myers conveyed his entire interest in the Bonner's Ferry ranch to his son. Both the senior Myers and Patrick became insolvent, and the Blankenships asserted a vendor's lien against the Bonner's Ferry property.

Although a lower court refused the lien on grounds that the Blankenships were not unpaid, the Idaho appellate court reversed. The appellate court stated, "if through no fault of the seller the seller never receives such consideration or collateral from the buyer, then the seller is unpaid and unsecured and has a vendor's lien." *Blankenship v. Myers*, 97 Idaho 356, 544 P.2d 314 (1975).

The term **vendor's lien** is used in several ways. In some situations, if the buyer does not pay the full purchase price, the seller reserves a lien in the deed. This is frequently referred to as an *express vendor's lien*. A lien of this type is very similar to a mortgage. It provides security for the unpaid seller just as a mortgage would. Like the mortgage, the express vendor's lien is the result of an agreement between the parties. Although most states allow express vendor's liens, they are not in common use in this country. The probable reason is that a mortgage to the unpaid seller provides greater protection because the buyer also signs a note for the debt. In a few states, however, the vendor's lien is an important element in real estate sales when the seller is not fully paid at the closing.

In a number of states, a vendor's lien arises by implication if the buyer does not pay the full price and the seller takes no other security. This is the type of lien involved in the Bonner's Ferry case. The *implied vendor's lien* exists without express agreement between the parties. It is based on the principle that a person who has acquired another's property should not be allowed to keep it without paying for it. An unpaid seller should be allowed to satisfy the debt from the proceeds of a foreclosure sale of the property. Courts in some states also justify the vendor's lien on the theory of *implied trust,* or *constructive trust.* These courts consider the buyer a trustee for the seller, holding legal title for the seller's benefit until the price is paid.

Courts and legislative bodies have often been critical of the implied vendor's lien. They consider the lien unfair because it is secret. They contend that third parties dealing with the buyer have no way of knowing of the lien's existence. Public records show that the buyer has legal title and that no security interests exist against the property. As a result, a third party might be induced to buy the property or grant credit with the property as security. Although the public record is clear, a seller might have a lien that could be a cloud on the title or take priority over a mortgage. To eliminate this injustice, many states, by statute or judicial opinion, hold the vendor's lien unenforceable against encumbrances or purchasers in good faith who do not know of the lien's existence. For example, if Ron Myers had sold the Bonner's Ferry ranch to a bona fide purchaser prior to the Blankenships' efforts to assert a vendor's lien, the property would no longer be subject to the lien. Even so, a vendor's lien is not without value; it may be asserted against the seller, the seller's heirs, or those who take from the seller with knowledge of the lien's existence.

Requirements. In those states in which it is recognized, the vendor's lien is created the moment the seller transfers legal title to the buyer. For the lien to exist, however, the seller must not have accepted some other type of security for the unpaid portion of the purchase price. For instance, if the seller takes back a mortgage, the lien is waived. Taking other land or personal property as security also waives the lien. In a number of states, a seller who agrees to pass a title free of encumbrances is not entitled to a vendor's lien unless one has been expressly reserved in the deed. Retention of possession by the vendor after passing title also generally negates a vendor's lien. The vendor, however, does not waive the lien by instituting an action to recover the unpaid purchase money.

Priority. As has been noted, in many states the vendor's lien has no priority against the interest of a bona fide purchaser from the vendee or security rights in the property given to a creditor without notice. In most states, the vendor's lien is also subject to a mechanic's lien for home construction, even if construction takes place after sale. These priority rules do not apply if an express vendor's lien is reserved in the deed and the deed is recorded. Under these conditions, third parties have a means of knowing that the lien exists. In any event, the vendor's lien does have priority over the claims of unsecured creditors.

In some sections of the United States, the interest of a person who sells real estate under a land contract is considered a vendor's lien. The vendor holds the legal title as security. If the vendee defaults, the vendor may foreclose the vendee's interest and apply the proceeds of the sale to the purchase price.

Tax Lien

■ *A lien imposed against real property for payment of taxes.*

The power of government to levy taxes is commonly coupled with the right to place liens on real and personal property to facilitate tax collection. Liens are encountered as part of the tax structure at all levels of government. In addition to federal and state governments, counties, cities, towns, and villages as well as nonpolitical units such as school and irrigation districts are authorized to use liens as security when taxes are unpaid.

Many types of taxes, when unpaid, create liens on property. These include both real and personal property taxes, income taxes, and estate taxes, as well as local assessments for sidewalks, sewers, and water distribution systems. Less frequently, liens may be used to collect contributions to unemployment funds, wages that have been withheld, and unpaid Social Security contributions.

Although **tax liens** may be placed against both real and personal property, liens on real property are generally more effective than those on personal property for several reasons. Personal property is easier to conceal than real property. Personal property may be moved from the taxing district or disguised with little difficulty. Real property's value is relatively stable, whereas many types of personal property deteriorate when used. As a result, personal property is often not of sufficient value to cover the delinquent tax.

Tax liens are not restricted to the property subject to taxation. In some jurisdictions, taxes assessed on personal property may be the basis for a lien on real property. A state may also collect taxes assessed against one parcel of real estate within its jurisdiction by proceeding against other parcels owned by the same person. A lien on property other than that against which the tax was assessed is limited to property owned when the taxes became collectible. Inasmuch as tax liens are statutory creations, the legislature has the authority to exempt certain types of property. Property exempt from tax liens varies considerably from state to state. Usually, the statutory provision establishing lien exemption parallels statutes exempting property from taxation in general.

Priority. People who are unable to pay a particular tax generally have other financial problems. Often, many claims exist against their property. These claims may have been the basis for liens for other taxes, judgments, or mortgages. The result is that litigation involving tax liens often concerns priority problems. Who has the first right to the proceeds produced by the sale of the property?

Legislative bodies have usually made real estate property tax liens superior to all other liens against the property, even those liens in existence before the tax lien. The rule of "first in time, first in right" does not ordinarily apply to tax liens.

TABLE 15.2	Types of Liens		
	Claimants	**Attachment to Real Property**	**Priority**
Mechanic's Lien	Those who perform labor or services in connection with real property	Detailed voluntary process	Superior over liens that attach after work commenced or materials furnished
Judgment Lien	Judgment creditors	Automatic on obtaining judgment	First in time, first in right
Vendor's Lien	Sellers	Express or implied on sale	Subject to mechanic's lien and bona fide purchaser for value
Real Estate Tax Lien	Taxing authorities	Simplified statutory procedure	Superior to most all other liens

CASE EXAMPLE

Graceland Savings and Loan held a mortgage on property owned by Ron Blue. The mortgage was recorded properly. Blue failed to pay his general property tax, and a lien was assessed against the property. The tax lien had priority over Graceland's mortgage.

State statutes ordinarily set forth any priorities existing between liens for different types of taxes. In the absence of a specific statute, the lien for general taxes is coequal with liens of other taxing units. Tax liens for general taxes are usually superior to liens for special assessments, even if the special assessment lien was prior in time. The reason is that the claim for the necessary support of government is a higher obligation than the demand for the costs of a local improvement. Maintenance of civil government is the first and paramount necessity for social order, personal liberty, and private property, and government cannot exist without revenue. Only on specific legislative direction will the priority of the sovereign claims of the state be denied.

Foreclosure of Tax Liens. Sale of tax liens on real property is one method commonly used in the United States to collect delinquent taxes. When taxes that are a lien against real property are in default, tax collectors in most states are authorized to sell the lien. These sales are usually by public auction. The successful bidder acquires the right to receive the overdue taxes and interest as these are paid. If there are no bidders, the taxing unit acquires the tax lien.

A successful bidder at a tax sale of the lien does not get title to the property but a lien against it. This lien is evidenced by a tax certificate. If the delinquent taxes are not paid after a period of time, the holder of the tax certificate may foreclose against the property. Usually, this period of time is two or three years. During this time, the property owner may redeem the property by paying the delinquent taxes, interest, and any penalties.

The purchaser at the foreclosure sale obtains title to the property. In most jurisdictions, the foreclosure procedure is very similar to that for a mortgage. A few jurisdictions continue to allow certain taxing units to conduct an absolute sale of real property

THE CHANGING LANDSCAPE

When purchasing a residence or property for commercial or investment purposes, it is important to obtain marketable title. *Marketable title* is what a reasonably prudent purchaser would accept and is often defined locally as a matter of custom. No one wants to find out that the largest purchase of his or her life is fraught with title problems because of unjustified liens. The determination of marketability and the existence of liens and priorities are legal questions that are too complex to be left to the lay buyer. For these reasons, title insurance is the great "savior." Through insurance principles companies are able to shoulder the risk for a premium that is set based on experience and state regulations. These title insurance companies do title examinations by examining the public records. Often, they have computerized records of the parcels accessible in their office that facilitate the examination.

The system, however, is far from foolproof. First, title companies exempt certain off-the-record liens and other encumbrances, leaving the new owner to self-insure against these liens. Then, title insurance companies are not immune from "going under," although state regulations substantially reduce this possibility.

The system of title insurance in place to guard against liens against title that undermine the marketability of real estate is a good one. Yet, it may need a little tweaking to cover up some cracks. Secondary insurance, not unlike supplemental health insurance, may be a way to further protect against loss, but to date, this type of insurance is not readily available. Another possibility is a federal or state guaranteed insurance program, not unlike the federal mandatory insurance program for banks and savings institutions. This could provide additional protection should a title insurance company become insolvent. Can you think of any other possibilities?

at public auction if taxes are delinquent. The highest bidder acquires immediate title to the property on payment of the bid and delivery of the deed.

Federal Tax Lien. The federal taxing authority uses liens against real property to aid in the collection of federal income, estate, and gift taxes. Federal tax liens for income taxes are not valid against a mortgagee, pledgee, mechanic's lienor, purchaser, or judgment creditor until a notice of lien is filed. Liens for federal estate taxes do not require recording or filing. They come into existence against all of a decedent's taxable assets automatically on that person's death. Relatively simple procedures have been developed to release a decedent's real property from the tax lien. These are designed to facilitate sale of the property. They ordinarily require a bond by the estate or partial payment of the tax. More information about tax liens is available at *http://users.erols.com/tax.atty/taxliens.html.*

Table 15.2 compares the types of involuntary liens discussed in this chapter.

■ KEY TERMS

attachment 334   lis pendens 333   tax lien 337

judgment lien 331   mechanic's lien 324   vendor's lien 335

lien 323   perfection of lien 328

■ INTERNET RESOURCES

For an overview of mechanic's lien, see

www.improvenet.com/adviceandresources/projectplanning/mechanics.html

■ REVIEW AND DISCUSSION QUESTIONS

1. When a contractor improves real property, the work is done on the basis of a contract with the owner. A contractor who is not paid may sue for breach of that agreement. Explain why a contractor should also be entitled to file a mechanic's lien against the property.

2. Mechanic's lien law differs appreciably from state to state. (a) Indicate at least five of these differences. (b) What public policy concerns might explain some of these variations?

3. Judgment lien law differs appreciably from state to state. (a) Indicate at least five of these differences. (b) What public policy concerns might explain some of these variations?

4. What is the chief criticism of the vendor's lien? Is this criticism justified?

5. For what reason does the tax lien enjoy a superior status? Do you agree that it should? Explain.

■ CASE PROBLEMS

1. Kile borrowed $15,000 from Chatfield, giving her a promissory note to cover the debt. The note was unsecured, but Chatfield knew that Kile owned substantial unmortgaged real property. A short time later, Hude won a judgment against Kile for $150,000. When Kile filed as a bankrupt, both Chatfield and Hude claimed priority in the real estate. Which of the two has the superior claim? Explain.

2. Wood owned several hundred acres of land in Texas. In 1952, he decided to explore for oil on the land and leased an oil-drilling rig from Cabot. Under the terms of the lease, Cabot was responsible for moving the rig to the Wood property. Cabot then

hired White Heavy Haulers to transport the equipment. White Heavy Haulers was not paid and filed a mechanic's lien against Wood's property. (a) Is the lien valid? Discuss. (b) Would your answer differ if under the lease the expense of moving the rig was to be borne by Wood? Explain.

3. Ransonne won a judgment against Sneed for $120,000. A certified copy of the judgment was filed in the office of the county recorder of Mesa County, a county in which Sneed owned real property with a market value of about $80,000. A short time later, Sneed contracted to sell this property for $82,000. Ransonne immediately sued to enjoin the sale on the basis of her judgment lien. She contended that the property would appreciate in value over the next few years and could then be sold to satisfy the judgment. Discuss the validity of her contention.

4. Jethro Construction Co., Inc. (Jethro), was the general contractor on two separate construction projects. Lasater Electric Co. (Lasater) was the electrical subcontractor on both projects. Lasater purchased its materials for its projects as well as others from Mac's Electrical Supply (Mac's). Lasater maintained an open account with Mac's. Over several projects, payments by Lasater to Mac's had been increasingly slow, and Mac's was worried about Lasater's ability to pay. What steps should Mac's take to ensure mechanics' liens against the projects if Lasater fails to pay?

5. A state statute created a mechanic's lien in favor of all persons "bestowing skill or other necessary service on . . . the construction . . . either in whole or in part, of any building, structure, or other work of improvement . . . ." In the course of supplying general engineering services to subdivide land into residential lots, Nolte located boundaries and set monuments in the ground to mark them. When Nolte was not paid, he filed a mechanic's lien. The owner argued that Nolte's lien was invalid because it was not related to any "building, structure, or other work of improvement," as the mechanic's lien statute required. Do you agree? Support your answer. *Nolte v. Smith*, 189 Cal. App. 2d 140, 11 Cal. Rptr. 261 (1961).

6. In 1980, Daniels invested $28,000 in the development of a condominium in Park City, Utah. He was to receive $80,000 for his share in the profits from the sale of condominium units. Additionally, he was hired to serve as general contractor for the project for which he was to be paid an additional $15,000.

The condominium was completed in July 1981, and Daniels was paid the $15,000, but he did not receive the $80,000. As a result, Daniels decided to file a mechanic's lien, but at the request of the owners who were trying to refinance, he did not immediately do so. Consequently, he did not file within 100 days of completion as required by state law.

On December 1, 1981, several water pipes in the condominium froze and Daniels was called in to make repairs. On February 3, 1982, he filed a notice of lien against the project for his $80,000. He listed December 1, 1981, as the last day labor had been performed. Deseret Federal Savings and Loan, the construction mortgagee, and CEN Corporation, an owner (defendants), moved for a summary judgment to declare Daniels' lien void. What are Daniels' arguments? What are the defendants' arguments? *Daniels v. Deseret Federal Savings and Loan*, 771 P.2d 1100 (Utah Ct. App. 1989).

7. Tabet Lumber Company supplied materials for a house being constructed for Richard and Jan Baughman. The Baughmans paid the contractor in full and moved into the house on October 25, 1985. On January 15, 1986, the contractor hung two mirrors in the bathrooms, installed handrails on the stairs, and weather-stripped two basement doors. These items were included in the original agreement. The contractor did not pay for all of the materials, and on April 15, 1986, Tabet filed a lien claim for the unpaid portion. The Baughmans asked the court to dismiss, contending that this filing was invalid as the state's mechanic's lien statute required filing within 90 days of completion. Their view was that substantial completion was sufficient and the 90-day period started running in October. Should the case be dismissed? Support your answer.

8. Any state requires that a subcontractor file a notice of furnishings to perfect a mechanic's lien. The notice provides a public record that the subcontractor is furnishing work and/or materials. The statute requires that it be filed within 21 days from the time that the subcontractor receives notice that work has commenced.

   Masonry, Inc., contracted with General Contractors, Inc., to do masonry work for The Southside Church. Masonry, Inc., did not file the notice of furnishings until the 30th day. General Contractors went bankrupt, and Masonry, Inc., was not paid. Masonry, Inc., looked to the church, who maintained that it paid General Contractors. The church insisted that Masonry, Inc., remove its filing. Masonry, Inc., refused to do so until the church paid it. What should Masonry, Inc., do and why?

9. The plaintiff, Askren, was the owner of a two-acre parcel of land in Indianapolis. He made a contract with Cardinal Industries, a hotel chain, to sell the parcel to Cardinal for $250,000. Half of the purchase price was to be paid in cash to Askren at the closing and the other half was to be paid in equal installments, together with 9 percent interest per year, on the first and second anniversaries of the closing. The agreement was on a printed form, but a clause had been typed in that Askren's "Security [for payment of the balance of the purchase price is] to be a Cardinal . . . promissory note." At the closing, Askren received $125,000 in cash plus a promissory note, the terms of which were identical to those specified in the agreement of sale. Cardinal borrowed a considerable sum of money to build a hotel on the parcel it had bought. The loan was secured by a mortgage on the real estate and its improvements. The loan and mortgage were later assigned to the principal defendant in this case, Third Savings and Loan Company. Cardinal went broke and failed to make either of the installment payments that it owed Askren. Does Askren have a vendor's lien on the parcel which would give him the right to bring a lawsuit to foreclose on the land? Explain. See *Askren v. 21st St. Inn,* 988 F.2d 38 (7th Cir. 1993).

16 Deeds

■ DEED

■ *A legal instrument conveying title to real property.*

The **deed** is the primary method of transferring title to real estate. Title is the totality of rights and obligations possessed by an owner. The term is also used in the sense of evidence of ownership. Therefore, the deed is one of the critical documents in the real estate transaction. Although problems involving deeds are ordinarily the concern of the attorney, the real estate professional needs to be familiar with the various types of deeds, the elements of a deed, and common restrictions imposed by some deeds.

The deed is a two-party instrument. One party, called the *grantor* (seller), conveys real estate to the second party, the *grantee* (buyer). Any written document containing the essential elements will be effective as a deed. Most states, however, have adopted statutory forms for the different types of deeds. The statutory forms are almost always short, often a single page, and all of the essentials are included. Although the statutory form is acceptable for all transactions, lawyers sometimes prepare a longer, more detailed document.

The use of statutory forms cuts the costs of recording and reduces the space necessary to preserve records and deeds. In some areas of the United States, especially heavily populated areas, space has become so acute a problem that many recording offices have turned to microfilm or microfiche storage or computerized systems to preserve the public records.

■ TYPES OF DEEDS

Several types of deeds are common in the United States. Ordinarily, in a real estate transaction, the type of deed that the seller uses is agreed on in the contract of sale. A seller is bound to furnish the type of deed stipulated by the real estate sales contract, even though another type of deed might provide the buyer more protection. The most common types of deeds are the warranty deed, bargain and sale deed, quitclaim deed, and fiduciary deed. (See Table 16.1.)

Warranty Deed

■ *A deed that conveys title and warrants that the title is good and free of liens and encumbrances.*

Custom often influences what type of deed will be agreed on in the contract. Real estate attorneys like to use the instrument that is in general use in a particular locality.

TABLE 16.1	Warranties		
Type of Deed		**Warranties**	**After-Acquired Title**
General Warranty		Yes	Yes
Special Warranty		Yes	Yes
Bargain and Sale		No	Yes
Fiduciary		Yes	Yes
Quitclaim		No	No

In some areas, one type of deed is standard for residential sales, whereas a different type of deed is used to convey commercial property. Parties should remember, however, that the type of deed is subject to negotiation at the time of contracting.

CASE EXAMPLE

Olvic's contract with Ziebarth called for a general warranty deed. At the closing, Olvic offered another type of deed customarily used in the area. Nonetheless, Ziebarth was entitled to a general warranty deed.

There are two types of warranty deeds—the general or full warranty deed and the special or limited warranty deed.

General Warranty Deed. The **general** or full **warranty deed** is most commonly used. A general warranty deed conveys the seller's title and contains covenants of title, or warranties. These covenants provide the buyer with some protection against claims that might interfere with ownership.

The covenants in a general warranty deed vary from one locality to another, but five covenants are customary: covenant of seisin, covenant against encumbrances, covenant of quiet enjoyment, covenant of warranty, and covenant of further assurances. (See Figure 16.1.) In some states, such as Illinois, these general warranty covenants are implied by statute by simply "warranting" the title. By California's use of a grant deed, and, in other states through the use of "statutory" deeds, the same result is accomplished. The warranties are implied. Still other states require express reference to the warranties.

By *covenant of seisin,* the seller guarantees his or her ownership of the property and existence of a right to convey. The covenant has also been construed to mean that the seller has an estate of the quantity and quality purportedly conveyed. This covenant is sometimes referred to as the *covenant of right to convey.*

The *covenant against encumbrances* is the seller's assurance that, at the time of conveyance, the property is free of encumbrances. Typical encumbrances are leases, easements, liens, and mortgages, discussed more fully in Chapters 7, 8, 9, 16, and 21. The covenant does not apply to those encumbrances specifically excepted in the deed because the buyer has agreed to accept them. In many states, encumbrances that are open and visible, or a matter of record, and that benefit the land are also excluded from the covenant against encumbrances.

| FIGURE 16.1 | General Warranty Deed |

General Warranty Deed

This general warranty deed is made the seventeenth day of May 2003, between Honus Grantor and Elsie Grantee.

Witness that Grantor, in consideration of $1.00 and other good and valuable consideration, paid by Grantee, does hereby grant and release to Grantee and assigns forever, the following described real estate, together with the appurtenances and all the estate and rights of Grantor in and to said premises:

[Insert description here]

And Grantor covenants as follows:

1. That Grantor is seised of said premises in fee simple, and has good right to convey the same.

2. That Grantee shall quietly enjoy the said premises.

3. That the said premises are free from encumbrances.

4 That the Grantor will execute or procure any further necessary assurance of the title to said premises.

5. That Grantor will forever warrant the title to said premises.

In witness hereof, Grantor has hereunto set his hand on the above date.

_____   _____

Witness   Grantor

_____

Witness

Acknowledged before me this 17th day of May, 2003.

_____

Notary Public

CASE EXAMPLE

Al Wilson purchased a lot from Bonnie McConnell. The lot and several others in the area were subject to certain building restrictions. At the time Wilson contracted he knew of these restrictions, but they were not mentioned in the contract. Wilson refused to accept a deed from McConnell on grounds that the restrictions violated the covenant against encumbrances. Because Wilson knew of the restrictions and they benefited the land, however, this argument was unsuccessful.

The *covenant of quiet enjoyment* and the *covenant of warranty* are very much alike. The covenant of quiet enjoyment warrants that the buyer will not be evicted by someone with a superior title. This covenant is not breached unless the buyer is actually evicted by a third party who has a superior title. The covenant of warranty warrants that the warrantor will defend title on behalf of the purchaser against all lawful claimants.

The practical implication of this warranty is that the warrantor must pay any litigation costs, including attorney fees, in addition to the damages sustained should the warrantee lose the property.

In some states the general warranty deed also contains a *covenant of further assurances*. This covenant obligates the grantor to perform all acts necessary to confirm the grantee's title, including the execution of any additional documents to accomplish the assurance.

The covenant of quiet enjoyment, the covenant of warranty, and the covenant of further assurances protect future purchasers as well as the immediate purchaser. They are regarded as future covenants and are said to *run with the land*. As a result, their breach may be the basis for suit by a remote buyer against a previous seller who has given a warranty deed. This suit may occur many years after the particular defendant sold the property. The phrase *run with the land*, discussed more fully in Chapter 9, is used because these covenants attach to the land and pass from one person to another as title is transferred.

> **CASE EXAMPLE**
> Several years after buying the property from Olvic, Ziebarth sold it to Lance Murphy. Ziebarth did not convey by a general warranty deed. Murphy's title was contested, and he was evicted from the property. Unable to sue Ziebarth, Murphy commenced an action against Olvic. Olvic defended on the grounds that he had not sold the property to Murphy. In this litigation, a court would find for Murphy on the grounds that the covenants of quiet enjoyment and warranty run with the land and extend to future owners.

Covenants in a warranty deed do not absolutely assure the buyer that the seller has title or guarantee any rights to the buyer. All they do is give the buyer a right to sue if a covenant is broken. Although they provide the buyer with some protection, that protection is limited by many factors. The seller who has given the covenants might become insolvent or leave the jurisdiction. In that case, any judgment against the seller would be difficult to obtain or of little value. Many states limit the seller's liability to the original purchase price. In these states, improvements or appreciation in value is not included as part of the buyer's losses. Not covered by the traditional covenants are invalid claims and threats of litigation. Because of the limited nature of the protection offered, a buyer should never rely solely on a warranty deed. Additional assurances such as title insurance, discussed in Chapter 19, should be obtained.

Special Warranty Deed. A **special** or limited **warranty deed** restricts the extent of the seller's warranties. In this type of instrument, the seller warrants only against acts that he or she has done that might adversely affect title. Of course, the deed conveys the seller's title to the property. The limited warranty deed then warrants that the grantor did not encumber the property; consequently, the grantor warrants to defend the title only against lawful claimants who took through the grantor.

> **CASE EXAMPLE**
> Ziebarth's conveyance to Lance Murphy was by a limited warranty deed. When Murphy discovered that Ziebarth's title was defective because of an undischarged mortgage given by Olvic, Ziebarth's seller, Murphy, brought suit against Ziebarth. Because the defect arose

before Ziebarth had acquired title, the limited warranty had not been breached. Murphy did, however, have a good cause of action against Olvic, who had conveyed by general warranty deed.

Bargain and Sale Deed

◼ *A deed that conveys title with no warranties.*

The **bargain and sale deed** conveys title but contains no warranties, the grantor's ownership and right to convey is implied. It may be used when, for example, there are some known encumbrances that the buyer will assume and that will be adjusted in the purchase price. Sometimes the bargain and sale deed contains covenants against the seller's acts. When this is the case, the bargain and sale deed has virtually the same effect as the limited or special warranty deed.

Quitclaim Deed

◼ *An instrument that transfers the grantor's interest only.*

Unlike the warranty deed and the bargain and sale deed, the **quitclaim deed** does not purport to convey title; it merely releases whatever interest the grantor possesses. If the grantor has title, the quitclaim deed conveys that title as effectively as a bargain and sale deed. A grantee who takes title by a quitclaim deed does not acquire any of the covenants that are given to a grantee accepting a warranty deed. When the contract does not mention the type of deed to be used, many states permit the seller to give a quitclaim deed.

One of the most common applications of the quitclaim deed is to transfer a spouse's interest in the marital residence to the other spouse as part of a divorce property settlement. That transfers exactly the interest the grantor-spouse has in the property, no more, no less. The quitclaim deed is also commonly used to clear a defective title by having a third person who has a possible claim on the realty convey whatever rights he or she has to the owner. The defect could be an outstanding lien, an easement, or a potential dower right, all of which are said to be "clouds on the title."

CASE EXAMPLE

Martin Russo contracted to sell property to Elmer Hunter. At the time, Russo was single, but he married before he signed and delivered the deed. Only Russo signed the deed. In their state, Russo's wife has a right of dower. On discovering the marriage, the attorneys for both parties asked Mrs. Russo to execute a quitclaim deed releasing all her rights to Elmer Hunter. In executing and delivering this instrument, Mrs. Russo would surrender any interest she might have in the property, including dower rights.

Sometimes a grantor delivers a deed to the grantee, and, in fact, the grantor does not have good title to the property that is the subject of the grant. Under the doctrine of after-acquired title, however, a title that is acquired after the transfer relates back to the date of the transfer. This is covered under land installment contracts in Chapter 22. Additionally, it would apply when a general or special warranty or bargain and sale deed is used. It would not, however, apply when a quitclaim deed is employed to transfer the property. Quitclaim deeds only convey the title the grantor has at the time of conveyance. (See Table 16.1)

Fiduciary Deed

■   *A deed that conveys title and contains no warranties except that the grantor has the authority to transfer title.*

A *fiduciary* is a person who has been placed by law in a position of trust regarding another's property, for example, the administrator or executor of a decedent's estate, treated in Chapter 18. The fiduciary might need to convey title to the decedent's real property but would not want to make guarantees or warranties concerning the title. In that case a **fiduciary deed**, a special form of deed similar to the bargain and sale deed, may be used. In it the fiduciary guarantees only that he or she has been properly appointed and authorized to sell and convey the property. For example, the estate executor may make an after-death transfer to the beneficiaries of the estate. The deed does not make any other warranties.

In many states it is customary to use a sheriff's deed to convey foreclosed property to the purchaser at public auction. This is a type of fiduciary deed. It warrants that the sheriff has the authority to transfer title to the purchaser.

■ ESSENTIAL ELEMENTS OF A DEED

A deed is a serious instrument that should be drafted by an attorney. A properly drafted and executed deed is critical to any real estate sale. Errors in a deed may cause problems not only for the current owner but also for future generations of owners. Sale of the property, financing, and even occupancy may be affected by errors that seem inconsequential. To help prevent these errors, the real estate salesperson needs some knowledge of the basic requirements of a valid deed. Because the deed should be drafted by an attorney, the salesperson's knowledge need not be extensive, but it should be sufficient enough to "flag" potential problems. With this background, the salesperson should be able to alert the drafter to issues that might lead to errors in the deed.

To be valid, a deed must include words of conveyance, a competent grantor, an identifiable grantee, and an adequate legal description. (See Table 16.2.) The instrument must be signed by the grantor, and notarized, and, in many states, witnessed. In addition, a valid delivery and acceptance must occur. State statutes may require other terms, for example, the name and address where the tax bill should be sent.

Words of Conveyance

The heart of a deed is the granting clause. A deed must contain words of conveyance sufficient to transfer an estate from one party to another. No particular words are necessary, provided that those used express an intention to convey title. Customary

TABLE 16.2	Essential Elements of a Deed

- Words of Conveyance
- Competent Grantor
- Identifiable Grantee
- Adequate Legal Description
- Proper Execution
- Delivery and Acceptance

words of conveyance include *grant, convey,* and *bargain.* A typical granting clause might read as follows: "Grantors do grant, bargain, sell, and convey to the said grantees forever. " The words *quitclaim* or *release* are words of conveyance commonly found in quitclaim deeds.

A deed without words of conveyance does not transfer title; the courts have, however, been indulgent in interpreting words in order to a give a deed effect when it was clearly the intent of the grantor to convey the property.

CASE EXAMPLE

Mary A. Searle conveyed land to her four children as tenants in common. Approximately seven years later, the four joined in the execution of an inartfully drawn instrument, which purported to change their rights as cotenants and to convey their interests to others.

The granting clause of this document stated, "Said premises are to be held so that as each of said parties shall die, the property shall vest in the survivors or survivor for their respective lives. . . ." Remainders were created using as granting words "to go," "to be his," and "shall go." In an action to establish who had title, plaintiffs argued that the operative words of grant, "are to be held," and the phrases used to grant the remainder interests were insufficient and that the instrument was not a valid deed.

The court did not agree, stating, "To be effective to transfer an interest in realty, a deed necessarily must contain words of present grant. . . . But no particular verbal formula is required under our rule of construction as previously given. The quoted words express an intention to create among the original cotenants new incidents of survivorship and power of sale, and to grant remainder interests to other persons subject to defeasance on the exercise of the power of sale. The instrument was not ineffective as a deed for lack of a sufficient granting clause." *Dennen v. Searle*, 149 Conn. 126, 176 A.2d 561 (1961).

Real estate may be transferred as a gift in which case no purchase money is paid. Ordinarily the transfer is predicated upon a sale.

Customarily, deeds will recite a nominal consideration such as "one dollar ($1.00) and other good and valuable consideration." This is done because buyers are often reluctant to have the actual purchase price shown, although the actual price paid is usually available through the auditor's office or some other public record. A recital of a nominal consideration is effective; if the question of actual consideration arises, the courts allow the parties to prove by extrinsic evidence the actual purchase price.

Competent Grantor

To be valid, a deed must have a competent grantor. Any natural person except, for example, one who is a minor, or who lacks mental capacity, may convey real estate by deed. Corporations and partnerships also have the capacity to convey real property.

Minors. Deeds made by minors are not void, but they are *voidable*, which means that the minor acquires the option of either ratifying or disaffirming the transfer.

The minor wishing to disaffirm a transfer by *deed* cannot ordinarily do so until reaching the age of majority, but a minor may void a *contract* to buy land at any time during minority and for a reasonable time after reaching majority. Today, in most states the age of majority is 18. Once having reached majority, the minor must institute proceedings to disaffirm within a reasonable time. If this is not done, the right is lost.

> **CASE EXAMPLE**
>
> John Spencer and his sister inherited land from their father. At the time, John was a minor. He attained majority five months later. John's sister was of full age at her father's death. Before John attained majority, he and his sister sold the property to Alpheas MacLoon. Shortly thereafter, MacLoon conveyed part of the property to the Lyman Falls Power Company and the residue to William Hutchins. Three years later the power company commenced substantial improvements on the land. John Spencer attempted to disaffirm. The company's attorney pleaded that Spencer had a right to disaffirm when he reached majority, but the right had been lost because he failed to assert it within a reasonable time. This argument was adopted by the court called on to rule on the issue.

Mentally Incapacitated. To cancel a deed for lack of mental capacity, evidence of a grantor's incompetency must be clear and convincing. The test of mental capacity to make a deed is the grantor's ability to understand the nature and effect of the act at the time the deed is signed.

> **CASE EXAMPLE**
>
> Florence Woodward owned a 120-acre farm near Verna, Oklahoma. When she was nearly 80, she became ill and moved to a nursing home. While a resident at the home, she conveyed the farm to a nephew. After Woodward's death, a niece contested the validity of the deed on grounds that the grantor was incompetent.
>
> Conflicting testimony was given at the trial concerning Florence Woodward's competency. Witnesses testified that prior to her hospitalization she was often confused and vague. Her concentration was described as poor. There was testimony that her home was untidy, and she often took care of her cattle at odd hours, such as midnight. A nurse from the nursing home testified that in her opinion Woodward would not have understood the effect of signing a deed, but she always recognized her nephews and would talk about her property. Other witnesses testified that Woodward was generally alert, competent, and normal.
>
> The court held the deed valid, stating that fragmentary evidence of isolated instances of failing memory or confusion is insufficient to overcome evidence that the grantor was competent. *Matter of Woodward*, 549 P.2d 1207 (Okla. 1976).

Corporations. A number of special rules apply to transfers of real property by corporations. The corporate officer who executes a deed must be authorized to do so. This authorization is obtained from the board of directors, which adopts a written resolution permitting the officer to act. In most states, if the corporation sells real estate that is a substantial portion of the corporation's assets, statutes require that the sale be approved by a designated portion of the shareholders, usually a supermajority, for example, two-thirds. Nonprofit corporations are often required by statute to obtain approval of a majority of members before selling real estate.

Partnerships. A partnership is not a legal entity for certain purposes—taxation, for example. However, all states have adopted the Uniform Partnership Act or a similar statute. These acts make it clear that a partnership is an entity for purposes of transferring title to real estate and holding title in its own name. Holding title in the name of the partnership avoids any problems associated with an interest in dower, because no dower attaches to a partnership interest.

Identifiable Grantee

A deed does not convey title unless it names an existing identifiable grantee. Of course, few transactions occur where the grantee does not legally exist. One example, however, would be a deed that designates an unincorporated association as the grantee. A deed naming this group would be invalid. It would need to name the legal trustees of the association. However, as the next case example illustrates, courts permit evidence outside of the deed to determine the identity of the grantee.

> **CASE EXAMPLE**
>
> I. A. Garraway and Mrs. I. A. Garraway signed a general warranty deed conveying to "The Trustees of Oak Grove Consolidated High School and Their Successors" a parcel of land. The deed was delivered and recorded. The trustees built a public school on the property and operated it for 28 years until the school was closed. The Perry County Board of Education succeeded to all rights of the former trustees of the high school. The Garraways' heirs sought to have the warranty deed declared null and void on the legal theory that no legal person was named as trustee in the deed. The trial court rejected the theory and the Supreme Court of Mississippi affirmed the trial court. The court stated:
>
>> In the first place, the Trustees of the Oak Grove Consolidated High School were indeed a corporate body politic. . . . In any event, the conveyance is effective because all our law requires is that the grantee be described in such terms that by reference to objective evidence otherwise available, his identity may be ascertained with reasonable certainty. . . . There are minutes before the court reflecting that . . . the Trustees of the Oak Grove Consolidated High School were W. A. Hegwood, Forrest Cochran, Arthur Breland, H. I. Breland and Charlie Herring. *Garraway v. Yonce*, 549 So. 2d 1341 (Miss. 1989).

Ordinarily, the determination of the proper designation of the grantee is a responsibility of the attorney or other person who drafts the deed. The real estate professional can aid the drafter by providing information of unusual circumstances regarding the name or marital status of the grantee. For example, during negotiations, the real estate salesperson may learn of the grantee's use of another name or a variation in spelling.

Adequate Legal Description

Problems involving descriptions in deeds are, like those involving designation of the grantee, not primarily the concern of real estate personnel but of legal personnel. Sales personnel, however, are apt to be aware of boundary controversies, which may result from, or indicate, description problems. Legal description and controversies involving boundaries are discussed in Chapter 17.

The salesperson who is aware of a boundary or description issue should urge the seller to obtain a solution before placing property on the market. This will save time and embarrassment as well as prevent hard feelings that arise when these issues come up after agreement is reached.

It is not difficult to inadvertently transpose words or omit portions of a description when copying it from one deed to another. Descriptions probably cause more litigation than any of the other formal requirements of the deed. The property to be conveyed must be described well enough in the deed to identify it with reasonable certainty. However, an imperfect description does not necessarily render a deed invalid. Presumably the grantor intended to convey something; the deed will usually be upheld unless the description is so vague or contradictory that the particular land cannot be identified.

Most courts interpret words of description liberally in order to uphold a conveyance. The basic rule in the construction of deeds is to ascertain and carry out the real intention of the parties. To accomplish this, courts first look to the document itself, but they will accept extrinsic evidence if the description furnishes a guide to identifying the property conveyed.

CASE EXAMPLE

Plaintiff and defendant owned adjoining land. A former owner of plaintiff's property had conveyed a ten-foot strip of ground to the township to be used as a drainage ditch. The ditch drained defendant's land as well as that of other landowners. The description in the deed to the township indicated a point of beginning and described the ditch as "running due south for 2,200 feet." For several years defendant had maintained the ditch, which was at the time of suit six feet wide.

Plaintiff commenced a trespass action against defendant, asking for an injunction prohibiting defendant from maintaining and using the ditch. Plaintiff argued that the deed to the township was ineffective because the description contained no boundaries. The court rejected this argument on the grounds that logically the line described was intended as the center of the ditch. The description thus furnished the means by which the property could be identified. *Franz v. Nelson*, 183 Neb. 122, 158 N.W.2d 606 (1968).

Land descriptions are covered in Chapter 17. Some legal descriptions are described by metes and bounds, which makes reference to compass directions, angles of degree, distances, monuments and landmarks. Regardless, a land description to be adequate must close, that is, when it is diagrammed it must not be open on any sides. Otherwise it is inadequate, and will not be given effect.

CASE EXAMPLE

Preoria sought to convey a portion of her farm property with the following metes and bounds description:

> Starting on the northeast end of the Miller-Hart Farm beginning at an iron pipe marked 1, and thence running southerly along the Hart Pond to a pin in the ground marked 2, and then westerly 112 feet to a pin marked 3. This is an inadequate description because it does not close.

> More modern descriptions refer to plats that are of public record in a town or subdivision which have been previously surveyed for accuracy. This avoids the closure problems.

Proper Execution

To be valid, a deed must be signed by the grantor; the grantee's signature is unnecessary. A few states require that a deed be signed at the end of the instrument. Otherwise the signature does not have to be in any particular place, but the signature must clearly apply to the entire instrument. Customarily, even when not required, a deed is signed at the end.

Signature may be by the grantor's mark or by any writing the grantor intends as a signature. When a grantor signs by a mark, the name should appear near the mark, and the act should be witnessed.

Attestation is the act of witnessing the execution of an instrument and subscribing as a witness. In general, the law does not require witnesses to a grantor's signature to establish a deed as valid. Witnessing and attestation, however, are traditional prerequisites to recording. The attesting witness subscribes the document for the purpose of verifying and identifying it. Usually, two witnesses are required. However, there is a statutory trend to eliminate the need for witnesses.

Acknowledgment is the act by which a grantor declares, before a duly authorized official (for example, a Notary Public), that a deed is genuine and executed voluntarily. Acknowledgment, like attestation, is in most states a prerequisite to recording rather than an essential requirement of a valid deed. The purpose of acknowledgment is to prevent forgery and fraud. The official witnessing the grantor's signature is charged with determining the grantor's identity. Each state, by statute, prescribes the officials before whom an acknowledgment must be made and the general form the acknowledgment must follow. Attestation and acknowledgment are discussed more fully in Chapter 19, which treats recording.

Power of Attorney. A general power of attorney is a written instrument authorizing a person, the attorney-in-fact, to act as agent on behalf of a principal. A general power of attorney ordinarily confers upon the attorney-in-fact the authority to do a variety of activities on behalf of the principal, including "all things which the principal could do." On the other hand, a special power of attorney ordinarily specifies one particular action the attorney-in-fact may do, for example, "signing a deed and transferring the real estate." (see Figure 16.2).

| FIGURE 16.2 | Special Power of Attorney |

Power of Attorney

I, Eberly Furston, do hereby invest my attorney-in-fact, Leroy Stutz, with full power and authority to sign a deed in my name and in my stead and on my behalf and to execute all other documents necessary to transfer title to my real estate located at 1100 Wilder Ave. N., Decatur, Illinois, to Francine Harbaugh for the purchase price of $125,000.

_____   _____
Witness   Eberly Furston

_____
Witness

Date: November 8, 2006

Eberly Furston, known to me, did execute this Power of Attorney on November 8, 2006.

_____
Notary Public

My commission expires on April 1, 2007.

A deed executed by an agent for the grantor, in the grantor's absence, is invalid unless the agent has a power of attorney. In a real estate transaction, the parties should use a special power of attorney instead of the all-inclusive general power of attorney. Courts strictly construe the power of attorney, and thus the power must specifically authorize the attorney-in-fact to convey the real estate. A general power to sell does not grant the power to convey. In some states, the *equal dignities rule* requires that a power of attorney in a real estate conveyance be executed with the same formalities required to execute the deed properly. In some states, a deed executed by a person with a power of attorney may not be recorded unless the power of attorney is also recorded.

Normally, a power of attorney may be revoked at any time. In most cases, the death of either the principal or the attorney-in-fact also revokes the power of attorney. Therefore, the purchaser taking a deed signed by an attorney-in-fact should be extremely cautious. The power of attorney should not be old, and the purchaser should require evidence that the principal is living. The purchaser should also insist that the power of attorney be recorded. This provides some protection because an unrecorded revocation is ineffective against a recorded power of attorney. Regardless, the seller's power of attorney may not be acceptable to parties involved in the transaction, for example, the mortgagee and the purchaser.

Delivery and Acceptance

A deed does not transfer title until delivered by the grantor and accepted by the grantee. Although manual transfer of the instrument is the common method of delivering a deed, this alone is insufficient to pass title. The grantor must intend to pass title and surrender control of the instrument. Unless these two components exist, the fact that the grantor has given up physical possession of the deed is of no consequence.

> **CASE EXAMPLE**
>
> Beatrice Curtiss executed a quitclaim deed to herself and to her granddaughter, Marilyn Feriss, as joint tenants. Although the deed was recorded, Mrs. Curtiss continued to occupy the property and paid all maintenance and insurance expenses. Both Mrs. Curtiss and other members of the family stated and acted as if Mrs. Curtiss were the sole owner. Mrs. Feriss was regarded and spoken of as "the inheritor." Mrs. Feriss never occupied the property or stayed there longer than a single night.
>
> In litigation involving the Feriss title, the appellate court stated that "the deed in question did not operate to pass an interest in the property . . . to Marilyn Feriss as the grantor did not intend for it to do so." *Curtiss v. Feriss*, 168 Colo. 480, 452 P.2d 38 (1969).

Conversely, even though physical transfer is the generally accepted procedure, delivery may be effective without it. Constructive or implied delivery, which is delivery without change of possession, is valid, although rare. As with actual delivery, the essence of constructive delivery is the intention of the parties, not the manual act of transfer. If the grantor, by words or acts, manifests an intention to be divested of title and for it to vest in another, the law in some jurisdictions recognizes that delivery is sufficient, even if the instrument itself (but not the right to control) remains in the hands of the grantor.

> **CASE EXAMPLE**
>
> On August 10, 1940, Frank and Elizabeth Agrelius, husband and wife, executed two warranty deeds, one deed conveying 80 acres of land to Clair T. Agrelius, the other deed conveying a nearby 80 acres to Paul Kenneth Agrelius. Neither deed was recorded during the lifetime of either grantor.
>
> On July 27, 1944, a safety deposit box was leased . . . in the names of Mr. and Mrs. Agrelius, who signed the lease at that time. Clair was also named as lessee, although he did not sign the lease contract until 1962. The deeds were placed in the safety deposit box. At some later time in 1944 . . . Mr. Agrelius told Clair of the two deeds executed in 1940. . . . At this time Mr. Agrelius handed Clair a key to the safety deposit box and said this would constitute delivery of the deed to him. After the death of Mrs. Agrelius in 1967, Clair removed the two deeds from the box and had them recorded.
>
> The trial court held that ". . . when Frank and Elizabeth Agrelius told Clair they had executed a deed conveying one 80-acre tract to him and another deed to the other 80-acre tract to Kenneth and placed the deeds in their lock box and then handed the key to the box to Clair, such actions constituted an effective constructive delivery of the deeds, and all the circumstances showed a purpose on the part of the grantors that there should be an immediate vesting of title in Clair and Kenneth, enjoyment only being postponed until the death of the grantors." See *Agrelius v. Mohesky*, 280 Kan. 790, 494 P.2d 1095 (1972).

Delivery is ineffective unless the grantor parts with legal control of the instrument. The grantor may not retain the power to recall the deed from either the grantee or a third party. Once a valid delivery has occurred, the deed may, however, remain in the grantor's custody or be returned to the grantor for safekeeping.

A deed may be effective even if it contains a provision that it is not to become operative until the grantor's death. Delivery must take place during the grantor's lifetime. Delivery may be made directly to the grantee, who holds the deed until the grantor's death. Whatever the situation, the grantor must be effectively divested of control of the deed. This does not occur if the grantor merely places the deed in a mutually accessible trunk, as the next case illustrates.

A grantor may deposit a deed with a third party to satisfy the legal requirement of

Matter of the Estate of Dittus
Supreme Court of North Dakota
497 N.W.2d 415 (N.D. 1993)

Background. Christ Dittus died without a will (intestate) January 15, 1975, survived by two sons and six daughters. Approximately two years before his death he signed two deeds, one in favor of his son Charles and the other in favor of his son Elmer. He placed the deeds in a safe-deposit box, told Charles about the deeds, and gave him a key to the safe-deposit box. Christ retained a duplicate key. Charles told Elmer about the deeds. During his life, Christ paid taxes and retained the income the property generated.

Charles and Elmer commenced an action to determine title to the properties. The trial court judge determined that the deeds were ineffective to transfer title during the decedent's lifetime and that they were intended to operate as testamentary transfers. The case was appealed to the Supreme Court of North Dakota.

Decision. The Supreme Court upheld the trial court decision.

Justice Levine. The interest transferred to a grantee by a deed does not vest until there is a delivery of the

deed by the grantor, and acceptance of the deed by the grantee. Therefore, a deed is of no effect unless it is delivered. But, delivery is of no avail unless the grantor effectuates it with the intent that the deed presently pass title to the grantee. Accordingly, "[i]f the intent is not to transfer the interest until the grantor's death, there is no present delivery and the conveyance is merely an ineffective attempt at a testamentary transfer."

* * *

We have previously addressed the issue of intent to presently transfer title in cases factually similar to this one. In *Frederick v. Frederick*, the grantor, joined by his wife, executed several deeds and placed them into a safe-deposit box. Sometime later, the grantees asked the grantor whether they could purchase a portion of his land and were told no purchase was necessary because the land had been deeded to them. The deeds, however, remained in the grantor's safe-deposit box until his death. The grantor also retained possession of the keys to the bank box until his death. Nearly a year after the grantor's death, his wife, in the presence of the grantees, removed the deeds and recorded them. Afterward, she returned the deeds to the safe-deposit box. The trial court determined that, under the circumstances, the deeds had been constructively delivered to the grantees.

We reversed, holding that there was "absolutely no evidence that the grantor intended to deliver the deeds to the grantees during his lifetime," that is, no evidence of an intent to relinquish

> dominion or control over [the] deeds or to vest title to the property in the grantees. In fact, the record is clear that his intention was exactly the opposite. He retained possession of the deeds in his bank box, retained the keys to the box in his own possession, and paid the taxes on the land for the intervening years until his death.

* * *

Charles and Elmer acknowledge that this case is similar to . . . *Frederick* in that Christ retained possession of the deeds in his safe-deposit box and paid the taxes on the real estate until his death. They assert, however, that . . . *Frederick* [is] distinguishable because the grantor, Christ, gave Charles a key to the safe-deposit box and told him that the Logan County real estate belonged to him and Elmer and that the deeds to the respective parcels could be retrieved by them any time thereafter. Charles and Elmer argue that these facts show that, although Christ did not relinquish control over his safe-deposit box, he did intend to relinquish control over the deeds within that box.

* * *

We agree that the record contains some evidence supporting Charles and Elmer's position. However, there is ample evidence supporting the trial court's decision that Christ did not intend to transfer title to the property to Charles and Elmer until he died and that the deeds, therefore, failed for lack of delivery. Christ retained a key to the safe-deposit box, retained the income generated by renting the property, and paid the taxes on the property. This evidence of Christ's exercise of dominion and control over the property strongly supports the inference that Christ did not, upon delivering the safe-deposit box key to Charles, presently intend to relinquish title to the Logan County farmland. Moreover, the delivery of but one of two keys to a safe-deposit box is inconclusive, without other evidence, of intent to presently transfer title.

. . . [T]he trial court concluded that Christ "intended the deeds to operate as testamentary transfers." We give due regard to a trial court's opportunity to assess the credibility of the witnesses and weigh the evidence.

The judgment is affirmed.

What should Christ have done to insure that the deeds would operate as an effective transfer?

---

delivery. This is an effective delivery if the grantor has surrendered all control over the instrument and is powerless to recall it. A deed delivered to a third party is effective from that time even if the grantor dies or becomes insane before the grantee obtains possession of the instrument.

Escrow. A means by which delivery may take place, escrow is a process where money and/or documents are delivered to, and held by, a third party until the terms and conditions of an escrow agreement are satisfied. Escrow is discussed in detail in Chapter 14. In a number of localities, real estate transactions customarily close through a third party called an *escrow agent* or *holder*. The escrow holder may be an attorney, a bank, a title insurance company, or an independent escrow agent.

Buyer and seller in an escrow closing agree to submit the necessary documents and funds to the escrow agent. The escrow agent is responsible for seeing that the transaction closes on the conditions agreed to by the parties. As stakeholder, the escrow agent retains the funds and mortgage documents submitted by the buyer. When the seller has delivered to the escrow holder a properly executed deed to the property and the holder is assured the seller is passing good title, the funds and mortgage documents are turned over to the seller.

■ DEED RESTRICTIONS

In addition to passing title, a deed may be used to regulate land use. This is accomplished through **deed restrictions**, a condition in the instrument or a covenant. (See Table 16.3.) Conditions must be included in the deed; covenants usually are, but a valid covenant may be created by a separate document.

Chapter 4 discussed the use of conditions to limit the use of an estate. That chapter indicated that, when a condition in a deed occurs, the owner's estate is subject to termination. In some instances, depending on the wording of the condition, termination is automatic; in others, termination depends on some action being taken by the person holding the reversionary or remainder interest.

Sometimes a purchaser of land will agree that it not be used in a particular manner. This type of representation is called a *covenant*. Although both a covenant and a condition limit land use, the legal effects of the two differ. When a condition occurs, the owner's interest terminates or is subject to termination. When a covenant is broken, the owner may be sued for damages or enjoined from breaking the covenant, but the owner does not lose title to the property.

Restrictive Covenant

■   *A provision in a deed limiting uses that may be made of the property.*

Restrictive covenants are an important tool used by developers to ensure consistency in land use. Persons selling a portion of their land also use them to prevent unde-

TABLE 16.3	Restrictive Covenants and Affirmative Covenants: Examples

Restrictive Covenants	Affirmative Covenants
Not build a fence	Build a fence
No commercial use	Only residential use
Minimum setback	Maintain a party wall
Maximum height for bushes	Provide bushes for screening light
Prohibit certain construction	Require certain construction

sirable uses of the property by the buyer. Restrictive covenants are, in effect, a private type of zoning regulation. By accepting delivery, the grantee is bound by restrictions in the deed.

Typical restrictive covenants limit property to residential use, provide minimum setback and acreage requirements, prohibit certain types of buildings, limit the number of structures, or set a minimum cost for housing to be constructed. Because restrictive covenants limit land use, courts do not always favor them. Today, however, most restrictive covenants will be enforced if they do not violate the constitution and/or public policy. An example of a covenant violating the constitution would be one restricting ownership of the land to members of a particular racial or religious group. Another example of a covenant violating public policy might be a covenant seeking to restrain someone from marrying.

Covenants, Conditions, and Restrictions

Covenants, conditions, and restrictions are commonly found in the bylaws of planned communities. Anyone purchasing a home in these communities is bound by their terms. They typically operate as requirements established by the ruling board of the community. Their purpose is to enhance and protect the value of the neighborhood as a whole and the property value of individual parcels. Violation of a requirement may result in fines or other sanctions, pursuant to the bylaws.

Architectural work done on the homes may also be controlled by the boards of these communities. There is typically an architectural control committee which must approve any modifications that are planned by a property owner. This may include not only construction but landscaping, as well.

Affirmative Covenant

Affirmative covenants are recognized in most states. Typical affirmative covenants involve agreements to build fences, maintain party walls, provide railroad crossings, and join and pay dues or an annual assessment to a homeowners' association for maintenance of, for example, roads, parks, or similar facilities. In a few states, affirmative covenants are not recognized as valid because they are too difficult to enforce.

CASE EXAMPLE

On February 16, 1911, 30 out of a total of 39 owners of property in a neighborhood signed an agreement which provided that, for the next 50 years, no tenant or owner of any race other than Caucasian would be permitted to reside in the neighborhood. On August 11, 1945, the Shelleys, an African-American couple, purchased a deed to a parcel of land in the neighborhood pursuant to a contract of sale. The Shelleys had no knowledge of the restrictive covenant. On October 9, 1945, owners of other property in the neighborhood sued to enforce the covenant. The Supreme Court held that courts could not enforce racially restrictive covenants because they violated both public policy and the Fourteenth Amendment to the Constitution. *Shelley v. Kramer,* 334 U.S. 1 (1948). In fact, since 1968, the federal Fair Housing Act makes it illegal to insert such a racial restriction.

Termination

Although many covenants are part of a planned pattern of land use, they also constitute a burden on the land. Frequently, buyers and sellers wish to terminate covenants because they interfere with more profitable uses of the property. A few states have passed legislation that provides for the elimination of stale restrictions after a fixed period of time, or when the limitation no longer substantially benefits those for whom it was created. Most states, however, do not have legislation of this nature. In these states, deed covenants often interfere with real estate development until they are eliminated.

Although several methods exist for eliminating covenants, each is either costly to accomplish or legally impractical. Covenants may be terminated by a release, by waiver, or by abandonment, but these methods are usually impracticable because several people often have the right to enforce a single covenant. Other methods are by acquisition of the property subject to the covenant by the owner of the property benefiting, or by litigation showing that conditions in the neighborhood have so changed as to nullify the benefits of the covenant. In the following case, a medical doctor sought to show just that.

Hewgley v. Vivo
Court of Appeals of Tennessee
1997 Tenn. App. Lexis 153

Background. Jose Vivo, a physician, converted one of his homes in a subdivision into a medical clinic. The subject property was in a subdivision containing 37 lots on the outskirts of Tullahoma. The deed to each lot contained a restrictive covenant limiting the use of the lots to residential purposes and authorized any of the subdivision's property owners to bring suit to enforce the covenants.

The subdivision has remained residential despite the development of the surrounding area. The golf course originally located to the west of the subdivision has been replaced by a high school. North Jackson Street has been expanded from two to five lanes. A hospital has been built in the area, and numerous commercial and retail establishments, including a shopping mall, have been constructed along North Jackson Street across from the subdivision.

Dr. Vivo was aware of the restrictive covenant in his deed when he purchased the lot. He believed that the noise, pollution, and traffic in the area rendered the location unsuitable for residential purposes.

Consequently, he had the property rezoned and began making alterations, including paving the front yard for a parking lot, building an additional room on the back of the house, and erecting an illuminated sign near North Jackson Street.

Neighbors filed suit seeking to enforce the restrictive covenant. The trial court upheld the validity of the covenant, and enjoined Dr. Vivo from using the property for commercial purposes. Dr. Vivo appealed.

Decision. The appellate court affirmed the ruling of the trial court.

Judge Koch, Jr. [Dr. Vivo argues] that the restrictive covenant no longer benefits the property because of the substantial changes in the character of the surrounding property. While extensive commercial development has occurred in the area surrounding the subdivision, we concur with the trial court's conclusion that enforcing the restrictive covenant will benefit the subdivision as a whole.

Persons who develop property may place restrictions on its future use for their own benefit and for the benefit of the other property owners in the development. These restrictions are commonly known as restrictive covenants. They need not have specific time limits, and are binding on remote grantees when they appear in the chain of title or when the grantee actually knew about the restrictive covenant when it acquired title.

In most circumstances, restrictive covenants cannot be released without the consent of the purchasers and grantees for whose benefit they were imposed. Restrictive covenants can, however, lose their force when they fail to serve a useful purpose. Thus, they may be rendered unenforceable if radical changes in the character of the entire neighborhood completely defeat the purpose of the covenant. When determining whether a restrictive covenant continues to derive any useful purpose, the courts must be concerned primarily with the continuing value of the restrictive covenant to the entire neighborhood, not the hardship to the parties attempting to avoid the restrictive covenant. While rezoning of property covered by a restrictive covenant is some evidence of a change in the character of the use of the property, rezoning alone does not require the courts to conclude that the restrictive covenant no longer serves a useful purpose.

During the past forty years, the City of Tullahoma has sprawled toward and past the subdivision involved in this case. Extensive commercial development has unquestionably taken place along North Jackson Street, and this development has affected the residential desirability of the houses facing North Jackson Street. But notwithstanding the development of the surrounding area, most of the property in the subdivision has retained its residential character.

The value of the protection afforded to residential property by restrictive covenants is reflected in the price of the property. Purchasers of residential property will pay a premium for the protections that restrictive covenants provide. While the value of the front-tier lots in a subdivision may decline because of the development of the surrounding property, this decline in value does not render the restrictive covenants unenforceable as to the front-tier lots if the surrounding development has not altered the residential character of the subdivision as a whole.

[Dr Vivo's] arguments . . . have two significant shortcomings. First, the commercial development along North Jackson Street has not altered the essential character of the entire subdivision. Second, the commercial development had already occurred by the time the [doctor] purchased the property. [He is] not entitled to . . . relief when [he] knew or should have known that the existing conditions would affect the residential use of [his] property and when [he has] already benefitted from the effects of the surrounding development by paying a lower price for the property.

Affirmed.

Construct a scenario whereby Dr. Vivo would prevail in his argument that the restriction is no longer valid.

THE CHANGING LANDSCAPE

Under the ancient tenurial system, evidence of transfers of real estate was by the "livery of seisin" ceremony. With external formalities both the grantor and grantee would come onto the land and the grantor would give a twig or clod of earth extracted from the land to the grantee. This was coupled with a formal declaration asserting transfer accompanied by a prescribed oath of allegiance made by the grantee. Witnesses were present; it was a day of festivities often accompanied by jousting and other sports of the time. Everyone remembered the day of pomp and ceremony and the land transfer, though there was no evidence by a writing.

Today, the evidence of land transfer is by recorded deed. We live in a society of "paper," and when it comes to something as important as a land transfer, there must be a formal writing that is recorded for the world to take notice. That writing is the deed, the subject of this chapter. Nonetheless, the trend is toward simplification. Most states have adopted a "statutory deed" or a short form that satisfies the requirement and is less costly to record.

The deed ordinarily does not contain much information beyond the names of the parties to the transfer transaction. It will contain a description that includes easements and other restrictions. However, most of the encumbrances and liens on the property are not contained on the deed but are found in other public records. Because the documents that affect the marketability of the property are spread out in various government offices, a search of the public records is quite demanding.

The Torrens system of registration, still in use in some places, is an attempt to ensure that all transactions that affect the title are contained in one instrument. This system is not in widespread use because it has proved to be very cumbersome. A second problem involving the recording of the deed is that many counties throughout the country have not computerized their deed records, and even when computerized they are not readily accessible to the public.

As we move deeper into the twenty-first century our challenge is to find a simpler, more cost-efficient method of transferring real estate, recording it, and finding all the transactions that affect the title. This solution appears simple, but although the technology is there, a couple of issues compound the problem. First, the paper is voluminous: to start computerizing the past would be not only a monumental task but a very, very costly one. Second, those who work in the county's recorder's office are often "political employees." Computerization would eliminate jobs. Do you have any suggestions that would make our records system more efficient while minimizing the associated problems?

■ KEY TERMS

affirmative covenant 361

bargain and sale deed 349

deed 345

deed restrictions 360

fiduciary deed 350

general warranty
 deed 346

quitclaim deed 349

restrictive covenant 360

special warranty deed 348

warranty deed 345

■ INTERNET RESOURCES

For general information concerning deeds, see

www.law.cornell.edu/topics/real_estate.html

For examples of deeds, visit

www.indiaproperties.com/vroot/link/legal/Legaldoc.asp

■ REVIEW AND DISCUSSION QUESTIONS

1. Explain the assurances provided a grantee by (a) covenant of seisin, (b) covenant of quiet enjoyment and (c) covenant of warranty.
2. Explain the difference between (a) a *general warranty deed* and a special or *limited warranty deed* and (b) a *bargain and sale deed* and a *quitclaim deed.*
3. What is the effect of a purchaser's failure to record a deed on (a) the purchaser's title and (b) a subsequent purchaser who relies on the seller's recorded title?
4. Name the essential elements of a deed and give an example of each.
5. List the difference between a covenant and a condition within the deed and the purposes of each.
6. Under what circumstances will a restrictive covenant no longer be enforceable?

■ CASE PROBLEMS

1. Dunlap owned a large farm, which he worked for many years with his son, Sam. Dunlap had a daughter, Celeste, who lived in the city. Dunlap had often told Sam, Celeste, and various relatives that Sam was to inherit the farm; nevertheless, nothing was ever done to ensure that it would happen. As Dunlap aged, he became senile and difficult to live with, but in lucid moments he talked about Sam's inheriting the farm. Because Sam knew that his father had no will, Sam had a deed prepared conveying the property to himself. Dunlap signed the deed. The execution of the instrument was done properly, according to state law. Two years later Dunlap died, and Sam had the deed recorded. Celeste has sued to have the deed declared invalid. What arguments should she make? What counterarguments should Sam make?
2. Everett Wine conveyed his property by deed to his son, Benjamin. He failed to read the deed before signing it. He was very old and suffered from lung disease, cirrhosis, and chronic brain syndrome. Concerning his mental capacity, his doctor wrote: "Mr. Wine's mental state fluctuated from psychotic to perfectly appropriate. There were times when Mr. Wine understood fairly well what he was doing, and there were times he was out of touch with reality." What additional evidence would you

like to pursue to determine whether Mr. Wine possessed the legal competency to sign a deed? See *Harper v. Rogers*, 387 S.E.2d 547 (W. Va. 1989).

3. Cossette Furr deeded land to Piedmont and Western Investment Corporation. At the time of the conveyance, Piedmont and Western Investment Corporation's charter had been dissolved by the Secretary of State for failure to file any report or return or to pay taxes or fees. Thereafter, the corporation was reinstated. Did the deed operate to convey title to the property? Explain. *Piedmont and Western Investment Corp. v. Carnes-Miller Gear Co., Inc.*, 384 S.E.2d 687 (N.C. Ct. App. 1989).

4. Harken intended to convey a portion of his property to his neighbor. He owned 100 acres but just desired to convey a sliver of the land along the east border with his neighbor, Prancy. The description read:

> Starting at the old Mulberry tree on the south side of the Harken Farm acreage going northerly parallel to the Prancy property 175 yards to the beginning of Old Feather Lake on the Harken Property.

What is the problem with this description? Comment on the adequacy of the description of the property. See *Haines v. Mensen*, 446 N.W.2d 716 (Neb. 1989).

5. Stephen Takacs and his son, John, purchased property as tenants in common. After sharing the costs of building a house, father, son, and the son's wife lived together on the premises for two years. During this period Stephen paid $40 per month for his room and board.

While the parties were living together in the home, the three went to the office of an attorney. The attorney, at Stephen's insistence, prepared a quitclaim deed conveying Stephen's interest to John Takacs and Mabel R. Takacs, John's wife.

At the time there was an understanding that the deed would become effective on Stephen's death and would not be recorded during his lifetime. The deed, however, was delivered to John. It was never in Stephen's possession, nor did Stephen reserve the right to recall it. Shortly thereafter, John died. Mabel Takacs recorded the conveyance and attempted to sell the property.

Stephen sued to set aside the deed. Will he be successful? Discuss. *Takacs v. Takacs*, 26 N.W.2d 712 (Mich. 1947).

6. On August 16, 1982, Alfred found a deed in his father's trunk. The trunk was located in the bedroom of his father's house, and was used to store valuable papers. Sanford Jones paid the taxes, collected the rent, and paid for repairs from December 7, 1981, until his death one and one-half years later. Has there been delivery? Explain. *Jones v. Jones*, 470 So. 2d 1207 (Ala 1985).

7. Chris Stevens, a farmer, owned 40 acres of land that he did not use. He leased the land for three years to Orlando Baron. The lease was for farming purposes. Before the lease expired, Stevens conveyed the property by general warranty deed to Morgan Kettlewell. Kettlewell planned to subdivide the property. He had no knowledge of the lease and believed the crops on the land were Stevens's. What right, if any, does Kettlewell have against Stevens? How could Stevens have protected himself?

Land Descriptions

■ LEGAL DESCRIPTION

■ *A description of a parcel of land that will be accepted by courts because it is complete enough to locate and identify the premises.*

This chapter deals primarily with descriptions found in real estate instruments. Boundary disputes are also discussed, as an intricate relationship exists between descriptions and boundaries. A description in a real estate instrument sets forth the physical dimensions of what is being conveyed. Boundaries are based on this description. They establish the property on the earth's surface. Often they are imaginary lines, but sometimes they are marked by objects.

With only a few exceptions, U.S. law requires a written instrument to transfer an interest in real estate. To be enforceable in a court of law, the written instrument must contain a valid description of the property involved. The courts will not enforce the written instrument if the description is incorrect or ambiguous. A seller or lessor who has agreed to transfer an interest in real estate is in breach of contract if the instrument executed does not properly describe the property. Even if the physical boundaries of a property are clear, no interest will pass if the property is not described properly.

The chief purpose of the description is to furnish a means for identifying a particular parcel of land. In addition, the description must describe an area that is bounded completely. In other words, the boundaries indicated by the description must close the parcel.

For a deed or other conveyance to be enforceable in a court of law, the description must make possible positive identification of the land. Courts consider this accomplished if a surveyor or other person familiar with the area can locate the property and determine its boundaries using the description in the conveyance. Although a description by street and number is not advisable, it passes title if the property is located in a municipality that has established a standard system of numbering and the property is identified to the exclusion of all others.

A technically accurate description that provides all the information necessary to locating land is preferable to one that needs clarification by other evidence. Courts, however, are exceedingly liberal in allowing outside evidence to clarify an ambiguous description. Testimony of the circumstances surrounding the transaction, the interpretation placed on the description by the parties, and statements of surveyors, neighbors, and public officials as well as the physical elements of the area may be introduced. What the courts are searching for is the intent of the parties.

CASE EXAMPLE

The Rogers owned a large piece of land. The land included a lake in which there were several islands. Seventy acres of land jutted into the lake, forming a peninsula. When the tides were high and the wind right, this peninsula was separated from the mainland by a watercourse. Boats could traverse the watercourse at these times. At other times, only an inch or two of water was in the watercourse.

The Rogers deeded all their mainland holdings to Inches and the islands to Burgess. A dispute arose between Burgess and Inches over ownership of the 70 acres. Burgess contended that the jutting piece of land was an island and belonged to him. Inches argued that it was part of the mainland and he was the owner. A court eventually resolved this dispute in favor of Inches. In doing so, it considered the testimony of fishermen who sometimes traversed the watercourse, aerial photographs, the original government survey (which didn't show the watercourse), a motion picture of a boat navigating the watercourse, and the testimony of surveyors. *Burgess v. Pine Island Corp.*, 215 So.2d 755 (Fla. 1968).

The description in the deed in this transaction was general, not specific. Almost all courts will try to sustain a deed even though it contains a general description. They are reluctant to declare the instrument void. Judges reason that the parties must have intended to do something or they would not have been involved in the transaction.

Butkovich v. Summit County
Supreme Court of Utah
556 P.2d 503 (1976)

Background. Summit County took title to the parcel in question as the result of a tax sale due to tax delinquency of a former owner. Subsequently, in July 1964 the Butkovichs purchased the land from the county, receiving a quitclaim deed. A year later the county issued a deed to correct the original quitclaim deed containing the following description: "All unplatted land in this Block (29 P.C.) and all land West of this Blk. and Pt. lot 1: Pt. lot A." Since that time the Butkovichs have held title and paid taxes on the property. Summit County argues that its quitclaim deed is invalid because it lacks an adequate description of the property. The trial court decided for the Butkovichs.

Decision. The Supreme Court of Utah affirmed the trial court's decision.

Justice Crockett. It is not to be questioned that in order to be valid, a deed must contain a sufficiently definite description to identify the property it conveys. But the rules which are generally applicable to controversies over the meaning of documents are also applicable to deeds. The problem lies in ascertaining the intent with which it was executed. It should be resolved, if possible, by looking to the terms of the instrument itself and any reasonable inferences to be drawn therefrom; and if there then remains any uncertainty or ambiguity it can be aided by extrinsic evidence. If from that process the property can be identified with reasonable certainty, the deed is not invalid for uncertainty.

The county's argument that the description in the deed is insufficient is based on the use of certain abbreviations therein as shown in the first two lines thereof: All unplatted land in this Block (29 P.C.) and all land West of this Blk. and Pt. lot 1: Pt. lot A.

No serious question is raised as to the commonly used abbreviations of Blk for "block," or Pt. for "part," of the named lots. The principal defect complained of is the use of the initials "P.C." which must be read as "Park City" to give the deed meaning and effect. Even if it be assumed that those initials might leave some doubt as to the designation of one of the main towns in the county, when it is aided by the later statement in the same deed referring to "the Park City Townsite," and is considered in the light of the rules herein above stated concerning the interpretation of deeds, it is our opinion that there is a sound basis for the trial court's conclusion that the description in the deed was sufficiently definite to convey the property in question to the defendants Butkovich.

Affirmed.

If you had a map of the Park City area, do you think that you could plot the Butkovichs' land from the description given in the quitclaim deed?

One type of general description that courts have consistently upheld conveys all the grantor's land in a particular area. This is sometimes referred to as a "Mother Hubbard" description. Similarly, if a deed describes a particular plot in fairly general terms but provides a clue to the land's location in a specific city, county, or state, the description is effective if evidence indicates the grantor owned no other land in the designated area.

Although courts are liberal in accepting outside evidence, a deed conveying land will be invalid if the description does not identify the specific parcel or at least provide a key to identifying property to the exclusion of all other sites.

CASE EXAMPLE

The City of Atlanta owned land at the foot of Climax Place. Berchenko owned all the land on the north of Climax Place, a frontage of 1,035 feet. Berchenko also owned a tract on the south, which had a frontage of 195 feet. Climax Place was only 22 feet wide, and the city wished to widen it to 50 feet.

To accomplish this, the city obtained from Berchenko a deed to "a 28-foot strip along Climax Place." The city then demanded that Berchenko remove a building that encroached on the north of Climax Place. Berchenko refused, claiming the deed invalid because the description was uncertain and insufficient. Both the lower court and the appellate court agreed. The appellate court stated, "no surveyor, however expert, could take the description contained in the instrument just mentioned, and by the aid of any extrinsic evidence, locate the precise body of land." See *City of Atlanta v. Atlanta Trailer City Trailer Park*, 213 Ga. 825, 102 S.E.2d 23 (1958).

■ REFERENCE TO OTHER DOCUMENTS

As illustrated by the *Burgess v. Pine Island Corp.* case, different kinds of outside evidence may be used to clarify a description. Included in this type of outside evidence are testimony, photographs, and original surveys. The most effective clarification is provided by a deed's reference to a survey, map, plat, or some similar document that correctly describes the land. The details of this extrinsic document become part of the description and can be used to resolve ambiguities or to locate the parcel. In fact, many deeds describe a parcel of land by reference to a master survey, plat, or map. This is a common practice that saves time and provides clarity.

Because of the complicated nature of boundaries and the economic importance of real property, the art of surveying has been in use since antiquity to establish and verify boundaries. The Babylonians, Assyrians, Egyptians, Hebrews, Greeks, and Romans perfected the art. In the Americas, the Indian peoples such as the Incas and Mayans were remarkable surveyors.

In the sophisticated technological world of today, surveys by trained professionals are an integral part of the real estate business. Although the basis of a real estate conveyance is what the parties agree to as the boundaries, agreement is seldom reached without the help of a survey. An agreed-on boundary cannot be changed by a survey, but a survey is generally used to establish new boundaries. Only in rare instances would a tract be subdivided without a survey or would unplatted land be sold without being mapped. In these situations, the surveyor's work is the basis for any description in a deed or other real estate instrument. Where title to land has been established, either through an informal survey by the parties or by a prior professional survey, the surveyor's sole function is to help determine the boundaries of the grant. In litigation involving this type of boundary problem, the surveyor often testifies as an expert witness, giving an expert's opinion as to what the grantor's intention was. The surveyor's work is a critical factor in each of the three types of descriptions discussed in this chapter and commonly used in the United States: metes and bounds, the rectangular survey, and plats and maps.

Metes and Bounds

■ *A method of describing land by specifying the exterior boundaries of the property using compass directions, monuments or landmarks where directions change, and linear measurement of distances between these points.*

As the eastern United States was settled and developed, probably the most common method of describing land was to name the parcel. For example, the property would be described as the Jacktown plantation or the Ebenezer Smith farm. Usually boundaries were indicated by naming the owners of adjoining property or by natural landmarks called *monuments*. An early nineteenth-century deed in a trespass case described the property as follows:

> A certain tract or parcel of land, including the mill-seat and mill known as the "Jethro R. Franklin Mill," the said tract situated in the county of Gates, embracing as far as the highwater mark, and bounded as follows: on the north by the lands of Richard E. Parker, Reddick Brinkley, and others, on the east by the lands of Harrison Brinkley and others, south by the desert road, west by the lands of Josiah H. Reddick and others.

A description based primarily on *adjoiners* (names of owners of contiguous property, a road or something similar) and monuments is still used if the costs of a survey are out of proportion to the amount of money involved. Descriptions of this nature may cause problems if some impermanent monuments are selected.

Metes-and-bounds descriptions provide a more sophisticated method of describing real property. A metes-and-bounds description is based on a survey that commences at a beginning point on the boundary of the tract and follows compass directions, called *courses*, and distances around the area to the point of beginning. Monuments are placed at the corners or at points where directions change. Monuments are visible objects, sometimes natural but often artificial. They can be posts, iron pipes, piles of stone, trees, streams, or similar objects. By following the courses and distances, a person should be able to walk the boundaries of the property.

A typical metes-and-bounds description follows:

> Beginning at an iron pipe marked A and thence running South 8 degrees 15 minutes East 75 feet to a pipe marked B thence North 78 degrees 27 minutes East 34 ³/₁₀ feet to a pipe marked C thence North 11 degrees 28 minutes West 74 ⁹/₁₀ feet to a pipe marked D thence South 78 degrees 27 minutes West 30 ²/₁₀ feet to the place of beginning containing 2410.7 square feet, more or less.

In reading a metes-and-bounds description, one always says "north" or "south" first and then announces the number of degrees east or west of that north or south line. The number of degrees east or west of the north or south line cannot exceed 90. Thus, to say "North 95 degrees East" as a designation for Line A in Figure 17.1 is incorrect. The correct reading is "South 85 degrees East."

FIGURE 17.1 Metes and Bounds

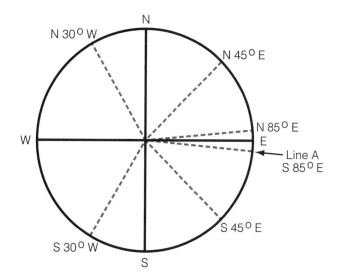

Metes-and-bounds descriptions based on a survey provide a very accurate method of designating the physical dimensions of a particular tract of land. When the land itself is supplied with permanent markers at each corner or angle, the parcel can be readily located for a long period of time. This method of describing land continues to be used extensively in the eastern United States. Metes-and-bounds descriptions are also used extensively in other areas of the country in conjunction with the rectangular survey to designate small parcels.

■ **Call.** *A term used to refer to the different monuments, courses, and distances that make up a metes-and-bounds description.*

Metes-and-bounds descriptions are not always based on a survey. Sometimes natural monuments used as **calls** are destroyed; in other instances, conflicting calls are the result of human error. To solve problems resulting from conflicting calls, courts have established a general order of preference to be given to calls when the intention of the parties is not clear. Natural monuments are preferred because they are considered more reliable than courses and distances. The general order of preference is:

1. natural monuments,
2. artificial monuments,
3. courses,
4. distances, and
5. quantity of acreage.

Adjoining landowners (adjoiners) are also important elements in some descriptions and receive a high degree of priority. Unless the adjoiner is clearly a mistake, it ranks with monuments, prevailing over courses, distances, and quantity of acreage.

CASE EXAMPLE

Jones and Morrison purchased contiguous parcels from a common grantor. The deed to Jones described the east line of his property as being from the center of Edison Street south to a bois d'arc tree, a distance of 79 feet. Morrison's deed described his property's east line as being from the center of College Street north to a bois d'arc tree, a distance of 210 feet. Actually, the distance from the center of Edison Street to the tree was 86 feet; from the center of College Street the distance was 207 feet, as shown on the map.

Morrison constructed a building on the property that encroached on what Jones believed was his land. Jones sued to require the removal of the encroaching portion of the building. In finding for Jones, the court stated, "[t]his makes the case a classic example . . . for application of the rule that courses and distances must yield to natural monuments. . . ." *Morrison v. Jones,* 58 Tenn. App. 333, 430 S.W.2d 668 (1968).

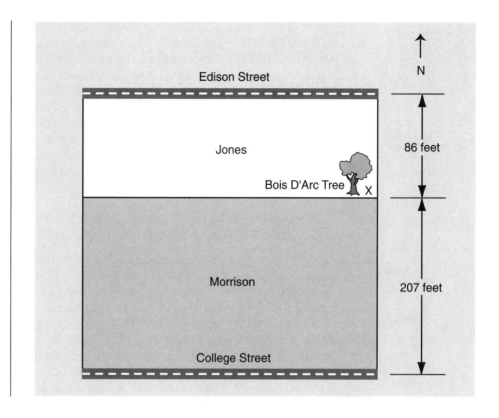

Rectangular Survey System

■ *System of land description that applies to most of the land in the United States.*

After the Revolutionary War, the United States acquired a vast area of land west of Pennsylvania and north of the Ohio River. This area, known as the Northwest Territory, was acquired when states ceded their claims to the United States as a means of paying their war debts. Faced with pressures from land speculators and settlers as well as the need for revenue, Congress in 1785 passed legislation to prepare these lands for disposal.

An important element of this legislation was the establishment of a **rectangular survey system**, also known as the *U.S. Government survey system*. Although the government survey was criticized and attacked by the private land companies, it eventually became the foundation on which vast areas of the West were surveyed and sold.

With the exception of Texas, land descriptions in all states west of the Mississippi, the five states formed from the Northwest Territory, and most of Alabama, Florida, and Mississippi are based on this massive survey. Eventually, the survey covered more than 2 million square miles in the continental United States. It has been extended to Alaska, where hundreds of thousands of square miles remain unsurveyed. Although modified by legislation from time to time over the 200 years that the system has been used, the fundamentals of the rectangular survey have remained fairly consistent.

Initially, a large area is selected for survey and a starting point is chosen. (See Figure 17.2.) This initial point is chosen by astronomical observation. A line called a *baseline* is run east and west through this point. A perpendicular line also runs north and south through the initial point. This is called the *principal meridian*. The survey for the entire district is based on these two lines. Over the long history of the government survey, 32 baselines and 35 principal meridians have been established.

Principal meridians and baselines are designated in various ways. At first they were numbered, but later they were given names. The first principal meridian is the western boundary of Ohio. The 41st parallel is its accompanying baseline. All land descriptions in a particular area surveyed with reference to a principal meridian will refer to it. The basic unit of the survey is the **township**.

■ **Township.** *An area of land approximately six miles square, containing as nearly as possible 23,040 acres and divided into 36 sections, each one mile square.*

Legislation guiding the surveyors required that a township be a square, as nearly as possible six miles on a side. Because the lines that run parallel to the principal meridian converge toward the north, townships in the north would be smaller than the required 36 square miles. To remedy this, correction lines are run parallel to a baseline at 24-mile intervals north and south. These lines are called *standard parallels* or *correction lines*. Lines called *guide meridians* are then surveyed east and west at 24-mile intervals with a standard parallel as a base. Although the townships in the north are slightly smaller than those in the south, the constant correction kept the difference at a minimum. Some early surveys established correction lines at intervals much greater than 24 miles, leading to substantial discrepancy in township size. Continuous establishment of guide meridians and standard parallels reduced the compounding effect of surveying errors.

Each guide meridian and standard parallel, as shown in Figure 17.3, is designated by numerical order and compass direction from the appropriate principal meridian and

---

FIGURE 17.2   Starting Point for a Survey

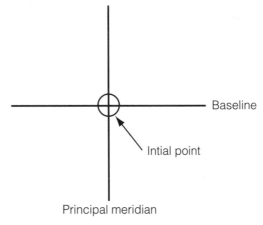

| FIGURE 17.3 | U.S. Public Land—Rectangular System of Subdividing |

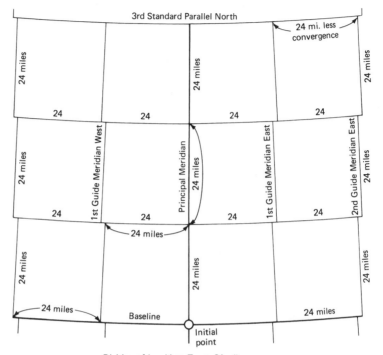

Division of Land into Tracts 24 miles square.

baseline. The intersections of guide meridians and standard parallels create square blocks or tracts 24 miles on each side. Townships are created by dividing these 24-mile tracts at six-mile intervals. The result is 16 township units approximately six miles square in each tract.

Although these 24-mile-square blocks are not a factor in describing real estate, townships are an integral part of a land description. Over an entire area surveyed, tiers of townships are numbered north and south from the baseline. They are also numbered consecutively east and west from the principal meridian. The east-west tiers are called *ranges*. Each township as a result has two numbers and two directions. These numbers and directions thus provide a specific designation for each. Because all townships and ranges are numbered in reference to a particular principal meridian and baseline, no two have the same designation.

The shaded unit in Figure 17.4 is tier 3 north, range 3 west of a principal meridian. This would be indicated as T3N, R3W. Townships are not only important elements in many land descriptions, they also are often important political subdivisions.

■ **Section.** *An area of land approximately one mile square, containing as nearly as possible 640 acres.*

FIGURE 17.4   Township Designations

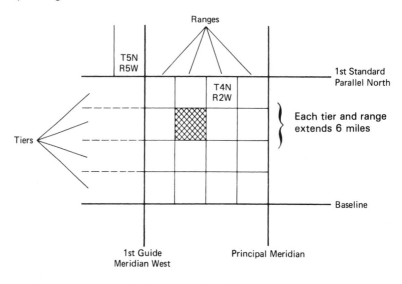

Each township of approximately six miles square is further divided into **sections**. A township thus contains 36 sections. The sections in a township are numbered consecutively, beginning in the northeast corner with the number 1. Six sections are numbered westerly along the far north of the township. Section 7, just south of section 6, commences a row numbered in an easterly direction. (See Figure 17.5.) This pattern of alternating west-east numbering is followed, with section 36 being the southeast unit in the township.

Although a different numbering system was used in some of the early surveys, most of the land surveyed has sections designated in this manner. As a result, the number of the section is also a key element in describing a particular parcel of land.

Commercial realities of land disposal often resulted in a need to divide each section further. Half sections, quarter sections, and even smaller units were needed. This division is readily accomplished by surveying and designating smaller units by their geographic location within the section.

A half section may be described as the north one-half of section 15 and a quarter section as the northwest one-quarter of section 15. As each section consisted of 640 acres, the number of acres in each of these smaller units is easy to determine. A half section is 320 acres; a quarter section is 160. Figure 17.6 indicates additional divisions of a section that are commonly used. As each township has a numerical designation in relation to a particular baseline and each section a number, any of these smaller plots is precisely located within the square mile of which it is a part.

The section designation of a description using the rectangular survey system might read as "the east ½ of the SW ¼." This would be the shaded portion of Figure 17.6. If the tract conveyed were in two quarters, the quarter-section designations would be joined by "and." For example, the description might be worded as "the east ½ of the northwest ¼ and the east ½ of the southwest ¼."

FIGURE 17.5 U.S. Public Land Survey—Typical Method of Numbering Sections

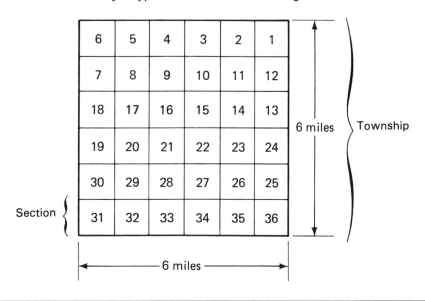

FIGURE 17.6 Divisions of a Section

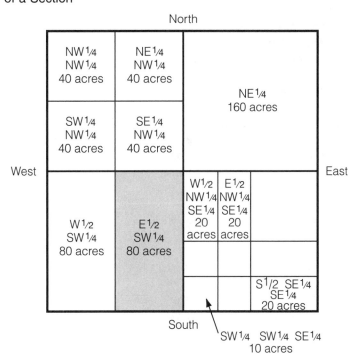

Governmental surveys were not made under ideal conditions. Errors often resulted because of weather, harsh terrain, hostile Indians, primitive equipment, and plain ineptitude. The prevailing legal rule, however, has consistently been that, once land has been conveyed on the basis of a government survey, the conveyance will not be disturbed even if error is found in the survey. This is indicated in the case that follows.

In most cases a survey does not create boundaries. Boundaries are created by the agreement of parties. The official government survey of the public land does, however, create boundaries. An original government survey, whether correct or erroneous, controls the boundaries of a section and parcels of land surveyed and platted from it. Courts feel that the parties who purchase property based on a plat from an official survey have a right to rely on it. If the survey is confirmed by the proper officials of the Department of the Interior, attack in the courts is no longer permitted when the property is sold.

Bishop v. Johnson
District Court of Appeals of Florida
100 So. 2d 817 (1958)

Background. Ralph and Francis Johnson (plaintiff, appellees) obtained title to a peninsula extending into Water Pen Lake. Their title was based on an official government survey and plat made in 1894. In 1949, a private survey of the lake showed a second peninsula just south of the first. This peninsula and adjacent land were conveyed to Wilbur Bishop (defendant, appellant).

Later it became clear that the official survey was erroneous. There was no peninsula as indicated on the official plat. The only peninsula was that indicated by the private survey. Both Bishop and the Johnsons claimed the peninsula and the Johnsons brought a suit to quiet title to the area. Their title was affirmed by the trial court and Bishop appealed.

Decision. The decree quieting title in the Johnsons was affirmed.

Judge Wigginton. Suit was brought by plaintiffs, the appellees here, to quiet title to portions of a certain peninsula of land which extends westerly from the eastern shore of and into the navigable waters of Water Pen Lake, commonly known as Cow Pen Lake, in Putnam County.

A copy of the map showing the contended location of the disputed lands is here inserted for convenience and clarity of explanation.

During the last quarter of the year 1849 an official federal government survey was made of lands now constituting Sections 20, 21, 22, 27, 28 and 29 of Township 10 S, Range 23 East. From this survey, and the field notes compiled as an incident thereto, an official township plat was constructed, approved and recorded.

This peninsula as it is identified by the government survey plat is depicted . . . by the letter "P", and consists of Lot 9 of Section 21, containing 12.10 acres, and Lot 3 of Section 22 containing 40.13 acres.

By patent dated November 18, 1903, the United States conveyed Lot 9 of Section 21 and Lot 3 of Section 22, both lying in Township 10 S, Range 12 E, to the State of Florida. Thereafter, on September 16, 1927, the Trustees of the Internal Improvement Fund conveyed both lots to one Phillip Bersch, who, on August 8, 1953, conveyed them to the appellees. It is under title thus dereigned that appellees based their claim.

Late in 1949 a private survey was conducted from which it was concluded that the peninsula, designated as Lots 9 and 3, was actually situated south and west of the point shown on the official plat. According to this private survey, the peninsula is appended to the mainland at the Northwest corner of Lot 1, in Section 27, as shown by the letter "E" on the . . . map. In reliance on this private survey, and under the mistaken belief that there existed a second peninsula, the Trustees of the Internal Improvement Fund issued to appellants as grantees a deed which purported to convey, by metes and bounds, the peninsula described in the aforementioned private survey. Some time after July 6, 1950, the date of the last mentioned deed, appellants acquired title to the northern portion of Lot 1, Section 27. Appellants rely on the deed of July 6, 1950, and the subsequent deed to Lot 1 in asserting their title to the disputed peninsula.

It is admitted by the parties hereto that there is, in fact only one peninsula extending westwardly from the east shore of the lake and into the waters thereof.

It is to be noted at the outset that the government survey of 1849 did not merely ascertain or identify the disputed lands, but created Lots 9 and 3, in Sections 21 and 22 respectively, being that peninsula lying in Township 10 S, Range 23 East. The mere fact that a subsequent private survey shows an error by the United States Deputy Surveyor in locating the peninsula on the official plat is immaterial, since the latter survey is not admissible in evidence to affect or change the lines or location of land sold in accordance with an official government survey and plat.

It is well settled that the description of land and plats from field notes of an original survey filed in the General Land Office are conclusive, and section lines and corners as laid down therein are binding on the General Government and all parties concerned. When lands described in a deed are by reference to or in accordance with a plat or survey, the courses, distances and other particulars appearing on the plat are to be as much regarded as if expressly set forth in the deed itself. The plaintiff and his prede-

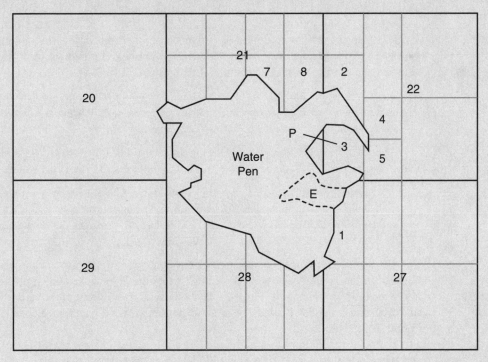

continued on next page

cessors in title acquired the land in question with reference to the official government plat which showed the property purchased to be a peninsula of land designated as lying in Sections 21 and 22, and extending from the eastern shoreline westward into the lake. The defendants are charged with knowledge, either actual or constructive, that the peninsula in question had been surveyed, platted and conveyed by the sovereign with reference to and in accordance with the official plat and that title thereto had become vested in the plaintiffs long before the defendants sought to acquire the lands by reference to a private resurvey. A resurvey that purports to change lines or distances or to otherwise correct inaccuracies and mistakes in an old plat is not competent evidence of the true line fixed by the original plat. Accordingly, it must be concluded that, as between the parties hereto, the government survey is paramount.

Accordingly, the decree appealed from must be and is hereby affirmed.

Affirmed.

Though it is clear in this case that there was only one peninsula, could a second peninsula have been formed between 1849, the date of the official survey, and 1949, the date of the private survey?

Plat

■ *A map showing items such as natural and artificial monuments, lots, blocks, and streets in a town or subdivision; generally drawn from a survey.*

A third method of describing land is by reference to a recorded **plat** or map. This method is used frequently in metropolitan areas. Usually it is used in conjunction with the rectangular survey or a metes-and-bounds description of a larger tract that is being divided. The property to be divided is surveyed and laid out in lots that are numbered in sequence. These lots are platted and when sold are described by their designated numbers. A description of this kind might read as follows:

> All of lot 8 in block 41 in Taylors Astoria, an addition within the corporate limits of the City of Astoria, Clatsop County, State of Oregon, as said addition was laid out and recorded by the Peninsular Land & Trust Company.

Although the deed does not contain the description of the entire survey, the United States Supreme Court in an early case supported this system. The court stated:

> . . . when lands are granted according to an official plat of the survey . . . the plat itself along with all its notes, lines, descriptions, and landmarks becomes as much a part of the grant or deed . . . as if such descriptive features were written out on the face of the deed . . . *Cragin v. Powell*, 128 U.S. 696 (1888).

The use of maps and plats of surveys has become an important means of describing land in the United States. Plats are readily available because almost all states and many localities require a developer, when subdividing property, to have the property surveyed and a plat of it made by a competent surveyor. A typical plat is shown in Figure 17.7.

Although requirements vary, the plat generally shows the proposed streets, blocks, and lots of the subdivision. The plat will also show such items as easements, rights-of-

FIGURE 17.7 Plat Adapted from *Davis v. DeVore*, 16 Ill. App. 334, 306 N.E.2d 72 (1974)

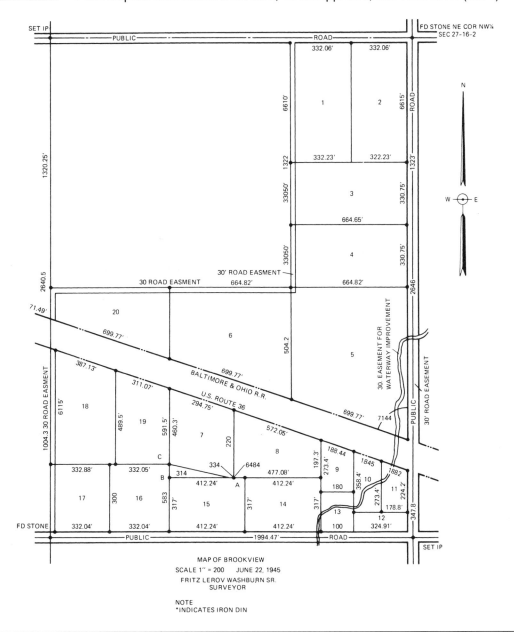

way, and topographical details, such as elevations, as well as other physical features. School sites and recreational areas are indicated on plats for larger developments. Blocks and lots are designated in some manner, usually by number but sometimes by letter.

In most areas subdivision plats must be approved by some governmental body before land is sold. Usually this is a local planning board or a designated official such as the county engineer. The approved plat is then recorded in a *plat book* as part of the public land records. The property in the subdivision is thus accurately described by reference to this record. In addition, recording of the plat serves to dedicate to public use land indicated on the plat as streets, parks, school and church sites.

In preparing land for a subdivision, the surveyor must carefully mark with permanent monuments physical boundaries of the parcels involved. The survey actually fixes the boundaries of the property, and these are reflected in the plat. If the plat and the boundaries fixed by the survey differ, the boundary as established by the physical monuments prevails.

■ BOUNDARY DISPUTES

Courts have adopted several rules in efforts to solve boundary disputes equitably. A fundamental principle is that the intention of the parties establishing a boundary should prevail. Although the plain meaning of the words used in a description is the best indication of intention, conflicting and ambiguous designations of boundaries must often be resolved by other rules. An example is the doctrine of "agreed boundaries."

For the doctrine of agreed boundaries to apply, the owners of adjoining property must be uncertain as to the true boundary. They must then agree as to what the true boundary is. This agreement does not have to be in writing. A minority of states require that there be some visible evidence of the boundary to be established. In any case, the boundary agreed on must be definite and certain. In a few states, the parties must continue to agree for a period equal to that required in cases of adverse possession. In most states, acquiescence for a shorter period is sufficient; however, the period varies greatly from state to state.

CASE EXAMPLE

Rouse owned a quarter section of land. In 1932 he sold the west portion to Cooper. In 1944 Rouse sold the east portion to Huggans. At the time of the sale to Cooper, the parties did not determine the exact boundary between the two properties but described the property using an old fence as one line. When Rouse conveyed the east parcel to Huggans in 1944, the description in the deed referred to the west boundary of the Huggans tract as the Cooper fence.

Huggans used the land up to the fence from 1944 until 1978. In 1978 the Cooper property was acquired by Weer. A survey at that time established the true property line 60 feet east of the fence. On acquiring the information, Weer attempted to remove the Cooper fence and Huggans petitioned the court for a temporary restraining order.

Huggans claimed that he had title to the 60-foot strip up to the fence, based on adverse possession and the doctrine of agreed boundaries. This claim was rejected by the court because he had not met statutory requirements for adverse possession and proof of an agreed boundary was not clear and convincing. *Huggans v. Weer*, 615 P.2d 922 (Mont. 1980).

Intention in many situations is determined by what courts presume or infer the parties probably desire to occur. An example is found in the common solution to the substantial litigation involving title to a public thoroughfare. When land abutting on a public road or street is conveyed, the grantee takes title to the centerline unless the description specifically excludes this area. This rule applies even if the description designates the tract as "bounded by" or "bordering on" the particular public way. The reason is that courts consider it unlikely that a grantor conveying land on a public way had any intention of retaining title to the area dedicated to public use. Because the grantor has conveyed the abutting property, the small strip of land is of little value to him or her. It is, however, important to the grantee, who now owns the adjacent land. On the other hand, if the conveyance specifically reserves the narrow strip for the grantor, the intention of the parties will be honored, as this intention is the most significant factor.

Sales Personnel and Property Description

Property description is an important element of almost every real estate transaction. Although it is ordinarily the concern of the real estate lawyer, all real estate sales personnel should be aware of its important legal aspects. If problems involving descriptions are discovered early in the proceedings, before the deed or other document involving the property is prepared, time can be saved and trouble averted.

Sometimes real estate personnel obtain information about boundary problems when listing property or drawing up a contract. These should be carefully noted and an effort made to have the owner resolve the problems before entering serious negotiations with prospective buyers. Because boundary disputes may indicate description problems, a sales associate who becomes aware of a boundary controversy when negotiating a sale of real estate should alert the seller's attorney so that the description can be verified.

THE CHANGING LANDSCAPE

As this chapter describes, when many people in the real estate chain are asked to describe a parcel of land, they think in terms of metes and bounds. Real estate brokers, attorneys, banks, surveyors, developers and builders are among these people. Having sat on a planning board for many years, and having asked the question of these professionals, "What is on the land?" unless there are buildings, the usual response is "nothing." Of course, "nothing" means no human development has taken place on the site.

If the same questions were asked of an ecologist, a geologist, a farmer, or an artist, one might get a very different response. The ecologist may see a complex forest ecosystem or a diverse wetland. The ecologist would see an existing community of soils, water, plants, and animals. The geologist would see signs of the stresses and development of the eons caused by fire, flood, glaciers, and inland seas. The farmer may see nutrient-rich soil that took thousands

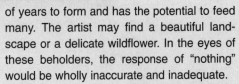

of years to form and has the potential to feed many. The artist may find a beautiful landscape or a delicate wildflower. In the eyes of these beholders, the response of "nothing" would be wholly inaccurate and inadequate.

If the parties in the real estate chain saw these diverse qualities of the land, would it affect how they did their jobs? Would the broker have a much more effective sales pitch? Would the developer include an area for a community garden so that some of the nutrient-rich soil could be saved and used? Would the builder try to design and construct homes that take advantage of the landscape vistas? If the bank saw the reactions of the developer and builder to this information, would it be willing to increase the size of the construction mortgage that it would be willing to provide?

Look out the window. What do you see?

■ KEY TERMS

call 374

metes and bounds 373

plat 382

rectangular survey
  system 375

section 378

township 376

■ INTERNET RESOURCES

www.outfitters.com/genealogy/land/land.html
(Legal land descriptions in the USA)

http://freepages.genealogy.rootsweb.com/~familyhistorypages/LegalLandDescription.htm
(How to read and understand legal land descriptions)

www.flatsurv.com/legaldes.htm
(An overview of legal descriptions of land)

■ REVIEW AND DISCUSSION QUESTIONS

1. Sketch an imaginary principal meridian and baseline and indicate the location of (a) Township 3 North, Range 3 East and (b) Township 1 South, Range 3 West.

2. Define the following terms and indicate their relationship to the rectangular survey system: (a) principal meridian, (b) baseline, (c) township, and (d) section.

3. The sketch below represents a section. Indicate the correct rectangular survey designation for the shaded portions labeled A and B.

4. Locate the following tracts of land in a section and indicate the acreage of each.

    (a) E ½ of the SE ¼

    (b) NW ¼ of the NW ¼ of the NW ¼

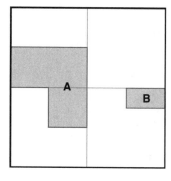

■ CASE PROBLEMS

1. A contract for sale of real estate described the property as follows:

   > Property of Greene D. Spillman located at Spillman, La., in Sections 48 and 49, T1S, R2W, West Feliciana Parish, La., and improvements. Bounded on the North by lands of Merrick, on the South by lands of Thoms and heirs of C. H. Bickham, on the East by Hwy. 967 and on the West by Mills Creek. The grounds measuring about 275 acres as per title for the sum of Sixty Thousand, Five Hundred Dollars.

   Engquist signed a contract to purchase this property. A survey indicated that the farm contained only 223.64 acres. When Engquist refused to perform, the owner sued for breach of contract. (a) Would the owner be successful? Support your answer. (b) What is the meaning of the terms T1S, R2W? *Adams v. Spillman*, 290 So.2d 726 (La. 1974).

2. Sketch the following parcel.

   > Beginning at a point 447.18 feet East of the N.W. corner of SE ¼ SE ¼, said Sec. 21; thence North 88 degrees 57' 30" East 402.00 feet; thence South 987.68 feet; thence North 89 degrees 56' West 401.93 feet; thence North 979.48 feet to the point of beginning. *LeBaron v. Crimson*, 412 P.2d 705 (Ariz. 1966).

3. Brasker, a real estate broker, claimed an interest in one and one-half acres in Lot 4 on the north end of Sapelo Island. Brasker supported his claim with a deed that included the following description: "All of that certain lot, tract or parcel of land situate, lying and being in the 1312 District, G.M., McIntosh County Georgia, at Raccoon Bluff on Sapelo Island, containing Twenty-One (21) acres, more or less and being Lot Four (4) of the Raccoon Bluff Subdivision of William Hillary. Said property being bounded Northerly by Lot 3; Easterly by Blackbeard Island River; Southerly by Lot 5; and Westerly by the lot line of Raccoon Bluff Tract. This being that same property conveyed to Ben Brown by deed and plat from William Hillary dated July, 1882 and recorded in Deed Book 'U' at Page 298 and 299, to which said deed and plat reference is hereby made for all intents and purposes."

   A plat showed one-acre and four-acre tracts out of Lot 4 established by a surveyor in 1882. The defendant argued that the deed was ineffective. Who is correct? Support your answer. [Adapted from *Brasker v. Tanner*, 356 S.E.2d 478 (Ga. 1987).]

4. Brasker also claimed an interest in a three-acre tract on Sapelo Island. The three acres were conveyed from a larger lot in a 1907 deed to Jack Handy. The defendants argued that the deed was ineffective because the tract's boundaries were not clear. The legal description from the warranty deed from Jack Handy's heirs was as follows: "that certain tract of land in McIntosh County on Sapelo Island, three (3) acres, more or less, and being in the 1312 District, and bounded on the North by Toni Handy and brothers, on the East by public Road, South by John Bailey and West by Sam Roberts."

Is the description adequate? What is the key factor in determining the description's adequacy?

18 Involuntary Transfers

The conveyance of real property by deed, sometimes called *voluntary alienation*, was discussed in Chapter 16. A conveyance by deed is generally the result of a mutual agreement set forth in a real estate sales contract. There are, however, several circumstances under which title to real property is transferred involuntarily.

■ INVOLUNTARY ALIENATION

■ *The transfer of title to land without the owner's consent.*

Involuntary alienation includes forced sales resulting from liens and foreclosures, discussed in Chapters 15 and 21. This chapter treats other forms of involuntary transfers: adverse possession, eminent domain, and transfers on death.

Adverse Possession

■ *Acquisition of title to real property by means of wrongful occupancy for a period of time established by statute.*

Adverse possession is based on the statute of limitations. As a general rule, a person in possession of realty has good title against everyone but the true owner. The true owner has a right to bring legal action to gain possession if the occupant wrongfully withholds it. The statute of limitations requires that this cause of action be brought within a certain time. The time varies from state to state but is commonly 12, 15, 20, or 21 years. Should the owner not sue within the statutory term, the adverse possessor, on meeting certain conditions, acquires title to the land.

Although the adverse possessor actually acquires title to the property, litigation is usually necessary to establish clear title before it can be sold. This is because the public records of land ownership show someone other than the adverse possessor as the owner.

Elements of Adverse Possession. A number of conditions must be met for a person to acquire title to land by adverse possession. Both case law and statutes establish requirements, although they differ from state to state and even from case to case. Some common qualifications are that such possession must be open, hostile, continuous, and exclusive. Other adjectives sometimes used are adverse, notorious, under claim of title, and under color of title. These requirements express a judicial and legislative intention that possession must be sufficiently evident to give the owner notice of what is happening.

CASE EXAMPLE

Marengo Cave Company owned land on which the only entrance to a large cave was located. The cave was occupied exclusively by the company for the statutory term and was used as a tourist attraction. When Ross, an adjoining landowner, discovered through a survey that a portion of the cave extended under his land, he brought a quiet title suit. The court found that, even though the company's possession was widely publicized in connection with the tourist business, it was still not "open and notorious" because an ordinary observer on the land could not have readily seen that the owner's rights were being invaded. Hence, Marengo Cave Company did not gain title by adverse possession. *Marengo Cave Co. v. Ross*, 212 Ind. 624, 10 N.E.2d 917 (1937).

The courts also require that possession be *exclusive and continuous* for the entire statutory period. This means that if the land is abandoned or the true owner reenters, either in the absence of the adverse possessor or simultaneously, the statutory term is interrupted and must start over again. A brief absence, such as a vacation, by the adverse possessor is probably not enough to defeat this requirement, however.

A related issue arises when there is a succession of adverse possessors. Most jurisdictions allow the *tacking* of one possessor's term to that of another if one acquired title directly from the other, as with a sale or transfer on death.

CASE EXAMPLE

Martin was the owner of a lot, but Boyer was in possession for five years from 1970 to 1975. Then Boyer purported to sell the lot to Lucas, who possessed it for eight years and devised it to Tenton in 1983. Tenton, however, did not enter the land. When Tenton died in 1986, his heirs took possession. They sued to quiet title in 1999.

The heirs would lose this suit in a jurisdiction with a 20-year statute because even tacking Boyer's term to Lucas's would bring the total to only 13 years. During the three years the lot was empty (1983 to 1986), possession reverted to Martin, the true owner. Adverse possession was not exclusive and continuous for the requisite 20 years. The heirs would win in a state with a 12-year statute, however, because their own entry and possession in 1986 would start the running of the statutory term.

When Adverse Possession Does Not Apply. Adverse possession does not apply when there is no "hostile use," that is, use against the will of the owner. Hence, permission to use will destroy the "adverse" element. Additionally, statutes and case law also often provide that in some situations statutes of limitations are prolonged or do not run at all. For example, adverse possession cannot be applied against the state or against one whose interest is not yet a possessory right, such as a holder of a future interest. It cannot be applied against those who have certain disabilities, such as minors and the mentally incompetent. For a disability to prevent the running of the statute, however, it must exist at the time a right to sue accrues, usually when the adverse possessor enters the land. In addition, the disability is personal to the owner and cannot pass to successors.

Purpose of Adverse Possession. To many, adverse possession seems like a legal way of acquiring land without compensating the owner, and some question whether, with modern legislation such as model title acts, recording acts, and the like, society needs this ancient doctrine. Nevertheless, public policy has historically supported the doctrine. Those who defend adverse possession argue that the state has certain duties to citizens:

- It should eliminate stale claims because evidence and witnesses may be unavailable.

- It should discourage *laches*—that is, delayed enforcement of one's rights.

- It should encourage full and efficient use of land.

- It should facilitate land transfer by providing a means to remove old title problems and thus quiet titles.

It seems likely that adverse possession will continue to be an aspect of property law for the foreseeable future. The prudent owner of vacant land held for development or investment will make periodic inspections of the property to check for adverse possessors. The mere posting of "no trespassing" signs is probably not sufficient to protect the owner's interest. The next case illustrates how acreage may be lost by the erection of a barbed wire fence.

Ebenhoh v. Hodgman
Minnesota Court of Appeals
642 N.W.2d 104 (Minn. Ct. App. 2002)

Background. Richard and Alma Tincher owned an 80-acre tract of farm property in Dodge County. The Tinchers deeded the north 40 acres to LeRoyal Sanders and the south 40 acres to Edward Ebenhoh. Edward constructed an east-west barbed wire fence dividing the two properties. Between 1942 and 1955 he repaired the fence every year so that the cattle would graze on the Ebenhoh parcel and not stray. In 1956 the cattle operation concluded, but Ebenhoh and his son planted crops close to the fence on a regular basis.

In 1968 Edward Ebenhoh sold the property to his son James, who continued to farm the parcel close to the barbed wire fence line from 1969 to 1984. In 1985 James leased the property. He acquired a new lessee from 1986 to 1996, a canning company cultivating asparagus. Beginning in 1996 James's son-in-law leased the property continuously, using it as farm property.

Frank Hodgman purchased the north 40 acres from his parents in 1976; they had purchased it from Sanders in 1955. A surveyor was retained in 1993 to survey the Hodgman parcel. The surveyor found the barbed wire fence to be located 11 feet north of the true boundary, thus excluding a portion of the Hodgman property.

Ebenhoh (appellant) brought an action to establish the boundary lines of the two parcels, maintaining that he had gained the disputed land by adverse possession. The trial court disagreed.

Decision. The court of appeals reversed and remanded.

Judge Anderson. Respondent Frank Hodgman testified that he purchased the Hodgman parcel from his parents in 1976, who had purchased the property from Sanders in 1955. He also testified that he

continued on next page

sold the Hodgman parcel to his brother, respondent Donald Hodgman, in 1993.

* * *

The district court concluded that although Ebenhoh showed that he openly and actually used the disputed tract for 15 years, he failed to show that his use was exclusive, continuous, or hostile. The court also concluded that Ebenhoh failed to show that the fence line constituted a boundary by practical location. This appeal followed.

Issue

Are appellants entitled to the disputed tract through adverse possession?

Analysis

Before title through adverse possession can be established, there must be clear and convincing evidence of actual, open, hostile, continuous, and exclusive possession by the alleged [usurper] for the statutory 15-year period.

* * *

Respondents do not challenge the district court's conclusions that Ebenhoh's use of the disputed tract was both actual and open; therefore, our review is limited to whether Ebenhoh's use of the disputed tract constituted, as a matter of law, exclusive, continuous, and hostile use of the disputed tract for the statutory 15-year period.

* * *

The exclusivity requirement is met if the [usurper] takes "possession of the land as if it were his own with the intention of using it to the exclusion of others."

The district court found that . . . other parties "continued to use the disputed area for hunting and fishing purposes throughout the years." Consequently, the district court concluded that Ebenhoh did not exclusively use the disputed tract for the statutory period.

* * *

The record, however, is clear that Ebenhoh, his father, and his lessees were the only individuals to use the disputed tract, save for the brief and insubstantial entries onto the property referenced by respondents. Ebenhoh testified that between 1942 and 1956 the fence prevented cattle from leaving the Ebenhoh parcel. It is also undisputed that for 30 years, between 1956 and 1986, Ebenhoh, his father, or his lessees planted crops as close as possible to the fence line. Respondent Frank Hodgman testified that during his ownership of the Hodgman parcel between 1976 and 1993 he *never* used the property abutting the fence line. It is also undisputed that it was not until 1998, 56 years after the fence was constructed, that respondent Donald Hodgman placed white flags in Ebenhoh's soybean field marking the 1993 survey line.

* * *

Adverse possession for any consecutive 15-year period is sufficient to establish continuity of use, and the statutory period must only be completed before bringing an adverse-possession action. "The possession of successive occupants, if there is privity between them, may be tacked to make adverse possession for the requisite period." "The possession of a tenant is, as to third parties, the possession of the landlord." . . .

The district court found that the canning company used most of the Ebenhoh parcel to cultivate asparagus between 1986 and 1996; the court also found that the canning company did not cultivate asparagus on the disputed tract, but rather used the disputed tract to move its machinery in and out of the field. The district court therefore concluded that the canning company's use of the disputed tract between 1986 and 1996 constituted occasional, not continuous use.

. . . Even if we were to accept the district court's highly questionable conclusion that the canning company's use of the disputed tract to move its machinery in and out of the Ebenhoh parcel did not constitute sufficient continuous use of the disputed tract between 1986 and 1996, the canning company's use of the disputed tract during that period is irrelevant. Ebenhoh's father cultivated crops and grazed cattle on the disputed tract between 1942 and 1956. Ebenhoh, his father, and his lessees cultivated crops, up to the fence line, between 1956 and 1986. By the time the canning company leased the Ebenhoh parcel in 1986, Ebenhoh, his father, and his lessees, had used the disputed tract continuously for 44 years.

* * *

The hostility requirement "does not refer to personal animosity or physical overt acts against the record owner of the property." To establish hostility of use, the [usurper] must "enter and take possession of the lands as if they were his own . . . with the intention of holding for himself to the exclusion of all others." Hostility is flexibly determined by examining "the character of the possession and the acts of ownership of the occupant."

* * *

Even though Sanders and Ebenhoh's father are deceased, and thus cannot explain why the fence was constructed or whether the use of the disputed

tract was originally permissive, that does not mean that Ebenhoh's father's undisputed use of the tract to cultivate crops and graze cattle between 1942 and 1956 is not relevant in determining hostility of use. Such logic could lead to an absurd legal rule where undisputed actual, open, continuous, and exclusive use of property for multiple decades could not result in adverse possession of that property because the original use of the property *may* have been permissive. It is also undisputed that after 1956 Ebenhoh, his father, and his lessees, continued to farm the disputed tract, as close as possible to the fence line, until at least 1998 when Ebenhoh's son-in-law began to honor the 1993 survey line.

Therefore, Ebenhoh's use of the disputed tract was hostile, in the sense that Ebenhoh and his father entered the disputed tract and took possession as if the tract was their own since 1942, with the intention of holding the tract to the exclusion of all others. . . .

Reversed and Remanded.

Why do you think Edward Ebenhoh erected a barbed wire fence? Does it matter?

Eminent Domain

■　*The power of government to take private property for public use with just compensation afforded to the property owner. (See Figure 18.1.)*

The power of **eminent domain** is one of the major attributes of sovereignty. In the United States, both federal and state governments are sovereign and may exercise this power. No specific constitutional grant is necessary for government to have the right to take private property for public use, although several state constitutions do contain provisions expressly conferring the power of eminent domain on the state.

Eminent domain is a power that the federal and state governments may delegate. The result is that eminent domain is often exercised by villages, cities, and counties, as well as by public bodies such as school boards and sanitation districts. The power may also be delegated to private corporations such as railroads, power companies, and other public utilities. On a proper delegation, eminent domain may be exercised by individuals and partnerships. For a delegation to be proper, the property must be devoted to a public use.

FIGURE 18.1   Eminent Domain Decision Tree

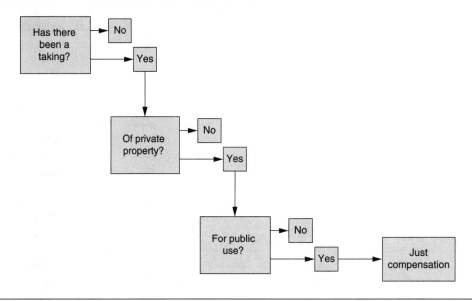

■ **Public Use.** *A use that benefits the community.*

The Fifth Amendment to the U.S. Constitution and the constitutions of the individual states require that property acquired through eminent domain be used to benefit the public and that just compensation be paid to the owners. Historically, in the United States, eminent domain has been used mostly to acquire land for public transportation systems and to satisfy government's need for space to conduct its business. As government has become increasingly involved in many aspects of life, the use of eminent domain has likewise increased. Today, government may use the power to acquire interest in land for diverse purposes such as parking lots to relieve congestion and traffic hazards, scenic beauty along highways, and public recreation.

CASE EXAMPLE

Before 1967 most of the land in Hawaii that was not owned by the state or federal government was owned in fee simple by 72 private landowners. These landowners, who had acquired their titles through the descendants of Polynesian chiefs, refused to sell land. They would only lease it on long-term leases. At the termination of a lease that was not renewed, the land and improvements reverted to the landowners.

In 1967 the Hawaiian legislature, using its power of eminent domain, enacted a Land Reform Act designed to extend the fee simple ownership of Hawaiian land. The act created a mechanism for condemning residential tracts and transferring ownership to existing lessees, while affording the landowners just compensation.

The owners of the fee simple estates challenged the constitutionality of the legislative action. They argued that their property was not taken for a public use or purpose because the government itself never possessed or used the land but transferred it to individuals. The United States Supreme Court determined that the statute was constitutional. The court stated that correcting inequities in the housing market satisfied the constitutional requirement that land be taken for a public use or purpose. *Hawaii Housing Authority v. Midkeff*, 467 U.S. 229 (1984).

Although land taken by eminent domain must be used for a public purpose, different interpretations exist as to what this means. A number of jurisdictions require that the property actually be used by the public. Even in these jurisdictions, the facility does not have to be open to the public, as long as some arm of government actually supervises the operation. Thus, public use is satisfied if a utility company acquires property by eminent domain, even though the general public cannot use the facility. A public utility commission supervises the overall business of the company and ensures that the property is used in the public interest.

In most jurisdictions, the public use requirement is met if some benefit to the public results from the acquisition of the property. The benefit does not have to be direct, nor does all of the public have to receive some advantage.

Courts have allowed the state to transfer lands acquired by condemnation to a private firm to build a plant that would increase employment in the area and to a developer to eliminate a slum. And, as the next case indicates, a physical invasion of the land is not necessary for a "taking" to occur.

■ **Condemnation.** *Legal proceeding by which the government exercises the right of eminent domain, acquiring private land for a public use.*

The Fourteenth Amendment to the U.S. Constitution prohibits state government from taking private property without due process of law, and the Fifth Amendment imposes like restraints on the federal government. As a result, some type of notice and some type of legal proceeding are required when a landowner is unwilling to convey property to a condemning authority for the price offered. Due process does not ensure any particular manner of proceeding, and federal and state law vary extensively as to the method and procedures that will be used. For example, many states use juries exten-

United States v. Causby
Supreme Court of the United States
328 U.S. 256 (1946)

Background. Appellant, the United States, repeatedly operated aircraft passing 83 feet over the respondents' (the Causbys) farm property. The aircraft passed 63 feet above their barn and 18 feet above the highest tree. Respondents claimed this amounted to a taking of their property and that they were entitled to just compensation. They sued and the U.S. Court of Claims agreed, awarding them damages. The government appealed to the United States Supreme Court.

continued on next page

Decision. The United States Supreme Court agreed with the Court of Claims that a taking occurred, but remanded the case to that court to determine precisely what property was taken and its value.

Mr. Justice Douglas. This is a case of first impression. The problem presented is whether respondents' property was taken, within the meaning of the Fifth Amendment, by frequent and regular flights of army and navy aircraft over respondents' land at low altitudes.

Respondents own 2.8 acres near an airport outside of Greensboro, North Carolina. It has on it a dwelling house, and also various outbuildings which were mainly used for raising chickens. The end of the airport's northwest-southeast runway is 2,220 feet from respondents' barn and 2,275 feet from their house. The path of glide to this runway passes directly over the property—which is 100 feet wide and 1,200 feet long. Since the United States began operations in May 1942, its four-motored heavy bombers, other planes of the heavier type, and its fighter planes have frequently passed over respondents' land and buildings in considerable numbers and rather close together. They come close enough at times to appear barely to miss the tops of the trees and at times so close to the tops of the trees as to blow the old leaves off. The noise is startling. And at night the glare from the planes brightly lights up the place. As a result of the noise, respondents had to give up their chicken business. As many as six to ten of their chickens were killed in one day by flying into the walls from fright. The total chickens lost in that manner was about 150. Production also fell off. The result was the destruction of the use of the property as a commercial chicken farm. Respondents are frequently deprived of their sleep and the family has become nervous and frightened. . . . The air is a public highway, as Congress has declared. Were that not true, every transcontinental flight would subject the operator to countless trespass suits. Common sense revolts at the idea. To recognize such private claims to the airspace would clog these highways, seriously interfere with their control and development in the public interest, and transfer into private ownership that to which only the public has a just claim.

If, by reason of the frequency and altitude of the flights, respondents could not use their land for any purpose, their loss would be complete. It would be complete as if the United States had entered on the surface of the land and taken exclusive possession of it.

* * *

There is no material difference between the supposed case and the present one, except that here enjoyment and use of the land are not completely destroyed. But that does not seem to us to be controlling. The path of glide for airplanes might reduce a valuable factory site to grazing land, an orchard to a vegetable patch, a residential section to a wheat field. Some value would remain. But the use of the airspace immediately above the land would limit the utility of the land and cause a diminution in its value.

* * *

The airplane is part of the modern environment of life, and inconveniences which it causes are normally not compensable under the Fifth Amendment. The airspace, apart from the immediate reaches above the land, is part of the public domain. We need not determine at this time what those precise limits are. Flights over private land are not a taking, unless they are so low and so frequent as to be a direct and immediate interference with the enjoyment and use of the land. We need not speculate on that phase of the present case. For the findings of the Court of Claims plainly establish that there was a diminution in value of the property and that the frequent, low-level flights were the direct and immediate cause. We agree with the Court of Claims that a servitude has been imposed on the land.

* * *

Since on this record it is not clear whether the [interest] taken is a permanent or a temporary one, it would be premature for us to consider whether the amount of the award made by the Court of Claims was proper.

The judgment is reversed and the cause is remanded to the Court of Claims so that it may make the necessary findings in conformity with this opinion.

Reversed and Remanded.

How would you approach evaluating the proper monetary award if the taking is deemed permanent? Temporary?

sively in **condemnation** cases. However, as long as the state legislature has provided a fair method of evaluation of eminent domain "takings" by providing the parties ample opportunity to be heard and to present evidence, due process is satisfied.

The United States Supreme Court has issued a number of rulings in the area of eminent domain. In *Penn Central Station v. New York City* the court refused to recognize a taking when a state historical landmark commission refused to permit Penn Central to build a high rise office tower on top of its Grand Central structure, even though it would not violate zoning regulations. The Court noted that Penn Central's existing use, unlike in *United States v. Causby,* was not thwarted. Moreover, the refusal qualified Penn Central for transfer development rights (TDRs) which gave it some economic consideration by allowing it to violate zoning and build on another property that was not a historical landmark. Or, it could sell the TDRs to another property owner interested in building in violation of zoning. Although this was not deemed just compensation, it did permit a reasonable return on Penn Central's investment. The investment-backed expectation test helped the Lucas's in *South Carolina Coastal Authority v. Lucas,* where investors purchased two plots of land on the beach. The Coastal Authority then passed a regulation prohibiting development of the coastal lands in order to maintain the aesthetic value of a free and uninterrupted view and walkway. In holding that this was a taking that demanded just compensation, the Supreme Court noted that the purpose of the purchase was to develop the land and hence these investment-backed expectations were thwarted, unlike Penn Central, which was still able to continue using its property as a train station as originally desired when purchased. For more treatment in the area of regulatory takings see Chapter 24.

■ **Just Compensation.** *The award the owner is entitled to, when property is taken by the government under its power of eminent domain, measured by the property's fair market value.*

The government and the landowner often dispute what constitutes proper compensation to the owner for a "taking." State constitutions and the U.S. Constitution require that such compensation be "just" or "reasonable." In each case, **just** or **reasonable compensation** must be determined by balancing the interests of the taxpaying public against those of the property owner to arrive at a result fair to both parties.

Compensation should not be more extensive than the owner's loss. The principal measure of the owner's loss is the fair market value of the property at the time. The U.S.

Supreme Court has held that market value and just compensation are synonymous. Market value is normally determined by what a willing buyer would pay in cash to a willing seller in an arm's-length transaction. The seller is entitled to have the property valued at its highest and most profitable use, even if the property is not currently being used in that manner.

CASE EXAMPLE

The state of Maryland condemned Kamin's property for a highway improvement project. The property was zoned as Rural-Agricultural (R-A). Based on the present use and zoning of the property, experts appraised the Kamins' property at about $136,000. Kamins produced evidence at the condemnation hearing that if the condemnation did not take place, the property could be rezoned to EIA, an Employment and Institutional use Area. A planning supervisor for the Maryland Planning Commission testified that had an application for a zoning upgrade to EIA been made, it would have been granted. Because the court concluded that there was a reasonable probability of rezoning of the property to EIA within a reasonable period of time, it assigned a value commensurate with that higher use ($500,000). *State Roads v. Kamins*, 572 A.2d 1132 (Md. App. 1990).

The most common method of determining value is to compare the property being taken with similar land recently sold. This information is generally presented to the courts through the testimony of expert witnesses. Real estate sales personnel are often expert witnesses in condemnation cases because they are familiar with the selling price of land. A good expert witness must be very familiar with the parcel of land involved as well as the selling price of comparable property.

Several states require that the condemning authority attempt to negotiate a voluntary settlement before commencing a condemnation action. Even when not a statutory requirement, this practice is followed in almost all cases. If the sovereign's offer is rejected, the most common procedure is to condemn by judicial proceeding. This action requires that the sovereign file a petition in court, giving notice to the owners and others having an interest in the land. Ordinarily, the condemning authority has the burden of establishing the right to acquire the property. Once this right is established, the owner must prove the value of the property taken and any additional damages. On the court's making the condemnation award, the interest necessary for the condemnor's purpose passes to the government authority involved. This interest may be an estate for years, an easement, or a fee simple absolute, but it may not exceed what is necessary to accomplish the public purpose for which the property was taken.

■ TRANSFER OF PROPERTY ON DEATH

When a person dies, title to that person's property may be transferred in one of two ways. When the decedent has made a valid "last will and testament," title to the decedent's property is transferred to the beneficiaries named in the will, subject to limitations imposed by the state. The person who has made a valid will is called a *testator* and is said to have died *testate*. A person who dies without making a valid will is said to have died *intestate*. State statutes direct to whom an intestate's property is transferred. For an introduction to estate planning see: *http://profs.lp.findlaw.com/estate/index.html.*

Intestate Succession

■   *Distribution of property of a person who dies without leaving a will or whose will is invalid.*

The general philosophy underlying the laws of **intestate succession** is that property should descend to those persons the intestate individual probably would want to own it. If the decedent expressed no preference by executing a will, it is assumed that the decedent would want the property to go to those closely related by blood or marriage. Society also benefits from this assumption because it keeps property within the family and tends to strengthen that important institution.

Laws of intestate succession are statutory. No one has a constitutional or natural right to a decedent's property. People inherit because the legislature says that they can. The law might direct that all property of an intestate decedent revert to the state, as it did in England immediately following the Norman Conquest. This system was opposed by powerful tenants of the king, however, and the English rulers were soon forced to recognize the principle of inheritance by members of the tenant's family.

In modern U.S. real estate law, the concept of inheritance by family members is integral to the succession to property on death. The idea that the state should acquire the property of an intestate is offensive to the sense of justice of almost all Americans. The state acquires title to the property only when the decedent has no relatives, an extraordinary occurrence discussed later in this section.

Historical Background. The origin of state statutes of intestate succession is found in English law. Primarily because of the importance of land to the political and social structure of England, English law treated the transfer of real property on the owner's death very differently from the transfer of personal property.

Until 1926 in England, when an owner died intestate, title to that person's real property passed directly to the heirs according to statutes of descent. Title to personal property passed initially to an administrator. After the administrator paid the claims against the estate, the personal property then passed according to the Statute of Distribution.

Currently, in England and a majority of jurisdictions in the United States, the laws of intestate succession no longer distinguish between real and personal property. Statutes, commonly referred to as *statutes of descent and distribution*, treat the two types of property in the same manner.

■   **Statutes of Descent and Distribution.** *Statutes that provide for the distribution of the property of a person who dies without a valid will.*

Every state legislature has determined the order of distribution to estate beneficiaries, in the absence of a valid will or other testamentary device. (See Figure 18.2.) Today in the United States, the distribution of the estate of an intestate is modeled, in a general way, on the English Statute of Distribution. Both current American and English statutes provide for distribution of the entire estate, not just personal property. American law also focuses primarily on provision for the surviving spouse and children.

A surviving husband or wife ordinarily is entitled to a half or a third share of the decedent's property. Many states increase this portion if the couple had no children.

FIGURE 18.2   A Statute of Intestate Succession

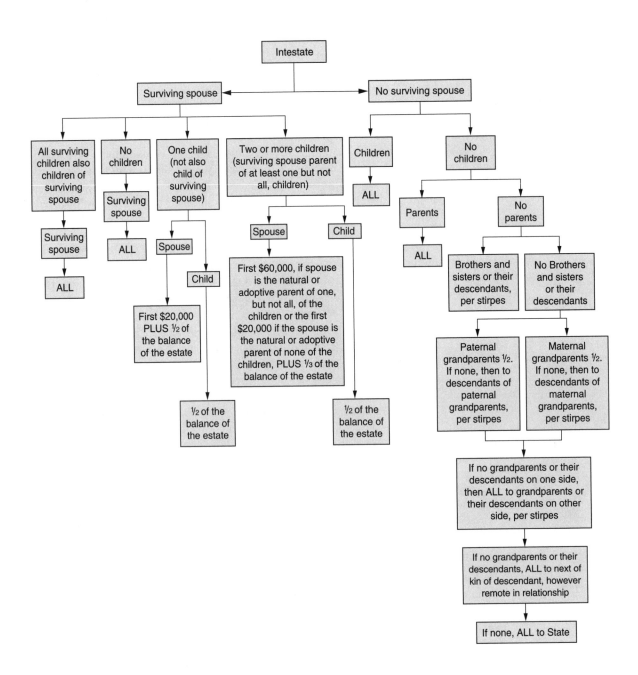

Some states give the surviving spouse a specific dollar amount and a fraction of the net estate exceeding that amount. Community property states normally differentiate between intestate distribution of separate property and that of community property.

In every state, a surviving spouse and children share all of the intestate's estate. The children take whatever remains after the spouse's share. If there is no surviving spouse, the entire estate passes to the children, who divide the assets equally.

■ **Per Stirpes Distribution.** *Distribution of intestate property to persons who take the share allocated to a deceased ancestor.*

A difficult question of fundamental fairness arises when a child who has children dies before a parent. When the grandparent dies, should the surviving grandchildren share equally with their aunts and uncles, or are they entitled only to the share of the deceased parent?

CASE EXAMPLE

Trent Hightower died intestate. His wife had predeceased him by many years. They had three children: Stephanie, Joseph, and Douglas. Stephanie and Joseph survived their father, but Douglas died before him. Douglas, however, left three children of his own: Trent, Jr., Eliza, and Anne. Trent Hightower's estate was divided into thirds, with one-third going to Stephanie, one-third to Joseph, and one-third to the children of Douglas. This allocation is *per stirpes* distribution. See Figure 18.3.

In some states, when the only distributees are grandchildren, distribution is by modified per stirpes. In these states each grandchild takes in his or her own right as in **per capita distribution.** The decedent's estate is divided equally by the *number* of grandchildren.

■ **Per Capita Distribution.** *Distribution of intestate property to persons who take equal shares as members of a class, not as representatives of an ancestor.*

CASE EXAMPLE

Jennie E. Martin died intestate, leaving as distributees three grandchildren: Alice E. Martin, Bourke Martin, and Ned Martin. Alice E. was the daughter of Earl Martin; Bourke and Ned were the sons of Charles Martin. Both Earl and Charles had died before their mother died. The court divided Jennie Martin's estate into three parts, giving one to each grandchild. Alice E. Martin argued that the distribution should have been per stirpes and that she should have received one-half.

The appellate court affirmed the lower court's action. The court stated, "We hold that it was the intention of the legislature that grandchildren, who alone survive the ancestor, should take equally. . . ." In other words, they should take as heirs, not by representation. *In re Martin's Estate*, 96 Vt. 455, 120 A. 862 (1923).

Order of Distribution. In the absence of a spouse or children, statutes generally distribute the intestate's property to parents. In a few states, brothers and sisters share with parents. Issue of deceased brothers and sisters take their parents' share, per stirpes.

Statutes ordinarily provide for the property to go to the "next of kin" if no specific relatives survive and in some states, if there are no relatives or next of kin, to stepchildren. Most states by statute provide a method for determining next of kin. Usually the

| FIGURE 18.3 | Intestate Example |

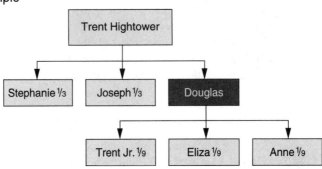

method is based on that used in England to determine kinship under the Statute of Distribution. Other than the surviving spouse, relatives by marriage ordinarily are not entitled to the intestate's property. (See Figure 18.2.)

■ **Escheat**. *Reversion of property to the state when a person dies intestate with no heirs or when property is abandoned.*

CASE EXAMPLE

Gene DiMond, who inherited property in St. Augustine from his only brother Henri, had no immediate surviving relatives. His parents were dead, and Gene had never married. Although he had one aunt, she had died many years before, leaving no children. On Gene's death, the state claimed the St. Augustine property because Gene had died without leaving a will and without heirs.

A decedent's property escheats to the state when the decedent dies intestate with no heirs. Because most decedents have heirs or make a will, **escheat** is not a common method by which a state acquires title.

Escheat is an incident of state sovereignty. Land should revert to the state ultimately for the people's benefit when no heirs exist. State constitutions in some instances contain provisions for escheat. Ordinarily, rules governing the details of escheat are statutory.

Some type of judicial proceeding is necessary to establish the state's right to the property. In a number of jurisdictions, title vests immediately in the state when a landowner dies intestate without ascertainable heirs. In these states, the judicial proceeding will be in the probate court, similar to proceedings to establish heirship. Other states require a more extensive action; in these states, title to escheated property does not vest in the state until a court so orders, after a hearing or trial. Escheat statutes are not favored by the courts and, as a result, are strictly construed.

Testate Succession

■ *Transfer of property when a person dies leaving a will.*

The right of an owner of property to direct to whom it should go on death has always been subject to significant limitations. Initially, the right to will one's property applied only to personal property. This right evolved in England shortly after the Norman Conquest in 1066.

Historical Background. It was not until the enactment of the Statute of Wills in 1540 that English law granted real property owners a limited right to transfer it by will. This right was curtailed substantially by dower, discussed in Chapter 4, as well as the customs and traditions of the English aristocracy. Many restrictions on the disposition of real property by will also existed in the United States. During the late nineteenth and twentieth centuries, these restrictions lessened. As land became less important as a source of wealth in relation to personal property, statutes in both England and the United States provided owners with comparable rights to dispose of both real and personal property by will. Today, in both countries, a person can dispose freely of both types of property by will. There are, however, limitations imposed by the state to protect the family. The law in the United States establishes a minimum amount, normally ⅓ or ½ of the estate, to which the surviving spouse is entitled. Thus, should the will leave less than the prescribed minimum, the surviving spouse is entitled to elect to take against the will, and claim his or her minimum statutory share. In addition, the law ensures that the debts of the decedent's estate are paid before beneficiary distributions.

■ **Will.** *A written instrument that permits distribution of an owner's property after death; it must contain certain elements to be legally enforceable.*

Our English legal heritage has had an extensive influence on requirements for making a valid will. As a result, similar requirements exist throughout the United States, although individual states deviate significantly from the common pattern. In most American jurisdictions, formality is a general characteristic of executing a will. Formality is predicated on a legislative desire to prevent fraud, undue influence, coercion, or a testator's impetuousness. Legislatures apparently believe that ceremony helps to prevent rash actions. In addition, formality helps to memorialize the transaction. To be valid, a will must ordinarily be signed by the testator and properly witnessed. (See Figure 18.4.) It need not be notarized. (See Table 18.1.) Additionally, the testator must possess a sound mind.

Sound Mind. A testator must possess a sound mind to have the capacity to execute a will. Sound mind requires that a person be able to appreciate the extent and value of his or her property; be able to formulate a plan for distribution; and know the natural objects of his or her affection. Sometimes a mental infirmity prevents the person from realizing these requirements; but, as the next case illustrates, even an Alzheimer's patient may execute a will during a lucid interval.

TABLE 18.1	Formalities of Executing a Will

✓ Written

✓ Signed by Testator at End

✓ Witnessed

✓ Acknowledged by Testator and Witnesses

  Notarized

Bye v. Mattingly
Supreme Court of Kentucky
975 S.W.2d 451 (Ky. 1998)

Background. Mr. McQuady's wife of 45 years died, leaving her entire estate to him. Because Mr. McQuady was unable to see and required assistance, he retained Mary Ruth Bye as his housekeeper.

In the summer of 1989 Mr. McQuady, along with Ms. Bye, visited an attorney. Mr. McQuady executed a new will that left all but $100 to Ms. Bye. Due to Mr. McQuady's failing health, a guardian was appointed in the spring of 1990. Mr. McQuady was diagnosed with Alzheimer's disease, which can be accentuated by poor health and poor treatment.

A petition, signed by Mr. McQuady, seeking to permit Mr. McQuady to marry Ms. Bye was filed and heard to determine whether it should be granted. At the hearing, Mr. McQuady insisted that he did not want to marry Ms. Bye and that he was afraid of her. He then terminated her services as housekeeper.

Five months later, in 1991, Mr. McQuady executed a new will, leaving all his property to his brother-in-law and a second cousin. The cousin drove Mr. McQuady to the law office where the new will was executed.

Mr. McQuady died in the summer of 1992. Ms. Bye brought an action challenging the validity of the 1991 will on grounds including lack of testamentary capacity. The jury found against Ms. Bye, thus upholding the new will. Ms. Bye, appellant, appealed the judgment and the Court of Appeals upheld the trial court decision.

Decision. The Supreme Court of Kentucky affirmed the Court of Appeals decision.

Chief Justice Stephens. . . . "Kentucky is committed to the doctrine of testatorial absolutism." The practical effect of this doctrine is that the privilege of the citizens of the Commonwealth to draft wills to dispose of their property is zealously guarded by the courts and will not be disturbed based on remote or speculative evidence. The degree of mental capacity required to make a will is minimal. The minimum level of mental capacity required to make a will is less than that necessary to make a deed. . . .

To validly execute a will, a testator must: (1) know the natural objects of her bounty; (2) know her obligations to them; (3) know the character and value of her estate; and (4) dispose of her estate according to her own fixed purpose. Merely being an older person, possessing a failing memory, momentary forgetfulness, weakness of mental powers or lack of strict coherence in conversation does not render one incapable of validly executing a will.

* * *

While a ruling of total or partial disability certainly is evidence of a lack of testamentary capacity, it is certainly not dispositive of the issue. This Court has upheld the rights of those afflicted with a variety of illnesses to execute valid wills. . . . We have not disturbed the testatorial privileges of those who believed in witchcraft, spiritualism or atheism. While none of these cases absolutely parallels the instant case, we recite them here to demonstrate how this Court has always taken the broadest possible view of who may execute a will no matter what their infirmity.

When a testator is suffering from a mental illness which ebbs and flows in terms of its effect on the testator's mental competence, it is presumed that the testator was mentally fit when the will was executed. This is commonly referred to as the lucid interval doctrine. Alzheimer's is a disease that is variable in its effect on a person over time. It is precisely this type of illness with which the lucid interval doctrine was designed to deal. By employing this doctrine, citizens of the Commonwealth who suffer from a debilitating mental condition are still able to dispose of their property.

The lucid interval doctrine is only implicated when there is evidence that a testator is suffering from a mental illness; otherwise the normal presumption in favor of testamentary capacity is operating. The burden is placed on those who seek to overturn the will to demonstrate the lack of capacity. . . .

In the present case there is no question that Mr. McQuady suffered from Alzheimers disease. However, under the doctrine he is presumed to have been experiencing a lucid interval during the execution of the will. The wisdom of this doctrine is demonstrated by Mr. McQuady's testimony during the hearing on the petition for marriage in Breckinridge District court. During that hearing Mr. McQuady was very lucid and demonstrated a complete grasp of the circumstances in which he found himself. Appellant has failed to offer this Court evidence which demonstrates that the testator did not have a lucid interval during which he executed the 1991 will. In sum, let it suffice to say that in the instant case a presumption of a lucid interval of testamentary capacity was appropriate.

Given this Court's consistent attitude toward the virtually absolute right of the citizens of the Commonwealth to make wills, it would be incongruous for us now to announce a new rule of law which restricted these rights which we have held in such high regard for so long. While the clear policy of the Commonwealth is that our citizens who are no longer able to fully care for themselves must be protected from the various societal predators, we will restrict their testamentary rights only when it is absolutely necessary and even then only to the degree required to defend their interests.

Affirmed.

Suggest evidence that would have overcome the presumption of testamentary capacity.

Written. All states require that a will be in writing, but a limited number of states do permit oral wills of personal property under limited circumstances. Generally, oral wills are valid if made by military personnel in actual service or under certain conditions by a person suffering a terminal illness. A will written entirely in the testator's own hand, known as a *holographic* will, is considered valid in a number of states, even if it lacks witnesses.

Signed. American courts are liberal in their interpretation of what constitutes a signature. A mark or an initial is sufficient if intended as a signature. Usually, the testator must sign personally, but someone else may if directed to do so by the testator. Usually, this must be done in the testator's presence. Generally, a signature any place on the document is sufficient if the intention is to validate the will. Some states require that the signature be at the end of the instrument. In those states, the entire document is invalid if the signature is in some other place.

FIGURE 18.4	Last Will and Testament

Last Will and Testament

of

Will B. Done

2100 Neil Ave.

Columbus, Ohio 43210

I, Will B. Done, over the age of twenty-one years, a legal resident of the county of Franklin, State of Ohio, and being of sound mind and memory and not acting under menace, duress, fraud, or undue influence, do make, publish, and declare this to be my Last Will and Testament, hereby revoking all other Wills and testamentary writings heretofore made by me.

Item I. I direct my executor to pay out of my estate all of my just debts and funeral expenses as soon as reasonably practical after death.

Item II. I hereby devise and bequeath all property of whatsoever kind, real and personal, wheresoever situate, to my wife, Ima, if she shall survive me.

Item III. In the event that my wife, Ima, does not survive me, I give, devise, and bequeath all the residue and remainder of my estate, real and personal, of whatsoever kind and wheresoever situate, absolutely and in fee simple to the children of our marriage, share and share alike, per stirpes.

Item IV. In the event my wife, Ima, does not survive me then I appoint Harold Greene and Sally Greene or the survivor as guardians over the person and property of said children under the age of twenty-one (21). Said guardians shall hold the money in trust for each minor until said child attains the age of twenty-one (21) and use such money until then for the support and education of the minor child. When each child attains the age of twenty-one (21), the guardians shall transfer the remaining funds held in trust for that child to said child and the guardianship of that child shall terminate.

Item V. I hereby appoint my wife, Ima, as executor of my Last Will and Testament if she survives me and is otherwise qualified; otherwise I nominate, constitute and appoint Rhesa Andrews, Columbus, Ohio. I hereby authorize and grant my executor full power without order of the Court to settle claims in favor of or against my estate, to sell at public or private sale for cash or credit, to mortgage, lease, or convey all or any part of my estate, real or personal, of whatsoever kind wheresoever situate, without application to or confirmation by any court or government agency.

Item VI. In the event that my wife and children do not survive me, then I give, devise, and bequeath all the residue and remainder of my estate, real and personal, of whatsoever kind, wheresoever situate, absolutely and in fee simple to my brother, Lance, my sister, Elgin, and my brother-in-law, Peter, share and share alike. I have intentionally not included my brother Conley because I know that adequate provision has already been made for him through other sources.

In testimony whereof, I have hereunto set my hand at Columbus, Ohio, this 15th day of August 2006.

_____

Will B. Done

Signed and witnessed in the presence of the testator and in the presence of each other.

_____   _____

Witness   Witness

Witnessed. Most state laws require only two witnesses for a will to be valid. Any competent adult may ordinarily act as a witness. In some states, a beneficiary under a will should not be a witness; a beneficiary's testimony may be sufficient to sustain the will in court, but he or she would then be disqualified to take under the will.

The common practice is for the testator to sign first in the presence of the witnesses. In many states the actual signing does not have to be viewed by the witness if the testator later acknowledges the signature.

Attested. Attestation is a requirement in all jurisdictions for most wills. *Attestation* means that the person must intend to act as a witness and must sign for the purpose of validating the will. In a very few states, the witness need not sign the instrument, but attestation is necessary even in those states. To validate the will, witnesses may be required to testify at a later date that the testator signed or acknowledged the signature in their presence.

In the vast majority of cases, a will includes an attestation clause. This clause appears at the end of the will following the testator's signature. Each witness signs the attestation clause, which recites the witness's observation of the formalities necessary for the proper execution of the will.

Family Protection. Prevailing public policy in the United States is to encourage provisions for spouse and children out of a decedent's estate. As noted earlier, if a person dies intestate, inheritance statutes in all states provide first for the decedent's immediate family. State laws also furnish some protection for the spouse and, to a lesser degree, the children of a person who fails to provide for them by will. Historically, many of these laws applied specifically to real estate. Dower rights, discussed in Chapter 4, is an example. Today, protection for a decedent's spouse in most states is accomplished by giving the spouse a right to elect a share against the will. The right of election applies to the entire estate, both real and personal property.

■   **Elective Share.** *A share of a deceased spouse's estate that a surviving spouse may claim if the decedent spouse's will did not provide at least this amount.*

Dower has been replaced in many states by the right of a surviving spouse to elect a share against the decedent's will. The right of election is based on statute, and the share varies from state to state. Inasmuch as the right of election is a relatively recent trend in the law, state legislation usually reflects modern developments for this purpose, such as the elimination of distinctions between real and personal property and similar treatment of husband and wife.

CASE EXAMPLE

Royce and Helen Hurley were married for many years. Early in their marriage Helen made a will leaving Royce $100,000. At the time, this was the bulk of Helen's estate. Over the years, Helen prospered but did not change her will. When Helen died in 1995, her net estate was more than $500,000. State statute gave surviving spouses a right to take under the will or to elect to take a one-half share against the will. Royce elected to take a one-half share ($250,000) instead of the $100,000 legacy.

The right of election is also influenced by past laws and customs. Many state legislatures regard it as a substitute for dower. Thus, the survivor's elective share is often set at a fractional amount, such as one-third of the decedent's estate. In a number of states, the share is less if the couple has children. However, children may be disinherited by their parents, and no state has a law that provides children an elective share.

■ ADMINISTRATION OF ESTATES

■ *A general term used to describe the management and settlement of a decedent's estate by a person appointed by the courts.*

Many of the procedures for settling the estate of a decedent are similar for both testate and intestate decedents. A very important initial step is the appointment of a personal representative to act for the estate. The person charged with administration of the estate of an intestate decedent is called an *administrator*; the person who is appointed to administer the estate of a decedent who dies testate is an *executor*. Sometimes the person nominated in a will as an executor is unable or unwilling to serve. Under these conditions, the court appoints an *administrator with the will annexed*.

The administration of a decedent's estate is ordinarily supervised by a special court, frequently referred to as a *probate* or *surrogate's court*. The appointment of a personal representative is an important element in administering a decedent's estate. In the will, the testator almost always nominates a personal representative. The personal representative may be either a person or an institution such as a trust company. The decedent's nominee is usually appointed by the court, unless that person or entity is not qualified or refuses to serve.

■ **Probate.** *Proof that an instrument is genuine and the last will and testament of the maker.*

In the vast majority of cases, **probate** is a straightforward procedure. Ordinarily, the person nominated in the will as personal representative files a written application or petition for probate. In many jurisdictions, the probate court supplies the proper forms for this procedure. The petition alleges the testator's death and domicile at the time of death. The will is usually attached to the petition unless it has been filed previously with the court. Usually the names, relationships, and residences of the heirs at law, as well as those receiving gifts under the will, must be included because they ordinarily will be notified of the proceeding.

When a petition is unopposed, the court may order probate on the documents filed. In some cases, a limited hearing is conducted in which the court takes testimony on the validity of the will. A number of states have developed shortened probate procedures for small estates, especially when no real property is involved.

Probate establishes that the will is valid and genuine. After the petition for probate is granted, the will can no longer be attacked on the ground of forgery, improper execution, or revocation except in a proceeding to set aside probate. Probate does not establish the validity or meaning of particular provisions of the will. If the court is satisfied that the nominated personal representative is qualified to serve, this person will be furnished with *letters testamentary* as evidence of authority to settle the estate.

State statutes prescribe the persons eligible for appointment as administrator and the order in which they must be considered. The order, based on relationship to the decedent, parallels the order of intestate inheritance in most states. Preference is given to the surviving husband or wife. If there is no husband or wife, the relative next entitled to distribution is selected as administrator. The court selects, from among those who stand in equal right, the person best qualified to manage the estate. Usually, preference is given to residents of the jurisdiction. The court grants *letters of administration* to the person appointed to administer the intestate's estate.

The personal representative, whether an executor or administrator, is authorized by the court to settle the decedent's estate. That representative is responsible for ensuring that assets are distributed in an orderly manner to those who are entitled to them. Although the personal representative has a wide variety of miscellaneous chores, four basic steps are integral to the settlement of the estate:

1. Collection of estate assets
2. Processing and payment of claims against the estate
3. Management of estate assets
4. Accounting and distribution of estate assets

Proof of Death. It is axiomatic that neither a will nor an inheritance statute is operative until a property owner dies. Ordinarily, the occurrence and time of death are easy to determine, but problems arise in at least two instances. One instance is a disaster in which several closely related people die at approximately the same time; another is a situation in which a property owner has been missing for an extensive period.

Many wills solve the problem of determining who has died first in a common disaster by including a provision in the instrument.

> **CASE EXAMPLE**
>
> Lance Beck and his wife, Hilda, were killed in a common disaster. Because of the nature of the accident, determining which one had died first was impossible. Lance's will left all his property to his wife if she survived him. If she did not, his estate was to go to his parents and to charity.
>
> Lance's will contained the following provision: "In the event my wife and I shall die under such circumstances that there is insufficient evidence to determine the survivor, it shall be conclusively presumed that I survived her." As a result of this provision, the estate went to Lance's parents and the charities that he had named, rather than into his wife's estate.

Most states by statute make special provisions for applying distribution rules when close relatives are killed under circumstances that make it impossible to determine the survivor. Almost all states have adopted the Uniform Simultaneous Death Act. In general, this act provides that in a common disaster each decedent's property shall be disposed of as if that decedent was the last survivor.

States also solve by statute the problem caused by a missing person. Generally, these statutes provide that a person whose absence is unexplained for a period of years, often seven, is presumed dead. The presumption, however, may be rebutted, if, for example, there is convincing evidence to believe that the person is alive.

THE CHANGING LANDSCAPE

Most people prefer to control their destiny—or, at least, their money. By writing a will, one avoids uncertainty and effects disposition according to desire. There is, however, a trend toward avoiding probate by establishing a trust. The trust "privatizes death" by removing it from the spectacle of public probate. Here, the trustor (settlor), the one creating the trust, names a trustee and beneficiaries. On death of the settlor, the trustee follows the instruction of the trust and makes the prescribed distributions to the named beneficiaries. The trustee may be a relative, a trusted friend, or an institution. In any event, costs of probate and delayed proceedings are avoided. An alternative approach to estate planning is to create the trust within a will, called a *testamentary trust*. Or the will may provide for the net estate to pour over into the existing "private trust," and, as in the living trust, the trustee is required to abide by the distribution guidelines.

With the increasing costs of nursing home care, and medicine extending lives, many are losing their accumulation of savings to the nursing homes. There is, of course, insurance, but expense and lack of foresight prevent this as a solution, at least, for now. Many are turning to the irrevocable *inter-vivos* trust or "Medicare trust," looking to it as a way to preserve the estate within the family and avoid the depletion of the family wealth. Through this "trust" technique, the settlor divests himself or herself of an estate and after a "look back" period, may have Medicaid, a federal program, provide for nursing home care. Should the family desire to upgrade or supplement the services they may do so, at their own expense. Is there a better alternative for providing for one's last illness without depleting the family wealth?

■ KEY TERMS

■ INTERNET RESOURCES

For comprehensive sites on wills and estate planning see:

www.nolo.com/index.cfm
(Drop-down menu for wills and estate planning)

For an estate planning overview see:

www.abanet.org/rppt/public/home.html

■ REVIEW AND DISCUSSION QUESTIONS

1. What are the major arguments for allowing a person to acquire title by adverse possession?
2. What are the advantages of writing a will, as opposed to dying intestate?
3. Explain the difference between per stirpes and per capita distribution.
4. Briefly indicate some of the limitations that exist on the transfer of real property by will.
5. Discuss the major duties of a person appointed to settle a decedent's estate.

■ CASE PROBLEMS

1. Kittrell owned four house trailers that were parked on the edge of his property. Unknown to Kittrell, the trailers extended a few feet onto his neighbor's property. This condition was discovered by a survey after the trailers had been there several years. At the time, Kittrell offered to buy the strip of land on which the trailers encroached. The owner refused to sell, but, because permanent plumbing had been installed, he did not order the trailers to be moved. Several years later the property was sold and the new owner demanded that Kittrell remove the trailers. Kittrell claimed ownership of the strip by adverse possession because the trailers had encroached on the land for more than ten years, the statutory period in the state. Discuss the validity of Kittrell's claim. *Kittrell v. Scarborough*, 287 Ala. 177, 249 So. 2d 814 (1971).

2. The Nollans purchased a beachfront lot in Ventura County, California. The lot contained a small bungalow, which was in disrepair. They desired to demolish the bungalow and replace it. They sought a permit to do so from the California Coastal Commission. The Commission granted the permit subject to the condition that the Nollans allow the public an easement to pass across a portion of their property to make it easier to get to a nearby county park. The Commission reasoned that the new bungalow would increase blockage of the view of the ocean and thus would prevent the public "psychologically" from realizing the benefit of a stretch of coastline. Is the condition constitutional? Explain. *Nollan v. California Coastal Comm'n*, 483 U.S. 825 (1987).

3. Berman owned a department store on property in a District of Columbia slum. The property was well maintained, and no building violations existed. Using the power of eminent domain, the District of Columbia Redevelopment Agency acquired Berman's property, along with that of others in the area. The purpose of the acquisition was for "the development of blighted territory." Berman argued that the taking was unconstitutional as his property was not substandard and, after redevelopment, was to be managed privately. Discuss the validity of Berman's contention. *Berman v. Parker*, 348 U.S. 26 (1954).

4. The Tahoe Regional Planning Agency (TRPA), an arm of the state of California and the state of Nevada in cooperation with each other, was created to regulate the development of the Lake Tahoe basin. While studying the environmental impact of the development, it issued two moratoria suspending residential development in the area. The first moratorium was for eight months and the second for 24 months. Landowners in the area filed suit claiming that this was a taking that required just compensation under the U.S. Constitution. Are the landowners entitled to compensation? How would that be computed? See *Tahoe-Sierra Preservation Council, Inc. v. Tahoe Regional Planning Agency,* 535 U.S. 302 (2002).

5. The statute of descent and distribution of the State of Y is as follows:

    If a person dies intestate, his or her real and personal property, if any, shall pass:

    (a) If there is no surviving spouse, to the children of the intestate or their lineal descendants, per stirpes.

    (b) If there is a spouse and one or more children or their lineal descendants surviving, the first $60,000 to the spouse, plus one-half of the remainder to the spouse and the balance to the children equally or to their lineal descendants, per stirpes.

    (c) If there are no children or their lineal descendants, the whole to the surviving spouse.

    (d) If there is no spouse and no children or their lineal descendants surviving, to the parents of the intestate equally or to the surviving parent.

    (e) If there is no spouse, no children or their lineal descendants and no parent surviving, to the brothers and sisters equally or their lineal descendants, per stirpes.

    (f) If there is no spouse, no children or their lineal descendants, no parents and no siblings surviving, to the next of kin.

    (g) If there is no next of kin, escheat to the state.

    Answer the following hypothetical questions based on this statute.

    a. Graham dies, leaving a valid will that bequeaths his entire estate to his sister-in-law, Ruth. He is survived by Ruth and by his mother, his grandson, and his brother. What is the result under the statute?

    b. Willis died intestate and is survived by his wealthy wife, Angela; his poverty-stricken mother, Rose; and his deserving second cousin, Ned. How will the estate be distributed?

c. Susan died intestate, survived by her son, Jack, and by three grandsons, Dennis, Randy, and Rob. Dennis and Randy are the sons of Susan's deceased oldest son, David, and Rob is the only child of Susan's deceased daughter, Cheryl. How will the estate be divided?

d. Rebecca died intestate, survived by her husband, Gus; her father, Bruce; her daughter, Nancy; and her grandchildren, Chuck and Jill, the children of her deceased son, Rick. The net probate estate is $50,000. How will it be divided?

6. Martha had two children, Peter and Mary. On Martha's death, neither Peter nor Mary were living. Mary left three children and Peter left two children. Assuming all of Martha's property was left to Peter and Mary, how much will each grandchild get if the property devolved per stirpes? How much if it devolved per capita?

7. Lindsey Henderson committed suicide at age 43. He had executed a will leaving all his property to Ms. Allison and Ms. Edge, no relations. He left out his closest relative, a brother, Larry Henderson.

The decedent lived with his mother until shortly before his death. He had a sketchy work record and some type of intellectual impairment. He had relied on his brother for assistance in handling his personal business.

Lindsey could read on a second-grade level. He had been diagnosed as being mentally retarded and suffering from an inadequate personality, anxiety neurosis, and perhaps delusional thinking.

The decedent met one of the beneficiaries, Ms. Edge, at a night club. They became friendly and she referred him to an attorney when he said he desired to make a will. She accompanied the decedent to the attorney's office but waited in another room while he talked to the attorney. The attorney noticed that the decedent was a "little strange," such that he asked him to return with a medical note stating that he was competent to make a will. This the decedent did not do. Nonetheless he returned the next day with two witnesses and the will was executed.

The decedent met the other beneficiary, Ms. Allison, at a club where she tended bar. They had a sexual relationship. The decedent's brother filed a will contest maintaining that his brother was under undue influence when he executed the will and that he lacked the mental capacity to execute a will. Discuss the issues and come to a conclusion based on the facts as to who should win the contest. See *Henderson v. Estate of Henderson*, 1997 Ark. App. LEXIS 334 (May 7, 1997).

8. John and Larue Morgan were married in 1960. In 1965 Larue disappeared. Although extensive efforts were made to locate her, she was never found. In 1973 John brought a legal action to have Larue declared dead. At the hearing, Larue's brother attempted to introduce as evidence a Christmas card that he had received from her in 1967. The judge refused to accept this evidence and declared Larue dead because she had been missing for more than seven years. Was the judge correct? Discuss.

19

Recording and Assurance of Title

■ RECORDING STATUTES

■ *Laws that require the entry into books of public record the written instruments affecting the title to real property.*

Under common law, deeds and other instruments affecting the title to real property were not *recorded*—officially entered into the public records. Problems arose for the owners when they lost or misplaced these deeds and other documents. Even more important, third parties had no way of knowing that a prior transaction had taken place. The person making a conveyance to an innocent third party may have previously conveyed to another and therefore had nothing to give to this subsequent party. These difficulties gave rise to the need for recording statutes. *The primary intent of these statutes is to protect third persons by giving them constructive notice that a prior transaction has occurred.*

The recording statutes that have been adopted by all states provide a means for notifying third parties as to the ownership or other interests existing in a given parcel of land. The recording takes place when a deed, mortgage, easement, or other legal instrument affecting the title to land is copied into the public record so that interested persons can discover the status of the title to the land. All entries regarding that title constitute the title history, also known as the *chain of title*.

Many centuries ago, land could be transferred by a symbolic gesture such as the giving of a handful of soil or a wild rose branch. Since England enacted its Statute of Frauds in 1677, however, a transfer of an interest in land must be in writing to attain legal recognition. The written document serves as proof of the transfer between the parties to the transaction—the buyer and the seller—and to anyone else who is aware of the writing. However, a prospective buyer unfamiliar with any prior transactions would have only the word of the seller as assurance as to what previously occurred. The buyer or the buyer's attorney can gain certainty about any prior transfer of an interest in the real estate by referring to the public records to find the recording of the transaction. If the transaction is duly recorded, one can rely on it with relative safety. (Limitations on reliance on the recording will be discussed later.) If the public records do not reveal that the seller owned the parcel, the prospective buyer would normally choose not to buy it. The risk is that the seller is not telling the truth or that some other interest is outstanding in the land. To take a conveyance under these circumstances is to invite a lawsuit; under normal conditions it is too great a risk to the buyer. Thus the purpose of the recording act is to give to the prospective buyer and to the public *legal notice* of the status of a particular property.

Legal Notice

■ *A knowledge of another's interest in real property sufficient to make the adverse interest legally binding on the prospective purchaser or any other party acquiring interest in the property.*

The public recording gives legal notice to third persons as to the existence of a transaction. Under the principle of *caveat emptor*, a prospective buyer or lender is charged with the responsibility of determining whether the seller holds title to the property and whether there are any encumbrances that would adversely affect the title. If an individual has legal notice of a defect or an encumbrance before acquiring an interest, he or she takes *title subject to those prior rights.* Legal notice may take the form of **actual notice**, implied notice, or constructive notice. (See Table 19.1.)

■ **Actual Notice.** *Title information that is acquired personally by the interest holder.*

A prospective purchaser may gain information from the seller or from other parties and from firsthand observation of the property.

> **CASE EXAMPLE**
> McCredy is negotiating an agreement to purchase Nagy's summer home. When McCredy inspects the premises, he finds several neighbors have been using a well on the property. If the neighbors have acquired and recorded an easement, that fact will appear on the record. If no easement is on the record, the users may have a prescriptive easement; that is, one imposed by law based on the extended use by the neighbors. If so, McCredy has actual notice of their easement.

TABLE 19.1	Legal Notice

Type	Example
Actual	Told by seller of disputed irrigation ditch; or on inspection views irrigation ditch crossing the land.
Implied	Quitclaim deed offered by seller to convey property (some states).
Constructive	Easement for irrigation ditch is recorded but records not examined; or irrigation ditch plainly visible but no inspection carried out.

An agreement between two parties gives *actual notice* to these two parties, even if it is not recorded. However, unless a third party has actual notice of the parties' interests, an unrecorded deed gives no legal notice to the third party. Likewise, when a prospective purchaser is shown a house that is being occupied by someone other than the seller, the purchaser is put on notice that the occupant may have some kind of interest. The purchaser is thus obligated, under the theory of actual notice, to ascertain the status of this third party.

■ **Implied Notice.** *Legal notice that is imposed by the law when conditions exist that would lead a reasonable person to inquire further into the condition of the title.*

If a prospective interest holder has **implied notice** of a possible claim, he or she is said to have legal notice of any interest that would be discovered during the course of a reasonable inquiry into the condition of the title. Failure to pursue such an investigation does not exempt the interest holder from notice.

Implied notice occurs in some states when the conveyance of property by quitclaim deed is a release of rights rather than a conveyance. In such states, use of a quitclaim deed is considered to give the purchaser *implied notice* that there may be defects in the title. In states where a quitclaim deed is considered a conveyance, no legal notice of adverse claims is implied merely by the existence of that type of deed.

■ **Constructive Notice.** *The knowledge of certain facts that might be discovered through a careful inspection of public records, provided that such information is within the history of title or discovered through an inspection of the premises.*

Under the concept of **constructive notice**, a prospective interest holder is considered to have legal notice of any information recorded within the history or chain of title, whether or not that individual has actual notice of the existence of the document.

Constructive notice also charges the prospective interest holder with any information contained within recorded documents. In addition, a person has constructive notice of all facts that would be revealed by an inspection of the property. For instance, constructive notice of an easement exists for a plainly visible drainage ditch that crosses the property. Notice occurs even if the person never visits the property or examines the public records, which may or may not reveal the existence of the easement.

CASE EXAMPLE

Sebastian leased land to Conley, who recorded the lease. The lease was for oil and gas exploration. Although the description in the lease was inaccurate, it did designate the land. Later Sebastian leased what he thought was adjoining land to Loeb. Part of the land leased to Loeb was the Conley parcel. Claiming that the record provided constructive notice of his interest, Conley sued to prevent Loeb from using the land. Both the lower court and an appellate court agreed that Loeb had constructive notice of Conley's interest and ordered Loeb to allow Conley access to the tract.

The appellate court stated as follows:

> The constructive notice furnished by a recorded instrument, insofar as the boundary of the land and every other material fact recited therein is concerned, is equally as conclusive as would be actual notice acquired by a personal examination of the recorded instrument, or actual notice acquired by or through other means. Every person must take notice of its contents to the same extent as if he had personal knowledge of every fact that it recites. This is the very purpose of our recording law. *Loeb v. Conley*, 160 Ky. 91, 169 S.W. 575 (1914).

In addition to notice of all items contained in the public records, prospective interest holders are also considered to have constructive notice of all taxes that attach to the property.

Types of Recording Statutes

Although all have a similar purpose, the recording statutes vary markedly from state to state. They are designed to give notice to parties who are considering acquiring an interest in land. Reliance on a warranty given in the deed is inadequate. The warranty gives the buyer the right to a lawsuit for damages but not to the land in which he or she is primarily interested. The two general types of recording statutes are **race-notice** and **notice**.

■ **Race-Notice Statutes.** *Statutes that provide that a subsequent buyer will prevail only if he or she has no notice of the prior transaction at the time of conveyance and he or she records first.*

Under these statutes the subsequent taker must get to the recorder's office before the predecessor does.

CASE EXAMPLE
Nagy conveys Laneacre to McCredy. Later, to acquire funds for his permanent relocation to South America, Nagy offers Laneacre to Brennan. Brennan does not know of the prior conveyance to McCredy, and the public record does not show that McCredy recorded his deed. Brennan decides to take the proffered conveyance and beats McCredy to the recorder's office.

Brennan would prevail if he recorded before McCredy *and* because he had no knowledge that Nagy had previously conveyed Laneacre to McCredy.

■ **Notice Statutes.** *Statutes that provide that the subsequent buyer prevails over all interested parties who have not recorded their interest at the time the buyer accepts the conveyance and pays consideration for the land without notice of the pre-existing conveyance.*

There is no *race* under these statutes. So long as the subsequent buyer takes without notice of the previous conveyance, he or she prevails over the previous conveyance. It is irrelevant that the first deed holder records thereafter or that the subsequent buyer never records.

It may seem unfair for the law to permit a grantor to make multiple conveyances of the same property. Theoretically, the grantor no longer owns the property after the initial conveyance and should be powerless to convey anything to another. This would be the case under the common law. Nevertheless, the impact of the recording statutes is to pry that title loose from nonrecording takers and to vest it in subsequent takers.

The recording statutes are chiefly geared to protect good-faith purchasers for value. Consequently, these statutes do not normally afford protection to persons who acquire the land through gift or inheritance. To attain the protection of the statutes, the purchaser must give consideration, that is, a value of some sort. The value need not be equal to the fair market value of the premises, but neither can it be nominal or merely recited in the deed without actual payment. It must be a real value. Why does the following case protect parties who inherited the land?

Roberts v. Estate of Pursley
Superior Court of Pennsylvania
718 A. 2d 837 (1998)

Background. In 1992, Roberts, the appellee, brought on action to quiet the title to parcels of land in Clinton County against the Estate of Pursley, the appellants. The parties can trace their titles back to 1854, but through different, conflicting chains of title. Though there was evidence of "ownership" being passed along over this period of time through wills and the like, no deed was properly recorded until 1964. In that year Milton and Mary Kelius purchased the disputed parcel and properly recorded the deed. In 1975, Roberts received the property through the wills of the Keliuses, and had a deed recorded. The predecessors of Pursley did not record their deeds until 1967. To further complicate matters, there was a flaw in the chain of title of Roberts due to an ineffective conveyance in 1901. Though disputing the title of Roberts at the time of the filing of this litigation, the appellants had had little or no involvement with the parcels prior to that time.

The litigation was prolonged and complex, but in this portion of it the trial judge found for the appellee, Roberts.

Decision. The Pennsylvania Superior Court affirmed the trial court's decision.

Judge Cirillo. Section 444 of the recording statute requires "all deeds made in the state to be acknowledged and recorded within ninety days." Deeds not conforming to this rule will be "adjudged fraudulent and void against any subsequent purchaser . . . for valid consideration."

The recording statute was intended to protect bona fide purchasers who give value for land. In order to qualify as a bona fide purchaser, the subsequent buyer must be without notice of a prior equitable interest.

If "legal title," within the Appellant's definition, were required for a subsequent purchaser to qualify as a bona fide purchaser, the recording statute would not further its intended goals. For instance, in the typical recording statute situation, a grantor sells land to a grantee who does not record the deed; then, a subsequent buyer purchases the same land from the first grantee. The subsequent grantee does not have "legal title" within the Appellant's definition because at the time the land was sold to him, the grantor did not have legal title to give such right. Yet, notwithstanding the fact that he does not have "legal title," he is a bona fide purchaser if at the time of the

continued on next page

sale he was without notice of an adverse interest and value was given for the purchase of the land. As evidenced here, imposing a requirement of "legal title" to the definition of a bona fide purchaser would nearly render the recording statute useless. We, therefore, find no merit in Appellant's argument.

Appellants' next contention is that Appellees cannot be protected under the recording statute because they inherited the disputed land parcel from their predecessors-in-interest, and have given nothing of value in return for title and are not in the position of bona fide purchasers. We extend protection to devisees and heirs who take from a bona fide purchaser. The purpose here is not to protect the heir or devisee, but to permit the bona fide purchaser to convey his land. Moreover, the application of this principle to heirs and devisees will further the policy of preventing the stagnation of property as well as the policies surrounding the bona fide purchaser concept. We are not, however, extending protection to heirs and devisees who take from one who has not acquired status as a bona fide purchaser. Extending such protection would not further the underlying purpose of the recording statute and the bona fide purchaser doctrine.

In the present case, the record indicates that Milton S. Kelius and Mary Kelius, Appellees' predecessors-in-interest, were bona fide purchasers for value without notice of Appellants' predecessors' claim. The record further indicates that, in 1964, the Keliuses recorded their deed in accordance with the Pennsylvania recording statute. In 1975, the parcel in dispute was devised to Appellees from the Kelius estate. At that time, Appellees properly recorded their interest. In accordance with the principle set forth above, Appellees acquired their interest subject to the protection afforded to their predecessors as bona fide purchasers. Because the Keliuses acquired title superior to that of Appellants' predecessors, Appellees have, therefore, acquired title superior to that of the Appellants.

Order affirmed.

If the appellants had little or no involvement with the disputed land prior to being sued by Roberts, why didn't Roberts "let sleeping dogs lie"?

■ THE RECORDING PROCESS

Although the name of the specific office and official will differ, deeds are recorded at a county office created for that purpose. The recorder will be authorized under state law to record deeds, mortgages, easements, contracts for sale and (in some states) leases, and any other transactions affecting the title to land. In addition, the recorder or some other county official will record notices of judgments, secured transactions, pending litigation, inheritance taxes, and other dealings that may also encumber the free transfer of land. Each document either conveys a part of the owner's property rights or creates an encumbrance or lien on the parcel.

CASE EXAMPLE

George sells the western half of Laneacre to Herman. In the deed of conveyance, George grants an easement to Herman to use George's driveway to get to and from the garage. To purchase the land, Herman borrows money from the bank and executes a mortgage for the western half of Laneacre to the bank to secure the loan. The deed conveys title to half of Laneacre and conveys an easement to Herman to use a part of the other half, and the mortgage to the bank is a lien on Herman's portion of Laneacre. Each of these documents is recorded to secure the rights of the party receiving an interest thereunder.

The early recordings under the recording statutes were handwritten, verbatim accounts of the deed or other instrument. Later these recordings were typed, and today they are in large measure photocopies of the original documents. The document presented for recording must be the original.

The recording process begins with the presentation of the instrument to the recorder, usually by the party seeking protection (for example, the buyer in a sales transaction). On payment of a recording fee and transfer taxes, the recorder stamps the instrument, showing the precise time it was filed with that office. Transfer taxes are imposed by the state, county, or local governments, and used for general revenue, or sometimes used for specific purposes, such as providing affordable housing or protecting open space. The instrument is later photocopied and entered into the deed books. These numbered books contain exact copies of all deeds ever filed in that county. Simultaneously, the names of the grantor and grantee are indexed in separate grantor and grantee index books, with a reference to the deed book number and page where a copy of the deed can be found. A similar procedure would be followed if the instrument were a mortgage, easement, or other document transferring an interest in the land.

Approximately ten states use a tract index that simplifies the title searching process. In addition to the grantor and grantee indexes, the tract index lists in a single place all the transactions that have occurred affecting the parcel concerning the searcher. Once the correct page is located, all deeds, mortgages, and other transactions are listed for the searcher's convenience. The title searcher can rely on this page (or pages) as containing all the relevant transactions affecting the concerned piece of property.

The act of recording in no way legitimizes an instrument. If a deed is forged or was never delivered, recording will not remove this impediment to its validity.

Chain of Title

■ *The recorded history of events that affect the title to a specific parcel of land, usually beginning with the original patent or grant.*

Documents filed at the recorder's office are within the **chain of title** if they concern the parcel and are recorded during the period in which each grantee has title to the parcel of land. If the title searcher were to begin the search anew today, the chain of title would begin with the present owner's deed (who is also the last grantee of record). That deed would contain a recital stating from whom the present grantee's seller got the parcel. Continuing the example above, the last recorded deed would have as grantor, Herman, to grantee, Isaac, and something like the following: "being all of the same premises conveyed on June 16, 1968, by George to Herman and being contained in Deed Book 202 at page 1121." Normally each deed in the chain of title contains a recital of this nature so that the searcher can trace the title back to the original patent or grant.

The attorney or other agent doing an original title search examines the grantor index from the day the present grantee got the parcel until the day the search is being done, to ascertain whether the present grantee conveyed any interest in the land to another. He or she follows the same procedure for each preceding grantee for the period of that grantee's ownership, as recited. Any conveyance in the grantor index during this time period must be checked to see whether it affects the concerned parcel. Similarly, the mortgagor index is examined to ensure that no mortgage is outstanding against the parcel. The county records must also be examined to determine whether there are any unsatisfied judgments, pending litigation, mechanics' liens, or secured transactions against the grantee. Each of these is an encumbrance on the land and normally must be satisfied prior to a buyer's acceptance of the deed.

If every transfer of property involved a title search going back to the original deed, title searches would be cumbersome and expensive. In many states the title is merely reviewed for transactions that have taken place since the last conveyance, inasmuch as the seller will supply his or her search for the previous title history.

Any transaction that is found within the chain of title is deemed to be constructively known by the buyer. Constructive notice is as valid a notice of the status of the parcel as that of which the buyer has personal knowledge. If a recorded transaction does not appear within the chain of title, however, the buyer is not charged with constructive notice of the facts contained therein.

CASE EXAMPLE

In 1984, George conveys to Herman, who does not record the deed. In 1985, George conveys the same parcel to Isaac, who records the deed. In 1986, Herman finally records his deed. Later that year, Isaac enters an agreement to sell the parcel to Jeremy. When Jeremy has a title search done, the deed from George to Herman is not in the chain of title. The title searcher does not examine the records for possible conveyances by George after 1985, when Isaac became the new owner. Because Jeremy is not charged with constructive notice of the deed to Herman, he takes the parcel free and clear of the prior deed to Herman. Herman has the right to sue George for damages but not for title to the land.

Some encumbrances on real estate do not appear in the chain of title, yet the buyer is charged with knowledge of them. These encumbrances include zoning laws, building restrictions, property taxes for the year of sale and subsequent years, and special assessments or taxes.

If the reconstruction of the chain of title reveals a gap or a flaw in the title, then the buyer is excused from the purchase agreement because the seller cannot deliver *marketable* or *unencumbered title*, for which the purchaser contracted. A *gap* occurs when the recorded documents do not indicate who owned the parcel during a given period. An example of a *flaw* in the title occurs when the buyer, in the purchase agreement, has been promised an unencumbered fee simple interest and a life estate is found outstanding in the title to the parcel. In either of these situations, it is said that there is a *cloud on the title*. A cloud on the title is created whenever doubt is created as to the validity of the grantor's title. The property is unmarketable so long as a cloud on the title exists. If the seller is willing, a *quiet title action* may be brought to get a judicial (court) ruling that the title is marketable. The seller joins as defendants all those parties who have a potential interest in the land. The plaintiff-seller requests that the court declare his or her title valid, thereby "quieting title" to the land. The buyer can then rely on the judicial assurances of good title and consummate the deal.

Acknowledgment

■ *A formal declaration by the person who executes an instrument that he or she is freely signing it; this signing is attested to by a public official, usually a notary public.*

The recorder does not pass judgment on the legitimacy of the instrument on recording it, nor does the fact of recording add any degree of validity to a document that is otherwise defective or void. Most states have, however, established some prerequisites that must be satisfied before a document is acceptable for recording. The chief requirement is that the deed or other instrument be *acknowledged*.

For instance, when preparing the deed, the seller of land may sign the deed and a separate **acknowledgment** before a notary public. The notary public then indicates in the acknowledgment that he or she has witnessed the seller's affirmation or signature. The witnessing of the signature by a disinterested public official gives reasonable assurance that the signature on the deed is that of the seller and not an impostor. Under the statutes, the deed is then acceptable for recording.

It should be noted that in most states the failure to have the deed acknowledged or to meet any other prerequisite for recording prevents the deed from being recorded and therefore serving as constructive notice to anyone. The rule seems to be overly technical and may be unfair because the subsequent purchaser doing a title search has notice of the conveyance and yet because of the mistake in the acknowledgment, can ignore it. As a result, some states have passed statutes to the effect that an unacknowledged or mistakenly acknowledged instrument will be notice to subsequent purchasers and to creditors.

The chief importance of the acknowledgment lies in the recording, not in the conveyancing itself. A deed need not be acknowledged to effectuate a conveyance because title will pass to the grantee on delivery and acceptance of the deed, whether it is acknowledged or not.

Mistakes in Recording

■ *Errors made by the recorder.*

The rule in most states is that a person who has properly presented an instrument for recording has satisfied his or her duty; the instrument will be constructive notice to a subsequent taker. The result is that a mistake made by the recorder initially falls on the future taker, even though that taker could not have discovered the instrument because of the mistake.

CASE EXAMPLE
Brownstein purchased a parcel of land from Peterson in 1951. In 1962, Brownstein conveyed a 20-foot drainage easement to the city. The city official presented the written easement for recording, but the recorder failed to enter Brownstein's name in the grantor index. In 1996, Brownstein conveyed the parcel to Jackson. Brownstein's conveyance to the city does not appear in the chain of title for the parcel. Jackson has no legal recourse against Brownstein or the city but would be able to recover against the recorder on that official's security bond.

A mistake by the recorder is a difficult dilemma for courts to resolve because neither the party presenting the instrument for recording nor the subsequent taker is at fault. A minority of courts, recognizing that the primary concern of the recording statutes is with good-faith purchasers for value, hold that the subsequent taker does have recourse against the grantor.

CASE EXAMPLE

Brownstein purchased a parcel of land from Peterson and presented the deed for recording. The recorder misplaced the deed and it was never recorded. Brownstein later enters a purchase agreement with Jackson in which he agrees to convey "good and marketable title" to him. When doing the title search, Jackson discovers that the deed by which Brownstein took title is missing. In some states Jackson would have a legal claim against Brownstein for breach of contract.

Regardless of which rule is adopted, the injured party has recourse against the recorder on his or her security bond.

Mistakes in the Instrument

■ *Errors made in the preparation of the instrument to be recorded.*

A mistake in the instrument recorded may affect the validity of the notice given. If the mistake is minor, it will not deter the instrument from being legal notice. For example, the grantor's name listed as Franc*is* Brown rather than Franc*es* Brown in a deed would be adequate notice to a third party. However, if the nature of the mistake is such that the instrument would no longer put the third-party searcher on notice to inquire further, the instrument will not be constructive notice. Thus, if the grantor's name is George Thomas but is typed in the deed as Thomas George, it will be listed in the grantor index under *G* for George and not *T* for Thomas. This deed will not be notice to a subsequent purchaser.

The following case illustrates a situation in which a failure of the grantees to record their deed did not cause them, or their successors in title, to lose their property interest. Why not? The case raises the issue of notice discussed earlier in the chapter.

Graham v. Lyons
Superior Court of Pennsylvania
546 A.2d 1129 (1988)

Background. In 1952, Paul and Helen Lyons delivered a deed conveying a parcel of land to Mr. and Mrs. Mitchell in exchange for $100. The deed was lost by the Mitchells and never recorded. In 1971, the Mitchells sold the land to Thomas and Laura Graham, who promptly recorded their deed. In 1968, before the Mitchells' conveyance to Grahams, the Lyons reconveyed the same parcel to their four sons. Many years later, the Grahams entered an agreement to sell the parcel, but during the course of the title search, the unrecorded deed was discovered. The Grahams sued the Lyons and their sons in a quiet title action to obtain a declaration from the court that their title was valid so that they could consummate the sale. The trial court decided in favor of the Grahams, and the Lyons appealed.

Decision. The Pennsylvania Superior Court affirmed the trial court judgment.

Judge Del Sole. Appellants (Lyons) who claim to be the rightful owners of the property in question, contend that the trial court erred when it failed to take into account the fact that Mr. and Mrs. Lyons had conveyed the subject property to William H. Lyons, Paul G. Lyons II, Lynn C. Lyons, and Samuel H. Lyons on October 28, 1968, the deed to which was recorded the next day. Appellants maintain that the Pennsylvania Recording Act protects their title since the conveyance was set down in writing and was recorded prior to the transfer of the property to appellees. (Grahams)

The argument advanced by Lyons must be dismissed since it is based on the faulty premise that the subject property was transferred in the 1968 conveyance. The deed conveying property from Mr. and Mrs. Lyons to their sons contains the following reservation:

Also, Excepting and Reserving five (5) campsites sold by Paul C. Lyons and Helen M. Lyons, his wife, to third parties totalling approximately eight (8) acres, more or less.

A title abstractor who testified at trial performed a title search and indicated that during his examination he discovered four recorded deeds transferring four different campsites. None of the four deeds consisted of a transferred campsite from Mr. and Mrs. Lyons to Mr. and Mrs. Mitchell. The trial court concluded that the unrecorded "lost" deed executed in 1952 to Mr. and Mrs. Mitchell was the fifth campsite which was "excepted and reserved" in the conveyance from Mr. and Mrs. Lyons to their sons. Although this conveyance was not recorded, the recording of a deed is not essential to its validity or to the transaction of title. The title to real estate may be passed by delivery of a deed without undertaking a recording since the recording is essential only to protect by constructive notice any subsequent purchasers, mortgagees and new judgment creditors. The question of whether Appellants had constructive notice that the property at issue was conveyed to the Mitchells is not at issue since Appellants' deed contains an exception which excludes this property from the description of the land transferred by the Lyons to their sons.

Since the property in question passed by means of a valid conveyance to Mr. and Mrs. Mitchell, who in turn transferred the property to Appellees (Grahams), and since the deed executed in 1968 from the Lyons to their sons excludes from its description the property at issue, the trial court properly ruled in favor of Appellees in this quiet title action.

Order affirmed.

Since the Mitchells did not record their deed, did they have good title?

Would title insurance discussed on page 429 have helped the Grahams in this case and saved them the trouble of litigating?

■ ASSURANCE OF TITLE

The average real estate buyer is not competent to determine on his or her own the status of the title to the parcel in question. Depending on the state, or often the local or county practice, the attorney hired by the buyer will have to provide evidence of the marketability of the title. This evidence of title may be provided by the lawyer's own research relating to the title. It is more often the case, however, that attorneys retain a title search firm or title insurance company to provide the necessary information. Specifically, evidence of title will be provided by abstract, by title insurance, or by certificate.

Abstract of Title

■ *A summary of all the recorded transactions, including deeds, mortgages, judgments, and the like, that affect the title to a specific parcel of land.*

The title searcher or abstractor will examine the chain of title, making a descriptive notation of all recorded transactions affecting the concerned parcel. Depending on local practice, the abstractor may be required to examine the title back to the original grant or only back to the preceding conveyance. The abstractor prepares for the party employing him or her a document—an *abstract*—that contains a description of the concerned parcel and a brief description in chronological order of all the instruments affecting the land that fall within the chain of title.

> **CASE EXAMPLE**
>
> The abstractor will examine the grantor index for the name George Lang for conveyances between the years 1994 and 2004, the period during which Lang was the record owner of Laneacre. Having noted the deed book pages of all such conveyances, the abstractor will look at the deeds to see whether they affect Laneacre in any way.

The abstractor similarly examines the mortgagor index and mortgage books for outstanding mortgages. He or she examines other books in search of easements, leases, judgments, mechanics' liens, secured transactions, tax liens, and pending litigation. A summary of each of these transactions is provided to the buyer or the buyer's attorney.

Attorney's Opinion. Based on professional judgment, the attorney states his or her opinion as to the condition of the title based on the facts revealed in the abstract. The abstractor makes no assertions as to the quality of the title but merely presents in the abstract the recorded events affecting the parcel. The attorney then examines the abstract and renders a professional judgment as to his or her opinion of title. The attorney does certify that all instruments pertinent to the parcel of land are included in the abstract. In large measure, the buyer can be expected to rely on this **attorney's opinion** of title. However, forged deeds or other errors in recording may well be undetected by the abstractor or attorney, and such imperfections may leave the buyer legally unprotected. Of course, if the abstractor or the attorney is negligent, the buyer would have a right to sue either or both for damages. A judgment for damages, however, is only as good as the ability of the judgment debtor to pay. If the attorney (judgment debtor) is financially sound, the buyer may recover the financial loss resulting from the attorney's professional error. If the attorney is not solvent, however, the money judgment may be uncollectible, and the buyer will not obtain financial satisfaction.

> **CASE EXAMPLE**
>
> Rite hired Pierson, an attorney, to represent him when he purchased Hilltop Acres from Jack Haney. Pierson performed the title search and provided Rite with an attorney's opinion assuring him that title was transferred to Haney. Mary Haney, Jack's sister, returned to town

and asserted an ownership interest in Hilltop Acres. The facts showed that their father left Hilltop Acres "to his children" and that Jack and Mary were his two children. Pierson had negligently failed to determine that Jack Haney, Rite's grantor, was not the only child. Rite may have to buy Mary's interest to get clear title but can then sue Pierson for damages because of his negligence in performing his professional duties. Recovery on the judgment by Rite will depend on the financial capacity of Pierson to pay.

Title Insurance

> ■ *A comprehensive indemnity contract that insures the titleholder against title defects and encumbrances that may exist at the time the policy is issued.*

To overcome the limitations arising from the methods just discussed, the practice of obtaining **title insurance** has arisen most everywhere. Title insurance has the advantage of insuring against loss caused by forged deeds and other undiscovered errors on the record. In the case of negligence it may also provide more financial security to the grantee-insured than would an individual attorney's opinion on the title. The title insurer pledges itself to defend—in court if necessary—the title of the insured and will pay for losses up to the maximum amount stated in the policy.

The title policy usually covers forged instruments, undisclosed heirs, misfiled documents, incorrect marital status, confusion over similarity of names, and mistaken legal interpretation of wills. Any of these defects will be defended by the title company.

Though title insurance does alleviate some of the shortcomings of the previous method, it is not a panacea. The title insurance company obtains an abstract of title for its review, and it excepts from its coverage all those defects discovered by the abstractor. In addition to discovered defects, the title policy usually excludes from coverage the rights of parties in possession, taxes and assessments not yet due or payable, zoning and other public regulations, and facts that would be revealed by a survey of the parcel. Many of these risks can be covered through policy endorsements for an additional fee. Also, title insurance only covers losses caused by events preceding the issuance date of the policy.

CASE EXAMPLE

Bloom purchased a title insurance policy when he obtained his parcel of land from Cedeno. Bloom can feel confident that if a deed in his chain of title described the grantor as single but his wife has suddenly been discovered, the insurer will pay off the wife up to the maximum policy amount. However, if the description of the parcel contained in the deed is unclear as to where the property line lies or the right of a neighbor to use a "common" driveway, his title policy will exclude these discovered defects from its coverage. Prior to the conveyance of the parcel, Bloom will have to decide whether he can live with these discovered defects.

The single-payment title policy will be required by the mortgagee for up to the amount of the loan. The mortgagee's policy does not protect the owner's equity in the property, the value above the mortgage amount. An owner's title policy should be obtained to cover the full value of the property at a relatively small additional cost. In some regions, the seller must pay for the insurance as part of the obligation to deliver good title to the buyer. In other areas, the buyer must absorb the cost. Also, it is advisable to have mechanic's lien coverage and an inflation guard. Coverage will continue until the titleholder or those heirs or devisees convey the property to another party. In short, courts have held that the title insurance coverage does not run with the land but ends when the interest of the insured terminates. Thus, a seller cannot transfer title insurance to a buyer.

Torrens Certificate

■ *A document issued under the Torrens system, a type of land title registration.*

In states where the Torrens system exists, it is not compulsory and exists along with the recording system previously described. The advantage of the system is that it eliminates the need for a title search, and the **Torrens certificate** shows the status of the title at any time.

The Torrens system can be used when a landowner applies in writing to the county court to have a title registered. A current title search is made and provided to the court, which holds a type of *quiet title action*. In this action, all parties who may have an interest in the parcel are notified and given a chance to be heard by the court. The purpose of the notice and hearing is to obtain assurance that all encumbrances to the title are known prior to issuance of a Torrens certificate. When the court is satisfied that the landowner is the titleholder and that all liens and encumbrances to that title have been revealed, it orders the certificate of title to the parcel to be registered.

Henceforth, the certificate of title will depict the exact state of the title. The original is filed with the recorder, and a copy goes to the owner. A party alleging to have an interest arising prior to the registration of the Torrens certificate will be precluded from attacking the present owner's or any subsequent owner's title unless his or her interest was recorded on the original certificate. To ensure that the Torrens certificate is always up to date, any conveyance, mortgage, lien, or other encumbrance on the parcel will not be valid until it is entered on the original certificate. Further, title does not pass until the registration takes place. If there is a defect of title, suit is usually against the state for the loss. A limited state fund is provided for such lawsuits.

As with the normal recording system, under the Torrens system it is usually necessary to go beyond the recorder's office (or the certificate) to determine whether there are unpaid taxes or special assessments, zoning and building restrictions, or federal court judgments that may affect the parcel.

For reasons not completely clear, the Torrens system has not been widely used. Perhaps the title searching apparatus already in place has successfully resisted the abolition of the title search. There is also the initial expense of having the title registered and the fact that the system is voluntary, both of which militate against its wide adoption. The Torrens system has been adopted to some degree by 15 states, but it does not seem to be spreading rapidly and is not likely to replace the present recording system in the foreseeable future.

Petition of Alchemedes/Brookwood
Minnesota Court of Appeals
546 N.W.2d 41 (1996)

Background. Beatrice Bell and Walter and Stella Kaluznick originally owned their apartments as condominiums. In 1985, the condominiums were converted to apartments. Bell and the Kaluznicks received leases with lifetime renewal options from the new owner, Brookwood Estates. The lease agreements were kept secret and not recorded in the certificate of title. The apartment complex is registered Torrens property.

In 1985, Brookwood granted a mortgage to Midwest Federal Savings & Loan Association (Midwest or Midwest Federal). The mortgage was registered on the Torrens title certificate, and applied to the whole apartment complex. The mortgage stated that "the premises are free from all encumbrances except as set forth on Exhibit B." One of the exceptions listed in Exhibit B was unrecorded leases, without further identification. Midwest went into receivership and the Resolution Trust Corporation (RTC) obtained the mortgage. Alchemedes purchased the mortgage from RTC. Later, Brookwood defaulted on the mortgage, and Alchemedes foreclosed. Subsequently, Alchemedes petitioned to have a new Torrens title certificate issued in its name. Bell and the Kaluznicks sought to have their leases memorialized in the new title certificate. The district court found that Midwest had actual and constructive notice of the leases, and that they should be recorded with priority over the foreclosed mortgage.

Decision. The Minnesota Court of Appeals reversed the District Court decision.

Judge Davies. Under the Torrens system, a party holding a certificate of title for property generally holds title free of all encumbrances except those memorialized on the certificate. This is to ensure that a person dealing with registered property "need look no further than the certificate of title for any transactions that might affect the land." The Minnesota Supreme Court has recognized one exception to the Torrens principle, that the Torrens Act does not do away with the effect of actual notice. Both parties agree that in determining whether there was actual notice, we examine the knowledge of Midwest Federal rather than that of Alchemedes. This case involves an apartment complex. Midwest Federal, therefore, knew that the property was subject to many leases. Midwest Federal undoubtedly made sure of that reality and even calculated the resulting cash flow. But, contrary to the district court ruling, that information did not provide notice of any long-term leases because leases of registered property for three years or more must be noted on the certificate. Thus, the district court erred in its conclusion that Midwest Federal's notice of "[u]nrecorded leases" constituted actual notice of the tenants' long-term leases. Midwest Federal could reasonably conclude that the leases of which it had actual notice and the leases referenced in Exhibit B were short-term leases. In addition, the Torrens law provides:

Neither the reference in a registered instrument to an unregistered instrument or interest nor the joinder in a registered instrument by a party or parties with no registered interest shall constitute notice, either actual or constructive, of an unregistered interest. This provision prevents the mortgage's reference to "unrecorded leases" from providing Midwest Federal with actual notice of any lease longer than three years. Midwest Federal's in-house counsel testified that at the time of the mortgage transaction, "no one knew about leases in excess of three years for this property." He also testified that if he had known of the leases, he "would not have allowed the loan to be closed. . . ." The record contains no contradictory evidence suggesting that Midwest Federal had actual knowledge of these specific leases.

continued on next page

Alchemedes argues that the district court erred in its determination that Midwest Federal had constructive notice of the unrecorded leases because the doctrine of constructive notice does not apply to Torrens property. In *Juran* [case], the court stated that the Torrens Act "abrogates the doctrine of constructive notice except as to matters noted on the certificate of title." Because the leases were not recorded on the certificate, the principle of constructive notice does not apply.

Alchemedes did not have actual notice that any lease was for a period beyond three years, neither from the reference to unrecorded leases in the mortgage nor on any other basis. The doctrine of constructive notice does not apply. The leases should not be memorialized on the new certificate.

Reversed.

Why did Brookwood Estates and the lessees keep the leases secret?

If you had your choice as a landowner, would you prefer the Torrens certificate or a typical recording statute? Why?

THE CHANGING LANDSCAPE

The process of recording deeds and other real estate instruments greatly facilitates the safe transfer of real property. The purchaser, having had a title search done, can feel secure that he or she owns the property purportedly conveyed and need not fear 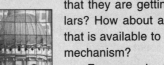 that other claimants will unexpectedly show up threatening his or her ownership. However, the information contained in a deed that is recorded describes the land only. There is seldom an indication in the deed of the development that has taken place on the land (e.g., house, factory, fences, barns). When land is developed, its predominant economic value is usually in the buildings and other structures on the land, not the land itself.

Buildings and other structures may look very similar to one another, but they may be very different in the value delivered to the purchaser. Those differences can run the gamut from the ability of the soil to permanently support the structures to the efficiency of the insulation in the building. These, and many other differentiating and value-delivering features, are not obvious to the naked eye or the inexperienced purchaser. Is it possible that we can create a recording system to better assure purchasers that they are getting fair value for their dollars? How about a computer-based system that is available to the public as the delivery mechanism?

For example, the buyer wants to know about the soundness of the structure and the operating costs of using the buildings. A ledger of information describing the soils on the site and their capacity for weight-bearing and stability, the rating of the insulation used, and whether single-, double-, or triple-paned, coated or uncoated windows were installed would help a prospective buyer. What materials were used in the construction? Are the indoor drywall and carpets free of toxins? Is the building very well ventilated? These questions are relevant in avoiding "sick building syndrome" and educating the building selection process.

Do you think that knowledge of these elements would add value to the real estate transfer process? What other elements should be recorded? Do you think that such a system might influence developers and builders to design and build higher quality structures? Do you think that such a system could be designed and operated conveniently and inexpensively?

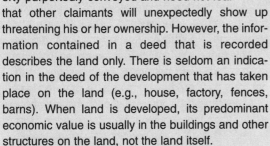

■ KEY TERMS

abstract of title 428	chain of title 423	race-notice statutes 420
acknowledgment 425	constructive notice 419	title insurance 429
actual notice 418	implied notice 419	Torrens certificate 430
attorney's opinion 428	notice statutes 420	

■ INTERNET RESOURCES

www.scottlawfirm.com/title.htm
(Overview of assurance of title)

www.co.ramsey.mn.us/et/docs/abstract.pdf
(Discusses abstract of title vs. torrens system)

www.mtgprofessor.com/title_insurance.htm
(Poses and answers questions about title insurance)

■ REVIEW AND DISCUSSION QUESTIONS

1. (a) Explain the purpose of recording statutes. (b) What must a plaintiff establish to be protected by this type of legislation?

2. Define *constructive notice* and explain how it might affect a person who purchases real estate.

3. What is the difference between a race-notice and a notice recording statute?

4. Describe the title searching process.

5. What are the prerequisites that must be met for an instrument to be recorded?

6. Explain why title insurance is often advisable even when the grantee receives a warranty deed.

7. What are the limitations in relying on title insurance for protection?

■ CASE PROBLEMS

1. Russell Ulrich claimed ownership of 38 acres of land through a chain of title dating back to a conveyance from the Loefler family to Ulrich's family in 1888. The Loeflers' claim to the land dates to an unrecorded deed prior to 1888. The Pennsylvania Game Commission (Commission) claims ownership to the same parcel through a conveyance from Handwerk. The origin of the problem is due apparently to a change in how land surveyors do surveys. The Commission argues that because the basis of Ulrich's claim is an unrecorded deed, his title is invalid. Does the Commission have a legitimate defense? *Commonwealth v. Ulrich*, 565 A.2d 858 (1989).

2. In an agreement dated March 9, 1964, Jaynes granted Lawing an option to purchase real property. The option was open for two calendar years. Before the option expired, Lawing took it up, but Jaynes refused to transfer the property. In April 1966, Lawing sued. Lawing's action was awaiting trial in March 1971 when Jaynes conveyed the property to McLean. When Lawing instituted his litigation in 1966, he filed a notice of his claim in the county registrar's office. The notice had been indexed improperly. In a suit by Lawing to have the deed from Jaynes to McLean declared void, what must McLean establish for a successful defense? *Lawing v. Jaynes*, 206 S.E.2d 162 (N.C. 1974).

3. Dowse sold land to Pender by warranty deed dated April 1, 1994. The deed was recorded on June 3, 1994. On May 29, 1994, Dowse fraudulently sold the same land to Petez. Petez recorded his deed on June 4, 1994. Petez had no actual knowledge of the deed to Pender. Between Pender and Petez, who has the superior claim in (a) a race-notice jurisdiction? (b) a notice jurisdiction? Explain.

4. Gagner purchased a parcel of land in 1969 after his attorney provided him with a certificate of title stating that the land was marketable and unencumbered by easements. In fact, a water district had previously been deeded a water pipe easement across the land, but the easement was not recorded until 1973. Although the easement was not in Gagner's chain of title, there were references in the chain indicating that the water district had certain rights in a larger parcel that included Gagner's land. The attorney relied on oral assurances from the seller, Crena, that these references did not affect the Gagner parcel. (a) Is the easement valid as to Gagner? (b) If it is valid, does Gagner have a remedy against the attorney? See *Gagner v. Kittery Water District*, 385 A.2d 206 (Me. 1978).

5. McDaniel discovered the existence of a utility easement along the eastern edge of his property that was not mentioned in his deed or noted in his title insurance policy. Because the title insurance policy purported to guarantee McDaniel fee simple ownership, he sued the title insurance company for the reduction in the fair market value of his land caused by the easement. The utility easement is recorded. Will McDaniel succeed? *McDaniel v. Lawyers' Title Guaranty Fund*, 327 So.2d 852 (Fla. 1976).

Closing the
Real Estate Transaction

■ CLOSING OR SETTLEMENT

■ *The final stage of the real estate purchase transaction during which the deed and the purchase money are exchanged.*

After the buyer and the seller sign a real estate purchase contract, they need time to prepare for the **closing**. The buyer ordinarily must search for financing, while the seller needs time to prepare evidence of title. Other documents need preparation as directed by the purchase contract, laws, and local customs. There is a deed to be drawn, inspection certificates to be obtained, expenses and income to be apportioned, and other preparatory matters to be completed. The interval between the signing and the closing date is intended to provide the necessary time to accomplish these matters.

The date of closing is normally specified in the contract. The date may be as early as two weeks from the date of the contract or as long as two months and occasionally even longer. One difficulty with a long interval is that lending institutions normally do not extend a loan commitment for more than 60 days without some additional cost to the borrower.

A postponement of the closing date does not result in a breach of the purchase contract, as long as the adjournment is reasonable. On the other hand, if the contract specifies that "time is of the essence," even a one-day postponement could be considered a breach for which the law would afford a remedy to the nonconsenting party (unless all parties agree in writing to the extension).

When the contract does not provide for a closing date, a reasonable time is implied. Because the purpose of the interval is to provide the necessary time to accomplish certain tasks, a reasonable time would be a period within which these tasks could ordinarily be completed.

The rights and obligations of the parties are defined by the contract. To a large extent, the contract governs the closing format. Local custom, to the extent that it does not contradict contractual provisions, also shapes the closing. Some localities, for example, customarily use the *escrow closing*, where the deed and purchase price are delivered to a third party, who is directed to close the transaction outside the presence of the parties. The escrow closing is the subject of Chapter 14. In other jurisdictions, the parties meet each other face to face at the closing. This conference type of closing is the subject of this chapter.

The object of the closing is to complete the transaction so that the purchaser is vested with title to the realty and the seller receives the purchase price. Various persons who may be responsible for the closing proceedings (other than the buyer and seller) include the real estate broker, attorney, and settlement clerk.

Broker

The real estate **broker** has an economic interest in the closing; at this stage, the real estate commission is paid by the broker's principal, who is normally the seller. For that reason, the broker usually participates in the closing preparation and is present at the closing.

State law varies concerning the broker's permissible role in the closing. Some states permit the broker actually to draw up legal documents, whereas other states relegate the broker to a more passive role. (See *Cultum v. Heritage House Realtors, Inc.*, on page 229.) Often the broker facilitates the closing by communicating with the lending institution, the purchaser, the seller, and/or their representatives on last-minute details. The broker may hand-deliver closing documents to the parties or to their legal representatives to minimize the risk of a breakdown in the critical last hours before closing. The broker may be responsible for reminding the parties what documents they need to bring to the closing. To the extent permitted by local law, the broker may even assist in the computation of prorations and the preparation of closing statements. In the absence of an attorney representing the seller, the broker will explain the closing process to the seller as it unravels, thus reducing anxiety and confusion at the closing table. (See Figure 20.1.)

Attorney

The **attorney's** role at the closing varies, depending on state law, the type of closing, and local custom. Although not every real estate closing involves attorney representation, when it does occur, purchasers are more apt to be represented than sellers. Perhaps this is because the lay seller is in a better position to recognize receipt of the full purchase price than the lay buyer is to ensure receipt of marketable title to the real estate.

At the ordinary closing, the attorney's role is routine, being confined to explaining the various documents to the client. Often, much of the attorney's preparation for the closing—examination of documents such as the deed, abstract or title insurance policy, mortgage, mortgage note, and closing statements—occurs in advance. If the attorney has

---

FIGURE 20.1	Closing

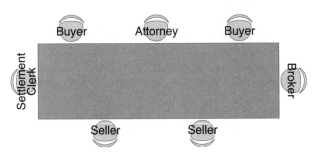

properly prepared in advance, the routine closing is normally smooth and may seem anti-climactic. An attorney has a more important role, however, in the rare closing where a difficult legal problem arises. Because no one can determine beforehand whether the closing will present an extraordinary problem, it is best for all parties to be represented by counsel. When parties are represented by attorneys, closings are likely to be smoother and less confusing; each party generally has confidence in his or her legal representative.

The seller is responsible for delivering a deed in conformity with the contract. For this reason, the seller must hire an attorney for the preparation of the deed or permit the lending institution's, or the settlement clerk's attorney to prepare it, in which event the fee will ordinarily be charged to the seller. The purchaser's attorney will examine the deed to ensure that the description of the property is accurate and that compliance with the necessary formalities for execution of the deed has occurred. The seller may be responsible, pursuant to the terms of the contract, for producing an abstract showing the history of the transactions that relate to the title of the property. An abstract may be prepared by the seller's attorney; in some jurisdictions professional abstractors who are not attorneys may perform this service. Based on the abstract, an attorney may be called on to provide a certificate or letter of opinion regarding the marketability of the title. An attorney who negligently renders a wrong opinion to the buyer will be liable for damages.

Settlement Clerk

◼ *The person who is designated to coordinate the execution of documents at the closing.*

The **settlement clerk** is responsible for ensuring that all documents are properly signed and delivered to the appropriate party. The settlement clerk may be an attorney, real estate broker, employee of the lending institution or title insurance company, or any other designated person. A few states require that the settlement clerk be licensed. The deed and other documents may require acknowledgment before a notary. Hence, it is advisable that the settlement clerk be a notary public. Otherwise, a notary public should be present.

Just how much a settlement clerk may do without violating statutes prohibiting the unauthorized practice of law has been the subject of legal disputes.

CASE EXAMPLE

First Escrow, Inc., does real estate closing services for banking institutions, title insurance companies, and others. It completes preprinted forms of documents, including deeds, notes, affidavits, settlement statements, IRS 1099 forms, and property inspection certificates. All forms are prepared or approved by a licensed attorney. It does not make any changes to the forms without an attorney's approval. It does fill in the blanks on the forms based upon information from the real estate contract, attorneys, title insurers, lenders, and the buyer and seller involved in the transaction. First Escrow charges a flat fee whether documents are prepared or not. A question arose as to whether this constituted the practice of law in violation of the prohibition to do so without a license.

The Supreme Court of Missouri reasoned that under the relevant statute in Missouri it did not constitute the unauthorized practice of law where the closing agent completes:

> Simple, standardized forms of documents, which, do not require the exercise of judgment or discretion, under the supervision of and as agents for a real estate broker, a mortgage lender, or a title insurer who has a direct financial interest in the transaction, or a licensed attorney who represents one of the parties in the transaction. See *In Re First Escrow, Inc.*, 840 S.W. 2d 839 (1992).

At the closing, a lot of paper changes hands. The closing is routine for the settlement clerk, who has undoubtedly performed numerous closings; for the buyers and sellers, however, it may be bewildering. Unless the settlement clerk is sensitive to that fact, the closing may be less than successful. Each document and transaction should be briefly explained to the parties, either by the clerk or by the attorney representing the client. Most problems that emerge at the closing can be remedied by thoughtfulness and a calm spirit.

■ PREPARATION FOR CLOSING

Preparation is the key to a successful real estate closing. Both the buyer and the seller need to take care of certain items preliminary to the closing. (See Table 20.1.) Failure to do so may result in a breakdown at the closing. The laws and customs that govern the buyer's and seller's conduct in preparation for closing do not vary greatly from state to state.

TABLE 20.1	Preparation for Closing
Buyer's Preparation	
Obtain Financing	
Examine Title	
Secure Hazard Insurance	
Determine Amount Needed at Closing	
Inspect Premises	
Seller's Preparation	
Obtain Evidence of Title	
Prepare Deed	
Remove Encumbrances	
Gather Utility Bills and Certificates	
Bring Sundry Certificates	

Buyer's Preparation

The buyer's preparation involves obtaining financing, examining the title, securing hazard insurance, calculating the amount needed at closing, and inspecting the premises.

Obtaining Financing. The buyer ordinarily lacks the available cash to pay for the property and must therefore search for a loan. The prudent purchaser selects a lending institution on the basis of the best buy available, comparing interest rates and other charges. A difference of one half of 1 percent in the interest rate may be very substantial over the life of the loan. A lending institution requires an application, a credit check, and an appraisal before it will approve a loan. Various federal laws related to the loan, discussed later in this chapter, place certain obligations on the lender.

The real estate contract is usually contingent on the buyer's obtaining a loan. If, after exercising good faith, the buyer is unable to obtain the necessary financing, the parties are discharged from any further obligations under the contract. The following case illustrates the concept of "good faith" in connection with seeking a loan.

Duncan v. Rossuck
Supreme Court of Alabama
621 So. 2d 1313 (Ala. 1993)

Background. The Duncans signed a contract to purchase a house from the Rossucks for $148,000. The contract stated in part: "This contract is subject to purchaser being able to obtain a suitable loan in the approximate amount of $118,400. The purchaser agrees to exert all reasonable effort and diligence to obtain such loan and to make application for such loan within 10 days." The Duncans sought financing at seven banking institutions, although they only applied in writing to one. Because they were experiencing difficulty in obtaining a loan, the Rossucks extended the closing date for 10 days. They also arranged for the Duncans to assume an existing mortgage on the property for about $79,000. A bank agreed to lend the Duncans the remaining amount on condition that they pledge additional property as security for the loan. The Duncans refused. The Rossucks then agreed to lend the Duncans the remaining amount on the same or more favorable terms as the bank. The Duncans would not agree. The Rossucks sued. The trial court found in favor of the Rossucks.

Decision. The Supreme Court of Alabama affirmed the trial court decision.

Justice Steagall. When the parties signed the contract, the Rossucks advised the Duncans that the term "suitable financing" meant that they must do their best to obtain the financing to purchase the real estate. The closing date was set for August 15, 1990.

In its order the trial court did not find any ambiguity in the term "suitable financing." The record shows that when the Duncans sought financing from the Bank . . . they specified their own terms in the written application and thus tailored their application to reflect what they considered to be a "suitable" loan. . . . The evidence contained in the record supports the trial court's conclusion that the term "suitable financing" was not ambiguous.

The Duncans next argue that, because the "suitable financing" provision was a contingency that did not come to fruition, their duty to perform under the contract never arose. This Court has previously held that a contract provision making the contract

continued on next page

subject to the procurement of a loan to finance the purchase price is a valid condition precedent to performance; however, the purchasers have the implied duty to attempt to obtain financing through a reasonable good faith effort. In this case, this duty was an express part of the contract.

In its order, the trial court specifically found that the suitable financing provision was a valid condition precedent to performance under the contract; however, the court found that the Rossucks offered such financing to the Duncans, and that the Duncans refused the financing solely because they wished to be relieved from performing under a contract that they had become disenchanted with. The Duncans' own testimony contained in the record fully supports the trial court's findings; thus, we find no merit in the buyer's argument on this point.

Affirmed.

What facts suggest that the Duncans failed to exercise good faith in obtaining a loan?

The institution that lends money to the buyer will require that the buyer sign a note promising repayment, plus a mortgage of the property, which secures repayment by giving the lender an interest in the property. At the closing, the lending institution will make sure that these instruments are signed by the buyer before disbursing the proceeds from the loan.

Examining Title. The contract may call for the seller to provide evidence of title in the form of an abstract, certificate of title, or title insurance, discussed more fully in Chapter 19. (In some jurisdictions it is the custom for the buyer to obtain and pay for evidence of title.) The buyer should insist on the evidence of title prior to closing so that an attorney may scrutinize the documents to ensure their reliability. An abstract should be up to date and contain no gaps in the chain of title. A certificate of title should be signed by an attorney. Title insurance policies should be checked to ascertain what encumbrances, if any, are excluded from protection. These exclusions may draw attention to title problems.

The purchaser is entitled to a marketable title in absence of a provision in the contract to the contrary. Marketable title is one for which a reasonable, prudent purchaser would be willing to accept and pay fair value. A marketable title is free from objections or encumbrances that would significantly interrupt the owner's peaceful enjoyment and control of the land or impair its economic value. To be marketable, it is not necessary that the title be free from every possible encumbrance or suspicion of encumbrance. It need only be free of a reasonable possibility of contentious litigation. Nobody wants to purchase a lawsuit, and, indeed, the law will not require a person to do so.

A defect that renders a title unmarketable may be in the chain of title. (See Chapter 19.) It may be discovered, for example, in tracing the title of a parcel of land, that the spouse of a grantor failed to sign the deed releasing dower. Or probate records may reveal that a previous grantor was incompetent at the time of transfer. A break in the chain of title may result from an inability to find a record of a previous owner ever having conveyed the property to a grantee.

The title may be rendered unmarketable because of an encumbrance on the property. An encumbrance is a charge on realty that impairs the use of the land, depreciates its value, or impedes its transfer. Liens, mortgages, easements, leases, tenancies, covenants, significant encroachments, and building restrictions are examples of encumbrances. Slight encumbrances that do not interfere with the use and enjoyment of the premises do not render a title unmarketable. A two-inch encroachment over a setback line is an example of a slight encroachment. Ordinary zoning and building code regulations do not render a title unmarketable. Nevertheless, a violation of either is deemed an encumbrance that does render the title unmarketable.

When the evidence of title is examined by the purchaser before closing, objections may be raised with the seller to be remedied before closing. If no time limitation is stated within the contract, the seller is entitled to a reasonable time to cure any defect. In some contracts the buyer possesses the specific right to cure the title and charge the cost to the seller. Under such a provision, the buyer may cure a defect out of the proceeds of the purchase price. If the defects cannot be remedied, or are not remedied, the purchaser may refuse title and sue the seller for breach of the contract.

Purchase contracts commonly require that the seller convey a title free of all encumbrances except "deed restrictions and easements of record." The purchaser should not sign such a contract until he or she knows what restrictions and easements, if any, are of record and is satisfied that they are immaterial. Otherwise, the purchaser may find out too late that the encumbrances excepted are of such a nature as to significantly reduce the property's value.

If the contract does not require that the seller provide evidence of title, the purchaser will undoubtedly desire to obtain such evidence. Obtaining that assurance before the closing is always better than winding up in a costly lawsuit because of title defects discovered later.

The contract may provide that the purchaser takes the property subject to tenants' rights: tenants are living on the premises, and the purchaser is required to honor their leases. Of course, the purchaser should examine the leases prior to signing the contract or require that the details of the leases be specified in the contract.

The purchaser should make sure that the seller prepares an assignment of the leases in the purchaser's favor and a letter notifying the tenants of the new ownership. At closing, the seller can sign the assignment and the tenants' letter, which can be delivered to the tenants along with a notice of where to send future rental payments.

Securing Hazard Insurance. It is important for the purchaser to secure hazard coverage on the property, well in advance of the closing date, to take effect on the day of closing. In fact, the mortgagee requires proof of coverage at the closing and will specify what type of evidence of coverage the purchaser needs to supply. Some mortgagees desire a copy of the policy; others require only a letter or binder evidencing coverage. Most mortgage instruments include a clause requiring that the mortgagor keep the premises insured in an amount at least equal to the balance due on the mortgage. Failure to do so constitutes a default. This failure is usually discovered when the insurance carrier notifies the mortgagee of a discontinuance of insurance coverage because of nonpayment, or otherwise.

Determining Amount Needed at Closing. The seller is entitled to the purchase price at closing, plus or minus any appropriate adjustments for conveyance fees, apportionment of taxes, insurance, and other proratable expenses. The purchaser usually pays closing costs, which include the loan origination fee, appraisal charges, the credit report fee, and other charges connected with the loan. Other miscellaneous fees for surveys, preparation of documents, and recording costs may be payable by the purchaser at closing. In addition, the lending institution may require that the purchaser deposit an amount for taxes and insurance into an escrow account. Normally, the settlement clerk collects one check from the purchaser and then writes checks for payments to the seller, seller's mortgagee, seller's broker, and any other parties entitled to funds. Determining the amount that the purchaser needs to bring to the closing necessitates a calculation that takes all of these factors into consideration. The lender should determine the amount in advance and communicate it to the purchaser in time for the purchaser to obtain the money needed. If a lending institution is not involved, either the real estate agent or the attorney for the purchaser can calculate the amount. In any event, the purchaser needs to review the amounts and calculations and be satisfied that they are accurate. The HUD Settlement Statement required in most transactions, and discussed later in this chapter, specifies the amount that the buyer needs to bring to the closing.

The purchaser needs to know what type of payment is acceptable; cashier's check, certified check, or money order is the customary form of payment. When the purchaser is a trusted customer of the financial institution handling the closing, the institution might accept a personal check drawn on that institution and then issue its own check to the seller.

Inspecting Premises. The real estate contract may afford the purchaser the right to inspect the premises prior to the closing. If so, the purchaser should arrange for an inspection to ensure that the condition of the premises is as stated in the contract and that the seller has made all repairs agreed on. In addition, the premises should be searched for zoning and building code violations, potential mechanics' liens, or any other encumbrances. Most buyers prefer that the inspection be near the closing date. If an inspection that is too near the closing date reveals objectionable defects, however, there may not be sufficient time before closing for the seller to remedy the problems. In absence of specific language in the contract granting the buyer the right to inspect, the buyer enjoys no such right. However, as a practical matter, the seller would not normally deny the buyer a preclosing inspection. In fact, it is not uncommon for the purchaser to have an expert do a full house inspection shortly after the contract is signed.

The purchaser may desire a survey, the contract may call for it, or the lender may require it. A surveyor or an engineer must be contracted to perform the task. Sometimes surveys raise questions concerning encumbrances.

Seller's Preparation

The seller's preparation involves obtaining evidence of title, preparing the deed, removing encumbrances, gathering utility bills and receipts, and bringing sundry certificates to the closing.

Obtaining Evidence of Title. The contract may require that the seller supply the buyer with the evidence of title in the form of an abstract or title insurance. The seller may have received an abstract on the property from the previous seller. In such an event, the seller must call on an attorney or abstractor to update it. If the contract calls for title insurance, the seller must select a title insurance company from which to purchase a policy.

Preparing the Deed. In most states, the preparation of the deed is the seller's obligation. Even if the seller is not represented by an attorney at the closing, the seller must hire an attorney or authorize someone else to employ an attorney to draw the deed. The basic content of the deed is prescribed by the purchase contract, state law, and local custom. Normally, the deed is signed at the closing. In the event the seller or anyone else who must sign the deed cannot be present at the closing, it must be properly executed beforehand.

Removing Encumbrances. The title search or inspection of the premises may reveal objectionable liens or other encumbrances not excepted in the contract, such as unrecorded easements, encroachments, or building code violations. Unless these encumbrances are removed, the closing is in danger of breaking down. The seller will ordinarily have an opportunity to remove any encumbrances. In the event the seller removes an encumbrance prior to closing, evidence of this removal should be produced at closing. The seller should obtain satisfaction of judgments, affidavits evidencing payment to laborers, or any other appropriate documents evidencing removal of the encumbrance. Sometimes the encumbrance is removed at closing when the seller deposits an amount of money necessary to discharge the encumbrance or authorizes a deduction for that purpose from the proceeds of the sale.

CASE EXAMPLE

Lone Star Development Corporation entered into a contract with Michael Miller and David Cross to sell certain realty in Pueblo County, Colorado, for $588,000. One thousand dollars was paid at the time of the agreement, and the remaining amount was to be paid at the closing on September 16, at which time Lone Star was to deliver a warranty deed and furnish a marketable title. There was an unpaid lien on the property in the amount of $479,756.71, of which all parties were aware. Lone Star intended to satisfy the lien out of the proceeds of the purchase price. Miller and Cross refused to tender the purchase price, maintaining that the unsatisfied lien rendered the title to the property unmarketable. Lone Star sued Miller and Cross for damages for breach of contract. The court held in favor of Lone Star and said that "a lien on real property which is going to be paid off from the proceeds of the sale of the property is not to be regarded as failure or inability to furnish a marketable title." *Lone Star Development Corp. v. Miller*, 564 F.2d 921 (10th Cir. 1977).

The property may be encumbered by an existing mortgage, a fact that will be revealed by a search of the title. The exact amount due on the mortgage as of the date of closing must be ascertained so that it may be satisfied out of the purchase price at closing. The seller should secure a statement from the mortgagee listing the outstanding balance due as of that date and the daily interest, in the event the payment is received later than the closing date. The institution handling the closing often takes care of securing this statement. The statement is produced at closing; the appropriate amount is deducted from the purchase price and sent to the seller's mortgagee.

Sometimes objections to title may be cured by the use of a quitclaim deed. A quitclaim deed has the effect of conveying to the grantee any interest the grantor has in the property. For example, a title search may reveal that a prior conveyance in the seller's chain of title was the subject of an incorrect legal description, which created a title defect. The defect may be cured by the previous grantor signing a quitclaim deed with the correct description in favor of the seller. Sworn statements verifying facts that satisfy the purchaser's and mortgagee's objections, as in the affidavit shown in Figure 20.2, are normally required and sufficient.

Gathering Utility Bills and Receipts. The seller should gather and bring to the closing, if requested, unpaid water, sewage, and other utility bills and receipts. Water and sewage charges are usually minimal, but they often cause the biggest problem and concern. Water companies read the water meter at intervals, and the exact amount owing at date of closing may be difficult to ascertain. Some homeowners elect to pay a standard monthly charge that is adjusted at the end of the year, making it difficult to determine the accrued charges or credits.

Some jurisdictions permit the imposition of a lien on property for unpaid water or sewer charges. Others treat them as a personal debt that does not run with the property, in which case judgment against the debtor would not encumber the property. Nonetheless, water companies do have the power to cut off one of life's necessities, and no new homeowner wants to litigate this issue.

Normally, the seller can arrange for a meter reading at or near closing. Based on an experience factor, the parties may agree to an amount at closing. In such a case, the seller should produce prior bills so that an experience factor may be derived. If all else fails, a sufficient amount to cover the seller's water bill for the interval may be escrowed at closing. The same principles hold for gas, electric, and other utilities. The seller should coordinate the turnoff date for the utilities; and the buyer should establish the utilities in his/her name at the appropriate time.

The contract usually calls for an apportionment of taxes as of the date of the closing. Ordinarily real property taxes are due at least twice a year. If the closing occurs on any date other than the dates taxes are payable, or if tax payments are for previous time periods, it is necessary to apportion the tax chargeable to the seller and the buyer. The seller may be required at the closing to produce receipts evidencing payment of taxes.

Bringing Sundry Certificates. The real estate purchase contract may require that the seller produce at closing a termite inspection certificate signed by a termite control inspector certifying that the premises are free from wood-destroying insects and damage from those insects. The contract may additionally call for a certificate from a gas company stating that the gas lines are free from leakage. Heating, plumbing, electrical, sewerage, or any other system may be the subject of required certificates showing the systems to be in good working order and free from defects. The seller should be prepared to produce the appropriate certificates at closing.

■ ACTION AT THE CLOSING

The place of the closing is controlled by local custom. Commonly the closing is conducted at the office of the lending institution where the purchaser has obtained financing to purchase the property. Other possible places of closing include an

FIGURE 20.2 Affidavit of Title

State of Ohio
County of Hamilton

Rod Ross, being first duly sworn, on May 1, 2006, deposes and says that:

1. He resides at 6415 Stover Avenue, in the City of Cincinnati, County of Hamilton, State of Ohio, and has resided at such place for approximately 10 years; he is a citizen of the United States, over the age of 18 years; he is the seller named in the contract of sale dated March 10, 1998, with Bert Haas as purchaser, and is the owner of the real property therein described.

2. He has been such owner since on or about July 1996, having acquired the same from Harry Blythe by deed; ever since his acquisition affiant has been in peaceful and undisturbed possession of such real property and neither his possession nor his title thereto has been disputed or denied by anyone.

3. Affiant's predecessor in interest was in peaceful and undisturbed ownership and possession of the same real property for approximately eight years prior to conveyance to affiant.

4. No use, tenancy exchange or occupancy of such real property or any part thereof has been such as to give rise to any claim of title or interest by adverse possession.

5. All taxes and assessments levied against the property have been paid when due, and such property is free and clear of any tax lien except for current taxes not yet due or delinquent.

6. The real property is free of any encumbrance by mortgage, deed of trust, or otherwise except restrictive covenants specified in the deed.

7. Plaintiff has not suffered any judgment or decree in any court and no judgment lien has ever attached against such property during affiant's ownership thereof, or during the ownership of affiant's predecessor in interest, to the best of affiant's knowledge and belief.

8. No lien for unpaid income taxes has been filed or is outstanding against the property.

9. No laborer has worked on the premises, nor has anyone supplied materials used on the premises who remains unpaid.

10. Affiant is not married.

11. In acquiring title to the real property described in the contract of sale, and in all subsequent transactions relating to the property, affiant has been designated and described only by the name subscribed hereto.

12. The reason for making this affidavit is to induce the purchaser named in the contract of sale to accept title to the real property therein described and pay the agreed purchase price therefor; the affidavit is made with the intent and understanding that each statement contained herein shall be relied upon.

_____   _____
Witness   Rod Ross, Affiant

_____
Witness

         Affirmed by Rod Ross, known to me this 1st day of May, 2006.

_____
Notary Public

attorney's office or the office of the real estate broker, title insurance company, or seller's mortgagee.

Both seller and buyer have responsibilities at the closing. Each is discussed below.

Seller's Actions

At the closing, the seller tenders the deed and provides evidence of title, if required. The seller is obligated to tender the deed to the buyer or to the settlement clerk for delivery to the buyer. The buyer should carefully check the deed to make sure its specifications are in accord with the contract. The deed should be of the type the grantor agreed to give. Any encumbrances that are excepted in the deed should be compared with the contract to ascertain whether they are found there. The description should be double-checked against the description contained in the survey, in the prior deed of conveyance, or another reliable source. The names of the grantor(s) and grantee(s) should be checked for accuracy. Even a minor misspelling of a name may cause future problems that will take time and money to remedy. Particular attention should be directed to the form of the execution to ensure conformity with state law. If, for example, the state law requires that the grantor subscribe the deed by signing an alphabetical signature, then a mark of the grantor should not be accepted. If the state law requires that two witnesses sign in the presence of each other, a deed otherwise witnessed is unacceptable. If the state law requires acknowledgment before a notary, the notary seal and notary commission expiration must appear on the deed.

The seller may be required to provide evidence of title in the form of an abstract or attorney's opinion, sometimes called a *certificate of title*, or title insurance, discussed in Chapter 19. Judgments or other encumbrances may intervene between the date of the abstract or attorney's opinion and the date of closing. For that reason, it is most advisable for the purchaser to make a final search of the title down to the moment of closing. Such a search is normally coordinated by the lending company or the title insurance company. Another way to protect the buyer who is unable to make a final search is to close in escrow, which is the subject of Chapter 14. Under this closing procedure, the settlement clerk or other escrow agent holds the executed deed and the purchase price pending a final check of the title. On notification by the buyer or buyer's attorney that the title is in order, the deed is transferred to the buyer and the purchase price to the seller. Sometimes the seller will be required to give the buyer an **affidavit of title** (as shown in Figure 20.2), which covers objections that might not appear in the title search.

Purchaser's Actions

At closing, the purchaser is obligated to tender the purchase price to the seller. Normally, in absence of an excuse by the seller, the purchase price must be produced and offered to the seller. It is normally not a sufficient tender for the purchaser to appear at the closing and maintain that the purchase money is available. The purchaser must actually make a show of the money with the intent to deliver it to the seller. This is not ordinary if the tender would be futile, for example, should the seller not appear at the closing.

Payment is usually made by some form of check, usually a cashier's or official check. However, whatever medium the contract calls for must be honored.

CASE EXAMPLE

Benjamin Chertok entered into a contract to purchase realty from Aroosiag Kassabian. Chertok made a deposit and agreed to pay the remainder in cash at the closing. At closing Chertok tendered a third person's certified check to Kassabian. Kassabian requested that he cash the check, and Chertok refused. After Kassabian refused to tender the deed, Chertok sought a return of his deposit. The court held that Chertok's tender was not the equivalent of payment in cash, and consequently he was in breach and not entitled to a return of his deposit. *Chertok v. Kassabian*, 255 Mass. 265, 151 N.E. 108 (1926).

Lending institutions charge closing costs, normally computed as a percentage of the amount borrowed. Closing costs are charged by the lending institution to cover the cost of services performed in connection with the loan and for servicing the loan. Closing costs vary among lending institutions.

If the buyer is financing the purchase through a new loan, the lender supplies a mortgage and a note for the borrower to sign at closing. Any existing mortgage on the property will be satisfied out of the purchase price, and a satisfaction of mortgage signed by the seller's lender will ultimately be recorded and sent to the seller.

In reality, most closings involve two distinct but related transactions. First, the sale of the property is closed between the seller and the buyer, with the seller receiving the purchase price and the buyer the deed. Second, the loan extended by the lending institution is closed between the lender and the borrower (buyer), with the borrower receiving the proceeds of the loan (which are used to pay the seller) and the lender receiving a note and mortgage from the borrower securing repayment of the loan. After the closing, the seller pays off the old mortgage and the seller's lending institution cancels the old mortgage. These transactions are illustrated in Figure 20.3.

■ REAL ESTATE SETTLEMENT PROCEDURES ACT (RESPA)

■ *A federal law that requires lending institutions to disclose certain information to purchasers of residential real estate and that prohibits those institutions from engaging in specified activities.*

A borrower who seeks a mortgage loan needs full information from lending institutions to select a lender prudently. RESPA requires that the lending institution make certain disclosures designed to help the borrower make informed judgments. Generally, RESPA is applicable to first mortgage loans made for the purchase of residential real estate. Residential real estate includes one-family to four-family properties. Cooperatives, condominiums, and mobile home lots can qualify as residential real estate. The act applies only to purchases where a lender (other than the seller) takes a purchase-money mortgage to secure the loan. A purchase-money mortgage in which the seller takes a mortgage back to secure the unpaid purchase price is not covered by RESPA. The requirements of RESPA are applicable only to lenders involved

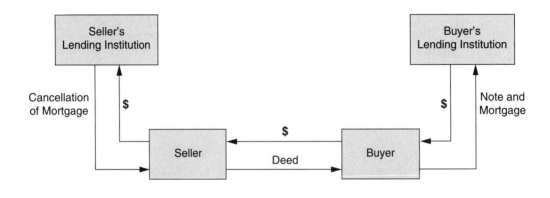

FIGURE 20.3   Transactions Involved in a Real Estate Closing

in a "federally related mortgage loan." The definition of *federally related* is very broad and includes any lending institution whose deposits are federally insured or regulated.

Settlement Costs Booklet

RESPA is administered by the Department of Housing and Urban Development (HUD). (See *www.hud.gov/offices/hsg/sfh/res/respa_hm.cfm* for more information.) HUD has prepared a **settlement costs booklet**. Every lender is required to provide an applicant for a mortgage loan with a copy of this booklet on the day of the loan application or, failing that, to deposit it in the mail to the applicant within three business days of the application. The booklet contains information about the real estate purchase process, including negotiating a sales contract and home loan financing. Under the heading "Selecting the Lender," the booklet suggests certain inquiries a borrower should make to compare lenders. For example:

■ Am I required to carry life or disability insurance? Must I obtain it from a particular company?

■ Is there a late payment charge? How much? How late may the payment be before the charge is imposed?

■ If I wish to pay off the loan in advance of maturity, must I pay a prepayment penalty? How much? If so, for how long a period will it apply?

■ Will the lender release me from personal liability if my loan is assumed by someone else when I sell my house?

■ If I sell the house and the buyer assumes the loan, will the lender have the right to charge an assumption fee, raise the rate of interest, or require payment in full of the mortgage?

■ Will I be required to pay monies into a special reserve account to cover taxes or insurance? If so, how large a deposit will be required at the closing of the sale?

In addition, the booklet contains information regarding homebuyers' rights and obligations, settlement services, and escrow accounts, as well as a sample work sheet to calculate the settlement costs.

Good-Faith Estimate

Another RESPA requirement is that the lender must provide the borrower with a good-faith estimate of settlement charges at the time of the application. These charges may be expressed as a range. A lender who fails to provide the required information on the date must deposit the information in the mail within three business days of the application. The good-faith estimates include the breakdown of the costs of settlement charges rendered by the mortgagee, for example, loan origination fee, credit report fee, appraiser's fees, title search charges, attorney fees, surveys, and document preparation. The complete schedule of all settlement charges is contained in Section L of the Uniform Settlement Statement. (See Figure 20.4.) The good-faith estimate does not have to include prepaid hazard insurance premiums or reserves deposited with the lender, such as escrow for taxes and insurance, because this information is not usually available to lenders at the application stage. Although the estimates must be made in good faith, they are subject to change as the market alters the costs of the various settlement charges.

Inspection of Uniform Settlement Statement

A closing or settlement statement is normally prepared by the settlement clerk handling the closing. The settlement statement (see Figure 20.4) consists of a summary of the buyer's (borrower's) and the seller's transactions, broken down into various categories. For some items it may be necessary to apportion income and expenses between the parties. For example, assume that the seller has paid the real estate taxes for six months in advance. Credit should be given to the seller for the portion paid that covers any period after closing. Apportionment of the taxes ensures that each person bears the expense only for the months that person had use of the premises. Other expenses often apportioned include water and sewer assessments, fuel, and insurance. Rental income may also be adjusted for unearned rentals received by the seller in advance.

RESPA requires that a lender permit the borrower a right to inspect the **Uniform Settlement Statement** (USS) one day before closing. The USS is a form settlement statement that contains a summary of the borrower's and seller's transactions and an itemization of the settlement charges as allocated to the borrower and seller. In the event that this information is unavailable the day before closing, the lender is relieved of the responsibility. In this case, the completed statement must be given to the buyer no later than the closing. This requirement may be waived by the buyer, but in the event of such waiver the USS must be mailed at the earliest practical date. Where there is a closing

FIGURE 20.4   HUD Settlement Statement

A.   **Settlement Statement**

U.S. Department of Housing and Urban Development

OMB Approval No. 2502-0265

B. Type of Loan

1. ☐ FHA   2. ☐ FmHA   3. ☐ Conv. Unins.
4. ☐ VA   5. ☐ Conv. Ins.

6. File Number: 7. Loan Number: 8. Mortgage Insurance Case Number:

C. Note: This form is furnished to give you a statement of actual settlement costs. Amounts paid to and by the settlement agent are shown. Items marked (p.o.c.) were paid outside the closing; they are shown here for informational purposes and are not included in the totals.

D. Name & Address of Borrower: E. Name & Address of Seller: F. Name & Address of Lender:

G. Property Location:

H. Settlement Agent:

Place of Settlement: I. Settlement Date:

J. Summary of Borrower's Transaction		
100. Gross Amount Due From Borrower		
101. Contract sales price		
102. Personal property		
103. Settlement charges to borrower (line 1400)		
104.		
105.		
Adjustments for items paid by seller in advance		
106. City/town taxes	to	
107. County taxes	to	
108. Assessments	to	
109.		
110.		
111.		
112.		
120. Gross Amount Due From Borrower		
200. Amounts Paid By Or In Behalf Of Borrower		
201. Deposit or earnest money		
202. Principal amount of new loan(s)		
203. Existing loan(s) taken subject to		

K. Summary of Seller's Transaction		
400. Gross Amount Due To Seller		
401. Contract sales price		
402. Personal property		
403.		
404.		
405.		
Adjustments for items paid by seller in advance		
406. City/town taxes	to	
407. County taxes	to	
408. Assessments	to	
409.		
410.		
411.		
412.		
420. Gross Amount Due To Seller		
500. Reductions In Amount Due To Seller		
501. Excess deposit (see instructions)		
502. Settlement charges to seller (line 1400)		
503. Existing loan(s) taken subject to		

| FIGURE 20.4 | HUD Settlement Statement *(cont'd)* |

202. Principal amount of new loan(s)	502. Settlement charges to seller (line 1400)
203. Existing loan(s) taken subject to	503. Existing loan(s) taken subject to
204.	504. Payoff of first mortgage loan
205.	505. Payoff of second mortgage loan
206.	506.
207.	507.
208.	508.
209.	509.
Adjustments for items unpaid by seller	**Adjustments for items unpaid by seller**
210. City/town taxes to	510. City/town taxes to
211. County taxes to	511. County taxes to
212. Assessments to	512. Assessments to
213.	513.
214.	514.
215.	515.
216.	516.
217.	517.
218.	518.
219.	519.
220. Total Paid By/For Borrower	**520. Total Reduction Amount Due Seller**
300. Cash At Settlement From/To Borrower	**600. Cash At Settlement To/From Seller**
301. Gross Amount due from borrower (line 120)	601. Gross amount due to seller (line 420)
302. Less amounts paid by/for borrower (line 220) ( )	602. Less reductions in amt. due seller (line 520) ( )
303. Cash ☐ From ☐ To Borrower	**603. Cash** ☐ To ☐ From Seller

Section 5 of the Real Estate Settlement Procedures Act (RESPA) requires the following: ✳HUD must develop a Special Information Booklet to help persons borrowing money to finance the purchase of residential real estate to better understand the nature and costs of real estate settlement services; ✳ Each lender must provide the booklet to all applicants from whom it receives or for whom it prepares a written application to borrow money to finance the purchase of residential real estate; ✳Lenders must prepare and distribute with the Booklet a Good Faith Estimate of the settlement costs that the borrower is likely to incur in connection with the settlement. These disclosures are manadatory.

Section 4(a) of RESPA mandates that HUD develop and prescribe this standard form to be used at the time of loan settlement to provide full disclosure of all charges imposed upon the borrower and seller. These are third party disclosures that are designed to provide the borrower with pertinent information during the settlement process in order to be a better shopper.

The Public Reporting Burden for this collection of information is estimated to average one hour per response, including the time for reviewing instructions, searching existing data sources, gathering and maintaining the data needed, and completing and reviewing the collection of information.

This agency may not collect this information, and you are not required to complete this form, unless it displays a currently valid OMB control number.

The information requested does not lend itself to confidentiality.

FIGURE 20.4   HUD Settlement Statement *(cont'd)*

L. Settlement Charges

		Paid From Borrowers Funds at Settlement	Paid From Seller's Funds at Settlement
700. Total Sales/Broker's Commission based on price $ @ % =			
Division of Commission (line 700) as follows:			
701. $	t	o	
702. $	t	o	
703. Commission paid at Settlement			
704.			
800. Items Payable In Connection With Loan			
801. Loan Origination Fee	%		
802. Loan Discount	%		
803. Appraisal Fee	to		
804. Credit Report	to		
805. Lender's Inspection Fee			
806. Mortgage Insurance Application Fee to			
807. Assumption Fee			
808.			
809.			
810.			
811.			
900. Items Required By Lender To Be Paid In Advance			
901. Interest from to @$ /day			
902. Mortgage Insurance Premium for months to			
903. Hazard Insurance Premium for years to			
904. years to			
905.			
1000. Reserves Deposited With Lender			
1001. Hazard insurance	months @$ per month		
1002. Mortgage insurance	months @$ per month		
1003. City property taxes	months @$ per month		
1004. County property taxes	months @$ per month		
1005. Annual assessments	months @$ per month		
1006.	months @$ per month		
1007.	months @$ per month		
1008.	months @$ per month		
1100. Title Charges			
1101. Settlement or closing fee	to		
1102. Abstract or title search	to		
1103. Title examination	to		
1104. Title insurance binder	to		
1105. Document preparation	to		
1106. Notary fees	to		
1107. Attorney's fees	to		

FIGURE 20.4	HUD Settlement Statement *(cont'd)*

1103. Title examination   to

1104. Title insurance binder   to

1105. Document preparation   to

1106. Notary fees   to

1107. Attorney's fees   to

(includes above items numbers:)

1108. Title insurance   to

(includes above items numbers:)

1109. Lender's coverage $

1110. Owner's coverage $

1111.

1112.

1113.

1200. Government Recording and Transfer Charges

1201. Recording fees: Deed $; Mortgage $; Releases $

1202. City/county tax/stamps: Deed $; Mortgage $

1203. State tax/stamps: Deed $; Mortgage $

1204.

1205.

1300. Additional Settlement Charges

1301. Survey   to

1302. Pest inspection to

1303.

1304.

1305.

1400. Total Settlement Charges (enter on lines 103, Section J and 502, Section K)

Previous editions are obsolete

form **HUD-1** (3/86)
ref Handbook 4305.2

without an appearance of the buyer or the buyer's agent, the lender need only mail the statement to the buyer as soon as practical after the closing. The lender need not provide a USS to the buyer when there are no settlement charges to the buyer or when the settlement charges are a fixed amount communicated to the borrower at the time of the loan application. However, here the lender must provide the borrower with an itemized list of services within three days after closing.

In all transactions covered by RESPA, the USS must be used. Otherwise, a statement resembling that form is normally used.

Abusive Practices

One reason Congress passed RESPA was because certain abusive practices had inflated closing costs. "Kickbacks" are one such practice expressly prohibited by RESPA. Kickbacks occur, for example, when a person or an entity gives a fee to another for business referrals.

> **CASE EXAMPLE**
> ABC Savings and Loan has an agreement with Alfred Hillman, attorney, whereby for every person ABC refers to Hillman for legal services in connection with real estate transactions, Hillman pays ABC 10 percent of the fees generated. This is an illegal kickback under RESPA. In addition, Hillman would be violating the attorney's code of ethics and would be subject to disciplinary measures.

There are similar prohibitions against the payment of a "phantom" charge, a fee that is given where no service has been performed. Both kickbacks and phantom fees may result in a violation for which criminal penalties may attach. Also, an aggrieved party may sue to recover three times the amount of the kickback or the phantom fee.

■ POSTCLOSING PROCEDURES

After the closing, the purchaser is the titleholder of the property, as evidenced by the deed. The deed must now be recorded to give constructive notice to the world of the new ownership and thus protect the buyer against rival claimants. The purchaser, purchaser's attorney, or, in some instances, the mortgagee presents the deed for recording in the proper office in the county courthouse. After receiving the appropriate fees, the clerk copies and records the deed and then returns the original to the purchaser. Satisfaction (cancellation) of the pre-existing mortgage must also be recorded. The new mortgage instrument that secures repayment of the loan is recorded by the mortgagee or the mortgagee's agent. After recording, the title insurer issues the title insurance policy in the name of the new owner and the mortgagee, if title insurance was purchased.

Any problems that may arise at the closing can be remedied by setting up an escrow and charging an escrow agent with the obligation of holding a portion of the purchase price necessary to ensure the resolution of the problem.

CASE EXAMPLE

At closing, Fred Thomas, seller, is unable to produce any paid receipts for water bills for the last year. Frank Hander, purchaser, is wary of closing without an assurance that any unpaid bills will be borne by the seller. An escrow account is set up with $400 funded from the purchase price, an amount everyone agrees would be more than sufficient to pay any unpaid water bills for a year. After closing, contact with the water company reveals an unpaid water bill of $90. The escrow agent will pay the amount out of the escrow funds and send the remaining $310 to the seller.

THE CHANGING LANDSCAPE

During most of the system of land tenure in England, there was no closing of the land transaction as we know it today. The ceremony of livery of seisin concluded both the transfer and the closing at the same time. Because of the value of land—its productivity and security—there had to be an immediate transfer, so that the land would not be in abeyance, but would always have someone attached to it. Hence, there was no interval between the sale and the closing.

In contrast, today, the conventional closing often occurs 30, 60, or 90 or so days after the parties have bound themselves by a real estate purchase contract. Moreover, the conventional closing today involves a number of persons beyond the buyer and seller and mounds of paperwork. Buyers and sellers normally sit in some anxiety as paper shuffles past them and they are obliged to sign document after document. Although each document is clearly titled and probably comes with a bit of oral explanation, not even the attorneys who may represent the parties read the documents completely.

Each year new forms are added to the cadre of documents. Federal mortgage regulations, state law, and the lender's policy continue to enlarge the heap of paper. There has to be an end to the paper mill, and there has to be a better way to accomplish the closing.

Although federal law requires that the real estate settlement form be in the hands of the purchaser at least 24 hours before the closing, this rarely happens. Thus, the parties and/or their attorneys are rushed at the closing and "pressured" to sign the documents as the settlement clerk instructs, oftentimes finding out too late that mistakes were made.

Is there a way that time may be saved at the closing while the parties can have time at home to read and perhaps sign the various documents? Could we combine a lot of the documents together and thus require fewer signatures? Should we dispense with the face-to-face closing altogether? What about the possibility of greater uniformity of the closing documents? Do any or a combination of these possibilities appeal to you?

■ KEY TERMS

affidavit of title 448

attorney 438

broker 438

closing 437

Real Estate Settlement
  Procedures Act 449

settlement clerk 439

settlement costs booklet 450

Uniform Settlement
  Statement 451

■ INTERNET RESOURCES

To learn more about escrow and real estate closings see

www.escrowhelp.com/articles.html

■ REVIEW AND DISCUSSION QUESTIONS

1. What is the role of a broker in a real estate closing?

2. What is the purpose for the interval between the signing of the real estate contract and the closing?

3. (a) What is the role of the settlement clerk at closing? (b) Who should act as a settlement clerk?

4. (a) Name five things the buyer normally must accomplish in anticipation of the closing and describe why each is important. (b) Name five things that the seller normally must accomplish in anticipation of the closing and describe why each is important.

5. What is the purpose of an affidavit of title?

6. (a) On whom does RESPA impose requirements? (b) What are those requirements?

7. List three documents that are normally signed at closing and describe each.

8. Why is it important for the deed to be recorded after the closing?

■ CASE PROBLEMS

1. Grace Zeigler and Harriet Milton entered into a contract for the sale of a parcel of land owned by Zeigler. The terms of the contract were established through negotiations between the parties. The contract did not make any provision for Zeigler to deliver an abstract of title. Zeigler neglected to furnish an abstract at the closing. Milton refused to pay the purchase price at the closing because Zeigler did not supply an abstract. (a) Is Milton's position sound? (b) Where should Milton look to determine whether Zeigler is bound to provide an abstract? (c) What can Milton do to ensure that she receives a clear title? See *Applebaum v. Zeigler*, 246 Ala. 281, 20 So. 2d 510 (1945).

2. The Maple Ridge Construction Company and Kasten entered into an agreement for the purchase of lots in a subdivision owned by Kasten. Maple Ridge encountered problems in obtaining financing and requested postponement of the settlement date. Kasten agreed to an extension of four months. Maple Ridge continued to try to obtain a suitable financing arrangement without success. Repeated requests for additional extensions were turned down by Kasten. The settlement date passed with neither party performing or demanding performance from the other. Five days after the expiration of the settlement date Maple Ridge informed Kasten that it was ready to perform. Kasten refused Maple Ridge's tender, claiming that the contract had expired. Maple Ridge commenced an action in specific performance against Kasten in an attempt to force Kasten to comply with the terms of their contract. Who wins? Discuss. See *Kasten Construction Co. Inc. v. Maple Ridge Construction Co. Inc.*, 245 Md. 373, 226 A.2d 341 (Ct. App. 1976).

3. Vega applied for and received a conventional mortgage loan from First Federal to finance the purchase of his residence. First Federal's deposits were insured by the Federal Savings and Loan Insurance Corporation (FSLIC). (a) Which federal statute should First Federal pay close attention to before completing its loan agreement with Vega? (b) What obligations are imposed on First Federal by this statute? (c) See *Vega v. First Federal Savings and Loan Association*, 433 F. Supp. 624 (D. Mich. 1977). (d) How would First Federal's obligations be affected if Vega sought to borrow money for the purchase of a commercial lot?

4. Mr. LaFond negotiated a contract with Ms. Frame whereby Ms. Frame agreed to sell to Mr. LaFond a parcel of land free from all encumbrances. The date for the conveyance of the deed and the possession of the land was set for one year from the date the contract was signed. The contract was silent regarding the payment of taxes on the property during the pendency of the contract. On the date set for conveyance, taxes assessed for the prior year were unpaid. (a) Who has the duty to pay these taxes? Why? (b) How could the parties have eliminated any uncertainty on this point? See *LaFond v. Frame*, 327 Mass. 364, 99 N.E.2d 51 (1951).

5. Jim Darrow has obtained an 8 percent, 30-year loan commitment from the Poplar Savings and Loan for $180,000 to purchase Liz Nodler's home at 1836 Cedarwillow, Columbus, Ohio. The sales price, pursuant to the contract previously entered into by the parties, is $200,000. The closing is to take place at the offices of the Poplar Savings and Loan on May 15. In addition to the purchase price of the house, Darrow has arranged to purchase the curtains for $300. County taxes on the property are $1,200 per year, payable semiannually. The county is six months behind on billing and collecting taxes; Liz's last payment was made January 15 of this year. The seller prepaid $200 on January 1 for hazard insurance, which covers the calendar year. The house is heated by oil; 50 gallons of home heating oil costing $1.50 per gallon remain in the tank on the day of closing. Seller's tenant has paid $600 advance rent for the month of May.

    Darrow is paying $20,000 as a down payment, which will be paid at the closing. The payoff by the seller of the first mortgage on the home, as of the date of closing, is $37,120.

Water and sewer assessments are payable quarterly at an even billing of $45 per quarter at the end of March, June, September, and December. Nodler made the March 31 payment. Every six months a reading is taken to determine the actual usage for the six-month period, and adjustments are made at the end of the year. Average adjustments for the last five years have resulted in an additional assessment of $40 at the end of the year.

A listing agreement with Decade Today REALTORS® requires that the seller pay a 6 percent commission. The loan origination fee was 2 percent. Seller, pursuant to the terms of the contract, was to pay two mortgage discount points (2 percent). The appraisal fee of $120 and $35 for a credit report was paid by Darrow at the time of the loan application. The survey fee of $175 to Survey Plat, Inc., is payable by the buyer at closing.

Assume that interest based on a 365-day calendar year is to be paid at closing for the 17-day period encompassing May 15 to May 31. Darrow will be required to deposit into escrow two months' taxes at closing. Attorney fees for preparation of the deed to be borne by the seller are $35. The buyer's attorney fees for services connected with the closing are $350, payable to Lincoln, Todd, and Harrison Law firm at closing. The seller obtained a joint title insurance policy, as required per contract, to fully cover the lender and the owner. The cost to the seller, to be disbursed at closing to ABC Title, Inc., is $500. The buyer's charge for recording fees for the deed and the mortgage amounts to $14 for each document. The seller must pay the recording fee for the release of the existing mortgage.

Additionally, a 0.01 percent county transfer conveyance fee is assessed against the seller. Seller, pursuant to the contract, agreed to pay for termite and gas line inspection costs. She employed Exterm Pest Control to do the termite inspection; the charge was $50 for the inspection and $240 for repair work. The seller employed the city to do the gas line inspection at a cost of $75. Using the HUD forms on pages 452 through 455, prepare the closing statement.

6. The Eisenbergs sought a $164,000 loan from Comfed to finance the purchase of a house being built for them. The loan was to be secured by a mortgage on the new home, and then it was to be assigned to Comfed's parent, the Bank. One provision required that the Eisenbergs pay 2½ percent of the face value of the loan as a "mortgage organization fee." Of that amount, ½ percent was to be paid to Comfed as a commission and the remainder to the Comfed branch manager and toward Comfed's overhead.

The Eisenbergs sued Comfed and its parent, the Bank, contending that the provisions allocating percentages were in violation of the anti-kickback provision of The Real Estate Settlement Procedures Act. Do you agree with the Eisenbergs? Explain. *Eisenberg v. Comfed Mortgage Co., Inc.* 629 F. Supp. 1157 (D. Mass. 1986).

7. On July 24, 2000, Gregory and Margaret Weizeorick closed on the sale of their house in Chicago. In connection with the closing and the repayment of the mortgage on the property, AAMG, as holder of the mortgage, provided the Weizeoricks and the closing company with a "Payoff Statement." The Payoff Statement included

a charge of $10 for a "Recording Discharge Release of the Lien Fee." The Weizeoricks paid this fee at the closing as part of the payoff of their mortgage. Also at the closing, the Weizeoricks were charged a "Release Fee" of $25.60 by the closing company, Attorneys' Title Guaranty Fund, as part of the "settlement charges" owed as the seller of the home. The Weizeoricks paid that fee as well.

The Weizeoricks sued AAMG, alleging that AAMG's charge of $10 for "recording services" at the closing violated the provision of the Real Estate Settlement Procedures Act (RESPA) that deals with "phantom charges." Do you agree with the Weizeoricks' allegations? Explain. See *Weizeorick v. ABN Mort. Group, Inc.,* 337 F.3d 827 (7th Cir. 2003).

 Go to the Student Study Guide CD-ROM and work through Case 4.

PART FIVE

Financing the Transaction

Mortgages

■ MORTGAGE

■ *A written instrument that uses real property to secure payment of a debt.*

A **mortgage** is used in a loan transaction in which real estate is the security. The purpose of the mortgage is to provide security for repayment of the debt. Without the existence of a debt, a mortgage has no effect.

CASE EXAMPLE

Anders Plumbing Company, Inc., owned a valuable building. The company needed money and desired to sell stock to Lance and Jean Billingham. To induce the Billinghams to purchase the stock, they were given a mortgage on the property.

Lee Sickles, a contractor, made improvements on the property. When he was not paid, Sickles attempted to enforce a mechanic's lien. The Billinghams argued that their mortgage had priority over the lien. In a suit by Sickles, the court would hold the mortgage invalid because it was not given as security for a debt.

For a helpful introduction to mortgages, visit *www.law.cornell.edu/topics/mortgages.html.*

Secured Debts

From the purchase of a family's modest first home to the million-dollar commercial sale, financing is the key to almost every successful real estate transaction. People and institutions lend money because lending is profitable; much of the profitability stems from the risk entailed. A lender's risk is reduced when its loan is a **secured debt**; that is, a loan that is secured by property—an automobile, real estate, a firm's inventory, or some other kind of valuable asset. When a loan is secured, the lender has a right to sell the security and apply the proceeds against the debt if the borrower fails to pay or violates some other term of the loan agreement.

In a mortgage relationship, the debtor is termed the *mortgagor*. The lender who takes the mortgage to secure repayment of the loan is referred to as the *mortgagee*.

The true nature of a mortgage, no matter what its form, is to establish a security right against a debtor's interest in real property. Most often the debtor's interest will be fee simple ownership, but legally mortgages may cover almost any interest in real estate that may be sold or assigned. Mortgages may be applied to rental income, life estates, estates for years, remainders, and reversions, as well as other valuable property rights. Mortgages are also used sometimes to secure obligations that are quite unrelated to the property mortgaged.

CASE EXAMPLE

Ray Adams wished to go into business for himself as a plumbing and heating contractor. He planned to hire one or two employees and open up a small showroom from which to sell plumbing fixtures. Although Ray had saved enough money to get started, he was advised by some of the manufacturers whose lines he wished to carry that he should have a line of credit with a local bank. Ray's bank was willing to give him a $45,000 line of credit; as security the bank asked for a mortgage against rental property that he owned.

Note

▦ *A written instrument signed by a borrower containing the provisions of a loan and a promise to repay according to the terms of the agreement between borrower and lender.*

In addition to security aspects, mortgage transactions often involve the borrower's personal liability to pay the debt. Usually the borrower makes the commitment by signing a note promising to pay the debt. In some states, the borrower signs a bond. The **note** or bond serves as evidence of the debt for which the mortgage is the security. The typical note contains the amount of the loan, the interest rate, and the time and method of repayment. This instrument is sometimes referred to as a *promissory note* or *mortgage note*.

The existence of the note and mortgage provide the lenders with two remedies if the debt is not paid: (1) to sue on the note and to obtain a personal judgment against the debtor or (2) to have the real estate sold and the proceeds applied against the debt. If the lender wins a personal judgment on the note, the judgment may be collected by attaching other property of the debtor or by garnishing the debtor's wages. In addition, if when sold the security does not generate enough to pay the debt, a personal action may be brought on the note. The two actions are ordinarily combined.

Title and Lien Theory

The historical theory that the mortgage conveys title to the mortgagee continues to be used in some states, referred to as **title-theory** states. Even in these states, however, although the mortgagee acquires title, the mortgagee does not acquire the right of possession unless the mortgagor defaults.

Most states recognize that in reality a mortgage is a lien. It is a device used by debtors and creditors to secure a debt. The mortgagee is interested primarily in having the security sold and the proceeds applied to the debt if the mortgagor fails to pay or violates some other mortgage provision. States taking this position are called **lien-theory** states.

In some states that consider the mortgage a lien, the mortgagee of real property has more rights than most other lienholders. Sometimes these rights are very similar to those a title holder would have. For example, in several states, by statute the mortgagee is entitled to oust a defaulting mortgagor from possession. Most other types of liens permit the holder only to have the security sold and proceeds applied to the debt. Since vestiges of title theory appear in the law of lien theory states and lien theory vestiges remain in some title theory jurisdictions, few states can be classified rigidly.

Content of Mortgage

Currently, the mortgage most commonly used in the United States is a two-party instrument. By its terms, one of the parties, the mortgagor, creates a security interest in property for the other, the mortgagee. Because historically the mortgage was a conveyance, the mortgage often has many provisions similar to those of a deed. In fact, in some states, it is called a *mortgage deed*. Legislative bodies in a few states have adopted statutory mortgage forms. Although they contain all elements essential to a valid mortgage, use of the statutory form is not required.

In general, for an instrument to be effective as a mortgage, it should include at least the following information:

- Names of the parties
- Legal description of the premises
- Language indicating that the instrument is given as security for a debt
- Statement of the debt secured
- Terms for repaying the debt

Additionally, the mortgage must be signed by the mortgagor and executed according to the laws of the state in which the property is located.

Most mortgages contain substantially more information than minimal requirements. Because the parties insert many provisions designed to protect their rights, mortgage instruments tend to be lengthy. The recording process is expensive and requires a great amount of storage space. A number of states have adopted statutes that allow mortgagees to record a *master mortgage* containing the desired covenants and clauses. This practice permits execution and recording of a short-form mortgage that incorporates by reference the provisions of the master mortgage.

Deed of Trust Compared

■ *A written instrument that transfers title to real property to a trustee as security for a debt owed by the borrower to the lender, who is a beneficiary of the trust.*

In an increasing number of states, the typical real estate security instrument involves three parties and is based on the law of trusts. Instead of executing a mortgage in favor of a lender, the borrower transfers title to a trustee through a **deed of trust**. The important difference between the mortgage and the deed of trust is that in a deed of trust, legal title passes to the trustee. The trustee holds this title for the benefit of both the borrower and the lender. When the debt secured by the deed of trust is repaid, the trustee must reconvey title to the borrower. By contrast, in a mortgage, title remains in the borrower. (See Table 21.1.)

TABLE 21.1	Mortgage and Deed of Trust: Comparison	
	Mortgage	**Deed of Trust**
Title	Legal title passes to buyer	Legal title passes to trustee
Default	Foreclosure in the event of default	Trustee may sell property on default
Lender	Lender is a matter of public record	Lender may remain anonymous
Discharge	Discharged by satisfaction of mortgage	Discharged by reconveyance by trustee to buyer

The trustee has the power to sell the property to satisfy obligations if the borrower fails to maintain payments on the debt or breaches some other condition of the loan agreement. This would include failure to keep the buildings insured, sale of the property, or by commission of waste. The power-of-sale provision makes judicial foreclosure procedure unnecessary, although the trustee usually may elect such procedure. Because judicial foreclosure can be avoided, collection from the security is more rapid and economical than through the court procedure. Additionally, the lender may remain anonymous in a deed of trust.

In most states a mortgage is discharged when the mortgagee executes a simple document called a **satisfaction of mortgage** or a *release of mortgage*. The deed of trust requires a reconveyance of the property by the trustee to the purchaser. The trustee will refuse to reconvey the property without assurance that the underlying obligation has been paid. Otherwise, the trustee would be personally liable to the lender for any amount still due. If the trustee is an individual, the problem of reconveyance may become especially acute because the individual trustee might be difficult to locate. For this reason, the preferred practice is to name a corporate trustee.

■ LOAN APPLICATION AND COMMITMENT

Today, most mortgage loans start with a printed application supplied by the lender, usually a standard printed Uniform Residential Loan application, if a residential loan. The application supplies the lender with information about the borrower necessary to decide whether the loan should be approved. Upon approval, the lender notifies the borrower and furnishes a formal commitment, often called a *loan approval.* The commitment is an offer to grant the loan subject to certain contingencies. At the point the commitment is made, there are still issues that must usually be resolved before the lender will actually fund the loan. For example, existing liens on the property may need to be cleared, a termite inspection showing no infestation supplied, and a survey showing no encroachments certificate obtained.

If the lender refuses to honor the contract, the borrower's damages are relatively easy to calculate. They are the increased cost of obtaining the loan from some other source. If the borrower does not use the funds, damages to the lender are very difficult to measure. In a number of cases, the courts have held that should this happen, the lender is entitled only to nominal damages. Because of problems associated with measuring the damages, many commitments for major loans contain provisions for a nonrefundable commitment fee paid by the borrower.

The following case illustrates the sanctity of the mortgage commitment.

Leben v. Nassau Savings & Loan Association
Supreme Court, Appellate Division
40 A.D.2d 830 (N.Y. 1972)

Background. The Lebens contracted with Smithtown Park, Inc., for a lot and a dwelling to be constructed by the seller. The contract provided that they were to apply for a mortgage loan from lending institutions designated by Smithtown. The mortgage was to be for $22,400, to run for 30 years and to bear interest at the rate of 6 percent per annum. A different provision of the contract provided that in the event the maximum allowable rate should change, the Lebens "will accept the . . . mortgage at the maximum rate which is in effect at the date of the closing of the permanent mortgage loan."

The Lebens applied to Nassau Savings for a mortgage loan. On December 6, 1967, Nassau Savings advised them by letter of its approval of the loan. The letter stated "Terms of this mortgage will be at the interest rate of 6%, in accordance with the terms of your contract, for a period of 30 years."

On October 4, 1968, the Lebens appeared at Nassau Savings for the closing of title. They were informed for the first time that the loan would bear interest at the rate of 7¼ percent. The Lebens had already moved into their new house and had canceled the lease on their apartment. They were told there would be no closing unless they acceded to the higher interest rate. To protect themselves, but over their objection, they signed an assumption, release, and modification providing for the increased interest rate, and title was closed.

Shortly thereafter they sued for a declaration that the mortgage agreement dated December 6, 1967, is a legal, binding commitment obliging

Nassau Savings to make the loan at 6 percent for 30 years. Additionally, they asked that the closing documents be reformed to comply with the December 6 letter of approval. The trial court dismissed their complaint and the Lebens appealed.

Decision. The appellate court reversed the trial court and ordered the documents reformed to comply with the terms of the letter of approval.

By the Court. In our opinion, the mortgage commitment agreement between plaintiffs and defendant clearly obligated defendant to make a mortgage loan at an interest rate of 6%. The addition of the phrase "in accordance with the terms of your contract" at best created an ambiguity and should be construed most strongly against defendant, the party who prepared it. Defendant is not named in the contract between the plaintiffs and Smithtown; nor does it appear that the provision with reference to the maximum allowable rate was made for its benefit.

In our opinion plaintiffs signed the assumption, release and modification agreement as the result of economic duress. The terms of that agreement . . . must be reformed to reflect the agreed on rate of 6%.

Reversed.

How could the commitment letter be altered to clearly permit an increase in the interest rate?

■ RIGHTS AND OBLIGATIONS OF PARTIES

A substantial amount of mortgage litigation involves disputes concerning the rights and obligations of the mortgagor and mortgagee. The well-drafted mortgage reduces the possibility of litigation by incorporating provisions that clearly indicate each party's rights and obligations.

Often a mortgage instrument that does not cover a problem arising between the parties will be used. When this is the case, public policy—reflected in legislation or case law—directs the parties. Inasmuch as questions involving possession, disposition of rents and profits and protection of the security are common, numerous legal rules exist to solve these problems.

Possession

■ *The right to occupy and control real estate to the exclusion of all others.*

The right to possession of mortgaged premises depends on the theory of mortgages followed in a particular state. In title-theory states, the common provision allows the mortgagor to remain in possession and enjoy the benefits of ownership until default. Several title-theory states have statutes prohibiting the mortgagee from taking possession until default.

In lien-theory states, the mortgagee has no right to possession. This principle, however, is frequently modified by a provision in the mortgage allowing the mortgagee to take possession on default.

As a general practice, either by statute or by mortgage terms, mortgagors have the right to remain in possession of mortgaged premises only until default. In a few states with statutory right-of-redemption laws, the mortgagor is allowed to remain in possession even after a foreclosure sale. This right to possession exists until the redemption period terminates unless limited by a provision in the mortgage.

The status of a mortgagor in possession differs from that of a mortgagee. Generally, the mortgagor in possession is entitled to all of the rights of ownership as long as the value of the security remains unimpaired. A mortgagee who takes possession has special, but limited, rights that revolve around protecting the security and applying proceeds to pay the debt.

Rents and Profits

Possession is an important factor in determining who has a right to rents and profits from the property. The well-established general rule is that a mortgagor who remains in possession is entitled to these earnings.

> **CASE EXAMPLE**
> Teal executed several mortgages to Walker on farmland and property in Portland, Oregon. The mortgages contained provisions allowing Teal to retain possession of the land but permitting Walker to take possession on default. When Teal defaulted, Walker demanded possession of the properties. Teal refused to yield possession, collecting earnings from the property until

ousted from possession by a foreclosure sale. As the proceeds of the sale fell far short of paying the debt, Walker sued for the rents collected after Teal's refusal to surrender possession. The United States Supreme Court . . . determined that the mortgagee was entitled to rents and profits only if actually in possession. *Teal v. Walker*, 111 U.S. 242 (1884).

A mortgagee who takes possession has a right to earnings from the property, but they must be applied to extinguish the debt. Amounts collected that exceed expenses are first applied to interest and then to principal.

Most mortgages that cover commercial property contain provisions in which the parties allocate rents, profits, and earnings. One approach is for the mortgagor to assign the rents and profits as additional security from the date of the mortgage. A more common provision allows the mortgagee to collect the rents on default. Until that time, rents go to the mortgagor. In both lien-theory and title-theory states, the mortgagee has a right to appoint a receiver to collect the rents and manage the property when there is a default. This right is based on either statute or the right to protect the value of the security.

Protecting the Security

A mortgagee has a right to protect the value of the security. Actions that have been held to impair the value of the security include cutting, removing, and selling timber; removing machinery; removing a dwelling; failing to pay liens; and failing to keep the property repaired. The mortgagee's right to protect the value of the security may be asserted against third parties as well as against the mortgagor.

Insurance. Hazard insurance is the best protection against many risks. The law is clear that both mortgagor and mortgagee have an insurable interest in the property. With a few exceptions, the law is equally clear that neither is required to insure for the other's benefit in the absence of an agreement to do so. Commonly, in the United States, a mortgagor agrees to insure for the benefit of the mortgagee. The typical proviso not only commits the mortgagor to insure but also authorizes the mortgagee to obtain insurance if the mortgagor fails to procure it, and to add the premium to the debt.

In addition to allocating responsibility for obtaining insurance, the mortgage should contain a provision covering the application of insurance proceeds. A standard approach is a requirement that the mortgagor obtain a policy, making loss payable to "mortgagor and mortgagee as interest may appear."

Taxes and Assessments

Taxes and assessments are the responsibility of the mortgagor. Mortgages frequently authorize the mortgagee to pay taxes if the mortgagor does not. The mortgagee may then add these payments to the debt. A tax lien takes precedence over a mortgage. In the event of foreclosure, the mortgagee recovers only after real estate taxes have been paid.

Financial institutions have adopted the practice of requiring mortgagors to pay a portion of taxes and insurance premiums each month, usually $\frac{1}{12}$ of the estimated yearly total. These funds are held in escrow by the mortgagee, usually without interest, to pay the annual insurance premium and property taxes as they come due.

■ PRIORITIES

Mortgage priority, sometimes called lien priority, problems generally occur when a debt is in default or probability of a default exists. Under these circumstances, each secured creditor attempts to ensure that its lien has first claim to the proceeds if the security must be sold. Sometimes the rank of a creditor will be determined by a provision in the security document. At other times the creditor's position is established by case law or, more often, by some statute.

The fundamental principle determining priority is "first in time, first in right," but modifications of this rule affect the mortgagee's position. As a result of the recording statutes treated in Chapter 19, the first-in-time priority generally belongs to the first party to deliver the security instrument for recording. In a majority of states, this priority is not accorded if the person recording has actual knowledge of a prior unrecorded claim. Some states do have "race to the court house" statutory provisions that apply to mortgages, as described in Chapter 19. Under these statutes, the first mortgage on the record has a superior right, even if the mortgagee knows of a prior unrecorded mortgage.

Mortgages and Leases

In general, the first-in-time rule applies to the priority relationship between mortgages and leases. When a lease is executed before a mortgage, the lease has priority. In a foreclosure sale, the purchaser would take subject to the lease. A lease entered into after a mortgage is subordinate to the mortgage if the mortgage has been recorded. In the event of a foreclosure sale, the purchaser of the property would take it free of the lease.

Mortgages and Mechanics' Liens

Litigation as to priority between mechanics' lienholders and mortgagees is widespread. Its outcome varies appreciably from state to state, even when the facts are similar. Although all state courts apply the fundamental rule of "first in time," state law differs as to when the mechanic's lien attaches, and it is time of attachment that establishes the first position. At least three different approaches are taken in the United States as to when the mechanic's lien becomes effective against other claims:

1. The lien, when properly filed, reverts back to commencement of construction, no matter when the claimant did the work or furnished the materials.

2. The lien, when properly filed, reverts back to the time the claimant began work or furnished materials.

3. The lien attaches when the claimant files his or her claim.

Mechanics' liens are discussed in Chapter 15.

■ DEFAULT

■ *Nonperformance of a duty or obligation accepted by either party as part of the mortgage transaction.*

The mortgagee cannot institute a foreclosure action until the mortgagor defaults. The most commonly recognized **default** is the failure to pay the interest or principal. Obligations other than the payment of principal and interest found in most mortgages include payment of taxes, assessments, and insurance. Often these commitments are worded in such a manner that failure to carry them out constitutes a default. Some mortgage instruments give the mortgagee the right to make the payment when the mortgagor fails to do so. The mortgagee may then add the amount to the mortgage debt and, in some states, consider the mortgagor in default.

Many mortgages are worded so that the mortgagor's failure to comply with statutes, ordinances, and government requirements affecting the premises constitutes default. Other relatively common provisions that may result in default are related to bankruptcy or the mortgagor's failure to keep the property repaired. Some mortgages provide that a mortgagor who files a voluntary petition in bankruptcy or makes an assignment for the benefit of creditors is in default. Permitting waste or allowing anything to be done on the premises that weakens the security of the mortgage are additional prohibitions often included in mortgages. If the covenant not to permit waste is breached, the mortgagor is in default.

Acceleration Clause

■ *A clause that makes the entire debt payable in the event of default.*

A critical legal question when default has occurred is the mortgagee's right to collect the entire debt. This problem arises when the mortgagor breaches a covenant that is not related to payment or when the debt is to be repaid periodically and a payment is missed. Under these circumstances to protect the investment, the mortgagee may elect to invoke the acceleration clause within the mortgage.

CASE EXAMPLE

Frederick defaulted on an installment of his $80,000 mortgage loan. The mortgagee, Northwest Bank, brought a foreclosure action and notified Frederick of its option to accelerate the entire debt. The notice stated that if Frederick paid the amount past due plus interest, he could cure the default. Frederick made no payment within the 30-day period. However, during the trial he proffered payment of the delinquent installments plus interest. Northwest refused to accept the amount, and Frederick moved to dismiss. The court refused to do so, holding that the notification of acceleration matured the entire debt, which was no longer payable in installments. *Northwest Bank v. Frederick*, 452 N.W.2d 316 (N.D. 1990).

Equity of Redemption

▨ *The right of the mortgagor or another person with an interest in the property to reclaim it after default but before foreclosure.*

In both title-theory and lien-theory states, the mortgagor has a right to redeem the property after default. Redemption may be accomplished by paying the full amount of the debt, interest, and costs. To be effective, the right of redemption must ordinarily be asserted prior to foreclosure. The purpose of foreclosure is to terminate the *equitable right of redemption*. Once the foreclosure sale has been confirmed, the mortgagor may no longer redeem the property, except in states in which statutes provide an additional period. This *statutory right of redemption* is discussed next.

Statutory Right of Redemption

▨ *The right of a debtor to redeem the property after a foreclosure sale.*

Legislatures in more than half the states have provided the mortgagor with a right to redeem after foreclosure. The creation of a statutory right of redemption is generally the result of political pressure by debtors during periods of economic distress. Although the first such statute was enacted in New York, most of the legislation exists in the western states. Agricultural interests have often been behind efforts to establish this right.

The period in which the former mortgagor may redeem varies from state to state. In some states, the period is short, and redemption may occur only in the few days or weeks' window between the date of the foreclosure sale and the date the sale is confirmed by the court. Other states permit a six-month to one-year period of redemption. Laws in some states also give some classes of persons a longer period of time to redeem than others. In a number of states, instead of granting the mortgagor a right to redeem after the foreclosure sale, state laws postpone the sale to provide a longer period of time to pay a debt that is in default. Except in a few states, any attempt by the lender to have the mortgagor waive redemption rights violates statute or public policy and is unenforceable.

▨ FORECLOSURE OF MORTGAGE

▨ *The legal procedure by which a lender who has advanced funds with real property as security recovers in the event of default.*

In the United States, mortgage foreclosure is accomplished in several ways. The two most common methods are judicial foreclosure and power-of-sale foreclosure. Strict foreclosure, a method important historically, is permissible in just a few states. (See Table 21.2.)

TABLE 21.2	Foreclosures: A Contrast		
	Judicial Foreclosure	**Strict Foreclosure**	**Power-of-Sale Foreclosure**
Theory	Lien	Title	Lien
Supervision	Court supervision	Court supervision	No court supervision
Cost	High	High	Low
Deficiency	May be deficiency on sale	No deficiency	May be deficiency on sale
Time	Slow	Fast	Fast

Judicial Foreclosure

■ *A legal procedure in which a court orders real estate sold to enforce the mortgagee's rights under the mortgage.*

Of the several methods of foreclosure, foreclosure by judicial action and sale is the most common. In a few states, it is the only method allowed. **Judicial foreclosure** is favored because a court supervises the entire procedure. As a result, the property is usually sold for close to its market value; in addition, chances for a defective foreclosure are reduced because the sale is based on a court order. On the other hand, this type of foreclosure is expensive and time-consuming.

Most jurisdictions regulate many aspects of the foreclosure procedure by statute. These regulations, which vary from state to state, must be followed closely or the sale will be invalid. Usually an action to foreclose must be brought in the county where the mortgaged property is located. Mortgagors and other interested parties are entitled to notice of the action and an opportunity to defend before an impartial tribunal having jurisdiction.

Foreclosure Sale. The chief purpose of a foreclosure action is to obtain a court order directing a public sale of the security. This sale terminates all parties' rights to redeem. The proceeds of the sale are allocated to pay expenses and the mortgage debt.

Various state laws regulate the method of conducting the sale. Usually it is carried out by the sheriff. In some states, a court-appointed master or referee conducts the sale. In any case, it will be supervised closely by the court.

Most states have some type of law attempting to ensure an *adequate sale price*. One common method is to require an appraisal by a group of disinterested persons before the property is auctioned. The sale must bring at least a portion—perhaps 60 to 75 percent—of the appraised value. Unless the final bid is at least that amount, the sale will not be consummated. Finally, a court may use its equity power to refuse to confirm a sale if the amount bid is grossly inadequate. Ordinarily, however, a properly conducted sale will not be set aside merely because of an inadequate price.

■ **Deficiency Judgment.** *Money judgment awarded to the mortgagee when funds obtained as a result of a foreclosure sale are insufficient to pay the debt.*

CASE EXAMPLE

Oscar Fong defaulted on a loan from Portland Trust. The loan was secured by a mortgage on real estate owned by Fong. At the time of default, the outstanding indebtedness was $75,000. The mortgage was foreclosed and the property ordered sold. The selling price at the fore-closure sale was $70,000. After this amount was credited, the bank commenced a personal action against Fong to collect the additional $5,000 plus all expenses.

Most states allow the mortgagee to collect any deficiency remaining after foreclo-sure. Usually the right to sue for a deficiency is provided in the court decree ordering foreclosure. The theory underlying the deficiency judgment is that the creditor has a right, based on the note, to collect the entire amount owed. This right exists independ-ent of the right to foreclose.

Deficiency judgments in residential foreclosures occur, but are somewhat unusual. Most residential loans are amortized on a monthly basis; the amount of the debt is con-stantly decreasing. Coupled with inflation and generally increasing property values, only sporadically will funds from the sale fail to cover the debt.

Nonjudicial Foreclosure

■ *Foreclosure based on terms in a mortgage, giving a mortgagee or third party the power to sell mortgaged property on default without resorting to judicial foreclosure.*

Legal complications, expense, and delay associated with judicial foreclosure have encouraged alternate methods of applying the security to the debt. Many mortgages contain provisions granting a mortgagee or third party the power to sell the real estate at a public sale if the mortgagor defaults. Generally, the sale is authorized without court intervention, but a few states require judicial confirmation, and many have statutes that prescribe procedures that must be followed.

Some states by specific legislation require foreclosure by judicial action. Statutes of this type effectively prohibit the use of a power of sale. Most states, however, do allow the **nonjudicial foreclosure**, also called power-of-sale foreclosure, and it is the prevailing practice in several states.

At one time, the nonjudicial foreclosure was touted as the solution to many of the problems of judicial foreclosure, but this expectation was not fulfilled. Lawyers repre-senting potential purchasers are wary of the process because the title acquired is not based on a judicial proceeding that establishes regularity. In addition, the purchaser's title is subject to attack because the sale does not have the official sanction of a court order. This attack may be made not only by the mortgagor but also by others who have an interest in the property.

Statutes in many states and case law in others provide some protection for the mort-gagor whose real property is subject to a power of sale. These statutes generally require notice, usually by advertisement, and a sale that is conducted fairly to produce a good price. A sale will not be valid if factors exist that tend to stifle competition among the bidders. In conducting the sale, the mortgagee is representing the mortgagor's interest as well as its own.

CASE EXAMPLE

Union Market National Bank held a $9,800 mortgage on property owned by Missak Derderian. The mortgage was in default, and the bank advertised a sale under a power included in the mortgage. The advertisement stated, in addition to a $500 cash down payment at the time of sale, "other terms to be announced at the sale."

At the sale, the auctioneer announced that a $500 deposit would be required of anyone prior to that person's bid being accepted. This was a very unusual condition, and Derderian's brother, who was planning to bid, refused to comply. The auctioneer as a result refused to accept his high bid of more than $10,000 and sold the property to the mortgagee for $8,500. All parties at the sale knew that Derderian's brother was financially responsible.

When Derderian challenged the sale as improperly conducted, an appellate court agreed with him. The court stated that "[a] mortgagee with the power to select the methods of sale must act as a reasonably prudent man would to obtain a fair price. . . . If the conditions announced at the sale . . . operate to prevent free bidding, it is the mortgagee's duty to change them." *Union National Bank v. Derderian*, 318 Mass. 578, 62 N.E.2d 661 (Mass. 1945).

Strict Foreclosure

■ *A judicial procedure that, by terminating the mortgagor's equity of redemption, gives the mortgagee absolute title to mortgaged real estate without a sale of the property.*

Judicial foreclosure and nonjudicial foreclosure are identified with the lien theory of mortgages. These procedures establish a mortgagee's right to have the property sold following default. The proceeds of the sale are used to pay the debt and expenses of the sale. If a balance remains, it is turned over to the mortgagor.

At common law, the mortgagee had a more extensive right. The mortgage gave the mortgagee a conditional or defeasible title. If the debt was not paid when due, the mortgagee's title became absolute. If the debt was paid when due, the mortgagor reacquired title.

Strict foreclosure is no longer common in the United States except in two or three states. Some states expressly prohibit strict foreclosure by statute; others accomplish the prohibition by requiring that the property be sold to compensate the creditor. The principal reason for the decline is that often strict foreclosure severely penalizes the mortgagor. At the same time the mortgagee has the potential for a windfall profit.

■ **Deed in Lieu of Foreclosure.** *A procedure in which the mortgagor conveys the mortgaged real estate to the mortgagee, who promises in return not to foreclose or sue on the underlying debt.*

> **CASE EXAMPLE**
> As security for a $50,000 loan, Naomi Tilson executed a mortgage to the Pike County National Bank. After making two payments on the loan, she defaulted. At the time of her default, the market value of the property was slightly in excess of $50,000. Because Naomi and her family were valued customers, the bank offered to accept a deed to the property instead of foreclosing. After discussing the consequences of this action with her attorney, Naomi agreed to convey the property to the bank.

The use of a deed in lieu of foreclosure is a common practice in the United States. In conveying to the mortgagee, the mortgagor surrenders any rights to a foreclosure sale and to redeem the property. In return, the mortgagee cancels the underlying debt and becomes the owner of the real estate.

Potentially, the transaction may benefit the mortgagor in a number of ways. For example, Naomi Tilson's credit rating would be protected. The conveyance would be carried out in the same manner as any sale, and adverse publicity that might accompany foreclosure would not exist. Economically, she could anticipate three important benefits. First, any obligation for taxes and assessments would terminate. Second, foreclosure costs would also be saved. Finally, and probably most important of all, she would not be responsible for any deficiency.

The deed in lieu of foreclosure is also advantageous to the mortgagee. Long delays usually associated with foreclosure by judicial sale are avoided. On the other hand, the mortgagee faces the problem of disposing of the security. Until the property is sold, the mortgagee has to maintain it, and expenses of the sale must be borne by the mortgagee because it now owns the real estate.

An important legal consideration involves junior liens on the property. The purchaser at a foreclosure sale takes title free of such liens, but a mortgagee who acquires title to real estate by deed in lieu of foreclosure is subject to these interests. If Naomi Tilson had not paid for improvements on the property and a mechanic's lien existed, the Pike County National Bank's deed would be subject to that lien. A deed in lieu of foreclosure is also subject to attack under the bankruptcy laws. Were Naomi to file for bankruptcy within a period of, say, 90 days after delivery of the deed to the bank, the bank could be treated as a preferred creditor. The deed would be set aside as a preferential transfer.

■ TYPES OF MORTGAGES

Fixed-Rate Mortgage

■ *A traditional fixed term mortgage that has a fixed-rate level payment plan and is fully amortized.*

Financial institutions, called private lenders, make conventional loans. Before the advent of private mortgage insurance (PMI) this type of loan required a minimum of 20 percent down payment by the borrower to reduce the lender's risk. As more and more borrowers looked to loan products with a lower down payment, the private lender, in an effort to stay competitive, began offering higher loan-to-value ratios if the bor-

TABLE 21.3	Types of Mortgages and Their Purposes

Type	Purpose
Adjustable-Rate Mortgage	To tie the market rate of interest to the mortgage rate on a periodic basis
Construction Mortgage	To provide financing for construction or renovation
Fixed-Rate Mortgage	To stabilize interest rate and payments over the life of the loan
FHA	To encourage lenders to extend credit with its federal loan insurance guaranty program
Open-End Mortgage	To permit the mortgagor to borrow additional funds as the mortgage is paid down
Package Mortgage	To permit the buyer to borrow more money and furnish the home by packaging real and personal property as security
Purchase-Money Mortgage	To provide financing for the purchaser of real estate and to grant the mortgagee priority over certain liens
Reverse Mortgage	To supplement the mortgagor's income
Rollover Mortgage	Ordinarily, to protect lenders against rising interest rates
VA	To provide economic incentives to veterans to purchase a house

rower provided the lender with mortgage insurance to eliminate the added risk involved with less down payment.

Due to the higher cost of housing in today's changing housing market, lenders are beginning to offer a 40-year fixed-rate loan in an effort to help borrowers qualify with a smaller monthly mortgage payment.

Adjustable-Rate Mortgage

■ *A mortgage that contains a provision permitting the mortgagee to adjust the interest rate based on an index contained in the mortgage.*

Adjustable-rate mortgages (ARMs) appeared in the '80s as an alternative to the traditional fixed rate mortgage with very high interest rates. Unlike a fixed-rate loan, the interest on an ARM is adjusted at the end of each adjustment period. There are three components to an ARM:

The index is the adjustable component. The index used is typically tied to a public reported index, such as a Treasury Security, with a similar period of maturity. For example, a three-year ARM might use a three-year treasury security rate as the index. The index used must be beyond the control of the lender and represent an average cost of funds.

The margin, or spread, is a percentage representing the lender's profit and cost of doing business. This percentage is calculated as basis points or a hundredth of a percentage point. For example, 250 basis points would be equal to 2.5 percent. The margin remains fixed and does not usually change over the loan period.

The adjusted rate is the index and the margin added together.

There are also annual and lifetime caps on an ARM. The **annual cap** (usually 2 percent) limits the amount of increase or decrease the rate could adjust in any one adjustment period. The **lifetime cap**, or aggregate, is the maximum a rate can adjust up or down over the life of the loan (usually 5-6 percent). So, for example, a one-year ARM with a start rate of 4.25 percent with 2/6 caps, can adjust no more than 2 percent or to 6.25 percent at the end of the first year even if the index increases to 2.5 percent. Regardless of how high or low the index goes, the loan will never go higher than 10.25 percent or back down no more than 6 percent to the original loan rate of 4.25 percent.

Today there are many variations of the basic ARM. These are sometimes called hybrid ARMs and often adjust early in the loan period and then settle into a fixed rate for the balance of the loan term.

Federal Housing Administration Mortgage (FHA Government-Insured Loan)

■ *A loan program that insures mortgage loans made by approved lenders.*

The National Housing Act of 1934 was responsible for the creation of FHA-insured loans to stimulate a depressed housing market. FHA is a government agency within the Department of Housing and Urban Development (HUD). This agency functions as an insurance company, insuring loans that are made by approved lenders. The borrower, as well as the property used as collateral, must meet stringent FHA underwriting guidelines before the loan will be fully insured.

FHA has loan insurance programs for several types of dwellings, the most popular being the Title II, Section 203 (b), a loan for an owner-occupied one-family to four-family dwelling unit with a fixed rate. They also offer several different types of loans to include home improvement, condominium units, and adjustable rate loans. FHA-insured mortgage loans:

■ have loan limits that vary from area to area based on the agency's perception of the differences in the cost of housing and local economy;

■ require a low cash investment from the borrower;

■ have competitive interest rates based on the market; and

■ have no prepayment penalty.

Borrowers pay a one-time up-front premium (UPMIP) at the time of closing which is a percentage of the amount borrowed. In addition, the borrower pays an additional premium per year that is added to the monthly mortgage payment. From these premiums the FHA accumulates reserves to cover expenses and losses on properties acquired due to borrower default.

Veterans Affairs Mortgage (VA or GI Loan)

■ *A loan program with a partial guarantee by the Department of Veterans Affairs available to lenders that finance home purchases by eligible veterans.*

In 1944 the GI Bill of Rights was passed to help returning veterans purchase a home. The act gave the Department of Veterans Affairs the authority to partially guarantee mortgage loans made to veterans by approved private lenders.

The guarantee, or entitlement, is the maximum amount of the loan the Department of Veterans Affairs guarantees a lender if the veteran defaults on the loan, with the balance due from the collateral. The guarantee amount changes periodically. In 2005 the guaranteed amount was $89,913 or 25 percent of the loan amount, whichever amount was less. While there is a guarantee limit, there is no loan limit as long as the borrower qualifies for the loan amount. A VA loan has several special benefits for the veteran:

■ no down payment required;

■ no prepayment penalty;

■ no mortgage insurance required;

■ no due-on-sale clause (the loan is assumable by any party qualified by the lender);

■ competitive interest rates based on the market; and

■ no mortgage insurance required.

The veteran pays a one-time funding fee (currently 2 percent of the loan amount) at time of closing. The funding fee can be financed in the loan under certain circumstances.

Purchase Money Mortgage

■ *A form of seller financing.*

A **purchase money mortgage** (PMM) is a mortgage given by a purchaser to the seller as part of the purchase price. The seller is financing part of the purchase price. The seller takes back a mortgage in lieu of cash as part of the consideration. The buyer makes payments to the seller until the PMM is satisfied. In most states the seller retains a lien on the property as security for the debt.

A buyer could also give a seller a PMM as part of the down payment and obtain a third party loan from a financial institution for the major portion of the sale price. In this instance, the financial institution would insist on having a priority lien position with the seller holding a second lien position.

The important protection provided by a purchase-money mortgage is illustrated by the following case.

Garrett Tire Center, Inc. v. Herbaugh
Supreme Court of Arkansas
740 S.W.2d 612 (1987)

Background. On April 26, 1984, Garrett Tire Center obtained a judgment against Robert Herbaugh. Garrett Tire was unable to collect on the judgment as no assets could be found. In 1984, Farmers and Merchants Bank made a purchase-money mortgage loan to Herbaugh. A purchase-money mortgage was filed on January 30, 1985, five minutes after the deed to Robert Herbaugh was filed.

In October 1986, Farmers and Merchants Bank filed for foreclosure on its purchase-money mortgage. Garrett Tire intervened claiming that its judgment lien was superior to the bank's mortgage. The bank moved for summary judgment and the trial court rendered judgment in its favor. Garrett Tire appealed.

Decision. The appellate court affirmed the summary judgment in favor of the bank.

Justice Purtle. The chancellor granted summary judgment in favor of a purchase money mortgagee over a prior judgment lien holder. The appellant argues that his judgment lien was superior because it attached before the appellee's mortgage lien. We hold that the appellee's purchase money mortgage had priority.

When a deed and a purchase money mortgage are a part of one continuous transaction, they are treated as being executed simultaneously. A prior judgment lien cannot attach because the purchaser never obtains title to the land, but acquires only an equity interest subject to the payment of the purchase money.

It is a general rule, to which there is little dissent, that a mortgage on land executed by the purchaser of the land contemporaneously with the acquirement of the legal title thereto, or afterwards, but as a part of the same transaction, is a purchase money mortgage, and entitled to preference as such over all other claims of liens arising through the mortgagor, though they are prior in point of time; and this is true without reference to whether the mortgage was executed to the vendor or to a third person.

The appellant argues that under [the Arkansas statute in question] a mortgage, including a purchase money mortgage, is not valid against a third party until recorded. Therefore appellant's judgment lien attached during the five minute space of time after the deed was filed and before the purchase money mortgage was recorded. Appellant relies on *Western Tie & Timber Co. v. Campbell*, where the state obtained a statutory lien on a defendant's real property for the criminal fines and costs adjudged against the defendant. Subsequently, the defendant simultaneously purchased land and executed a purchase money mortgage on it. The purchase money mortgage was recorded eight months later. The priority between the state's lien and purchase money mortgage became the issue on appeal.

The *Western Tie* court correctly stated the law as follows:

> It is quite well settled by the authorities that a mortgage, given at the time of the purchase of real estate to secure the payment of purchase money, whether given to the vendor or to a third person, who, as part of the same transaction, advances the purchase money, has preference over all judgments and other liens against the mortgagor.

Nonetheless the court held that the legislature intended to give the state a lien against an unrecorded mortgage; so, under the circumstances the prior state lien was superior to the purchase money mortgage.

Despite the result in *Western Tie*, there is no dispute that a purchase money mortgage, executed as a deed as part of one continuous transaction, and recorded within a reasonable time to prevent detrimental reliance by a third party, is superior to any other lien. In the present case appellee Farmers and Merchants Bank obtained a promissory note secured by a purchase money mortgage as part of one transaction and recorded its lien within a reasonable time. The appellant did not in any way rely on the deed before the purchase money mortgage was recorded. The fact that the purchase money mortgage was filed five minutes after the deed was recorded did not affect the validity of the mortgage. We hold that the deed was encumbered by the purchase money mortgage at the time it was filed.

Affirmed.

What is the policy reason behind the rule announced by the court?

Construction Mortgage

■ *A mortgage given to secure funds advanced to construct or improve a building.*

Construction loan is a term frequently used in the real estate industry. Like many common terms, it has a variety of meanings. Sometimes people use it in a general sense when discussing sources of funds to remodel or make relatively minor improvements. More specifically, the term refers to a number of industry practices that provide substantial funding for construction or renovation. A common characteristic of these practices is that the lender agrees to advance a total sum but supplies the funds over a period of time as work progresses. The loan is secured by a construction mortgage.

On completion of the work, the lender carries the mortgage as a permanent investment or assigns it to another lender. Some financial institutions will not make short-term construction loans, either based on internal decisions or because they are prohibited from making these loans by law. If financing through one of these institutions, the property owner first must obtain a short-term loan from an interim lender. When construction is completed, permanent financing, called a construction perm loan, is arranged. Usually this is based on a prior agreement made by the permanent mortgagee to provide long-term financing.

Both the construction mortgage and the mechanic's lien look to the property as security. The periodic advances made by the lender are secured by the increased value of the property stemming from the completed work. At the same time, if those working on the structure are not paid, they have a right to a lien against the real estate. The time when the mechanic's lien attaches is critical to the rights of the parties. For example, in a number of states, a mechanic's lien dates back to the start of construction. If a construction mortgage is not recorded until work commences, the mechanic's lien is superior even if perfected later. A number of states separate buildings from the land when attempting to adjust the interest of the construction mortgagee and the mechanic's lienholder. In these states the mechanic's lien has superior rights in the building even if a construction mortgage has been recorded against the property. Other states have different rules relating to time of attachment.

To establish the priority right of the construction mortgagee and to ensure that workers will be paid, state statutes provide the lender with a preferred position in the security if provisions for disbursing funds are followed. The construction mortgagee must be certain to follow these provisions exactly. Usually they involve two steps: obtaining detailed statements from contractors and subcontractors of the work that has been done and, when funds are disbursed, obtaining proper waivers from the parties to whom payments have been made. Not all states have statutes regulating construction loans. In those that do not, the construction mortgagee must develop procedures to ensure that the mortgage rights will be superior to the mechanics' liens.

Open-End Mortgage

■   *A mortgage that permits the mortgagor to borrow additional funds, usually up to the original amount of the debt.*

Traditionally, in most American jurisdictions, a mortgage to secure future advances provides the lender with priority over liens intervening between the recording of the mortgage and the future advance. This principle is especially well established when the future advance is obligatory.

CASE EXAMPLE

Midge and Tony McLaughlin, a young married couple, executed a $25,000 mortgage to United National Bank for funds advanced to purchase a small house. Midge and Tony planned to have a family and knew that additions would have to be made to the house. When they explained this to the loan officer, he suggested an open-end mortgage. A provision was included in the mortgage requiring the bank to lend them additional funds up to the original amount of the loan.

Several years later, Midge and Tony requested those additional funds. During the intervening years, a judgment had been entered against Midge as a result of an automobile accident. Despite this judgment, United National advanced the money; the original mortgage provided security for the additional funds.

In most open-end mortgages, the mortgagee is not required to advance the additional funds. If the mortgagee has this option, the priority of the lien over an intervening encumbrance in most states depends on notice of the intervening claim. If the mortgagee has actual notice of an intervening lien and elects to advance the funds, any lien that results is inferior to that of the intervening claimant. In the previous example, if the mortgage was nonobligatory and United National had knowledge of the judgment against Midge, a lien resulting from any later advance would be inferior to the judgment lien.

Balloon Payment Mortgage

■   *A mortgage that allows the mortgagor to make smaller regular payments than are required to completely amortize the loan.*

Partially amortized mortgages require a payment that includes both principal and interest, but the payment is not enough to pay off the loan. The balance still owing at the end of the term is called a balloon payment. The borrower either pays the loan off with proceeds from the sale of the property, or some other resource, or refinances the balance at perhaps more competitive terms.

Package Mortgage

■ *A mortgage secured by both personal and real property.*

Package mortgages are used today primarily in financing commercial and industrial ventures. The mortgage covers not only the real property but also personal property essential to the operation of a business. In a mortgage covering a motel, for example, most lenders would require a lien on the furniture and other items necessary to operate the business. In the event of a foreclosure, the security would be much more valuable if it included equipment necessary for operation.

Many underwriters will not approve a package mortgage on residential property. The concern is that they must justify the value of the personalty as collateral over the life of the loan. Because that is difficult to do, the underwriter will often exclude personalty from the collateral as having no value. In the event of a foreclosure, it is difficult to assure that the personal items will remain.

In the instance a lender writes a package mortgage for a residential loan, usually a newly constructed home, the mortgagor is able to finance appliances at the same rate of interest as the mortgage. This rate is usually lower than the rate of a consumer loan and the price of the appliance can be spread over the entire term of the mortgage. The chief argument against the package mortgage is that the buyer, in paying for the appliances over the term of the real estate mortgage, is paying for them long after their useful life has expired.

Reverse Annuity Mortgage

■ *A mortgage loan in which the mortgagee advances funds to a homeowner based on the homeowner's equity in the real estate.*

The reverse annuity mortgage is designed to allow elderly (age 62 and older) homeowners to convert the equity in their home into cash without having to give up the home. They exchange the equity over a period of years for a monthly payment from the lender based on the borrower's life expectancy, the value of the property, and the interest rate.

■ MORTGAGE INSURANCE

■ *Insurance provided by certain government agencies or private corporations protecting mortgage lenders against loss caused by a borrower's default.*

Authorities estimate that more than 25 percent of real estate mortgage loans are covered by some type of mortgage insurance. Mortage insurance provides *liquidity*—the ease with which an asset may be converted to cash. Insured mortgage loans are much more liquid than those that are not insured. Liquidity is greater because firms initiating insured loans must follow established standards and procedures. These procedures include an approved appraisal of the structure as well as approval of the creditworthiness of the borrower. When a loan is insured, not only the lender but also the insurer must be convinced that the property value covers the loan and the borrower has the ability to repay.

Another benefit of mortgage insurance is a reduction in the number of foreclosures. When an insured loan is in default, the insurer pays the debt and takes over the property. The insurer then attempts to sell the property to cover its losses. Today, two federal agencies and several private firms share the mortgage insurance business.

Conventional Mortgage Insurance

Most conventional lenders are restricted to loan-to-value ratios of 80 percent (80 percent loan, 20 percent down payment), unless the increased loan amount is insured. In such cases, the borrower pays the premium called Private Mortgage Insurance (PMI). The monthly premium is included in the monthly mortgage payment. The Homeowners Protection Act of 1998 (HPA) provides for the cancellation of PMI when the loan balance reaches 78 percent of the original value of the home at time of loan closing, provided the loan is current.

FHA Insurance

■   *Insurance provided to lenders under Title II of the National Housing Act.*

The Federal Housing Administration, an organization of HUD, fully insures loans that have met required underwriting criteria. For all FHA loans originated after January 1, 2001, the annual mortgage insurance premium (MIP) is subject to automatic cancellation when the loan-to-value ratio reaches 78 percent, providing the borrower has paid the premium for at least five years. The insurance, however, will remain in force for the life of the loan. Because the borrower of a condominium loan does not pay an up-front mortgage insurance premium, and the loan is based on term of the loan and the interest rate, here the monthly MIP is paid for the life of the loan.

■ REGULATIONS AFFECTING MORTGAGE LOANS

Both state and federal regulations influence mortgage lending. Usually these regulations favor borrowers as legislators recognize that the borrower's bargaining position is weaker than the lender's. Usury statutes, the Truth-in-Lending Act, and the Equal Credit Opportunity Act are examples of regulations with which lenders must contend.

Usury

■   *The practice of charging interest on a loan in excess of a rate allowed by law.*

Religious disapproval of interest resulting in usury laws has influenced relationships between borrowers and lenders for centuries. The importance of usury laws depends to a large extent on economic conditions. When money is scarce, lenders are able to charge higher rates for loans, and usury becomes a factor that they must consider. Almost every state has laws prohibiting lenders from charging excessive interest. These statutes vary appreciably from state to state. Not only do the permissible rates differ, but major differences exist in the transactions that are covered and the penalties levied against the usurious lender.

The impact of usury laws has been limited by federal legislation, to some extent. The Depository Institution Deregulation and Monetary Control Act (DIDMC) eliminated state interest ceilings on first mortgage loans made by financial institutions and secured by residential real estate, with some exemptions.

Truth-in-Lending

▪ *The popular name given to part of the Consumer Credit Protection Act of 1968, the federal statute that requires lenders to disclose the cost of consumer credit so that users may better compare terms available from different sources.*

The purpose of the Truth-in-Lending Act is to foster the informed use of consumer credit, that is, credit extended to an individual to be used primarily for personal, family, or household purposes. This legislation in no way fixes maximum or minimum charges for credit.

Real estate credit is only one of many types of credit covered by the act. To come within the scope of the act, real estate credit must be extended to a natural person and be granted to finance acquisition or initial construction of the borrower's principal dwelling. Thus, mortgage loans to corporations and to individuals for business purposes are excluded. Credit extended to the owner of a dwelling containing more than four units is also exempt.

The key to understanding Truth-in-Lending is *meaningful disclosure*. Provisions of both this act and of Regulation Z, the Federal Reserve Board's interpretations of the act, require that borrowers be furnished with the facts they need to make intelligent decisions on the use of credit. To accomplish this, information must be presented using terminology specified in the act and Regulation Z. This information must be clear, conspicuous, and in writing. Generally, the information must cover all costs of credit and include, in most cases, the finance charge and the annual percentage rate.

▪ **Finance Charge.** *Dollars-and-cents total of all charges a borrower must pay, directly or indirectly, for obtaining credit.*

Prior to Truth-in-Lending, some lenders presented credit to borrowers in a manner that concealed or even misrepresented costs. Although institutions furnishing real estate credit were not generally as flagrant in this practice as other suppliers of consumer credit, some confusing practices did exist in the mortgage lending market. A relatively common practice was to charge a borrower for extras, loan fees, service charges, or points that were not quoted with the interest rate. The Truth-in-Lending Act requires that lenders disclose the dollar total of *all costs* of credit. Extra charges cannot be tallied separately if they are a cost of credit. They must be included in the finance charge.

Costs that a buyer would pay regardless of whether credit is extended need not be included in the finance charge. Items such as title examination fees, title insurance premiums, survey costs, and legal fees fit into this category. These costs must be itemized and disclosed to the borrower separately if included in the total financed.

■   **Annual Percentage Rate.** *The relationship between the total finance charge and the amount to be financed in annual percentage terms.*

Disclosure of the annual percentage rate (APR) allows consumers to compare finance charges among lenders, making shopping for the cost of credit more understandable. Based on a time period of a year, the APR is similar to simple annual interest, a concept with which many consumers are familiar.

Credit Advertising. Regulation Z defines *credit advertising* broadly. The definition covers commercial messages that either directly or indirectly promote a credit transaction. Thus, developers or real estate brokers are subject to the act if their advertisement includes terms to be granted by a creditor. Although the definition of *advertising* includes oral as well as written communication, it does not encompass a broker's or developer's responses to a buyer's questions about available credit.

Yield Spread Premium

■   *A fee a lender pays a mortgage broker for securing a customer who borrows at an interest rate above market.*

The mortgage brokerage industry has grown to where it originates nearly 50 percent of all residential real estate loans in the United States. The mortgage brokerage business acts as a middleman bringing the borrower and the lender together. A mortgage brokerage business does not make loans; they accept a loan application from a borrower and then find a wholesale lender willing to make a loan to the borrower. The broker is compensated from either the borrower, the lender, or from both for facilitating the transaction.

The mortgage broker or retail lender gets paid a fee from the wholesale lender, called a yield spread premium (YSP), for originating and processing the loan. The amount of the YSP is based on the amount of the loan and the rate offered and accepted by the borrower. Each day a mortgage broker or retail lender receives rate sheets from the various wholesale lenders. The rate sheet indicates their PAR rate, the rate the lender charges with no points to the borrower because it gives the lender the yield they want for 30 years. The higher the interest rate above PAR rate, the higher the YSP paid to the broker. If the borrower accepts the PAR rate or a rate above PAR, the wholesale lender will pay the broker the corresponding YSP.

This indirect fee is paid to the mortgage broker or lender at the time of funding the loan. In some states the amount of the fee must be disclosed to the borrower at the time of closing. In addition to the YSP, the broker receives other fees directly from the borrower as an application fee or at the time of closing. The fees required directly from the borrower must be used in calculating the borrower's APR (annual percentage rate). The YSP is not a fee from the borrower so it is not used in the calculation of the APR.

Equal Credit Opportunity Act

■ *Federal statute that prohibits lenders from refusing credit based on race, color, religion, national origin, sex, marital status, age, public assistance income, or other classifications protected by the act.*

In addition to the Equal Credit Opportunity Act (ECOA), the Federal Credit Reporting Act (FCRA) requires the lender to provide the borrower with the name, address, and phone number of the credit reporting agency that provided the information on which the lender based their adverse action. In order for the government to monitor the lender's compliance with ECOA, applicants are asked to furnish information regarding race, ethnicity and sex at the time of application. This information appears on the Fannie Mae residential loan application, but the applicant is not required to furnish the information, and the refusal to answer will not jeopardize the loan application.

An individual who is denied credit and can establish that the creditor has violated the Equal Credit Opportunity Act may recover actual damages plus punitive damages up to $10,000. The plaintiff who brings a successful action under ECOA is also entitled to reimbursement for court costs and reasonable attorney fees.

Real Estate Settlement Procedures Act (RESPA)

■ *Enacted in 1974 to ensure that buyers are informed in regards to the amount and type of charges they will pay at settlement.*

RESPA requires (among other things) that the lender:

■ Must provide the loan applicant the Special Information Booklet *Buying Your Home* within three business days of receipt of the loan application

■ Must provide the borrower with a Good Faith Estimate of the borrower's anticipated settlement costs which also include the lender's fees

The USA Patriot Act

The USA Patriot Act (Uniting and Strengthening America by Providing Appropriate Tools Required to Intercept and Obstruct Terrorism Act of 2002) was enacted by the U.S. Congress in October 2001, as a response to 9/11. The USA Patriot Act gives a wide range of new tools to combat money laundering, terrorist financing, identity theft, and other forms of fraud. This act requires lenders to obtain the following identifying information from an applicant at the time of loan application: name, date of birth, address, and their taxpayer identification number. This would be a Social Security number for U.S. citizens or other government-issued identification numbers such as a passport. The act specifies that documents used to verify an applicant's identity include unexpired government-issued identifications that show the applicant's nationality or residence and a photo, such as a driver's license or passport.

The Fair and Accurate Credit Transaction Act

The Fair and Accurate Credit Transaction Act (Fact Act), signed into law December 2003, extends national standards for consumer credit reporting. An important purpose of this law is to reduce identity theft and make it easier for consumers to obtain their credit rating information. The Fact Act requires lenders to provide consumer credit scores, and the four reason codes, as well as a National Credit Score Disclosure form. The four reason codes identify the main factors that affect the borrower's score. The disclosure form explains to the applicant that other factors are considered in the approval of their home loan in addition to the credit score. The lender provides the applicant with a copy of their credit report and score along with the disclosure. The consumer is encouraged to review the information for accuracy.

The act also allows consumers to receive a free copy of their credit report once a year. This is to help prevent identity theft and assist victims in repairing their credit histories.

Predatory Lending Practices

■ *A term used to describe a wide range of unfair financial practices usually occuring in the "sub-prime" mortgage market.*

Nearly all states have some form of a "fair lending" law to protect consumers from predatory lending practices. These practices most often target certain groups of people such as minorities, the elderly on fixed incomes, and lower income individuals, with the intention of outright fraud and abuse. The lender depends upon their lack of education, understanding of financial terms, and sometimes their desperate financial situations.

Predatory practices include:

■ Lending to borrowers who do not have the ability to repay the loan

■ Refinancing the loan repeatedly without regard to an actual benefit to the borrower

■ Charging large prepayment penalties when the borrower pays off the loan or refinances the loan before the term of the loan is over

■ Offering loans with one set of terms at time of application but then pressuring the borrower to accept lesser terms at time of closing

■ Offering a loan product that has an unreasonably high payment due at the end of the term

■ Offering high sub-prime interest rates and massive fees to an unknowledgeable borrower who otherwise qualifies for a prime loan

In an effort to protect the consumer against predatory lending practices, many states now require disclosures from the lender to borrowers alerting them to many of these unfair practices.

■ SALE OF MORTGAGED REAL ESTATE

> **CASE EXAMPLE**
>
> Hal Zenick owned a home encumbered with an $85,000 mortgage at 9 percent interest. The mortgage was held by the Harper Hill Savings and Loan Association (Harper Hill). Hal, who had purchased the property for $98,000, had lived there for about a year when he was transferred and forced to sell. During the year, interest rates had risen considerably in Hal's area, and the broker with whom he listed the property suggested that Hal might sell his home more quickly and for a better price if the mortgage were retained. The buyer would not have to finance at the higher interest rates and might save in other ways.

Whether Hal lives in a title-theory or a lien-theory state, he has an interest in the property that he can sell. He cannot, however, escape personal liability for the mortgage debt unless Harper Hill, the mortgagee, releases him. In addition, the property remains subject to Harper Hill's lien. Nothing that Hal can do short of paying the underlying debt can eliminate the lien. And, Hal's right to sell his interest without discharging the mortgage may be restricted by a clause in the mortgage instrument, referred to as a *due-on-sale clause*.

Due-on-Sale Clause

■ *A provision found in most mortgages requiring that the mortgagor pay off the mortgage debt if the property is sold.*

A **due-on-sale clause** limits the mortgagor's right to convey the real property without discharging the mortgage. The clause treats the sale of mortgaged premises as a default; because almost all mortgages also contain a clause making the entire debt due on default, the mortgagee may call the loan when the mortgagor sells the property. Of course a mortgagee such as Harper Hill can negotiate a modification of the debt with the mortgagor and the grantee and not call the mortgage. In Hal's case, Harper Hill might do this if the grantee were willing to pay interest at a rate that was closer to what the association was obtaining on new loans.

If Hal's mortgage does not contain a due-on-sale clause, two major approaches exist to the manner in which he may sell the property without discharging the mortgage. The property may be sold with the grantee agreeing to "assume and pay" the mortgage, or the property may be sold "subject to" the mortgage.

Assumption

■ *A contract between a grantor-mortgagor and a grantee in which the grantee agrees to assume responsibility for the mortgage debt.*

Assume that Hal's broker found a buyer who was willing to pay $100,000 for Hal's residence. The buyer had $15,000 in cash and was anxious to assume the mortgage. The purchase offer that the buyer submitted to Hal contained the following provision:

"Buyer assumes and agrees to pay the obligation secured by mortgage to Harper Hill Savings and Loan Association recorded according to the terms of the mortgage and the note accompanying it." When Hal accepted this purchase offer, a contract was created, one provision of which was the buyer's promise to pay the mortgage debt. This is a typical assumption agreement. (See Figure 21.1.) Ordinarily, agreements of this nature originate in the contract of sale, but they may be made in a separate instrument.

In some states, an oral assumption, if provable, is binding, although certainly oral assumptions are not a preferred practice, and several states by specific statute require assumption to be in writing. In many cases the deed also contains an assumption clause. This binds the grantee on acceptance of the deed, even when only the grantor signs the instrument.

The assumption agreement does not relieve the mortgagor/grantor of personal liability for the debt. Hal continues to be responsible to Harper Hill, but he has acquired the right to sue the buyer if the debt is not paid. This right is based on the contract between them in which the buyer has assumed the debt. However, if the buyer and Harper Hill Savings modify the terms of the loan, Hal is released from liability for the debt.

Implicit in the assumption agreement is the buyer's commitment that the seller may look to the land for reimbursement if forced to pay the debt. For Hal, additional monetary responsibility exists only if the land becomes less valuable than the debt.

The land, however, remains subject to the mortgage, and if the debt is not paid, the mortgagee may foreclose. In addition, the mortgagee without foreclosing may sue the buyer on the assumption. The mortgagee's right exists in spite of the fact that it was not a party to the assumption agreement.

Novation

■   *A mutual agreement in which a creditor agrees to discharge an existing debt and to substitute a new obligation and a new debtor in its place.*

A novation differs from an assumption to which the mortgagee has consented. (See Figure 21.2.) In the assumption, the original mortgagor has a secondary liability even after the property is sold. In a **novation**, the original mortgagor is discharged and the old debt is extinguished. Few mortgagees will consent to a novation during periods of increasing interest rates unless the new debtor agrees to pay interest at the prevailing rate.

"Subject To"

■   *Refers to a sale in which buyer agrees to purchase property subject to the lien of the mortgage.*

Perhaps the buyer found by Hal's broker would not be willing to assume the mortgage debt. Under these circumstances, the buyer would pay Hal for his equity in the property. Any interest acquired by the buyer is subject to the lien of the mortgage. If there is a default, the property will be foreclosed, but the buyer has not agreed to become personally liable.

FIGURE 21.1   Assumption

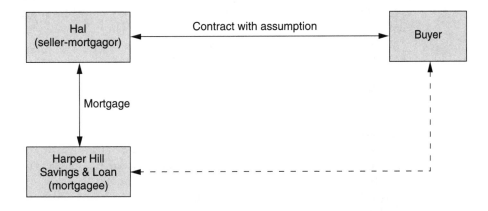

FIGURE 21.2   Novation

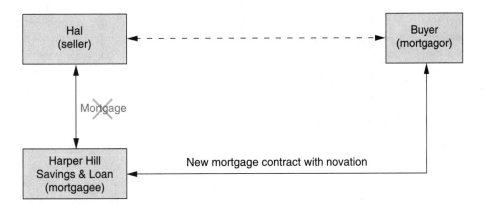

As noted, a buyer who takes property subject to the mortgage has no personal obligation. Both the mortgagee and the seller/mortgagor must look to the land to collect the debt in the event of default. If proceeds from a foreclosure are not sufficient, the deficiency is the seller/mortgagor's responsibility. A number of states have, however, extended the buyer's responsibility with the *doctrine of implied assumption*. In these states, the buyer is personally liable, even when no promise to assume exists, when the amount of an existing mortgage is deducted from the purchase price and the buyer pays the difference.

CASE EXAMPLE

Metcalf contracted to sell property to Lay for $29,000. The property was encumbered with a $20,000 mortgage. The contract did not mention the existing mortgage because Lay anticipated financing without it. This financing did not materialize, and the salesperson for the seller suggested that Lay merely purchase the equity. Lay agreed. Lay never talked with the seller, and no express assumption was discussed. At the closing, the price of the property was clearly shown as $29,000 with a $20,000 credit for the mortgage. The deed to Lay excepted the existing mortgage. When the debt was not paid, the mortgagee foreclosed. Not realizing enough from the sale to pay the debt, the mortgagee sued Metcalf, who in turn sued Lay. Lay would be held personally liable, although he had not assumed the mortgage, if the court applied the *doctrine of implied assumption*.

THE CHANGING LANDSCAPE

Mortgages make it possible to purchase real estate. People usually cannot afford to pay cash for such a large purchase; hence, they must borrow money to do so. Because the mortgage acts as security for repayment of the debt, lenders are willing to extend a mortgage loan. The purchase-money mortgage is particularly safe for lenders because it gives priority over certain existing liens. The area of mortgages is controlled, in part, by federal and state laws and regulations, which change from time to time.

Mortgage interest rates rise and fall, as determined by certain economic indicators, thus making purchases of homes either more or less affordable. Interest rates for existing adjustable-rate mortgages may rise or fall during the life of the mortgage, as calculated by a predetermined formula. Fixed interest rate mortgages are set for a specified number of years and do not change during the life of the mortgage.

It is important to keep a good credit record because the best mortgage interest rates go to those with the best credit rating scores. These scores are determined by credit bureaus that gather information on consumers. This information includes debt repayment history and other credit information. The difference between a *very high* credit score and a *high* credit score could mean a 1 percent difference in the mortgage interest rate, which is a substantial amount of money over the life of the loan.

It is not uncommon for credit bureaus to make mistakes when compiling credit information; hence, borrowers should scrutinize their credit report when seeking a loan and bring to the lender's attention any wrong information. Consumers have the legal right to have the credit bureau correct the information.

Do you think that there should be a uniform method of compiling the credit score, given the importance of the score? Do you think that the formula for compiling the credit score should be clearly revealed? What benefit would this provide?

KEY TERMS

adjustable-rate mortgage 479

annual cap 480

annual percentage rate 488

assumption 491

construction mortgage 483

deed in lieu of foreclosure 477

deed of trust 467

default 473

due-on-sale clause 491

Equal Credit Opportunity Act 489

equity of redemption 474

judicial foreclosure 475

lien theory 466

lifetime cap 480

mortgage 465

nonjudicial foreclosure 476

note 466

novation 492

open-end mortgage 484

package mortgage 485

purchase money mortgage 481

satisfaction of mortgage 468

secured debt 465

strict foreclosure 477

title theory 466

Truth-in-Lending 487

usury 486

INTERNET RESOURCES

Learn about the government-chartered mortgage corporation Freddie Mac by visiting

www.freddiemac.com

REVIEW AND DISCUSSION QUESTIONS

1. Explain how the legal rights given to a mortgagee by a mortgage differ from the legal rights given by a note.
2. Discuss the difference between the lien and title theories of mortgages.
3. Explain the differences between a mortgage and a deed of trust.
4. Explain the rights and privileges of a mortgagee that takes possession of mortgage premises on the mortgagor's default.
5. (a) List the three different approaches taken in the United States as to when a mechanic's lien becomes effective. (b) In your opinion which of these is the most equitable? Why?
6. What is a foreclosure by power-of-sale? How does it differ from judicial foreclosure?
7. The terms *finance charge* and *annual percentage rate* (APR) are important in Truth-in-Lending legislation. Explain what each means.
8. What is a due-on-sale clause? Explain why this clause has become increasingly important in recent years.
9. Distinguish between an "assumption" and "subject to" purchase.

■ CASE PROBLEMS

1. Tom Hildebrant purchased a four-unit rental property for $175,000. River National Bank lent him $155,000 to complete the purchase. The loan was secured by a mortgage on the property. Because of a severe recession in the area caused by closing of several steel mills, Hildebrant was unable to consistently rent all of the units, and he defaulted on the debt. As a result the bank foreclosed. At the foreclosure sale, the property sold for $145,000. Does Tom have any liability on the unpaid portion of the debt? Discuss.

2. McCorriston purchased rental real estate in a lien-theory state. The purchase was secured by a mortgage loan from the First Bank of Crooksville. When McCorriston defaulted, the bank attempted to collect the rents from the property to be applied against the loan. The mortgage did not contain a provision allowing it to do so. However, the bank argued that as McCorriston had defaulted, it was entitled to the rents. Was the bank correct? Support your answer.

3. Able, Baker, and Charlie purchased a farm for investment. They took title as tenants in common. Part of the purchase price was secured by a purchase-money mortgage on the property. The mortgage and note were signed by Able and Baker but not Charlie. When the parties defaulted, the seller joined the three in a foreclosure action. Charlie defended on grounds that she did not sign the mortgage and note. Would she be successful? Support your answer.

4. Oellerich and his wife sold real estate that they owned. The purchasers assumed the mortgage. The assumption agreement provided that the Oellerichs were not released from liability on the original debt if the purchasers defaulted on the note. Shortly thereafter the lender and purchasers executed a modification agreement that increased the interest on the note. The Oellerichs were not parties to this agreement. Did the modification agreement affect the rights of the parties? Explain how and why. *Oellerich v. First Fed. Sav. & Loan Assn.*, 552 F.2d 1109 (5th Cir. 1977).

5. Albert owns real property worth $35,000. He borrows $28,000 from Martin and executes a mortgage on the property in Martin's favor. The term of the mortgage is 15 years. Seven years later, Albert sells the property to Bobb for a cash amount with the mortgage remaining on the property. What difference, if any, will it make to Bobb if the deed from Albert states "subject to a mortgage indebtedness of _____" or "subject to a mortgage indebtedness of _____, which said indebtedness the grantee assumes and agrees to pay"?

6. Larson owned a commercial building that he had inherited from his mother. The original mortgage on the building had been satisfied. In January 1974, Larson leased a portion of the building to Hutchins for a five-year term. The lease was immediately recorded. In March 1975, Larson borrowed $75,000 from the Belville Bank, giving it a mortgage on the property. The mortgage was for a term of ten years. It was recorded on April 11, 2000. The $75,000 was used to renovate the property. In 1977, because the debt was not paid, the bank foreclosed.

(a) Kane, the purchaser at the foreclosure sale, wished to use the entire building and brought an action to eject Hutchins. Would Kane be successful? Discuss.

(b) Assume that, on March 27, Anderson began electrical work that was part of the renovation. The work was not completed until June. When Anderson was not paid, he filed a mechanic's lien. What are Anderson's rights vis-à-vis the Belville Bank? Discuss.

7. Smith agreed to purchase property from Layton. As part of the contract, Smith assumed and agreed to pay the existing mortgage. Smith immediately contracted to sell the property to Young. Layton agreed to convey directly to Young, who assumed the mortgage in the deed to him. Smith never had title to the property. The mortgage was not paid, and the foreclosure took place. There was a deficiency, and the mortgagee sued Smith. Would the mortgagee be successful? Discuss.

8. Lon Gabele is the president of Gabele Builders as well as its chief salesperson. Fredericktown Savings agrees to finance homes built by Gabele at a rate of 10½ percent if the buyer makes a $2,500 downpayment. Gabele places an advertisement in the local paper indicating that homes can be purchased at $2,500 down. The only other information in the advertisement is the offering price, Gabele's name, and the location of the development.

Prior to the advertisement's appearance, a number of buyers visited the homes that Gabele had for sale. When asked about financing, Gabele informs them that it is available at 10½ percent. He provides no additional information but refers them to Fredericktown Savings. Has Gabele violated the credit advertising provisions of the Truth-in-Lending Act? Support your answer.

22

Land Installment Contracts

■ LAND INSTALLMENT CONTRACT

■ *A legally enforceable agreement between a buyer and a seller whereby the buyer promises to make periodic installment payments to the seller toward the purchase price of real property and the seller promises to convey title to the property on receipt of the last installment.*

Chapter 11 considered the real estate purchase agreement, which is the ordinary contract for the sale of real estate. That agreement defines the rights and duties of the seller and buyer in preparation for the closing of the transaction, which is discussed fully in Chapters 14 and 20. Between the signing of the purchase contract and the closing, there is a short interval ranging from about one to three months. During this interval, the seller is expected to obtain title insurance or secure other evidence of title, while the buyer attempts to secure financing, typically through a lending institution.

Sometimes the buyer is unable to obtain financing from a lending institution. Lacking the necessary cash, the buyer may be forced to defer the purchase while awaiting improved finances. Several alternatives are open, however, that may enable the buyer to purchase the property. If the seller is willing to extend financing to the buyer for the purchase price, one alternative is the seller-financed purchase-money mortgage, which is discussed in Chapter 21. Under that method, the seller transfers the deed to the property to the buyer and the buyer signs a mortgage in the seller's favor. The mortgage secures the remaining unpaid purchase price owed to the seller. The **land installment contract**, also known as a *land contract* or *contract for deed*, is another method of seller financing.

For the buyer, the land installment contract is a method of financing a real estate transaction through the seller; for the seller, it secures the payment of a debt. The rules that attach to ordinary contracts also apply to land installment contracts. The agreement must be supported by consideration and entered into by parties who possess the requisite capacity. Nevertheless, some obvious distinctions separate the land installment contract from the ordinary real estate purchase contract. In an ordinary real estate purchase contract, the buyer's right to possession is deferred until closing or thereafter. Under a land installment contract, possession is normally immediate and does not await final payment. In addition, the relationship between the parties to a real estate purchase agreement is of rather short duration, usually ceasing at the closing, when title is conveyed. The legal relationship of the parties to a land contract lasts longer. Such a contract may endure for as long as the seller is willing to extend the financing, perhaps 20 years or more, although shorter periods are more common. Often the seller extends a payment schedule based on a 20-year to 30-year amoratized payback period, but requires that the entire balance be paid in full after a shorter period, for example, three to five years. The final payment is known as a *balloon payment* and normally requires that the buyer find outside financing to meet the payment. Before final payment, the seller holds legal title, whereas the purchaser is normally in possession of the property and enjoys *equitable title*.

Title Problems

On completion of all terms of the contract, including payment of the last install-ment, legal title passes to the buyer, and the deed can be recorded in the buyer's name. Until the last installment is paid, the property remains in the seller's name. During this interval, the seller may encumber the property with mortgages or other liens. Unless the buyer is protected, he or she may pay the entire purchase price and find the property totally encumbered. By recording the land installment contract, however, the buyer may secure protection against most future encumbrances. Recording places all prospective mortgagees and lienors on notice of the buyer's interest in the property, and title prob-lems are less likely to arise.

When the contract is unrecorded and the seller encumbers or sells the property, the installment contract buyer may be without remedy. A claim against the seller for damages will not necessarily help the buyer should the seller be insolvent. Sellers often discourage or impede the recording, because it is easier to resell the property on the buyer's default if the contract is not recorded. Some states by statute require that a land installment con-tract be recorded. However, the law is not always sufficient to insure compliance.

Liens that attach before the creation of the installment contract may go unnoticed if the buyer fails to investigate the title beforehand. Title insurance protects the buyer's interest in the property. This form of assurance is normally required when a third-party lender is involved. In land installment contracts, however, there is no third-party stim-ulus because the seller finances the transaction. The uneducated buyer may fail to have the title examined. The prudent buyer should require proof of title in the seller as a con-dition of entering into the contract, should be sure the contract is immediately record-ed, and should require a clause within the contract clarifying that the seller agrees to tender a deed to the property free of all liens and other encumbrances.

After-Acquired Title

In some cases, the seller does not have title at the time of entering into the contract but subsequently acquires it. In this event, the buyer is entitled to **after-acquired title** when the time comes for the deed to be transferred to the buyer.

CASE EXAMPLE

Jim Ferguson, seller, enters into a land installment contract with Bill Hodd, buyer, whereby Ferguson is to tender a free and unencumbered deed to 20 acres of farmland designated as the Hill property, on Hodd's completion of 60 monthly payments of $300 each. At the time the contract was entered into, Ferguson possessed only a leasehold interest. Thereafter, how-ever, he acquired the property in fee simple absolute from the lessor. On completing the last installment payment, Hodd is entitled to the fee under the doctrine of after-acquired title. See *Bull v. Goldman*, 30 Md. App. 665, 353 A.2d 661 (1976).

Should the buyer learn, after signing the contract, that the seller does not possess marketable title, in some jurisdictions the buyer may rescind the contract and seek return of the installment payments previously paid.

Contract Terms

Basic rules of real estate purchase contracts treated in Chapters 10 and 11 also govern land installment contracts. Because a land contract involves an interest in land, it must comply with the Statute of Frauds, which requires that the contract be supported by a written memorandum. Normally, the land installment contract must be properly executed before it can be recorded. State statutes vary and should be consulted to ascertain the particular requirements for proper execution. Ordinarily, it must be signed, witnessed, and notarized. Some jurisdictions, however, dispense with the witness requirement.

The parties are free to agree on the terms of the land contract, and the courts will enforce those terms to the extent that they do not offend public policy. Over the years, certain typical terms have emerged. Generally, the specifics of the terms reflect the relative bargaining strength of the buyer and seller. It appears that the seller has traditionally possessed the upper hand. Nonetheless, the courts will give effect to the intent of the parties. The following case well illustrates the necessity of making that intent clear within the writing.

McKone v. Guertzgen
Supreme Court of Wyoming
811 P.2d 728 (Wyo. 1991)

Background. McKone sold his land to the Guertzgens under an installment contract. The contract provided that the Guertzgens would have possession of the property, but that the deed would not pass until all payments had been made under the contract.

The Guertzgens converted the property from a service station into a liquor store/lounge. The Chief of the town's fire department ordered the removal of the underground fuel tanks because they violated the fire code. Each party argued that it was the responsibility of the other to undertake the expense of removal.

The purchaser brought an action against McKone, the vendor, seeking to hold him liable for the removal. The trial court judge found the vendor responsible. The vendor appealed.

Decision. The trial court decision is affirmed.

Justice Cardine. . . . [W]e acknowledged that the purchaser under a contract for deed has an "equitable interest" in the property. Thus, we agree that the Guertzgens fit the Code's definition of owner because their equitable interest in the property is also a contingent interest, which the Code includes under the definition of owner. The parties' agreement provides that the warranty deed remains in escrow until the Guertzgens have made all the payments under the agreement and the warranty deed is conveyed to them.

Professor Rudolph has summarized the legal principles of the contract for deed:

continued on next page

The contract [for deed] typically provides for the payment of the purchase price in installments over a period of years and for retention of title in the seller until the purchase price is fully paid, but gives the buyer a right to possession from the execution of the contract.

. . . Until there has been a conveyance of the warranty deed, McKone continues to hold legal title and remains the legal owner of the property.

. . . [W]e hold that McKone is the party responsible for the removal of the tanks because he was the owner of the property when they were abandoned.

Affirmed.

Chief Justice Urbigkit dissenting. When . . . McKone entered into a transaction with . . . [the Guertzgens] to sell a business lot . . . none of them expected that abandoned underground petroleum tanks would come back to haunt both the seller and buyers. Events change rapidly in this society in which we live and society came back to them to look with disdain, suspicion and active antagonism on the abandoned underground petroleum product storage tanks.

The buyers bought the property "as is, where is." Unfortunately, in acceptance of an invalid legend of the advantages of the escrow deed arrangement for installment contract for sale . . . the parties were faced with events occurring since sale which have severely impacted the property's value—abandoned underground petroleum product storage tanks.

The buyers paid promptly and properly on the installment contract for about eight years until notice by the fire marshal of current law changes and regulations regarding abandoned underground petroleum product storage tanks. . . .

We are now faced . . . with society's imposition of an expensive cost on the landowner and are asked who is to pay—the seller or the buyers? I would really like to believe that some part of the responsibility should be placed on whoever advised these parties to use the installment sale technique

. . . instead of a note and mortgage, but those other parties are not here before us. We have a seller, buyers and an imposed cost by the government.

For this case I would hold that the buyers, by their agreement, bought problems of future governmental action with land purchased in specific accord with the "as is, where is," provisions of the written agreement. I would reverse the district court's judgment. . . . Further, I would determine that the unknown and unforeseen go with the risk of purchase and do not remain with the equity of retained sale price obligation. The owner of the premises should be the possessor with rights to the property, not the holder of a security device for purchase payment.

Justice Golden dissenting. I respectfully dissent. When resolving this sort of dispute this court looks first to the parties' agreement. If the writing was unambiguous it expresses and controls the parties' assignment of rights and obligations. I believe we need go no farther than the language of the written agreement to decide this case.

The majority applies this principle, but finds the provisions asserted by McKone do not address this particular contingency, and looks beyond the agreement language to determine liability for the cost of removing the abandoned tanks. In his dissent Chief Justice Urbigkit also looks to the agreement and resolves the issue to his satisfaction by applying "as is, where is" provisions of the written agreement.

I agree with the majority that the provisions McKone relies on do not allocate the burden of removal costs, but do note they evidence the intent of the parties that the Guertzgens would shoulder all responsibilities connected with the property when they assumed possession. I cannot identify an "as is, where is," provision, but I find that another agreement term does assign responsibility for removing the tanks in a manner consistent with the delegations in the provisions offered by McKone. . . .

We are not concerned here so much with allocation of risk of loss as we are with determination of which party is responsible for compliance with laws.

The agreement assigns this responsibility to the Guertzgens where it states that buyer agrees to purchase and take property SUBJECT TO easements, reservations and restrictions of record and to Zoning and other laws.

Restate concisely the position of the majority and each dissent. Which opinion do you prefer? Explain.

Price. Normally the buyer pays a down payment and periodic installments. The installment payments include principal and interest. The installments may be payable monthly, quarterly, annually, or at any other agreed-on interval. Unless otherwise stated, taxes and insurance are the seller's responsibility because the seller is the legal owner of the property until the entire purchase price is paid. However, neither statute nor custom prevents an allocation of taxes and insurance to the parties on the basis of their respective interests in the property. In most cases, however, the bargaining position of the seller is strong enough to require that the buyer assume the whole burden of these charges. This is not an unreasonable burden, considering that the buyer receives the present beneficial use of the property and expects full ownership in the future.

Waste, Removal, and Inspection. The buyer is normally in possession of the premises in an installment contract. Consequently, the installment buyer is in the best position to maintain the premises and keep it in good repair. Customarily, the parties include a clause in the contract that makes the buyer responsible for the maintenance of the property. Similarly, the installment contract may include a clause prohibiting **waste** or removal of fixtures or improvements without the consent of the seller. The failure of a buyer to comply with these clauses is a breach of the contract that gives rise to various remedies discussed later in this chapter.

The seller needs the right to inspect the premises to police these provisions. For that reason, a clause similar to the following is often included: "Seller shall have the right to enter on and inspect the property and the buildings and improvements thereon after giving reasonable notice to do so."

■ **Indemnification**. *The act of compensating another in the event of loss.*

In the event that the buyer fails to keep the property in repair or causes waste, damages may result from either loss of property value or consequent injury to occupiers of the property. Mechanics' liens (discussed in Chapter 15) may also encumber the property if the purchaser fails to pay workers or suppliers for renovations, repairs, improvements, or other authorized work. An **indemnification** clause such as the following may be included for the seller's protection:

> Buyer shall hold seller free and harmless from any and all demands, loss, or liability resulting from the injury to, or death of, any person because of the negligence of the buyer or the condition of the property at any time after the date possession is delivered to the buyer. Buyer shall further indemnify seller for the amount of any and all mechanics' liens or other expenses or damages resulting from any renovations, alterations, building repairs, or other work ordered by the buyer.

Should the buyer fail to pay the tax assessments or insurance as agreed on, the seller's security is jeopardized. The government, deprived of its taxes or assessments, may place a tax lien on the property and even foreclose for failure to pay. The seller's security would also be jeopardized should the property be destroyed by fire unless hazard insurance is maintained. If there is a mortgage on the property, the mortgagee may foreclose in the event that taxes, assessments, and/or insurance payments are in arrears. To protect the seller against these risks, the seller may require that a clause be included within the installment contract as follows:

> Should buyer fail to pay any amount pursuant to this contract for taxes, assessments, or insurance within ten (10) days before that amount becomes delinquent, the seller may pay the amount and buyer agrees to repay to seller the amount paid by the seller together with interest at the rate of ten (10) percent per annum.

Assignment. In the absence of a provision in the contract prohibiting assignment, the buyer is free to transfer his or her interest in the land contract. Assignment does not, however, relieve the installment buyer of the obligation to continue making installment payments to the seller. The seller may desire to limit the buyer's right of assignment, being concerned that the assignee (one to whom the property is transferred) may be more likely to jeopardize the seller's interest in the property than the installment buyer. For this reason, the installment contract normally includes a provision prohibiting assignment without the seller's written consent. In absence of such a clause, the buyer may assign the contract, and the seller must respect that assignment.

CASE EXAMPLE

Wayne and Lucille Hickox entered into a written agreement for the sale and purchase of 864 acres of real estate with Barbara and Billy Bell. The purchase price was $700,000, payable $50,000 as a down payment and the remainder in installments. Under the contract, the purchasers had the option, as payments were made, to have the sellers sign a warranty deed in favor of buyers to such land as paid for based on $815 per acre. The Bells faithfully made payments the first four years and then assigned the contract to the Hesses, who made payments thereafter. The Bells requested that the Hickoxes execute a warranty deed conveying 83.67 acres based on the amount of principal paid to date. The Hickoxes refused to credit any amount of the payments made by the Hesses because it was not paid by the Bells.

Finding in favor of the Bells, the Illinois Appellate court said:

> [W]hen a valid assignment is executed, the assignee (1) acquires all of the interest of the assignor in the property that is transferred and (2) stands in the shoes of the assignor. . . . [We] find that the money paid by the Hesses under the contract is to be credited to the Bells as payment under the contract.

See *Hickox v. Bell*, 195 Ill. App. 3d 976, 55 2 N.E.2d 1133 (1990).

At any time before title passes, the seller is free to transfer the property to someone other than the installment buyer. Installment payments are then directed to the new owner. The sale is subject to the rights of the installment buyer, who still remains entitled to the property on fulfillment of the terms of the installment contract. The seller's power to assign may be limited by agreement, but normally it is not because of the purchaser's weaker bargaining position.

Mortgage. Mortgages are discussed in detail in Chapter 21. A typical clause regarding the seller's right to mortgage the property, pending the full payment of the purchase price, is often included within the land contract. A clause similar to the following is not uncommon: "The seller may mortgage the property, but in no event may such mortgage exceed the amount of the balance due on the contract."

> **CASE EXAMPLE**
> Norma Livingston sells real property to Howard Kessler on a land installment contract for $120,000, payable $20,000 down and $5,000 principal annually thereafter, plus 10 percent interest for 20 years. After five years, Livingston desires to borrow money and gives a mortgage in the property to the Second National Bank as security for the loan. Livingston may mortgage the property up to $75,000, the balance due on the installment contract.

In addition, the buyer may be contractually safeguarded against the consequences of a seller defaulting on a mortgage by inclusion of a clause similar to the following:

> The seller shall keep any mortgage on the property in good standing, and if the seller defaults on any mortgage, the buyer may pay the delinquency and receive credit toward payment due under the terms of the contract.

An installment buyer who desires to borrow money from a bank or other lending institution may use as collateral the realty that is the subject of the land contract. Unless the contract expressly states otherwise, the buyer is entitled to mortgage the property to the extent that its value exceeds the amount owed on the land installment contract. A provision in the contract prohibiting assignment does not prevent the installment buyer from mortgaging his or her interest.

> **CASE EXAMPLE**
> Jaurel and Edna Fincher entered into a land contract whereby Lester Stacey and his wife agreed to purchase a one-half acre tract of land from the Finchers. The purchase price was $1,200, payable $200 down with the remainder payable in installments of $47.50 per month. Paragraph seven of the contract provided that the "Buyers may not assign their rights hereunder in whole or in part." Later, the Staceys entered into an agreement with Miles Homes to purchase a precut home for erection on the tract for $6,378. The Staceys made a down payment and signed a promissory note for the balance due. The note was secured by a mortgage on the tract of land purchased. Miles Homes delivered the materials to the site in accord with the contract. The Staceys made payments to the Finchers but defaulted after the death of Mrs. Stacey. Similarly, the Staceys defaulted on their obligation to pay Miles Homes. The Finchers canceled the contract (with the consent of Mr. Stacey), reacquired possession of the land, and sought a judicial order determining that the Miles Homes' lien was invalid. The court concluded that the prohibition against assignment did not prohibit the Staceys from entering into a valid mortgage and that the Finchers owned the property subject to the Miles Homes' lien. *Fincher v. Miles Homes*, 549 S.W.2d 848 (Mo. 1977).

If the buyer mortgages the property and then defaults on obligations under the land installment contract, a serious question arises concerning the mortgagee's rights. The seller must notify the mortgagee of the default before taking any action regarding the property. In some jurisdictions, the mortgagee is entitled to acquire title to the property by paying the seller the amount due under the installment contract. In this circumstance, the mortgagee may receive more value than the balance due on the mortgage loan. Other jurisdictions limit the mortgagee's recovery to the amount of the mortgagor's indebtedness due by requiring the mortgagee to invoke foreclosure, as discussed in Chapter 21. Under such an action, the property is sold. The land installment seller is paid first from the proceeds an amount necessary to satisfy the amount due on the land contract. The remaining proceeds are used to satisfy the mortgagee's indebtedness, and the installment buyer receives the balance of any remaining monies. In a few states, the mortgagee is obligated to pay the balance of the indebtedness owed to the seller before the foreclosure sale.

CASE EXAMPLE

Toble sold Randomacre to Hillside on land contract. Hillside mortgaged the property, and when he defaulted, he owed $40,000 on the land contract and $20,000 on the mortgage. The property was foreclosed and sold at public auction for $70,000. The proceeds were distributed as follows:

Toble:	$40,000
Mortgagee:	20,000
Hillside:	10,000
Total:	**$70,000**

Conveyance. The buyer's ultimate objective is to receive good title to the property. On performance of the contractual obligations, including payment of the last installment, the seller is obligated to give good title to the property by conveying the deed to the buyer. This requirement is normally reflected in a clause that reads as follows:

> When the buyer has paid the full purchase price with interest due and in the manner required by the terms and conditions of this contract; and, if the buyer performs all other provisions required of the buyer by the terms and conditions of this contract, seller agrees to convey the above described property to the buyer by deed of general warranty, with release of dower, if any.

■ ADVANTAGES AND DISADVANTAGES

As described in the beginning of this chapter, land installment contracts have features not available in ordinary real estate purchase contracts. They also present their own advantages and disadvantages to both buyer and seller. (See Table 22.1.)

Advantages to the Buyer

Most purchasers are not financially able to raise the entire purchase price in one lump sum; consequently, they must obtain financing to purchase the realty. A buyer, how-

TABLE 22.1	Advantages/Disadvantages of Parties to Land Installment Contract	
	Buyer	**Seller**
Advantages	Make property purchasable	Attract buyers
		Tax break
		Incidents of ownership
Disadvantages	Death of seller	High risk of default
	Transfer problems	
	Failure to record	

ever, may not be able to secure financing from a lending institution because of an inability to meet down payment requirements or because of an unsatisfactory credit rating; or the lender may refuse to extend credit because of the marginal value of the property.

The principal advantage that the installment contract offers to buyers is the ability to purchase the property. For little or no down payment, buyers are able to gain an interest in, and derive the benefit of, the property. The land installment contract increased in popularity as a financing tool in the early 1980s, when high interest rates decreased the borrowing power of many people. Its usage continued even in the face of declining interest rates.

Advantages to the Seller

The land installment contract may also benefit the seller. Such benefits may include attraction of buyers, tax advantages, and continued incidents of legal ownership.

Attract Buyers. The main advantage to sellers is that the land installment contract provides a means for increasing the demand for property by attracting buyers who could not otherwise purchase the property because of an inability to secure outside financing. The ability to set the schedule of repayment so that it is affordable to the buyer often places the seller in a position to adjust the purchase price and the interest rate upward or downward. The more attractive the terms, the greater the likelihood of selling unattractive property. Yet, the seller will certainly want to set a payment that will at least cover the mortgage payments.

Tax Break. Under an installment contract, the seller does not receive the entire purchase price in one lump sum. Payments are extended over a period of years. Under an Internal Revenue Code section, a seller may elect to partially defer tax treatment for gains in an installment sale transaction. A taxpayer who elects the installment method of reporting need only report as income, in a given year, the proportion of the installment payments that the gross profit bears to the total contract price. Consequently, income is spread over a period of time. As a result, the seller may defer taxable income to a future time when overall income may be less. The seller consequently receives a welcome tax break.

CASE EXAMPLE

Barry Martin sells property to Sheila Cable for $100,000, payable $25,000 down with the remainder to be paid over 15 years at payments reducing the principal $5,000 a year. Martin had previously purchased the property for $75,000. His gross profit is $25,000 ($100,000 contract price – $75,000 original purchase price). Cable pays the $25,000 down payment. The proportion of the gross profit to the total contract price is 25 percent (25,000/100,000 = 25%). Martin, by electing the installment method, need report as income in the year of sale only $6,250 (25 percent of $25,000 down payment) and $1,250 in each succeeding year (25 percent of $5,000).

Incidents of Legal Ownership. The land installment contract secures the payment of the buyer's indebtedness and gives the seller certain incidents of legal ownership. As discussed earlier, the seller may assign the property subject to the contract, or mortgage the property up to the total amount of indebtedness. This is attractive to a seller, who may reap the benefits of incidents of ownership while involved in a sale of the property.

Disadvantages to the Buyer

The land installment contract may present certain disadvantages to the buyer. These disadvantages may arise should the seller die, fail to transfer good title or neglect to record the contract.

Problems Created by the Death of the Seller. Although the land contract is enforceable against the seller's heirs on death, as a practical matter enforcement may be very costly. The buyer may be forced to hire an attorney to accomplish the transfer. The beneficiaries may be difficult to locate, and the property may be tied up in probate for years. Should there be a large number of beneficiaries, the situation becomes more laden with concurrent ownership interests and difficulties. Because minor and incompetent beneficiaries may require the appointment of a guardian, resolution may be even further complicated and delayed. Similar problems are present when the seller assigns the installment contract to another, who then dies.

Unwillingness or Inability to Transfer Good Title. The seller might refuse to transfer the title to the buyer after fulfillment of the contract. The buyer, who is legally entitled to the deed, may be forced to file a suit seeking specific performance. Even worse, after the buyer pays the installments in conformity with the contract, the seller may not have good title. Normally, the seller has agreed to convey title to the buyer on receiving the final payment. By prevailing authority, the seller is not required to maintain marketable title during the pendency of the contract, although a few jurisdictions have taken a contrary view. The buyer could obtain protection by insisting on a contract provision requiring the seller to maintain marketable title or by obtaining title insurance.

Failure To Record. As stated earlier, the installment contract should be recorded to protect the buyer's interest. Sellers may try to discourage buyers from recording because in the event of default, less difficulty attends to quieting title in their name if there has been no recording. In fact, some contracts may contain *in terrorem* clauses that prohibit recording at the expense of forfeiture. Although their validity is dubious, they undoubtedly discourage some buyers from recording. Some states by statute require that the installment contract be recorded and provide penalties for failure to do so, such as rescission of the contract.

If the installment contract is recorded, the majority of states give the buyer's contract priority over most subsequent purchasers and lienors because they are on, at least, constructive notice of the buyer's interest. Further, the land installment buyer usually has priority over subsequent purchasers and lienors who have knowledge of the buyer's interest, even if the contract is unrecorded. In many jurisdictions, the fact that the buyer is in possession gives subsequent purchasers constructive knowledge of the buyer's interest, even if the contract is not publicly recorded.

Disadvantages to the Seller

From the seller's viewpoint, the land installment contract is often a compromise, sometimes negotiated as a result of an inability to sell the property conventionally. Three reasons may exist for this inability: high market interest rates may make it impractical for purchasers to obtain conventional financing, the purchaser's financial status may prevent him or her from obtaining a loan from a lending institution, or the property may be undesirable in appearance. Because the land contract often attracts buyers who are otherwise not able to purchase the property because of their financial status, risk of default is high.

Default may result in the buyer's forfeiture of all rights in the property, and the buyer's interest may then revert to the seller. In this case, the seller is burdened with the property once again and must reenter the real estate market, necessitating additional brokerage costs and perhaps attorney fees and other operating expenses. In some jurisdictions, forfeiture is not an available remedy. Instead, judicial foreclosure of the property is necessary to cut off the buyer's interest. The cost of foreclosure makes it a burdensome remedy for the seller.

■ REMEDIES

As with other contracts, it is possible that breach or default may occur in a land installment contract. Should this happen, certain remedies are available, described in the following sections. (See Table 22.2.)

TABLE 22.2	Land Contract: Remedies	
Seller's Remedies	**Buyer's Remedies**
Forfeiture	Specific performance
Foreclosure	Foreclosure
Rescission	Rescission
Damages	Damages

Sellers' Remedies

A seller possesses several remedies against a buyer who fails to pay or who otherwise defaults under the terms of the installment contract, including specific performance of the contract, damages, rescission, forfeiture, and foreclosure. These remedies were covered generally in Chapter 10. Forfeiture and foreclosure remedies, however, deserve special attention as seller's remedies under the land installment contract.

Forfeiture. Often included within the terms of a land contract is a **forfeiture** clause, which provides that, in the event the buyer fails to abide by the terms of the contract, the seller has the right to terminate the contract, retake possession of the property, and retain all prior payments. Traditionally, these forfeiture clauses have been upheld by the courts. When enforced, the defaulting buyer loses all equity in the property, and the seller often receives a substantial windfall. The forfeiture penalty may be very severe to a defaulting buyer.

> **CASE EXAMPLE**
>
> In 1971 Sellmer, the seller, entered into an installment sale contract with Donaldson, the buyer, for the purchase of a summer cottage on the Ohio River. The purchase price was $16,500 at the rate of 8 percent per annum for ten years. The contract called for a $2,000 down payment, and the monthly payments were $175. Donaldson, on several occasions, failed to make timely payments and failed to make three monthly installments in 1973. Donaldson failed to keep the property insured, contrary to a provision in the installment contract to do so. Additionally, Donaldson failed to keep the property in repair and left the property in an uninhabitable condition. Sellmer sued Donaldson, seeking a forfeiture and termination of the contract. The court held that because "Donaldson had wholly failed to perform his obligation to acquire adequate insurance and had allowed the property to deteriorate to such an extent that substantial repair was necessary before the house would even be habitable," forfeiture was a proper remedy. Consequently, the court ordered that more than $7,000 in payments made by Donaldson be forfeited to Sellmer and that the contract be terminated. *Donaldson v. Sellmer*, 166 Ind. App. 60, 333 N.E.2d 862 (1975).

Most states have departed from automatic approval of the forfeiture remedy, and all states have mitigated its harshness by statute or judicial decision. Some states require a "grace period," within which the buyer may cure any breach. In those jurisdictions, forfeiture is permitted only after compliance with procedural technicalities. The seller must notify the buyer of the intention to invoke forfeiture and of the grace period. If the buyer fails to correct the default within the specified period that the statute permits, forfeiture is proper. The lengths of these grace periods vary from 30 days to a year. Some states graduate the grace period depending on the portion of the contract price the buyer has paid. In the event the seller affords the requisite statutory notice and there is no response by the buyer to cure the defect, some states permit forfeiture without judicial proceedings. Others require court action.

Another state statute softens the hardship of forfeiture by eliminating forfeiture as a remedy under certain circumstances; for example, when the purchaser has paid a specified percentage of the purchase price. Still another statutory approach eliminates forfeiture altogether by providing that the seller of a land installment contract shall be deemed to be a mortgagee and shall be subject to the same rules of foreclosure and to the same regulations, restraints, and forms that are prescribed in relation to mortgages.

Even when there is no statutory modification, courts are reluctant to uphold a forfeiture clause and often employ various rationales to relieve the defaulting buyer from a harsh result. If, for example, a seller consistently accepts late payments from the buyer and thereafter seeks forfeiture for delinquent payment, a court may hold that the seller has waived any rights under the contract for forfeiture by failing previously to object to delinquent payment. Other jurisdictions analogize a defaulting buyer in a land installment contract to a defaulting mortgagor and recognize an "equity of redemption period." In those jurisdictions, courts determine the period of grace through tests of fairness and reason.

CASE EXAMPLE

In April 1967, the Allens (purchasers) entered into a land installment contract with the Ulanders (sellers) for the purchase of real estate. Under the terms of the contract, the Ulanders agreed to convey the real estate to the Allens after payment of $9,700 at the rate of $85 or more per month at 7 percent interest per annum. The contract further provided for forfeiture in the event the purchasers failed to make timely payments. Over a period of 7½ years, the Allens paid more than $7,500 in principal and interest and built up an equity of $1,583. They also made improvements to the property, adding two bedrooms, a bathroom, and paneling. The Allens failed to make five payments in 1974 and 1975, and the Ulanders instituted an action in forfeiture. The court, applying equitable notions, allowed the purchasers 30 days to deposit with the court a sum equal to five months' payments to avoid forfeiture. The court held that "where a purchaser under an installment land contract has acquired a substantial equitable interest in the property, the court has discretion to utilize a remedy similar to that permitted in foreclosure actions." *Ulander v. Allen*, 37 Colo. App. 279, 544 P.2d 1001 (1976).

Other equitable rationales may be invoked to support a refusal to recognize forfeiture. Some courts hold that if the buyer would sustain a substantial net loss as a result of forfeiture, then forfeiture would be unconscionable; in that case, the buyer is entitled to restitution. Under this view, if the seller's actual damages, based on the fair market rental value of the property and other damages, are less than the buyer's payments, the buyer would be entitled to the difference.

CASE EXAMPLE

Mr. and Mrs. Hoyle, under an installment contract for the purchase of a motel, make total installment payments of $120,000 on a $345,000 purchase price. Additionally, they expend $30,000 on repairs and improvements to the premises. After four years, the Hoyles default on their installment payments and vacate the premises. The reasonable rental value of the motel is $30,000 per year. Under an equitable approach, because the $150,000 expenditure on payments and improvements is substantial, the buyer is entitled to restitution in the amount of $30,000, computed as follows: Buyer's total expenditures are $150,000, consisting of payments in the amount of $120,000 and improvements in the amount of $30,000. The reasonable rental value of the property is $30,000 × 4 years (the period of time in which the Hoyles occupied the premises), or $120,000. The difference between the total payments and the reasonable rental value is $30,000 payable to the Hoyles.

Finally, some courts have struck down the forfeiture clause simply on the basis that it constitutes an unconscionable penalty.

Foreclosure. As noted, some states by statute provide for foreclosure as the proper remedy for a seller against a defaulting installment buyer. Only a few states have recognized foreclosure by judicial decision as a seller's remedy in the event of the buyer's default. Indiana is one such state. In Indiana, the courts reserve the remedy of forfeiture for cases of absconding or abandoning buyers or where only a minimum amount has been paid by the buyer while the seller is making expenditures for taxes, insurance, and maintenance. In all other cases in that jurisdiction and in some other jurisdictions, the courts recognize judicial foreclosure as the proper remedy. In Ohio, foreclosure is required when the buyer has paid at least 20 percent of the purchase price or has faithfully made payments for at least five years.

Buyers' Remedies

The buyer possesses several possible remedies against a seller who fails to convey title or otherwise defaults under the terms of the contract. The remedies of specific performance, rescission, damages, and foreclosure will be examined.

Specific Performance. A buyer who completes the requirements under the installment contract, including payment of the last installment, is entitled to the deed. If the seller does not convey the deed, a court may award specific performance, mandating that the seller execute a deed in the buyer's favor. Refusal to abide by the court judgment may result in contempt of court and punishment. The court may also execute a deed in the buyer's favor, or the very judgment may act as the instrument that passes title to the buyer.

Rescission. Another remedy for an installment buyer on a seller's default is to elect rescission—that is, to have the contract terminated and the contract payments returned. In this instance, fairness often requires that a value for rental of the property be deducted from the amount due the buyer. The remedy of rescission is designed to return the parties to their original position. This remedy is especially desirable for the buyer when the subject real estate has depreciated in value below the contract price.

Damages. The installment buyer, in reliance on the contract, may have expended money to improve the property. If the seller breaches under these circumstances and is unable to convey a marketable title, the buyer may prefer to sue for damages. A judgment for damages, when properly certified and filed, becomes a general lien on all real property the seller owns until the judgment is satisfied. As a lienor, the buyer may foreclose on any of the seller's real property to satisfy the judgment. Other means of satisfying the judgment include attachment and sale of the seller's personal property and garnishment of the seller's wages.

Foreclosure. The installment buyer has an equitable interest in the property. As such, the buyer possesses an equitable lien on the property securing the buyer's interest. Consequently, the buyer may foreclose on the property in the event of the seller's default and recover the purchase payments.

THE CHANGING LANDSCAPE

The land installment contract is a creative tool that facilitates a sale. During times of high mortgage interest rates it is especially popular. The due-on-sale clause in the seller's mortgage would ordinarily be triggered by the land contract. However in reality, it seldom comes to the mortgagee's attention as long as mortgage payments are current.

One downside of the land contract is that on default, the seller may have to institute suit to clear the title. Another is that on satisfaction the seller may not convey the title to the buyer, thus requiring that the buyer sue to gain title. Still a third is that the seller may encumber the property before the deed is transferred to the buyer. This poses a problem to the buyer, particularly when the land contract was not previously recorded.

To avoid these problems, the deed of trust or long term escrow may be employed. In these devices, a third-party trustee holds the deed and has legal title. Then, on the occurrence of certain events, in accordance with the trust document the trustee responds accordingly. For example, on default, the document may require that the trustee convey legal title back to the seller or, on satisfaction, to the buyer.

In summary, the land contract is a creative financing tool that enables buyers who cannot buy under a conventional method to buy. An alternative is for the seller to extend financing through a purchase-money mortgage, under which title passes to the buyer. Finally, there is the deed of trust, where title is held by a trustee. As a buyer, which method do you prefer: deed of trust, purchase-money mortgage, or land contract? Will your answer be different if you are a seller? Can you suggest any other creative techniques by which the buyer may purchase property, while the seller maintains security for repayment of the debt?

■ KEY TERMS

after-acquired title 500
forfeiture 510
indemnification 503

land installment
  contract 499
waste 503

■ INTERNET RESOURCES

For a link to the contents of a land installment contract see

http://janus.state.me.us/legis/statutes/33/title33sec482.html

■ REVIEW AND DISCUSSION QUESTIONS

1. Describe the differences between a land installment contract and an ordinary real estate purchase contract.

2. Who is helped by the doctrine of *after-acquired title*? In what ways?

3. (a) What is the primary advantage to a buyer who buys property on a land installment contract? (b) What are the advantages to a seller?

4. (a) What is the primary disadvantage to the buyer who sells property on a land installment contract? (b) What are the disadvantages to the seller?

5. What are some acts that might be considered a buyer's breach of a land installment contract?

6. Describe the seller's remedy of forfeiture and explain how the states have softened the impact of that remedy.

7. Describe the buyer's remedies in the event the seller defaults on a land installment contract.

■ CASE PROBLEMS

1. Donald Reed and LaVonne McAdow entered into a land installment contract for the sale of a parcel of land owned by Reed. The contract was never recorded. Subsequently, Reed assigned his entire interest in the land to Ohio Mortgage Company, which was unaware of the contract between Reed and McAdow. The assignment was not recorded. After the assignment of the land, Kagey Lumber Company obtained a judgment against Reed and is now in the process of placing a lien on the property. (a) Will Kagey's judgment become a lien on the property? Why or why not? (b) What are Kagey's rights in the property? Describe. (c) Is Ohio Mortgage Company subject to the provisions of the contract between Reed and McAdow? Discuss. See *Butcher v. Kagey Lumber Company*, 164 Ohio St. 85, 128 N.E.2d 54 (1955).

2. Moorman and Whitman signed a land installment contract for the sale of real estate owned by Moorman. The contract stated that the land consisted of three tracts totaling 460 acres. Whitman assigned his interest in the contract to Maxwell. The assignment, expressly authorized by the contract, contained a description of the land similar to that in the land installment contract. After three years, Maxwell paid Moorman the entire balance due under the land installment contract and received the deed to the property. Maxwell then attempted to sell the property to Fentress. Before the deal was consummated, Fentress notified Maxwell that the property contained only 355.9 acres rather than 460 acres, as stated in their contract. Maxwell and Fentress agreed to a reduction in the purchase price, and the contract was signed. Maxwell then attempted to persuade Moorman to return to him approximately 23 percent of the purchase price he paid. Moorman refused. (a) Can Maxwell successfully maintain an action against Moorman for return of the disputed portion of the purchase price? Explain. (b) Does Moorman have a cause of action against Whitman? Explain. See *Maxwell v. Moorman*, 522 S.W.2d 441 (Ky. Ct. App. 1975).

3. Newman entered into a land installment contract with Mountain Park Land Company to purchase a tract of timberland. After Newman paid approximately

one-half of the money due to the company under the contract, the company, without the consent of Newman, cut down trees from the land and sold a substantial amount of the timber. As a result of the actions of Mountain Park, the land decreased in value. (a) Does Newman have a cause of action against Mountain Park? (b) If so, what is that cause of action and what are his possible remedies? See *Newman v. Mountain Park Land Co.*, 85 Ark. 208, 107 S.W. 391 (1908). (c) What if Newman had harvested the trees, inflicting the damage to the property during the pendency of the installment contract? Would Mountain Park have a cause of action against Newman? Explain. See *Reynolds v. Lawrence*, 147 Ala. 216, 40 So. 576 (1906).

4. Ben Schottenstein and Jack J. Devoe entered into a land installment contract. The terms of the contract stipulated that certain property would be conveyed in fee simple absolute by Schottenstein to Devoe in return for $21,500 payable in installments over a ten-year period. After signing the contract, Devoe learned that Schottenstein did not have legal title to the property at the time of the contract signing. Devoe therefore seeks to void the contract. (a) May he do so? Explain. (b) What is Schottenstein's counterargument? (c) What could Devoe have done if he knew of the state of Schottenstein's title prior to signing the contract? See *Schottenstein v. Devoe*, 83 Ohio App. 193, 82 N.E.2d 552 (1948).

5. Purchasers under a land installment contract made only four out of 12 monthly payments, failed to pay taxes and maintain insurance, and failed to pay sewer and water charges. In absence of a statute, what factors are relevant to determine the proper remedy available to the land installment seller? Explain. See *Grombone v. Krekel*, 754 P.2d 777 (Colo. Ct. App. 1988).

6. Doris Blackburn entered into a land installment contract with the Smiths. After several late payments by Blackburn, the Smiths served a notice that the contract would be forfeited and thereafter instituted a suit seeking forfeiture. Ohio Revised Code section 5313.07 says that when the vendee of a land contract has paid 20 percent of the purchase price, the vendor's remedy for default lies in foreclosure and not in forfeiture.

   The land contract was executed on a printed form that did not contain the words *purchase price*, but Blackburn agreed to pay $20,000, with $2,000 down and $204.85 per month at 9 percent interest for 12 years. At the time of trial, it was stipulated that Blackburn had made the following payments: a down payment of $2,000; 23 monthly payments of $204.85 ($4,711.55 total) as per the contract to cover principal and interest; insurance premiums for two years of $320; and real estate taxes for 1984 and part of 1983 in the amount of $571.61. Is forfeiture appropriate? Explain. *Smith v. Blackburn*, 511 N.E. 132 (Ohio App. 1987).

7. Szaleski and Goodman entered into a land installment contract. Szaleski made several payments under the contract. Later, Szaleski discovered discrepancies in the description of the land in the contract and the actual condition of the land. He sued Goodman and asked the court to declare the contract void. The court found the contract to be void and ordered that the payments made by Szaleski to Goodman be

returned to Szaleski. Should the fair rental value of the property for the time he occupied the property be withheld from the amount that Goodman returns to Szaleski? Discuss. See *Szaleski v. Goodman,* 260 Md. 24 (Md. Ct. App. 1970).

 Go to the Student Study Guide CD-ROM and work through Case 5.

PART SIX

Government
Regulation

Fair Housing Laws

■ FAIR HOUSING

■ *The term used to describe a national policy against most types of discrimination in housing.*

The recent decades have seen increasing involvement of government in housing in the United States. Types of housing regulations discussed elsewhere in the text include zoning and subdivision regulations, rent controls, and mortgage regulations. During the same period, government has exhibited an interest in ensuring, through legislation, that no member of our society is refused an opportunity to obtain decent housing. (See Figure 23.1.)

Equal Protection

■ *The constitutional mandate that all people be treated equally under the law.*

In the late 19th-century case of *Plessy v. Ferguson*, 163 U.S. 537 (1896), the U.S. Supreme Court affirmed the doctrine that "separate but equal" was the law of the land. This concept was used to separate the races in many sectors of American life, including public transportation, education, and accommodations. In housing, some state and local governments passed laws confining blacks and whites to separate sections of cities for residential living. This practice was considered constitutional as long as both black and white sections were provided. Economic and social pressures also were factors separating the races in residential areas.

The separate-but-equal doctrine provided equality in theory, but it has been well documented that it had little relationship to equality in fact. Black and white schools were equal neither in physical plant nor in the quality of education children obtained in them. In housing as well, the quality and locations were not equal for blacks and whites.

In 1954, beginning with the school desegregation cases, the separate-but-equal doctrine was laid aside, and **equal protection** became the constitutional mandate. In these cases, the plaintiffs were black children who, pursuant to statutes in Kansas, South Carolina, Virginia, and Delaware, attended schools segregated on the basis of race. In each of these states, with the exception of Delaware, federal district courts had denied relief to the plaintiffs, citing the separate-but-equal doctrine of *Plessy v. Ferguson*. In the Delaware case, the state supreme court adhered to the doctrine, but ordered plaintiffs admitted to the white schools because of their superiority to the black schools. Plaintiffs appealed to the U.S. Supreme Court, which rejected the language of *Plessy v. Ferguson*. In an important decision the court stated:

| FIGURE 23.1 | Evolution of Fair Housing Protection |

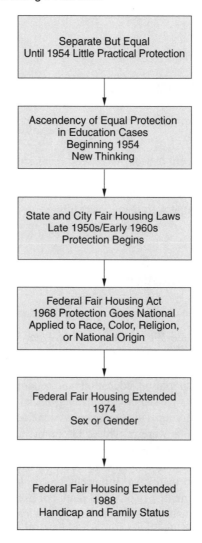

We conclude that in the field of public education the doctrine of "separate but equal" has no place. Separate educational facilities are inherently unequal. Therefore, we hold that the plaintiffs and others similarly situated for whom the actions have been brought are, by reason of the segregation complained of, deprived of the equal protection of the laws guaranteed by the Fourteenth Amendment. *Brown v. Board of Education*, 347 U.S. 483 (1954).

After the decision in *Brown v. Board of Education*, the country began the slow process of racially integrating society. In the late 1950s and early 1960s, several states and cities enacted fair housing laws with varying degrees of coverage. These statutes were a prelude to the entry of the federal government into the fair housing arena. Because the federal government is now the focus for regulation of discrimination in housing, the remainder of this chapter will concentrate on several federal legislative enactments.

■ FEDERAL FAIR HOUSING LEGISLATION

It was more than ten years after *Brown v. Board of Education* before Congress became active in enacting the fair housing statute.

Fair Housing Act (1968) as Amended

There are two major pieces of federal fair housing legislation. In 1968, Congress enacted the first comprehensive fair housing law in Title VIII of the Civil Rights Act of 1968, known also as the Fair Housing Act. The law prohibited discrimination and imposed liability on those who discriminated against persons seeking to buy or rent housing. One could not discriminate based on race, color, religion, or national origin. In 1974, Congress added sex or gender as a protected category. The Fair Housing Act of 1988 extended the categories of protection to include handicap and familial status. It should be noted that states have fair housing laws too, and those laws may include additional protected classes.

Coverage. Most housing is covered by the Fair Housing Act. Some exceptions are single-family housing sold or rented without the use of a broker (as well as other requirements that must be met), owner-occupied buildings with no more than four units, and housing operated by religious organizations and private clubs that limit occupancy to members.

Prohibited Actions. In the sale or rental of housing, no one may take any of the following actions based on race, color, national origin, religion, sex, familial status, or handicap:

- refuse to rent or sell housing;
- refuse to negotiate for housing;
- make housing unavailable;
- set different terms, conditions, or privileges for sale or rental of a dwelling;
- provide different housing services or facilities;
- falsely deny that housing is available for inspection, sale, or rental;
- for profit, persuade others to sell or rent (blockbusting); or
- deny anyone access to or membership in a facility or service, such as a multiple listing service, related to the sale or rental of housing.

In the providing of a mortgage, no one may take any of the following actions based on race, color, national origin, religion, sex, familial status, or handicap:

- refuse to make a mortgage loan;
- refuse to provide information regarding loans;
- impose different terms or conditions on a loan;

- discriminate in appraising property;

- refuse to purchase a loan; or

- set different terms or conditions for purchasing a loan.

Also, it is illegal for anyone to:

- threaten, coerce, intimidate, or interfere with anyone exercising a fair housing right, or assisting others in exercising such rights;

- advertise or make any statement that indicates a limitation or preference based on race, color, national origin, religion, sex, familial status, or handicap. The prohibition against discriminatory advertising applies to single-family and owner-occupied housing otherwise exempt from the law. (See Coverage above).

CASE EXAMPLE

Pevorus, a single person, owned a large house with an attached casita. He lived on the first floor of the house and rented the second floor to Nowery. He also rented the attached casita to Farley. After giving proper notice, Nowery vacated the second floor at the end of the lease. Pevorus, embittered by his Vietnam War experience, refuses to rent to anyone of Asian extraction. Chai, a Korean-American and a prospective tenant, challenges the legality of Pevorus' discriminatory refusal to rent to him.

Because Pevorus has only two rental units, and assuming he does not advertise his discriminatory preferences or use a broker to find a tenant, he is exempt from the prohibitions of the federal fair housing laws in renting the second floor and the casita. He must also be aware that state fair housing laws may be more restrictive than the federal law and may not provide the same exemptions.

Aggrieved Parties. The Fair Housing Act allows any aggrieved party to file a complaint for discriminatory practices. The term "aggrieved party" is broadly defined to include a victim, corporations, fair housing groups, testers, real estate professionals, local governments, and the Secretary of HUD.

Equal Opportunity Posters. The act was amended in 1972 by a requirement that equal opportunity posters be displayed at brokerage houses, model home sites, mortgage lender offices, and similar locations. The poster must contain the slogan "Equal Housing Opportunity" and must carry a brief equal housing opportunity statement. Failure to display such a poster will be treated as prima facie evidence of discrimination; that is, in the absence of evidence to the contrary it will be presumed that the broker discriminates in violation of the law.

As noted above, *Representation* that a dwelling is not available for inspection, sale, or rental, when in fact it is available, is also illegal. Other discriminatory acts explicitly made illegal under the law include *blockbusting*, *redlining*, *discriminatory advertising*, and *steering*. The following case presents an example of a situation where the facts are misrepresented by the agent of the lessor to a minority person seeking housing.

Asbury v. Brougham
U.S. Court of Appeals, Tenth Circuit
866 F.2d 1276 (1989)

Background. Rosalyn Asbury tried to rent an apartment or a townhouse from Brougham Estates in Kansas City. The specific facts surrounding the refusal are discussed later in the case. Asbury charged that Brougham violated §1982 of the Federal Procedural Code and a section of the Fair Housing Act (1968) (FHA) by refusing to give her the opportunity to rent, to inspect, and to negotiate a rental of an apartment or townhouse because of her sex or race. Asbury was awarded $7,500 compensatory damages and $50,000 punitive damages by the jury at trial. Brougham contended that the evidence did not support the compensatory damages because Asbury failed to prove a discriminatory intent. Brougham challenged the punitive damages also because discriminatory motivation must be proven under §1982 to gain punitive damages. Brougham appealed to the Court of Appeals.

Decision. The Tenth Circuit Court of Appeals affirmed the trial court.

District Judge Parker. §1982 and the FHA both prohibit discrimination on the basis of race. In order to prevail on a claim made under these statutes, plaintiff must prove a discriminatory intent. A violation occurs when race is a factor in a decision to deny a minority applicant the opportunity to rent or negotiate for a rental, but race need not be the only factor in the decision. In addition, the FHA specifically prohibits dissemination of false information about the availability of housing because of a person's race. Accordingly, failure to provide a minority applicant with the same information about availability of a rental unit or the terms and conditions for rental as is provided to white "testers" results in false information being provided and is cognizable as an injury under the FHA.

The three-part burden of proof analysis established in *McDonnell Douglas Corp. v. Green* has

been widely applied to FHA and §1982 claims. Under the *McDonnell Douglas* analysis, plaintiff first must come forward with proof of a prima facie case of discrimination. Second, if plaintiff proves a prima facie case, the burden shifts to defendants to produce evidence that the refusal to rent or negotiate for a rental was motivated by legitimate, non-racial considerations. Third, once defendants by evidence articulate non-discriminatory reasons, the burden shifts back to plaintiff to show that the proffered reasons were pretextual.

The proof necessary to establish a prima facie case under the FHA also establishes a prima facie case of racial discrimination under §1982. In order to establish her prima facie case, plaintiff had to prove that:

(1) she is a member of a racial minority;

(2) she applied for and was qualified to rent an apartment or townhouse in Brougham Estates;

(3) she was denied the opportunity to rent or to inspect or negotiate for the rental of a townhouse or apartment; and

(4) the housing opportunity remained available.

A review of the evidence in this case shows that plaintiff establishes her prima facie case. Defendants stipulated that Asbury is black. Plaintiff testified that on February 23, 1984, she went to Brougham Estates with her daughter to obtain rental housing. At the rental office at Brougham Estates, Asbury encountered Wanda Chauvin, the manager, and explained to Chauvin that she was being transferred to Kansas City and needed to rent housing. Asbury told Chauvin that she needed to secure housing by the middle of March or the beginning of April. In response, Chauvin said there were no vacancies, but told Asbury she could call back at a later time to check on availability. Chauvin provided no information concerning availability of rental units that would assist Asbury in her efforts to rent an apartment or

continued on next page

townhouse at Brougham Estates. Asbury asked for the opportunity to fill out an application, but Chauvin did not give her an application, again stating that there were no vacancies and that she kept no waiting list. Asbury also requested floor plans or the opportunity to view a model unit, and Chauvin refused. Instead, Chauvin suggested Asbury inquire at the Westminister Apartments, an apartment complex housing mostly black families. Although Chauvin did not ask Asbury about her qualifications, plaintiff was employed with the Federal Aviation Authority at a salary of $37,599. Based on her salary, defendants concede that Asbury would likely be qualified to rent an apartment or townhouse at Brougham Estates.

Defendants argue that Asbury was not rejected because Chauvin courteously invited her to call back. However, there is ample evidence in the record to support the jury's finding that defendant's failure or refusal to provide Asbury the opportunity to rent or inspect or negotiate for the rental of a townhouse or apartment constituted a rejection because of her race cognizable under §1982 and the FHA.

Defendants testified that families with a child are housed exclusively in the townhouses at Brougham Estates, and that there were no townhouses available on the date Asbury inquired. Asbury introduced evidence suggesting that both apartments and townhouses were available and, in addition, that exceptions previously had been created to allow children to reside in the apartments.

On February 24, 1984, the day after Asbury inquired about renting, Asbury's sister-in-law, Linda Robinson, who is white, called to inquire about the availability of two-bedroom apartments. The woman who answered the telephone identified herself as "Wanda" and invited Robinson to come to Brougham Estates to view the apartments. The following day, February 25, 1984, Robinson went to the rental office at Brougham Estates and met with Wanda Chauvin. Chauvin provided Robinson with four plans of one- and two-bedroom apartments at Brougham Estates. Robinson specifically asked Chauvin about rental to families with children, and

Chauvin did not tell Robinson that children were restricted to the townhouse units. Robinson accompanied Chauvin to inspect a model unit and several available two-bedroom apartments. On inquiry by Robinson, Chauvin indicated that the apartments were available immediately and offered to hold an apartment for her until the next week.

Asbury also provided evidence indicating that townhouses were available for rent. On February 1, 1984, Daniel McMenay, a white male, notified Brougham Estates that he intended to vacate his townhouse. On April 4, 1984, Brougham Estates rented the townhouse vacated by McMenay to John Shuminski, a white male.

Since Asbury met her burden of proving a prima facie case of racial discrimination, the burden shifted to defendants to prove a legitimate, non-discriminatory reason for denial of housing.

Defendants claimed their legitimate, non-discriminatory reasons for rejecting Asbury arose out of the policies at Brougham Estates that families with one child could rent townhouses but not apartments, and that families with more than one child were not permitted to move into Brougham Estates. Defendants contended that in accordance with these rental policies, no appropriate housing was available for Asbury when she inquired. However, plaintiff introduced evidence indicating that exceptions to these rules had been made on several occasions; families with children had rented apartments, and families with more than one child had been permitted to move into Brougham Estates. The jury could therefore find that defendants' reasons for denying Asbury the opportunity to negotiate for rental were not legitimate and non-discriminatory.

Defendants also argue that evidence of a high percentage of minority occupancy in Brougham Estates conclusively rebuts the claim of intentional racial discrimination. Although such statistical data is relevant to rebutting a claim of discrimination, statistical data is not dispositive of a claim of intentional discrimination. Moreover, there was other evidence from which the jury could have determined that race was a motivating factor in defendants' decision to refuse to negotiate with Asbury for a rental unit.

Having reviewed the record in this case, we find that there was substantial evidence supporting and a reasonable basis for the jury's verdict awarding both compensatory and punitive damages, and we affirm the district court's decision to deny defendants' motion for a new trial.

Affirmed and remanded.

Given a high rate of minority occupancy, doesn't that clearly indicate nonracial motivation in turning Asbury down? Suppose Brougham Estates had three reasons for refusing to rent to Asbury. She had a "bad attitude," her child was unruly, and her race. Would that be illegal?

■ **Blockbusting.** *Practice by which real estate agents attempt to exploit racial tensions, as when African-Americans move into a previously all white neighborhood, through repeated solicitations for the sale of homes.*

CASE EXAMPLE

Bowers and a number of other real estate firms in Northwest Detroit conducted solicitation campaigns in Northwest Detroit involving fliers, telephone calls, and door-to-door canvassing. As part of their campaign, fliers were allegedly delivered to "Resident." One flier contained the legend "We think you may want a friend for a neighbor . . . know your neighbors." Another mailing also addressed to "Resident" purported to carry "neighborhood news." It announced that a real estate agency had just bought a house at a specific address in the recipient's neighborhood, that the named sellers had received cash, and that the recipient might receive the same service. The recipients lived in changing neighborhoods. This conduct was judged to be illegal. *Zuch v. Hussey*, 394 F. Supp. 1028 (D. Mich. 1975).

■ **Redlining.** *Denial of a loan by a lending institution or the exacting of harsher terms for loans in certain parts of a city. Redlining also applies to insurance companies.*

CASE EXAMPLE

The Laufmans, a white couple, purchased a home in a predominantly black neighborhood. When financing was denied by the Oakley Building and Loan Company, the Laufmans sued. They argued that the defendant had redlined areas in the community in which minority group families were concentrated.

The defendant moved for summary judgment. The court denied the motion. In denying the motion, the court stated that "although not altogether unambiguous, we read this [Sec. 3604 and 3605 of the Civil Rights Act of 1968] as an explicit prohibition of 'redlining'." *Laufman v. Oakley Building and Loan Co.*, 408 F. Supp. 489 (1976).

■ **Steering.** *Channeling by a broker or salesperson of prospective home buyers toward, or away from, certain areas, either to maintain homogeneity or to change the character of that area, usually for the purpose of enhancing sales opportunities.*

CASE EXAMPLE

The Village of Bellwood and six individuals brought suit against two real estate firms for steering black homebuyers to one area of the Village, and white homebuyers to another area. The real estate firms argued that the Village and the individuals, who were admittedly testers and not prospective homebuyers, were not economically injured and could not sue under the Fair Housing Act.

The U.S. Supreme Court held the conduct of the real estate firms was illegal steering under the Fair Housing Act and that the plaintiffs' contention that they were being denied the opportunity to live in an integrated community was adequate economic injury to bring the suit. *Gladstone Realtors v. Village of Bellwood,* 441 U.S. 91 (1979).

■ IMPLEMENTATION OF THE FAIR HOUSING ACT

Fair Housing Act and the Handicapped

Handicap-based discrimination was made illegal by the Fair Housing Act amendments of 1988. The protection applies broadly to those with a physical or mental disability that substantially limits one or more major life activities. Three categories of discrimination are recognized: direct discrimination, reasonable modification, and reasonable accommodation. Direct discrimination, by which a housing provider openly refuses a rental based on a physical or mental handicap, needs no further amplification.

Reasonable Modification. A landlord is required to permit a tenant, at the tenant's expense, to make a **reasonable modification** of the living space in order to have full use and enjoyment of the premises. A modification may be installing grab bars, ramps, and alarms, and/or widening doorways. The modifications can go beyond the living unit itself, and include the laundry room or the garage.

The tenant must obtain the landlord's consent prior to making a modification. The landlord can withhold consent only where the modification is unreasonable owing to the financial or administrative burden it imposes. If the modification would interfere with the landlord's or the next tenant's enjoyment of the premises, the handicapped tenant may be required to restore the premises to its original condition on leaving.

There are special rules that apply to multifamily dwellings built after March 13, 1991. A multifamily dwelling is defined as a building with four or more living units if the building has an elevator or a ground floor dwelling with four or more units. Such a multifamily dwelling unit is required to have full handicap accessibility to common areas, and all entrances must be wheelchair accessible. Within individual units the law requires accessibility to all switches and environmental controls, reinforcement of bathroom walls to allow for future installation of grab bars, and sufficient widths in kitchens and bathrooms to afford wheelchair maneuverability. The statute provides that compliance with the American National Standards Institute standards for providing accessibility and usability for physically handicapped people is satisfactory.

Reasonable Accommodation. The Fair Housing Act mandates that a landlord or housing provider make reasonable accommodation of its rules, policies, practices, and services for a handicapped person to enjoy the unit. In contrast with a reasonable modification, the housing provider may be required to take affirmative measures to meet the reasonable accommodation specification. The handicapped person is entitled to an equal opportunity to use and enjoy the dwelling unit. The concept of reasonable accommodation is also used in applying section 504 of the Rehabilitation Act of 1973.

A housing provider may have to waive its "no pet policy" to accommodate a service or companion animal such as a "seeing-eye dog" for a blind person. Another example is that parking rules may have to be adjusted to accommodate a person with a mobility-related disability. In reasonable accommodation lawsuits, the courts have applied a type of balancing test. It will balance the needs of the handicapped person against the financial burden placed on the housing provider. The housing provider may be required to incur reasonable costs but will not have to assume an undue financial burden. In applying the balancing tests, the courts appear to favor the handicapped person, except under extreme circumstances.

Group Home Accommodations. The Fair Housing Act prohibits local governments from applying laws and regulations that discriminate against group homes of nonrelated persons. Land use regulations, including zoning provisions and special use permits, cannot effectively prohibit groups of disabled individuals from living in the residence of their choice. If the purpose or effect of the law is to exclude or restrict group homes, it violates the reasonable accommodation provision.

As with the reasonable accommodation provision that applies to disabled individuals, the courts use a balancing test in group home cases. The courts seek to decide if the accommodation of its law to the group home imposes an undue hardship on the municipality. It will examine variables such as crime and safety concerns, negative impacts on real estate values, and the financial burden placed on the parties.

There is an exemption in the Fair Housing Act for restrictions regarding the maximum number of occupants permitted in a dwelling. The courts in interpreting the exemption have carefully confined it to regulations solely limiting the number of persons residing in a unit. The following case is an example of that narrow construction.

City of Edmonds v. Oxford House, Inc.
Supreme Court of the United States
115 S. Ct. 1776 (1995)

Background. Oxford House operates a group home in the City of Edmonds, Washington, for 10 or 12 adults recovering from alcoholism and drug addiction. The City's zoning code provides that occupants of single-family dwelling units must compose a "family." It defines a family as either persons, regardless of number, related by genetics, adoption, or marriage or a group of five or fewer unrelated persons. The city cited Oxford House for violation of this zoning code provision. Oxford House asserted reliance on the Fair Housing Act provisions protecting handicapped persons from discrimination. The definition of a handicapped person is broad enough to include the residents of Oxford House. The District Court found that the zoning regulation was within the Fair Housing Act exemption. The Court of Appeals reversed, finding for Oxford House, and holding that the exemption was inapplicable to this zoning restriction.

continued on next page

Decision. The United States Supreme Court affirmed the Court of Appeals decision.

Justice Ginsburg. The Fair Housing Act (FHA or Act) prohibits discrimination in housing against persons with handicaps. Section 3607(b)(1) of the Act entirely exempts from the FHA's compass "any reasonable local, State, or Federal restrictions regarding the maximum number of occupants permitted to occupy a dwelling." This case presents the question whether a provision in petitioner City of Edmonds' zoning code qualifies for §3607 (b)(1)'s complete exemption from FHA scrutiny. The provision, governing areas zoned for single-family dwelling units, defines "family" as "persons [without regard to number] related by genetics, adoption, or marriage, or a group of five or fewer [unrelated] persons."

The defining provision at issue describes who may compose a family unit; it does not prescribe "the maximum number of occupants" a dwelling unit may house. We hold that §3607(b)(1) does not exempt prescriptions of the family-defining kind, i.e., provisions designed to foster the family character of a neighborhood. Instead, §3607(b)(1)'s absolute exemption removes from the FHA's scope only total occupancy limits, i.e., numerical ceilings that serve to prevent overcrowding in living quarters.

Discrimination covered by the FHA includes "a refusal to make reasonable accommodations in rules, policies, practices, or services, when such accommodations may be necessary to afford [handicapped] person[s] equal opportunity to use and enjoy a dwelling." Oxford House asked Edmonds to make a "reasonable accommodation" by allowing it to remain in the single-family dwelling it had leased. Group homes for recovering substance abusers, Oxford urged, need 8 to 12 residents to be financially and therapeutically viable. Edmonds declined to permit Oxford House to stay in a single-family residential zone, but passed an ordinance listing group homes as permitted uses in multifamily and general commercial zones.

The sole question before the Court is whether Edmonds' family composition rule qualifies as a "restrictio[n] regarding the maximum number of occupants permitted to occupy a dwelling" within the meaning of the FHA's absolute exemption. In answering this question, we are mindful of the Act's stated policy "to provide, within constitutional limitations, for fair housing throughout the United States." We also note precedent recognizing the FHA's "broad and inclusive" compass, and therefore according a "generous construction" to the Act's complaint-filing provision. Accordingly, we regard this case as an instance in which an exception to "a general statement of policy" is sensibly read "narrowly in order to preserve the primary operation of the [policy]."

Land use restrictions designate "districts in which only compatible uses are allowed and incompatible uses are excluded." These restrictions typically categorize uses as single-family residential, multiple-family residential, commercial, or industrial.

Land use restrictions aim to prevent problems caused by the "pig in the parlor instead of the barnyard." In particular, reserving land for single-family residences preserves the character of neighborhoods, securing "zones where family values, youth values, and the blessings of quiet seclusion and clean air make the area a sanctuary for people." To limit land use to single-family residences, a municipality must define the term "family"; thus family composition rules are an essential component of single-family residential use restrictions. Maximum occupancy restrictions, in contradistinction, cap the number of occupants per dwelling, typically in relation to available floor space or the number and type of rooms. These restrictions ordinarily apply uniformly to all residents of all dwelling units. Their purpose is to protect health and safety by preventing dwelling overcrowding.

Section 3607(b)(1)'s language—"restrictions regarding the maximum number of occupants permitted to occupy a dwelling"—surely encompasses maximum occupancy restrictions. But the formulation does not fit family composition rules typically tied to land use restrictions. In sum, rules that cap the total number of occupants in order to prevent overcrowding of a dwelling "plainly and unmistakably," fall within §3607(b)(1)'s absolute exemption from the FHA's governance; rules designed to preserve the family character of a neighborhood, fastening on the composition of households rather than on the total number of occupants living quarters can contain, do not.

Turning specifically to the City's Community Development Code, we note that the provisions Edmonds invoked against Oxford House, are classic examples of a use restriction and complementing family composition rule. These provisions do not cap the number of people who may live in a dwelling. In plain terms, they direct that dwellings be used only to house families. Captioned "USES," ECDC §16.20.010 provides that the sole "Permitted Primary Us[e]" in a single-family residential zone is "[s]ingle family dwelling units. "Edmonds itself recognizes that this provision simply "defines those uses permitted in a single family residential zone." A separate provision caps the number of occupants a dwelling may house, based on floor area:

> Floor Area. Every dwelling unit shall have at least one room which shall have not less than 120 square feet of floor area. Other habitable rooms, except kitchens, shall have an area of not less than 70 square feet. Where more than two persons occupy a room used for sleeping purposes, the required floor area shall be increased at the rate of 50 square feet for each occupant in excess of two.

This space and occupancy standard is a prototypical maximum occupancy restriction. Edmonds nevertheless argues that its family composition rule, ECDC §21.30.010, falls within §3607(b)(1), the FHA exemption for maximum occupancy restrictions, because the rule caps at five the number of unrelated persons allowed to occupy a single-family dwelling. But Edmonds' family composition rule surely does not answer the question: "What is the maximum number of occupants permitted to occupy a house?" So long as they are related "by genetics, adoption, or marriage," any number of people can live in a house. Ten siblings, their parents and grandparents, for example, could dwell in a house in Edmonds' single-family residential zone without offending Edmonds' family composition rule.

Family living, not living space per occupant, is what ECDC §21.30.010 describes. Defining family primarily by biological and legal relationships, the provision also accommodates another group association: five or fewer unrelated people are allowed to live together as though they were family. This accommodation is the peg on which Edmonds rests its plea for §3607(b)(1) exemption. Had the City defined a family solely by biological and legal links, §3607(b)(1) would not have been the ground on which Edmonds staked its case. It is curious reasoning indeed that converts a family values preserver into a maximum occupancy restriction once a town adds to a related persons prescription "and also two unrelated persons."

Edmonds' zoning code provision describing who may compose a "family" is not a maximum occupancy restriction exempt from the FHA under §3607(b)(1).

Affirmed.

Recraft the City of Edmonds zoning code to come within the exemption under the Fair Housing laws.

Fair Housing Act and Familial Status

Unless a building or community qualifies as housing for elderly persons, it is illegal to discriminate based on familial status. **Familial status** refers to a family with one or more children under 18 years of age with a parent or other legal custodian. Familial status may be the least well known to the public category of discrimination. Examples of a few recent cases may help to illustrate.

CASE EXAMPLE

In August 2004, the owner of a mobile home attempted to sell the home to a couple with children. Rennels Property Management, the owner and manager of Marlin Court where the mobile home was located, informed the couple that Marlin Court was an adult-only community. The sale fell through, and the mobile home owner was unable to buy their intended new home.

The Court ordered Rennels Property Management to pay the mobile home owner $32,000 because they were the indirect victims of familial status discrimination.

CASE EXAMPLE

In May 2004, Isabel Luna attempted to rent an apartment from New Cambridge Apartments. New Cambridge informed Luna that because the apartment she was interested in would require her children of the opposite sex to share a room, it was not available. New Cambridge had a policy of requiring children of the opposite sex sleep in separate bedrooms. During a subsequent investigation it was also revealed that New Cambridge had a policy banning children from living on the fourth floor of the apartment complex. Both policies were found to constitute familial status discrimination, and New Cambridge was ordered to pay Luna $15,000.

There is an exemption from the familial status provision for housing for the elderly. To take advantage of this exemption, the owner must prove that:

- the HUD Secretary determined that the housing is specifically designed for and occupied by elderly persons under a federal, state, or local government program; or

- it is solely occupied by persons 62 or older; or

- it houses at least one person 55 or older in at least 80 percent of the occupied units, and otherwise adheres to a policy showing an intent to house persons 55 and older.

Under the latter provision the property would continue to be exempt if some of the 20 percent of the housing not occupied by persons 55 and older were families with children.

Statutory Remedies

It is in the area of remedies provided by the Fair Housing Act that the amendments of 1988 make their most significant changes. There are three distinct avenues open for redressing housing discrimination under the new law: administrative enforcement, Attorney General litigation, and private litigation. (See Figure 23.2.)

Administrative Enforcement. An aggrieved party may file a complaint of discrimination with HUD any time up to one year after its occurrence. The administrator will either transfer the complaint to a state or local agency or begin an investigation. If the state or locality where the alleged discriminatory activity took place has a HUD-approved "substantially equivalent" fair housing program, the complaint is assigned to the nonfederal authorities.

FIGURE 23.2   Administrative Enforcement

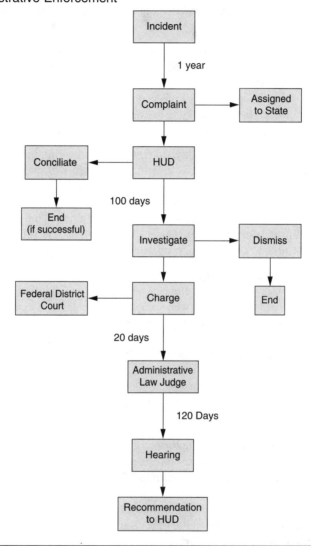

If there is no substantially equivalent nonfederal program, HUD has 100 days to carry out an investigation of the complaint and to file a report of its findings. During the 100-day period, HUD must begin a process of conciliation attempting to obtain an agreement ending the dispute. Note that a state program must be substantially equivalent to the federal so that when a complaint is referred to the state a similar procedure is followed.

If no conciliation agreement is reached during the 100-day investigatory period, HUD must dismiss the complaint or file charges. If HUD files charges, the aggrieved party has 20 days to exercise an election to take this matter to federal court for a jury trial. If the aggrieved party does not choose to go to federal court, the case stays in the administrative arena and is assigned to an administrative law judge (ALJ).

CASE EXAMPLE

Fleming, a prospective tenant, visited a property owned by Fredricy. While showing the rental property to Fleming, Fredricy stated that her children would be prohibited from playing outside in the front yard. Fleming filed a complaint. After conciliation failed, Fleming opted to sue Fredricy in federal court claiming that the remark was familial status discrimination. In June 2003, the federal court found that the policy prohibiting the children from playing in the front yard was discrimination and awarded $23,064 in damages.

The ALJ has 120 days to commence a hearing on the charges filed. At the conclusion of the administrative hearing, the judge will make recommendations to HUD for resolution of the dispute. It is highly likely that HUD will accept the recommendations. The ALJ can award the complainant actual damages, an injunction, or other equitable relief, and/or assess substantial civil penalties. The judge can also award the complainant attorney's fees. Once HUD approves the ruling, the parties have 30 days to appeal the case to the appropriate Federal Court of Appeals.

CASE EXAMPLE

Blackwell, a white, refused to sell his house to a black couple (Herrons). Instead, Blackwell leased the house to a white couple. The Herrons filed a complaint with HUD. The ALJ found for the Herrons, granting them $40,000 in actual damages and granting $20,000 to the white couple who leased the house for their embarrassment and economic loss; he also assessed a civil penalty of $10,000 against Blackwell.

The Eleventh Circuit upheld the ALJ on all the relief granted. This is the first case decided by an ALJ under the 1988 Fair Housing Act Amendments enforcement procedures. Notice the flexibility the ALJ has in granting relief. *Secretary, HUD ex rel. Herron v. Blackwell*, 908 F.2d 864 (1990).

Attorney General Litigation. If, after HUD files a charge of discrimination, the aggrieved party exercises the election to have a jury trial, HUD will notify the Attorney General; the Attorney General has 30 days to file a civil action in federal court on behalf of the complainant.

In this type of litigation, the court may grant any relief that is available in private litigation (discussed in the next section), including actual and punitive damages, injunctions, and other appropriate equitable remedies.

In addition to this type of civil action aimed at redressing a specific discriminatory action, the Attorney General may file suit where there is a pattern or practice of discrimination or there is a discriminatory denial of rights to a group of persons, raising issues of public importance.

Finally, the Attorney General has the authority to bring actions to enforce a conciliation agreement reached by the parties under the administrative process of the act.

Private Litigation. An aggrieved party may bring a private enforcement action in federal district court within two years of the discriminatory action. The private lawsuit can be filed even though an administrative complaint is filed with HUD. If a conciliation agreement is entered on the HUD-filed complaint, or if a hearing commences before the ALJ, the private lawsuit must be terminated.

There are several advantages to the private litigation avenue for the complainant. The judge can appoint an attorney for the complainant when he or she is unable to retain one and can waive statutory costs and fees if complainant is financially unable to bear them. More important, the court can grant unlimited actual and punitive damages and can more liberally require the defendant to pay the aggrieved parties' attorney's fees.

THE CHANGING LANDSCAPE

Undoubtedly, we have come a long way in our laws regarding racial issues. Just before the turn of the 20th century the law of the land was "separate but equal." In principle the words exude fairness, but in practice it doomed racial minorities to a status of legal and social inferiority. As chronicled in this chapter, the past 50 years have seen giant strides in the law to remedy past discriminatory policies. Certainly, spurred in significant measure by these legal changes, there is a great deal more racial fairness today in our society.

One could reasonably expect the outcome of the fair housing laws discussed in this chapter to be greater integration in our residential neighborhoods.

There has been some improvement, but do you sense that the races continue to live apart? Why? Is the fundamental purpose of the fair housing laws to integrate neighborhoods or to prevent discrimination in the housing market? Depending on your answer, have the laws succeeded? Suppose the owner of a large multiple-family housing complex sets a quota on the number of minorities it will allow in the complex. The purpose is that if the quota is exceeded, history teaches that there will be "white flight." If white flight occurs, the complex will not be integrated. However, if a family is denied rental based on race, that is discrimination. What should the purpose of the Fair Housing laws be?

■ KEY TERMS

blockbusting 525

equal protection 519

fair housing 521

familial status 529

reasonable
modification 526

redlining 525

steering 525

■ INTERNET RESOURCES

www.pueblo.gsa.gov/cic_text/fed_prog/disability-laws/disrits.htm
(A guide to disability rights law–Fair Housing Act)

http://dir.yahoo.com/Society_and_Culture/Issues_and_Causes/Housing/Fair_Housing/
(Fair housing site listings)

www.usdoj.gov/kidspage/crt/housing.htm
(Law and history of housing—redlining explained)

www.hud.gov/offices/fheo/index.cfm
(HUD site with links to many other sites and topics)

www.fairhousing.com/legal_research/regs/
(Fair Housing Regulation)

http://ut.essortment.com/realestatehou_rjbj.htm
(Understanding the Fair Housing Act)

■ REVIEW AND DISCUSSION QUESTIONS

1. Compare the theory and the reality of the policies of "separate but equal" with "equal protection."

2. Has discrimination in housing been completely banned by law?

3. Differentiate between blockbusting and steering.

4. Distinguish between reasonable modification and reasonable accommodation in protecting disabled persons from discrimination under the Fair Housing Act. Which one is likely to involve more disputes? Why?

5. From the perspective of an aggrieved party, how did the Fair Housing Act amendments of 1988 provide a greater incentive to redress discriminatory treatment?

■ CASE PROBLEMS

1. D. C. Williams and his wife, a black couple, wished to purchase lots in a subdivision being developed by the Matthews Company. The subdivision was not integrated. When they made an offer to purchase, a company official informed them that lots were sold only to builders. Although generally this was the case, some lots had been sold to individuals.

   Williams and his wife approached several white builders. Each of them refused to purchase and build for the Williams family, stating that they would get no more business in that area if they built for a black. Eventually Anderson, a black builder, agreed to purchase a lot and build the house that Williams and his wife wanted. The Matthews Company informed Anderson that it would not sell him the lot because he was not on the company's approved builder list. When Anderson attempted to find out what he had to do to become approved, he was informed that only the company president could do this and he was out of the country on a trip to the Orient for two months. The company had no policy for approval of builders but it did have an office memo indicating support for integration of the subdivision. The memo also indicated a belief that the issue was a sensitive one and should be handled at the level of company president.

No public announcement had ever been made of the company's commitment to integration, and no black person had ever acquired property in the subdivision. Has the Matthews Company violated any of the federal civil rights statutes? Discuss. *Williams v. Matthews Co.*, 499 F.2d 819 (8th Cir. 1974).

2. Greenwood was a sales associate in an office visited by Bago, a prospective buyer. Bago expressed an interest in a property in a specific area of Detroit. Greenwood told Bago that she had some nice property listed outside the city. She stated, "The school system is poor in Detroit." Later she asked, "Do you read the newspapers? Even the police are afraid to live in the area, and they are supposed to protect us." Greenwood gave Bago several listings in Detroit and a suburb and suggested that he compare prices, indicating that prices were lower in Detroit because blacks lived there. Greenwood further indicated that she would sell him any property he was interested in, wherever it was located. What, if any, violation of fair housing legislation has Greenwood committed? Support your answer.

3. The Wilsons owned an apartment building and advertised for tenants over a several month period in the local newspaper. The ads had language such as "ideal for single older person," and "ideal for one." Testers went to the building posing as prospective tenants and were routinely asked about their family status. Some were told that "lots of elderly and retired people" live in the building. On one occasion the Wilsons missed an appointment with a single mother and ignored all attempts to reschedule the meeting. Did the Wilsons violate the Fair Housing Law? Explain.

4. Swanner owned several rental properties in Anchorage. On several occasions, he refused to rent to couples who intended to cohabit but were unmarried. Swanner contended that couples living together outside marriage were likely to engage in fornication, and that was repugnant to his religious beliefs. If you were Swanner, what would you argue in court? Does Swanner's conduct violate the Fair Housing Acts? *Swanner v. Anchorage Equal Rights Com'n*, 874 P.2d 274 (1994).

24

Land Use:
The Constitution
and the Plan

The basic tenets of U.S. property law can be traced back to feudal times in England. Between the king and the lowest serf was the great mass of landholders. The landholder was not an owner but had the right to use a parcel of land. In exchange for that right of use, certain duties were owed to the superior on the feudal scale. These duties might include providing military service or a portion of the crops grown on the land. Our system of private property has evolved from this scheme, in which each landholder owed certain obligations in exchange for the right of use, but the legal notion of private property in America took its own peculiar twist.

As in England, the landholder's *rights* gradually expanded into what we refer to as *ownership*. These rights eventually gave the owner almost absolute and unfettered control over his or her grant of land. William Blackstone, the great 18th-century authority on the common law, referred to a person's property right as "that sole and despotic dominion," thereby depicting the extensive freedom that accompanied land ownership. A person's ownership rights were never quite as absolute as Blackstone alleged, but the wide range of rights he visioned became indelibly etched in the minds of landowners in England and America.

The American difference applied not to the "rights" side of the equation but to the "duty" side. Almost from the inception of this country, a landowner owed no duty to anyone except to refrain from acts on the property that would significantly interfere with another landowner's use of his or her property. Once the purchase price was paid, the buyer of land owed no additional duty to the seller. Our concept of property has always emphasized the landowner's rights over any duties arising from that ownership.

Though most Americans still cling tenaciously to the idea of absolute ownership rights in land, those rights eroded sharply in the twentieth century. The subdivider of land usually places a significant number of restrictions on use in the deed to the new homeowner. Municipal codes place an array of restraints on an owner's property rights. For instance, zoning laws limit an owner's use of the land. Other statutes or local ordinances require that an owner hook up to a sewer, desist from playing loud music late at night, refrain from keeping farm animals, and get a permit to build an addition to the house, to name only a few. This chapter will describe some of the traditional private restrictions on an owner's use of real property. It will then discuss constraints created by the Federal Constitution. Finally, it will discuss the planning process that must precede most regulations.

■ PRIVATE RESTRICTIONS ON LAND USE

Many limitations on the use of land are the result of agreements between buyers and sellers. These limitations are often referred to as *private restrictions*. The term *private restrictions* is also used to refer to limitations on land use imposed by the common law.

Restrictive Covenants

■ *Private agreements, usually placed in the deed by the seller when conveying land to the buyer, that restrict future use of that land.*

Parties to a real estate transaction are free to enter into any legal agreement that suits their particular situation. An agreement restricting the future use of the land is called a **restrictive covenant**.

A restrictive covenant is said to run with the land if it attaches to the land and is not dependent on the continued ownership of the parties to the original deed. The buyer's successors in title would be bound by the covenant, and the seller's successors in title would continue to benefit from the covenant.

> **CASE EXAMPLE**
>
> Baum, as the original grantee of a subdivided parcel, covenanted in the deed to accept and pay for a seasonal water supply provided by the original grantor. Eagle Enterprises, the successor to the original grantor, sued Gross, the successor to the grantee Baum, to enforce the restrictive covenant relating to the supplying of water. Eagle Enterprises argues that the covenant attaches, or "runs with the land," thereby binding all subsequent owners to pay for supplying the water. Gross responds that the covenant bound only Baum and did not run with the land.
>
> The court held that a restrictive covenant will run with the land if it meets three conditions: (1) the original parties must intend that it run with the land; (2) there must be privity of estate between the parties; and (3) the covenant must touch and concern the land. Although the court found that this particular covenant was personal and did not "touch and concern" the land, any covenant that meets the threefold test will be held to run with the land. *Eagle Enterprises, Inc. v. Gross*, 39 N.Y.2d 505, 349 N.E.2d 816 (1976).

Privity of estate is a phrase used to express the successive relationship of the parties to the land. For example, privity of estate exists between the grantor and grantee of an easement. The term *touch and concern the land* relates to the determination of whether the purported easement is peculiarly tied to the land itself or is rather a personal agreement between the parties and only incidentally concerns the land. The distinction between a personal covenant and one that touches and concerns the land is not always clear.

The restrictive covenant may carry a time limitation such as: "This covenant shall run with the land and be in effect for 20 years from the date of the conveyance." Usually, however, no termination period is stipulated, and the covenant lasts indefinitely.

Over the years, restrictive covenants have not been favored by the courts because they constituted an encroachment on the free transferability of land. Courts have never been enthusiastic about permitting land to be tied up with restrictions on use; when any doubt exists as to the meaning of the covenant, courts often find against the party placing the restriction in the deed. Despite the clear intention of the parties in the *Eagle Enterprises* case described above, note the reluctance of the court to bind future parties where grounds existed for relieving the land from the restriction.

The use of restrictive covenants and the attitude of courts toward them may be shifting. Today a substantial amount of residential development takes place in the form of subdivisions. The developer usually places a broad range of restrictive covenants in the plat plan or the individual deeds of the homebuyers or both. The purpose of the restrictions is to protect other landowners in the subdivision from losing some of their property value because of the unorthodox activity of a neighbor in the subdivision. For example, a restrictive covenant might prohibit the landowners from raising pigs or other farm animals. To avoid conflicts caused by questionable land use during development or immediately after the subdivision is completed, developers are inclined to include restrictive covenants against everything not narrowly confined to normal single-family use. The developer thereby makes every subdivision owner the third-party beneficiary of the restrictive covenants in the deeds of the other homeowners in the tract. The covenants generally are part of the deed or are filed with the general plat plan for the development and then recorded, thereby giving notice to all parties having an interest in the land in the future. The covenant is now part of the chain of title and runs with the land indefinitely.

Traditionally, the person selling part of his or her land subject to restrictive covenants has the right to enforce the covenant in the courts. Similarly, any owner in the subdivision as the third-party beneficiary of the developer-homeowner contract has enforcement rights in the court. However, a modern practice is for the developer to create a group such as an architectural committee to administer the covenant procedure. The developer and some associates often constitute the committee. The committee is authorized to handle complaints and (sometimes) to permit deviations from the restrictions in the covenants. For example, the restrictive covenant may bar all buildings from the land except the house and attached garage, unless approved by the architectural committee. On request, the committee may permit the homeowner to build a small toolshed on the property.

One problem may arise from this practice when the developer conveys all the parcels in the tract and does not provide for transfer of membership on the committee to the local subdivision residents, creating a hiatus. Theoretically, any homeowner *can* enforce the covenant. If the courts follow their traditional inclination of disfavoring restrictive covenants, however, enforcement may be impossible. It is arguable that the covenantor intended the *committee* to be the mechanism for enforcement, but the committee is now defunct.

An additional problem is that when restrictive covenants proliferate, people tend to ignore them. County or local zoning and building codes reduce the need for restrictive covenants by controlling major use changes or construction on residential land.

CASE EXAMPLE

Rachel assembles a four-foot by six-foot metal shed on her property to store her lawnmower and garden tools. Although the building is prohibited (without permission) by the restrictive covenant in Rachel's deed, it is common in her subdivision to own these sheds; in other words, "everyone ignores the covenant." The courts may not enforce the restrictive covenant on request by a neighbor because the homeowners have acquiesced in this noncompliance.

However, there are instances where Rachel will clearly be subject to the restrictive covenant and probably to a building code. When Rachel decides to build a second house on her lot, the covenant is violated and a building permit is required. The building inspector, to offer some measure of protection to other residents, oversees her plans. The building code, rather than the restrictive covenant, will probably become the enforcement mechanism.

Nevertheless, the restrictive covenants still provide a mechanism for an unhappy neighbor to complain, even concerning minor alterations like the small metal storage shed.

Restrictive covenants can be terminated in several ways. *All* the concerned parties may agree in writing to the termination. This approach may prove infeasible where the number of parties to the covenant is large. The covenants can also be terminated through condemnation of the land by a public agency having the power of eminent domain.

A common method of extinguishing these covenants is through nonuse or misuse. The character of the neighborhood may change, making continuation of the restrictions meaningless.

CASE EXAMPLE

William and Mae Pelster filed suit to enjoin the Millsaps from constructing a house on a lot in the plaintiffs' neighborhood. A restrictive covenant prohibited owners from subdividing their lots. The lot that Millsaps proposed to build on was a subdivided lot. The Millsaps argued that the character of the neighborhood had substantially changed over time, as many of the original lots had been subdivided.

The court stated that a restrictive covenant is unenforceable if clear and convincing evidence exists that (1) a substantial change in the character of the neighborhood existed; (2) enforcement of the restriction would not restore the neighborhood to its prior character; and (3) enforcement would impose greater hardship on the Millsaps with minimal benefit to the Pelsters. The court decided that the restrictive covenant in this case was unenforceable because numerous lots had been split previously, many current residents favored the splitting of this lot, and the Millsaps had signed a house construction contract unaware at the time that the restrictive covenant existed. *Pelster v. Millsaps*, 2001 Ohio App. Lexis 4556 (2001).

■ PUBLIC RESTRICTIONS ON LAND USE

In the 20th century, private restrictions were eclipsed in importance by public restrictions. Land use and development is controlled predominantly by legislation adopted at the state and local levels. Initially, control was by zoning codes; more recently, there has been a wide variety of other types of regulations.

Zoning and other regulatory legislation is examined in the next chapter. The remainder of this chapter is confined to three preconditions for a valid regulation. Any land use legislation must be a valid exercise of the police power, conform to federal and state constitutional limitations, and be preceded by a certain degree of planning.

The Police Power

The authority to regulate land use is almost exclusively provided by the police power. The **police power** is the inherent right of the state to regulate to protect the pub-

TABLE 24.1	Police Power and Eminent Domain: Comparison	
	Police Power	**Eminent Domain**
Source	Inherent in state	Inherent in state
Purpose	Public purpose (health, safety, or welfare)	Public use (coterminus with public purpose)
Financial Implications	No government payment	Government pays just compensation
Impact on Ownership	Private party retains ownership	Government physically takes land

lic health, safety, or welfare of its citizens. The grant of authority under the police power is very broad, and it can be delegated to local governments.

To be a valid exercise of the police power, the legislative body must have a legitimate police power purpose, that is, a public health, safety, or welfare reason for its enactment. It must prove also that there is a substantial connection, or nexus, between the legislatively stated purpose and the regulation enacted. For instance, if the law's stated purpose is highway safety, it must substantially promote highway safety.

Unlike the exercise of the power of eminent domain, the legislature regulating under the police power does not take the regulated property, nor does it pay just compensation to the property owner. (See Table 24.1.) Though the U.S. Supreme Court in the following case discusses the situation as if it were a regulatory takings case (see next section), one can see from the test it applies that it involves the issue of a valid exercise of the police power.

Nollan v. California Coastal Commission
U.S. Supreme Court
483 U.S. 825 (1987)

Background. James and Marilyn Nollan leased a small beachfront bungalow in Ventura County, California. Subsequently, they entered into a contract to purchase the land from the owner, but the agreement was contingent on their ability to demolish the bungalow, now fallen into disrepair, and to replace it with a larger house. To achieve this end, they needed a permit from the California Coastal Commission (Commission). The Commission's function was to protect the coastal area from harmful development. The Commission granted the permit, but conditioned it on the Nollans' willingness to grant a public easement across the near-ocean portion of the lot. The Commission had conditioned all permit requests in the area in this fashion, apparently with the expectation of linking easements for public access along the shore and between two parks lying north and south of Nollan's land. The parks are about one-half mile apart.

The justification given by the Commission for the easement condition was that the new, larger house would further block the view of the ocean and worsen the public's ability to see that there was nearby public access to the beach. Also, it argued that the new house would further privatize the shorefront.

continued on next page

The Nollans sued, contending that the permit condition violated their property rights. The trial court found for the Nollans because there were inadequate facts to support the request for an easement. The Court of Appeal reversed the trial court.

Decision. The United States Supreme Court reversed the California appellate court, ruling in favor of the Nollans.

Justice Scalia. Had California simply required the Nollans to make an easement across their beachfront available to the public on a permanent basis in order to increase public access to the beach, rather than conditioning their permit to rebuild their house on their agreeing to do so, we have no doubt there would have been a taking. To say that the appropriation of a landowner's premises does not constitute the taking of a property interest but rather, "a mere restriction on its use," is to use words in a manner that deprives them of all their ordinary meaning. Indeed, one of the principal uses of the eminent domain power is to assure that the government be able to require conveyance of just such interests, so long as it pays for them. We have repeatedly held that, as to property reserved by its owner for private use, "the right to exclude [others is] 'one of the most essential sticks in the bundle of rights that are commonly characterized as property.'"

Given, then, that requiring uncompensated conveyance of the easement outright would violate the Fourteenth Amendment, the question becomes whether requiring it to be conveyed as a condition for issuing a land use permit alters the outcome. We have long recognized that land use regulation does not effect a taking if it "substantially advance[s] legitimate state interests" and does not "den[y] an owner economically viable use of his land." Our cases have not elaborated on the standards for determining what constitutes a "legitimate state interest" or what type of connection between the regulation and the state interest satisfies the requirement that the former "substantially advance" the latter. They have made clear, however, that a broad range of governmental purposes and regulations satisfies these requirements. The Commission argues that among these permissible purposes are protecting the public's ability to see the beach, assisting the public in overcoming the "psychological barrier" to using the beach created by a developed shorefront, and preventing congestion on the public beaches. We assume, without deciding, that this is so.

If the Commission attached to the permit some condition that would have protected the public's ability to see the beach notwithstanding construction of the new house—for example, a height limitation, a width restriction, or a ban on fences—so long as the Commission could have exercised its police power (as we have assumed it could) to forbid construction of the house altogether, imposition of the condition would also be constitutional. Moreover, (and here we come closer to the facts of the present case), the condition would be constitutional even if it consisted of the requirement that the Nollans provide a viewing spot on their property for passersby with whose sighting of the ocean their new house would interfere. Although such a requirement, constituting a permanent grant of continuous access to the property, would have to be considered a taking if it were not attached to a development permit, the Commission's assumed power to forbid construction of the house in order to protect the public's view of the beach must surely include the power to condition construction on some concession by the owner, even a concession of property rights, that serves the same end. If a prohibition designed to accomplish that purpose would be a legitimate exercise of the police power rather than a taking, it would be strange to conclude that providing the owner an alternative to that prohibition which accomplishes the same purpose is not.

The evident constitutional propriety disappears, however, if the condition substituted for the prohibition utterly fails to further the end advanced as the justification for the prohibition. The essential nexus is eliminated.

The Nollans' new house, the Commission found, will interfere with "visual access" to the beach. That in turn (along with other shorefront development) will interfere with the desire of people who drive past the Nollans' house to use the beach, thus creating a "psychological barrier" to "access." The Nollans' new house will also, by a process not altogether clear from the Commission's opinion but presumably potent enough to more than offset the effects of the psychological barrier, increase the use of the public beaches, thus creating the need for more "access." These burdens on "access" would be alleviated by a requirement that the Nollans provide "lateral access" to the beach.

Rewriting the argument to eliminate the play on words makes clear that there is nothing to it. It is quite impossible to understand how a requirement that people already on the public beaches be able to walk across the Nollans' property reduces any obstacles to viewing the beach created by the new house. It is also impossible to understand how it lowers any "psychological barrier" to using the public beaches, or how it helps to remedy an additional congestion on them caused by construction of the Nollans' new house. We therefore find that the Commission's imposition of the permit condition cannot be treated as an exercise of its land use power for any of these purposes. Our conclusion on this point is consistent with the approach taken by every other court that has considered the question, with the exception of the California state courts.

Justice Brennan argues that a person looking toward the beach from the road will see a street of residential structures, including the Nollans' new home, and conclude that there is no public beach nearby. If, however, that person sees people passing and repassing along the dry sand behind the Nollans' home, he will realize that there is a public beach somewhere in the vicinity. The Commission's action, however, was based on the opposite finding that the wall of houses completely blocked the view of the beach and that the person looking from the road would not be able to see it at all. Our cases describe the condition for abridgment of property rights through the police power as a "substantial advanc[ing]" of a legitimate State interest. We are inclined to be particularly careful about the adjective where the actual conveyance of property is made a condition to the lifting of a land use restriction, since in that context there is heightened risk that the purpose is avoidance of the compensation requirement, rather than the stated police power objective.

Reversed.

Can you persuasively make the argument that the condition in the permit does substantially advance a legitimate state interest?

Constitutional Limitations

The most important constitutional limitation in the land use area pertains to *eminent domain*. Theoretically, the government has the inherent power to take land from private owners for its own use. The federal and state constitutions, however, place constraints on that power. They provide that a taking of property by government, or an exercise of eminent domain, must have a public purpose and that the government must pay just compensation. When the government exercises its power of eminent domain, it physically takes the land away from its former owner. It is not merely regulating use as it does when using the police power.

The government's power to *regulate* under the police power and its power to *take* land under eminent domain appear at first blush to be distinct and separate. The courts have found, however, that there can be conflict in the exercise of the two powers. A regulation under the police power may be so restrictive of the private owner's use of the land that a court may hold that it constitutes a *regulatory taking*. In a regulatory taking, the court declares that the attempt to regulate went beyond the police power and crossed the constitutional line of the eminent domain or takings clause. It requires the government therefore to withdraw the regulation or to pay the landowner just compensation.

The courts are clear that an attempted exercise of the police power can be found to be an unconstitutional regulatory taking. Drawing the line between valid and invalid regulations has proven to be a struggle for courts. Some courts declare that a law that prevents a harm to the public is a valid regulation and one that confers a benefit on the public is an invalid regulatory taking. Is a regulation that requires that a residential land developer dedicate part of the land for parkland to serve the needs of future homeowners preventing harm (e.g., congestion) or conferring a benefit (e.g., giving them extra and unnecessary land without paying for it)? There is no inherently correct answer, and therein lies the frailty of the rule. In the *Lucas* case, appearing later in this chapter, the U.S. Supreme Court expressly rejects this line of reasoning.

Some courts argue that a regulatory taking occurs when all reasonable use of the land is taken by the law. Is the "all reasonable use" test a purely economic analysis? If so, how much of the economic value of the land must be taken? Alternatively, when land has little economic value but significant natural resource value, such as a wetland, must the rule encompass more than the economic value of the land? No significant agreement exists among the federal and state courts as to how to perform the regulatory takings analysis.

The U.S. Supreme Court, while acknowledging the ad hoc nature of the analysis, has settled on a largely economic analysis. The court makes clear, however, that a physical invasion of the land is a regulatory taking, regardless of the economic implications.

CASE EXAMPLE

Teleprompter placed a one-foot-wide cable television box on the rooftop of a building owned by Loretto. The cable television company obtained the authority to do this from a state law permitting the placing of cable boxes and wires on private land. Loretto challenged the law as an unconstitutional regulatory taking of a part of her land.

The U.S. Supreme Court ruled for Loretto, stating that a "permanent physical occupation authorized by government is a taking without regard to the public interest it may serve." It is noteworthy that the rule applies only to permanent physical occupations; it is a per se rule, however, applying regardless of the extent of the public interest served by the state law or the slight degree of economic injury to the landowner. *Loretto v. Teleprompter Manhattan CATV Corp.*, 458 U.S. 419 (1982).

Without a permanent physical occupation created by the regulation, the court scrutinizes the full economic impact of the law on the value of the land, or the so-called diminution in value test. The court has never defined where the diminution line should be drawn. Perhaps it is no more precise than being at the point at which all reasonable economic use is confiscated. The court makes clear in the *Lucas* case that destroying *all* economic value is a regulatory taking, unless there is some justification under prior law. The court seldom finds regulatory takings under the diminution in value test.

A second economic-based test appears to be a modification of the diminution in value test, though both are applied in the same cases. The court looks to see if the reasonable investment-backed expectations of the landowner are frustrated. If the landowner continues to obtain a reasonable return from the land despite the regulation, the court is unlikely to find that the reasonable investment-backed expectations were frustrated. No significant clues beyond this have emerged from the court as to how these reasonable expectations are determined.

Some courts have shied away from using a solely economic rationale in deciding regulatory takings cases. These courts contend that land is in part a public natural resource so fundamental to human existence on this planet that decisions about it cannot be made examining only a law's economic impact on its current owner. The continued validity of this position is brought into question by the following case and other U.S. Supreme Court decisions.

Lucas v. South Carolina Coastal Council
Supreme Court of the United States
112 S. Ct. 2886 (1992)

Background. David Lucas purchased two lots in a residential subdivision on the Isle of Palms, South Carolina, for $975,000. Lucas, a house builder, subsequently sought a permit from the South Carolina Coastal Council (Council) because the lots were located in a "critical area." When Lucas purchased them in 1986, the lots were not in a critical area. In 1988, a major hurricane, Hugo, blasted the South Carolina coastal island and redistributed the sand on the Isle of Palms. Such a redistribution of sand is common when major storms strike barrier islands like the Isle of Palms. Historically, critical area demarcations had often shifted in response to shifting sands caused by storms. The Beachfront Management Act (Act) (1988), the law that brought the Lucas lots within the designated critical area, sought to set a baseline seaward from which the land was highly erodible and not appropriate for houses.

The Council denied Lucas' permit request, and Lucas sued claiming a regulatory taking. The trial court ruled that the permit denial deprived Lucas of all economic use of the lots and awarded him $1.2 million in "just compensation." The Supreme Court of South Carolina reversed, holding that the Act was designed to prevent a serious public harm. Given the validity of the Act's purpose, no compensation

was due regardless of its effect on the land's economic value.

Decision. The U.S. Supreme Court reversed, again ruling for Lucas.

Justice Scalia. Prior to Justice Holmes' exposition in *Pennsylvania Coal Co. v. Mahon* (1922), it was generally thought that the Takings Clause reached only a "direct appropriation" of property, or the functional equivalent of a "practical ouster of [the owner's] possession." Justice Holmes recognized in *Mahon*, however, that if the protection against physical appropriations of private property was to be meaningfully enforced, the government's power to redefine the range of interests included in the ownership of property was necessarily constrained by constitutional limits. If, instead, the uses of private property were subject to unbridled, uncompensated qualification under the police power, "the natural tendency of human nature [would be] to extend the qualification more and more until at last private property disappeared." These considerations gave birth in that case to the oft-cited maxim that, "while property may be regulated to a certain extent, if regulation goes too far it will be recognized as a taking."

continued on next page

Nevertheless, our decision in *Mahon* offered little insight into when, and under what circumstances, a given regulation would be seen as going "too far" for purposes of the Fifth Amendment. In 70-odd years of succeeding "regulatory takings" jurisprudence, we have generally eschewed any set formula for determining how far is too far, preferring to "engage in . . . essentially ad hoc, factual inquiries." We have, however, described at least two discrete categories of regulatory action as compensable without case-specific inquiry into the public interest advanced in support of the restraint. The first encompasses regulations that compel the property owner to suffer a physical "invasion" of his property. In general (at least with regard to permanent invasions), no matter how minute the intrusion, and no matter how weighty the public purpose behind it, we have required compensation.

The second situation in which we have found categorical treatment appropriate is where regulation denies all economically beneficial or productive use of land. As we have said on numerous occasions, the Fifth Amendment is violated when land-use regulation "does not substantially advance legitimate state interests or denies an owner economically viable use of his land."

We have never set forth the justification for this rule. Perhaps it is simply, as Justice Brennan suggested, that total deprivation of beneficial use is, from the landowner's point of view, the equivalent of a physical appropriation. "For what is the land but the profits thereof?" Surely, at least, in the extraordinary circumstance when no productive or economically beneficial use of land is permitted, it is less realistic to indulge our usual assumption that the legislature is simply "adjusting the benefits and burdens of economic life," in a manner that secures an "average reciprocity of advantage" to everyone concerned.

On the other side of the balance, affirmatively supporting a compensation requirement, is the fact that regulations that leave the owner of land without economically beneficial or productive options for its use—typically, as here, by requiring land to be left substantially in its natural state—carry with them a heightened risk that private property is being pressed into some form of public service under the guise of mitigating serious public harm.

We think, in short, that there are good reasons for our frequently expressed belief that when the owner of real property has been called on to sacrifice all economically beneficial uses in the name of the common good, that is, to leave his property economically idle, he has suffered a taking.

It is correct that many of our prior opinions have suggested that "harmful or noxious uses" of property may be proscribed by government regulation without the requirement of compensation. "Harmful or noxious use" analysis was, in other words, simply the progenitor of our more contemporary statements that "land-use regulation does not effect a taking if it 'substantially advances legitimate state interests'. . . ." The transition from our early focus on control of "noxious" uses to our contemporary understanding of the broad realm within which government may regulate without compensation was an easy one, since the distinction between "harm-preventing" and "benefit-conferring" regulation is often in the eye of the beholder.

When it is understood that "prevention of harmful use" was merely our early formulation of the police power justification necessary to sustain (without compensation) any regulatory diminution in value; and that the distinction between regulation that "prevents harmful use" and that which "confers benefits" is difficult, if not impossible, to discern on an objective, value-free basis; it becomes self-evident that noxious-use logic cannot serve as a touchstone to distinguish regulatory "takings"—which require compensation—from regulatory deprivations that do not require compensation.

Where the State seeks to sustain regulation that deprives land of all economically beneficial use, we think it may resist compensation only if the logically antecedent inquiry into the nature of the owner's estate shows that the proscribed use interests were not part of his title to begin with. It seems to us that the property owner necessarily expects the uses of his property to be restricted, from time to time, by various measures newly enacted by the State in legitimate exercise of its police powers.

Where regulations prohibit all economically beneficial use of land, any limitation so severe cannot be newly legislated or decreed (without compensation), but must inhere in the title itself, in the restrictions that background principles of the State's law of property and nuisance already place on landownership.

On this analysis, the owner of a lake bed, for example, would not be entitled to compensation when he is denied the requisite permit to engage in a landfilling operation that would have the effect of flooding others' land. Nor would the corporate owner of a nuclear generating plant, when it is directed to remove all improvements from its land on discovery that the plant sits astride an earthquake fault. Such regulatory action may well have the effect of eliminating the land's only economically productive use, but it does not proscribe a productive use that was previously permissible under relevant property and nuisance principles. The use of these properties for what are now expressly prohibited purposes was always unlawful.

The "total taking" inquiry we require today will ordinarily entail (as the application of state nuisance law ordinarily entails) analysis of, among other things, the degree of harm to public lands and resources, or adjacent private property, posed by the claimant's proposed activities, the social value of the claimant's activities and their suitability to the locality in question, and the relative ease with which the alleged harm can be avoided through measures taken by the claimant and the government (or adjacent private landowners) alike. The fact that a particular use has long been engaged in by similarly situated owners ordinarily imports a lack of any common-law prohibition (though changed circumstances or new knowledge may make what was previously permissible no longer so). So also does the fact that other landowners, similarly situated, are permitted to continue the use denied to the claimant.

It seems unlikely that common-law principles would have prevented the erection of any habitable or productive improvements on petitioner's land; they rarely support prohibition of the "essential use" of land. South Carolina must identify background principles of nuisance and property law that prohibit the uses he now intends in the circumstances in which the property is presently found. Only on this showing can the State fairly claim that, in proscribing all such beneficial uses, the Beachfront Management Act is taking nothing.

Reversed.

Suppose there is no physical invasion by the government, and some economic value remains after the government regulation. Can there be a regulatory taking?

It should be noted that the holding of the *Lucas* case is a narrow one. It holds that a regulatory taking occurs when all reasonable and beneficial economic use is denied the landowner; and then only when the proposed use was not already restricted by the state's nuisance and property law. It did make clear, however, that the harm/benefit type of analysis used by prior courts was no longer appropriate in a *Lucas*-type situation.

The Lucas reasoning suffered another blow in the case *Tahoe-Sierra Preservation Council v. Tahoe Regional Planning Agency (2002).* In the *Tahoe* case the U.S. Supreme Court made clear that unless there is a "permanent obliteration" of value the *Lucas* reasoning did not apply. So, even a 95 percent reduction in value would not constitute a *Lucas*-type taking. Remember in *Lucas,* the Court concluded that there was a taking of total economic value, even though it is hard to imagine that land on a barrier island off the South Carolina coast was without any economic value. Tahoe also affirmed the rule that in determining the value of the landowners property the court would examine the whole parcel and not merely the restricted portion of the property.

CASE EXAMPLE

Edlyn Associates proposed to build 80 homes on a 100 acre parcel it owned in Easton. The Easton Planning Board informed Edlyn Associates that 60 acres of the land were regulated wetlands and could not be developed for residential structures. Edlyn Associates sued the Planning Board contending that the regulation obliterated the entire value of the 60 acres of wetland since it could not build on them.

A court would rule that in assessing the value of the land in a regulatory takings case it would examine the parcel as a whole (100 acres). Since Edlyn Associates had 40 acres that it could develop, there was no "permanent obliteration" of the value of the parcel. If the court were so inclined, it might try to ascertain whether the 60 acres of wetland retained some economic value.

By far the most important constitutional limitation in the land use area is the prohibition against regulatory takings. There are, however, other constitutional limitations that have played a lesser role in land use litigation, such as the equal protection clause. Most regulations attacked in court with an equal protection argument were adopted for economic reasons. In economic-based equal protection cases, the courts permit a regulation to differentiate between classes of persons (e.g., married and unmarried), but the classification must be reasonable and bear a rational relationship to a permissible state objective (e.g., public safety). In short, regulators may differentiate between classes but cannot discriminate against a group. It should be noted that this rational basis test does not apply in cases involving certain types of differentiations, such as those based on race or color. Differences based on race or color are subjected to a more rigorous test and are unlikely to survive judicial scrutiny.

Some state courts review land-use regulations using a substantive due process standard. These courts examine the legislation under attack to see if in their view it is reasonable. So the courts actually second-guess the wisdom of the legislature in passing the law. The courts balance the benefit that the law can be expected to attain against the cost it will impose on society or individuals. Ideally, this is a repetition of the exact balancing process that the legislature carried out before adopting the law.

The federal courts and many state courts reject the notion of reviewing cases under a substantive due process standard. They contend that the wisdom of a law is within the purview of the legislative body and should not be overturned by a court unless it is arbitrary in nature. Whether these courts always refrain from reviewing the wisdom of land-use laws despite what they say is a matter of some debate.

Planning

The cornerstone of any land-use regulation is a plan. The law provides that regulations, especially zoning codes, must be based on a comprehensive plan. The regulator may organize, restrict, or even prohibit development for public health, safety, and welfare purposes, so long as the regulation is not arbitrary and is adopted pursuant to a plan.

There is no clear definition of what constitutes a comprehensive plan. Some state courts in zoning cases contend that the comprehensive plan need not be in writing, but may be inferred from the zoning map and the community's traditional land-use patterns. In reality these courts pay only lip service to the planning requirement. It is a rare community that relies on a zoning map and past development patterns and develops in a truly planned fashion. Despite this fact, many states continue to minimize the planning requirement.

The Comprehensive Plan. Some states and municipalities take the planning requirement seriously and mandate the preparation and adoption of a bona fide comprehensive plan. A **comprehensive**, or master, **plan** has some standard characteristics. It deals with future physical development of the community, contains a textual statement of land-use policies, and has a set of descriptive maps. The plan and maps are general in nature. A zoning code and map are usually adopted to make the plan operational and to add precision to the broad policies and maps contained in the plan.

LaBonta v. City of Waterville
Supreme Judicial Court of Maine
528 A. 2d 1262 (1987)

Background. Shaw's Realty Company sought to locate a 170,000-square-foot shopping center on a parcel of land adjacent to Kennedy Memorial Drive in Waterville. A strip of land 800 feet deep along the drive was zoned for commercial use. The back portion of the parcel was zoned for residential use. Shaw petitioned the city council to rezone 8.1 acres of the land from residential to commercial. After holding public hearings on the proposed rezoning, the city council amended the zoning code by affirming Shaw's zone change request.

Robert LaBonta and a group of neighbors to the parcel filed suit to have the zone change overturned. They argued that the amendment was inconsistent with the city's comprehensive plan. In particular, it was inconsistent with the goal of protecting residential neighborhoods. The trial court found for the city.

Decision. The Supreme Court of Maine affirmed the trial judge's opinion in favor of the city.

Chief Justice McKusick. The comprehensive plan, that section 4962(1)(A) requires every municipality to have as a prerequisite to zoning, is by definition "a compilation of policy statements, goals, [and] standards" with respect to issues relevant to land use regulation. The Waterville comprehensive plan sets forth a number of goals relevant to the rezoning requested by Shaw's, of which the protection of residential neighborhoods is but one. Particularly pertinent is the plan's emphasis on the need to expand economic opportunity in Waterville and to provide adequate space for commercial development. Even more specifically, the plan sets as a zoning goal for the City the commercial development along three arteries including Kennedy Memorial Drive, by stating the following:

"Commercial growth should continue to follow its present pattern of development with relation to three major traffic arteries of the City.

"Firstly, College Avenue has been, for years, the traditional node for newer commercial development. The present state of development and large volumes of traffic on that street preclude other types of use. Main Street, south of Route 95, and Kennedy Memorial Drive also have very large traffic volumes. While these streets do not have a long history of commercial development, their present state of rapidly progressing development has established them

continued on next page

as major areas of commercial land use outside of the downtown area.

"By allowing for commercial development to occur in a coherent pattern in these areas of the City, other areas may be completely exempted from the pressures of this type of land use. . . ."

From the transcript of the hearings conducted by the city council, it is clear that the council recognized and acted on its responsibility to amend the zoning ordinance only in a way consistent with the comprehensive plan and the multiple goals stated therein. Faced with the multiple goals of protecting residential neighborhoods and promoting economic opportunity and commercial development along Kennedy Memorial Drive, the city council was not required to refrain from permitting any intrusion whatever on an area previously zoned residential. Rather it had the job of accommodating these multiple goals in a way to advance the overall best interests of the City and its people as defined by the comprehensive plan read as a whole.

The test for the court's review of the city council's rezoning action is whether "from the evidence before it" the city council could have determined that the rezoning was in basic harmony with the [comprehensive] plan. In making that review of the record before the city council, the court will not substitute [its] judgment for that of the duly elected legislative body, the city council. The parties challenging the council's action have the burden of showing inconsistency between the rezoning and the comprehensive plan.

On the basis of the evidence before it, the city council is justified in concluding that the zoning change was in basic harmony with the comprehensive plan because the change struck a reasonable balance among the City's various zoning goals. On the one hand, the goal of promoting commercial development along Kennedy Memorial Drive (with the creation of *additional* job opportunities and the attraction of consumer dollars to Waterville) could not be fully achieved by the proposed shopping center within the 800-foot strip previously zoned commercial. The development of "one-stop shopping" means that a retail shopping area to be competitive must be large enough to offer customers a substantial variety of stores; and significant traffic flow advantages accrue to a deeper shopping center layout as compared to strip development. Also, recently imposed environmental regulations require the construction of a storm water retention basin, which in turn requires an additional area for a commercial establishment. On the other hand, the area that the city council rezoned commercial had been zoned residential for 58 years and still at the time of the rezoning no house had been built within it. The residents challenging the Waterville rezoning fail to persuade us that the city council's conclusion was not adequately supported by the evidence before it.

Judgment affirmed.

What is the relationship between the comprehensive plan and the zoning code and map?

Planning boards that make land-use decisions often consult the zoning code but seldom have cause to refer to the comprehensive plan. Does that make sense?

Generally, state legislation enables municipalities to enact zoning codes and other land use regulations, but makes comprehensive planning a precondition. In short, the planning and regulating are done locally under state authorization. There is a trend, however, for the states to become more involved in the land use planning and regulating process. During the 1970s, some state legislatures became dissatisfied with local planning and rescinded local power to do so. The rescission was usually for reasons of environmental protection and often applied to limited areas of the state. For example, New York placed land-use control over the Adirondack Mountain region in the hands of a state-appointed regional agency, and California created the San Francisco Bay Conservation and Development Commission to plan and regulate future land use for the Bay Area.

This trend toward state control continues and is broadening. Some states have enacted comprehensive planning and land-use systems applicable to the entire state, not confining them to environmental protection purposes.

Growth Management Systems. Several states have enacted comprehensive legislation setting up a system of **growth management** directed by the state. The leading state in this type of planning is Oregon. Oregon's system established a set of statewide planning goals and policies within which localities must operate. It established the state Land Conservation and Development Commission to oversee and guide the localities in this process. There are 19 goals with accompanying guidelines. The goals run the gamut from citizen involvement to land-use planning to forest lands to energy conservation. Each locality must devise a land-use plan and process consistent with these statewide goals.

Other states, including Delaware, Tennessee, Florida, Vermont, Georgia, Maine, Maryland, Rhode Island, Washington, and New Jersey, have enacted similar legislation applying to a portion of the state, for example, a coastal area, or to the entire state.

Community-Based Strategic Planning. Though the precise legal changes that will ensue are uncertain at this time, a different type of planning evolved in the 1990s. Though it is **community-based planning**, it does not appear to be emanating from the bureaucracy of local government as in the past. Civic leaders in some metropolitan areas gathered together broad segments of the community for the purpose of planning the future of land development and other activities.

The civic leaders conducted a strategic planning process similar to that used in business. After gathering representatives from all segments of the community to participate in the process, the group developed a community vision, conducted an inventory and assessment of community resources, set and prioritized goals, and established benchmarks to measure progress. Communities such as Chattanooga, Tennessee; Seattle, Washington; Portland, Oregon; Pattonsburg, Missouri; and Buffalo, New York, actively engaged in this planning process. The process is strongly promoted by the President's Council on Sustainable Development in its 1996 report entitled *Sustainable America*.

This planning process lays heavy emphasis on human scale development, environmental protection, and redevelopment of brownfields (i.e., old, rundown, and contaminated industrial sites). These are not the roots of current planning and zoning. The result may be an *increase* in mixed-use zoning with a return to a village-type setting. With the current emphasis on sustainability in development, planning may lead to greater weight being given to durability; energy conservation; protection of aesthetic, cultural, and historical qualities; minimizing and reusing building materials; and increased use of native plants that reduce the need for fertilizer, pesticides, and water. As these elements appear in community plans, it is likely to lead to changes in zoning and building codes.

■ **Ecological Constraints on Development.** *Ecology is the science that deals with the relationship of organisms and their environment. "The basic insight of ecology is that all living things exist in interrelated systems; nothing exists in isolation. The world system is weblike; to pluck one strand is to cause all to vibrate; whatever happens to one part has manifestations for all the rest. Our actions are not individual but social; they reverberate throughout the whole ecosystem."[1]*

Slowly, humans are coming to realize that they are part of the natural systems and that these systems have definable limits to their capacity to serve human needs. Thoughtless abuse of the elements within natural systems, such as the land, air, and water, inevitably spread throughout the system, causing harm far beyond the source of the abuse.

In some measure, these **ecological constraints** differ from other constraints. Laws are usually the product of social value judgments made by government. For example, deciding that 65 miles per hour is the best speed limit on a highway is a value judgment. Arguably, some other number might have been selected at a different time, like 55 miles per hour. To a certain extent, ecologically based laws are the product of the natural and physical sciences and not social policy determinations. For example, it is known that when the amount of oxygen in a stream is reduced due to pollution, certain residents (fish) of the stream ecosystem will die. There is no value judgment in that. If we make the value judgment that the fish must be protected, minimum oxygen levels in the water must be maintained. Whether it is the protection of fish or humans that concerns us, certain ecological imperatives must be met. The earth and its ecosystems have definable limits.

Development on land in the floodplain increases the chances of subsequent flooding destructive to human life and property and to the ecosystem. Filling a wetland for development reduces wildlife habitat and destroys major incubators for important food supplies for humans. Cutting of forests reduces the natural systems' ability to buffer against the buildup of carbon dioxide, causing global warming. The connection between land development and natural systems is significant and undeniable.

Today, a great deal of information about the impact of development on natural systems is known. Many jurisdictions mandate that an environmental assessment be done prior to development to ensure that the ecological impacts are known to the decision maker.

■ **Environmental Impact Assessment.** *A statement detailing environmental data and analyzing that data regarding a proposed land development action.*

About one half of the states now require some type of environmental impact review when considering a development proposal. Most of these state statutes and regulations are patterned after the National Environmental Policy Act (NEPA). NEPA requires the preparation of an environmental impact statement (EIS) for federal actions that may significantly affect the quality of the environment. The equivalent state laws, or little-NEPAs, require EISs for state actions. State action in many of these states includes private action requiring any type of state approval. In these states, significant development proposals, such as those large in size or those to be located in an environmentally sensitive area, must be accompanied by the preparation of an EIS.

An EIS is a detailed, analytical document that describes the action being proposed, portrays the state of the environment in the area where the action is proposed, and analyzes the environmental impact that the proposal is likely to have on the existing environment. The purpose of the EIS is to provide the decision maker (government agency) and the public with all the relevant environmental data prior to making the decision to approve or disapprove the development.

In most states, the environmental impact law is a procedural law and cannot mandate a particular result. The law compels the agency to generate and analyze the environmental information but does not compel the agency to disapprove the development proposal based on the bad environmental news. The decision maker must consider the environmental data along with the economic, technological, social, and political data regarding the proposal. A few little-NEPAs create substantive law and can compel the agency to disapprove the development proposal.

The preparation of an EIS has become more manageable in recent years. Some communities have developed natural resource inventories that provide the scientific data to assist in preparing EISs. Many areas have private contractors available who specialize in preparing EISs.

Ultimate responsibility for preparing EISs lies with the government agency. The normal procedure is that the agency makes the threshold decision of whether to prepare an EIS. This decision may be facilitated by consulting the agency's EIS regulations, which will list projects necessitating EISs and those not requiring an EIS. For the types of actions not listed in its regulations, often called *unlisted actions*, the agency prepares an environmental assessment. The environmental assessment (EA) is a mini-EIS whose purpose is to decide whether the proposed development action may have a significant effect on the quality of the environment. If the EA reveals that significant environmental impacts will not result, it terminates the process by issuing a "negative declaration." If the EA indicates that there may be significant environmental impacts, the agency must prepare an EIS. The preparation of the EIS is often preceded by a process called *scoping*. During scoping, the agency consults with all interested parties to determine what the significant impacts are likely to be (e.g., water pollution) and what the scope of those impacts is (e.g., within the Black River drainage area).

The EIS is initially prepared in a draft form called a *DEIS*. The DEIS is circulated to relevant parties and is made available to the public. All parties have a specified period of time to respond to the DEIS. The agency then prepares a final EIS, known as an *FEIS*. The FEIS must address any shortcomings in the DEIS and respond to any reasonable comments made to the agency during the DEIS comment period. The FEIS is then considered by the agency decision maker along with other relevant information in determining whether to disapprove or to go ahead with the proposal.

■ NOTE

1. Science Action Coalition, with A. Fritsch, *Environmental Ethics: Choices for Concerned Citizens*, 3–4 (1980).

THE CHANGING LANDSCAPE

If you refer back to "The Changing Landscape" at the end of Chapter 2, there is a discussion of a shift in the rights-responsibilities equation for landowners. Government regulation has tempered the almost absolute freedom of landowners over their property. It even suggests that some duty of stewardship of the land might emerge over time. Similarly, in Chapter 3, the discussion is about Aldo Leopold's vision of a need for a land ethic wherein humans value the natural characteristics of the land and make development decisions based on environmental and aesthetic values as well as economic values.

Contrast these views with the one espoused by the U.S. Supreme Court in the *Lucas* Case. On page 546, column 1, 14 lines from the bottom, Justice Scalia quotes the following: "For what is the land but the profits thereof?" The majority of the justices on the 1992 court clearly see land solely as an economic commodity. It is little different from a share of stock, a turret lathe in a machine shop, or a slab of sheet rock.

Justice Hallows, writing for the Wisconsin Supreme Court in 1972, *Just v. Marinette County*, 201 N.W. 2d 761 (1972), expressed a contrasting view. He noted that swamps and wetlands were once considered wasteland, undesirable and not picturesque. By 1972, "even to the unitiated," there was, he said, an appreciation for their vital role in nature, their capacity to purify water, and their possession of special beauty.

Which view do you identify with? Having stood on the south rim of the Grand Canyon, having witnessed the sights and smells of autumn leaves in upstate New York, having seen the flittings of a vermilion flycatcher in early spring along the San Pedro River in Arizona, having listened to elk bugle and bison thunder in Yellowstone Park, and having seen, heard, and felt so many other wonders of land and the creatures of the land, it is hard to think of it as an ordinary "commodity"? Why is the divide between these opinions so broad?

■ KEY TERMS

community-based
  planning 551

comprehensive plan 549

ecological constraints 552

environmental impact
  assessment 552

growth management 551

police power 540

privity of estate 538

restrictive covenant 538

■ INTERNET RESOURCES

http://ohioline.osu.edu/cd-fact/1262.html, click on land trusts
(Land trusts)

www.fwlaw.com/takings.html
(Government restrictions on land use—implications of Takings Clause)

www.toolkit.cch.com/pops/P99_04_1071_03.asp
(Private restrictions on land use defined)

www.epa.gov/greenkit/case.htm
(Maintenance of a sustainable level of land use—various case studies)

■ REVIEW AND DISCUSSION QUESTIONS

1. Explain the rationale used for permitting one homeowner in a subdivision to sue a neighbor asserting a restrictive covenant in the neighbor's deed.

2. Why are courts unfavorably inclined toward restrictive covenants?

3. At this time which is the more important land use control factor—restrictive covenants or zoning? Why?

4. Distinguish between the power of eminent domain and a police power regulation.

5. Why do many courts refuse to review cases under a substantive due process standard?

6. When will a "regulatory taking" occur?

7. Discuss the purpose behind environmental impact assessment.

■ CASE PROBLEMS

1. Since 1921, the landowners' property was used as a golf course. The owner decided to try to develop a part of the land for residential use. This plan was thwarted by the town when it rezoned the land for recreational use only. The justification for the rezoning was to combat overdevelopment and to preserve community open space. The rezoning permits the continued use of the property as a golf course. The landowner sued the town, contending that rezoning was a taking under (1) the *Nollan* case, and (2) the *Lucas* case. Can you distinguish those cases from this one? *Bonnie Briar Syndicate, Inc. v. Town of Mamaroneck*, 721 N. E. 2d 971 (1999).

2. Unlimited, Inc., applied for a building permit to construct a convenience store. Kitsap County granted the permit subject to two conditions: that Unlimited (1) provide an easement to owners of nearby commercially zoned property to facilitate the development of their land; and (2) dedicate, or give to the County, a strip of land for a county road extension. Unlimited sued the County contending that the conditions affected a taking of their property without just compensation. Discuss. *Unlimited v. Kitsap County*, 50 Wn. App. 723, 750 P.2d 651 (1988).

3. The City of Seattle adopted a greenbelt ordinance that required that landowners preserve from 50 to 70 percent of their land in its natural state without paying them compensation. The City asserted a valid police power purpose for the law. What test must be applied to these facts to determine whether a taking without just compensation has occurred? Discuss. *Allingham v. City of Seattle*, 109 Wn. 2d 947, 749 P.2d 160 (1988).

4. A developer in New York City proposed to build a highrise luxury condominium. New York State has a little-NEPA mandating the preparation of environmental impact statements (EISs) for some projects. The EIS examined the project's effects on the physical environment and found none that were significant. The EIS was challenged, however, because it did not discuss the impact that the project would have on the existing patterns of population concentration, distribution, growth, or neighborhood character. The preparer of the EIS contended that these factors were not within the term *environment*. Discuss the pros and cons of the parties' positions in this case. *Chinese Staff and Workers Ass'n v. City of New York*, 68 N.Y.2d 359, 502 N.E.2d 176, 509 N.Y.S. 449 (1986).

25

Regulation of Land Development

Early in the 20th century, state and local governments strayed to some degree from their laissez-faire attitude toward private land ownership. Though landowners never had quite the absolute rights alluded to by Blackstone (on page 537), little land regulation existed. This system of nonregulation faded as the congestion, noise, pollution, and other urban ills manifested themselves to city dwellers.

The chief tool selected to address these problems early in the century was zoning. The adoption of zoning codes proliferated after the U.S. Supreme Court, in the 1926 case *Village of Euclid v. Ambler*, 275 U.S. 365, found constitutional a system that divided the community into use zones. Zoning has retained its primacy as a land-use regulatory mechanism. Many modern zoning codes are not confined to separating land uses but address problems like protecting prime agricultural lands.

Zoning is no longer alone, whatever its form, in regulating land use. Americans realized that zoning codes were not protecting the land from environmental degradation. Wetlands, prime agricultural lands, historical heritage, and wildlife habitat were being lost at an alarming rate despite zoning. The result was legislation, in addition to zoning, addressing the special problems of environmental degradation.

This chapter discusses traditional zoning and its modern nuances. It describes some of the problems created by development for special types of land areas and discusses regulatory tools used to cope with these problems.

■ ZONING

■ *The regulation by the government, usually a municipality, of structures and uses of land within designated zones.*

In its simplest form, traditional **zoning** divides the municipality into districts for residential, commercial, and industrial uses. Within each of these districts, limitations are placed on the size and height of buildings, the location of the buildings on the parcel, the density of development in the area, the minimum size of the parcel, and perhaps the type of structure permitted on the site. The purchaser of a parcel of land must be aware not only of the restrictions revealed by a title search but also of the limitations placed on the land by the zoning code.

The power to zone is expressly given to each locality (municipality or county) by the state through **enabling legislation**, by which that state authorizes the locality to regulate in the area of land-use control. That legislation requires that the zoning code adopted by the locality be consistent with a plan for development. The zoning districts are to be placed on a map pursuant to that plan, for the purpose of maintaining property values, matching designated use to the character of the land (low-density development in unsewered areas with relatively impermeable soil, for example), and promoting the environmental, cultural, and economic welfare of the area in any other way.

Some courts have been lenient in approving zoning codes when the question pertains to the existence of a plan. They have not required a truly comprehensive plan in the modern sense. Often a zoning code and map drawn up by a qualified firm and adopted by the town has met with judicial approval, even though review of how to optimize local development or nondevelopment is lacking.

One reason for this judicial leniency has been that sparsely populated localities cannot reasonably afford to develop a comprehensive plan. Thus, the economic ability of the locality to generate a more comprehensive plan becomes relevant. The courts are not explicit on this point, but this economic constraint seems to underlie many decisions.

The three basic zoning classifications of *residential*, *commercial*, and *industrial* have tended to proliferate. It is not uncommon now for localities to have 15 to 20 or more zones. The use permitted within a zone is often more narrowly confined, with separate zones for single-family houses on one acre, single-family houses on one-half acre, condominiums, garden-type apartments, double houses, and so on. Separate zones are designated for shopping centers, office buildings, personal service shops (e.g., beauty parlors), and gas stations. For industry, the developer has to select the correct zone from among heavy manufacturing, light manufacturing, warehousing, and the like. With this multitude of zones, the locality is able to exercise tighter control over the location of development. Careful examination of local zoning code definitions and requirements is essential because they tend to be highly variable.

One intrinsic problem with zoning that is magnified by the multiplication of zones is inflexibility. Theoretically, the municipality periodically studies the needs of the locality and develops a zoning code or makes amendments to the existing codes based on those needs. Those needs may change before the municipality undertakes to assess them, so that zones may be outdated and discourage more appropriate development.

In some areas of the country when condominiums came into vogue, there were no appropriate zones to accommodate them, and their development was therefore hindered. Other localities acted promptly to create special districts for condominiums, only to find them a passing fad and economically infeasible for the area. The result was that districts zoned for condominiums were then classified inappropriately.

A major advantage of this inflexibility is that it tends to make land values more stable. Potential uses of the land are known, and within general limits the market value of the land is known. The apparent inflexibility of traditional zoning does not tell the entire story. There are several ways in which uses are permitted to exist despite their inconsistency with the zoning code restrictions.

Nonconforming Use

■ *A legal use that was established prior to zoning or prior to the present zoning classification and is permitted to continue despite its nonconformance with the current zoning code.*

Most zoning codes are superimposed on partially developed localities. There is no guarantee that all development prior to zoning took place on optimal sites, as seen by the present drafters of the zoning code. These **nonconforming uses** present a problem. The owners cannot be ordered to discontinue an otherwise legal use immediately unless they are paid full value for their land. To do otherwise may constitute an unconstitutional taking of their land. The traditional solution was to permit the nonconforming use to continue and hope that it would eventually disappear.

The law regarding nonconforming uses has not left that disappearance purely to chance, however. The nonconforming user cannot enlarge that use. Whether the use has been enlarged will be a question for the fact finder (jury or judge). Similarly, a landowner who discontinues the nonconforming use will not be able to resume it later.

CASE EXAMPLE

In 1968, Patrick Gilbertie constructed a house on a one-acre parcel. He conducted a plumbing repair and supply business from his residence, which was a legal use under the town regulations in existence at that time. In 1972, the town regulations changed to prohibit the combined residential and business use. By 1988, Gilbertie's business was booming, and the town ordered him to cease operations because his legal nonconforming use was now illegal because the amount of business being done had significantly increased.

Gilbertie sued and the court found for him. The court determined that the type of nonconforming use had not materially changed, and the fact that the amount of business had increased was not an illegal expansion of the nonconforming use. *Gilbertie v. Zoning Board of Appeals*, 581 A.2d 746 (1990).

The nonconforming use is said to run with the land and not with the individual owner. The nonconforming user may convey his or her land to another, and the buyer can continue the nonconforming use. If the nonconforming building is substantially destroyed, it cannot be rebuilt in noncompliance. From the perspective of the mortgage lender, a nonconforming use presents an element of risk. If the building is destroyed, it cannot be rebuilt. Generally, nonconforming uses will not receive maximum financing for that reason.

Despite the precautions taken under the law to encourage the disappearance of nonconforming uses, they do not always fade away.

CASE EXAMPLE

Susan Wilson purchased a grocery store in an area subsequently zoned residential. As residential development occurs, Wilson will enjoy a virtual monopoly as a grocer because residential zoning has excluded grocery competition. Of course, Wilson will not be able to expand her store under current zoning.

Some localities have taken more direct steps to ensure the discontinuance of nonconforming uses. Ordinances have been passed placing a limit on the length of time the nonconformity will be permitted. So long as the time limitation is reasonable, such ordinances will be upheld by the courts. An important factor in determining reasonableness will be the life expectancy of the nonconforming structure. However, even though there are many examples of ordinances limiting the time allowed for nonconformity of advertising signs, the authorities have been reluctant to apply similar time limitations to other structures.

Zone Change

■ *A zoning amendment made by the legislative body that enacted the zoning code.*

The apparent inflexibility of the zoning code is mythical in most localities, although the uses permitted in a given zone may be inflexible. As previously mentioned, the zoning code is created to implement a plan—master plan, comprehensive plan, or some less specific plan—but none of these plans is intended or can be expected to reflect entirely the future needs of the community. The plan may soon become dated. In addition, some areas of the locality may be zoned not so much for the anticipated use but as a holding zone until more definite decisions can be made. For instance, the northern one-half of a community could be zoned A-1 for agricultural use. The reason for this zoning would not be that this part of the town would be used for agriculture indefinitely, but that because development in the area was years away, the A-1 classification would create a holding zone. This approach would permit the town to postpone its ultimate zoning decision until the time for development was closer and it could better perceive the community needs. In addition, any attempt to use the land for other than agricultural purposes would require a **zone change**, which would allow the town to monitor closely any development in the interim.

The zone change technique employed by communities is a method for keeping their plans current and for reducing the inflexibility of the zoning code. Most jurisdictions treat zone changes as legislative matters requiring that the legislature act to change them. A few states contend that zoning is an administrative decision and zone changes on individual parcels can be made by the appropriate agency, for example, the planning board.

Although a local government can initiate a zone change, generally the moving party is a landowner or developer, who tries to convince the legislative body that the proposed use makes more sense than the use designated in the zoning code. When granting a zone change, the legislature must be careful to establish the reasons for the change. The change must be presented as being justified by the current needs of the community. In this way, the zone change is assured of being consistent with the notion that the locality is continuing to plan for its land use.

Variance

■ *Permission obtained from the appropriate governmental authorities to deviate in a minor way from the specific requirements of the zone under the zoning code.*

In contrast to a zone change, a **variance** is not actually a change in the law. A variance is generally a modest deviation from the requirements of the zoning code. For instance, a landowner may gain a variance to allow him to set his proposed house back only 25 feet from the street rather than the 30 feet required under the zoning law. His parcel of land would continue to be zoned R-1 as it was before the variance.

Use variances can also be granted. Because they could permit a commercial use in a residential zone, however, they are more destructive to the local plan and are less likely to be granted.

F.S. Plummer Co., Inc. v. Town of Cape Elizabeth
Supreme Judicial Court of Maine
612 A.2d 856 (1992)

Background. Prior to 1981, F.S. Plummer Co., Inc. (Plummer), purchased several undeveloped lots in an existing subdivision. The lots were zoned Residential A District. In 1981, the Town of Cape Elizabeth (Town) enacted comprehensive zoning amendments. As a result four of Plummer's lots were rezoned Resource Protection District (RPD), making it impossible to develop them for residential use. Plummer applied for a zone change, but the Town Council denied the application. Plummer sued the Town alleging a denial of due process, a lack of substantial evidence to support the denial of the application, and an abuse of discretion. The trial court agreed with Plummer and ordered the Town to reclassify the lots as residential.

Decision. The Supreme Judicial Court of Maine reversed the trial court's decision.

Justice Rudman. The ordinance itself is presumed to be constitutional. The burden is on Plummer to show by "clear and irrefutable evidence that it infringes on paramount law" and to establish "the complete absence of any state of facts that would support . . . the ordinance." In order for the ordinance to be a valid exercise of the Town's police power it must 1) provide for the public welfare, 2) use means appropriate to the desired ends, and 3) not be exercised in an arbitrary or capricious manner.

Among the goals of the RPD is the protection of the environment and water quality. This goal provides for the public welfare and is a valid object of the exercise of the Town's police power. Restricting development in wetland areas is an appropriate means of achieving those objects.

Under the Town's zoning ordinance, the RPD consists of:

All other areas so designated on the official zoning map, and any apparent wetlands contiguous thereto . . . unless the applicant for a permit for use or development of any land within the foregoing descriptions shall demonstrate by way of an on-site survey that the land does not constitute either "wet-

lands" . . . or "Sebago Mucky Peat" type soil, or coastal dunes.

Plummer's property was designated as part of the RPD on the official zoning map. The ordinance provides a reasonable mechanism for landowners who feel their property was improperly included in the RPD to petition for its reclassification. Although Plummer was able to demonstrate that its property did not contain Sebago Mucky Peat, the Town found, and Plummer concedes the fact, that its property contains wetlands. Therefore, the Town Council's adoption of the ordinance cannot be said to be arbitrary or capricious and the Town's amendment of its zoning ordinance, the effect of which was the reclassification of Plummer's property, was a valid exercise of its police power.

To successfully challenge the Town Council's denial of its zone change request Plummer must show that the Town's decision was inconsistent with the comprehensive plan. The Town Council found that these lots contained wetlands, and that filling the lots could create runoff and flooding problems. The comprehensive plan states that "certain areas of the community should be excluded from development because of the natural conditions of the land. Where these conditions can be shown to have a substantial relationship to the public's health, safety and welfare (i.e., flood hazard or ability to support a subsurface disposal system) severe restrictions on development can and should be sustained." The comprehensive plan further contemplates that no development will occur in the RPD. We conclude that the Town Council's denial of Plummer's zone change request was in basic harmony with the comprehensive plan.

Reversed.

The court in Lucas v. South Carolina Coastal Council *(p. 545), decided in the same year (1992), might argue that this was simply a case of the town attempting to preserve green space without paying for it. What do you think?*

Variances are granted by an administrative body in the locality. It may be called a *zoning board of appeals*, a *board of adjustment*, or some similar title. To obtain a variance, the applicant must prove that the failure to grant it will cause unnecessary hardship. In addition, the applicant must show that the new use will not reduce the value of surrounding properties, that the granting of it is within the public interest, that it is not contrary to the spirit of the zoning code, and that the cause was not created by the applicant.

CASE EXAMPLE

The Town of Hampstead's zoning ordinance prohibits residential buildings higher than 1½ stories. The purpose of the regulation is to retain the view of and from the lake and to maintain the beauty and countrified atmosphere of the town. Alexander applied for a variance to put an additional full story on his one-story home. His variance application was denied by the town, and he sued to overturn the denial.

The court held that the denial of the variance was based on protecting the lake view and was therefore not arbitrary. It went on to state that to obtain a variance, the applicant must prove the following: (1) no reduction in the value of surrounding properties would be suffered; (2) granting the permit would benefit the public interest; (3) denial of the variance would create unnecessary hardship for the applicant; (4) granting the permit would do substantial justice; and (5) the use must not be contrary to the spirit of the ordinance. *Alexander v. Town of Hampstead*, 525 A.2d 276 (1987).

The rule of law states that no one has a *right* to a variance, so courts will not overturn the administrator's decision to deny it unless the decision is arbitrary. This narrow scope of judicial review permits the zoning board wide latitude in approving and disapproving variances. Unless the zoning board strictly requires that the applicant meet the burden of proof mentioned above and unless it keeps foremost the goals intended to be accomplished in the zoning code, its wide latitude can lead to an undermining of the land-use goals established for the locality.

Grey Rocks Land Trust v. Town of Hebron
Supreme Court of New Hampshire
614 A.2d 1048 (1992)

Background. William Robertie owned 35 acres of land on which five buildings were clustered near the town road. The land was along a channel, and Robertie operated a marina on it. The buildings were used for boat storage, boat repairs, and boat-related retail sales. The land was zoned Lake District and uses were limited to those that protected scenic, recreational, and environmental values or the natural and scenic resources of the town. The specifically stated permitted uses did not include a marina. In 1987, Robertie applied for an expansion of his commercial use of the property. The Town of Hebron denied the application because the marina was a nonconforming use and could not be expanded. The marina predated the zoning ordinance. In 1988, Robertie applied to the Zoning Board of Adjustment (ZBA) for a variance to build a boat storage building. The ZBA granted the variance.

Grey Rocks Land Trust (Grey Rocks) is an abutting landowner whose land is used for recreation and residential purposes. After losing their argument opposing the variance, Grey Rocks sued to overturn the granting of the variance because Robertie had failed to prove that its denial would create an unnecessary hardship. The Superior Court upheld the ZBA.

Decision. The New Hampshire Supreme Court reversed the decision concluding that the grounds for a variance had not been satisfied.

Justice Johnson. "To obtain a variance under RSA 674:33 I(b), an applicant must satisfy each of five requirements: (1) that a denial of the variance would result in unnecessary hardship to the applicant; (2) that no diminution in value of surrounding properties would occur; (3) that the proposed use would not be contrary to the spirit of the ordinance; (4) that granting the variance would benefit the public interest; and (5) that granting the variance would do substantial justice."

This court has further defined the requirement that a denial of a variance [would] result in unnecessary hardship. The standard for establishing hardship is narrow. "For hardship to exist under our test, the deprivation resulting from application of the ordinance must be so great as to effectively prevent the owner from making any reasonable use of the land." Furthermore, the hardship must arise from "some unique condition of the parcel of land distinguishing it from others in the area. . . ." "The uniqueness of the land, not the plight of the owner, determines whether a hardship exists."

In order for the ZBA to have concluded that a hardship existed, it would have to have found that literal enforcement of the ordinance bars any reasonable use of the land. Thus, a showing that Robertie was making a reasonable use of the land at the time of the application for a variance would preclude a finding of hardship.

The uncontroverted fact that the Marina had been operating as a viable commercial entity for several years prior to the variance application is conclusive evidence that a hardship does not exist. The defendant Robertie was clearly making a reasonable use of his property prior to his application for a variance. A viable, nonconforming business fails to meet the strict standard for a finding of hardship established by cases such as *Governor's Island*.

In addition to failing to find that denying the variance would preclude any reasonable use of Robertie's property, the ZBA also failed to find that Robertie's land was unique. The ZBA stated in its submission of fact findings to the court that "[t]he Newfound Lake Marina is the only Marina located within the Town of Hebron." A nonconforming use, however, may not form the basis for a finding of uniqueness to satisfy the hardship test. The nonconforming use that is presently located on Robertie's land has nothing to do with the land itself. Therefore, because the record fails to reflect any other basis for finding that Robertie's land is unique, we hold that the ZBA erred as a matter of law in finding that Robertie satisfied the uniqueness prong of the hardship requirement.

The defendants next argue that, independent of the hardship requirement, the owner of a nonconforming use has a right to "[develop] [the] nonconforming use in a way that results in a mere intensification of the use that reflects a natural expansion and growth of trade."

"[I]n order to determine how much a nonconforming use may be expanded or changed, we must look to the facts existing when the nonconforming use was created. We must also consider the extent to which the challenged use reflects the nature and purpose of the prevailing nonconforming use, whether the challenged use is merely a different manner of using the original nonconforming use or

continued on next page

whether it constitutes a different use, and whether the challenged use will have a substantially different impact on the neighborhood."

We have never permitted an expansion of a nonconforming use that involved more than the internal expansion of a business within a pre-existing structure.

In the instant case, it is apparent from the aerial photographs, and the defendants concede in their brief, that the new building is located 450 feet closer to Grey Rocks than the five pre-existing buildings. Thus, the new building clearly has a greater aesthetic impact on the abutting property than the other five buildings. In this case, we hold that the new building will have "a substantially different impact on the neighborhood."

Any expansion of a nonconforming use must be evaluated in the context of the zone in which it is located. The Lake District is intended to protect "scenic, recreational and environmental values" and to "encourage only such further development as will not harm the environment or destroy this district or any part thereof as a natural and scenic resource of the Town." We hold as a matter of law that the construction of a new building, such as the one proposed by the Marina, would substantially impair the natural scenic, recreational, and environmental values of the surrounding property, contrary to the purposes of the Lake District, and is therefore beyond the scope of the "natural expansion," to which the Marina is entitled.

Reversed.

If Robertie can show that he has been losing money on the marina for several years, would that change the outcome of the case?

Exceptions in Zoning

■ *Permitted uses provided for in the ordinance that are inconsistent with the designated zone.*

Unlike variances or zone changes, exceptions are built right into the zoning ordinance. For instance, an R-1 (residential) zone may permit by exception the construction of a church, school, or park within that district. The uses by exception are different from the uses allowed by the zoning code but are considered to be compatible with those uses. No special administrative permission is necessary. So long as the proposed use coincides with the exception detailed in the zoning code, the landowner will be allowed to construct the excepted use.

Special-Use Permit

■ *A system whereby special exceptions to the zoning ordinance are granted by the land-use administrator under a permit arrangement set forth in the zoning ordinance.*

It has become common in zoning codes to omit certain uses from any of the zoning classifications. These uses are allowed only by getting a permit, which entails obtaining the approval of local zoning officials. Hospitals, churches, schools, recreational facilities such as golf courses, and cemeteries may be handled in this fashion. Some of these uses may not be offensive in any specific zone, but the permit process retains control for community officials over their location in those situations where they may be objectionable. The **special-use permit** provides for flexibility in locating these uses for the applicant and maintains public control at the same time.

The special-use permit can be attacked on the basis that it is spot zoning, that is, unplanned zoning. However, this approach can be distinguished in several ways. Generally, special uses are enumerated as such in the zoning ordinance, giving rise to the notion that they may be appropriate uses in an array of zones, depending on surrounding conditions. Many of the uses are not intrinsically offensive; they are singled out for the special-use permit process so that they can be blended into the community in a planned way. This is the antithesis of spot zoning.

Even where the permitted use has greater potential for offending the area residents, such as a cemetery, jail, or gas station, the purpose of segregating these uses in the zoning code is to ensure that they are placed on sites consistent with community needs.

■ VARIATIONS AND SPECIAL USES OF TRADITIONAL ZONING

The original purpose of traditional zoning was to keep different uses of land separate so that, for instance, an industrial use did not become a nuisance for nearby residential homeowners. Communities discovered that separating uses alone did not eliminate all their problems, nor did it provide them with ideal living conditions. Zoning, and variations of it, are being used to attack a wide variety of urban and suburban ills.

Large-Lot Zoning

■ *A zoning classification that requires a minimum of one acre or more of land for each single-family house that is constructed.*

The selection of one acre as the minimum size for **large-lot zoning** is somewhat arbitrary. Other writers may contend that it should be slightly larger or smaller. What size lot constitutes a questionable zoning classification may depend on the location of the property. For instance, city lots tend to be small, and rural lots tend to be much larger. In any event, at some point, depending on the location, the minimum lot size may be so large that it raises a legal question as to whether or not the size can be justified under the police power.

Advantages. In many areas of the country, it is not uncommon to have zoning classifications requiring a minimum lot size of one, two, or even five acres. Several legitimate public policy reasons can be given for mandatory lots of that size. Where municipal sewers and water are not available, the soil and geologic conditions may necessitate sparse development for nature to function adequately in supplying water and for cleansing wastewater. In some states where it is recognized as a salient reason for zoning, and in other states where it may be used merely as an additive reason, aesthetics may be offered as a reason for large-lot zoning. Sparse development on large, generously landscaped lots is attractive to almost everyone.

Large-lot zoning, despite the language contained in the purpose clause of a local code, may have a hidden motivation. Wealthy people prefer to live on large lots, which give better assurance of privacy in tranquil surroundings. The greater the financial means of the owner, the larger the residential lot is likely to be. It is quite natural for someone who can afford it to select a dream home in suburbia. Similarly, the desire to have amenities as well as to retain the market value of their properties causes others to desire comparable high-priced housing nearby.

A second purpose for this type of zoning is that sparse development on large lots tends to be less expensive in terms of the cost of public services. Though municipal sewer and water facilities, if available, may be more expensive, other community services, such as schools, fire, and police, tend to be less expensive. A major share of municipal property taxes goes for schools, and taxpayers usually wish to keep these taxes down. Statistically, well-to-do people have relatively few children, and restricting developments to large lots enables residents to reduce school taxes.

Disadvantages. Hidden motivation may represent the negative side of large-lot zoning. The intent of such zoning, or at least a residual result, is discriminatory. Even when the intent of large-lot zoning is for the socially laudatory purpose of permitting people to enjoy the "fruits of their labor," one effect of such zoning is to exclude the poor and less financially advantaged.

Excluding the financially disadvantaged usually results in the exclusion of minority groups as well. A municipality that caters to the wealthy with large-lot zoning may be steering low-income and middle-income housing and the resulting higher public service taxes into nearby communities. A community may feel that exclusive use of large-lot zoning will help prevent higher taxes, crime, and congestion. These social ills do not go away, however; they are merely concentrated in communities that do not exclude through large-lot zoning.

Judicial Responses to Large-Lot Zoning. Though not yet widespread, there is a growing tendency among state courts to reject large-lot zoning as unconstitutional. The Pennsylvania and New Jersey courts led this movement.

> **CASE EXAMPLE**
>
> The zoning ordinance in the Town of Concord required a minimum lot size of one acre along existing roads and three acres on the interior. Kit-Mar Builders were denied a request to rezone their property lots smaller than mandated by the code. Kit-Mar sued Concord, contending that the large-lot zoning was an unconstitutional taking of its property.
>
> The Pennsylvania Supreme Court held that a zoning provision of this type is unconstitutional if either its purpose or its result is exclusionary. The only exception would be where the municipality can show some extraordinary justification for requiring large lots. An extraordinary justification would be where the natural conditions of the soil, for instance, cannot handle denser population and there is no other reasonable, nonexclusionary method of resolving the problem. *In re Kit-Mar Builders, Inc.*, 439 Pa. 466, 268 A.2d 765 (1970).

Most Pennsylvania communities would be hard-pressed to satisfy the judicial burden of proving extraordinary justification.

The New Jersey courts went a step further. The New Jersey Supreme Court, in an opinion that has implications beyond large-lot zoning, has declared that developing communities must provide for their fair share of the low-income and middle-income housing needs of their region. *South Burlington County N.A.A.C.P. v. Township of Mt.*

Laurel, 67 N.J. 151, 336 A.2d 713, *appeal dismissed*, 423 U.S. 808 (1975). Taking a cue from the Pennsylvania courts, the opinion permits an exception when "peculiar circumstances" can be shown. *Peculiar circumstances* sounds very much like extraordinary justification. The legal basis of the court's ruling is that under state law citizens have a right to decent shelter, and rampant large-lot zoning could effect a denial of this right.

In short, large-lot zoning will be unacceptable where the community has not otherwise provided the housing, or potential for housing, for its share of the region's less financially advantaged people. The adoption of a regional approach to land-use decision making has long been espoused by scholars and planners but had not previously received broad judicial approval.

If the New Jersey approach were broadly adopted, it would not sound the death knell for large-lot zoning. So long as a community is able to provide for its share of the regional housing needs elsewhere, it may continue to have large-lot zoning. In addition, there is nothing that prevents a developer from voluntarily building houses on large lots to satisfy a demand for such housing.

The U.S. Supreme Court, in *Agins v. City of Tiburon*, 447 U.S. 254 (1980), seemed less concerned than the above states about the potential disadvantages to large-lot zoning. It held that a regulation that limited an owner to as few as one house on a five-acre lot was legal. The court stated that where a regulation promoted a police power purpose and did not deny the owner all reasonable economic use, no regulatory taking occurred. Also, New Jersey has since created an administrative mechanism for coping with the fair share housing program. The Pennsylvania courts have been circumspect in recent years about striking down large-lot zoning.

Planned Unit Development (PUD)

■ *An "overlay" zoning concept that enables a developer to obtain a higher density and more mixed use than the underlying zoning would allow, with more generous provision for green space.*

This definition of a **planned unit development** (PUD) is necessarily vague. As it has evolved, the PUD has become many things. It is a term used to describe a development that clusters houses on undersized lots to provide more open space to the residents. The term is used to depict a development that permits various types of housing within the same tract, such as townhouses, apartments, and single-family housing. In another community, it may be flexible enough to allow mixed uses, such as residential, commercial, and even light industry (such as warehouses). Some zoning maps designate areas of the community as PUD zones, while other communities adopt a *floating-zone* concept in which the PUD becomes affixed to a particular land area when an appropriate proposal for mixed use is made to the community officials. Whichever cloak PUD wears, it provides the land use decision maker with additional flexibility in planning for growth within the community.

Procedurally, the developer usually needs community approval for the total PUD at the inception of the project. This general approval both authorizes the PUD as such and sanctions the overall design concept of the development presented. Because the PUD is usually a large development, it will be constructed in sections over several years. As the developer plans each section of the PUD, community approval will need to be obtained for the specifics of that section. A few years into the PUD construction, market conditions may change, causing the developer to seek an alteration of the general plan. For example, condominiums may not be selling in the community; the developer, seeking approval for Section 4, which was previously approved for condominiums, may seek to amend the PUD to put two-family homes in Section 4.

Because the floating PUD is more common than the fixed-zone approach, the PUD plan must obtain the approval of the planning board along with a zone change from the local legislative body. This dual clearance, added to the planning board's approval of each individual section, affords the community the opportunity for closely controlling the development. The key word is *opportunity*. The major criticism of PUDs is that this very flexibility offers too much chance for abuse. Sometimes a beautifully integrated PUD concept is undermined when the developer annually changes the proposal on the section-by-section approvals to take advantage of the short-run market for a given type of development. The result is a hodgepodge that gives the appearance of no planning. The antidote is a planning board, which presses the developer to retain the original plan unless there is an extraordinary reason for change or the change will enhance the overall design of the project.

The original PUD concept was intended to provide for large-scale, relatively self-sufficient development on the order of a new town. A large PUD has the potential for creating an integrated community. It provides for generous quantities of open space in exchange for an increase in density in the living areas, with total density remaining the same. Because the size of the project necessitates development over several years, it permits medium-range community planning with continuous updating through the section-by-section approvals. Where integrated multiple uses are permitted, it can provide for more proximity between residents and services and for a reduction in car miles and energy consumed. The major drawback, however, cannot be overemphasized. A PUD is only as good as the public administrators require it to be.

Performance Standards Zoning

One specialized zoning technique that is growing in popularity is **performance standards zoning**, which establishes certain standards that must be met by any user of land within the zone. Performance standards have been set for such things as noise, vibrations, odors, toxic wastes, signs, and heat emanating from a site. For instance, a standard may provide that no odor is allowed beyond the property line. Most of these standards have been established to ensure that industrial operations do not interfere with surrounding land uses.

Performance standards are especially appropriate for multiple-use situations, such as those that exist in PUD developments. The concept of performance standards may also be useful for controlling adverse impacts in traditional, commercial, and residential zones. For instance, they can be used to regulate impacts on drainage, visual sensitivity, and traffic congestion.

Agricultural Lands Zoning

▓ *Lands that are actively being used for grazing and crop production.*

Prime agricultural lands have been shrinking at an increasingly rapid rate, especially around the country's population centers. A report of the Council on Environmental Quality estimates that prime farmland is being lost at the rate of a million acres per year, or more than four square miles per day. People have become aware that regional shortages of farm crops are inevitable if farmlands continue to be lost to development and abandonment at this rapid rate.

Several factors have caused the shrinking of agricultural lands near metropolitan areas. Farmlands have been assessed for property taxes at development rates, which many farmers cannot pay out of profit from the farm operations, causing them to sell out. The inducement of high land prices has enticed many farmers to sell off their land for development. Further, the demands of farm life appeal to fewer and fewer young people as our society becomes more mobile and leisure-oriented.

Many states have undertaken measures to slow the decrease of farmland. Several states use a form of private contract to protect farmland. The farm owners agree to continue to use their land for agricultural purposes for a specific period of time (e.g., eight years, subject to renewal). The state agrees to fix real property tax assessments at agricultural land levels, rather than letting taxes increase as market values increase due to nearby development. This type of approach has been modestly successful in slowing farmland loss.

A technique with more long-run potential is zoning. Under traditional zoning, communities created a use zone for agricultural purposes. This agricultural zone in developing communities, however, is merely a holding zone awaiting a permanent classification when community leaders better understand its development needs for that area. This is not zoning for agricultural use.

Some communities now zone areas for farmland use and consider it to be the planned permanent use of that land. They determine that farm purposes are the highest and best use of the land, and sharply limit subdividing of agriculturally zoned land. In short, farmland is already developed.

As noted in Chapter 9 on easements (page 190), a tool called **conservation easements** can be used for multiple social purposes. When an owner gives a conservation easement to another, he or she surrenders the right to develop the land. A farm protection organization may solicit a conservation easement from a farm owner. Under the conservation easement the farm owner would cede the right to develop the land for any use other than for a farm. The farm protection organization may pay the farm owner for the grant of "development rights," or the farm owner may be willing to donate the rights in order to assure that the land is used for farming in perpetuity. Although changes to the law are currently being debated in Congress, there are income tax benefits that can accrue to the farm owner upon conveyance of the development rights.

A conservation easement is also a valuable tool for protecting wetlands, floodplains, and other open space uses. In addition to the income tax benefits mentioned above, the landowner will have a corresponding reduction in local property taxes due to the reduced economic value of the land.

Subdivision Regulations

■   *Restrictions on the division of a parcel of land into two or more units. A subdivision will require prior approval by an administrator such as a planning board.*

The zoning code controls only the use and siting of construction on the land. **Subdivision regulations** control the size and location of streets and sidewalks, the placing of sewer and water lines and mandated drainage facilities, and the location of parks and open spaces. When the subdivider presents a plat plan to the planning board, the board determines whether the streets, sewers, and so forth meet the conditions necessary for maintenance of the public health, safety, and welfare.

Subdivision regulations generally take the form of standards, specifications, and procedures set for street signs, streetlights, street trees, fire hydrants, storm drains, sanitary sewers, curbs, gutters, and sidewalks. The regulations may require that the developer post a performance bond to ensure compliance with these rules. The final plat, or subdivision map, submitted by the developer will illustrate in detail all the improvements required under the subdivision rules.

CASE EXAMPLE

Sowin Associates applied to the Planning and Zoning Commission for subdivision approval of a plan for 11 lots on a ten-acre parcel. The parcel was zoned residential. The Commission denied subdivision approval because the development could cause off-site traffic congestion, decrease property values, and was in disharmony generally with the area. The Associates' plan was apparently in conformity with the Town's subdivision regulations. Sowin Associates sued to reverse the Commission's denial.

The Court reversed the Commission's denial because Sowin Associates' plan conformed to the town's subdivision regulations. It stated that traffic congestion, decrease in property values, and area disharmony are relevant considerations in a zoning matter determining the use of the land but not in a subdivision matter. *Sowin Associates v. Planning and Zoning Commission*, 23 Conn. App. 370, 580 A.2d 91 (1990).

Subdivision Exactions and Impact Fees. Subdivision exaction is a requirement that a subdivider dedicate part of its land, or an in-lieu-fee payment, to the community to serve site-specific needs created by the subdivision.

An **impact fee** is a device requiring a subdivider to fund major, off-site infrastructure expansion that serves the community at large as well as the subdivision residents.

Approval of the developer's plat plan usually coincides with the community's agreement to accept title to all streets, streetlights, and so forth, when completed. Herein lies the *quid pro quo*, the equal exchange that enables the community to regulate a subdivision closely. The developer agrees to comply with the various subdivision regulations and expects in return that the community will accept a *dedication*, or transfer of title, of the infrastructure facilities, including roads, sewers, hydrants, and drainage structures. The transaction relieves the developer of continuing responsibility for maintaining these facilities.

One dedication, or *subdivision exaction*, that is becoming common now is one for parks or open space. The planning board may insist that the developer dedicate a percentage of its land, or money in lieu of parkland, prior to granting approval of the final plat. This type of dedication has been approved as a reasonable extension of the transaction discussed previously.

States take different approaches to how closely the need for the parkland must be tied to the demand created by the residents in the developer's subdivision. In states with a more flexible rule, the planning board can exact land based on future, as well as present, needs of the subdivision residents; that is, ten years from now 15 acres of open space per thousand people will be the standard rather than the present ten acres per thousand.

As sources of funds for community improvement have disappeared over recent decades, communities are striving to create new tools to fund needed projects. The subdivision exaction tool addresses needs created by and within the subdivision. A new subdivision, along with other development in the area, generally creates the need for the construction or expansion of areawide off-site improvements. Many communities authorize the collection of user impact fees from subdividers for such improvements as widening of nearby highways, expansion of water and sewage treatment facilities, and construction of landfills. The user impact fee resembles payment in lieu of land fees used in subdivision exactions. Some differences between the two are in-lieu fees finance on-site improvements, and user impact fees finance off-site projects; in-lieu fees are generally assessed based on the subdivision's acreage or number of lots, and user impact fees are based on the square footage of the proposed buildings or the number of bedrooms; and in-lieu fees are confined to residential subdivisions, while user impact fees are often applied to other types of development, too.

As with subdivision exactions, care must be taken to tie the size of the fee to the share of the cost of the improvement created by the subdivider. This caution is especially important in light of the U.S. Supreme Court case, *Nollan v. California Coastal Commission*, 107 S.Ct. 3141 (1987). The Court decided that there must be a "substantial" connection between the government's stated purpose and the regulatory action. In this case, that means that there must be a substantial connection between the needs created by the subdivision and the specific subdivision's exaction or user impact fee. Insertion of the word *substantial* into the usual test for valid regulations provides the courts with the power to second-guess the regulators.

■ LAND ETHIC: ECOLOGICAL IMPERATIVES AND VALUE CHOICES

There is a growing awareness that humans are part of a larger community. This community includes not only the other humans who inhabit the planet but the flora (plants) and fauna (animals) that share our living space. Human life and that of the plants and other animals cannot exist without certain essential ingredients, including clean air and water, sunlight, livable habitat, and the ozone layer, to mention a few. Humans, other animals, plants, and these essential ingredients are all bound together in an intricate and inseparable web of relationships called *ecosystems*. Humans are important, but not the sole participants, in life on this planet.

The quality of life on the planet depends in large measure on the sensitivity and respect with which humans make decisions. No decisions are more important than those made about land. Land provides humans with their habitat, and it provides the habitat for the animals and plants that provide humans with the essential ingredients of existence, food, and air.

During this past century, humans have been less than sensitive and discreet in their decisions about land. In the long view, this insensitivity threatens life itself. In the future, protection of some types of lands from development—such as wetlands, prime agricultural lands, floodplains, coastal areas, and wildlife habitat—is an **ecological imperative**. Beyond these imperatives lie some important value choices about other types of land. The quality of human life seems to depend on retaining our history through preservation of landmarks and historical areas, protecting aesthetically pleasing areas and retaining diversity of land types.

The remainder of this chapter discusses some regulations aimed at protecting these "ecological imperatives" and **environmental value choices**. These regulations evidence an emerging land ethic that places future emphasis in land-use decisions on environmental harmony. Protection of wetlands, the floodplain, the coastal zone, and other critical areas, including prime farmland (discussed earlier), are ecological imperatives. Preservation of historical culture and scenic areas are community value choices.

Wetlands

■   *Lands that have groundwater levels at or near the surface for much of the year or that are covered by aquatic vegetation.*

Historically, **wetlands**, including treed swamps and grass-dominated marshlands, have been treated as wasteland. They were considered inaccessible areas whose major function was the breeding of insect pests. In recent years, however, we have begun to see wetlands in a different light. True, wetlands are breeding areas for mosquitoes, as is any depression that retains water, such as residential drain spouts. Nevertheless, wetlands are also an important natural resource.

Wetlands provide areas for storm waters to gather for their slow return to the groundwater and air. Therefore, they are important as flood control areas. High groundwater and storm waters do not disappear on the development of a site or on the laying of drainpipe. Drainpipe merely concentrates the water, shifting the wetness problem farther downstream in the watershed. Wetlands provide this retention function naturally.

In addition, wetlands provide highly productive wildlife habitats. Hunters, fishermen, birders, trappers, and other recreationists find wetlands extremely important in supporting their leisure time habits. Wetlands provide an outdoor classroom for amateur and professional scientists and are aesthetically pleasant to many people. With public recognition of these resource values, and the setting aside of the traditional view of wetlands as areas to be filled and developed, legal methods for protecting these areas have evolved.

Many states passed legislation to control development in wetland areas. The technique generally adopted has been a permitting process. Prior to filling, dredging, or otherwise substantially modifying a wetland area, the landowner must get a federal, state, regional, or local permit. Permits are not issued where development will cut deeply into the resource value of the wetland area, unless there is a strong counterbalancing reason for doing so. The state wetland protection systems vary, but they generally involve the preparation of wetlands inventories and maps and the issuance of guidelines or regulations for controlling the process of issuing permits. It should be realized that a permit process does not *automatically* curtail development on all wetlands, but it *may* result in a landowner's being unable to make full economic commodity use of his or her land.

The federal Clean Water Act of 1972, as amended, created a permit system administered by the U.S. Army Corps of Engineers for most dredging and filling activities in wetlands connected with navigable waters. The term *navigable waters* has been defined broadly under the statute to include any waters that have the capability of affecting interstate commerce. Prior to the issuance of any permit, the corps must prepare an environmental impact statement (EIS) that analyzes all environmental factors. One remedy the corps has utilized against landowners who fill without a permit is to compel the removal of the fill and the restoration of the wetland, an undertaking that can be extremely expensive. A controversy continues under federal law as to the technical definition of a wetland. The broader the definition of a wetland, the more land that will be subject to the permit system and to the possibility of restriction on development.

Some states and localities have used a zoning approach to control development in wetlands. These zones, which might be called *conservation and recreation districts*, allow only uses consistent with retaining the character of the wetland. Prior to 1970, the zoning approach, which lacked the flexibility of a permit system, was uniformly held to be an illegal taking without due process of law. The judicial rationale was that this type of zoning denied landowners all *reasonable* economic use of their land. Fishing, boating, and hunting, which might have been allowed, were not "reasonable" uses.

More recently, most of the states' wetland measures, as well as the federal wetland permit procedures, have been upheld under judicial scrutiny. In addition, some life has been breathed into the zoning approach for controlling wetland development.

The one constant in "takings" analyses is the rule that the landowner cannot be deprived of all reasonable use. A serious question is raised as to whether or not filling for development is a reasonable use of a wetland. Also, what is reasonable in this area is a time-related notion, so yesterday's unreasonable use may become reasonable one day.

Wetlands are being controlled as special environments in most states where they are numerous. The techniques for control vary somewhat, but judicial approval for all the approaches seems to be growing.

Palozzolo v. Rhode Island
U.S. Supreme Court
121 S.Ct. 2448 (2001)

Background. Anthony Palozzolo owns a 20-acre parcel in the town of Westerly. In 1971, the Rhode Island Coastal Resources Management Council (Council) designated almost all of the property as coastal wetlands. Palozzolo made several proposals for developing the parcel. At one point he proposed to subdivide the land into 74 building lots; most recently, he proposed a private beach club. The proposed development would require 11 acres to be *continued on next page* filled, with some areas needing as much as six feet of fill. All of Palozzolo's development proposals were rejected by the Council. A landowner wishing to fill a salt marsh needed a "special exception." To attain a special exception the proposed development had to serve "a compelling public purpose which provides benefits to the public as a whole as opposed to individual or private interests." Following Palozzolo's final rejection, he sued the Council claiming that it had unconstitutionally deprived him of all economically beneficial use of the property. He sought $3.15 million in damages. The Rhode Island state courts found for the Council.

Decision. The United State Supreme Court affirmed the Rhode Island courts on the "takings" issue.

Justice Kennedy. We have before us the ground relied on by the Rhode Island Supreme Court. It held that all economically beneficial use was not deprived because the uplands portion of the property can still be improved. On this point, we agree with the court's decision. Petitioner accepts the Council's contention and the state trial court's finding that his parcel retains $200,000 in development value under the State's wetlands regulations. He asserts, nonetheless, that he has suffered a total taking and contends the Council cannot sidestep the holding in *Lucas* "by the simple expedient of leaving a landowner a few crumbs of value."

Assuming a taking is otherwise established, a State may not evade the duty to compensate on the premise that the landowner is left with a token interest. This is not the situation of the landowner in this case, however. A regulation permitting a landowner to build a substantial residence on an 18-acre parcel does not leave the property "economically idle."

In his brief submitted to us, petitioner attempts to revive this part of his claim by reframing it. He argues, for the first time, that the upland parcel is distinct from the wetlands portions, so he should be permitted to assert a deprivation limited to the latter. This contention asks us to examine the difficult, persisting question of what is the proper denominator in the takings fraction. Some of our cases indicate that the extent of deprivation effected by a regulatory action is measured against the value of the parcel as a whole, but we have at times expressed discomfort with the logic of this rule. A sentiment echoed by some commentators. Whatever the merits of these criticisms, we will not explore the point here. Petitioner did not press the argument in the state courts, and the issue was not presented in the petition for certiorari. The case comes to us on the premise that petitioner's entire parcel serves as the basis for his takings claim, and, so framed, the total deprivation argument fails.

The court did not err in finding that petitioner failed to establish a deprivation of all economic value, for it is undisputed that the parcel retains significant worth for construction of a residence.

Affirmed.

Is it possible that a subsequent court would accept the idea of dividing the land into upland and wetland for "takings" analysis on the issue of deciding "all economically beneficial use"?

If Palazzolo acquired the land in 1978 and the Council's regulation went into effect in 1971, is he prevented from arguing that the regulations "take" his property? (See Lucas *case.)*

Floodplains

■   *Areas near waterways that are prone to flooding.*

Human beings have always tended to settle near streams, lakes, and other bodies of water. The body of water provided a drinking supply, fishing, and a convenient means of transportation. The first permanent settlements were made with a wary eye toward the ravages that a flood-swollen stream could cause. High, sheltered places near the water were favored over lower-lying areas that were more susceptible to flooding.

People slowly seemed to lose this sensitivity to the forces of nature. Settlements became more numerous in low-lying, flood-prone river valleys. Floods were either tolerated or, in more recent history, controlled by capital construction projects such as dams, levees, and dikes that alleviated the problem. In recent years it has become clear that, although dams and dikes may postpone or prevent some floods, sooner or later the dike weakens or the dam is not massive enough to handle a severe storm, and a flood ensues.

The cost of removing people from the **floodplains** throughout the world is prohibitive. Many people would not be willing to leave even if economic constraints did not prevail. In recent years, governments have undertaken measures to protect those living on the floodplain and to discourage others from building new structures or from repairing flood-damaged structures within the floodplain.

Some communities have used zoning as a method of controlling growth on the floodplain. A *floodplain district* would prohibit building new structures or filling or damming within the floodplain. It would prohibit any residential use. The purposes of this zoning would be to protect people who might choose to live on the floodplain unaware of the hazards of doing so, to protect those near the floodplain who would be injured by obstructions in the flow of floodwater, and to protect the public at large, who must bear the cost of disaster relief when persons on the floodplains lose their property because of flooding.

The legal question raised again is whether this type of regulation, which permits very limited economic use, denies all reasonable economic use of the land and thereby constitutes a taking. One could conclude that a purchaser of land within the floodplain should not expect to develop the land in a manner that would increase the risk of flooding for ones' neighbors. The background principles of a state's nuisance and property laws may preclude such development, so that a total ban on development would be legal under the *Lucas* rationale. In addition, protective regulation may be effective in many instances without eliminating all economically viable use.

Although this regulatory trend is aimed at keeping people out of the floodplain, the federal government is involved in protecting its residents. The national Flood Insurance Program makes flood insurance available to landowners in flood-prone communities, where such insurance was previously exorbitantly expensive or simply unavailable. In essence, unless an individual in a flood-prone area has flood insurance, he or she will not be able to get a mortgage from the bank. If a community does not participate in the flood insurance program, federal aid or loans for use within the federally described flood hazard area will not be made available. An additional regulatory hook in the system is that a community must agree to establish land-use controls for the flood-prone area before it is able to participate in the insurance program. In short, the expectation is that insurance will replace disaster relief in some measure, and new construction on the floodplain will be discouraged. A contrary argument can be made, though. By subsidizing insurance for those who live on the floodplain, the federal program encourages people to continue to live there.

Beverly Bank v. Illinois Department of Transportation
Supreme Court of Illinois
144 Ill.2d 210, 579 N.E.2d 815 (1991)

Background. Beverly Bank (Bank) owns two lots in the Village of Flossmoor, located in the Butterfield Creek floodway. The 100-year floodway is a model based on a statistical projection of the land that would be flooded by a worst storm likely to occur within any 100-year period. The lots are zoned for single-family use. In 1988, the Bank's application for an extension of a construction permit was denied because section 18(g) (state law) prohibits all new residential construction in the floodway. Bank sued and was successful in the lower court.

Decision. The Illinois Supreme Court reversed the lower court, deciding for the defendant Department of Transportation.

Justice Cunningham. Before the General Assembly enacted section 18g, the law required that any new construction in the 100-year floodway may only be permitted if it would not increase the flood level. Section 18g prohibits all new construction which is not an appropriate use. The legislation was enacted in the wake of severe flooding which occurred in the Chicago metropolitan area in September 1986 and August 1987.

The General Assembly specifically determined what would and would not be an appropriate use of the floodway:

"(3) 'Appropriate use of the floodway' means use for (i) flood control structures, dikes, dams and other public works or private improvements relating to the control of drainage, flooding or erosion; (ii)

structures or facilities relating to the use of, or requiring access to, the water or shoreline, including pumping and treatment facilities, and facilities and improvements related to recreational boats, commercial shipping and other functionally dependent uses; and (iii) any other purposes which the Department determines, by rule, to be appropriate to the 100-year floodway, and the periodic inundation of which will not pose a danger to the general health and welfare of the user, or require the expenditure of public funds or the provision of public resources or disaster relief services. Appropriate use of the floodway does not include construction of a new building unless such building is a garage, storage shed or other structure accessory to an existing building and such building does not increase flood stages."

Plaintiff further argues that this court must not give "blind deference" to the General Assembly's express prohibition of new, nonappropriate construction, but must balance the individual hardships imposed on plaintiff by application of section 18g against the benefit to be gained by the public. According to plaintiff, this court must engage in a case-by-case factual inquiry to determine whether section 18g is unconstitutional as applied to any given piece of property in the 100-year floodway on which the property owner wishes to construct a new residence.

If the court were to review, as plaintiff urges, the constitutionality of section 18g as it applies to a particular piece of property by engaging in an ad hoc factual determination, the court would, in effect, be holding the class-wide prohibition on new residential construction unconstitutional on its face for failing to provide for a variance or special use. The court may not judicially create exceptions to this prohibition by engaging in individual factual evaluations with regard to each parcel of land which lies within the floodway in each instance in which a property owner desires to build a house.

"It is well established that reasonable restraints on the use of property in the interest of the common good and bearing a real and substantial relation to the public health, safety, morals and general welfare constitute a valid exercise of the police power."

Defendant identifies several legitimate State interests, any of which, it argues, provide a reasonable basis for the prohibition of new residential construction in the 100-year floodway. In addition to the interest of reducing flood damage, defendant argues that the prohibition protects the health and welfare of those who would live in the new houses, reduces the expenditure of public funds, and limits the extent of emergency relief services required by the periodic inundation of flood waters.

Even if plaintiff were to successfully build the two proposed houses in the floodway at an elevation which would not flood, defendant points out, the homes would still be surrounded by moving water during the 100-year floods. Emergency vehicles would not have access to the homes, and the residents could find themselves stranded without food, clean water, or electricity. In such a situation, defendant points out, the residents would very likely need to relocate temporarily to emergency shelters provided by the State's disaster relief services. Defendant argues that each and all of the above rationales justify the challenged flood control legislation and sustain its validity.

We agree with defendant that the General Assembly has the authority to prohibit all new residential construction in the 100-year floodway. It is reasonable for the General Assembly to rely on the extensive research contained in the Governor's flood control task force report which documented the demographic and land use changes which have contributed to the increased flooding in the 100-year floodway. It is reasonable for the General Assembly to accept the recommendation of the task force that a central part in the response to the severe flooding which may occur in a 100-year flood event is the prohibition of all new residential construction in the floodway. It is also reasonable for the General Assembly to rely on the scientific study contained in the report which emphasized the importance of maintaining existing natural storage areas in the watershed to reduce flood damage.

Finally, plaintiff argues that defendant's refusal to grant the permit extension constitutes a taking of plaintiff's property without just compensation in violation of the Fifth Amendment to the United States Constitution.

As plaintiff acknowledges, the Fifth Amendment's prohibition of the taking of private property for public use without just compensation does not preclude the State from taking private property, but only requires the State pay compensation. The Fifth Amendment does not require that just compensation be paid in advance of, or even contemporaneously with, the taking. "If the government has provided an adequate process for obtaining compensation, and if resort to that process 'yield[s] just compensation,' then the property owner 'has no claim against the Government' for a taking."

We agree with defendant that the Court of Claims Act provides a constitutionally adequate mechanism by which plaintiff may obtain compensation should the facts reveal a taking of plaintiff's properties in the 100-year floodway. As defendant states, plaintiff has not been denied compensation; plaintiff has not sought compensation through the appropriate means.

Reversed.

Do you think that the regulations in this case create a regulatory taking of the Bank's two lots?

Coastal Zone

■   *The area including coastal waters and the adjacent shorelands.*

The **coastal zone** environment is an extremely fragile area. It is an ecosystem of interconnected marshes, mudflats, beaches, and dunes. Human activities that create pollution and siltation can destroy these fragile ecosystems and the quality of the coastal waters generally. To prevent this type of destruction, the federal and state governments have enacted regulatory schemes protecting the coastal zone.

The primary regulation in the area is the federal Coastal Zone Management Act of 1972 (CZMA). The purpose of the CZMA is to establish a fairly uniform system of state controls for coastal lands, including the Great Lakes. The program is administered by the National Oceanic and Atmospheric Administration. Participation in the program by the states is voluntary.

The CZMA requires that the states undertake coastal lands planning and develop management programs for protection and development of these lands. The act provides for annual grants of up to 80 percent of the cost of the development and implementation of coastal zone management programs. The state programs must identify the boundaries of the coastal zone, define the permissible uses within the zone, and establish the regulatory agencies and controls that will implement the plan. The program must identify procedures for designating specific areas for preservation or restoration due to their "conservation, recreational, ecological, and esthetics values."

The CZMA was broadened in several ways by legislation enacted in 1980. The act expanded protection "to significant natural systems, including wetlands, floodplains, estuaries, beaches, dunes, barrier islands, coral reefs, and fish and wildlife habitat," within the coastal zone. The act expands the CZMA purposes "to minimize the loss of life and property" in flood-prone areas within the coastal zone.

This new law created Resources Management Improvement Grants, available to states for developing deteriorating urban waterfronts, for preserving and restoring important natural areas, and for providing public access to beaches and other coastal areas.

In addition to federal regulatory activity in coastal areas, several states are active in coastal zone protection separate from the CZMA program. For instance, under state legislation, New Jersey and Delaware regulate certain industrial activities in the coastal area. In a separate development, the New Jersey Supreme Court in *Matthews and Van Ness v. Bay Head Improvement Assoc.,* 471 A.2d 355 (1984), held that the public has a right of access to and use of the dry sand beach areas shoreward of the wet sand area generally recognized as public land.

Critical Areas

■   *Areas legislatively identified as containing natural limitations, or ones that are important to maintaining the ecosystem.*

Beyond zoning codes, the normal approach toward regulation is a piecemeal one, that is, to adopt separate controls for wetlands, others for the flood-prone areas, and still others for prime agricultural lands. A more systematic approach is to regulate all sensitive areas under a single, comprehensive set of rules. Some communities have adopted critical area controls to accomplish this end.

The first task that must be undertaken by a community prior to enacting **critical area** controls is to make policy determinations as to what types of lands or resources have special value to the community. The legislature then adopts a critical area controls system aimed at protecting these lands and resources. Normally, these include lands that have natural limitations for development (floodplains, steep slopes, lie on an earthquake fault), lands that are ecologically important (wetlands, habitat for endangered or threatened species of animals and plants), and lands that are prized by the community because of their economic value, scarcity, or uniqueness (prime farmland, scenic vistas, historical sites). It should be noted that some of the areas identified as critical fit the category of ecological imperatives (wetlands), while others are products of community value choices (historical sites). The controls may contain a variety of types of regulations, including acquisition of some lands, zoning, and permits.

Once the types of lands to be protected are identified and the regulatory scheme is established, the specific geographic locations of the critical area sites must be identified. Usually, these sites are mapped. The critical area map can be overlaid onto the zoning map for use by the agency administering the critical area controls.

The advantages of critical area controls are that they are comprehensive and systematic. Prospective developers are put on notice as to those lands that are incompatible with development, thereby avoiding poor land investments and lost time.

The concept of critical area controls is not confined to local communities. Some states—including Florida, Maine, Maryland, Minnesota, Nevada, North Carolina, Oregon, Vermont, and Wyoming—have enacted laws that make use of the concept. Other states—including New Jersey (Pinelands) and New York (Adirondack Mountains)—have singled out regions of the state for critical area controls. The Federal Land Policy and Management Act (1976) provides that the Bureau of Land Management identify critical environmental areas and promulgate regulations giving them special protection.

The use of critical area controls is growing, and they appear to provide a systematic addition to traditional land use regulations for protecting lands valued by the community.

Historic Preservation

■ *The preservation of buildings, and perhaps archaeological sites, from destruction by new development.*

Though the **historical preservation** concept is applied more broadly, it is usually applicable to buildings in urban areas. In some regions of the country, communities have designated certain areas historic districts because of their economic and cultural significance. In effect, this is a type of zoning. Within historical districts, permits have to be obtained prior to making a significant change in the facade or structure of a building. Because the historical district usually enhances the economy of the affected area, and change is controlled only by a permit system rather than prohibited, the courts are unlikely to find a regulatory taking exists.

Historically significant buildings do not normally constitute an entire district but are scattered among other urban developments. Many cities have designated landmarks in the community and have established a regulatory scheme for preserving their historical significance. The landmark designation differs from a historical district in that in the former the burden falls unevenly on a limited number of landowners. Also, the benefits of the landmark designation may accrue to the area in general and not solely to the landmark owner. In a historical district, the burdens and benefits, at least theoretically, fall equally on all landowners within the district.

One approach to landmark protection, adopted by New York City, utilizes a concept known as **transferable development rights** (TDRs). The TDR concept is somewhat variable and complex, so it will be oversimplified here. Each tract of land has a certain number or amount of development rights that attach to the land and are transferable. A landowner proposing to build a high-rise residential unit does not obtain enough development rights with the deed to develop to the maximum permitted by the zoning code. These rights, or TDRs, have to be purchased from other landowners—in this case, the ones who own the landmarks and are prohibited from fully utilizing the TDRs on their own property. In this fashion, the economic burden of owning a landmark (or a wetland, a scenic vista, or an archaeological site) does not fall solely on the shoulders of the landmark owner. Landowners simply go into a ready market to purchase or sell TDRs.

Historical preservation is a relatively new concern in this country, and the law pertaining to it is evolving. Reasonably designated historical districts seem secure from judicial consternation. Landmarks legislation is legal and has found a potentially useful tool in the use of TDRs, but questions as to their legality and as to whether a convenient market arrangement will evolve for their purchase and sale create some uncertainty. Whatever the limitations, a growing number of communities are making the value choice to preserve the best of their historical heritage.

Aesthetics

■   *Originally, regulation to retain visual and scenic beauty.*

Traditionally, **aesthetics** is associated with a community's goal of maintaining its visual and scenic beauty. Regulation for aesthetic purposes may include a ban on billboards, set-back requirements for buildings in a zoning code, or fencing for junkyards. In recent years, two questions have occupied courts in reviewing aesthetic regulations. One is whether a regulation based solely on aesthetic purposes is a valid exercise of the police power, and the second question pertains to the precise meaning of the term *aesthetics*, because it appears to be broadening from its initial definition.

The validity of aesthetic regulations has evolved over the course of the 20th century. During the early part of this century, the courts indicated that a regulation based partially or exclusively on aesthetics was invalid. The main problem was that the courts perceived controls based on beauty and good taste to be too subjective for institutions that demanded objective standards. Toward the middle of the century, judicial attitudes shifted. Though aesthetics could not be the sole basis for a regulation, it was acceptable as a reason among other traditional reasons for regulating. If a community banned billboards because they threatened public safety and because they were ugly, an otherwise reasonable regulation was valid. Though the aesthetics—based part of the purpose was treated with suspicion and was referred to often as an *unimportant makeweight*, aesthetics clearly gained legitimacy as a regulatory purpose during this era.

Currently, another shift in judicial attitude toward aesthetics is occurring. It appears that a majority of state appellate courts have accepted aesthetics alone as a legitimate reason for exercising the community's police power. Communities can regulate billboards for the solitary purpose of improving the appearance of the area. The groundwork for the courts accepting aesthetics as a full-fledged regulatory purpose was laid by the U.S. Supreme Court in the case of *Berman v. Parker*, 348 U.S. 26 (1954). The Court declared that the concept of public welfare in the police power was broad enough to encompass aesthetic regulations. In regard to public welfare, it states that the "values it represents are spiritual as well as physical, aesthetic as well as monetary. It is within the power of the legislature to determine that the community should be beautiful as well as clean, well-balanced as well as carefully patrolled."

The New York Courts were among the earliest to accept the principle that aesthetics can stand alone as a basis for regulation.

CASE EXAMPLE

McCormick owned 39 acres of land on Oseetah Lake in the Adirondack Mountains. McCormick applied to the Adirondack Park Agency (APA) for a permit to develop 32 lots on the tract. The APA granted the permit subject to a restriction against placing any boat houses on the shoreline of the lake. The sole basis for the restriction was that boat houses would interfere with the rustic or aesthetic quality of the area. McCormick protested the restriction in court.

The court upheld the APA decision, affirming a previous position that aesthetics alone could substantiate a zoning regulation. The court noted that a "regulation in the name of aesthetics must bear substantially on the economic, social, and cultural patterns of the community or district." *Matter of McCormick v. Lawrence*, 83 Misc.2d 64, 372 N.Y.S.2d 156 (1975).

This latter language regarding community economic, social, and cultural patterns may simply be recognizing that an aesthetics regulation must be supported by a public health, safety, or welfare reason, or it may be an attempt to provide some criteria for reviewing the reasonableness of this type of regulation. Regardless, aesthetics as the primary reason for a regulation is an expansion of the limitations existing under prior law.

Now that the judicial mist is beginning to clear around the question of whether aesthetics can stand alone, the mist is reappearing on another front. The definition of aesthetics as used by communities in their regulations, and by the courts in validating those regulations, seems to be expanding. The aesthetics language being used by legislatures and courts is not confined to visual beauty. The courts continue to wince at the potential for abuse of such a subjective concept.

One writer who has analyzed the cases has opined that aesthetics is a concept referring to our "shared human values" and has nothing to do with visual beauty. Historical buildings and wetlands are not preserved because they are visually beautiful, but because the community cherishes them, beautiful or not. Another writer analyzing the recent cases suggests that aesthetics is being used to express the desire of humans to live in harmony with their physical environment. Protection of coastal areas and wildlife habitat is a reflection of the attitude that humans must share the planet by necessity with their fellow creatures.

Whatever its precise definition, the concept of aesthetics provides communities with significant latitude for adopting controls to protect and preserve the natural environment.

THE CHANGING LANDSCAPE

"City Limits: Putting the Brakes on Sprawl" (Worldwatch Paper #156, June 2001) cites some interesting and unnerving facts. In 1999, it was estimated that Americans in the 68 cities studied spent 4.5 billion hours of extra travel time and burned 6.8 billion gallons of fuel due to traffic delays, at a whopping cost of $78 billion. Another study indicated that the average American spends 72 minutes a day driving, more than twice the time that average parents spend with their children. Of those children, ages 5-15, only 10 percent walk to school. Medical people tell us we have a burgeoning obesity problem among our children. Is there a connection? Researchers note that 1 million people worldwide, mostly pedestrians, lose their lives in automobile accidents annually. These vehicles contribute 73 percent (1997) of the carbon emissions, evidently helping to cause global warming. On and on the article recites disturbing facts, but you get the picture.

Good or bad, news is news and life goes on; unless someone acts. The article argues that in large measure these ills are caused by sprawl. Sprawl is a product of conscious, well-intended decisions with unintended consequences. An initial reaction might be to act by building more highways to alleviate traffic jams. Michael Replogle of Environmental Defense says that, "adding highway capacity to solve traffic congestion is like buying larger pants to deal with a weight problem."

Copenhagen, Denmark, chose a different path. As traffic began to mushroom in the 1960s, rather than widening roads, officials closed streets to cars, making a better and safer situation for pedestrians. Officials made walking and bicycling more attractive by creating bike lanes and devoting the city center to pedestrians. The result is that between 1970 and 1996 bicycle use in the central city area increased by 65 percent. Officials developed a "safe routes to school" program so that students could walk and bicycle to school. British cities are now emulating the Copenhagen program. An overall result of all of this is that the total number of kilometers driven by motor vehicles in Copenhagen has dropped by 10 percent since 1970. During the same period in the United States, miles driven has quadrupled to 4 trillion miles.

With some continued dedication in the United States, we could be on our way to dramatic reductions in pollution from cars. Unfortunately, cleaner cars do not mean fewer cars or miles driven. Are the measures used in Copenhagen transferable to the United States? Can we develop and redevelop our cities and suburbs to focus on people (pedestrians) rather than cars? Do we want to? If not, where will the rapidly increasing miles driven and their resulting traffic jams take us?

KEY TERMS

aesthetics 582

coastal zone 580

conservation
  easements 571

critical areas 581

ecological imperative 574

enabling legislation 559

environmental value
  choices 574

floodplains 577

historic preservation 581

impact fee 572

large-lot zoning 567

nonconforming use 561

performance standards
  zoning 570

planned unit
  development 569

special-use permit 567

subdivision regulations 572

transferable development
  rights 582

variance 562

wetlands 574

zone change 562

zoning 559

zoning exceptions 566

INTERNET RESOURCES

www.cyburbia.org/directory, click on land use and zoning
(Land use—zoning issues discussed and includes examples of zoning ordinances of
all states in the United States)

www.plannersweb.com/articles/are015.html
(Open space zoning—clustering and benefits)

freeadvice.com/law/592us.htm
(What is zoning?)

www.epa.gov/owow/wetlands/
(federal wetlands protection)

www.lta.org/conserve/options.htm
(land trust alliance discusses various use of conservation easements)

REVIEW AND DISCUSSION QUESTIONS

1. The courts that have rejected large-lot zoning have retained an exception to their
    declaration of illegality. They have said that large-lot zoning is all right if there is
    some "extraordinary justification." What would constitute such a justification?

2. Why have courts been reluctant to approve regulations that are based solely on
    visual beauty?

3. If the floodplains are dangerous places to live, then we should have a policy against
    people living there. Discuss the implications of such a policy.

4. Contrast a zone change request with a variance request.

5. If a community wanted to permanently restrict the use of its prime farmland to agricultural use, can it legally do it? Support your answer.

■ CASE PROBLEMS

1. The Town of Preston passed a sign control ordinance. Section 8 of the ordinance stipulated that all existing signs within the town must conform to the sign ordinance within five years from the date of its enactment. Marvin Miller has a large, flashing, nonconforming sign that he does not wish to remove. What arguments should Marvin assert? Would he be successful?

2. S. Volpe & Company petitioned the board of appeals for a special permit to construct a golf course on its land. Golf courses were one of the specially permitted uses allowed under the Town of Wareham's zoning ordinance. The board denied the permit because the land included salt marshes and the golf course would destroy the ecology of the region and harm local fishing. What will be the result in court? *S. Volpe & Co. v. Board of Appeals of Wareham*, 370 Mass. 868, 348 N.E.2d 807 (1976).

3. Rogers owns a large single-family house in the suburbs. She plans to move to a more expensive house in a nearby suburb. To afford the new house, Rogers wants to convert her present home into a two-family apartment. The zoning classification for her house is R-2, that is, single-family house on a minimum lot size of 20,000 square feet. Advise Rogers on how to proceed. Is she likely to be successful under your suggested procedure?

4. Ima Nactivist, councillor for the Town of Riverview, introduced legislation at the town board meeting that, if enacted, would require the removal of all structures now existing on the floodplain in Riverview. The legislation included an array of dates on which types of structures would have to be removed, ranging from 1 to 15 years. Older and less valuable structures would be removed earlier, and newer and more valuable ones would be eliminated later. Cyrus Caselaw, town attorney, informed Ima that the proposed law was clearly unconstitutional. Ima retorted that Cyrus was misinformed. Discuss.

5. Ka-Hur owned property in a residentially zoned district. The buildings were a pre-existing nonconforming use. It was originally used as a fuel storage and distribution facility. For two years that business become ancillary to a fishing and truck repair business. Provincetown contended that Ka-Hur lost the protection of its legal nonconforming use. Ka-Hur argued that the businesses were very similar. What do you think? *Ka-Hur Enters., Inc. v. Zoning Bd. of Appeals of Provincetown*, 424 Mass. 404, 676 N.E. 2d 840 (1997).

Environmental Law

Since the early 1970s, numerous federal laws have been enacted advocating protection of the physical environment. Several of these laws directly or indirectly affect real estate transactions. The impact of the Comprehensive Environmental Response, Compensation, and Liability Act (CERCLA) is the most dramatic; however, the Clean Water Act, the Clean Air Act, the Resource Conservation and Recovery Act, the National Environmental Policy Act (discussed in Chapter 24), the Coastal Zone Management Act, and several others affect real estate decisions. Each of these federal laws may be paralleled or complemented by similar state laws.

■ COMPREHENSIVE, ENVIRONMENTAL RESPONSE, COMPENSATION, AND LIABILITY ACT (CERCLA)

■ *A statute whose purpose is to provide a regulatory mechanism for cleaning up inactive waste sites that release hazardous substances into the environment.*

The **CERCLA**, or Superfund Law, was enacted in 1980. It was significantly amended by the Superfund Amendments and Reauthorization Act, or SARA, in 1986. The purpose of CERCLA and SARA is to establish a regulatory mechanism for dealing with abandoned or inactive hazardous waste sites.

The public health and safety problem created by inactive hazardous waste sites was first brought to the public's attention by the discovery of significant health impacts of the Hooker Chemical site at Love Canal in New York. Since that time, literally thousands of inactive hazardous waste sites have been identified in every region of the country. Many of these sites leak hazardous materials into the water, air, and soil in the surrounding area.

Superfund

CERCLA mandated that a national inventory of hazardous waste sites be made. The inventory identified and assessed 41,400 inactive hazardous waste sites. The Environmental Protection Agency (EPA) identified those sites in the inventory that merited remedial action and placed them on the National Priority List (NPL). A site is listed on the NPL if it receives a minimum score, currently 28.5, under a technical listing procedure called the *Hazardous Ranking System* (HRS). The major effect of being put on the NPL is that the site will be cleaned up and is eligible for the use of Superfund monies to facilitate the cleanup.

The Hazardous Substances Response Fund, or **Superfund**, was established to provide a source of funds for cleaning up hazardous waste sites. Under the law to date, Congress has made available over $12 billion to conduct cleanup activities. Approximately 87 percent of the Superfund monies comes from taxes on industry, principally the petroleum and chemical industries, which are the major sources of hazardous waste. The remainder of Superfund monies comes from Congressional appropriations from other federal tax revenues. Superfund can be used to pay for expenses incurred in planning for site cleanup and for the cleanup itself. Many states have their own version of Superfund that may provide additional cleanup funds.

Implementing the Cleanup

Cleanup activities or response costs can be incurred by federal or state officials or private parties. If the party incurring the response costs wishes to be reimbursed by Superfund, by state funds, or by the parties responsible for the hazardous waste, it must follow the **National Contingency Plan** (NCP).

The NCP originated in the Clean Water Act for cleaning up oil spills. Under CERCLA, it was adapted for use in cleaning up hazardous waste sites on land. The NCP provides a step-by-step procedure that must be followed in carrying out a removal action or a remedial action at the site. (See Figure 26.1.) A removal action is immediate, and interim measures are used to neutralize an imminent threat from the site. For example, a removal action may involve removing barrels that are leaking waste into a stream or putting up a security fence to protect the public from the hazardous nature of the site. A remedial action is the permanent action taken to eliminate the threat created by the site to public health or safety or to the environment.

A goal of CERCLA is to get the parties responsible for disposing of the hazardous waste to clean up the site. To date, the EPA has entered private party settlements valued at more than $18 billion. Unfortunately, the responsible parties may be unknown to the EPA or be unwilling to clean up the site. The EPA determines, however, who will conduct the cleanup action. The EPA may choose to clean up the site itself using Superfund monies, or the EPA may negotiate an agreement with the state by which the state will carry out the cleanup activities. The EPA may insist that the responsible parties clean up the site. Where the EPA cleans up the site using Superfund money, it subsequently seeks reimbursement (contribution) from the responsible parties. It currently recovers about 70 percent of its Superfund expenditures. Most of the remaining 30 percent covers the cost of orphan sites, those sites where the responsible parties cannot be identified.

Liability

Any party who has incurred response costs from either a removal action or a remedial action may recover all or part of those costs from potentially responsible parties. To succeed, the plaintiff must prove five elements:

1. The place involved is a facility.
2. The facility caused a release or threat of a release of a hazardous substance.
3. The defendant is a potentially responsible party.
4. The damages sought were the necessary costs incurred responding to a release.
5. The plaintiffs followed the NCP.

FIGURE 26.1 Steps for Cleaning Up a Superfund Site

Site Discovery
Process begins when a hazardous substance release (e.g., spill, abandoned site) is identified and reported to EPA.

CERCLIS
Site is listed in the Comprehensive Environmental Response Compensation and Liability Information System (CERCLIS), which inventories and tracks releases providing comprehensive information to response agencies.

Preliminary Assessment (PA)
This is the first stage of a site assessment. Preliminary Assessments are conducted to determine if an Emergency Removal Action is necessary, and to establish Site Inspection priorities.

Site Inspection (SI)
The second stage of a site assessment involves on-site investigations to ascertain the extent of a release or potential for release. The Site Inspection usually involves sample collection and may also include the installation of groundwater monitoring wells.

Removal Action
A short-term, fast-track federal response to prevent, minimize, or mitigate damage at sites where hazardous materials have been released or pose a threat of release. Removal Actions may occur at any step of the response process.

Hazard Ranking System (HRS) Package
Site assessment information is then used in the Hazard Ranking System (HRS). HRS is a screening system to evaluate environmental hazards of a site.

NPL Listing
The NPL is a list of abandoned or uncontrolled hazardous substance sites that are the national priorities for long-term cleanup, making them eligible for federal cleanup funds.

Remedial Investigation/Feasibility Study (RI/FS)
Once a site has been placed on the NPL, a Remedial Investigation (RI) and Feasibility Study (FS) are conducted. The purpose of the RI is to collect data necessary to assess risk and support the selection of response alternatives. The FS is a process for developing, evaluating, and selecting a remedial action.

FIGURE 26.1 Steps for Cleaning Up a Superfund Site *(cont'd)*

Record of Decision (ROD)

Once an RI/FS is completed, a Record of Decision (ROD) is generated, which outlines cleanup actions planned for a site.

Remedial Design (RD)

The Remedial Design (RD) is the set of technical plans and specifications for implementing the cleanup actions chosen in the ROD.

Remedial Action (RA)

Remedial Action (RA) is the execution of construction and other work necessary to implement the chosen remedy.

Construction Completion

Construction completion is when physical construction of all cleanup remedies is complete, all immediate threats have been addressed, and all long-term threats are under control.

Operation and Maintenance (O&M)

Operation and Maintenance (O&M) are activities conducted at a site after remedial construction activities have been completed to ensure the cleanup methods are working properly.

Deletion from NPL

When EPA, in conjunction with the state, has determined that all appropriate response actions have been implemented and no further remedial measures are necessary, a Notice of Final Action to Delete is published in the Federal Register. If the EPA receives no significant adverse or critical comments from the public within the 30-day comment period, the site is deleted from the NPL.

Abstracted from *www.epa.gov/superfund/action/20years/ch4pg2.htm*

First, the party must prove that the place involved in incurring the costs is a facility. The courts have broadly interpreted facility to be a typical hazardous waste disposal site but have also held such places as horse stables and spraying trucks to be facilities.

Second, there must be a release or the threat of a release of a hazardous substance from the facility. In addition to its own definition of what substances are hazardous,

CERCLA uses the hazardous definitions contained in the Clean Water Act, the Resource Conservation and Recovery Act, and other environmental laws. The release of the hazardous substance can be to any medium, including the soil, the groundwater, or the wind.

Third, the defendant from whom response costs are sought must be a person covered by the law, or a **potentially responsible party** (PRP). PRPs are broadly defined to include past or present owners or operators of the facility, past or present generators of the waste disposed at the facility, and past or present transporters of waste to the facility, if the transporter selected that facility. It should be noted that a PRP does not have to participate in, or even know about, the disposal of the hazardous waste. Merely being an owner or operator at the time the hazardous waste was deposited on the site qualifies one as a PRP.

It is the broad definition of PRPs and the extent of their legal liability that has markedly changed real estate transactions in recent years. Owners may be lessors who knew nothing of the activities on the site or (in limited circumstances) lenders to the owners of the facility that have foreclosed on a defaulted mortgage and taken title to the land to protect their investment, or parent corporations that participated in the management of a subsidiary corporation that was the facility owner.

When a PRP is held liable for response costs under CERCLA, the liability is strict, and joint and several. Strict liability means that the plaintiff need not show fault on the part of the defendant but only that they come within the definition of a PRP. Joint and several liability means that the plaintiff can sue any one or more of the PRPs without including all of them, and the PRPs sued are responsible for the total response costs. If the defendant PRPs know that other PRPs exist, it is up to them to bring them into the litigation. It is possible for a defendant PRP to prove that its waste is severable or divisible from all other waste at the facility. In the event that the defendant PRP can prove divisibility, it can only be held liable for the contribution of its waste to the response costs.

To hold a PRP liable for response costs, the plaintiff does not have to prove that the PRP's waste actually caused the release; only that a waste of the type deposited by the PRP was released. With the broad definition of PRP, the restrictive nature of strict liability, joint and several liability, and the requirement that the plaintiff does not have to prove causation, CERCLA casts a wide, almost impenetrable, net.

The fourth element that the plaintiff must prove is that costs it seeks to recover were reasonably necessary to remedy the threat created by release from the facility. Finally, the plaintiff must follow the National Contingency Plan in expending the funds to clean up the site.

The following case explores the remedies available to the current owner of a hazardous waste site against those who owned the site when the waste was actually deposited.

Cadillac Fairview/California Inc. v. Dow Chemical Co.
Ninth Circuit Court of Appeals
840 F.2d 691 (1988)

Background. In 1976, Cadillac Fairview purchased a site in Torrance, California. Later it learned that hazardous waste was deposited on the site and that it had migrated to the underlying soil and was a threat to cause substantial environmental and health problems. At the request of state officials, Cadillac Fairview hired engineers to do chemical testing at the site and to evaluate the hazards posed by the contamination. In addition, it erected a fence around the site and posted guards to keep trespassers off the site. It spent $70,000 on these removal activities.

The site had been purchased by the federal government in 1942 and a rubber-producing plant had been constructed on it. Dow Chemical operated the facility under a contract with the government; that contract authorized Dow to dump hazardous by-products of its production processes on the site. In 1955, Shell Oil purchased the site; it also deposited hazardous waste on the site until 1972. Cadillac Fairview purchased the site from a successor in title of Shell Oil.

Cadillac Fairview sued the federal government, Dow, and Shell to recover its response costs and for an injunction ordering that all remedial action and costs of that action were the responsibility of the federal government, Dow, and Shell. The federal district court dismissed Cadillac Fairview's suit for failure to state a cause of action.

Decision. The Ninth Circuit Court of Appeals held that Cadillac Fairview was entitled to response costs for its removal action, but was not entitled to the injunction.

Circuit Judge Wallace. Section 107-(a)(2)(B) of CERCLA expressly creates a private claim against any person who owned or operated a facility at the time hazardous substances were disposed of at the facility for recovery of necessary costs of responding

to the hazardous substances incurred consistent with the national contingency plan. Cadillac Fairview alleged that it incurred "necessary costs" of response within the meaning of section 107(a), and that Dow, Shell, and the federal defendants owned or operated the Site at the time that hazardous substances were deposited there. Despite these allegations, the district court dismissed Cadillac Fairview's suit against the private defendants for failure to state a claim under section 107(a).

The district judge based his decision to dismiss Cadillac Fairview's damages claims on its failure to await governmental action with respect to the Site before bringing suit. The court held that in order for a private response action to be "consistent with the national contingency plan," it must be "initiated and coordinated by a governmental entity, and not by a private individual acting alone." The court also stated that the costs incurred by Cadillac Fairview were not compensable response costs under section 107 because they did not constitute "cleanup costs" within the meaning of the national contingency plan.

Though the national contingency plan describes the role of lead agencies in examining information and determining appropriate responses to environmental hazards, we hold that such provisions do not constrain private parties seeking to recover response costs under section 107(a). We concluded that this reading of section 107(a) was supported both by "the lack of any procedure whereby a private party could seek to obtain prior governmental approval of a cleanup program" and by CERCLA's broad remedial purpose to promote private enforcement actions "independent of governmental actions financed by Superfund." In *NL Industries*, we reaffirmed our holding in *Wickland*, and rejected the argument that response costs cannot be deemed "necessary" in the absence of lead agency approval of the cleanup.

Shell argues that although no federal involvement is necessary, some significant state or local governmental action must precede a response action for which recovery is possible under section 107(a).

Shell, however, cites no authority for the proposition that significant state or local governmental action is a necessary prerequisite to a private action under section 107(a). Nor is there any mention of such a requirement in either section 107 or in the national contingency plan. We are thus reluctant to read a state or local governmental action requirement into the statute absent some strong indication that Congress intended that private parties await action by a state or local government before commencing a response action. Our examination of CERCLA's provisions leads us to conclude that significant state or local governmental action need not precede a response action for that action to be either "necessary" or "consistent with the national contingency plan."

Dow argues that without preliminary governmental action, a defendant can be forced to pay for cleanup actions that are inadequate or ill-conceived. This argument ignores the plain language of the statute. Section 107(a) does not allow recovery of any and all costs of response that a private party incurs. To recover costs under section 107(a), the party undertaking the response action must prove that the costs it incurred were "necessary" and that it incurred those costs in a manner "consistent with the national contingency plan." A response action is consistent with the plan for purposes of section 107 only if it satisfies criteria set forth in pertinent regulations.

We conclude, therefore, that the district court erred in ruling that some governmental entity must authorize and initiate a response action for that action to be necessary and consistent with the national contingency plan.

As an alternative ground for the dismissal of Cadillac Fairview's damages claims, the district court held that Cadillac Fairview failed to allege that it incurred "cleanup" costs within the meaning of

section 107(a). We rejected the distinction between investigatory costs and on-site cleanup costs in *Wickland*. Section 107(a)(2)(B) allows recovery of "costs of response," which includes costs incurred "to monitor, assess, and evaluate the release or threat of release of hazardous substances," and costs of actions "necessary to prevent . . . damage to the public health . . . [including] security fencing or other measures to limit access." The testing and security expenditures alleged by Cadillac Fairview fall within the ambit of those defined by the section. The district court thus erred in holding that Cadillac Fairview failed to state a claim for recovery of those costs under section 107(a)(2)(B).

Cadillac Fairview also pleaded a claim for injunctive relief ordering Dow, Shell, CC&F, and the federal defendants to undertake appropriate response actions with respect to the Site in a manner consistent with the national contingency plan. The district court examined CERCLA's provisions and found that the only private remedy provided in CERCLA is the private cause of action for response costs described in section 107(a). Under section 107(a), the United States, a State, an Indian Tribe, or any other person may recover necessary costs of response incurred consistent with the national contingency plan. There is no mention of a right to injunctive relief in section 107(a). In contrast, under section 106(a), the President may require the Attorney General to seek injunctive relief "when the President determines that there may be an imminent and substantial endangerment to the public health or welfare or the environment." The district court concluded that the failure to provide for injunctive relief in section 107(a), coupled with the absence of any provision for a private right of action under section 106(a), mandated the conclusion that Congress did not intend to create a private cause of action for injunctive relief under CERCLA.

We conclude, therefore, that CERCLA 107(a) does not provide for a private right to injunctive relief against owners and operators as defined by section

continued on next page

107(a)(2). Section 106(a) and 107(a) indicate that when Congress wished to provide for injunctive relief under CERCLA, it knew how to do so and did so expressly. The district court's dismissal of Cadillac Fairview's claims for injunctive relief against Dow, Shell, CC&F, and the federal defendants is affirmed.

Affirmed.

What are the economic/business implications of the CERCLA provisions holding PRPs responsible for cleanup of inactive hazardous waste sites, rather than having the federal government clean up the site?

Defenses

The defenses for a PRP are few and narrow. The PRP may defend by proving that the release of a hazardous substance was caused by an act of God or of war. The law includes a "third-party" defense, which is equally narrow. If the PRP can prove that the release was caused solely by a third party having no contractual relationship to the PRP and that the PRP used due care with respect to the hazardous substance, including taking adequate precautions to prevent harm, it is not liable under CERCLA. Proving the lack of any contractual relationship, such as a lease, a deed, or a shipping contract, is unlikely, unless the PRP is the victim of a midnight dumper.

SARA added a defense, called the **innocent landowner defense**, that is broader in nature. If the hazardous waste was placed on the site before the defendant PRP became the owner and the defendant did not know or have reason to know that the waste was on the site at the time of acquisition, or if the PRP is a government agency that obtained the land involuntarily (e.g., nonpayment of taxes) or is a person who acquired through inheritance or bequest, the defendant is not liable.

To meet the test "did not know or have reason to know," the defendant must undertake at the time of acquisition "all appropriate inquiry" into previous ownership and uses of the property consistent with good commercial and customary practice in an effort to minimize liability. All appropriate inquiry includes consideration of the specialized knowledge or experience of the defendant, the relationship of the actual purchase price to the market value of the property (if not contaminated), the obviousness of the presence of the hazardous waste, and the ability to detect hazardous waste through appropriate inspection.

It appears that, at a minimum, the defendant at the time of acquisition must have visually inspected the property, checked government records concerning past ownership and uses of the property, and made further inquiry if the purchase price was distinctly lower than the market prices of other property in the vicinity. In practice, it appears that a Phase I environmental site assessment (ESA) by a qualified professional is becoming the standard. The Phase I ESA is used to determine the environmental conditions on the property. It consists of a records review, site reconnaissance, interviews with current owners and occupants of the property and with local government officials, and a report.

If the PRP cannot meet the "all appropriate inquiry" test but is a minor contributor to the waste at the facility, the EPA may enter a *de minimis* settlement with the otherwise innocent purchaser. The statute authorizes a de minimis settlement when the purchaser did not know of, conduct, or permit the generation, transportation, storage, treatment, or disposal of any hazardous substance at the site and did not otherwise contribute to the release of the hazardous substance. In the de minimis settlement, the PRP is required to pay a proportionately higher amount of the estimated response costs in exchange for avoiding the costs of litigation and the uncertainty of delay in settling the matter.

The following case includes a critical evaluation of CERCLA when it is applied to real estate owners and transactions. It points out some of the problems incurred when the government tried to affix liability for hazardous waste cleanup on the "potentially responsible parties" rather than letting it fall onto the taxpayers. As you read the case it might be enlightening to ask who should pay for cleaning up hazardous waste sites from the perspective of fairness, economic efficiency, and environmental protection.

United States v. A&N Cleaners and Launderers, Inc.
Federal District Court
854 F.Supp. 229 (1994)

Background. Berkman, Petrillo, and the Custos (Berkman defendants) each hold a one-third interest in a parcel of land as tenants in common. A&N Cleaners and Launderers, Inc. (A&N), operate a dry cleaning establishment in a building on the parcel. A floor drain traversed the entire length of the interior building and emptied into a dry well. The Village of Brewster well field was used to extract 300,000 to 400,000 gallons of water per day from the aquifer. In 1982, the well field was placed on the National Priorities List due to the presence of volatile halogenated organic compounds (VHOs) in the groundwater. The remedial investigation/feasibility study (RI/FS) revealed that the dry well was a significant source of the VHO contamination. The United States sued the Berkman defendants for costs incurred as owners of the site causing a release of hazardous substances.

The Berkman defendants argued that they were third parties who did not cause the release, and alternatively, that they were innocent landowners. These defenses are provided for in CERCLA.

Decision. The Federal District Court found that the Berkman defendants could not rely on the two CERCLA defenses.

District Judge Sweet. Under the "Third-Party Defense" set forth in CERCLA §107(b)(3), a defendant is not liable if it establishes that the release or threatened release was caused solely by:

(3) an act or omission of a third party other than an employee or agent of the defendant, or than one whose act or omission occurs in connection with a contractual relationship, existing directly or indirectly, with the defendant.

The second defense relevant to this case, the "Innocent Landowner Defense," is actually a special case of the Third-Party Defense. In 1986 Congress created an exception to the "no contractual relationship" requirement of the Third-Party Defense, thereby making it available to some owners who acquired the relevant property after the disposal or placement of hazardous substances occurred. CERCLA defines "contractual relationship" as including "land contracts, deeds or other instruments transferring title or possession," unless:

the real property on which the facility concerned is located was acquired by the defendant after the disposal or placement of the hazardous substance on, in, or at the facility and. . . . [a]t the time the defendant acquired the facility the defendant did not know and

continued on next page

had no reason to know that any hazardous substance which is the subject of the release or threatened release was disposed of on, in, or at the facility.

To qualify as an Innocent Landowner one must have undertaken "all appropriate inquiry into the previous ownership and uses of the property, consistent with good commercial or customary practice" at the time of transfer. "Good commercial or customary practice" is not defined in the statute, and the relevant legislative history is vague, indicating that "a reasonable inquiry must have been made in all circumstances, in light of best business and land transfer principles." In deciding whether a defendant has complied with this standard, courts consider any specialized knowledge or expertise the defendant has, whether the purchase price indicated awareness of the presence of a risk of contamination, commonly known or [from] reasonable information about the property, the obviousness of the presence of contamination at the property, and the ability to detect such contamination by appropriate inspection.

Landowners who meet the requirements will not be found to be in a "contractual relationship" with the party responsible for the release of hazardous substances at the property.

CERCLA's liability scheme was intended to ensure that those who were responsible for, and who profited from, activities leading to property contamination, rather than the public at large, should be responsible for the costs of the problems that they had caused.

In addition, Congress intended CERCLA's liability scheme to provide incentives for private parties to investigate potential sources of contamination and to initiate remediation efforts.

The imposition of strict liability solely on the basis of property ownership, however, does something other than cause handlers of dangerous substances to be responsible for the hazards they create. It transfers the costs of the national problem of remediating abandoned contaminated sites onto the shoulders of individuals involved in real estate transactions, many of whom had never violated any environmental regulation, thereby negating Congress' intention

of making those responsible for causing contamination pay for its remediation.

CERCLA's narrow affirmative defenses do little to alleviate the unfairness of the statute's liability scheme, particularly in cases where liability is predicated solely on property ownership. By restricting the application of the Defenses to those that have complied with a series of ill-defined due care and investigatory requirements, CERCLA in practice imposes the costs of the public problem of ferreting out contaminated sites onto the private individuals involved in real estate transactions and ownership without even providing reasonable guidance on what these property owners must do to meet their obligations.

The only blameworthy activity that many property owners facing CERCLA liability have engaged in is the failure to comply with the host of amorphous and undefined due care requirements necessary for establishing CERCLA's affirmative defenses. Also, as demonstrated by the present case, the Government's access to the highly technical information necessary to identify contamination is often superior to that of the ordinary landowner. Rather than preventing blameworthy defendants from escaping liability, shifting the burden of proof of causation to defendants merely helps ensure that the Government will recoup their Response Costs, "at the cost of imposing liability on some individual defendants who caused no harm, but are unable to prove it by a preponderance of the evidence."

In addition to its unfairness, the liability structure of CERCLA is counterproductive. PRPs faced with disproportionate liability litigate tenaciously, prolonging or postponing remediation of contaminated sites and increasing dramatically the costs of remediation.

If Congress must shift the costs of ferreting out contamination from the general public to those involved in real estate transactions it should, at a minimum, define the scope of the required investigation.

Were the Berkman Defendants to have had a clear, intelligible mandate from Congress or the EPA regarding the investigation they should have conducted prior to purchasing the Property and the monitoring that they should have conducted since its purchase, it is doubtful that they would be before the Court at this time.

However, since the Berkman Defendants' liability is predicated on their unwitting ownership of contaminated property, rather than on any disposal of waste which might have occurred on the Property since they purchased it, they bear the burden of showing that a totally unrelated third party is the sole cause of the release of hazardous substances in question.

The Berkman Defendants have failed in this burden. This conclusion precludes the application of either of the Defenses to the Berkman Defendants.

If you were a Congressman amending CERCLA, what specific type of inquiry would you require of a person to take advantage of the innocent landowner defense?

Damages

Any person can recover response costs, including costs of assessing and planning the cleanup. The government can get an injunction to halt a release of a hazardous substance or ensure an administrative order compelling a PRP to conduct the cleanup. If a PRP refuses to obey the administrative order to clean up, the government can recover punitive damages up to three times the actual cost of the cleanup. The federal government may also assess civil penalties of up to $25,000 per violation.

CERCLA places an affirmative obligation on federal and state governments to seek to recover **natural resource damages** caused by the release of a hazardous substance. The term *natural resources* is broadly defined to include injury to public "land, fish, wildlife, biota, air, water, groundwater, drinking water supplies," and other natural resources owned or held in trust by the federal and state governments. The President and the governor of the relevant state must identify a trustee for natural resources. The trustees must agree on the natural resource damage and seek recovery against the PRPs. Superfund monies cannot be used to pay natural resource damages.

Brownfield Initiative

Many former industrial sites in urban communities have fallen into disuse and decay. These areas, referred to as **brownfields**, are often contaminated with hazardous waste. Due to the high cost of decontaminating brownfield sites, and the uncertainty caused by the CERCLA process, businesses are reluctant to locate new facilities on brownfield sites. These unproductive industrial areas add little to the tax base and economic life of the urban communities in which they are located.

Businesses tend to locate their new facilities on previously undeveloped sites in the suburbs or in rural areas. These previously undeveloped sites, or greenfields, already provide community services, as agricultural land, scenic areas, wetlands, floodplains, or open space. Arguably it makes more sense to redevelop the unproductive brownfield sites than to expand into greenfield areas.

Sensitive to these needs, the federal government is trying through administrative regulation to revitalize urban communities by encouraging the cleanup and redevelopment of brownfield sites. The Brownfields Initiative provides grants to communities as seed money to encourage redevelopment. The seed money is used for assessing contamination on abandoned sites, resolving liability concerns, and attracting redevelopers who will invest in the brownfields. The federal EPA is in the process of removing 27,000 low-priority urban sites from the Superfund inventory, removing a stigma that may discourage redevelopers. In short, unproductive urban real estate may be in for a period of revival, as the strictures of CERCLA are applied by the government in a less adversarial fashion and with a sharper focus on reducing public health and environmental risk.

The Business Liability Relief and Brownfield Revitalization Act (2001) was enacted to promote cleanup and reuse of brownfield sites. It provides some liability protection for certain prospective purchasers, lenders, and property owners. It also has provisions to enhance state response programs. The Brownfield Tax Incentive Act (1997, amended 2000) allows responsible parties to treat cleanup costs as deductible expenses, rather than capitalizing them. Congress and the EPA have been very active in recent years in trying to remove CERCLA as a barrier to brownfield redevelopment.

■ STATE CERCLA-TYPE STATUTES

Several states—including California, Connecticut, Illinois, Iowa, Missouri, and New Jersey—have enacted CERCLA-type laws that often focus on real estate transactions. Many other states have adopted laws to make the real estate transaction a trigger that sets off an inquiry into the possible existence of hazardous waste on the site. For example, the California Torres Act requires that an owner of nonresidential property who knows or has reasonable cause to believe that a release of a hazardous waste from the site has occurred must give written notice to the buyers or lessees prior to concluding a real estate transaction with them. Failure to do so may result in civil penalties.

The model that most states appear to be following is New Jersey's Industrial Site Recovery Act (ISRA), which went into effect in 1983. The law applies to any industrial establishment, including manufacturing firms, warehousing businesses, utilities, repair operations, and transportation and communication services. It applies when the industrial establishment engages in any conveyance of real estate experiences, changes in ownership or operation, is acquired or taken over, has a lease expire, or goes into bankruptcy or ceases or transfers operations.

If the industrial establishment engages in one of the above activities, it must undertake an environmental audit to determine if its site is contaminated by hazardous waste. If contamination is found, the firm must develop a cleanup plan, which is subject to review and approval by a state agency. The transaction cannot be concluded until the state agency signs off on the audit or the cleanup plan. The firm must provide financial assurances equal to the anticipated cost of the cleanup to guarantee that cleanup actually occurs.

Failure to comply with the statute makes the real estate or other transaction voidable by either the state or the transferee. The industrial establishment may be liable for up to $25,000 per day in fines and is strictly liable for all cleanup and related costs.

Notice that the New Jersey law has as its trigger a real estate or some other business transaction. Under federal CERCLA, the trigger is the release of a hazardous substance from the site.

■ CLEAN WATER ACT

■ *A statute whose purpose is to cleanse, maintain, and enhance the quality of the nation's water resources.*

The Clean Water Act amendments, adopted in 1972 and amended several times since then, use a system of effluent and water quality standards to limit pollution in the nation's surface waters. The chief focus of the law through 1987 was on regulating point sources of pollution. A point source is a discrete conduit (pipe) used to dispose of wastes.

Statutory Structure: Industrial Dischargers

Effluent standards are technology-based standards imposed on major industrial sources of water pollution. Major industrial sources were categorized by industry (e.g., chemical) or subcategory of industry (e.g., chemical-sulfuric acid). Each source within the designated category of industry was to adopt "best practicable technology" by 1977 and a stricter "best available technology" or "best conventional technology" by 1983. In some cases, these dates were extended by subsequent amendments to the 1972 law.

Water quality standards are ambient standards based on a use of the body of water designated by the state. The state determines that a stream, or portion of it, should be used to supply drinking water to a municipality or as a trout stream or for some other designated use. To use the stream for the state-designated purpose, certain types of pollution (e.g., fecal coliform) cannot exceed established levels. The established level is the water quality standard needed to maintain the quality of the receiving water.

A point source of water pollution must conform to the stricter of the effluent standard or water quality standard. In reality, the source must adopt the effluent standard, but if necessary, due to the high quality demanded by state-designated use (drinking water) or stream conditions (many other sources of mercury in the stream) or other factor, the source must adopt the stricter water quality standard. The enforcement mechanism is that each major pollution source must get a permit that states a specific number limitation on each type of effluent.

At this time, most industrial sources have adopted the technology necessary to meet the effluent standard. Two significant areas of water pollution are inadequately addressed by the point source, technology-based standard approach. Due to a prior lack of understanding and to limitations on existing technology, toxics dumped into the water are only now beginning to be regulated. Nonpoint sources of pollution, those not emanating from a discrete conduit, are also by and large unregulated. Nonpoint sources of pollution come mainly from agricultural runoff, mining and timbering waste, and construction and road runoff.

In 1987, Congress, recognizing the continuing problems of toxic and nonpoint source pollution, amended the law to refocus attention on these pollution sources. The EPA must identify those waters that fail to meet water quality standards due to toxics and nonpoint sources of pollution. The states must then develop management programs to systematically eliminate the nonconformity of the identified waters to the water quality standards.

The effluent standards do not have a direct effect on land use, as they only designate the technology that must be used by a new industrial pollution source. However, the water quality standard, which concerns itself with the quality of the ambient water, may affect the location of water pollution sources. Industrial sources will have to be relatively clean in order to locate on a stream whose use is designated for drinking water or swimming. Others will be forced to locate on streams with lower water quality standards.

■ CLEAN AIR ACT

■ *A statute whose purpose is to cleanse, maintain, and enhance the quality of the nation's air resource.*

The Clean Air Act, adopted in 1970 and amended in 1977 and 1990, mandates that the EPA regulate pollutants that are harmful to public health and welfare. The country is divided into air quality control regions for purposes of administering the act. The EPA assembled the full body of relevant information about pollutants it chose to regulate and issued the information as a *criteria document*. Based on these criteria, the EPA promulgated national ambient air quality standards (**NAAQS**) for what came to be called the **criteria pollutants**. There are six *criteria pollutants:* sulfur dioxide, nitrous oxide, carbon monoxide, ozone, particulates, and lead.

There are two types of NAAQS. Primary standards are intended to protect public health; secondary standards are stricter than primary standards and exist to protect public welfare. Public welfare includes protecting soil, water, vegetation, wildlife, visibility, and the like.

The states were to formulate state implementation plans (**SIPs**) for meeting the NAAQS. Primary standards were to be met by 1975 and secondary standards within a reasonable time (1977 was designated by the EPA). These dates were extended, and 25 years later, many regions continue to have trouble meeting one or more of the standards.

In the 1977 amendments to the Clean Air Act, Congress ordered the air quality control regions to be divided into those that attained and those that did not attain NAAQS. The regions are referred to as **PSD** (prevention of significant deterioration) **regions** (attainment) and nonattainment regions. An industrial source of air pollution seeking to locate in an area needs to know whether it is a PSD region or a nonattainment region.

If the region is a clean air area, or PSD region, the law mandates that the air quality cannot be *significantly* deteriorated. The law divided PSD regions into three categories based on the anticipated economic growth in the area. In the Class I region, little to no additional criteria pollutants are allowed. In a Class II region, moderate increases are allowed, and in Class III regions, greater increases are permitted. The regional increments, or allowed deterioration, are specific number limitations and are permanent. In no case, however, may the pollution exceed NAAQS, regardless of the allowed regional increment.

Any major industrial developer seeking to locate in a PSD region must obtain a permit, agree to use best available control technology as defined by the EPA to limit its emissions, and prove that the NAAQS and the PSD regional increment will not be exceeded. The industrial applicant for a permit to pollute the air is required to do a full year of site monitoring prior to construction to determine existing levels of the pollutants in the area, to ensure that the PSD increment will not be exceeded.

If the industrial source tries to locate in a nonattainment region, it must obtain a permit. Although pollution sources are permitted to locate in a nonattainment region, it may be difficult to do so because the region must make regular progress toward achieving the NAAQS. Thus, the new source must find an offset for its pollution in the region and must adopt control technology that achieves the lowest rate of emission required of any source of its type in the country (called LAER). The source also runs the risk that it will be required to achieve greater control in the future because the NAAQS must ultimately be met.

In 1990, Congress passed major amendments to the Clean Air Act. The amendments address four continuing problems: urban smog, motor vehicle emissions, acid rain, and toxic air pollutants. At least two of these areas of regulation may affect the industrial real estate developer. The urban smog provisions apply to the remaining nonattainment regions. These regions must make annual progress toward achieving the NAAQS and must meet the standards within 3 to 20 years, depending on the severity of the current urban air pollution problems. A new industrial facility in a nonattainment region must show that its level of pollutants will be offset (and more) by reductions of other sources of pollution in the region in order to continue this region's progress toward meeting the NAAQS.

The acid rain provisions establish a permanent cap for sulfur dioxide emissions that is less than one-half of the 1980 level of emissions. The mechanisms chosen to achieve the necessary reductions are controls on electricity-generating power plants. It does not appear at this time that the acid rain provisions will directly affect other industrial facilities, but they may be indirectly affected by increases in the cost of energy or limits on its availability.

■ OTHER LEGISLATION

There are many other statutes—federal, state, and local—that directly or indirectly affect real estate transactions. The National Environmental Policy Act (NEPA) requires the preparation of environmental impact statements; the National Flood Insurance Act mandates protection for floodplain areas; and the Coastal Zone Management Act protects coastal regions from unwise development; these are discussed in Chapters 24 and 25. The Resource Conservation and Recovery Act (RCRA) regulates active hazardous waste sites and underground storage tanks. The Endangered Species Act protects the habitat of endangered or threatened species of plants and wildlife. The Federal Insecticide, Fungicide and Rodenticide Act (FIFRA) regulates the application of these substances to the land and to the environment generally. The Safe Drinking Water Act establishes minimum standards to protect the quality of municipal drinking water supplies. These and other federal environmental laws are often complemented by similar or more restrictive state laws. A careful review of the array of environmental legislation is necessary to safely conclude real estate transactions today.

■ INDOOR POLLUTION

■ *Pollution within buildings that may come from many sources and is now recognized as a serious health problem.*

Indoor pollution sources release gases or particles into the air. Several recent studies point to indoor air pollution as the number one environmental human health risk. Inadequate ventilation, high temperature, or humidity can increase concentrations of these pollutants. The sources of indoor pollution are many. Among the most prominent are radon, asbestos, tobacco smoke, formaldehyde, lead, pesticides, and household products.

The health risks created by indoor pollution are magnified because people spend approximately 90 percent of their time indoors, and those likely to spend the most time indoors—the young, the elderly, and the chronically ill—are the most susceptible. The adverse effects range from headaches and fatigue to cancer and heart disease.

As the case for indoor pollution is substantiated and the information regarding its risks is more widely communicated, the likelihood that builders, architects, employers, and landlords will incur legal liability increases. The legal theories likely to be used are negligence, breach of express or implied warranties, strict product liability, fraud or misrepresentation, and a host of others.

Environmental Tobacco Smoke (ETS)

Scientific studies estimate that **environmental tobacco smoke** (ETS) accounts for 62,000 deaths from coronary disease in the United States annually to smokers. According to the EPA, exposure to tobacco smoke in the environment can cause lung cancer in nonsmokers. In 1992, the EPA concluded that ETS causes serious respiratory problems in children, including severe asthma attacks and lower respiratory tract infections. A large U.S. study indicates that maternal exposure to ETS during pregnancy and postnatal exposure increases the risks of sudden infant death syndrome (SIDS). The EPA classifies ETS as a group A carcinogen—known to cause cancer in humans. The macabre tale could go on.

In response, numerous legal avenues are being used to regulate ETS. Some court cases applying common law rules found a duty for employers to provide nonsmoking employees with protection from proven health hazards. In 1997, President Clinton signed an executive order making federal worksites smoke-free. The Pro-Children's Act (1994) prohibits smoking in facilities where federally funded children's services are provided on a regular or routine basis. By 1999, 45 states had a variety of smoking regulations ranging from restricting smoking on public transportation to comprehensive restrictions on worksites and public places. Over 40 states limit smoking on state worksites. Thirty-one states regulate smoking in restaurants. Involuntary exposure to ETS is preventable and the nation's governments are acting in a wide variety of ways to protect against the risks of ETS.

Drinking Water

The Safe Drinking Water Act was amended in 1986 to require the use of lead-free pipe, solder, and flux in the installation of public water systems and in the plumbing of buildings connected to public water systems. In 1996, the law was amended to require that drinking water suppliers provide an annual report to all customers that identifies the level of contaminants in the water supplied and a description of the health risks associated with those contaminants. A prospective homebuyer will probably expect to see a copy of this report.

Radon

Radon is an odorless, colorless, radioactive gas that results from the natural decay of uranium below ground. It has been linked to lung cancer. In 1988, Congress amended the Toxic Substances Control Act with an act called the Indoor Radon Abatement Law. Although the law specifically states that it does not create a legal cause of action, it brings nationwide attention to the radon problem. The law sets the long-term goal of reducing indoor radon levels to that of the outside ambient air. The EPA is ordered to publish periodic updates on radon health risks and information on the methods available to measure and reduce those risks. The EPA has developed model construction standards and techniques for controlling radon levels. The statute provides money to assist states in developing programs to promote public awareness of radon risks and in developing feasible measures to mitigate the risk. Tests are now available for determining radon levels in buildings. A radon test is becoming a fairly common request by real estate purchasers.

Asbestos

Asbestos use in commercial building products began in the early 20th century and was common for many years. Asbestos can cause asbestosis (a scarring of lung tissue) and forms of lung and stomach cancer. Regulations promulgated by the Occupational Safety and Health Administration (OSHA) place significant responsibilities on building and facility owners, managers, and lessors. Among the responsibilities for commercial builders are due diligence surveys and disclosures about presumed asbestos-containing materials. Otherwise, regulation of asbestos removal and disposal are controlled by state law.

Lead-Based Paints

Historically, lead was added to paint to facilitate drying and endurance. It is a toxic metal that is linked, even in small amounts, to severe health and environmental risk. Lead-based paints were banned from use in residential units in 1978. Regulations that took full effect in 1996 apply to all residences built before 1978. The regulations require that real estate agents and property owners disclose to purchasers and new tenants (including renewing tenants) all known lead-based paint and lead-based paint hazards in the residence. In addition, the agents and owners must provide a pamphlet, "Protect Your Family from Lead in Your Home," which contains low-cost tips for identifying and controlling lead-based paint hazards. Notification and disclosure language must appear in the contract or lease, and parties must verify in writing that the regulations requirements were met. Finally, homebuyers will have ten days to conduct a lead-based paint inspection or risk assessment at their own expense before the contract becomes final. The right to inspect can be waived by the buyer.

THE CHANGING LANDSCAPE

We live our lives in a very linear fashion. One of our primary social values is "progress." For many of us, progress means having more *stuff*, more convenience, and more generally than the prior generation. Progress, or the "more" paradigm, plays havoc with the need to feel satisfied or happy. Progress is linear, endless, and cannot, if we take it seriously, lead to happiness.

Our industrial system is linear. Industry extracts raw materials from the earth and heats, beats, and treats these materials to make salable products. The heating, beating, and treating processes are not perfectly efficient, so there is waste that is redeposited into the earth. Most of the salable products soon become obsolete waste, and depending on the way in which they are disposed, their materials are returned to the soil, air, and water. The waste has much of its utility spent, so much of it will not be useful to future generations. Are these linear systems the wisest approach?

Perhaps there is a research lab or a wise old teacher we can consult on the wisdom of linear systems. There is! Earth has been evolving through trial and error experimentation for billions of years. Oddly, Earth's natural systems are circular, not linear. If linear systems ever prevailed on this planet, they have long since been tossed onto the scrap heap of failed experimentation. Should we reorient our personal value systems and our industrial systems to be circular rather than linear?

What would that mean for industry, which is the object of most of the regulation discussed in this chapter? In an article, "A Road Map to Natural Capitalism" (*Harvard Business Review*, May-June 1999), the authors suggest that we need to undertake a four-step program to cure our polluting industrial habits. First, we need to dramatically increase the productivity of natural resources (reduce waste) by designing industrial systems as a whole and not piecemeal and by developing innovative technologies (e.g., new power systems for automobiles). Second, we need to redesign production by mimicking biological (circular) models. In essence, we should "close-loop" our systems and eliminate waste altogether. Third, we need to change the current business model so that producers of products retain responsibility from birth to grave. Perhaps more leasing of products rather than selling them would achieve this goal with some products. Finally, beyond the first three, we need to restore, sustain, and expand our own natural habitat and resource base. It is not enough to simply slow our use of the natural resource base by increasing our productivity; we actually need to increase the existing resource base. The article and the book by the same title discuss many ways to achieve each of the four steps.

If you were a farmer, a rancher, a real estate developer, an electricity generator, or a landowner, rather than a manufacturer, would the four-step program contain some wisdom for you?

■ KEY TERMS

■ INTERNET RESOURCES

www4.law.cornell.edu/uscode/42/ch103.html
(CERCLA statute)

www.epa.gov/superfund/action/law/cercla.htm
(CERCLA overview)

www.epa.gov/oar/oaqps/peg_caa/pegcaain.html, click on 2.
(Plain English guide to Clean Air Act)

www4.law.cornell.edu/uscode/42/ch85.html
(Clean Air Act)

www.epa.gov/ebtpages/water.html
(water and its regulation)

www.americanheart.org/presenter.jhtml?identifier=l1223
(more on smoking regulation from an advocate group

■ REVIEW AND DISCUSSION QUESTIONS

1. Discuss how the Hazardous Substances Response Fund, or Superfund, is used to pay for cleaning up hazardous waste sites.
2. If a business is going to purchase a site that was previously used by an industrial firm, what precautionary steps would you suggest to avoid CERCLA liability?
3. If a party wants to recover money spent on response costs under CERCLA, what must it prove to win in court?
4. Can an innocent landowner be held liable for response costs under CERCLA? Discuss.
5. What are the chief problems left to be addressed to make the nation's water quality safe for public health and safety? Who is most likely to be affected by regulations addressing these problems?
6. How can air pollution controls affect real estate transactions?

7. What are the main sources of indoor pollution? Why is it critical that the problem of indoor pollution be remedied?

■ CASE PROBLEMS

1. Idarado Mining Co. operated a mine for the extraction of several metals, including zinc, lead, silver, and gold. The operation of the 16-square-mile site created hazardous waste in the form of tailings, mine drainage, and waste rock. The State of Colorado submitted several alternative plans to a court for cleaning up the site under CERCLA. The court approved one of the state's plans, stating that it was consistent with the National Contingency Plan, and authorized the State to incur removal and remedial costs of nearly $2 million. The State completed the cleanup and sued Idarado for the response costs. Idarado contested some of the costs, including the costs of preparing the plans not approved by the court and the cost of restocking a stream with fish. Idarado's waste previously destroyed the stream's fishery. Is Idarado likely to be successful in challenging these response costs? Explain. *Colorado v. Idarado Mining Co.*, 735 F.Supp. 368 (1990).

2. Complaints by neighbors near a site formerly owned by Bell Petroleum Services, Inc. (Bell) about discolored drinking water caused an investigation by the Environmental Protection Agency (EPA). The investigation revealed that the aquifer from which the drinking water was drawn was contaminated by chromium, a hazardous waste. The State of Texas and the EPA cooperatively cleaned up the site and then sued Bell for response costs. Bell denies responsibility because it no longer owns the site and because the governments did not prove that it was Bell's chromium waste that caused the contamination. Bell does not deny that it deposited chromium waste on the site. Discuss. *U.S. v. Bell Petroleum Services, Inc.*, 734 F.Supp. 771 (1989).

3. Belvidere Steel Co. is seeking a site to expand its operations. It finds an apparently ideal site on the Little Lehigh River in northeastern Pennsylvania. The technical people have certified to the board of directors that the site is free of contamination from hazardous waste, has an excellent transportation system, and is otherwise ideally located for the manufacture of specialty steel. At this stage, you are called before the board to discuss the site as the technical expert on air and water pollution. What issues are you going to discuss with the board?

4. Ruth Arones, a real estate broker, has an "exclusive right to sell" contract to sell a house owned by Karl and Nan Lipper. The Lippers tell Arones that the house is airtight and therefore extremely energy efficient. Arones notices that the inside of the house has not been painted in some time and that the paint is chipping badly. Arones knows also that some houses in the vicinity have shown high levels of radon when tested. Arones has a young couple, who have two small children, interested in buying the house. You are a senior broker in Arones's firm and she relates these facts to you, seeking your advice on how to proceed. There are no applicable state statutes. How would you counsel Arones?

Green Development

In 1992 in Brazil, at the United Nations-sponsored Conference on the Environment, the nations of the world in attendance determined that they would seek "sustainable development" of their economies, environments, and societies in the future. **Sustainable development** means that the current generation of people can use the resources of the planet to satisfy their needs as long as that does not interfere with the ability of future generations to do the same. Each nation was to take this general definition of sustainable development home and determine specifically what it meant for that particular nation. The President's Council on Sustainable Development issued the United States' initial response in 1996, with a follow-up report in 1999. In these reports, the authors emphasized that to create a sustainable society, future decisions had to be based on the "triple bottom line." When making decisions, developers in all sectors of society had to balance economic, environmental, and social factors—the **triple bottom line.**

New ideas like sustainable development and triple bottom line often come and go within a relatively short time frame. These ideas, however, seem to have staying power because they address basic dissatisfactions in society. Today, concern is expressed repeatedly over issues like the loss of a sense of community, undue destruction of natural land areas, inadequate and ill-advised housing for poor people, pollution of the air and water, traffic jams, and destruction of scenic sites. All of these detract from the quality of people's lives. Much of the blame for these conditions is laid at the door of a market-based system that encourages decisions based solely on economic factors. The usual reason given is that environmental and social considerations are likely to cost more money and therefore subtract from the value of the investment. Green development is an example of an application of triple-bottom-line thinking to the area of real estate development.

■ GREEN DEVELOPMENT

■ *A form of development of land that integrates economic, environmental, and social considerations in projects of any size.*

Green development is not an idealistic pursuit carried out by developers willing to lose money to achieve environmental or social goals. It is a pursuit intended to reach financial goals along with environmental and social ends. It is a win-win-win pursuit. The primary focus in this chapter is on minimizing negative environmental impact without sacrificing financial success.

The green aspects appropriate for an individual project are highly variable. The green features can be energy conservation, minimizing water usage, encouraging recycling, reducing impact on land ecosystems, limiting the need for automobile travel, maximizing green space surrounding the development, and so on. There are a couple of movements in the United States that promote some form of green development.

Smart growth advocates promote investing resources to restore a sense of community and vitality to older city centers and suburbs. With new development, smart growth emphasizes a pedestrian-centered orientation and a greater mix of residential and commercial uses. It also looks to preserve open space and protect the environment in general. The smart growth advocates have a vision as to what the community should be and builds that into their development decisions.

New urbanism, or neotraditional development, is an approach that seeks to create more livable communities by designing them to resemble and function like traditional small towns. The development is designed on a pedestrian-oriented scale where people can walk to basic services. It includes narrow streets to control traffic speed, less paved area, and public and semipublic spaces, front porches, and limited front yard setbacks to encourage neighborliness.

Green development, smart growth, and new urbanism share many similar attributes and goals. The precise parameters of each are likely to merge over time as the successful attributes are retained, and the others discarded. New urbanism seems to share less emphasis on environmental factors than green development contains. All seem to recognize the fact that post–World War II urban-suburban style development has struck a discordant note with a large segment of society.

■ ELEMENTS OF GREEN DEVELOPMENT

The book *Green Development: Integrating Ecology and Real Estate*, produced by the Rocky Mountain Institute, identifies several elements or "common threads" shared with many green development projects.[1]

Environmental Responsiveness

Much of our modern real estate development has a bulldozer mentality. The natural state of the land is irrelevant; the construction equipment can easily modify what naturally exists on the land to fit whatever development is proposed. Little concern is exhibited about retaining the natural terrain, destroying wildlife habitats, or building over prime agricultural soils.

Green development stresses sensitivity to the existing land environment in siting buildings, drainage, roads, or retained open space. It usually makes good environmental and financial sense to build into or with the existing environment. Siting the building to avoid cold winds or afternoon exposure to the sun can save on the size of the heating and air-conditioning equipment installed and reduce energy used and the cost needed to operate the equipment. Allowing mature trees to survive the bulldozer may further reduce severe exposure to the weather and the BTUs necessary to sustain indoor comfort. By retaining any existing wetland on the site, the developer may be able to save money on man-made drainage facilities and preserve wildlife at the same time. Natural plantings are less expensive and better adjusted to a site than those purchased at the local nursery.

Resource Efficiency

Because the resources needed for economic development come from the earth, they are undeniably limited. The utility and scarcity of resources are, however, highly variable. In the massive global economy, it is uncertain what or how much of various natural resources will be necessary to sustain that economy. Prudence dictates that resources should be used conservatively. Prudence is also mandated by the definition of sustainable development cited at the beginning of the chapter.

Resource efficiency is easier to understand when examined through multiple lenses. It can be described as getting more productivity from each unit of resource used. For example, this can be done through reuse and recycling. In many cases resource efficiency can be seen as the mirror image of waste. Waste occurs because the process or system used does not make optimum use of the resource inputs, and waste is the result; therefore, lower resource efficiency is achieved.

In developing real estate, resource efficiency is relevant at every stage. It drives planning, site preparation, infrastructure installation, construction of buildings, and subsequent use and maintenance of buildings. Each stage provides opportunities for improved resource efficiency. Increased resource efficiency means using less; using less means lower costs.

One study estimates that 60 percent of the electricity used in the United States is for lighting buildings. Careful design to maximize the use of daylighting can significantly reduce the need for artificial lighting. Tools like reflective ceilings and walls, dimmable lights, and larger, well-insulated windows can enhance the daylighting available. In addition to improving energy efficiency, studies indicate that high-quality lighting significantly reduces worker absenteeism.

Community and Cultural Sensitivity

For many people the suburban subdivision, mall-based development that has been predominant over the past half-century is satisfactory. There are, however, growing numbers of people who are intensely unhappy with a living style that does not create a sense of community. The lack of community is signified by a loss of the sense of belonging to a place and to people. In many suburban subdivisions neighbors barely know each other and have little or no interaction. Such subdivisions are literally bedroom communities where one sleeps but carries on few social functions outside the house. There are some who contend that these subdivisions are designed primarily for the automobile and not for the people who live in them. If one reflects on how garages and driveways dominate the fronts of houses, one can find some credibility in this view.

In some measure a sense of community will arise only if the area is designed for it. One tactic supported by advocates of new urbanism and others is "traffic calming." Residential streets tend to be wider than necessary to maximize traffic safety. Research now shows wide, straight roads encourage speed, and speed is the primary cause of traffic accidents. Traffic calming proposes narrowed residential streets and the use of roadside trees and shrubs that create a feeling of narrowness. The result will be slower driving, safer roads, less land consumed for roadways, and perhaps, a return to the use of streets for multiple purposes. It is likely to increase *communications* among neighbors and consequently their sense of *community*. It is better environmentally because less land is paved, and more is available for open-space and storm-water retention. It is better financially because it reduces infrastructure costs. If narrowing streets lead to safer streets, more communication between neighbors, environmental protection, and less development cost, it sounds like a win-win situation.

It is estimated that Earth is 3.8 billion years old. During this unfathomably long period of time, it has been going through a process of evolution. What has evolved is what works; that which does not work has been discarded into the waste bin of history. As we develop real estate it makes sense to examine what has evolved over that time to decide how we can develop land in a sustainable fashion.

The earth works through systems; its closed-loop processes effectively use and reuse waste generated by the systems. Nothing exists in isolation. A goal of green development is to establish and reinforce connections "between people and place, between people and nature, and between buildings and nature" (*Green Development*). The elements discussed in the previous three sections give life to those connections.

Architects talk about designing their buildings to blend into the existing built community so that they complement and enhance the character and quality of the neighborhood. That perspective can be broadened to assure that built projects are in harmony with the existing natural environment. First, this requires a careful, upfront assessment of what is already on the site. Second, there must be a projection as to what parts of the natural environment are likely to be affected. Third, the development plan must show how potential negative impacts will be minimized and how natural site characteristics can be used to enhance the project. Preserving existing trees and vegetation, protecting vistas, taking advantage of exposure to sun and wind to minimize artificial heating and cooling needs, saving wildlife habitat, and using natural drainage patterns are examples of opportunities to protect the environment, improve the quality of life for the inhabitants, and reduce infrastructure costs. This is a triple-bottom-line approach to development.

■ BENEFITS AND DRAWBACKS OF GREEN DEVELOPMENT

Many of the benefits of green development are noted above, and they are similar to arguments made to encourage industrial and service firms to be environmentally proactive. First, reductions in capital costs and in operating expenses can be realized. Development that conforms to the natural contours of the land, reduces width of roads, and uses existing wetlands in the drainage plan can reduce capital costs. Many of the energy-conserving measures discussed in prior sections will cut operating expenses. If buildings are constructed so as to provide clean and uncontaminated air, insurance premiums, workers' compensation payments, and reductions in time lost from work can all further reduce operating expenses.

The old cliché that time is money is surely the case for land developers. The process of getting the array of governments' approvals to complete a project can be extremely time-consuming. Plans for a green development that have done a thorough site assessment, leading to a project that melts into the existing environment, and have adopted measures to promote a sense of community within the project are likely to run into less opposition in the approval process. Less opposition means quicker approval. Quick approval reduces costs.

Many other benefits can be cited that would foster green development. (See Table 27.1.) The question that arises then is why, that with all the benefits, would not all development be green? There are barriers. *Green Development* cites these barriers, among others: Green development is new and the benefits of it are not widely known. This type of development dictates more time and sometimes more money upfront. A first-class site assessment requires a team of experts working together on a plan for the project. Finally, developers and financial institutions are risk-averse. Wading into untried or murky waters creates an aura of risk. Only time and experience will fully address the risk factor. None of the barriers to green development are fatal, and most are due to the relative newness of the idea.

■ GREEN DEVELOPMENT AND THE LAW

The actions of the various levels of government in adopting laws and regulations significantly influence the type of real estate development that will follow. When the federal government in 1956 passed the National Interstate and Defense Highway Act, it took a significant step in launching the suburban sprawl that subsequently blanketed the nation. When the interstate highway act is coupled with federal laws underwriting the expansion of water and sewer lines and individual home mortgages, a future of sprawl was ensured. Further, failure of the national government to coordinate the activities of agencies dealing with land use, the environment, and transportation promoted a future of sprawl. Some of these laws continue to deter the growth of green development. Beyond federal law, traditional laws that zone for uses that must be kept separate promote a car-oriented society built on existing open space or "greenfields." There are mechanisms available, however, that can facilitate green development as an alternative to traditional development.

TABLE 27.1	Benefits of and Barriers to Green Development	
Benefits		**Barriers**
Lower capital cost		Not widely understood
Lower operating expenses		More money and time upfront
Faster approvals		Skeptical financial institutions
Blend with natural environment		
Enhanced community		

Cluster Development

In traditional zoning in a single-family residential zone, the code generally provides that each home must have a minimum-sized lot (e.g., one-half acre). In addition, there will be minimum setbacks from each lot line (e.g., 30 feet from front and back lines and 20 feet from side lot lines). Developers are generally free to create as many lots as they can gerrymander into an acreage after providing for necessary infrastructure (e.g., roads, drainage).

Cluster development allows the developer to use smaller lots than required under the zoning code (e.g., one-half acre per house) as long as the density of houses does not exceed that which is permitted under the traditional zoning. The land not developed is set aside as open space for the benefit of the community. Therefore, it is environmentally and socially better because green space is left undisturbed, and the area is available for the physical and visual enjoyment of people in the neighborhood. Clustering can produce financial value for the homeowners in the form of higher property values, and for the developer through lower infrastructure costs. If the green space set aside in one development can be linked to green space in other developments, it will form a contiguous corridor that is beneficial to wildlife and suitable for walking trails, and will generally multiply its value to the community.

Bayswater Realty & Capital Corporation v. Planning Board of the Town of Lewisboro
Court of Appeals of New York
560 N.E. 2d 1300 (1990)

Background. Bayswater Realty, owner of 227 acres of land, sought approval of a subdivision. It involved the Town's cluster zoning provision (§281) in placing the 115 lots permitted under the conventional subdivision provisions for the area. The clustering of the lots resulted in 60 acres of open space to be dedicated to the Town under the clustering provisions. The 60 acres consisted of 7 noncontiguous parcels, 90 percent of which was wetland used for the development's storm water retention and other drainage facilities. The remainder of the land was steep slopes. The Planning Board approved the subdivision subject to the dedication of the 60 acres of open space, including a foot-trail system. The approval was also conditioned on the payment of a "recreation fee." This fee was authorized by Section 277 of Town Law, which empowered the Planning Board to show park, playground, or recreational areas on the plat. Under Section 277, if the parcel does not contain appropriate lands for a park, etc., area, the Planning Board can mandate payment of a fee in lieu of land. The in-lieu fee was placed in a trust fund to support neighborhood park, playground, and recreation purposes, including the acquisition of property for those purposes.

Bayswater sued to annul the part of the approval that required it to pay the in-lieu recreation fee. It argued that the 60 acres required under the clustering's provisions satisfied the demand for recreation land under Section 277.

Decision. The Court of Appeals of New York affirmed the lower court's decision in favor of the Planning Board.

Judge Hancock. The power of the Planning Board to require that a plat show park, playground or recreational areas under section 277 is not equivalent to the power it possesses under section 281 to attach conditions to the ownership, use or maintenance of open lands when exercising discretion to modify minimum lot area standards in the clustering process. While both section 277 and section 281 are intended to serve the general aim of fostering the preservation of open lands, the provisions are designed to address different societal needs. While they may be employed simultaneously, they operate independently.

Section 277 gives the Planning Board an additional planning control device to be used as a means of reserving lands needed by the broader community for park and recreational purposes. The section represents a legislative reaction to the threatened loss of open land available for park and recreational purposes resulting from the process of development in suburban areas and the continuing demands of the growing populations in such areas for additional park and recreational facilities. The park and recreational needs which section 277 is designed to meet are those of the town or the community at large—not the isolated needs, within the subdivision, itself.

In exercising its powers under section 277, the Planning Board, in approving a conventional subdivision, may, in a proper case, require that the plat itself show parklands suitable for playground or other recreational use. When, however, a particular subdivision does not have land of sufficient size or of the proper character to be set off and committed for the town's recreation and playground requirements, section 277 provides that the developer may be directed to pay a sum of money "in lieu" of such commitment. It is significant that if such "in-lieu" payment is permitted, the statute specifies that the sum paid "shall constitute a trust fund to be used by the town exclusively for neighborhood park, playground or recreation purposes including the acquisition of property." From this provision, it is evident that the primary concerns addressed by section 277 are the present and anticipated future requirements of the town or broader community, not the subdivision alone.

In contrast, the conditions which the Planning Board is empowered by the Town Board to attach under section 281 relate to the open space inside the subdivision resulting from the exercise of the Planning Board's authority to modify the conventional subdivision plat by reducing the minimum area and other requirements for individual lots. The concern is with assuring that the open lands thus created within the proposed plat through clustering are preserved as such and not built on and that if any of such lands are available "for park, recreation, open space, or other municipal purposes directly related to the plat" that they be kept open and maintained for such purposes.

The authority granted under section 281 gives the Planning Board a means of establishing permanent control over the open lands generated by the clustering process by attaching "conditions on [their] ownerships, use, and maintenance" in return for the Planning Board's discretionary relaxation of the zoning restrictions which makes the clustering possible. Not surprisingly, since the focus of section 281 is on the preservation of open lands within the subdivision and not with meeting the present and future requirements of the broader community, the Planning Board is not authorized under section 281 (as contrasted with section 277) to allow payment of money in lieu of setting aside the open space created by the cluster.

Obviously, if it were otherwise and the statute permitted the Planning Board to accept money in return for freeing the open lands for development by waiving any controls of restrictions it might otherwise impose under section 281, the Board could increase the permitted density of the subdivision in contravention of section 281.

Thus, we conclude that the Planning Board's powers under section 281 to attach conditions to

continued on next page

open lands and to require under section 277 that a plat show parklands available for playground or other recreation purposes are not mutually exclusive.

Before the Planning Board may exercise its authority to impose a payment requirement in lieu of setting aside lands under section 277, it must make two determinations with respect to the proposed plat: (1) that a "proper case" exists for requiring the developer to show on the plat "a park or parks suitably located for playground or other recreational purposes," and (2) "that a suitable park or parks of adequate size [to meet the requirement] can not be properly located in any such plat or is otherwise not practical."

In the ordinary situation where a conventional subdivision plat is submitted, the Planning Board first determines whether there is a "proper case" for requiring the developer to show parklands "suitably located for playground or other recreational purposes" (§277) within the boundaries of the subdivision. Such determination requires an evaluation of the present and anticipated future needs for park and recreational facilities in the town based on projected population growth to which, of course, the particular subdivision development will contribute.

Assuming that it finds that the town needs additional park and recreation space, the Planning Board must then decide whether to make the developer provide such space within the proposed plat (thus reducing the number of permitted lots in the subdivision) or pay money as a substitute. This determination necessarily entails an assessment of the size and suitability of any areas within the subdivision plat which could be possible locations for park and recreation facilities as well as the consideration of practical factors including whether there is a need for additional facilities in the immediate neighborhood.

Affirmed.

Explain how cluster development of residences promotes the triple bottom line?

How does cluster development save money for developers?

Incentive Zoning

Local legislatures can create **incentive zoning**, a system of zoning incentives that are granted to developers when they provide certain benefits to the community. The incentives may take the form of allowing greater density than otherwise permitted under the zoning code or waiving an array of other zoning code requirements. In exchange, the developer may be required to provide affordable housing or other amenities that will benefit the residents of the community. It is not unusual for localities to mandate the payment of impact fees or even dedication of part of the land by developers to offset costs created by the development, such as the need for parks, new roads, or drainage systems. Under the law the fees and other dedications required to be paid must bear a rough proportionality to the impacts caused by the particular new development. In the following case the court decided that the requested dedication of land was not justified by the situation.

Dolan v. City of Tigard
U.S. Supreme Court
512 U.S. 374 (1994)

Background. The State of Oregon enacted legislation that required that all municipalities adopt comprehensive land use plans. The City of Tigard adopted a plan that included a Central Business District (CDC). The CDC requires that landowners leave 15 percent of the site as open space. The city also adopted a plan for a pedestrian/bikeway pathway that would encourage shoppers to limit their use of cars for short trips. New development within the CDC would be required to dedicate land for the purpose of the pathway. In addition, the city adopted a Drainage Plan to protect against flooding along Fanno Creek, which runs through the CDC. The Plan proposed a series of channel improvements and keeping the floodplain free of structures.

Florence Dolan, who owns a plumbing and electric supply store in the CDC, applied for a permit to replace the existing store with a new one. The new store would be twice the size of the original and have a 39-space paved parking lot. The Planning Commission granted the permit subject to the conditions that development not take place either on or adjacent to the floodplain. In essence, it required that Dolan dedicate the floodplain land and a 15-foot strip adjacent to the floodplain for a pedestrian/bikeway pathway. The dedication would encompass roughly 10 percent of the Dolan site.

The Planning Commission justified the request for the dedication of land because it was reasonable to assume that customers and employees would utilize the pathway for transportation and recreation needs, and relieve the increase in traffic congestion caused by Dolan's expansion of the store. The floodplain dedication was justified by the increase of impervious surface due to the larger building and the paved parking lot.

Dolan appealed the conditions in the permit to the state Land Use Board of Appeals (LUBA). She argued that the proposed dedication was not related to her proposed development, and consequently was a taking of her property without just compensation in violation of the Fifth Amendment. LUBA disagreed, holding that the dedication had a reasonable relationship to her development. The Oregon Court of Appeals and the Oregon Supreme Court affirmed LUBA's conclusion.

Decision. The U.S. Supreme Court reversed the Oregon Supreme Court ruling in favor of Dolan.

Chief Justice Rehnquist. The Takings Clause of the Fifth Amendment of the United States Constitution, made applicable to the States through the Fourteenth Amendment, provides: "[N]or shall private property be taken for public use, without just compensation." Without question, had the city simply required petitioner to dedicate a strip of land along Fanno Creek for public use, rather than conditioning the grant of her permit to redevelop her property on such a dedication, a taking would have occurred.

On the other side of the ledger, the authority of state and local governments to engage in land use planning has been sustained against constitutional challenge as long ago as our decision in *Euclid v. Ambler Realty Co.* (1926). A land use regulation does not effect a taking if it "substantially advance[s] legitimate state interest" and does not "den[y] an owner economically viable use of his land." The conditions imposed were not simply a limitation on the use petitioner might make of her own parcel, but a requirement that she deed portions of the property to the city. Under the well-settled doctrine of "unconstitutional conditions," the government may not require a person to give up a constitutional right—here the right to receive just compensation when property is taken for a public use—in exchange for a discretionary benefit conferred by the government where the property sought has little or no relationship to the benefit.

continued on next page

In evaluating petitioner's claim, we must first determine whether the "essential nexus" exists between the "legitimate state interest" and the permit condition exacted by the city. If we find that a nexus exists, we must then decide the required degree of connection between the exactions and the projected impact of the proposed development. Undoubtedly, the prevention of flooding along Fanno Creek and the reduction of traffic congestion in the Central Business District qualify as the type of legitimate public purposes we have upheld. It seems equally obvious that a nexus exists between preventing flooding along Fanno Creek and limiting development within the creek's 100-year floodplain. Petitioner proposes to double the size of her retail store and to pave her now-gravel parking lot, thereby expanding the impervious surface on the property and increasing the amount of stormwater run-off into Fanno Creek.

The same may be said for the city's attempt to reduce traffic congestion by providing for alternative means of transportation. In theory, a pedestrian/bicycle pathway provides a useful alternative means of transportation for workers and shoppers: "Pedestrians and bicyclists occupying dedicated spaces for walking and/or bicycling . . . remove potential vehicles from streets, resulting in an overall improvement in total transportation system flow."

The second part of our analysis requires us to determine whether the degree of the exactions demanded by the city's permit conditions bear the required relationship to the projected impact of petitioner's proposed development. The city required that petitioner dedicate "to the city as Greenway all portions of the site that fall within the existing 100-year floodplain [of Fanno Creek] . . . and all property 15 feet above [the floodplain] boundary." In addition, the city demanded that the retail store be designed so as not to intrude into the greenway area. The city relies on the Commission's rather tentative findings that increased stormwater flow from petitioner's property "can only add to the public need to manage the [floodplain] for drainage purposes" to support its conclusion that the "requirement of dedication of the

floodplain area on the site is related to the applicant's plan to intensify development on the site."

"The distinction, therefore, which must be made between an appropriate exercise of the police power and an improper exercise of eminent domain is whether the requirement has some reasonable relationship or nexus to the use to which the property is being made or is merely being used as an excuse for taking property simply because at that particular moment the landowner is asking the city for some license or permit."

We think a term such as "rough proportionality" best encapsulates what we hold to be the requirement of the Fifth Amendment. No precise mathematical calculation is required, but the city must make some sort of individualized determination that the required dedication is related both in nature and extent to the impact of the proposed development.

We turn now to analysis of whether the findings relied on by the city here, first with respect to the floodplain easement, and second with respect to the pedestrian/bicycle path, satisfied these requirements. It is axiomatic that increasing the amount of impervious surface will increase the quantity and rate of storm-water flow from petitioner's property. Therefore, keeping the floodplain open and free from development would likely confine the pressures on Fanno Creek created by petitioner's development. In fact, because petitioner's property lies within the Central Business District, the Community Development Code already required that petitioner leave 15% of it as open space and the undeveloped floodplain would have nearly satisfied that requirement. But the city demanded more—it not only wanted petitioner not to build in the floodplain, but it also wanted petitioner's property along Fanno Creek for its greenway system. The city has never said why a public greenway, as opposed to a private one, was required in the interest of flood control.

The difference to petitioner, of course, is the loss of her ability to exclude others. As we have noted, this right to exclude others is "one of the most essential sticks in the bundle of rights that are commonly characterized as property." It is difficult to see why recreational visitors trampling along petitioner's floodplain easement are sufficiently related to the City's legitimate interest in reducing flooding problems along Fanno Creek, and the city has not attempted to make any individualized determination to support this part of its request.

The city contends that a recreational easement along the Greenway is only ancillary to the city's chief purpose in controlling flood hazards. The city wants to impose a permanent recreational easement on petitioner's property that borders Fanno Creek. Petitioner would lose all rights to regulate the time in which the public entered onto the Greenway, regardless of any interference it might pose with her retail store. Her right to exclude would not be regulated, it would be eviscerated.

We conclude that the findings on which the city relies do not show the required reasonable relationship between the floodplain easement and the petitioner's proposed new building.

With respect to the pedestrian/bicycle pathway, we have no doubt that the city was correct in finding that the larger retail sales facility proposed by petitioner will increase traffic on the streets of the Central Business District. The city estimates that the proposed development would generate roughly 435 additional trips per day. Dedications for streets, sidewalks, and other public ways are generally reasonable exactions to avoid excessive congestion from a proposed property use. But on the record before us, the city has not met its burden of demonstrating that the additional number of vehicle and bicycle trips generated by the petitioner's development reasonably relate to the city's requirement for a dedication of the pedestrian/bicycle pathway easement. The city simply found that the creation of the pathway "could offset some of the traffic demand . . . and lessen the increase in traffic congestion." No precise mathematical calculation is required, but the city must make some effort to quantify its findings in support of the dedication for the pedestrian/bicycle pathway beyond the conclusory statement that it could offset some of the traffic demand generated.

Reversed.

How would the city go about proving that the pedestrian/bicycle pathway was justified?

Overlay Zoning

To protect natural resources, such as a wetland, mountain view, or watershed, the legislature may resort to **overlay zoning** and design an overlay district. To protect a natural resource, the regulation superimposes additional restrictions on the existing zoning district. It may limit density, mandate additional setbacks on buffer areas, or limit the height of buildings. As long as the overlay district is created to protect natural resources and does not single out particular property owners to bear unreasonable burdens, it is likely to satisfy a legal challenge.

This is a brief sampling of a few of the regulatory tools that can be used to facilitate green development. Other tools, such as planned unit developments, agricultural zoning, and transferable development rights are discussed in Chapter 25. "(I)t will require a paradigm shift to move society from the thinking that the best it can do is minimize impact, toward a view in which development is seen as both contributing to the growth of healthy human communities, while simultaneously restoring (not merely sustaining) the natural environment" (*Green Development*).

THE CHANGING LANDSCAPE

For social change to occur, a certain critical mass of support for action must form. For more than 30 years we have heard discussions about making a dramatic shift away from using the internal combustion engine to power motor vehicles. The engines use huge amounts of oil, a nonrenewable natural resource, and are a major source of pollution that harms public health and the environment. It now seems that the critical mass for change has been reached with the introduction of hybrid cars and with the expectation that fuel cell cars will be on the market by the end of this decade. It has taken a long time, but the change is likely to be dramatic.

A critical mass of support must form as well for most developers and builders to think of green building as the norm. As with motor vehicles, the shift is highly likely to take place. The questions are when, and what will trigger it? The easiest way to foment change in a market economy is for the innovation desired to be competitive in price. Another way is for the government to subsidize or tax activities to encourage the desired result. So the government could provide tax credits to builders who use green methods or materials, or the credits might flow to the homeowners who would then choose to buy green houses. Public education, espousing the benefits of green development, might affect the mix of considerations weighed by homeowners or commercial and industrial buyers to shift in favor of green building purchases. The education approach has been effective against tobacco use and, to a lesser degree, with illegal drugs.

If a person were a policymaker, what mix of strategies would he or she use to promote green building as the norm? If the policymaker changed hats and became a developer/builder, would he or she propose the same mix of strategies? Suppose a policymaker and a developer/builder got together. What strategies would they be likely to agree on?

■ NOTE

1. Reproduced with permission of the Rocky Mountain Institute. Excerpts from *Green Development: Integrating Ecology and Real Estate.*

■ KEY TERMS

cluster development 616
green development 611
incentive zoning 618

new urbanism 612
overlay zoning 621
smart growth 612

sustainable
 development 611
triple bottom line 611

■ INTERNET RESOURCES

www.usgbc.org
(Describes activities of industry Green Building Group)

www.ebuild.com
(Guide to green building products)

www.MBDC.com
(Discusses green solutions to buildings and materials design and use)

www.RMI.org/sitepages/pid13.php
(Green information for building and real estate professionals)

■ REVIEW AND DISCUSSION QUESTIONS

1. How does the concept of sustainable development differ from the way we are currently developing?
2. What is the "triple bottom line"?
3. How does the development approach of the "new urbanists" enhance the opportunity for forming closer-knit communities?
4. Contrast the natural processes of the earth with modern industrial processes.
5. What are some of the barriers to green development? Can they be overcome?

■ CASE PROBLEMS

1. Del Monte Dunes at Monterey, Ltd. (Del Monte), a developer, applied numerous times for approval of an oceanfront multiunit residential complex on a site zoned for that use. Each time the city of Monterey rejected the proposal for various environmental and other concerns. On the final try for approval, though Del Monte had satisfied previous concerns, the proposal was again rejected. Del Monte sued the city, claiming an unconstitutional taking of its property. Del Monte argued that the "rough proportionality" test of the *Dolan* case should be applied. It contended that the city could not justify the denial under that rule of law. Can and should the Dolan ruling be applied or should it be distinguished? *City of Monterey v. Del Monte Dunes at Monterey, Ltd.*, 119 S. Ct. 1624 (1999).

2. Anderson applied to change a zoning classification on 30 acres of undeveloped land within an area called the Pine Bush in the city of Albany. He wanted to build five two-story buildings on the site. The pine barrens are the only remaining large pine barrens on inland sand dunes in the United States. The barrens support rare plant and animal species. The city decided that the Pine Bush should be open to commercial development, but also that the ecological integrity of the area should be preserved. The city created a C-PB zone within the Pine Bush that could be sought by a developer-applicant to allow development, but subject to special review standards to protect its integrity. What kind of a regulation is this an example of? Is this an effective way of protecting the Pine Bush? *Save the Pine Bush, Inc. v. City of Albany*, 512 N.E. 2d 526 (1987).

3. Sydney Athans, a recent college graduate, is asked by her father to take over his real estate development business. Sydney agrees on the condition that she will be free to develop land and construct buildings in a manner sensitive to the environment. Her father agreed. Sydney has 500 acres to develop into a single-family or mixed-use (with a zone change) development. She hires you to provide ideas and parameters for making her development "green." What types of things would you recommend? Why?

 Go to the Student Study Guide CD-ROM and work through Case 6.

GLOSSARY

A

abstract of title A summary of all the recorded transactions, including deeds, mortgages, judgments, and the like, that affect the title to a specific parcel of land.

acceleration clause A provision in a mortgage giving the mortgagee the right to declare the entire debt due and payable on default.

acceptance Assent to the terms of an offer.

accession Gradual increase in riparian or littoral property as a result of deposits of sediment made by a body of water.

accord An agreement to substitute a different kind of performance for that originally contracted.

accretion The rights and principles the law uses to deal with changes in the size and shape of land due to natural causes.

acknowledgment In conveyancing, the act by which a person who has executed an instrument, before an authorized officer, usually a notary, declares that the instrument is genuine and executed voluntarily.

action for rent or damages When a landlord seeks money damages against a tenant for injury.

actual notice Title information that is acquired personally by the interest holder.

adjudicated insane Has been declared insane by a court.

adjustable-rate mortgage (ARM) A type of flexible-rate mortgage.

administration of estates A general term used to describe the management and settlement of a decedent's estate by a person appointed by the courts.

administrative remedies Remedies provided by administrative agencies based on power granted in an enabling act.

administrator A person charged with administering the estate of an intestate decedent.

adverse possession Acquisition of title to real estate by means of wrongful occupancy for a period of time established by statute or common law.

aesthetics Regulation to retain visual and scenic beauty.

affidavit of title A sworn statement verifying facts that satisfy certain objections to title.

after-acquired title Title acquired by a grantor subsequent to conveyance to a buyer; this ordinarily invests the buyer with the "after-acquired" title.

agency A legal relationship in which one party, called the *principal*, authorizes another, called the *agent*, to act in the principal's behalf.

agency coupled with an interest An agency that cannot be revoked by the principal.

agricultural lands Lands that are actively being used for grazing and/or crop production.

alienation Transferring ownership, title or interest in real estate from one person to another.

allodial system A system in which land is owned without obligation to pay rents; private ownership.

alluvion Land created by sediment left by a body of water.

amortization Repayment of a debt in periodic installments of interest and principal over a period of time.

annual cap Limits the amount of increase or decrease a rate could adjust in any one adjustment period (usually 2 percent).

annual percentage rate (APR) As defined in the Truth-in-Lending Act, the percentage that the total finance charge calculated on an annual basis bears to the amount of the loan or credit.

anticipatory breach A breach of contract that occurs as a result of repudiating a contract before the date due for performance.

appeal Process in which a higher court reviews alleged legal errors made by a lower court or an administrative agency.

architect A professional person who prepares the plans and specifications for the construction of a house.

assessments The regular monthly payments for upkeep of the common elements, as well as payments required for special expenses or improvements to those common elements.

assignee A party to whom a right is transferred.

assignment Transfer of a property right from one person (the assignor) to another (the assignee).

assignor A party who transfers a right.

assumption A contract between a grantor/mortgagor and a grantee in which the grantee agrees to undertake responsibility for the mortgage debt.

attachment (1) The process by which a secured party acquires a security interest in collateral. (2) The act of seizing a defendant's property by legal process to be held by a court to ensure satisfaction of a judgment that might be awarded.

attestation The act of witnessing the execution of an instrument and subscribing as a witness.

authority Term used in the law of agency denoting the agent's power to perform acts authorized by the principal. (*See also* express authority; implied authority.)

B

balloon payment The final payment under a contract, which is substantially larger than the previous installment payments.

bargain and sale deed A deed that conveys title but makes no warranties.

bilateral contract A contract involving a promise in exchange for a promise.

blockbusting Inducing (for profit) the sale or rental of any dwelling by indicating that a particular class of person (for example, nonwhite) has entered or will enter the neighborhood.

breach of contract The unexcused failure to perform an obligation under a contract.

broker An agent who facilitates a transaction between parties.

builder *See* contractor.

building code compliance Protects the public health, safety, and welfare by regulating building and construction standards.

buyer's broker A broker who has contracted to locate real estate for a buyer.

bylaws The rules governing the internal operation of a condominium development.

C

call Term used to refer to the different monuments, courses, and distances that make up a metes-and-bounds description.

capacity The legal ability to enter into a contract.

caveat emptor Let the buyer beware.

caveat venditor Let the seller beware.

certificate of title A statement of opinion by an attorney that describes the status of the title to a parcel.

certiorari, writ of A legal document in which a higher court orders a lower court to supply the record of a case that the higher court wishes to review.

chain of title The recorded history of events that affect the title to a specific parcel of land, usually beginning with the original patent or grant.

Clean Air Act A statute whose purpose is to cleanse, maintain, and enhance the quality of the nation's air resource.

Clean Water Act A statute whose purpose is to cleanse, maintain, and enhance the quality of the nation's water resources.

closing The final state of the real estate purchase transaction, when the deed and the purchase money are exchanged.

cluster development Permits housing density greater than required by the zoning ordinance in order to increase community open space.

coastal zone Area including coastal waters and the adjacent shorelands.

codification Collection and organization of judge-made law into a code or statute.

cognovit A confession of judgment that permits the landlord, on default by the tenant, to obtain a judgment against the tenant without the need for formal legal proceedings.

commitment Used in mortgage financing to designate the lender's promise to loan a specified amount of money at an agreed-on rate of interest.

common elements The parts of the development property that are necessary or convenient for the residents of a condominium and are owned in common by all the condominium residents.

common law (1) Law based on written opinions of appellate courts (*see* judge-made law). (2) The traditional nonstatutory law of England and the United States.

community property A form of co-ownership between husband and wife in which each has a one-half interest in property acquired through the labor of either during marriage.

Comprehensive Environmental Response, Compensation, and Liability Act (CERCLA) A statute providing for cleanup of inactive waste sites that release hazardous substances into the environment.

comprehensive plan A prerequisite for regulating land use. Its contents can range from a thorough master plan to a zoning code and map.

condemnation Legal action by which government acquires private property for a public use; based on the right of eminent domain.

condominium The fee simple ownership of one unit in a multiple-unit structure, combined with an ownership of an undivided interest in the land and all other parts of the structure held in common with the owners of the other individual units in the structure.

condominium association The organization stipulated by statute to administer the operation of the common elements of the condominium.

conservation easements The conveyance of development rights to the grantee to protect the current use or nonuse of the land.

consideration A promise, act, or forbearance bargained for and given in exchange for a promise, act, or forbearance.

construction mortgage A mortgage given to secure funds advanced to construct or improve a building.

constructive eviction An occurrence that results when the actions of the landlord so materially interfere with the tenant's enjoyment as to make the premises uninhabitable.

constructive notice The knowledge of certain facts that might be discovered by a careful inspection of public records, provided that such information is within the history of title, or discovered by an inspection of the premises.

contingency clause A provision within a contract that makes performance under the contract conditional on the occurrence of a stated event.

contract A promise or an agreement that the law will enforce.

contract for a deed *See* land installment contract.

contractor The person or firm that undertakes to construct a house at a given price.

contract zoning Zoning in which an applicant will be granted a requested zone change only after contracting with the community to comply with certain covenants.

cooperative A form of ownership in which the land and buildings are (usually) owned by a corporation; individual unit residents own stock in the corporation and have a proprietary lease in a specific unit or apartment.

co-ownership Ownership of real estate in which two or more people have undivided interests.

correlative right, doctrine of A legal doctrine that prohibits depletion of a common pool of oil or gas, sometimes applied to water.

cotenancy *See* co-ownership.

counteroffer A new offer made as a response to a person who has made an offer.

covenant of fitness of the premises An assurance that the premises are fit for habitation.

covenant of quiet enjoyment A warrant by the landlord that the tenant will have the premises free from interference by the landlord or anyone claiming better right to the premises than the landlord.

covenant to deliver possession The landlord's promise to deliver the right of possession to the tenant at the time the lease is scheduled to start.

critical areas Areas legislatively identified as containing natural limitations, or ones that are important to maintaining the ecosystem.

curtesy A common-law estate that provided a husband with a life interest in all his wife's real property at the time a child was born of the marriage.

D

damages Money recoverable by one suffering a loss or injury due to breach of the contract.

decisional law Law that evolves from published opinions of appellate courts. (*See* judge-made law.)

declaration A document required by state law, which must accompany, and be recorded with, the master deed for the condominium development.

dedication The grant of real property such as a public street to a governmental unit for public use.

deed A legal instrument that conveys title to real property on delivery and acceptance by the grantee.

deed in lieu of foreclosure A deed in which a mortgagor conveys mortgaged real estate to the mortgagee, who promises in return not to foreclose on the mortgage debt, which is in default.

deed of trust A legal instrument in which a borrower transfers real property to a trustee as security for a debt. The lender is the beneficiary of the trust.

default Nonperformance of a duty or obligation as part of the mortgage transaction.

defeasible fee *See* fee simple defeasible.

deficiency judgment A money judgment awarded to the mortgagee when funds obtained as a result of a fore-closure sale are insufficient to pay the debt.

delivery Surrender of possession and control of a docu-ment to a third party.

Department of Veterans Affairs (VA) loan guarantees Guarantees provided by the VA to lenders that finance housing construction and purchases by veterans.

developer The person or firm that subdivides a parcel of land and prepares the site for construction.

disavow Avoid a contract.

discharge The release of contractual obligations.

diversity jurisdiction Power of federal courts to hear cases involving citizens of different states.

dominant estate The parcel of land that benefits from an easement appurtenant; also called *dominant tenement*.

dower Life estate of a widow in one third of any real estate to which her husband had legal title during marriage. (*See also* inchoate dower.)

dual agency A transaction in which an agent represents both principals.

due-on-sale clause A provision found in some mortgages requiring that the mortgagor pay off the mortgage debt if he or she sells the property.

duty to repair Tenant's obligation to leave premises in about the same condition as when received, reason-able wear and tear excluded.

E

earnest money A cash deposit evidencing a good-faith intention to complete a transaction.

easement A right to use another's real property for a par-ticular purpose.

easement appurtenant The right of an owner of a parcel of land to benefit from the use of another's land. (*See also* dominant estate; servient estate.)

easement by necessity An easement that permits the owner of a landlocked parcel to cross a parcel of land of which the landlocked parcel formerly was a part.

easement in gross An easement that exists as a personal right apart from a dominant estate.

ejectment A legal action to recover possession of real property.

elective share The share of a deceased spouse's property that the surviving spouse may claim if the decedent left no will or the decedent spouse did not will the minimum specified by law to the surviving spouse.

eminent domain Right of the state to take private prop-erty for public use. Just compensation must be paid to the owner.

enabling legislation State statutory authorization granting a local government the right to regulate in a specific area.

environmental impact assessment A statement describ-ing and analyzing the environmental impacts of a proposed action.

environmental tobacco smoke Refers to the exposure of smokers and nonsmokers to the unhealthy effects of tobacco smoke in various environments.

Equal Credit Opportunity Act Federal statute prohibit-ing discrimination in an applicant's credit transaction.

equal protection The constitutional mandate that all peo-ple be treated equally under the law.

equitable title The buyer's right to obtain ownership of real property on payment of the purchase price.

equity of redemption The right of a mortgagor or another person with an interest in real estate to reclaim it after default but before foreclosure.

escheat Reversion to the state of title to property of a per-son dying without heirs or leaving a will.

escrow A process by which money and/or documents are held by a third party until the terms and conditions of an agreement are satisfied.

escrow agent The third party who is the depositary in an escrow transaction.

escrow agreement An agreement that directs the escrow agent regarding terms and conditions under which the deed or other instruments are to be delivered to the parties and the disposition of the deed or other instruments on default.

estate The extent and character of a person's ownership interest in real property. (*See also* future estate; life estate.)

estoppel certificate A statement by a mortgagor that he or she has no defense against paying the mortgage debt; it also indicates the amount that remains unpaid.

eviction by the landlord The term usually associated with the legal procedure by which a landlord has the tenant removed from the premises because the tenant has breached the lease agreement.

evidence of title A document verifying ownership of property.

exceptions in zoning Permitted uses provided for in the ordinance that are inconsistent with the designated zone.

exclusive agency A listing in which the seller gives one broker authority to procure a buyer for property but also retains the right to sell the property without the broker's services.

exclusive right to sell A listing in which the seller gives one broker authority to procure a buyer for property, but the broker is entitled to a commission if the seller procures the buyer.

exculpatory clause A lease clause by which the landlord attempts to be excused from liability for negligence in maintaining the leasehold premises.

executed A promise that has been performed.

executor Person appointed in a will to administer the estate of a decedent who died testate.

executory An unperformed promise.

exemptions Transactions that would otherwise meet the definition of a security but that have been statutorily excused from the law's restrictions.

express authority Authority a principal confers on an agent explicitly; it may be conferred orally or in writing.

express grant An easement created by an owner expressly granting in a deed a specific right to another to use the owner's property.

express reservation Where a property owner conveys title to another by deed specifically reserving within the deed an easement for himself or a third party.

F

fair housing The term used to express a national policy against most types of discrimination in housing.

familial status Refers to a family with one or more children under 18 years of age with a parent or other legal guardian.

federal question A legal dispute that involves the U.S. Constitution, a treaty, or a federal statute. Federal question cases are heard by federal courts.

fee simple (absolute) The most extensive estate in real property that an owner can possess.

fee simple defeasible A fee simple estate that terminates on the occurrence of a specified condition; also called a *qualified fee*.

fee simple determinable A defeasible fee that terminates automatically if a stated act or event occurs.

fee simple subject to condition subsequent A fee that may be terminated by the grantor when a certain condition is fulfilled.

feudal system A system in which landowners pay rents to a superior.

FHA insurance Insurance provided to lenders under Title II of the National Housing Act of 1943.

fiduciary duty A trustee's responsibility to act solely in the best interests of the owner or beneficiary of the trust.

finance charge Defined in the Truth-in-Lending Act as the monetary total of all charges a borrower must pay the lender for credit or a loan.

fixture An item that was once personal property but now because of the nature of its relation to the property is deemed permanently affixed and thus treated as part of the realty.

fixture filing A section of the Uniform Commercial Code that allows a security interest to persist in goods (personal property) that later become fixtures.

flexible-rate mortgage A mortgage that contains a provision permitting the mortgagee to adjust the interest rate upward or downward in a manner specified in the mortgage.

floodplains Areas near waterways that are prone to flooding.

foreclosure A procedure in which property used as security for a debt is sold in the event of default to satisfy the debt.

foreclosure of mortgage Legal procedure by which a lender that has advanced funds with real property as security recovers in the event of default. (*See also* judicial foreclosure; power-of-sale foreclosure; strict foreclosure.)

forfeiture The loss of the right to a down payment on real estate as a result of a breach of contract; a buyer's loss of an interest in property under a land installment contract, due to breach of the contract.

fraud A deceptive act or statement deliberately made by one person in an attempt to gain an unfair advantage over another.

freehold estate An interest in real property created to last for an uncertain period of time.

future estate An interest in real property that will become possessory in the future.

G

general lien A lien that applies to all property that a person owns.

grantee Person who acquires title to real property by deed.

grantor Person who transfers title to real property by deed.

green development A form of development that integrates financial, environmental, and social considerations in projects.

gross lease A lease in which a flat or fixed amount of rent is paid by the tenant.

ground lease A specialized type of net lease in which the lessor leases a piece of vacant land to the lessee, usually with the stipulation that the less*ee* at his or her own expense will construct a building thereon.

growth management plans Comprehensive growth plans that dictate both when and where growth will occur.

H

historic preservation The preservation of buildings, and perhaps archaeological sites, from destruction by new development.

holdover tenant One who failed to vacate or surrender possession of the premises on the ending date of a term tenancy.

homestead laws Laws that provide heads of families some exemptions from creditor's claims.

I

implied authority An agent's authority to do those acts necessary and proper to accomplish the express terms of the agency.

implied notice Legal notice that is imposed by the law when conditions exist that would lead a reasonable person to inquire further into the condition of the title.

implied warranty of habitability A warranty imposed by law on the landlord by which he or she represents that a residential property is safe and sanitary and fit for living at the time the tenant enters and during the period of tenancy.

incentive zoning A system of incentives given to developers that provide certain community benefits in their projects.

inchoate dower The expectant interest of a wife to dower.

indemnification The act of compensating another in the event of loss.

independent contractor A person who is retained to do a job, using his or her own judgment as to how the work will be done.

individual unit deed The deed for each individual condominium unit in the development.

indoor pollution Pollution within buildings that is recognized as a health problem.

innocent misrepresentation An unintentional misstatement of a material fact that induces justifiable reliance to the detriment of a party.

in pari delicto At equal fault.

interpleader A legal procedure whereby a party deposits money into court so that the court may distribute it to the rightful owner.

in terrorem clause A clause in an installment contract that prohibits recording at the expense of forfeiture.

inter vivos trust A trust that takes effect during the life of the creator.

intestate A person who dies without leaving a will.

intestate succession Distribution of property of a person who dies without leaving a will or whose will is invalid.

intrastate offering An exemption from registration under federal securities law where the offering is made solely to residents of the state by a resident offeror doing business in the same state.

involuntary alienation The transfer of title to land against the owner's wishes.

J

joint tenancy Co-ownership in which the entire estate passes to the survivor on the death of the other joint tenant or tenants.

joint venture A business entity in which two or more persons agree to carry out a single undertaking for profit.

judge-made law Law based on the written opinions of appellate courts, called *precedent*.

judgment creditor A plaintiff who has won a monetary judgment that has not yet been paid.

judgment lien A lien that attaches to real property of a defendant when a plaintiff wins a judgment in the jurisdiction in which the property is located.

judicial foreclosure A foreclosure ordered by a court.

judicial remedies Remedies provided by the courts.

jurisdiction The power of a court to hear a case.

just compensation The award to the owner when property is taken by the government through eminent domain.

L

land installment contract A contract in which the buyer pays the purchase price on an installment basis. The seller/owner retains title until the purchase price is paid; also called *contract for a deed*.

landlord's lien A common-law lien known as the *right of distress*; it provides the landlord with a lien on the personal property of the tenant where there is a failure to pay rent.

large-lot zoning A zoning classification that requires a minimum of one acre or more of land for each single-family house that is constructed.

lease A contract, either written or oral, that transfers the right of possession of the premises to the less*ee* or tenant.

leasehold estate An estate created when the owner of property, known as the *lessor* or *landlord*, conveys a possessory interest in the real property to another, known as the *lessee* or *tenant*, for a specific period of time in exchange for the tenant's payment of rent.

legal description A description of a parcel of land complete enough to locate and identify the premises.

legal notice A knowledge of another's interest in real property sufficient to make the adverse interest legally binding to the prospective purchaser or any other party acquiring interest in the property.

license A personal privilege to enter another's property for a specific purpose.

licensing laws State laws that require that a person obtain a license to act as a real estate broker or sales associate and regulate the conduct of those who act as brokers or sales associates.

lien A claim against another's property securing either payment of a debt or fulfillment of some other monetary charge or obligation. (*See also* general lien; specific lien.)

life estate An ownership interest in real property created to last for a person's life.

lifetime cap The maximum a rate can adjust up or down over the life of a loan (usually 5–6 percent).

limited partnership A partnership formed according to the provisions of a state limited partnership act. The liability of a limited partner is limited to the amount invested.

limited warranty deed A deed in which the seller warrants against acts that he or she has done that might affect title; also called *special warranty deed*.

lis pendens, notice of A notice filed for the purpose of warning people that legal action has been taken that might affect title or possession of specified real property.

listing A contract between a seller and a broker authorizing the broker to find a buyer for real property on specified terms in return for a fee if the broker is successful. (*See also* open listing.)

littoral lands Lands that border on an ocean, a sea, or a lake.

long-term escrow A financing device that combines the land installment contract and the escrow.

M

marketable title Title that is free of liens or other encumbrances that interfere with the peaceful enjoyment of the property.

mechanic's lien The right of one who renders services or supplies materials in connection with improvements to real property to seek a judicial sale of the realty to satisfy unpaid claims.

memorandum A writing that contains essential terms in satisfaction of the statute of frauds.

metes and bounds A method of describing land using compass directions, monuments or landmarks, and linear measurements.

mistake Unintentional error.

mistakes in recording Errors made by the recorder.

mistakes in the instrument Errors made in the preparation of the instrument to be recorded.

mobile home A transportable structure built on a chassis and designed for year-round living.

mortgage A document that uses real property to secure payment of a debt.

mortgagee A lender who acquires an interest in a borrower's real property as security for repayment of a loan.

mortgage insurance Insurance provided by government agencies or private corporations protecting mortgage lenders against loss caused by a borrower's default.

mortgagor A borrower who gives a lender an interest in the borrower's real property to secure payment of a loan.

multiple-listing service An organization among brokers who have contracted to agree to share listings with each other.

N

negative amortization A mortgage where periodic payments on the amortized loan do not cover all the interest that is due; the unpaid amount is added to the principal.

NEPA A statute requiring the preparation of a document detailing environmental data and analyzing that data regarding a proposed government action.

net lease As contrasted with the gross lease, a type of lease in which the tenant agrees to pay the taxes, insurance, repairs, and other operating expenses of the premises.

new urbanism A development movement that seeks to create more livable communities designed to resemble and function like traditional small towns.

nonconforming use A legal use that was established prior to zoning or prior to the present zoning classification and is permitted to continue despite its nonconformance with the zoning code.

nonjudicial foreclosure Also known as the power-of-sale foreclosure. Foreclosure based on terms in a mortgage giving a mortgagee or third party the power to sell the security if the borrower defaults.

note The borrower's written promise to repay a loan according to its terms.

notice statutes Statutes that provide that the subsequent buyer prevails over all interested parties who have not recorded their interest at the time the buyer accepts the conveyance and pays consideration for the land without notice of the preexisting conveyance.

novation An agreement in which a creditor agrees to discharge an existing debt and to substitute a new obligation and a new debtor in its place.

nuisance An unreasonable interference by one party with another's use or enjoyment of his or her land.

O

offer A proposal intended to create a contract on acceptance by the person to whom it is made.

open-end mortgage A mortgage that permits the mortgagor to borrow additional funds, usually up to the original amount of the debt.

open listing A brokerage agreement that entitles the broker to a fee only if his or her activities bring about the sale. The property may be listed with several brokers.

option contract A contract that gives a person a designated period of time to buy or lease real property at a specified price.

optionee One who is the recipient of an option.

optionor One who agrees not to revoke an offer.

overlay zoning A set of additional restrictions to protect natural resources, such as a wetland or scenic vista.

P

package mortgage A mortgage debt secured by both personal and real property.

parol evidence Oral or other evidence extraneous to a written contract.

parties' tort liability A civil duty to third parties to maintain premises in a reasonably safe condition.

partition A legal action in which a co-owner obtains a division of real property, terminating any interest of other co-owners in the divided portion. Each former co-owner's share is now owned individually.

partnership An association of two or more persons to organize a business venture and divide the profits.

party wall A single wall on the boundary of adjoining properties; it serves as a common support for buildings on each of two parcels.

per capita Distribution of an intestate's property in equal shares to persons who have the same relationship to the decedent without reference to the share an ancestor would have taken.

percentage lease A lease whose rental is based in part on the gross sales made by the tenant on the premises.

percolating water Water that passes through the ground, not flowing in a clearly defined underground stream or supplied by streams flowing on the surface.

perfection Legal steps necessary to establish a valid mechanic's lien; acts by which a secured party establishes priority in collateral over claims of third parties.

performance standards zoning Standards set to limit the adverse off-site impact of an owner's use. For example, standards can be established for odors, noise, and signs.

periodic tenancy An estate continuing from period to period until terminated by proper notice from one of the parties.

personal property Property that is not real property; generally characterized as having substance and being movable.

per stirpes Distribution of an intestate's property to persons who take only the share that an ancestor would have taken.

planned unit development (PUD) A concept involving a development larger than a traditional subdivision, generally permitting mixed uses within the develop-

ment and attempting to provide a maximum amount of land for open space.

plat A map of a subdivision indicating boundaries of individual properties; it also includes details such as lot numbers, blocks, streets, public easements, and monuments.

possession The right to occupy and control real estate to the exclusion of all others.

possibility of reverter A possibility that an estate based on a condition may revert to the grantor if the grantee or those who take through the grantee breach the condition.

power of attorney A document authorizing a person, the attorney-in-fact, to act as agent on behalf of another as indicated in the instrument.

power of termination The future interest that a grantor of an estate subject to a condition subsequent has to terminate the estate if the condition occurs; also called *right of reentry*.

precedent A published opinion of an appellate court that serves as authority for determining a legal question in a later case that has substantially similar facts.

predatory lending A term used to describe a wide range of unfair financial practices usually occuring in the "sub-prime" mortgage market.

prescription Acquisition of an easement through wrongful use of another's land for a period of time designated by statute.

prior appropriation Water rights doctrine giving primary rights to first users of water.

private offering An exemption from registration under federal securities law for offerings made to knowledgeable investors who have adequate information to evaluate fully the risks in the transaction.

probate The legal proceeding that establishes the validity of a will.

profit à prendre A nonpossessory interest in real property that permits the holder to remove part of the soil or produce of the land.

promissory estoppel A doctrine that prevents a party from denying that a promise is supported by consideration.

property Legal rights that a person possesses with respect to a thing; rights that have economic value.

prorate To divide or allocate proportionately.

prospectus A written document containing all the information necessary for an investor to make an independent and intelligent decision regarding a securities offering.

public use A use that benefits the community.

puffing Statements of opinion made by a seller to induce the purchaser to buy.

punitive damages Damages awarded as a punishment to the wrongdoer; punitive damages are beyond compensatory damages incurred.

purchase-money mortgage A mortgage given to a lender to secure part of the purchase price of real property, delivered contemporaneously with the transfer of title to the buyer.

Q–R

quitclaim deed An instrument that conveys the grantor's interest in the property.

race-notice statutes Statutes that provide that a subsequent buyer will prevail only if he or she has no notice of the prior transaction at the time of conveyance.

ratify Approve a contract.

ready, willing, and able Capable of present performance.

real estate escrow *See* escrow.

real estate investment trust (REIT) A tax shelter that exempts certain qualified real estate investment syndications from corporate taxes where 90 percent or more of the ordinary income is distributed annually to the beneficiaries or investors, and other income and asset tests are met.

real estate purchase contract An agreement whereby a seller promises to sell an interest in realty by conveying a deed to the designated estate for which a buyer promises to pay a specified purchase price.

real estate sales associate A person employed by a real estate broker who lists and sells real estate.

real estate securities Any arrangement whereby a person invests money in a common enterprise involving real estate with the expectation of attaining profits from the efforts of a promoter or some other third party.

Real Estate Settlement Procedures Act (RESPA) A federal law that requires that lending institutions disclose certain information to purchasers of residential real estate and prohibits those institutions from engaging in certain fraudulent activities.

real property Land, buildings, and other improvements permanently affixed to land.

real property rights Ownership or proprietary rights in land and anything permanently affixed to land.

recording statutes Laws that require the entry into books of public record the written instruments affecting the title to real property.

rectangular survey system System of land description that applies to most of the land in the United States.

redlining Denial of a loan by a lending institution or the exacting of harsher terms for loans in certain parts of a city for unlawful discriminatory reasons.

reformation A court remedy ordering a change in a lease or a contract.

registration of securities The listing of an issuance that meets the definition of a security—and is not otherwise exempted—with the SEC and (perhaps) with state officials.

regulatory taking A regulation that deprives the owner of all reasonable use of the land; constitutes a de facto taking of the property without due process of law under the Fifth and Fourteenth Amendments to the Constitution.

rejection An offeree's refusal or failure to accept an offer.

relation back A legal doctrine whereby the title acquired by a deed relates back to the moment of the first delivery to an escrow agent.

release of mortgage *See* satisfaction of mortgage.

reliction Land created when water recedes.

remainder A future interest in real estate created when a grantor conveys less than a fee simple and by the same instrument directs another estate to arise immediately on the termination of the prior estate.

rent The compensation paid by the less*ee* for the possession of the leased property.

rent paid in advance Rent payments due prior to the beginning of the lease period.

rent withholding The practice, allowed in a few states under limited circumstances, in which the tenant withholds rent as an inducement to force the landlord to perform repairs.

rescission A cancellation of a contract that results in the parties being restored to the position they were in before the contract was made.

respondeat superior, doctrine of The legal doctrine that an employer is liable for the wrongful acts of employees committed within the scope of their employment.

restrictive covenant A provision in a deed limiting the uses that may be made of the property.

reversion A future interest in real estate created by operation of law when a grantor conveys a lesser estate than he or she possesses.

revocation An offeror's act of withdrawing an offer.

right of reentry *See* power of termination.

right of survivorship A characteristic of some forms of co-ownership by which the surviving cotenant acquires the entire estate.

riparianism Water rights doctrine based on the idea that all owners of riparian lands are entitled to share equally in the use of water.

riparian lands Lands that border on a stream or watercourse.

rollover mortgage A mortgage that must be refinanced every few years to adjust the interest rate up or down in response to prevailing market conditions.

rule of capture A legal principle of oil and gas law allowing a landowner the right to all oil and gas from wells on his or her land, including oil and gas migrating from the land of others.

run with the land Rights in real property that pass to successive owners.

S

satisfaction The performance of an agreement to substitute a different kind of performance for that originally contracted.

satisfaction of mortgage A written statement by the mortgagee that the debt secured by the mortgage has been paid; also called a *release of mortgage*.

scienter In fraud action, knowingly making a false statement or asserting that something is true without actual knowledge.

S corporation A corporation that has elected to be treated as a partnership for tax purposes.

section An area of land approximately one mile square, containing as nearly as possible 640 acres.

secured transaction A transaction in which the parties agree that personal property or fixtures will secure a loan or the purchase of an item on credit.

security deposit Money deposited by the tenant, usually at the inception of the lease, over and above the advance payment of rent for the security of the landlord.

segregation in housing The voluntary or enforced separation of one group from another in residential location based on religious association, ethnic background, race, or a combination of these factors.

seisin Ownership of real property.

"separate but equal" facilities A concept that permitted the state to enforce separation of the races so long as each race was provided with "equal" services or facilities.

separate property In community property jurisdictions, property owned by either spouse prior to marriage and property acquired during marriage by gift, inheritance, or will.

servient estate The parcel of land that is subject to an easement appurtenant; also called *servient tenement*.

settlement *See* closing.

settlement clerk The person who is designated to coordinate the exchange of documents at the closing.

smart growth A development movement that emphasizes a pedestrian orientation, mixed residential and commercial uses, and protection of the environment.

special-use permit A system whereby special exceptions to the zoning ordinance are granted by the land-use administrator under a permit arrangement.

specific lien A lien that applies only to a designated property.

specific performance A court decree mandating that a party perform according to the contract.

spot zoning A zone change permitted by the local legislature that is not in harmony with the comprehensive plan for that area.

statute of frauds A statute that necessitates that certain contracts, to be enforceable, be supported by a written memorandum and signed by the party against whom enforcement is sought.

statutes of descent and distribution A statute that provides for the distribution of an intestate's personal property; it is patterned after the English Statute of Distribution.

statutory law Law enacted by local and state legislative bodies and by Congress.

statutory right of redemption The right of a mortgagor to redeem the property after a foreclosure sale.

steering Channeling of prospective homebuyers to, or away from, certain areas.

strict foreclosure A judicial procedure that terminates the mortgagor's equity of redemption and establishes the mortgagee's absolute title to mortgaged real property.

subdivision regulations Restrictions on the division of a parcel of land into two or more units. A subdivision will require prior approval by an administrator such as a planning board.

subject to As used in financing the purchase of real property, a sale in which an existing mortgage on the property is not paid off, the buyer paying only for the seller's equity.

sublease A transfer of part of the leasehold interest of the tenant, with the tenant retaining a reversionary interest.

subordination agreement As used in mortgage financing, an agreement in which a mortgagee surrenders a priority lien and accepts a junior position in relationship to other liens or claims.

substantial performance The extent of compliance under the terms of a contract that discharges a party from further obligation although failing to perform totally under the contract.

syndicate A group of investors who pool their resources to develop, manage, or purchase real estate.

T

tax lien A lien imposed against real property for payment of taxes.

tenancy at sufferance A tenancy created when a person is wrongfully in possession of another's land without a valid lease.

tenancy at will A tenancy that exists until either party chooses to terminate it.

tenancy by the entirety Co-ownership of real property by husband and wife. The right of survivorship is a characteristic of a tenancy by the entirety.

tenancy in common A form of co-ownership in which each owner possesses an undivided right to the entire property. Shares of co-owners need not be equal, and no right of survivorship exists.

tenancy in partnership A form of co-ownership in which each partner owns partnership property along with all other partners.

tender An offer of money or property as required by the contract.

tenure A historic system of holding lands, a characteristic of which was the possessor's subordination to some superior to whom the possessor owed certain duties.

term tenancy An estate for a specified period of time that has a specific beginning date and a specific ending date. When the ending date arrives, the estate is terminated without notice by either party.

testamentary trust A trust that does not take effect until the death of the creator.

testate succession Transfer of property when a person dies leaving a will.

testator A person who dies leaving a will.

third-party beneficiary A person who is allowed to enforce a contract although not a party to it.

third-person guaranty of rent The requirement that a third person guarantee performance on a rental agreement.

title The totality of rights and obligations possessed by an owner; evidence of ownership.

title insurance The comprehensive indemnity contract that insures the titleholder against title defects and encumbrances that may exist at the time the policy is issued.

Torrens certificate A document issued under the Torrens system; a type of land title registration.

township An area of land approximately six miles square, containing as nearly as possible 23,040 acres and divided into 36 sections.

trade fixtures Items added to land or buildings by a tenant to be used in the tenant's trade or business.

traditional zoning Zoning based on classifying land into use districts, such as residential, commercial, and industrial uses.

transfer development rights A system of land controls that permits the transfer of the right to develop from sites that are desired to be preserved to sites on which maximum development is desirable.

trespass A wrongful, physical invasion of the property of another.

trust A legal relationship in which a person transfers legal title to property to a trustee who manages it for the beneficiaries of the trust. (*See also* inter vivos trust; testamentary trust.)

trustee The person responsible for managing a trust.

Truth-in-Lending Federal statute that requires that lenders disclose the cost of consumer credit.

U

underground streams Subterranean waters that flow in clearly defined channels discoverable from the earth's surface.

undivided interest Interest of a co-owner that gives him or her the right to possession of the entire property along with other co-owners. (*See* co-ownership.)

undue influence The exertion of dominion over another person that destroys that person's ability to exercise independent judgment.

Uniform Partnership Act A model act that establishes the legality of the partnership form of ownership.

Uniform Settlement Statement A closing statement required for all federally related residential first mortgages.

unilateral contract A contract involving a promise in exchange for an act.

usury The practice of charging interest on a loan in excess of a rate allowed by law.

V

variable-rate mortgage A type of flexible-rate mortgage.

variance Permission obtained from the appropriate governmental authorities to deviate somewhat from the designations under the zoning code.

vendor's lien The right of a seller to a lien against land conveyed for any unpaid or unsecured portion of the purchase price.

voidable A contract that may be voided or validated at the option of a party.

W

waiver Intentional surrender of a known right or privilege.

warranty deed A deed that conveys title and warrants that title is good, free of liens and encumbrances, and that the grantor will defend against lawful claims. (*See also* limited warranty deed.)

waste Damage caused by the tenant, including failure to protect the premises from decay and ruin caused by the natural elements.

wetlands Lands that have groundwater levels at or near the surface for much of the year or that are covered by aquatic vegetation.

will A written instrument that permits distribution of an owner's property after death.

wraparound mortgage A second mortgage covering an existing mortgage that the lender agrees to service.

wrongful abandonment The tenant's vacating of the premises without justification and with the intention of no longer performing under the terms of the lease.

wrongful eviction An act that occurs when the landlord without justification deprives the tenant of the possession of the premises.

Y

yield spread premium A fee a lender pays a mortgage broker for securing a customer who borrows at an interest rate above the market.

Z

zone change A zoning amendment made by the legislative body that created the zoning code.

zoning The regulation by the public, usually a municipality, of structures and uses of land within designated zones.

CASE INDEX

CASE SUBJECT INDEX

INDEX